D1045090

Political Opposition and Local Politics in Japan

THIS BOOK IS BASED ON A CONFERENCE SPONSORED BY THE JOINT
COMMITTEE ON JAPANESE STUDIES OF THE AMERICAN COUNCIL OF
LEARNED SOCIETIES AND THE SOCIAL SCIENCE RESEARCH COUNCIL

Political Opposition and Local Politics in Japan

edited by
KURT STEINER, ELLIS S. KRAUSS,
AND SCOTT C. FLANAGAN

PRINCETON UNIVERSITY PRESS
Princeton, New Jersey

To KITTY, *for her forbearance and moral support*
To RACHEL, *born in Kyoto without opposition*
To RITA, *for her love and encouragement*

CONTENTS

vii

Contents

ACKNOWLEDGMENTS

In June 1976 a group of scholars met in Wilmington Beach, North Carolina for a workshop on local opposition in Japan. The editors of the present volume alternated in chairing the sessions of the workshop, which reflected the structure of the work that has resulted. In addition to the writers of the papers presented in the following text, the participants were: Susan J. Pharr, the University of Wisconsin, Madison; Bradley M. Richardson, Ohio State University; Richard J. Samuels, Massachusetts Institute of Technology; George O. Totten III, University of Southern California; Taketsugu Tsurutani, Washington State University; James W. White, University of North Carolina; and Michio Yanai, Seikei University, Tokyo. All of them contributed most usefully to the discussion, and the editors and authors would like to express their gratitude for these contributions. To Susan Pharr goes our special thanks also for making the necessary arrangements in her then-capacity as Staff Associate of the Social Science Research Council. Richard Samuels served ably as rapporteur for the session.

We acknowledge our indebtedness to the Joint Committee on Japanese Studies of the American Council of Learned Societies and the Social Science Research Council, which sponsored the workshop and provided the support that made the entire enterprise possible. To the Bureau for Faculty Research of Western Washington University we are thankful for the typing of the completed manuscript.

Many of the writers of the papers incurred additional debts to organizations or individuals. These debts are gratefully acknowledged by them individually in the beginning of their papers.

KURT STEINER
SCOTT C. FLANAGAN
ELLIS S. KRAUSS

PART ONE

INTRODUCTION

CHAPTER I

TOWARD A FRAMEWORK FOR THE STUDY OF LOCAL OPPOSITION

Kurt Steiner

THIS volume has two main purposes: to describe and analyze the spectacular developments in Japanese local politics over the last decade and a half and to contribute to theory building in a relatively new subfield of comparative politics, namely comparative local politics. Up to now the literature in this subfield tended to concentrate on Europe on the one hand and on the Third World on the other hand. By adding the case of Japan, we hope to facilitate a broader comparative analysis; by focusing on the relationship between local politics and political opposition, we want to add a new dimension to the ongoing enterprise of theory building.

The relationship between local politics and political opposition periodically attracts public attention. Partisans greet with hope or view with alarm increases in the number of local communities controlled by the Italian Communists, the French Left, the Japanese "Progressives," the Christian Democrats in West Germany, or whoever may be in opposition in the country at a given time. But a scholarly, objective analysis of the relationship in cross-national terms is rarely attempted. As the title of this essay indicates, we propose to take some exploratory steps in that direction. Although the results are likely to be tentative and the emerging comparative framework may turn out to be a partial one because not all possible variables are taken into account, we feel that the attempt has to be undertaken and that it is inherently worthwhile.

THE END OF THE "CONSERVATIVE PARADISE" OF LOCAL GOVERNMENT IN JAPAN

This study was prompted by questions that arose in our consideration of recent developments in Japanese politics. That these developments have been significant becomes clear when we view them against their historical background. Before and during the Second World War, the local government system of Japan was highly centralized, both in

3

law and in practice. After the war, the Allied Occupation of Japan promoted local autonomy as part of its overall effort to democratize the country. Thus the Constitution of 1947 provided for the direct election of local chief executives, from prefectural governors to village mayors, as well as of local assemblies. This opened up new possibilities for political competition at all subnational levels. However, for nearly twenty years after the reform, local government remained a "conservative paradise." Of course, during nearly all of this time conservative governments were also in power at the national level; but there the progressive opposition managed to capture at least one-third of the seats in both houses of the Diet. By comparison, inroads of the opposition at the local level were negligible. From time to time, progressive governors held office in four or five of the forty-six prefectures, but, with the notable exception of Governor Ninagawa of Kyoto prefecture, elected in 1950 and in office for twenty-eight years thereafter, they showed little staying power. Progressive mayors of large cities elected in the first postwar elections experienced a similar fate.[1] By and large, progressive chief executives at both levels faced conservative majorities in their assemblies. Smaller cities, many of them results of recent amalgamations fostered by the central government, and the great mass of towns and villages were the province of the independent mayors and the independent assemblymen, most of them of conservative leanings.

To understand this conservative near-monopoly at the subnational level, it is well to remember that the proportion of voters living in rural areas and employed in primary industries was high. These voters continued to adhere to traditional patterns of attitudes and behavior, based on collectivity orientation and particularistic interpersonal relations. These patterns, benefiting conservative candidates, were of greater effect in local than in national elections, and thus local governments remained under conservative control.[2] The opposition parties showed little interest in local politics, and consequently they made few efforts to overcome this conservative advantage, for example by building up local organizations. They were also hampered much more than the conservatives—many of whom ran as independents—by the notion of nonpartisanship in local politics, which influenced many voters.

[1] On the situation before 1965, see Kurt Steiner, *Local Government in Japan* (Stanford: Stanford University Press, 1965), especially Chapters 15 and 16; on subsequent developments, see Chapters 3 and 9 of this volume.

[2] In 1950, about 48 percent of the labor force was engaged in primary industries; only 26 percent of the population lived in cities of 100,000 or more. By 1970, the respective figures were 19 percent and 52 percent. See Chapter 5.

The fact that the conservatives were in control of the national as well as of most local governments had implications for the scope of local autonomy. The Occupation's efforts at increasing local autonomy notwithstanding, the central government controlled local governments through a number of channels, some formalized, some informal, some official, some semiofficial or unofficial, and this "guidance" was widely accepted without questioning its legal basis or binding quality. A number of factors contributed to this situation: the lack of a clear definition of independent local functions, the general dependence of local governments on financial grants from the center, and the practice of delegating national functions to local entities or their chief executives, often without providing the requisite financial support, which placed an "excess burden" on the financially strapped local governments. Considering the reasons for the gap between the constitutional ideal of local autonomy and the reality of central control, the following statement seemed appropriate in 1965:

> On the one hand, the institutional reforms of the Occupation remained a halfway house, especially in the area of functions and finances; on the other hand, attitudes inherited from the past—such as the persistence of hierarchial notions in the minds of national bureaucrats and local office holders and the slight regard for the legal process as a means of solving problems of inter-governmental relations—prevented the local entities from assuming the role that the reforms supposedly assigned to them. Local autonomy did not fail in Japan; it was never fully established.[3]

In the early sixties, the conservative national government gave great emphasis to plans for national economic development.[4] It provided incentives for local governments to induce new industries to establish themselves in their areas by providing them with land as a gift, by granting them temporary property tax exemptions, and by constructing supportive public facilities for them. Used to following guidance from above, hard pressed for financial resources and thus attracted by promises of grants-in-aid and bond permits from the national government, and persuaded by the argument that new industries would broaden the tax base in the future, local governments actively competed with each other to lure industries to new locations. Somewhat paradoxically, this conservative policy of economic development was one

[3] Steiner, *Local Government*, p. 470.

[4] The National Development Plan and the New Industrial Cities Construction Law of 1962 are examples. A forerunner was the National Land Comprehensive Development Law of 1950. See Chapter 10.

of the factors that weakened the conservative hegemony in local government. The new industries, with the concomitant siphoning off of workers in the primary sector of the economy and the immigration of workers in the secondary and tertiary sectors into rural areas, accelerated and broadened the spread of urbanization. This in turn meant a shrinkage of the hitherto secure electoral base of conservative politicians at the various levels.[5]

As already noted, during much of this time, the leftist opposition concentrated its attention on national elections, in part because the chances of success seemed better and in part because the stakes were higher. Their most immediate and important purpose was to stem the "reverse course" of conservative governments, and above all, to prevent a revision of the constitution. While the Socialist parties routinely referred in their platforms to the need of "democratization" of local government, in actuality they showed relatively little interest in local elections and devoted few resources to them. But, having reached the "one-third barrier" in national elections and having become aware of the need for mobilization at the local level during the security treaty struggles of 1960, they turned their attention increasingly to local politics.

Under the impact of these and other factors yet to be noted, the landscape of local politics changed drastically in the late sixties and early seventies. Progressive local governments proliferated so that some 40 percent of the population lived in areas with progressive chief executives. By 1975, the number of progressive governors had increased to nine, including those of Kyoto, Tokyo, and Osaka. While the Liberal Democrats and conservative independents still held a majority of seats in most prefectural assemblies, this was no longer the case in seven of the forty-seven prefectures.

Progressive successes at the city level—and particularly in the big cities—were equally spectacular. About 130 of the 643 city mayors were considered to be progressive, including the mayors of the most important urban centers such as Yokohama, Nagoya, Kyoto City, Osaka City, and Kobe. Again, conservative majorities existed in the assemblies of most cities as well as in town and village assemblies throughout the country. However, this was no longer the case in all "designated cities" (major cities designated by the Diet and thereby

[5] See Chapter 2. The conservatives attempted to make up for the slack by increased emphasis on their "direct pipeline to the center." Aqua, following Muramatsu, sees in this blatant partisan appeal the transition from a "cohesive" to a "cooperative" pattern. (See also Chapter 10.)

granted the exercise of certain prefectural functions), nor was it the case in a number of suburban and satellite cities in the Tokyo and Osaka metropolitan areas and in some medium-sized regional cities.

Another factor that is generally assumed to have contributed to the progressive successes in local politics was also a result of national action in pursuit of economic growth. As industry spread, the negative effects of economic growth in the form of environmental deterioration and of pollution-induced illnesses led to the emergence of a new political phenomenon, namely of citizens' movements that were organized in rural and in urban Japan. The actual relationship between these movements and progressive politics at the local level is quite complex, as will be shown in Part Three of this volume. But, since local governments became a major target of protest and since progressive local chief executives were prone in the beginning to show their responsiveness to these new pressures from below, the potential of the movements in their totality (as distinguished from the often ephemeral individual movements) of having an impact on local politics is clear.

All of these developments have naturally attracted the attention of the mass media in Japan. The quantity of the output of Japanese scholarship on related matters is also quite impressive. In the United States, too, research on Japanese local government and politics has proliferated and, in contrast to the past, when rural Japan was the main focus of attention, much of it deals with urban Japan.[6] As stated at the outset, one of the purposes of the present volume is to contribute to that body of literature.

VIEWS ON THE LINKAGES BETWEEN
NATIONAL POLITICS AND LOCAL POLITICS

Another purpose of this volume is to contribute to theory building in the field of comparative local politics. Such an effort must be based on the recognition of the wide variety of local-extralocal linkages. We are interested here in local-national linkages of a specifically political nature and, more particularly, in situations in which the content of that linkage-channel may be characterized as opposition. In other words, we focus on situations in which the political forces in control

[6] On research in the United States, see Jack G. Lewis, "Comparative Perspectives on Japanese Urban Politics," a paper prepared for the 1975 National Conference of the American Society for Public Administration in Chicago. An example of recent American scholarship in this field is Gary Allinson's *Japanese Urbanism* (Berkeley: University of California Press, 1975).

of local units are in opposition to the predominant forces at the national level, whether this be an opposition in terms of party, political tendency, or policy.[7] As noted above, such situations are quite frequent.

Politicians are aware of the potential importance of local opposition for national politics. Thus opposition parties, successful in a local election, may claim that their victory indicates a trend permitting predictions regarding the next national election—a claim usually denied by the government party; the government may view a victory of the opposition in subnational units with alarm, anticipating that it will use its power to resist national policies (such as a policy for economic development) and thus hamstring their implementation; or an opposition party, devoid of hope for a national takeover in the near future, may take heart from its local successes, which permit it to maintain its strongholds or, perhaps, to establish new beachheads. But while the phenomenon is relatively frequent in reality, until recently little consideration has been given to it in the literature, much of which deals with national-local relations in general and depoliticized terms.[8]

Some of the classics in the field of comparative politics and democratic theory saw in local politics not so much a source of potential opposition as an agent for socialization into politics in a democracy. Thus de Tocqueville wrote of the town meetings of New England as "grammar schools of liberty" and Lord Bryce, concurring, considered the practice of local self-government "the best school of democracy." Implicit both in the preference of these writers for local independence and diversity and in their aversion against centralization and standardization is the assumption that a certain antagonism between the national government and the local governments—the type of antagonism in intergovernmental relations that I will later refer to as "institutional opposition"—is natural and legitimate. On the other hand, Bryce condemned the type of opposition with which this volume deals, that is,

---

[7] By "opposition in terms of party" we mean situations in which a party that is in opposition at the national level controls a local government. "Opposition in terms of political tendency" exists when parties or other groups sharing a basic political view and thus belonging to the same "political family" or "tendency"— such as the "Left" in France or the progressives in Japan—are in local control but in opposition at the national level. "Opposition in terms of policy" encompasses cases in which the local government, regardless of its political coloration, opposes specific national policies or their local implementation.

[8] Exceptions are, for example, Robert H. Evans, *Co-existence: Communism and its Practice in Bologna, 1945-1965* (Notre Dame, Indiana: University of Notre Dame Press, 1967); Mark Kesselman, *The Ambiguous Consensus: A Study of Local Government in France* (New York: Knopf, 1967), and other works by the same author; and parts of Donald Blackmer and Sidney Tarrow, eds., *Communism in Italy and France* (Princeton: Princeton University Press, 1975).

"political opposition," as disturbing and harmful. He felt that such an opposition is based on questions, foreign to the sphere of local government, and that the intrusion of such questions negates what he considered to be an advantage of local self-government, namely its insulation from national politics. Where such insulation exists, conflict in individual local units need not coincide with partisan political conflict: "When local discontents arise," he wrote, "it is better for them to find vent in the local arena rather than encumber the central authority." Similarly, de Tocqueville felt that a decentralized system has the advantage of resolving many issues short of recourse to the national government and thus of reducing political tension and increasing political stability.[9]

Subsequent social and political developments did not favor the insulation of local government from national politics that had been considered desirable and possible by these writers of an earlier day. The self-sufficient community, which was their ideal, hardly exists anymore. Local systems are—to borrow a term from the literature on international relations—"penetrated systems." Changes in patterns of political participation and in the character of political parties produce a tendency toward an increased "nationalization of local politics."[10] National and local politics no longer move in separate orbits.

While local-national linkages of a political nature have become more salient since de Tocqueville and Bryce expressed their concern about them, the literature tends to treat national politics and local politics in isolation from one another. Thus the recent literature on political opposition deals almost exclusively with opposition between parties at the national level and does not give any detailed consideration to local political opposition.[11] In this volume we discuss local political opposi-

[9] Alexis de Tocqueville, *Democracy in America*, Borzoi edition (New York: Knopf, 1945), 1:60-65; James Bryce, *Modern Democracies* (New York: Macmillan, 1921), 1:133; 2:435-436, 492-493.

[10] The quotes refer to James Rosenau, "Pre-theories and Theories of Foreign Policy," in *Approaches to Comparative and International Politics*, ed. R. Barry Farrell (Evanston, Ill.: Northwestern University Press, 1966), pp. 27-93, and to Douglas E. Ashford, "Parties and Participation in British Local Government and Some American Parallels," *Urban Affairs Quarterly* 11 (1975): 58-81. See also Richard J. Samuels, "Extralocal Linkages and the Comparative Study of Local Politics," *Comparative Urban Research* 5 (1978): 24-43.

[11] See, for example, Robert A. Dahl, ed., *Political Oppositions in Western Democracies* (New Haven: Yale University Press, 1966) and Dahl, ed., *Regimes and Oppositions* (New Haven: Yale University Press, 1973). In the former book, Dahl recognizes in passing the possibility that subnational political systems may be a site for encounters between government and opposition (p. 340), and he suggests that

tion in one country, Japan, but we also want to call attention to the need for a comparative and theoretical analysis of the relationship between national and subnational politics in general.

For a long time the literature on local government and politics also failed to deal with that relationship. In the American literature, local government was long considered as a field for the application of administrative theory. In political science departments of American universities, courses on state and local government were usually part of the offerings in the field of public administration. As Lawrence Herson so eloquently demonstrated in 1957 in his article "The Lost World of Municipal Government," the textbooks on city government dealt with local administration descriptively, and although they often prescribed reforms for greater efficiency, they paid little attention to local political processes and to local policies. The underlying premise was that "after all, there are only two ways of paving a street or enforcing quarantine regulations—a right way and a wrong way" and that "the right way, of course, is known only to the expert." This premise naturally led to the neglect of "the democratic issue where the streets are to be paved."[12]

A second characteristic of the American literature was the neglect of extralocal linkages.[13] This tendency was reinforced by the literature on community power structures and community decision making. While in contrast to earlier works this literature emphasized local political processes, it did so largely under the unwarranted assumption that the locality was an autonomous arena of political action. The

---

a study of patterns of opposition in local government might be highly instructive. The chapter by Val Lorwin on Belgium (pp. 147-187) and the chapter by Hans Daalder on the Netherlands (pp. 188-236) occasionally refer to linkages between local and national politics without exploring them systematically. A perusal of the journal *Government and Opposition* confirms this neglect of consideration for local oppositions.

[12] *American Political Science Review* 51 (1957): 330-345.

[13] An exception was Arthur Maas's *Area and Power* (Glencoe, Ill.: Free Press, 1959). This work not only considered extralocal linkages but also attempted to introduce comparative perspectives. In his introductory article, Maas considered "areal division of power" as one of the two divisions of power in a democracy, the other being, of course, the separation of power between the three branches of government at the center (or what Maas called "the capital division of power"). Implicit in this view of the power of subnational units as a constraint on the national government was a linkage from below to above in the form of local opposition, but this notion was not developed, and the book failed to stem tendencies in the literature in an opposite direction.

parochial American "autonomous tradition" handicapped serious consideration of extralocal influences.[14]

In the literature dealing with local government and politics in other Western countries and particularly in countries in which the issue of centralization or tutelage was important, there was normally some consideration of national-local linkages. This consideration was, however, normally limited to formal intergovernmental linkages of a legal, administrative, or financial character, and even these linkages were considered only in the direction from above to below. Since linkages in the opposite direction and the behavioral aspects of such linkages were usually disregarded, there was also little concern for partisan local opposition, although in reality such opposition existed in many of these countries.

As American political scientists became interested in the politics of developing societies, the resistance of the traditional sector of these societies to penetration by the state building and nation building elite at the center attracted some attention. Since tradition was seen as highly localistic, it was recognized that national-local tensions were inherent in the modernization process.[15] But the comparative cross-national and cross-historical implications of political development for national-local relations have not, as yet, been fully developed.

The literature on local politics that strives for comparative analysis is of relatively recent vintage. In its comparative emphasis, it has shed the various previously noted parochialisms and avoided their pitfalls. Above all, it fully recognizes that local systems are not closed systems, so that we need to talk about "local level politics" rather than about "local politics," that local-extralocal linkages are not merely of an institutional nature but also involve extragovernmental actors, and that

[14] For a discussion of this problem, see Mark Kesselman and Donald Rosenthal, *Local Power and Comparative Politics*, Comparative Politics Series, vol. 5 (Beverly Hills: Sage Publications, 1974), and Richard J. Samuels, "Extralocal Linkages." It should be noted that some works of the community power literature give consideration to extralocal linkages. Examples are Ronald L. Warren, *The Community in America* (Chicago: Rand McNally, 1963), and Arthur J. Vidich and Josef Bensmen, *Small Town in Mass Society* (Princeton: Princeton University Press, 1958). Robert O. Schulze, "The Bifurcation of Power in the Satellite City," in *Community Political Systems*, ed. Morris Janowitz (Glencoe, Ill.: Free Press, 1961) is noteworthy for its consideration of extragovernmental linkages.

[15] Traditional local resistance to penetration by a modernizing elite confronts many Western writers with the value dilemma of modernization versus local autonomy or even of modernization versus democracy. For an attempt to solve this dilemma see Henry Maddick, *Democracy, Decentralization and Development* (Bombay: Asia Publishing House, 1963).

linkages flow not only from above to below but also in the opposite direction.[16] The present volume aims at making a contribution to this newer tendency in the literature. As already stated, its distinctiveness lies in its emphasis on one specific content of the local-national linkage channel, namely political opposition, and in its attempt to link the fields of local politics and political opposition.

THE HOMOGENIZATION OF POLITICS

We noted that the possibility of local opposition is inherent in the state-building process. The underlying cleavage is that between a centralizing and standardizing elite at the center and its bureaucracy, on the one hand, and the local elites at the periphery, on the other hand. The local elites perceive the encroachment of the center as a threat to their own power as well as to the cultural identity of their territorial communities.[17] If local resistance to integration has been unsuccessful, the opposition is reduced to a single issue, namely that of centralization versus autonomy. This underlying issue may find expression in a number of ways. In the process of state building and nation building itself, the outcome of the conflict may determine the terms of integration of the periphery, for example through the establishment of a federal system or a system of local self-government or, conversely, by the destruction of traditional communities and the establishment of central administrative units without reference to primordial loyalties. But the issue is likely to linger on beyond the initial state building and nation building stage. That is to say, even when the institutional arrangements between the state and subnational units are in place, a certain tension persists in their relations. At issue is the scope of what is often called "corporate autonomy," the right of subnational units to administer their own affairs.[18] This tension may find expression in opposition regarding various aspects of intergovernmental relations between officials at the national level and officials below the national level who represent single units or all units at a given level. When all local units similarly situated establish a common front in the opposition to central government

[16] Marc Swartz, *Local Level Politics* (Chicago: Aldine, 1968). In this section, I have relied on the previously mentioned article by Samuels, which presents an analytical scheme of these linkages.

[17] This formulation is based on the introduction, "Cleavage Structure, Party Systems and Voter Alignments," to *Party Systems and Voter Alignments*, ed. Seymour M. Lipset and Stein Rokkan (New York: Free Press, 1967), pp. 1-64.

[18] "Corporate autonomy" is analytically distinguished from "civic autonomy," that is, the right of the local citizens to determine the will of the local unit (local democracy).

policy in a field of intergovernmental relations—for example, when all cities or all big cities demand more autonomy in the form of a greater scope of independent functions or of independent financial resources —the institutional character of the opposition becomes particularly clear.[19]

This type of institutional opposition has its basis in cleavages that are, in the last analysis, divisions along a territorial or center-periphery axis. In the course of the industrial revolution, other divisions arise along a functional axis cutting across the territorial units. These cleavages lead to conflicts over allocation of resources, such as those between agricultural and industrial interests, between tenants and owners, or between workers and employers. In due time, these cleavages and conflicts may well tend to undermine the inherent solidarity of the established territorial communities, as Lipset and Rokkan state. But it is important to note that their thrust is normally first felt at the national rather than at the local level, precisely because of the inhibiting character of the inherent solidarity of established territorial communities. The impact at the local level is uneven. The solidarity is first undermined in communities most strongly affected by industrialization rather than in rural communities. In rural communities local notables and officials may defend the communal solidarity against the impact of these new divisions and conflicts that threaten the basis of their power and run counter to their value system. A conservative national leadership may also view the emergence of conflict resulting from functional cleavages (such as class cleavages) with some alarm. It may consider the formation of parties reflecting the new divisions—and in particular the rise of class-based opposition parties—to be potentially destabilizing at the national level. In the hope of preventing functional opposition from engulfing local government as well, it may attempt to keep the local government insulated from national partisan politics—depoliticized. In such attempts, it may find a willing ally in conservative local notables.[20]

In Japan, this way of thinking was exemplified by Yamagata Ari-

---

[19] The big city movement described in Steiner, *Local Government* (pp. 177-182), is a typical example.

[20] We may note that the view that local government has only the function of providing efficient administrative services (which I mentioned previously in connection with the American literature but which is also to be found elsewhere) may under certain conditions serve as a rationalization for conservative efforts to keep local governments depoliticized and to make these efforts more palatable to the general public. It is no coincidence that this way of thinking is reflected in the writings of Lord Bryce or de Tocqueville, who feared the influence of mass politics on the state and, in this sense, may be seen as conservatives.

tomo, the architect of Japan's local government system during the Meiji period. Considering the formation of parties at the national level as inevitable, he was determined to guard local government against their encroachment. He did not object to a grant of participation in such a depoliticized local government—especially to notables, property owners, or tax payers. On the contrary, as long as there was no linkage to partisan politics, such a grant of participation recommended itself to him as a sop to those who clamored for participation on the national level, as a training ground for them, or as a way to deflect discontent and opposition from the national to the local level.[21]

In urban centers strongly affected by the industrial revolution, however, the insulation of local politics from national politics may not be a promising scheme. A different strategy seems indicated. Recognizing that politicization cannot be stemmed in these cities, the central government may want to keep their control firmly in its own hands. This means that centralization and bureaucratization are escalated and that the grant of political participation is limited in these areas. Typically, big cities in Japan had no mayor of their own until 1898, and until 1926, town and village assemblies elected their mayor, but city assemblies were only permitted to nominate three candidates for one position to be appointed by the Home Minister. In 1943, under wartime conditions, the Japanese government reverted to this type of thinking when it abolished Tokyo City, comprising the areas of the present wards, as an administrative unit and incorporated it into a larger unit, Tokyo Metropolis, which was administered by a government-appointed governor.[22] The distrust of conservative governments against the politically restive and opposition-prone politicized urban units can also be illustrated elsewhere: we need only think of Paris being administered by government-appointed prefects from 1871 to 1977 in the absence of an elected mayor.[23]

It is doubtful whether the general scheme for depoliticization of local government can be successful in the long run because in time the tendency towards the "homogenization" of politics at the center and

[21] Steiner, *Local Government*, pp. 20-30.

[22] Similarly, the Law for Tokyo Metropolis of 1943 made the ward chiefs appointed officials. On subsequent developments, see Chapter 9.

[23] The French Minister of the Interior in 1884, Waldeck-Rousseau, expressed this rationale by stating that "in Paris there reigns either riot or insurrection, and the revolution in Paris turns into revolution or counter-revolution throughout the whole of France." The first election for a mayor of Paris took place in March 1977. The Prefect of Police remains under the jurisdiction of the Minister of the Interior.

at the periphery is likely to prevail.[24] The tempo and extent of the politicization of the periphery is influenced by a number of factors, and it accordingly varies among and within countries. Cultural factors, such as a high valuation of harmony, may inhibit the emergence of political conflicts even at the national level;[25] a conscious national policy of "insulating" local government from national politics may be particularly effective in such a setting. The tendency among officials and inhabitants to consider the local government in terms of administration rather than politics and thus to see a linkage with national party politics as inappropriate and potentially dysfunctional also inhibits the process of politicization. Within countries the speed of the process may be uneven in industrialized and in rural areas, with the former entering it sooner and progressing faster and the latter lagging behind because the traditional value system retains its hold longer in the countryside. Thus in rural areas, local politics may long remain patron-client politics, based on particularistic personal relationships.[26] Local notables seeking election for a local office may not need and thus disdain linkages to parties at the center and prefer to run as independents. In such settings, partisan appeals that necessarily would have to cut across community and particularistic solidarities are relatively ineffectual, and the penetration of partisanship into politics in general and into local politics in particular is impeded.[27]

On the other hand, in some areas urbanization and industrialization lead to concentrations of blue-collar workers, the natural clientele of leftist parties, thus enabling such parties to form there. It follows from their overall ideological goals that their primary partisan appeal is directed toward political changes at the national level. But they may also recognize the possibility of capturing control of localities with

[24] See Hans Daalder, "Parties, Elites and Political Development in Western Europe," in *Political Parties and Political Development*, ed. Joseph La Palombara and Myron Weiner (Princeton: Princeton University Press, 1966), p. 64.

[25] In his contribution to Robert Dahl's *Regimes and Oppositions*, Michael Leiserson notes the absence of a word in Japanese that expresses adequately the meaning of the English word *opposition* and the absence of the Western notion that opposition is an intrinsic part of politics rather than being inherently subversive ("Political Opposition and Political Development in Japan," p. 346).

[26] For the case of Japan, see Steiner, *Local Government*, pp. 376-377, 423-424, 432-435; Scott C. Flanagan, "Voting Behavior in Japan: The Persistence of Traditional Patterns," *Comparative Political Studies* 1 (1968): 391-412.

[27] We may note that the conflict between agrarian and industrial interests in some countries in the West led to the formation of agrarian parties. For a number of reasons this did not happen in Japan, and the inhibiting influence of the traditional value system in the countryside may have been one of the reasons.

heavy concentrations of their clientele. This promotes a homogenization of politics and, if successful, engenders political local opposition.
We may think of the examples of England, where Labor captured
local positions early in the century, of France with its "red belt" around
Paris going back to the 1920s, of Austria, where Vienna became a "red
bastion" at about the same time, and of similar situations in Italy with
its "red belt" of Emilia Romagna.

It should be noted that the "homogenization" of politics at the center
and the periphery creates a new type of local-extralocal linkage, those
between nongovernmental actors or institutions, such as local party
organizations and their national party apparatus. The strength of these
linkages varies among different countries and among parties. It depends, among other things, on the organizational characteristics of
individual parties and especially on their general articulation and centralization, which in turn may be related to their ideology, clientele,
and other factors.[28]

In Japan, the politicization of local government was long delayed. To
the end of the Second World War, the laws regarding local government reflected the policy of depoliticizing local government. Cultural
factors, such as the stress on particularistic relations and on orientation towards areal collectivities, impeded the process of politicization especially in the countryside, where even the territorial opposition
lost its salience as a result of the convergence of interests between a
conservative central government and conservative local powerholders.
In urban areas, the leftist parties, which otherwise may have spearheaded the process of politicization and the emergence of local political opposition, were weak, poorly organized, and disinterested in
local politics. The recent developments that are the subject of this
volume are particularly significant because they constitute a break-
through in the process of politicization of local government.

LOCAL INSTITUTIONAL OPPOSITION AND
LOCAL POLITICAL OPPOSITION

Local political opposition does not replace other forms of local-national
opposition, but it adds a new dimension to them. Among other things,

---

[28] Samuels calls these linkages "extragovernmental" and discusses some of the
literature dealing with them. For the concepts of general articulation and centralization, see Maurice Duverger, *Political Parties* (New York: Wiley, 1954), pp. 40-
60. While the linkages between party organizations at various levels are the most
obvious extragovernmental linkages and those most germane to our discussion,
they are not the only ones, as Samuels points out.

it heightens the salience of institutional local opposition. When sub-national units are depoliticized or are under the control of the party governing at the national level—when political local opposition is absent—the saliency and strength of institutional opposition tends to be depressed: in spite of the tension inherent in their mutual positions, bureaucrats at both levels dealing with each other over time in a stable system of intergovernmental relations tend to come to understandings with each other, based more on cooperation than on antagonism; demands by individual local units or by national organizations, representing all local units of the same level, tend to take the form of lobbying or petitioning for grants; open conflict tends to be the exception rather than the rule. On the other hand, local political opposition gives a new impetus and reinforcement to institutional opposition: a local political opposition will attempt to expand local autonomy in order to more fully exploit the possibilities inherent in its control of local power positions, while the government's interest in such a situation lies in restricting local autonomy and in utilizing all available control mechanisms;[29] the demand for more local autonomy or the resistance to attempts at increased centralization may be used to depict the nationally governing party as unresponsive or undemocratic and thus to embarrass it; the issue of centralization versus autonomy, normally grist for the mills of institutional opposition, becomes politicized. In the 1950s when Japanese cities resisted the recentralization of the police, they found a natural ally in the opposition parties in the Diet, whose determined though unsuccessful struggle to keep police under municipal control led to some of the most riotous scenes in Japan's parliamentary history.[30]

[29] One of these control mechanisms in Italy is the dissolution of communal or provincial administrations. A table in P. A. Allum, *Italy: Republic Without Government?* (New York: Norton, 1973), shows that such dissolutions were common during the fascist regime and that they reached another height of more modest proportions in 1956-1958, a period that included the Zoli government, which had to rely on rightist support (p. 223). The author comments that this strategem can be used as much for political as for legal reasons and that "intervention and other controls are weapons that the Prefect can use against the opposition parties, as they were against the Communist Party throughout the Cold War" (p. 225). Other control mechanisms may be brought into play when local entities controlled by the opposition get into financial difficulties. Note that Kyoto prefecture was at one time subjected to financial controls by the center as a "finance reconstruction entity" and that Mishima City was threatened with a similar step. See Chapters 8 and 11.

[30] Steiner, *Local Government*, pp. 255-259. Another example for the politicization of the issue of local autonomy may be taken from recent Italian political history. The establishment of the so-called "ordinary regions" called for in the con-

As a matter of fact, political leaders on both sides often anticipate the emergence of local political opposition and attempt to prepare for it. As far as central governments are concerned, the previously-mentioned establishment of a special and restricted system of self-government for areas that they deem more likely to fall into the hands of the political opposition (such as for the big cities, including the capital city) may be seen as a move in this political game, although it may be rationalized in different terms. On the other hand, political opposition parties may champion local autonomy in an anticipatory way, regardless of the ideological or programmatic fit of that stance, even before they actually achieve local power. Thus the platforms of various leftist parties in prewar Japan frequently contained demands for more local autonomy, although, given their weakness, this could be only the expression of a pious hope.[31] Today the demand for the retention or expansion of local autonomy has become a recurrent theme in platforms and action programs of leftist opposition parties in Japan. The present endeavors of progressive local governments in Japan to enlarge the scope of local policy agenda, their exploitation of hitherto unused provisions of the Local Autonomy Law, and their use—in a departure from longstanding tradition—of lawsuits against the central government to resist "excess financial burdens" show that the institutional opposition between levels of government is strongly reinforced by political opposition. The present situation contrasts sharply with the relatively quiescent attitudes of local governments at the time when local government was a "conservative paradise."

In the absence of political opposition, the legal structure may be a fair reflection of intergovernmental relations as they exist in reality. The existence of political opposition at the local level creates tensions that may lead to a greater degree of autonomy in reality than the legal structure would lead one to expect. Thus the present local government structures of France and Italy are nearly as centralized as was that of prewar Japan, for example, in the control exercised through a centrally appointed official (prefect) over the intermediate level (department, province) as well as over the municipalities. In spite of this, local gov-

---

stitution was long postponed by successive Christian Democrat-dominated governments, afraid that some regional governments might fall under Communist control and that the Communist Party would then use them as a springboard for national politics. The regions were established in 1970 under pressure from the Socialists, formerly in opposition, whose collaboration in a "Center-Left" alliance was now needed (See Allum, *Italy*, p. 226).

[31] Steiner, *Local Government*, p. 42.

ernments in the hands of the opposition in these countries have for a long time engaged in experimentation, provided a variety of noncompulsory services, and generally created a scope of local decision making unknown in Japan even after the centralizing framework there was loosened by the occupation reforms, until local opposition in the form of progressive local governments became important.[32]

One problem for local oppositions is inherent in the ambiguous character of local entities as self-governing bodies, on the one hand, and as subdivisions in a hierarchical system of administration, on the other hand, with all the downward linkages that the latter character involves. These linkages include the cases of delegation of central government functions to local chief executives who actually may serve and may be accountable to two masters at the same time. The tensions inherent in this situation are subdued as long as the political coloration of the central government and of the local governments does not differ. An apolitical local electorate or one that is of the same coloration as the national government will expect its elected chief executive to be responsive to and to avoid frictions with the central government, partly in the hope that this harmonious relationship with the center will be of benefit to the locality by inducing the center to provide more grants to it in general or for the delegated functions in particular. In this situation a candidate for the office of chief executive, adhering to the ruling party, may plausibly stress his "pipeline to the center" in his campaign. But local candidates, associated with the political opposition and relying on progressive voters for their chances, cannot plausibly use that slogan. They thus may shift the emphasis to their relations to the other master, the local people, and to their desire to be responsive to them. Local opposition candidates are thus likely to stress their greater "pipeline to the people," thus highlighting the tensions created by the institutional arrangements. When progressives are then in power, the stress on the "pipeline to the people" may be given institutionalized mechanisms that provide for an increased two-way flow of communication between the local executive and the general public. While the term "pipeline to the people" is taken from the vocabulary of recent Japanese local politics, the phenomenon described is not unknown elsewhere. Thus in Bologna, long in opposition hands, neighborhood branches of city hall in various parts of the city have been established

[32] Mark Kesselman, "Overinstitutionalization and Political Constraint: The Case of France," *Comparative Politics* 3 (1970): 29-44, shows the obverse side of the coin—the ability of local governments to resist state pressures in the face of a centralized system.

to facilitate more effective communication of the citizens with the communal administration.[33]

LOCAL POLITICAL OPPOSITION AND CITIZENS' MOVEMENTS

The type of local political opposition discussed in the foregoing section can emerge only after mass suffrage has been granted at the various levels of government. In other words, it has its basis in elections —in mass participation in the form of voting. In Japan and elsewhere, recent events have drawn our attention to other forms of political participation, namely participation in social movements with political goals. The goals may range from radical social change to the rectification of specific social injustices or to the change of specific policies.[34] Nevertheless, all or at least most of the groups of this type share some common characteristics. One of these is a disillusionment with the effectiveness of the customary forms of participation through parties and established interest groups, such as labor unions. Related to this is a preference for mass protest activities and direct action. Finally, most of them derive their original motivation from an intense concern with particular causes, problems, and issues. This accounts for the profusion of these groups and, in many cases, for their ephemeral nature. A prominent cause in Japan is related to the ecological problems created by industrialization. Our concern here is with the so-called "citizens' movements" that arose in Japan in the mid-sixties to protest the rapid economic growth policies of the national government and their consequences at the local level.

The inclusion of a section dealing with these movements in a book on local opposition requires a word of explanation. After all, their immediate target may not be the national government (as is the case in the oppositions previously discussed) but rather a polluting corporation or the local government; also, their immediate aim may not be

[33] Raphael Zariski, *Italy: The Politics of Uneven Development* (Hinsdale, Ill.: Dryden Press, 1972), p. 133 and Terry E. MacDougall, "Political Opposition and Local Government in Japan: The Significance of Emerging Progressive Local Leadership" (unpublished dissertation, Yale University, 1975), pp. 334-348. Where localism is strong, the emphasis on responsiveness to the local people rather than to the central government allows progressive chief executives to broaden their appeal beyond opposition voters as shown by Krauss in Chapter 11 of this volume.

[34] Examples are the civil rights movement in the United States and the students-workers movement in 1968 in France. In Japan, the movements against nuclear bombs and against the Mutual Security Treaty with the U.S. may be mentioned in addition to the ecology-oriented movements discussed in Part Three. On the latter movements, see especially Chapter 6.

the control of local governments in the sense in which opposition parties attempt to control local governments. Yet they are intricately, if subtly, related to both types of local opposition.

Most citizens' movements are closely tied to local communities.[35] Typically they seek to aid the victims of past pollution or to prevent further environmental deterioration in a locality. It is true that their activities are often directed against an already established polluting industrial plant or company (as is normally the case of the pollution victims movements) or against the establishment of a potentially polluting industrial plant. But the ultimate thrust is against the implementation of the national government's policy of economic growth at any price, and their political effect is felt at that level, as when the Diet enacts such laws as the Basic Law for Environmental Pollution Control or the Law for Relief of Victims of Environmental Pollution or when it establishes the Environmental Agency.[36] The local government almost inevitably becomes involved. Pressure is exerted on it to side with victims groups rather than with the polluting company with which local government may have been connected, especially in the case of company towns. The pressure of preventive movements is often directed at inducing or forcing the local government to oppose the establishment of a plant or industrial complex in the area. What is demanded of the local government is that it resist the customary guidance from above and instead utilize the available scope of corporate autonomy. Recall movements against the mayor or the assembly may be initiated for this purpose, or the issue may be made salient in the next election. The results may be a restructuring of power within the community. Of course, this restructuring does not put the local governments in control of citizens' movements, and this is indeed not normally one of the goals of the movements. But citizens' movements and their local allies do exert an influence on elections and on policy making. In terms of policy, the implicit and often explicit thrust of this influence is a strengthening of local autonomy vis-à-vis the central government, that is, local institutional opposition.

The relationship of citizens' movements to local political opposition is analyzed in Part Three of this volume, but some preliminary remarks

[35] An exception is what Margaret McKean calls the "roving ombudsman citizens' movements," but even "they devote their efforts to the more typically residentially-based citizens' movements." See Chapter 7.

[36] The dates of these measures were 1967, 1969, and 1971, respectively. See for example, Cynthia H. Enloe, *The Politics of Pollution in a Comparative Perspective* (New York: McKay, 1975), pp. 229-232, and Norie Huddle and Michael Reich, *Island of Dreams* (New York: Autumn Press, 1975), pp. 256 ff. See also Chapter 8 of this volume.

are in order here. There is some controversy about this relationship among observers. There are, on the one side, those who see in these movements only peasant uprisings in modern garb—a view to which we do not subscribe. At the other extreme there are those who see in citizens' movements purposely created auxiliary organizations of progressive parties—old wine in new bottles, new fronts for the old Left[37]—but there are a number of reasons why this view also has to be rejected.[38] One of these reasons is that the movements arose precisely because the leftist parties and also the trade unions had not been alive to the issues of environmental pollution and its consequences. These issues are too remote from both the socio-economic issues of the allocation of resources between the main functional groups and from the partially related cultural issues that form the raison d'être of the Japanese Left. As is often pointed out, they are cross-stratal and "post-industrial" in nature, while the interest of leftist parties remains fixed on stratal and industrial issues.[39] Equally important, most citizens' movements consciously attempt to remain independent of parties and to project a neutral partisan image, as their frequent basis in existing community organizations indeed requires.

This is not equivalent to stating that there is no relationship at all between these movements and the political opposition by progressive local governments. A certain affinity is only natural because both the movements and the progressive local governments oppose policies of the national government and protest their effects. It would also be surprising if the "colonization efforts" of the leftist parties would be utterly without effect, and we know that in some movements opposition parties or leaders are involved. On the other hand, leaders and participants are by no means exclusively or even predominantly on the Left. Rather, the movements cut across traditional socio-economic and political cleavages. As Krauss and Simcock note, this is a consequence

[37] This view may be partly a legacy of the leftist origin of the "idea" of citizens' movements. See Chapter 6.

[38] It is useful in this context to compare the lack of mass organizations of the Japan Socialist Party at both the national and the local level with the thriving organizational life of the Italian Communist Party in Bologna as depicted by Evans, *Co-existence*, pp. 95-97. It should be noted that citizens' movements also challenge policies or individual actions of progressive local governments, thus confirming the existence of a certain independence. In such cases the reaction of individual progressive local chief executives may differ, as shown by the cases of Minobe in Tokyo and Ninagawa in Kyoto. See Chapters 6, 9, and 11.

[39] This is a major theme in Taketsugu Tsurutani, *Political Change in Japan: Response to Postindustrial Challenge* (New York: David McKay Company, Inc., 1977), especially pp. 192-211.

of the areal and cross-stratal impact of the pollution problem as well as of the organizational substructure of most of the movements.[40]

The relationship of citizens' movements to local political opposition is, therefore, quite complex. This complexity is reflected in the restructuring of power within the communities. It is easy to see that this restructuring loosens the hold of conservative community power brokers who in the past often dominated local politics and who in some cases still dominate the local assemblies, but it is not so simple to state who replaces them and what role citizens' movements play in their replacement or, in other words, in the creation and maintenance of a political local opposition in a given locality. The complexity of the relationship is also reflected in the ambiguity of the mutual attitudes of movements and established progressive administrations. The study by Jack Lewis (Chapter 8) deals with the former aspect of the question, using the important case of Mishima as an example; the study by Ellis Krauss (Chapter 11) refers to the latter aspect in the case of Kyoto prefecture. The political role played by the movements also calls for further clarification of the term "local political opposition" and for an analysis of the characteristics and forms of that phenomenon. We now turn to this task.

LOCAL PARTY SYSTEMS AND LOCAL POLITICAL OPPOSITION

In the foregoing, we defined "local political opposition" somewhat loosely as situations in which political forces at the local level are in opposition to the predominant forces at the national level, whether this be an opposition in terms of party, political tendency, or policy. The definition calls our attention to the relatively neglected subject of political constellations at the various subnational levels and in individual subnational entities. We are familiar with the diversity of party systems at the national level, but little research has been done on local "party systems." The work that has been done in this area indicates that there is a great variety of local party systems within countries and that these local party systems are not often a replica of the national party system. In other words, local government is an arena of political contestation with some degree of autonomy.

For example, the term "predominant party system" has been coined with regard to the national level. But "predominant parties" exist also at subnational levels in countries that at the national level may have a two-party system or a multiparty system.[41] Thus in England, "on

[40] See Chapters 6, 7, and 8.
[41] On the typology of party systems in general and on predominant party sys-

some councils one party has a monopoly of all the seats" and "on others, an opposition party exists, but it may be small and destined to be permanently in opposition."[42] An example from another two-party system, Austria, would include the capital city, Vienna, administered by Socialists who had an absolute majority in the city council ever since 1919.[43] Predominant party systems at the local level also exist in countries with multiparty systems at the national level, such as France. Kesselman gives the example of the red belt around Paris, where cities have been ruled by Communist mayors without interruption (except during the Occupation) since the 1920s, and of a number of other cities, including "a mining town in the southwest [that] recently celebrated its 75th straight year of socialist rule."[44] The existence of "local predominant party systems" in which the locally predominant party is a party in opposition at the national level is only one—and a rather extreme—example of the autonomy of the local political arena.

Of course, cases can also be found in which the control of the main decision-making organs in a subnational unit alternates between political parties. However, in general, local control by a single political party appears to be more the exception than the rule. As Kesselman notes, in France "most local governments are ruled by coalition of diverse forces, rarely by a local branch of a national party" that has been able to "colonize" a local government. In Italy only a few of the larger communities have single-party majorities on their councils; most majorities are the result of local coalition building. Administration by coalition is also the rule in the municipalities of Belgium and the Netherlands.[45]

---

tems in particular, see Giovanni Sartori, *Parties and Party Systems: A Framework for Analysis* (Cambridge: Cambridge University Press, 1976), especially pp. 192-201a. For an attempt at classifying local party systems in England and Wales, see J. G. Bulpitt, *Party Politics in English Local Government* (New York: Barnes and Noble, 1967), pp. 104-130.

[42] R. M. Punnett, *British Government and Politics* (New York: W. W. Norton, 1968), p. 396 and sources cited there.

[43] The authoritarian and Nazi interludes from 1934 to 1945 interrupted Socialist administration in Vienna. After 1945, the city was administered for more than two decades by a grand coalition following the pattern then existing at the national level, although with a different distribution of influence. Throughout this time and since then the position of mayor was always held by a Socialist.

[44] Mark Kesselman, "Political Parties and Local Government in France: Differentiation and Opposition," in *Comparative Community Politics*, ed. Terry N. Clark (New York: John Wiley and Sons, 1974), p. 114.

[45] For France, see Kesselman, "Political Parties and Local Government in France," p. 114. For the other countries see Allum, *Italy*, pp. 213-214; Lorwin in Dahl, *Political Oppositions*, p. 177; and Galen A. Irwin, "Party, Accountability,

Such local coalitions require local conditions (including a local party system) that provide an "opportunity structure" for their formation.[46] Whether a coalition is actually formed and what partners are included may be determined exclusively by local decision makers. However, the decision may also be influenced by extralocal actors, such as party headquarters at a higher level. The existence or strength of this influence depends on a number of factors, including the organizational type of the individual parties and their organizational reach. Even in the case of Communist parties—where the potential for such influence is strongest—actual influence varies significantly between countries and over time.[47] As we move toward the center of the political spectrum and toward looser organizational structures, such influence tends to diminish. Thus Socialist mayoral candidates in France decide on the "list" they propose to head, as do candidates from other parties. In Italy, the "opening to the Left" at the local level (for example, in form of DC-PSI coalitions) antedated the "opening to the Left" at the national level, and PSI-PCI alignments as well as alignments from the DC to the Right occur at the local level.[48]

In general, more often than not municipal coalitions form and fall apart with little reference to national coalitions patterns. It thus happens that local coalitions include parties that oppose each other at the national level. Even where a single party forms the national government, its local adherents may form a coalition with parties in opposi-

---

and the Recruitment of Municipal Councilmen in the Netherlands," in *Elite Recruitment in Democratic Politics*, ed. Heinz Eulau and Moshe M. Czudnowski (New York: John Wiley & Sons, 1976), p. 166. In some cases—including those of the larger Italian communities and of the municipalities in Belgium and the Netherlands—the local councils are elected by proportional representation. This influences both the local party system and the need for coalitions.

[46] For a definition of "opportunity structure" and an application of that concept to a local coalition, see Jack G. Lewis, "Hokaku Rengō: The Politics of Conservative-Progressive Cooperation in a Japanese City" (unpublished dissertation, Stanford University, 1975), pp. 82-83, 107-119.

[47] On France and Italy, see Jerome Milch, "The PCF and Local Government: Continuity and Change," in Blackmer and Tarrow, *Communism in Italy and France*, p. 340; also Sidney Tarrow, "Party Activists in Public Office: Comparisons at the Local Level in Italy and France," in *ibid.*, pp. 143 ff. In Chapter 11 of the present volume, Ellis Krauss relates a case in which the National Committee of the Japan Socialist Party refused to sanction a local decision not to enter an electoral alliance at the prefectural level.

[48] On France, see Kesselman, *The Ambiguous Consensus*, pp. 119 ff., and Denis Lacourne, "Left-Wing Unity at the Grassroots," in Blackmer and Tarrow, *Communism in Italy and France*, p. 330. On Italy, see for example, Dante Germino and Stefano Passigli, *The Government and Politics of Contemporary Italy* (New York: Harper & Row, 1968), p. 175.

tion to it. This raises the question of whether such a coalition should be considered a "local political opposition" or not and whether the hypothesized reinforcement of institutional opposition by local political opposition comes into play in such cases. Although a generally valid answer to this question may well not be possible, the very formation of such a coalition is an indication of a weak or fractionalized structure of the nationally governing party and of the independence of the local party organization, and therefore some reinforcement of local opposition is likely to take place. In Japanese cities in which the mayor is supported by such a coalition, his membership on the National Association of Progressive Mayors is a good indication of local political opposition.

We previously referred to local party systems and to the potential differences between them and the party system at the national level. In our example, we stressed the differences in the relationship between the same parties at the two levels; but it should also be noted that there is sometimes a difference of the parties encompassed by the national party system and by the local party system. Some national parties may not be part of a local party system, and, conversely, there may be "parties" that exist only in some localities and that have no specified national connections. In Wilhelminian Germany, such parties were called "city hall parties" (Rathausparteien); in the Netherlands and elsewhere they are subsumed under the category of "local lists." As Irwin notes, some of these groups, commonly dubbed "community interest party," are organized by individuals who feel that the basis for the party structure at the national level is not appropriate for local politics; other groups represent local conflicts within national parties or reflect personal rivalries or the rivalry of subunits within a city or town. In England and Wales, such labels as chamber of trade, owner-occupier, ratepayers, municipal, and progressive are used.[49] Where individuals rather than lists compete for election, local notables do not need to organize a group, however loosely structured, but are able to run as independents. In this case, a de facto local coalition may consist of partisans of a party plus a number of independents. In smaller units such as towns and villages the relationship is likely to be the reverse: the great majority of candidates for the assembly may be independents and only a few may be partisans.[50]

[49] Galen Irwin in Eulau and Czudnowski, *Elite Recruitment*, p. 167; J. G. Bulpitt, *Party Politics*, p. 109.

[50] This is the case in most Japanese towns and villages. In 1973 there were five prefectures, including Tokyo, Kanagawa, and Osaka, without any town or village assemblymen elected as Liberal Democratic Party (LDP) candidates. It should be

We referred earlier to the relationship of the citizens' movements in Japan to political parties. We rejected the view that the movements are nothing but fronts of progressive parties, but it would be equally doubtful to consider them as completely unrelated to these parties. A first step in illuminating the relationship is to recognize the variety of types encompassed by the general term "citizens' movements," as is attempted in the introduction to Part Three and in the various chapters included in that part. In the present context, our focus is on the question, What role do these citizens' movements play in the formation and maintenance of local coalitions that constitute a local opposition? Here a distinction must be made between sponsored and independent movements. The sponsored movement is not an autonomous partner, motivated for reasons of its own to join a coalition; it is rather a device to mobilize support for an incumbent administration. Our interest is in independent movements, which form the great majority. They are spontaneously created, and they evince a strong tendency to maintain a distance from political parties and to resist "colonization" by them.[51]

As we stated earlier, a certain affinity of goals between these movements and progressive parties is natural. Such an affinity is lacking in their relationship to the conservative parties. On the other hand, we also noted that ecological issues may cut across normal cleavages and that the citizens' movements, often based on traditional community organizations, include conservative party identifiers among their leaders and members. The participation of a citizens' movement in a progressive coalition is thus by no means a foregone conclusion. Even where a local ecological issue naturally arrays a citizens' movement with a progressive candidate for the position of mayor in common opposition to local implementation of the economic growth policies of the conservative government, a catalyst may be needed. It is often provided by an intellectual who commands general respect in the community— a "man of culture" or *bunkajin*—who may steer the movement into electoral support for the progressive candidate.[52] As Krauss and Sim-

---

noted that even where the nonpartisan ethos favors the candidacy of independents, a sort of latent partisanship may be involved. Japanese newspapers divide independent candidates and office holders into those who are "conservative," "progressive," or "pure." Traditionally the first group is most numerous. The prevalence of "conservative independents" in town and village assemblies may explain the absence of LDP assemblymen in these five prefectures.

[51] See Chapters 6 and 7.

[52] There are many variations of this pattern. In Kamakura, the steps were the creation of an "Association to Protect Kamakura's Natural Landmarks and Na-

cock note, the potential of citizens' movements for bringing about political realignments is perhaps their most significant impact on local politics.[53]

At any rate, progressive local governments in Japan often come into being through electoral coalitions of a variety of groups, including citizens' movements. Often these coalitions are based on a formal agreement. In some cases the coalition is institutionalized in a roof organization, resembling to some extent Duverger's model of "indirect parties." At the gubernatorial level, *Minkyo* and *Fushimindantai*, the institutions that kept the opposition in power in the Kyoto prefecture for more than a quarter of a century, may serve as examples. In Tokyo, Governor Minobe referred to the less institutionalized, broad front of organizations that supported him as the "Metropolitan Peoples Party" (*Tomintō*). This technique of adding other groups to a coalition of parties permits the candidate to appeal to voters who might not be willing to vote for a candidate representing only a coalition of parties, including voters alienated from the parties in general, voters with strong localist loyalties, or even conservative voters who, nevertheless, find the progressive candidate attractive for a variety of reasons. Typically, the candidate does not run under a party label but as an independent candidate. Often—as in the case of Minobe of Tokyo, Ninagawa of Kyoto, and Kuroda of Osaka, all of them one time professors —he is a respected intellectual of the type that at the city level serves as a catalyst for coalition formation.[54] While there are certain institutional and cultural factors that may play a role in the Japanese case,

---

ture," leading to the formation of a citizens' party that was originally to compete independently in the election but ultimately entered into a coalition with the Japan Socialist Party and the Japan Communist Party. In his dissertation (see note 46), Jack Lewis analyzes the formation and maintenance of the coalition in Mishima between maverick conservatives and the progressives in which environmental issues and citizens' movements played an important role, and in Chapter 8 of this volume he describes the complex interplay between the citizens' movements, established associational life, parties, and interest groups. In this case, too, a respected intellectual served as the initial link.

[53] See Chapter 6. Joji Watanuki suggests that the hitherto powerful triangle of LDP, bureaucracy, and big business may in the future meet more and more resistance from a loose tripartite coalition of opposition parties, urban local governments, and citizens' movements. See his "Japanese Politics in Flux," in *Prologue to the Future*, ed. James W. Morley (Lexington, Mass.: Lexington Books, 1974), p. 82.

[54] On party coalitions and on the importance of groups concerned with ecological and other urban problems, see MacDougall, "Political Opposition and Local Government," pp. 236-252.

it may be that cross-national research will show parallels in other countries. The question remains to be explored in a systematic fashion.

As we said earlier, local coalitions are the result of local political conditions, including the local party system. It is clear that "local party system" has to be defined broadly to encompass not only parties existing at the national level but also more or less loose groupings in the locality that adopt a label for election purposes. The fact that electoral coalitions may also involve other groups (such as citizens' movements in Japan) confuses the picture still further, as does the presence of independents who avoid any common labeling.[55] It may be expected that a clarification of "local party systems" would throw some light on the patterns of coalitions in local governments—both electoral coalitions (which have been our main concern in the foregoing) and legislative coalitions. It is only when this groundwork of clarification has been completed that we will be able to give a more systematic picture of the many forms that local political opposition can take. We can only console ourselves at this time with the hope that we have laid bare a complex of long neglected but important questions that, it seems to us, are a fruitful object of cross-national research in the area of comparative local politics.

ELECTORAL TRENDS, CITIZENS' MOVEMENTS, AND PROGRESSIVE ADMINISTRATIONS: AN OVERVIEW

The articles following in this volume are grouped into three parts dealing respectively with electoral trends, citizens' movements, and progressive administrations. In each part, an attempt is made to answer some broad and important questions raised by recent developments in Japanese local politics. Thus we ask whether recent trends in local elections, resulting in successes by the progressive opposition and in the proliferation of progressive local administrations, are likely to be a temporary or a permanent phenomenon. An answer to this question requires an analysis of the correlation of these trends with demographic and socio-economic changes and with attitudinal changes related to voting behavior. The differences found in voting patterns between

[55] In *Party Politics*, Bulpitt admits that any definition of local party systems can only be a very imperfect one, and (for the purpose of his article, which deals with councils) restricts the term to local governments where party representatives comprise a majority of the council membership or where, although independents form a majority of the council, more than one party group is represented on the council and this party representation forms at least 30 percent of the total council membership (p. 109).

national and local elections raise the question of whether electoral trends at the local level are likely to have significant ramifications for national politics. More particularly, who are the voters who vote for progressive candidates at the local level and for conservative candidates at the national level? What factors, aside from the large-scale changes just noted promote or inhibit progressive successes at the local level? Most of these questions emerge in Part Two, but some of them are also dealt with in the other two parts.[56] Thus, Part Three attempts to analyze not only the character of citizens' movements but also their significance and their impact on local elections and on the formation of progressive administrations. Similarly, in Part Four, Ellis Krauss's study of the development and maintenance of leftist government in Kyoto prefecture deals, among other things, with the techniques of mobilization successfully used there and suggests explanations for some progressive successes elsewhere.

The topic of Part Three, citizens' movements, has been the subject of a number of articles. Much of this writing has been nothing short of euphoric, hailing the movements as the beginning of a new political culture in general and of local grass-roots politics in particular. In addition to evaluating that literature, we ask such questions as the following: What is the relationship between these movements and established community organizations, traditionally part of conservative mobilization networks? Who are the leaders and followers? What effect does active involvement in these movements have on the political attitudes of participants? What is the relationship of the movements to political parties and to the establishment and maintenance of progressive administrations? Not surprisingly, an attempt to answer such questions requires that various types of citizens' movements be distinguished from each other. Again, while most of these questions emerge in Part Three, some—such as the questions regarding the relationship between citizens' movements and established progressive administrations—are also discussed in Part Four.

Progressive local administrations emerge as the result of the electoral trends analyzed in Part Two, where Terry MacDougall's contribution focuses on the big cities. The phases of that emergence more generally are traced in Part Four. The case study of Kyoto prefecture in that part specifies the distinct stages of the development of the progressives' most durable local stronghold in Japan. By dealing with techniques

---

[56] This is only partly because the subject matters of the three parts overlap to a certain extent. Striving for an integrated volume, the editors at an early stage presented to the contributors a set of guiding questions to be dealt with wherever applicable.

of support mobilization on the one hand and with the goals, accomplishments, and limitations of policy making on the other hand, it raises questions regarding the role of ideology, of interest group politics, and of localism in a dual context. Ronald Aqua's study deals specifically with questions of policy. Do progressive local administrations of medium-sized cities have policy priorities that differ from those of the national administration and from those of conservative local administrations? In other words, does partisanship matter in regard to outputs? An antecedent question is whether existing patterns of central-local relations allow a leeway for the setting of policy priorities by cities. The answers to these questions are based on aggregate data and, particularly, budgetary data. It is thus important that the Kyoto study calls our attention to outputs of a nonbudgetary, more symbolic nature.

The example just given highlights the variety of methodologies in this volume. Such a variety is required by the variety of the questions asked. Some questions—such as Margaret McKean's questions about the socialization of participants in citizens' movements and about the effect of behavior on attitudes—deal with microlevel phenomena; others—such as the questions raised in Scott Flanagan's contribution—deal with phenomena on the macrolevel. It is thus natural that analysis is in some cases based on voting data (for example, MacDougall, Flanagan, Krauss) or on other aggregate data (Aqua), while in other cases it is based on interview data (McKean, Lewis, Allinson, Flanagan, and Krauss).

A characteristic of the volume is the inclusion of a case study in each of its three central parts. In Part Two, Allinson comparatively examines the context in which progressive office holders are elected —or fail to be elected—in two suburbs of Tokyo of which one has been under progressive control for some time, while the other remained under conservative control. In Part Three, Jack Lewis uses the important case of Mishima City to analyze the characteristics of leaders and participants of the citizens' movement there as well as the characteristics of the movement's organization and decision making and to provide new insights into the relationship between citizens' movements and conventional local politics. In Part Four, Ellis Krauss analyzes the power base, the mobilizational techniques, the stages of development, and the policies of the Ninagawa administration in Kyoto. None of these case studies is merely descriptive; none limits itself to factors that are merely idiosyncratic. It is our belief that case studies of this type can make a valuable contribution not only in terms of closing the gap between analytic and experiential knowledge but also in terms of analysis itself by strengthening or weakening established

generalizations and, in the latter case, potentially leading to their refinement.

Each of the three parts is introduced by an essay contributed by
one of the editors. These essays are meant to perform a variety of
functions: for the reader interested primarily in the contribution the
Japanese case might make to the field of comparative local politics,
they provide the background for the recent developments in Japanese
local politics, they provide a more comprehensive coverage of the
topics of the three parts by filling in the gaps between individual
articles within a given part; they link the findings of the analytical
studies and the case studies in each part; and they also provide links
between the three parts.

Chapters 1 and 12, the general introduction and conclusion, integrate
the study of political opposition and local politics with broader concerns of the field of comparative politics and its fledgling subfield,
comparative local politics. The introduction calls attention to the concept of local political opposition. Such an opposition is, of course,
the result of the politicization of local government. In our conclusion, we take a new look at that phenomenon and discuss its effect
on local autonomy and on the larger political system. Beyond the
question of whether local opposition victories allow predictions regarding national elections, loom larger questions of the role of a viable
opposition in a democracy and of the relationship of local political
opposition to the performance of that role.[57]

[57] The local opposition in Japan with which we are dealing in this book happens
to be largely identified with parties, politicians, or movements to the left of the
ruling conservative party on the ideological spectrum. For this reason the favorable assessment of the effect of the rise of local opposition presented in the conclusion may appear to involve a leftist bias. However, such an impression would
be erroneous. Our discussions and conclusions do not assume any inherent supe-
riority of the Left. In addition to discussing the accomplishments of leftist opposition at the local level, we have endeavored to point out the limitations of the
leftist rule, the self-interested motivations behind some leftist programs and opposition demands, and the opportunities that conservatives have for using the politicization of local politics to their advantage. We consider it quite likely that the
respective positions on the question of local autonomy would be reversed if the
present roles of the Left and Right in Japan were reversed, with the progressives
forming a hegemonic central government and a conservative trend towards power
at the local level. We feel that our assessment that the politicization of local politics and the rise of local opposition has functional consequences in the context
of Japanese democracy would hold true for such a situation as well.

PART TWO

ELECTORAL TRENDS

CHAPTER 2

ELECTORAL CHANGE IN JAPAN: AN OVERVIEW

Scott C. Flanagan

ELECTORAL trends are giving rise to a new politics in Japan. The cumulative magnitude of changes in partisan support over the last thirty years has been very substantial. Moreover these trends have recently brought the conservative-progressive electoral balance to the brink of a critical threshold that if crossed may potentially bring about a fundamental realignment of the party system and a dramatic reorientation in Japanese foreign and domestic policy. Thus an analysis of Japanese electoral trends is an important study in and of itself. It is particularly fitting, however, to conduct this analysis in the context of a study of political opposition and local politics because of the peculiar pattern that the trends have assumed. As we shall see, the consistency of these trends coupled with their unevenness across levels (national and local) draws attention to two important facets of political change in Japan: the underlying socio-economic causes of the growth of political opposition in a rapidly modernizing one-party dominant system and the emergence of a "dual politics" that heightens the significance of local elections and local governments.

In this introduction to the electoral trends section, we shall discuss these two important facets of political change to set the stage for the three succeeding analytic chapters. The cast of players—the political parties—and the rules of the game—the electoral systems for the different types and levels of election—will also be introduced to acquaint the reader with the basic descriptive information necessary to understand the context in which political competition takes place. Finally, a thorough understanding of local electoral trends requires a comparison with national election trends. Since the following chapter by Terry MacDougall supplies the basic descriptive information on local trends, this chapter will focus on national developments in order to facilitate our understanding of the comparisons between levels that are to follow.

THE GROWTH OF PROGRESSIVE ELECTORAL SUPPORT

One of the most striking features of voting trends in Japan has been the gradual long-term growth of support for the opposition parties.

35

This gradual increase has occurred across all types and levels of election. Thus we find a parallel rise in the percent of the vote polled by the progressive parties in both types of local election—assembly and chief executive—and on all three election levels—national, prefectural, and municipal. In our terminology, both the prefectural and municipal levels are designated as local. To portray the general pattern of growing progressive support here, however, we will present the voting data for the House of Represesntatives election to the national Diet. Because the House of Representatives or Lower House of the Diet is by far the more powerful and politically significant house, it is the appropriate choice for an analysis of national trends, although we will make some mention in the course of this chapter of the parallel trends that have been taking place in the House of Councillors or Upper House. This national data not only supplements the local data employed in the following chapter but is particularly useful for the discussion of dual politics developed herein. It should be kept in mind, however, that the national trends described here are closely paralleled by those found on both levels and in both types of local election.

We have in Japan an unusually long and stable period of one-party dominance. Outside of a brief seventeen-month interlude in the early postwar period when the leading progressive party played a major role in a coalition government, the progressive parties have been completely shut out of power on the national level. Total conservative dominance was reasserted in the fall of 1948 and subsequently was virtually guaranteed when the two postwar conservative parties (the Liberal Party and the Democratic Party) merged to form the Liberal Democratic Party (LDP) following the 1955 national Diet election.

Conservative dominance, however, has not gone unchallenged. As shown in Table 1, the combined progressive vote has grown in the House of Representatives (HR) elections over the last twenty-five years from 24 to 48 percent. Perhaps this trend could best be described as a decline in the universal appeal of conservative parties and candidates. In the 1952 election, the conservatives captured almost three-quarters of the total vote. By 1976, the LDP's share of the vote had dropped to 42 percent and the total conservative vote to 52 percent.

It is the consistency of the conservative decline in electoral support that is so arresting. This consistency strongly suggests that the trend has been largely independent of short-term influences such as the rise and fall of political issues, corruption scandals, and appealing candidates and party leaders. The 1960 "crisis of parliamentary democracy," the "black mist" scandals of 1966, and the "Tanaka Watergate" and Lockheed scandals of 1974 and 1976 that assumed massive proportions

Table 1

House of Representatives Elections, 1952-1976

	1952	1953	1955	1958	1960	1963	1967	1969	1972	1976
Popular Vote (%)										
RIGHT										4 (NLC)
LDP	(66)	(66)	(64)	58	58	55	49	48	47	42
Indep.	7	4	3	6	3	5	6	5	5	6
Total Conservative Vote	73	70	67	64	60	60	54	53	53	52
CENTER										
CGP	—	—	—	—	—	—	5	11	8	11
DSP	—	—	—	—	9	7	7	8	7	6
LEFT										
JSP	(21)	(28)	(30)	33	28	29	28	21	22	21
JCP	3	2	2	3	3	4	5	7	10	10
Total Progressive Vote	24	30	32	36	39	40	45	47	48	48
Total Progressive Seats (%)	25	31	35	36	35	37	41	38	42	44
Progressive Seat/Vote Ratio	1.0	1.0	1.1	1.0	.90	.92	.91	.81	.88	.92

NOTE: The progressive seat/vote ratio is the combined percentage of progressive party HR seats won, divided by the percentage of the total vote received. The vote percentages in parentheses for the years 1952-1955 represent the combined percentages received by those parties that merged to form the LDP and JSP respectively following the 1955 election. Rounding of percentages makes the figures for total conservative vote slightly higher or lower than the addition of the figures for the votes for individual parties.
SOURCE: *Japan Statistical Yearbook*, 1952-1977 editions.

in the media seemed to have provoked barely a ripple at the polls. There were no sharp conservative losses in those election years, but rather a continuation of the incremental erosion of conservative support that has characterized the entire postwar period. On the other hand, the popularity of Prime Minister Ikeda and his "income doubling" plan and the Okinawa reversion agreement failed to reverse the pattern of LDP decline in 1963 and 1969. Thus, the gradual long-term transfer of electoral support from the conservative to the progressive camps seems to be virtually independent of these kinds of short-term political influences.

Bradley Richardson's important recent analysis of stability and change in Japanese voting behavior has shown that in comparison to the United States, there is far greater stability from one election to the next in the percentage of the vote received by each party in Japan.[1] Richardson reports an average net partisan change of 5.1 percent in Japan between successive HR elections over the years 1958-1972 compared to an average change per election of 10.1 percent in the United States for the years 1956-1968. In other words, compared to American voters, only half as many Japanese are switching their votes from one party to another between successive elections despite the fact that there are many more parties to choose between in Japan. In the United States, however, these rather sizable fluctuations have not introduced any discernible trend. In contrast, the far smaller shifts from election to election in Japan have cumulated to produce long-term changes of considerable magnitude.

Indeed as Richardson demonstrates, the aggregate data mask even sharper cumulative changes in the patterns of partisan support that have occurred in some (mainly metropolitan) constituencies. After 1960, as the aggregate rate of descent in LDP support in HR elections began to decrease, the Liberal Democrats' decline in some large urban constituencies appeared to accelerate. Richardson reports that thirty of the HR constituencies (about one-fourth of the total) experienced a net partisan change of over 25 percent between the years 1960 to 1972, while in almost half of these the change was in excess of 30 percent.

It appears that these changes in partisan support are closely related to the urbanization process. In Table 2, we note that there is a close association between the rate and timing of urban growth and the decline in the conservative vote. In those prefectures that have experienced the most rapid rates of population growth (Tokyo and Osaka), we find the sharpest rise in opposition support (from 42 to 66 percent

[1] Bradley M. Richardson, "Stability and Change in Japanese Voting Behavior, 1958-1972," *The Journal of Asian Studies* 36 (1977): 675-693.

Table 2

Population Growth and Progressive Vote in House of Representatives Elections
for Selected Types of Prefectures

Prefectures by Type	Percent Population Growth		Percent of Total Vote for All Progressive Parties			
	1950–60	1960–70	1955	1960	1967	1972
ALL	12	11	32	39	45	48
Mature Urban—High Growth (Tokyo, Osaka)	50	25	42	53	63	66
Mature Urban—Low Growth (Hokkaido, Fukuoka)	16	2	46	49	54	55
New Urban—High Growth (Saitama, Chiba)	11	53	29	32	41	45
Rural—Low Growth (Ibaraki, Tochigi, Gumma, Yamanashi)	-1	4	29	33	33	36
Rural—Negative Growth (Shimane, Saga, Kagoshima)	4	-12	23	28	27	29

NOTE: Population growth and progressive vote figures are based on combined total population and voting figures across all prefectures in each category rather than on prefectural averages.
SOURCE: *Japan Statistical Yearbook*, 1950-1974 editions.

between 1955 and 1972). In contrast, Fukuoka and Hokkaido represent a very different pattern of urban development. These are prefectures that displayed strong population growth throughout the prewar years and up through the 1950 to 1955 period. Since that time, however, their growth has decreased sharply. Thus, while progressives emerged in the early postwar period with substantial levels of support in these areas, their rate of expansion has been slow, consistently under the national average. This slow rate of progressive growth, then, seems to be correlated with the low rates of in-migration following 1955.

Similar kinds of differences are found in the more rural areas. Saitama and Chiba were originally largely rural prefectures that have experienced phenomenal rates of in-migration, especially since 1960.[2] As a result, the progressive vote has risen very sharply within these new urban prefectures since then, namely from 32 percent in 1960 to 45 percent in 1972. In response to the late timing of this growth, the ratio of progressive-vote increases in these prefectures compared to those in the country as a whole has climbed successively from 0.5 to 1.4 to 1.8 in the 1955-1960, 1960-1967, and 1967-1972 periods respectively. In other words, during the first of these periods (1955-1960), the combined progressive vote in these two prefectures was increasing at half the national average, while by the third period, it was expanding at nearly twice the national rate. In contrast, it appears that the rate of growth in the support for progressive parties is beginning to level off in Tokyo coinciding with a decline in the rate of population growth in that prefecture, a decline that began only after 1965. The large population increases have now shifted from Tokyo to the "suburban" prefectures of Saitama and Chiba, and as a result, in the future we might expect the greatest increases in progressive support to occur there.

If we move out one more tier from the central Tokyo metropolitan hub, we come to the more heavily rural prefectures of Ibaraki, Tochigi, Gumma, and Yamanashi. Population growth in these areas has been very low, and it appears that the spread of urban development out from the center is only just beginning to reach them. Thus the development of a viable opposition has lagged in these areas, and yet most recently the progressives have scored significant advances, especially in Ibaraki and Tochigi. Our last group of prefectures are composed of those that

[2] For instance, between 1955 and 1975 the percentage of the labor force engaged in agriculture and related primary industries dropped from 46 to 9 percent in Saitama and from 56 to 15 percent in Chiba, while the percent of the population living in cities 100,000 and over rose from 23 to 48 percent in the former and from 20 to 57 percent in the latter. Bureau of Statistics, Office of the Prime Minister, *Japan Statistical Yearbook*, 1958 and 1976 editions (Tokyo: Japan Statistical Association).

have experienced the largest rates of negative growth since 1960. Rural depopulation has finally become a reality in some areas of Japan. We hypothesize that the effect of depopulation has been to prolong the existence of the status quo as the younger and iconoclastic depart for the freer and more economically promising environment of the cities. Indeed it is in these areas that the opposition parties have experienced the most intractable resistance to their growth, remaining unable to garner even 30 percent of the vote as late as 1972.

Table 2 strongly suggests that urbanization and other related processes of change are intimately associated with the growth of a political opposition in Japan.[3] While we have used the national HR election data here to illustrate this trend, the succeeding chapters will present the corresponding prefectural and municipal election trend data to confirm that this gradual expansion of opposition strength over time is a generalized phenomenon that extends across all levels and types of elections. We have in the Japanese case, then, a singular opportunity to study the effects of the long-term processes of economic development and modernization on the increase of political competition and the rise of an opposition as an effective political force on both the national and local levels. A study of electoral trends in Japan should thus reveal some very important insights into the relationships between macrosocietal processes of demographic and political change, both on the individual (voting behavior) and institutional (party system) levels.

THE NATIONAL-LOCAL DUALITY OF POWER

While Table 1 draws our attention to the long-term continuities in the process of partisan change in Japan, Table 2 alerts us to the unevenness of this process. This uneven pattern of electoral change highlights a second important facet of political change in Japan—namely the emergence of a dual politics. In many of the largest and nationally most visible metropolitan constituencies, the LDP has for the last decade been reduced to minority status, polling less than one-third of the votes in both national and local assembly elections. In spite of the party's clear rejection by the most mobilized and articulate segment

[3] A detailed analysis of the changes associated with the urbanization process that promote higher levels of opposition voting is presented in Chapter 5. It should also be noted that there has been a persistent strain of rural radicalism in Japan dating from the prewar era, such that in certain rural areas (for instance in Nagano and more recently in parts of the Tōhoku) the Japan Communist Party has done rather well. See George O. Totten, "The People's Parliamentary Path of the Japanese Communist Party: Part I, Agrarian Policies," *Pacific Affairs* 46 (1973): 193-217.

of the Japanese mass public, however, it has been able to maintain a majority in both houses of the Diet and hence sole control of the national government.

We have, then, an emerging imbalance in the power of the progressive parties between the national and local levels. On the national level it is business as usual—continued conservative control of the government. But on the local level, the administration of prefectural and municipal governments is increasingly coming under the control of progressive chief executives. In fact, Terry MacDougall has calculated that as of 1974, over 41 percent of all Japanese lived in prefectures or cities having progressive chief executives.[4] This growth in local progressive power has been further magnified by the fact that progressive victories have been disproportionally concentrated in the industrial and cultural centers of Japan. For many urban progressive supporters, therefore, years of frustration and defeat in national level politics have recently been joined by expanding rates of success in local level elections.

There is, then, an emerging duality of political power in Japan in the form of a persisting conservative dominance on the national level and growing progressive power on the local level. This concept of a duality of power needs to be carefully qualified, however, for a close examination of election data confronts us with a strange paradox—namely, How do we explain the phenomenon of greater progressive power at the local level when the progressive parties consistently poll a higher percentage of the vote in national as opposed to local assembly elections?

The explanations for this seeming paradox are twofold. First the progressives' power on the local level is primarily derived from their success in chief executive rather than assembly elections. While the progressive parties continually draw fewer votes in local as opposed to national assembly elections, they frequently match or better their national support levels in the local chief executive elections. Thus if the local chief executives were elected by the local assemblies in a manner similar to the election of the prime minister by the Diet or, worse yet, if the local chief executives were appointed by the national government as they were in the prewar period, the asymmetry in the national-local balance of progressive strength would not have appeared.

There are several reasons for the progressives' better showing in local chief executive as opposed to local assembly elections. The most per-

[4] Terry MacDougall, "Japanese Urban Local Politics: Towards a Viable Progressive Opposition," in *Japan: The Paradox of Progress*, ed. Lewis Austin (New Haven: Yale University Press, 1976), p. 42.

suasive of these centers around the notion of election district "size" as discussed in Chapter 5 of this book. In the election of the prefectural governors and the city, town, and village mayors, the local entity as a whole serves as the election district, and its inhabitants directly elect their chief executives. In the case of the prefectural assembly elections, the prefecture is divided up into multiple districts that are coterminous with the city (*shibu*) and county (*gunbu*) administrative boundaries, with each district electing one or more members proportional to the district's population.[5] The number of fixed seats in the prefectural assemblies range from 41 to 125, with an average of about 60 members. This means that many more votes are required to gain the office of governor than to win election as a prefectural assemblyman.

In the case of the municipal assembly elections, the great majority of assembly members are elected on an at-large basis from a single city, town, or villagewide district. There are a fair number of exceptions to this general pattern: in the big cities, the administrative wards serve as election districts, and a number of other cities, particularly the amalgamated cities, have opted to establish election districts as well.[6] As in the case of the prefectural elections, however, the important variable here is the wide disparity in the number of votes necessary to elect a mayor as opposed to a municipal assemblyman. The typical city assembly averages a little under thirty-five members, and the town and village assemblies average slightly less than twenty members. Given the Japanese single-entry ballot system, the same vote that elects the prefectural and municipal chief executives respectively must be divided among a far larger number of candidates in the prefectural and municipal assembly races. The impact of this substantial difference in the number of votes required for victory on the percentage of the vote gained by the opposition parties in chief executive as opposed to assembly elections is treated in considerable detail in the discussions of areal representation and district size in Chapters 3 and 5.

Not only do the progressives poll a higher percentage of the vote on the average in chief executive as opposed to local assembly elections

[5] The county (*gun*) was actually abolished as a separate administrative level of government in 1926, but it still holds some territorial meaning. Traditionally all areas outside the cities were divided into counties that in turn were divided into towns and villages. Thus while each city constitutes one prefectural assembly district, a county area election district is composed of a number of towns and villages. For example Figure 4 in Chapter 5 gives an example of the ten towns and villages that make up one of the prefectural assembly election districts in Miyagi prefecture. See Kurt Steiner, *Local Government in Japan* (Stanford: Stanford University Press, 1965), p. 46.

[6] Ibid., pp. 378-382.

but there are also several factors associated with the "presidential" character of the chief executive elections that enhance progressive power on the local level.[7] One of the major sources of weakness within the progressive camp in Japan has been the growing fragmentation of the opposition party vote. While the assembly elections encourage competition among the progressive parties, the chief executive elections induce them to try to cooperate and concentrate their forces behind a single joint candidate. Thus the opposition may assume a stronger, more coherent expression in chief executive elections. But an even more important advantage stems from the character of these chief executive offices. The offices of governor and mayor are the only executive posts in Japan that are directly elected by the people. This fact gives the local chief executive a special personal mandate from the people to which the prime minister cannot lay claim. This populist dimension to the office provides an important added resource that is particularly advantageous for reformist chief executives and has in several instances enabled them to expand the exercise of the powers of their office beyond its legally prescribed limits.

If progressive power on the local level is largely a function of the executive type of local election, it must also be qualified by the fact that it is largely limited to urban areas. Herein we find our second explanation for the seeming paradox in the national-local duality of power. While progressive power assumes its strongest and most visible expression on the local level, in much of the countryside local government remains a conservative paradise. It must be kept in mind, therefore, that the national-local dualism is a function of Japan's urban-rural dualism—in the urban areas the progressive parties command electoral

---

[7] Not only do the larger district sizes associated with chief executive elections favor the progressive vote, but such factors as candidate image and incumbency can also potentially balloon the progressive vote in these elections far above its normal levels in the corresponding local assembly elections. As demonstrated in a number of the other studies presented in this book, the progressive parties have frequently been able to find attractive candidates with considerable popular appeal to run as mayors and governors, and candidate image seems to be a particularly important voting criterion in the chief executive type of election (see Chapter 5). Moreover incumbent local chief executives in Japan almost always draw an added measure of voting support from the occupancy of their office regardless of which political camp they are associated with. This incumbency effect can, of course, penalize progressive candidates as well, especially in a context in which the majority of chief executives are conservatives. If we control for the effects of incumbency and party coalition patterns in these elections, however, it would appear that on the whole the larger district sizes and appealing candidate images have enabled progressive candidates to do somewhat better in chief executive as opposed to local assembly elections.

majorities on both the national and local levels, while in the rural areas conservative candidates gain majorities on both election levels. Thus it was progressive pockets of strength, chiefly in metropolitan areas, that first enabled the opposition parties to gain administrative power on the local level.

By 1977, however, the electoral strength of the dominant conservative party had declined to such an extent that it had become clear that if Japan had a presidential type of system on the national level, the country would have a progressive president.[8] The implications of this statement direct our attention to the other side of Japan's duality of power—namely the fact that for roughly the last decade, the national dominance of the LDP has been artificially sustained by the electoral system. To fully understand the emergence of the national-local dual politics, therefore, we must now turn to a discussion of the basis of conservative dominance on the national level and its projected longevity. In the context of this discussion, we will introduce the major outlines of the changes in the behavior of Japanese voters that have been taking place in Japan's party system over the last two decades.

NATIONAL ELECTORAL TRENDS

There are three important factors that have contributed to the Liberal Democrats' prolonged success in national level elections. First, the electoral system has consistently overrepresented rural districts and, as was shown in Table 2, these constituencies remain to this day heavily conservative in their voting preferences.[9] Second, Table 1 shows that the LDP has enjoyed a more or less stable 5 percent cushion in the form of the independent vote. In HR elections, the independent vote is largely a disguised LDP vote. Most independents are aspiring LDP party representatives who have failed to receive official party endorse-

[8] In both the 1972 and 1976 HR elections, the four major progressive parties (the Japan Socialist Party, the Japan Communist Party, the Democratic Socialist Party, and the Clean Government Party) polled 48 percent of the vote. In both the 1974 and 1977 House of Councillors local constituency elections, these same four parties polled 55 percent of the vote. Here we see the effects of the larger district sizes that obtain in House of Councillors compared to House of Representatives elections. Given the even larger district size that would pertain to the direct election of a Japanese president—that is, the entire nation as one district electing one man—we should expect a progressive majority to potentially be even greater than it has been in recent House of Councillors elections.

[9] Rural voters are further overrepresented by the fact that they turn out to the polls at much higher rates than do urban voters. Thus even within districts with mixed urban-rural populations, the rural sections contribute a higher proportion of the actual vote relative to their proportion of the elegible voters.

45

ment. This is because the electoral system for the House of Representatives election requires that the voter cast a single nontransferable vote in a multimember constituency for a specific candidate rather than for a party. Too many candidates in a given electoral district will split a party's vote, and this can result in the defeat of all its candidates. For this reason, the number of officially recognized party candidates in each district is "rationed," and some conservative hopefuls have to run as independents. Successful independent candidates, however, are almost always welcomed into the party fold as official LDP Dietmen immediately following the election. Thus, whereas the LDP has failed to gain 50 percent of the vote in HR elections since 1963, the independent vote, in essence, kept the party above the 50 percent level up until 1976 (see Table 1).

Finally, the electoral system has served to reward the LDP with bonus Diet seats in response to the increasing fragmentation of the opposition vote. During the 1950s, Japan seemed to be moving towards a two-party system, but particularly since 1963 that trend has given way to a development towards a multiparty system. Thus the decline in the LDP vote has been matched by a decline in the vote of the leading opposition party, the Japan Socialist Party (JSP), such that the LDP's roughly two-to-one advantage over the JSP in electoral support has been mantanied throughout the 1955 to 1976 period.

The Socialists suffered their first decline with the defection of several right-wing factions that formed the Democratic Socialist Party (DSP) prior to the 1960 election. A second wave to this decline occurred in the late 1960s and the early 1970s in response to the emergence of the Buddhist Clean Government Party (CGP), the political arm of Japan's fastest growing "new religion,"[10] coupled with the impressive advance of the Japan Communist Party (JCP). This does not mean that these three minor parties have drawn their support exclusively or even largely from the JSP. A substantial portion of their electoral gains have come from former conservative voters, new voters, and from those who previously were only infrequent or nonvoters. The effect of the rise of the minor parties, however, has been to erode both the LDP's and the JSP's share of the total vote.

The fragmentation of the opposition vote is clearly apparent from Table 1. In the 1958 election, the JSP polled 92 percent of the total

[10] This "new religion," the Sōkagakkai or Value Creating Society, was actually organized in 1937 as a lay sect of Nichiren Buddhism, but it was not until after the war that the society began to increase rapidly in membership, growing from five thousand households in 1950 to over seven million households in 1970. See James W. White, *The Sokagakkai and Mass Society* (Stanford, Calif.: Stanford University Press, 1970).

opposition party vote. By 1976, its share of the opposition vote had dropped to 44 percent. The HR electoral districts are "medium sized," with all but one of the present 130 constituencies electing three to five representatives. While the system does allow a maximum potential of five parties to gain some representation on a national basis, it also serves to disproportionally reward the largest party at the expense of the small parties, particularly in the three member districts. The opposition parties are in this sense competing against themselves. In any district where an opposition party cannot achieve the necessary threshold of victory, all opposition votes cast for that party are wasted. Thus the greater the number of parties that divide the opposition vote, the more opposition votes will be wasted. The electoral system, therefore, has rewarded the conservative camp for its greater unity and conversely has penalized the progressive fragmentation with unfavorable seat-to-vote ratios for the opposition since 1958 (see Table 1).

The overrepresentation of rural areas, the cushion of votes for independents, and the fragmentation of the opposition have all helped to bolster the Liberal-Democrats' Diet strength in the face of declining electoral fortunes. For instance, in the 1969 election, the LDP gained only 48 percent of the votes but won 59 percent of the seats. Moreover, immediately following the election, twelve of the sixteen successful independents were hastily inducted into the party, raising the LDP strength to a commanding 62 percent of the seats. It would appear, therefore, that the LDP has been able to capitalize on the electoral system to artificially prolong its dominance on the national level.

The Liberal Democrats' continued control of the Diet, however, is not guaranteed. Indeed there are several reasons to believe that the growing number of progressive victories on the local level may be a harbinger of a progressive government on the national level. First, there is a limit to how far the overrepresentation of rural areas will be allowed to go. Twice now, in the mid-1960s and the mid-1970s, partial reforms have been introduced by carving out new HR districts in heavily populated metropolitan areas and thereby expanding the number of seats allotted to urban constituents. Since these changes have not been coupled with a reduction of seats in those rural constituencies that are declining in population, the additional seats have resulted in increasing the total membership of the Lower House first by nineteen seats and most recently by another twenty seats. Thus over the last decade, metropolitan districts have been awarded an additional 8 percent of the total house membership. While this does not fully compensate for the changes in the distribution of the population, it does eliminate the worst inequities.

Secondly, the closer the LDP comes to slipping below the magic 50-percent-plus-one command of Diet seats, the more attractive secession becomes to dissident internal party factions. The LDP is comprised of a loose alliance of some eight to twelve parliamentary factions based on patterns of personal loyalty and financial dependency between faction leaders and their followers rather than on policy differences. The LDP has managed to hold itself together for twenty-five years because of the realization that so long as the party commanded a majority, each faction's power aspirations (that is, each faction's desire to secure cabinet positions) could best be served by remaining within the party.

In the 1974 Upper House election, however, the LDP managed to gain only half the seats. Directly following the election, one independent joined the party, and so majority control was assured, but the margin of victory was perilously thin. It was thus perhaps only a matter of time before some dissident LDP factions would bolt the party and try their luck at establishing themselves as an independent conservative force. The first break in the dike came with the 1976 secession of six young LDP Dietmen led by Kono Yohei to form the New Liberal Club (NLC). While the NLC represented an extremely small group of junior party members with little seniority to lose, it did surprisingly well in the December 1976 HR election. Kono was able to assemble twenty-five candidates to run under the NLC banner, and while this enabled the party to enter less than one-fifth of the district races, it gained 4.2 percent of the nationwide vote and seventeen seats, thereby equaling the number of seats won by the long-established JCP. The New Liberal Club's overnight success has proven the feasibility of defecting from the LDP, and it may pave the way for more departures in the future.

For the time being, however, the LDP remains in control of the government. Although the party emerged from the 1976 election with seven fewer seats than necessary for a majority, it was again able to recruit enough independents to command a slim three-vote margin. Thus the Liberal Democrats have assured their control of the cabinet, at least until the next HR election, for it is the Lower House in Japan that elects the prime minister. Moreover, there is no guarantee that the LDP will continue to lose support at the polls. In fact, a careful analysis of Table 1 shows that the rate of transfer of votes from the conservative to progressive camps on the national aggregate level has steadily decreased from an average rate of 1.6 percent per year in the 1952-1960 period, to 1.0 percent per year for 1960-1967, to .4 percent per year for 1967-1972, and most recently dropping to an almost imperceptible

.06 percent per year for 1972-1976.[11] In other words, it appears that the recent furor over the Lockheed scandal rebounded mainly to the advantage of the New Liberal Club and that the lines between the progressive and conservative camps, at least on the national level, may be stabilizing.

Furthermore, the success of the NLC as a splinter party on the right has not, at least in the short run, encouraged other LDP defections. If anything, NLC successes appear to have stimulated further fragmentation on the Left. Thus in the 1977 House of Councillors (HC) election, three new minor parties joined the fray: the Socialist Citizens' League, created by the secession of moderate JSP faction leader Eda Saburo;[12] the United Progressive Liberals, composed largely of mass media celebrities of a leftist hue; and the Japan Women's Party, an outgrowth of the women's liberation movement. Like the NLC, these new parties have tried to capitalize on the voters' disenchantment with all the established parties and to appeal to the expanding floating vote, particularly in urban areas. For instance, in forming the Socialist Citizens' League, Eda had repeatedly stressed that the League's emphasis was to be on "citizens" rather than "socialist," and in general these new minor parties have vocally proclaimed their independence from all established ideologies.[13]

The LDP hailed the results of the 1977 HC election as a victory, but it can be viewed as such only in light of how bad the party had expected the outcome to be. The LDP won half the seats up for election, and when three successful independents were brought on board and the party's preelection strength added in, it was able to hold onto the same slim majority (127 seats) that it had attained in the preceding 1974 election. An evaluation of these results requires that we take note of the HC election system. The 252 members of the Upper House sit for six-year terms with half the membership standing for election every three years. Voters cast two ballots, one in a single nationwide constituency electing 50 seats and the other in forty-seven local constit-

[11] These figures are actually more accurate than could be computed from the information given in Table 1, as they are based on vote changes in the conservative camp (LDP + NLC + Indep.) carried to two decimal places with the intervals between elections rounded to the nearest whole year and taking into consideration the month in which each election was held.

[12] In May of 1977, Eda died suddenly prior to the HC election. However, his son, Eda Satsuki, ran in his place and, in fact, was the only Socialist Citizens' League candidate to be elected. *The Japan Times*, 12 July 1977, p. 2.

[13] "Increased Fluidity in Japanese Politics," *Japan Times Weekly*, 12 July 1977, p. 2.

uencies that are coterminous with the prefectures and elect a combined total of 76 seats.

Once again, it was the electoral system rather than the voters that came to the LDP's rescue. As in the HR election, rural voters are over-represented, and the many one- and two-member local constituencies strongly favor the conservatives.[14] Thus while the LDP won half of the seats, its voting percentages continued to decline. In the HC local constituency elections, the trend has been from a 52 percent share of the vote in 1959, to 44-45 percent shares in the mid-to-late 1960s, to 39.5 percent in 1974, and to a further very slight decline in 1977. In the HC national constituency elections, however, the LDP has polled some-what higher than these levels since 1965, due perhaps to its introduction of celebrity candidates. But in 1977 its national constituency vote dropped precipitously from 44 percent in the previous two elections to 35.8 percent.

Many commentators have interpreted the results of this election as a rejection of the Left and the Right and a move towards the Center. Indeed both the CGP and DSP made significant gains, with the JSP and especially the JCP realizing the greatest declines. The real significance of this election, however, probably lies elsewhere. Typically the bulk of Japanese voters have been tied to one of the five main parties either through personal or organizational loyalties. These attachments are what has accounted for the high levels of stability that Richardson has found in Japanese voting behavior, with low levels of fluctuation in the aggregate party vote from one election to the next. To some extent in 1976 but very clearly in 1977, we have witnessed the appearance of a new phase in the multiparty trend—the emergence of flash parties. Flash parties typically accompany periods of political instability or political transition. The appearance of a new wave of minor parties is, at least in part, a function of the impending change from a one-party dominant system to some other kind of party balance.

In addition, the appeal of these new parties for the voters clearly does reflect a widespread discontent with the established parties and a search for alternatives to the Left and the Right. Indeed the HC na-tional constituency vote suggests the emergence of a centrist third force: 36 percent voted LDP, 26 percent for the JSP or JCP on the Left,

[14] In both the Upper and Lower House elections there is about a three-to-one ratio between the number of votes necessary for victory in a number of urban and rural districts. For instance, in the 1977 HC local constituency election, over half a million votes were necessary for victory in several urban districts whereas in some rural prefectures such as Tottori only 160,000 votes was sufficient. "LDP's Relative Victory," *Japan Times Weekly*, 23 July 1977, p. 3.

while the two center parties collected 21 percent of the vote and the NLC and other minor parties an additional 10 percent. In other words, the more moderate party groupings won almost one-third of the national constituency vote.

At this juncture, however, the emergence of the flash parties heralds the advent of a new mode of electoral behavior more than it does a new political alternative. Indeed immediately following the election, the Japan Women's Party quietly folded its tent and dissolved, and by March of 1978 the Socialist Citizens' League had joined with four other dissident JSP Dietmen to form a new party, now labeled the Social Democratic League.[15] Moreover, it is doubtful that the United Progressive Liberals or even the New Liberal Club will endure for very long, at least in their present forms. What the appearance of this new wave of minor parties suggests is a substantial growth in the proportion of unattached, floating voters, particularly in large metropolitan areas, who are available for instant recruitment by new political currents and movements. What we are likely to see, therefore, is not only the rise and fall of minor flash parties but also an increased ebb and flow in the fortunes of the five established parties. Thus, for instance, in the 1972 HR election, the JCP tripled its seats, while in the 1977 HC election that same party lost roughly half of its seats that were up for reelection. As Gary Allinson describes so well in the introduction to Chapter 4, what we are seeing in Japan is the appearance of a new kind of Japanese voter who is motivated neither by traditional attachments to personalities or organizations nor by the old ideological slogans that have defined national politics throughout the postwar period.

THE DUALITY OF POLITICAL STYLES

The suggestion that not only the Japanese party system but also the behavior of Japanese voters is changing leads to a final point—namely that the concept of a dual politics in Japan has a second important dimension. We have discussed the duality of power phenomenon in some detail, noting that it has two sides: growing levels of progressive success at the local level, primarily in urban areas and in the executive type of election, and a tenacious conservative grasp of the national reigns of power that seems almost immune to the decline in the LDP vote in HR and HC elections and that, even in the face of this growing weakness at the polls, draws renewed strength from the absence of a coherent alternative to continued LDP rule at the national level. In ad-

[15] "A Post-Mortem on Chupiren," *Japan Times Weekly*, 30 January 1977, p. 12; "Former JSP Men to Form Party," *Japan Times Weekly*, 28 January 1978, p. 2.

dition to this emerging national-local duality of power, however, there is a continuing duality in political styles. This second dimension to the dual politics concept also defines the parameters of the conservative-progressive competition, but here the contrast is between the way the political game is played rather than the stage (national or local) on which it is acted.

The notion of dual political styles has several related aspects. First we find a clear distinction between the old conservative policies that have continually stressed economic growth at any cost and capital intensive public works projects and the new progressive policies that place more emphasis on welfare, environmental, and quality of life issues. Second there is the contrast between the old politics that stresses personalistic ties and the dispensing of favors and gifts to individual constituents and local community groups and the new politics that emphasizes mass organizations and movements, national issues, and media appeals. Finally, there is the distinction between what we might call the old political consciousness and the new. We find increasingly that Japanese citizens, especially in metropolitan areas, are shedding the old attitudes of deference, apathy, and parochialism and are taking a more active, participant role in political affairs through citizens' movements and other such activities.

To the extent that there is a congruence between the duality of power and the duality of style, we find conservative national governments adhering to the old politics and progressive local administrations pursuing an innovative, new politics course. A word of caution, however, is necessary to alert the reader to the fact that there is not always a one-to-one relationship between progressives, local power, and the new politics on the one hand and conservatives, national power, and the old politics on the other. We have already pointed out that although the progressives control many of the key, urban gubernatorial and mayoral posts, they are very far from holding anything like a majority of these offices. Similarly the new politics is not synonymous with progressive public officials. Indeed many progressive and conservative politicians seem to blend the old and new politics in different ways. Perhaps a more accurate metaphor would be to suggest that the Japanese electorate is composed of two galleries—a gallery of traditionals and a gallery of moderns. In general, the conservatives have been far more successful in playing to the traditionalist gallery, but some have also learned how to appeal to the modern type of voter as well. Conversely, progressive politicians have also been known to exploit traditional appeals. Nevertheless, we can say that the progressive parties have served as a vehicle for reorienting political concerns on the local level, and as a result there is an increasing difference in tone and priorities between local and national governments.

In the following three chapters of the electoral trends section, the authors analyze the causes for the rise in opposition strength at the polls and its uneven urban-rural and national-local pattern of development. Terry MacDougall's chapter focuses on the seven largest cities in Japan where the progressives have made their most impressive advances. He delineates the shifting fortunes of the various parties and the dynamics involved in these changes. Through his utilization of descriptive statistics, he illustrates the phenomenon of a national-local gap in levels of opposition voting, but he also shows that in the big cities the trend has been towards convergence. He presents several hypotheses to account for this pattern of lower levels of progressive support in local assembly elections and convergence in the urban centers. He also discusses a number of important features of the gubernatorial and mayoral elections, including the backgrounds and attributes of the candidates in big city executive elections over the last thirty years and the patterns of party coalitions in candidate endorsements.

Gary Allinson presents an engaging case study of two suburban Tokyo cities that are similar in many ways, including the fact that both have had strong progressive majorities in national elections since at least 1960. On the local level, however, the progressives dominate in only one of these two cities, while in the other we find a persistent pattern of conservative control. By employing this "most similar systems" design, he demonstrates that factors other than level of urbanization and socio-economic structure profoundly influence local electoral behavior.[16] In particular, his analysis illustrates the important role that a community's organizational infrastructure, pattern of historical development, and timing of urban growth can play in voting behavior at the local level.

In the final chapter of Part Two, I attempt to test several of the central hypotheses raised by the other chapters in the electoral trends section. In the first part of the chapter, survey data are used to investigate the demographic and attitudinal correlates of opposition voting. Support is found for each of five hypotheses that link phenomena associated with the urbanization process to increased political competition. Finally, the technique of path analysis is employed to illustrate the interaction of the five identified phenomena in stimulating higher levels of opposition voting. The remainder of the chapter is devoted to testing two hypotheses that are believed to account for the national-local gap

[16] Adam Przeworski and Henry Teune, *The Logic of Comparative Social Inquiry* (New York: Wiley-Interscience, 1970).

in levels of progressive voting. The first of these, the district size hypothesis, is raised in MacDougall's chapter, and the second, the district age hypothesis, emerges from Allinson's analysis. Several tests employing aggregate data and some supplementary survey data lend convincing support to both of these hypotheses.

CHAPTER 3

POLITICAL OPPOSITION AND BIG CITY
ELECTIONS IN JAPAN, 1947-1975

Terry Edward MacDougall

ELECTORAL politics in Japan's big cities has undergone dramatic changes in the past two decades. Conservative electoral support in the country's major urban areas—Tokyo, Yokohama, Nagoya, Kyoto, Osaka, Kobe, and KitaKyushu—has dropped from the fifty and sixty percent ranges in national and local elections up to the early sixties to a third or a quarter of the vote in the mid-1970s. Although the urban electoral decline of the conservatives has not affected the ability of the Liberal Democratic Party (LDP) to hold onto the reins of the national government, it has ended LDP and conservative independent absolute majorities in the Tokyo Metropolitan Assembly (TMA) and in the assemblies of the six "designated" large cities.[1] Also, at some point since 1963, candidates backed by the Japan Socialist Party (JSP), alone or jointly with one or more of the other opposition parties, have been directly elected as governor of Tokyo and mayor of each of the large

I would like to express my gratitude to the ACLS-SSRC Foreign Area Fellowship Program for its support under which research for this article was initiated and to the University of Virginia's Summer Grant Committee, which provided support for further research and writing. I would also like to thank Gary Allinson, Jack Lewis, and Scott Flanagan for their helpful comments on an earlier draft, and Key Kobayashi of the Orientalia Division of the Library of Congress who assisted in the location of data on big city assembly and executive elections.
[1] "Designated cities" are established by action of the National Diet in accordance with the provisions in Article 252, paragraphs 19-21 of the Local Autonomy Law. A city must have a population of at least 500,000 to be so designated. Once designated, a city forms administrative and electoral wards, carries out a number of welfare, planning, and other functions normally reserved for the prefectures, and receives similar treatment to that of the prefectures in the allocation of local bonds. Yokohama, Nagoya, Kyoto, Osaka, and Kobe have been designated cities throughout the period of this study. KitaKyushu was designated in 1962 after its formation out of a number of smaller cities. Sapporo, Kawasaki, and Fukuoka were added in the autumn of 1971. "Big city" will be used to refer to both the designated cities and Tokyo Metropolis, which in fact has the status of prefecture and includes cities, towns, and villages as well as the twenty-three wards from the old city of Tokyo.

cities. Today, among these seven extremely important urban local governments, only KitaKyushu is without a progressive executive head. Electoral success, which has eluded the opposition parties at all levels of government throughout the postwar years, appears at last to have been attained in the major urban areas.[2]

My primary aim in this chapter is to present documentation on the electoral fortunes of opposition parties and candidates in local assembly and local executive elections in Japanese big cities from 1947 to 1975. For this purpose, I have compiled virtually complete data on postwar elections to the TMA and governorship, large city assemblies and mayorships, and House of Representatives (HR) seats in the same areas. For comparison and in order to put the electoral developments within the big cities into the context of national patterns and trends, less complete supplementary data will be used for other prefectural and city elections throughout the country. I shall also present a number of hypotheses to try to account for big city electoral patterns and trends and for some of their similarities to and differences from those in the remainder of the country. Later chapters in this volume will present more detailed evidence that can serve as a basis for rejecting, revising, or maintaining these hypotheses. One question guides the present inquiry: Is the current appearance of opposition success in the big cities solidly based and likely to be a permanent phenomenon?[3]

PREFECTURAL AND CITY ASSEMBLY ELECTIONS

Japanese local politics is often described as a "conservative paradise." Although less apt today than it was a decade or more ago, this catch-phrase still has some basis in fact. In the 1975 local elections, conservative candidates for Japan's forty-seven prefectural assemblies received close to 60 percent of the vote and 63 percent of the seats (see Table 1). Independents predominate in city, town, and village assemblies;

[2] Throughout this chapter, "conservative" will be used to refer to the Liberal Democratic Party and to local independent candidates who share a similar political orientation (if not formal affiliation) with the LDP, and "progressive" will be used to refer to all four of the opposition parties, to the labor unions that support them, and to the local independent candidates backed by them. A distinction will at times be made between the "left-progressives" (Japan Socialist Party and Japan Communist Party) and the "moderate-progressives" or "Center" parties (Clean Government Party and Democratic Socialist Party).

[3] I shall not be concerned in this chapter with the substantive differences between progressives and conservatives. For details on that aspect of progressive local government, see later chapters in this volume and also my study, *Localism and Political Opposition in Japan* (New Haven: Yale University Press, forthcoming).

Table 1

Percent Distribution of Prefectural and
City Assembly Seats, 1975

	Prefectures[a]	Designated Cities[b]	Other Cities[c]
LDP	52.6	31.7	9.0
Independents	14.3	10.0	63.2
Conservative	(10.5)	(8.8)	
Neutral	(1.9)	(0.3)	
Progressive	(1.9)	(0.9)	
Others	1.8	0.0	0.3
DSP	3.7	9.9	2.6
CGP	7.1	18.3	8.3
JSP	16.1	16.6	10.1
JCP	4.4	13.5	6.5
Total percent	100.0	100.0	100.0
Total seats	2,864	650	20,086

[a] These figures include the 1972 Okinawa, 1973 Tokyo, and 1974 Saitama prefectural assembly elections, vacant Tokyo Metropolitan Assembly seats filled in April 1975, and April 1975 elections for all other prefectural assemblies.
[b] Included are the results of the 1973 KitaKyushu City Assembly election and those for all other designated cities in April 1975. The other cities are Sapporo, Kawasaki, Yokohama, Nagoya, Kyoto, Osaka, Kobe, and Fukuoka.
[c] These figures include April 1975 elections for 390 cities, elections earlier in 1975 for 19 cities, and the distribution of seats for 234 other cities as of the end of 1974. The total number of cities, excluding designated cities, is 634.
SOURCES: *Mainichi shinbun*, 15 April 1975 and 2 May 1975; *Asahi shinbun*, 30 April 1975.

most of them are conservative in orientation, if not of formal affiliation. LDP and independent candidates held a combined total of 71 percent of city assembly seats throughout the country in 1975. Conservative independents are even more dominant in town and village assemblies.

Viewed in a national perspective, the persistence of conservative electoral success is extremely impressive at all levels of government. In the House of Representatives, the LDP still maintains an absolute majority.[4] Only seven of the forty-seven prefectural assemblies—Tokyo, Kanagawa, Nagano, Kyoto, Osaka, Fukuoka, and Okinawa—are without majorities of LDP and conservative independent members, and even in these the LDP is the largest party. Most city, town, and village assemblies also have conservative or nonpartisan majorities.

But the exceptions to this picture of conservative dominance are im-

[4] This majority, however, was reduced to a razor thin advantage in HR elections in December 1976 as a result of LDP intraparty conflict, the Lockheed scandals, and the addition of twenty new seats in the metropolitan areas.

portant ones. They include the seven prefectures named above, all designated cities, an increasing number of suburban and satellite cities in the Tokyo and Osaka metropolitan areas, some medium-sized regional cities, and, less importantly, several small mining cities. In all of these assemblies, conservative absolute majorities have been replaced by a more fluid situation in which no single party or political tendency dominates.

In this chapter I shall concentrate on these exceptions, particularly Tokyo Metropolis and the designated cities of Yokohama, Nagoya, Kyoto, Osaka, Kobe, and KitaKyushu. These big cities are important in their own right; they account for slightly over one-fifth of the country's population and for far greater concentrations of its productive capacity and financial, administrative, and cultural assets. Tokyo, the nation's capital, is particularly important because of its media exposure and its role as a pace setter for the country. The political significance of the loss of conservative majorities in big city assemblies has been magnified by the direct election of progressive executive heads for each of these local governments. Big city progressive governments are new and conspicuous symbols of the long-term conservative electoral decline and a possible base of operation for the opposition to challenge conservative local and national political dominance and policy priorities.

Characteristics of Big City Assembly and HR Elections

Five characteristics of big city assembly and HR elections are of particular interest to us: (1) conservatives have traditionally been considerably stronger in local assembly than in HR elections in these areas, the opposite being the case for the progressives; (2) support for conservative candidates in big city assembly elections has dropped sharply since 1959 and moved towards convergence with the (more slowly declining) level of support conservatives receive in HR elections in the same areas; (3) JSP support in HR elections has declined to the point of convergence with its level of support in big city assembly elections; (4) since the mid-1960s, the Japan Communist Party (JCP) has grown rapidly and fairly steadily in both national and local elections, and it has surpassed the JSP in votes or assembly representation in some of the big cities; and (5) the Clean Government Party (CGP), whose support grew even more rapidly than that of the JCP in the 1960s, has become overall the largest opposition party in the big city assemblies. Each of these points merits some elaboration.

Conservative support since 1947 has always been higher in local than in national elections. Figure 1 illustrates that nationwide it has been consistently close to ten percentage points higher in prefectural assembly than in HR elections.[5] Nationally, there is no sign that this difference in rate of conservative support by kind of election is diminishing. The situation is otherwise in the big cities, where the difference by kind of election has been greatly reduced over the postwar years. For example, conservatives received 71 percent of the vote in the big city assembly elections of 1947 but only 52 percent of the HR vote in the same areas—a difference of 18 percent. Even as late as 1959-1960, the difference was still 18 percent. But it was reduced to only 5 percent in recent big city assembly and HR elections, when the conservative vote fell to 37 and 32 percent respectively (see Table 2). The same kind of changes can be found in the individual cities.

Extremely sharp declines in the conservative share of the big city assembly vote since 1959 account for this convergence of rates of conservative support by kind of election. These changes can be viewed in greater detail in Table 3, which presents complete postwar data on the Tokyo Metropolitan Assembly elections and is fairly typical of the pattern found in all of the big cities.[6] The greatest decline in conservative support occurred between 1959 and 1963 with the appearance of the CGP and the separation of the Democratic Socialist Party (DSP) from the JSP. These moderate-progressives (or center) parties also cut into the left-progressive vote in 1963. But whereas the Left resumed its upward momentum in subsequent elections, the conservatives continued to decline. As shown in Table 2, conservative support in HR elections also dropped sharply between 1960 and 1972—from 46 to 32 percent. However, the rate of conservative electoral decline in big city elections has been greater at the local than the national level, resulting in the pattern of convergence previously noted.

Support for the Left in big city HR elections has been relatively high since 1947, when the combined JSP-JCP vote was 44 percent. That year the two parties polled an average of only 27 percent of the vote in assembly elections in the same districts—a difference of 17 percent (see Table 2). Since the emergence of the center parties in the early 1960s, however, the leftist vote, like that of the conservatives, has converged. By the early 1970s, the leftist vote in the assembly and HR elections averaged 38 and 40 percent respectively.

Convergence in the case of the left is largely a result of its slow and

[5] The difference would be far greater if city elections were compared with HR elections, but because so many of the candidates in the former run as independents, the data would not be entirely comparable.

[6] Tokyo is atypical only in the extreme weakness of the Democratic Socialist Party, which does somewhat better in all the other big cities.

Figure 1

House of Representatives and Prefectural Assembly Elections [a]

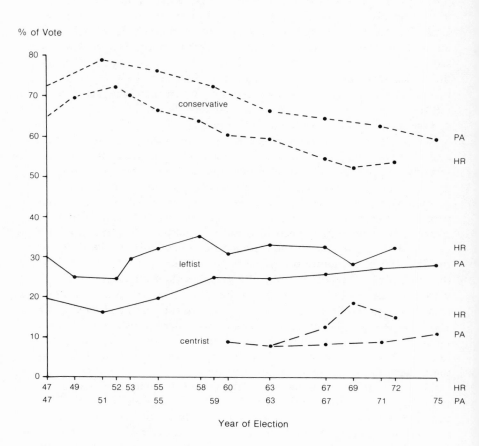

% of Vote

Year of Election

NOTE: "Conservative" includes the LDP, its pre-1955 predecessors, and independents; this slightly overestimates conservative strength, since a few progressive independents are included. "Leftist" refers to the JSP and JCP. "Centrist" refers to the DSP and CGP. PA stands for Prefectural Assembly. HR stands for House of Representatives.

SOURCES: PA elections: *Asahi shinbun* and *Mainichi shinbun*, selected issues, 1947-1975. HR elections: Kōmei Senkyo Renmei, *Shūgiin giin senkyo no jisseki: Dai-ikkai-dai-sanjukkai* (Tōkyō Senkyo Renmei, 1967) and *Asahi shinbun*, selected issues, 1967-1972.

Table 2

Party Support in Selected Big City Assembly and HR Elections, 1947-1975
(percentage of vote by party)

	1947[a] Assem.	1947 HR	1959 Assem.	1960 HR	1963 Assem.	1963 HR	1975 Assem.	1972[b] HR
LDP[c]	54	47	50	45	43	41	32	28
Independents	17	5	14	1	8	2	5	4
Conservative Total	(71)	(52)	(64)	(46)	(51)	(43)	(37)	(32)
DSP	—	—	—	13	9	14	8	11
CGP	—	—	—	—	10	—	17	16
Center Total	—	—	—	(13)	(19)	(14)	(25)	(27)
JSP	24	37	30	33	24	34	20	20
JCP	3	7	4	7	5	9	18	20
Left Total	(27)	(44)	(34)	(40)	(29)	(43)	(38)	(40)
Other	2	4	1	—	1	—	—	—
Total[d]	100	100	99	99	100	100	100	99

NOTE: The Big City Assemblies include the Tokyo Metropolitan (Prefectural) Assembly and those of the following designated cities: Yokohama, Nagoya, Kyoto, Osaka, and Kobe.

[a] No data could be located for the 1947 Kobe City Assembly election; 1951 data are substituted.

[b] In 1972, the JCP did not run a party endorsed candidate in Nagoya but supported Tanaka Michiko, an independent who joined the party only after her election. Votes for Tanaka are included under the JCP's total and not under the total for independents.

[c] The LDP was formed in 1955 out of previously existing conservative parties; 1947 data refer to these parties.

[d] Rounding error makes some columns add up to less than 100 percent.

SOURCES: Kōmei Senkyo Renmei, Shūgiin giin senkyo no jisseki: Dai-ikkai-dai-sanjukkai (Tōkyō: Kōmei Senkyo Renmei, 1967); Shūgiin jimu-kyoku, Dai-33-kai shūgiin giin sōsenkyo ikkan (Tōkyō: Okurashō, 1973); and Asahi shinbun.

Table 3

Tokyo Metropolitan Assembly Elections 1947-1973
(percentage of vote by party)

	1947	1951	1955	1959	1963	1965	1969	1973
LDP	55	56	55	54	48	30	33	34
Independents[a]	12	20	16	13	3	10	6	4
Conservative Total	(67)	(76)	(71)	(67)	(51)	(40)	(39)	(38)
DSP	—	—	—	—	5	7	5	4
CGP	—	—	—	—	11	13	17	18
Center Total	—	—	—	—	(16)	(20)	(22)	(22)
JSP	26	21	25	30	28	28	24	20
JCP	4	2	3	3	4	10	14	20
Left Total	(30)	(23)	(28)	(33)	(32)	(38)	(38)	(40)
Others[b]	3	1	1	—	—	2	—	—
Total[b]	100	100	100	100	99	100	99	100

NOTE: The LDP was formed in late 1955 out of previously existing conservative parties; 1947-1955 LDP data refer to those parties. Similarly, the Socialists underwent a series of splits and reorganizations, but all their votes are included under the JSP. The CGP was established in 1964, but it was preceded by the Clean Government Association, which ran candidates in the 1963 election. These are included under the CGP.
[a] Almost all the independent vote went to conservatives, but in a couple of elections some progressive independents or neutral candidates received a small part of it. Conservative strength is only slightly overestimated by including all independent vote in that category.
[b] Rounding of percentages makes some of the columns add up to slightly more or less than 100 percent.
SOURCES: *Asahi shinbun* and *Mainichi shinbun*, selected issues, 1947-1973.

intermittent growth in support in local elections combined with major setbacks for the JSP in HR elections. The JSP received the major share of the increased leftist vote in the 1955 and 1959 local elections, but since the late 1960s, leftist gains in local elections have been almost entirely by the JCP.

Today the JSP and JCP nearly equally divide the leftist vote in big city assembly and HR elections (see Tables 2 and 4). Between 1963 and 1975, the JCP vote approached or surpassed that of the JSP in Tokyo, Kyoto, Osaka, Kobe, and KitaKyushu assembly elections. During the same period, its assembly seats in the seven big cities in Table 4 increased from 22 to 92 while those of the JSP declined from 120 to 93. The shifting fortunes of these two left-progressive parties in local assembly elections parallel those found at the HR level. In the nationwide prefectural assembly and HR elections, a similar shift of lower magnitude has occurred, giving the JCP about one-third of the leftist vote.

Table 4

JSP and JCP Support in Big City Assemblies
(percentage of vote and number of seats)

	JSP				JCP			
	1963		1975		1963		1975	
	Vote	*Seats*	*Vote*	*Seats*	*Vote*	*Seats*	*Vote*	*Seats*
Tokyo[a]	27.8	32	20.5	20	4.5	2	20.2	24
Yokohama	19.1	16	23.9	19	3.3	0	12.3	11
Nagoya	24.6	22	23.2	17	3.9	0	9.2	5
Kyoto	19.1	13	15.9	8	12.5	8	23.5	20
Osaka	16.7	12	13.5	9	8.5	5	19.2	15
Kobe	21.8	16	16.4	10	4.2	1	13.8	10
KitaKyushu[b]	17.0	9	14.6	10	7.3	6	15.5	7

NOTE: The total number of assembly seats increased between the two elections from 120 to 125 in Tokyo, 72 to 88 in Yokohama, 68 to 72 in Kyoto, and 85 to 94 in Osaka. It remained constant at 76 in Nagoya, 68 in Kyoto, and 64 in KitaKyushu.
[a] Tokyo elections were in 1963 and 1973.
[b] KitaKyushu elections were in 1965 and 1973.
SOURCES: *Asahi shinbun* and *Mainichi shinbun* selected issues, 1963-1975.

The long-term growth in leftist support in local elections has been interrupted by two major setbacks: in 1951, following the Socialists' disappointing experience in national coalition government, the red purge and the outbreak of the Korean War; and in 1963, the emergence of the centrist parties. Also in 1975, continued advance by the CGP and a fairly strong performance by the conservatives slowed or reversed the Left's most recent growth in support.

Particularly in the big cities, the CGP has played a pivotal role in the movement towards national-local vote convergence for both the Left and the Right. Although it has drawn support away from both sides in the big city assembly and HR elections, it cut relatively more deeply into the bloated LDP-conservative independent vote in local assembly elections and, to a lesser extent, into the always sizable leftist vote in HR elections.[7] Indeed, the emergence of a center in big city politics may be one of the most important, although little explored, developments in the past decade.

In 1963, the DSP and the Clean Government Association (forerunner of the CGP) made their first appearance in the big city assembly elections capturing 9.1 and 9.9 percent of the vote respectively. Since then, the DSP has had mixed fortunes, declining in Tokyo, Yokohama, Kyoto, and Osaka and increasing in Nagoya, Kobe, and Kita-Kyushu. The CGP however, has made steady advances in all these cities. In the last big city assembly elections, it averaged nearly 18 percent of the vote, with a high of 21 percent in Osaka. Even in Kita-Kyushu and the three newer large cities in Sapporo, Kawasaki, and Fukuoka, it received only slightly smaller shares of the vote. Its total number of assembly seats in these ten big cities is larger than that of either the JSP, JCP, or DSP (see Table 1).

Like the JCP and DSP, the CGP has its strongest base of support in the big cities. Of the three, the DSP is the one most limited to specific pockets of strength. The CGP has considerable support in the urban prefectures and many regional cities, but it has not grown as rapidly or as evenly outside the big cities as has the JCP.

The appearance of the CGP, the Socialist split, and the growth of the JCP have resulted in the emergence of a national multiparty system and, in some areas, local multiparty systems. The impact on national politics so far has been to fragment the opposition rather than to wrest the reins of government away from the conservatives. In the big cities, however, the growth of a Center has cut deeply into conservative strength and has also impeded the possible development of a leftist majority. Nationally, if the long-term decline of the LDP in HR elections continues, an accommodation among some of the parties and a

---

[7] Although these changes in party preferences have never been adequately explored, they are apparent in Table 2. In the 1970s, the Fair Election League has done some good studies of more recent changes. See, for example, Kōmei Senkyo Renmei, *Seiji ishiki ni kansuru chōsa hōkokusho, 1972* (Tōkyō: Kōmei Senkyo Renmei, 1972), pp. 77-97.

coalition government would seem to be inevitable. In the big cities a similar, although not identical, situation now prevails. Interparty accommodations are necessary to get some items of legislation through big city assemblies and to avoid immobility. In these assemblies, the CGP and the DSP—in most cases, the CGP alone—have enough seats to swing the vote in a conservative or leftist direction. Under these conditions one might expect the DSP and CGP to be courted by both the Right and the Left for support within the assemblies and in the executive elections.

Explaining the Character of Big City Assembly Elections

At least four factors have contributed to the early weakness of the Left in urban local politics: (1) a prewar legacy that impeded grass roots organization; (2) the Left's lack of interest in local politics; (3) the principle of nonpartisanship in local politics; and (4) the electoral systems for local assemblies.

The prewar legacy is detailed in George Totten's study of the Japanese social democratic movement.[8] The urban male labor force with stable industrial employment was small in size and scattered among numerous small-scale industries; these circumstances made unionization difficult. An appeal to class consciousness conflicted with strong local loyalties and the dominant value of social harmony. Police surveillance of the labor and socialist movements was constant; oppression was intermittent. Also, both the labor and socialist movements that did develop showed far greater interest in national than in local politics, since only the former provided the authority and power to resolve the questions—including the legal status of labor—with which they were concerned. As in the postwar period, prewar proletarian parties consistently received a higher share of the vote in national elections than at the local level.

Despite the rapid organization of labor unions in the immediate postwar years, the JSP failed to bring large numbers of workers or others into a party organization. Seldom has the JSP had as many as 50,000 members, and only a fraction of those have been committed activists. Local branches have remained skeletal organizations with intermittent activities. Unions could be mobilized, but, as in the prewar years, this was easier in national politics, which labor has identified as the more relevant site for its political activities. To the Left, even questions of

[8] George O. Totten, *The Social Democratic Movement in Prewar Japan* (New Haven: Yale University Press, 1966), especially pp. 3-15. This paragraph is based largely on Totten's description.

local autonomy tended to call for national political struggles rather than local ones, since the perceived threat came more from the moves of the conservative national government to recentralize police, education, and other functions than from local abuses of them. Almost all Socialists felt that their limited resources should be concentrated on national politics in order to defend and, it was hoped, to enlarge the opposition's one-third share of HR seats needed to prevent conservative revision of the postwar constitutional system.

Possibly the strongest appeal of the JSP was in terms of its defense of the new democratic political system; in this role it could elicit support in national politics. Without strong grass-roots party or candidate organization, however, the JSP tended to be removed from the concerns of local politics, which have traditionally centered on concrete benefits—a new school, road, bridge, or the like—for the community. In effect, local politics was abandoned to the conservatives who had long been entrenched in positions of community leadership and had the additional advantage of close contacts with the party in power.

A principle of nonpartisanship has pervaded local politics in most areas of the country. In part, this reflects the kind of center-periphery gap in speed and level of politicization found in West European countries that was, perhaps, aggravated in the Japanese case because of the skeletal nature of local party organization.[9] In addition, tight community organization and a value system that supports group cooperative activity provide positive incentives for communities to seek local political representation without regard to partisan differences that might divide members in national politics. *Areal representation*, in which a candidate runs for election with the explicit backing of one or more communities on the understanding that he will uphold their interests in the local assembly, therefore, has had a strong appeal. Although it is far more complex today than it once was, voter mobilization based on an appeal to areal representation still functions through recommendations of a candidate by community associations (which are ubiquitous) or through his close identification with community interests.[10]

[9] Stein Rokkan, "Electoral Mobilization, Party Competition, and National Development," in *Political Parties and Political Development*, ed. Joseph LaPalombara and Myron Weiner (Princeton: Princeton University Press, 1966), pp. 241-265.

[10] For a study of rural political behavior in which areal representation is a central feature, see Richard H. Beardsley, John W. Hall, and Robert E. Ward, *Village Japan* (Chicago: The University of Chicago Press, 1959), pp. 349-397. For a recent study of urban communities, community associations, and association heads that includes their political functions, see Tōkyō Shisei Chōsa kai, *Tōkyō ni okeru chiiki shakai soshiki* (Tōkyō: Tōkyō Shisei Chōsa kai, 1971). For a national survey

A major alternative or supplement to areal representation, necessitated by the amalgamations of towns and villages and the increasing diversity of urban neighborhoods, is the *individual candidate support group (kōenkai)*.[11] People are drawn into such a group on the basis of areal, family, business, occupational, educational, and other particularistic ties with the candidate or with someone close to him. Members may benefit from vicarious participation in the candidate's career, his concern for the members' well-being (expressed through cards and gifts), group activities, and, for the areal groups, community representation in the assembly.

Conservative local politicians have been very successful in using these means of mobilizing electoral support without resort to the LDP label. Their strength as local politicians does not depend on the LDP so much as on the trust that they can inspire in the voters and the impression that they will work for community benefits. Persons well-known through community association, fire squad, and other local leadership roles need not appeal to partisan slogans or causes in order to mobilize support for themselves or others. Although such local leadership roles are not closed to progressives, they have been dominated by the conservatives. In short, the dominant modes of local political representation and voter mobilization, built on the nonpartisan principle, militated against a strong progressive presence in local assemblies.[12]

The electoral systems for city, town, and village assemblies help perpetuate the preceding kind of particularistic and nonpartisan local politics. In almost all municipal assembly elections, with the exceptions of those in the large cities and a few medium-sized cities that have adopted district systems by local ordinances, candidates run on an at-large basis rather than from specific districts. All candidates must com-

---

of the political role of community associations, see Kōmei Senkyo Renmei, *Dai-7-kai tōitsu chihō senkyo to yūkensha II* (Tōkyō: Kōmei Senkyo Renmei, 1972), pp. 182-189.

[11] See Gerald L. Curtis, *Election Campaigning: Japanese Style* (New York: Columbia University Press, 1971); Bradley M. Richardson, "Japanese Local Politics: Support Mobilization and Leadership Styles," *Asian Survey* 7 (1967): 860-875; and observations in this article concerning the 1971 local elections in the Tokyo metropolitan area.

[12] For a more detailed description of modes of voter mobilization and political representation in Japanese local politics, see the following two chapters in this volume by Allinson and Flanagan. For an earlier discussion of nonpartisanship, particularistic contacts between candidates and voters and how these practices work to the advantage of the conservatives in local level elections, see Scott C. Flanagan, "Voting Behavior in Japan: The Persistence of Traditional Patterns," *Comparative Political Studies* 1 (1968): 399-410.

pete with each other, since there are no lists and each voter has a single-entry ballot. A strong candidate can therefore draw support away from a weaker one of the same party causing him to be defeated. Independent candidates running with the backing of specific communities or their own support groups do not face this difficulty: Since these mechanisms are effective for electing conservative candidates, it is generally not necessary for them to seek an LDP endorsement or for the LDP to offer one. In contrast, fewer progressive candidates have the advantage of community recommendations or their own support groups. Thus they are more likely to run with a party endorsement and thus to become vulnerable to the bias of the system.

Areal representation and individual candidate support groups depend on intense and particularistic contacts between a candidate and his backers. The at-large kind of electoral system facilitates these modes of voter mobilization by keeping the threshold for success low. Under this type of system, the locally prominent candidate can physically and financially maintain close personal contact with enough persons to assure his election without resort to a party label. Indeed, the party label could be a hindrance, particularly if the candidate's campaign is based on a promise of areal representation, since he will have to appeal across the conservative-progressive division.[13]

The electoral system for large city assemblies (and prefectural assemblies) is similar to that for the HR, but with a far lower threshold of votes needed for election.[14] The large cities have a number of multimember districts corresponding to their administrative wards. A voter casts his single vote for a given candidate, not a list. A larger number of votes is needed for election from a district in a large city than is the case in other cities. For example, in Yokohama's eleven-member Tsurumi Ward district—containing approximately 200,000 people—a candidate needed at least 6,054 votes to be elected to the city assembly in 1967, four times the number needed in the case of Hachioji City, which also had a population of 200,000.

Particularistic and nonpartisan politics, which favor the conservatives, may be more difficult, although not impossible, to maintain when so

[13] For a similar argument concerning the impact of a multimember district, multiple plurality system on the appeal of candidates, see Lester Seligman, "Oregon Politics: The Eve of the Campaign," in *A State Chooses Its Lawmakers*, ed. Lester Seligman et al. (Chicago: Rand McNally, n.d.), pp. 46-47.

[14] The number of city assembly seats to be filled by a district of a designated city varies considerably. Sometimes it approaches the three-to-five level of HR districts but at other times it is well over ten. The designated city district is really intermediate between the HR and city assembly in this respect.

many votes are necessary for election. Under these circumstances, candidates may begin to see an advantage in using a party label to reach and to appeal to the larger number of voters that they would have to attract in order to win. Thus, the kind of electoral system may provide a partial explanation of why the large cities are far more politicized —that is, with fewer independents elected to the assemblies—than other cities and why progressive candidates have done better there than elsewhere. The fact that politicization has proceded least rapidly in large cities such as KitaKyushu and Fukuoka where the number of persons elected from each district is highest and the threshold for election lowest is supportive of this line of reasoning.

But even the higher thresholds needed to be elected to assemblies in large cities like Osaka are far lower than those needed for election to the HR. This may account in part for the continued, although diminished, use of traditional methods of voter mobilization in local elections even in the big cities, in contrast to the development of newer forms of candidate support groups, media campaigns, and other methods of mobilization for HR elections. Candidates for national office, of course, generally have better access than do local politicians to the resources of funds and connections necessary to develop these alternative modes of mobilization.[15]

I would contend, then, that the kind of electoral system is a crucial intervening variable in shaping the style of local politics, making it relatively easy to continue nonpartisan and particularistic politics outside the big cities. If this hypothesis is correct, we should not expect progressive majorities in local assemblies just because the progressive parties receive large majorities of the vote in prefectural or national elections in any given area or because a progressive is elected as mayor.

Conservative electoral decline in big cities. Conservative electoral decline in Japanese big cities is closely related to the rapid economic growth that has transformed these areas since the late 1950s. Elsewhere I have shown in an analysis based on aggregate data that greater degrees of industrialization, community instability, and population concentration in Japanese cities are positively correlated with the vote for the opposition parties as a whole.[16] In a later chapter in this volume, Scott

15 The great importance of this difference in available resources for local and national candidates as a factor in the continued use by the former of more traditional modes of voter mobilization was suggested to me by Jack Lewis based on his observations in Mishima City.

16 These relationships held at significant levels even when each of the variables was controlled for the others. See Terry Edward MacDougall, "Political Opposi-

Flanagan finds a similar relationship between the socio-economic changes characteristic of economic growth and the erosion of conservative support using survey data. In effect, economic growth has contributed to the conservative electoral decline in the urban areas by weakening a crucial basis of conservative support—the solidarity of local communities—and by creating new problems for the cities that cannot be handled adequately through the old pattern of areal representation.[17]

Survey data reported in Table 5 reveal the impact of new urban problems on altering the public policy priorities of Tokyo residents. Between 1958 and 1972, the problems of road improvement, unemployment, and provision of educational facilities have declined in salience. In contrast, traffic, consumer, and pollution problems have newly emerged, and social welfare concerns have reemerged. Most of the problems that have diminished in salience are ones that are amenable to solution through the particularistic kind of representation characteristic of a conservative style in local politics—bringing special benefits to a community. Those that have become more salient are structural problems in the society and economy that cannot be solved simply by enlarging and dividing the pie.

The conservative electoral decline in the urban areas, especially the big cities, may in part be explained as a reaction against the conservative government's one-sided emphasis on economic growth and as a search for alternative answers to the new problems that have arisen as a result of that growth. Whether the emergence of new issues and the questioning of old policies have changed the political consciousness of urban residents in any fundamental ways and whether conservatives or progressives are providing appropriate answers to the new problems are questions addressed in later chapters of this volume.

Growth of the CGP and JCP. Organization has been a crucial variable in the advances made in urban areas by the CGP and JCP. Sōkagakkai, the lay association of Nichiren Shōshū Buddhism, grew phenomenally in Japanese cities in the 1950s and 1960s to over six million households by appealing to those who were relatively left out in Japan's

---

tion and Local Government in Japan: The Significance of Emerging Progressive Local Leadership" (unpublished dissertation, Yale University, 1975), pp. 122-173. Hereafter cited as MacDougall, *Dissertation*.

[17] Allinson's chapter in this volume delineates the principal socio-economic changes in urban areas that have tended to weaken community solidarity, including the extension of transportation networks into formerly isolated areas, increased residential mobility, and the influx of young white-collar workers.

Table 5

Public Policy Issues of Concern to Tokyo Residents
(by percentage of respondents)

	1958	1965	1972
Road improvement	35	15	7
Unemployment	21	1	n[a]
Educational facilites	18	2	n
Housing	17	25	16
Sewer construction	13	9	8
Traffic policy	—[b]	11	12
Consumer policy	—	11	12
Social welfare	12	2	13
Public hazards (pollution)	—	1	15
Others	73	40	17
Total	189	118	100

NOTE: Only the top five named issues in either of the years are included in this table; their frequency of citation for the other two years is also given. In 1958, respondents were asked to name two issues; in 1965, one or two; and in 1972, one.
[a] Data were available for only the top seven issues.
[b] This item was not listed in 1958.
SOURCES: For 1958-1969: Tōkyōto, *Tosei seiron chōsa* (Tōkyō: Tōkyōto, 1958-1969). For 1970-1972: Tokyo Metropolitan Government, *Tokyo Municipal News* 23, no. 3 (April 1973).

rush toward prosperity, especially to new migrants to the cities and to older residents employed in smaller enterprises.[18] As an outgrowth of the political arm of Sōkagakkai, the CGP therefore has both a strong grass-roots organization in Sōkagakkai and a natural concern for urban problems. By the late 1960s, the JCP also emerged as a significant force in urban politics. It enhanced its acceptibility at that time by its moves toward gaining independence from both the Soviet Union and China, criticism of student violence, professions of a desire to work within the parliamentary sysem, and scrupulous attention to such problems as day care centers and welfare facilities.

These two parties have adopted similar electoral tactics: when weak, avoid intraparty competition by placing only a single candidate in a district; when running more than a single candidate in a district, divide the district or city territorially among the party candidates and have each candidate restrict his or her campaigning to an assigned area— for example, by placing posters and operating a sound truck only

[18] On Sōkagakkai, see particularly James W. White, *The Sōkagakkai and Mass Society* (Stanford: Stanford University Press, 1970).

71

within the allotted territory. The tactics of the two parties diverge insofar as the CGP tends to place candidates only in those cities or districts where they are almost certain of victory, whereas the JCP runs candidates in many areas where they have no hope of immediate success. In this manner, the CGP has put a higher premium on creating the impression of being a winner even within a limited area, while the JCP has been more concerned with the constant demands of building party organization throughout the country.

Since CGP votes come in large numbers from Sōkagakkai members, the latter's meetings and activities offer opportunities beyond the formal campaign to learn which candidate to support. In addition, the CGP's mass base in Sōkagakkai and its daily contacts with the electorate through numerous CGP complaint and consultation centers give it the necessary grass-roots contact to make an accurate assessment of its level and distribution of support. For the JCP, similar functions are performed through the daily activities of its 300,000 member party organization, other more loosely related groups, and its mass circulation newspaper, *Akahata (Red Flag)*.[19] Strong organizations have enabled these parties to make better assessments of the levels and distribution of their support than the JSP and LDP. Consequently, they have experienced fewer cases of their candidates' defeating each other.

Organizational strength, improved public images, and close attention to urban problems have been the bases of CGP and JCP growth. That growth, however, is not without its limits. Sōkagakkai growth has slowed or even levelled off, and the CGP is faced with the difficult task of appealing for support beyond this assured base. Unlike the Communist parties of Italy and France, the JCP is still far weaker than the Socialists among the labor unionists. Also, much of the JCP vote seems to be based on disillusionment with the established LDP and JSP rather than on agreement with communist ideology. Some of it may flow back to the Socialists if the JCP gets closer to actual governmental power.

Changes in Big City Assembly Elections

Three changes in big city assembly elections stand out in the preceding analysis: the degree of politicization, the growth in opposition electoral support, and the convergence in a party's level of support between assembly and HR elections.

[19] For details on the membership, finances, and party organs of the various parties, see *Seiji handobukku* (Tōkyō: Seiji Kōhō Sentā, 1975).

Big city assembly elections today are far more politicized—measured by the percentage of vote going to party candidates—than are similar contests in other cities. Independents receive only 5 percent of the vote in Tokyo, Yokohama, Nagoya, Kyoto, Osaka, and Kobe assembly elections, 15 percent in Sapporo and Kawasaki, and 30 percent in Kita-Kyushu and Fukuoka. By comparison, in prefectural assembly elections, nationwide independents still receive over 15 percent of the vote, while in small- and medium-sized city assembly elections they continue to receive a *majority* of votes and seats.

A relatively high level of politicization has existed for the big city assemblies since 1947 when independents received only 17 percent of the vote (see Table 2). In the 1950s, this percentage increased in some of the cities but decreased in others. The first uniform and sharp drop in the share of independent vote occurred in 1963 when the big city assembly average was only 8.3 percent. That year the LDP greatly increased its number of endorsements of assembly candidates in response to advances made by the Left in 1955 and 1959 and, even more importantly, to the challenge from the Center. For the first time, conservative independents found themselves in competition with moderate candidates from the CGP and DSP who might cut into the conservative electoral base more easily than leftist candidates. Their response was to take refuge in the LDP label.

Thus, there are two principal reasons for the high level of politicization of big city assembly elections and for the virtual elimination of significant independent candidacies by the mid-1960s: the kind of electoral system and the highly competitive political conditions of the big cities. The large number of votes needed for election in the multimember districts of the big cities as opposed to the small number needed in the citywide at-large elections elsewhere made it more difficult from the start to base a successful campaign simply on a promise of areal representation or the support of an individual candidate support group. These techniques were, and continue to be, used in the big cities, but they are usually supplemented by use of the party label to attract the votes of those who cannot be reached through personal contact. Also, because of a potentially large leftist electoral base, the relatively competitive political conditions of the big cities may have further convinced the conservatives of the desirability of using party endorsements. Today there is virtually no difference in level of politicization between big city assembly and HR elections.

Opposition electoral support for big city assemblies grew from 27 percent in 1947 to 63 percent by 1975 (see Table 2). I have suggested, or implied, at least four reasons for this huge change in voting patterns. First, today there is a wider spectrum of opposition parties from which the big city voter might choose, including the CGP and DSP, which must be considered "moderate-progressive" rather than "left-progressive" parties. This enlargement of the range of choice to include moderate parties among the opposition has permitted voters to express their dissatisfaction with the LDP without supporting the leftist parties. Second, the opposition parties have become more interested in urban local politics than they were earlier. Increased interest is a result of: (1) the failure of the JSP to sustain its earlier growth in HR elections and its subsequent turn to the local level in hopes for revival; (2) growth of Sōkagakkai as an urban socio-religious movement of the lower and lower-middle classes whose social and welfare interests could not be realized without political representation; and (3) a discovery of a wide range of urban discontents that could be exploited to attack the LDP.[20]

Third, opposition candidates and parties have become more active in organizing the urban electorate. I have emphasized the growth of CGP and JCP *party* organization, but as Gary Allinson shows so clearly in his chapter, it is also vital to consider the enormous socio-economic changes of the past three decades that have given opposition spokesmen (and women) more equal access to the local leadership positions so useful as an avenue of advancement into local politics. Large-scale inmigration to the big cities, growth of new suburbs, extension of transportation networks to older neighborhoods, and the like have multiplied the number of local leadership posts (in community associations, civic groups, PTA, etc.), created some communities (especially those dominated by young white-collar workers in huge apartment blocks) in which progressives have easy access to these posts, and diversified and enlarged formerly isolated communities so that the older conservative local leadership might be challenged by energetic opposition candidates appealing to the new residents (or even older ones) on the basis of new urban issues.

These new issues are a fourth reason for the growth of opposition support in the big cities. No longer are urban residents concerned foremost with road improvement, sewer construction, educational facilities, and other such direct and tangible benefits that conservative assembly members so often promised and brought to their constituents.

[20] For details on the increased interest of the opposition in local politics, see MacDougall, *Dissertation*, pp. 285-298; Matsushita Keiichi, *Shibiru minimamu no shisō* (Tōkyō: Tōkyō Daigaku Shuppan kai, 1971), pp. 247-249; Nihon Shakaitō, *1961 shakaitō no shinrosen* (Tōkyō: Nihon Shakaitō, 1961), especially pp. 35-36.

Rather, they are more often disturbed by air, water, and noise pollution, traffic accidents and congestion, and continued inadequacies in social services and housing. By and large, these new concerns cannot be met simply by the old formula of enlarging the pie and dividing the benefits. Indeed, the problems themselves may be attributed in large measure to the past priority given by a conservative national administration with the ready compliance of conservative local authorities to rapid economic development at the expense of social services and measures to protect the living environment.[21] It is both to the widespread disillusionment with the ruling party and to these specific issues that opposition candidates have begun to appeal with so much success.

Today each of the parties receives approximately the same percentage of the vote in big city assembly elections as it does in HR elections in the same areas, in contrast to the relatively stronger performance by the Right in assembly elections and the Left in HR elections in the late 1940s and 1950s (see Table 2). The meaning of this pattern of convergence in partisan support levels in the big cities is not entirely clear. On the one hand, recent surveys indicate that as much as 40 percent of the big city electorate does not support any party and that those with a strong party identification are a small minority.[22] On the other hand, our data indicate that, in aggregate, voting patterns in the two kinds of legislative elections do not significantly differ. They suggest the *possibility* that big city voters may be making fairly consistent partisan choices in assembly and HR elections.[23]

[21] Some progressive local authorities also put a high priority on economic development, but because they were relatively few in number and because until recently they did not hold office in many of the more important cities, they were less conspicuous. Also, some of them, such as the JSP mayors of Kushiro and Yokohama, took important initiatives to assure closer supervision of industrial expansion from the early 1960s. The progressive governor of Kyoto provides a similar example. See Ellis Krauss's contribution to this volume on the governor of Kyoto. On the other two cities, the following works are most useful: Yamaguchi Tetsuo, *Toshi no jikken* (Tōkyō: Keisō Shobō, 1969), and Asukata Ichio, *Kakushin shisei no tenbō* (Tōkyō: Shakai Shinpo, 1967).

[22] For example, polls taken by the Fair Election League in Tokyo Metropolis, Nagoya City, Kyoto City, KitaKyushu City, and Fukuoka City in July-August 1974 all indicate that in the big cities as a group and in the individual cities just named approximately 40 percent of the respondents would not or could not name a party they support, although about a quarter of these (or 10 percent of the total) indicated some preference between progressive and conservative. Kōmei Senkyo Renmei, "Dai toshi ni okeru senkyo keihatsu no kisōteki kenkyū shiryō 1," February 1975. For extensive survey findings on the degree of party identification and support, see Kōmei Senkyo Renmei, *Seiji ishiki ni kansuru chōsa hōkokusho, 1973* (Tōkyō: Kōmei Senkyo Renmei, 1973), pp. 93-145.

[23] In one survey after the April 1967 local elections, voters were asked about

The contradiction may be more apparent than real. In the big cities, widespread discontent with all parties is combined with highly politicized elections in which the voter has little choice but to pick among them. Even if a voter lacks a strong party identification, he may still have a partisan preference when pressed to make a choice. In big city assembly and HR elections he is in fact pressed to that point, since the only serious candidates are official party candidates. Supporting this interpretation is the fact that big city voters cite "party" as opposed to "the individual" about twice as frequently as voters in other cities when explaining their choice in city assembly elections.[24]

If I am right, future changes in voting patterns at one level of legislative election in the big cities are likely to be reflected in similar changes at the other level. It may also follow that such changes will be

---

their voting behavior in both the January 1967 HR elections and the recent local elections. Results follow for Tokyo Metropolis. Only those respondents who voted in both elections are included.

Partisan Choices in Elections in Tokyo Metropolis, 1967

Partisan Choice in Municipal Assembly Elections	N	Partisan Choice of Same Respondents in HR Election (by percentage)						
		LDP	JSP	DSP	CGP	JCP	Indep/ Other	No Answer
LDP	217	83.4	7.8	3.2	0	0	0.5	5.0
JSP	155	7.0	84.5	1.3	0.6	2.6	0	3.9
DSP	19	15.8	15.8	57.9	0	0	5.3	5.3
CGP	38	2.6	2.6	2.6	86.8	2.6	0	2.6
JCP	20	0	25.0	0	0	70.0	0	5.0
Indep/Other	75	33.3	34.7	14.7	1.3	0	6.7	9.3
No Answer	60	10.0	16.7	0	1.7	1.7	3.3	66.7

Note the very high rate of consistency in partisan choices between the two kinds of election—HR election and elections for the assemblies of cities, towns, villages, and wards within Tokyo Metropolis. In the more politicized election for the Tokyo Metropolitan Assembly or for the assemblies of large cities an even higher rate of consistency might be expected. The levels of consistency are particularly impressive, since they predate the full development of the pattern of convergence I have described. The table is recalculated from Kōmei Senkyo Renmei, *Dai-6-kai tōitsu chihō senkyo to yūkensha II* (Tōkyō: Kōmei Senkyo Renmei, 1972), p. 328.

[24] This is as would be expected because the big city elections are more politicized. But even when those in the big cities who indicate a preference for "the individual" are asked what it is about the individual that leads them to support him, they are about twice as likely as those in other cities to name such factors as "his policy," "he's the candidate of the party I support," and other such reasons close to party support. See, for example, Kōmei Senkyo Renmei *Dai-7-kai tōitsu chihō senkyo to yūkensha II* (Tōkyō: Kōmei Senkyo Renmei, 1972), pp. 174-182.

smaller in the future than in the past, unless there is a wholesale re-organization of political parties, since big city legislative elections are now fully politicized and present the voter with the full spectrum of party choices available in the country. In the future, changes in partisan preferences, not simply mobilization of uncommitted or marginal backers of the older established parties, will be necessary before a party can make significant gains in the big cities. One will have to look more to the suburban, satellite, and regional cities than to the big cities for evidence of further growth in opposition strength in assembly elections. Even that growth, however, may be limited because of the citywide at-large kind of electoral system that has generally been more masterfully exploited by local conservatives than by progressives. Although the avenue for opposition advancement in these assemblies may be narrowed by the nature of the electoral system, it will definitely not be closed. Insofar as they can increase their efforts in organizing the electorate through party activities or individual candidate groups, they may be able to exploit some of the same opportunities that have allowed them to advance in the big cities.

GUBERNATORIAL AND MAYORAL ELECTIONS

Gubernatorial and mayoral elections in most areas of Japan have been no less a "conservative paradise" than local assembly elections. In 1975, approximately 72 percent of the prefectural governors and the same percentage of mayors of small- and medium-sized cities could be considered as "conservatives" and another 8 percent of each as "neutrals" (see Table 6). Only 20 percent were "progressives" including 9 of the 47 governors and 132 of the 634 mayors of small and medium-sized cities. Nevertheless, these figures represent the greatest numbers and percentages of progressive executives ever.[25] It is especially in large cities that progressive successes in executive elections have been most marked: six of the nine designated cities have progressive mayors. Indeed, it is precisely the election of progressives to mayoral and guber-

---

[25] See Table 6, note "a" for source and method of classification of progressive, conservative, and neutral mayors. Calculations of numbers of progressive mayors always involve some element of judgment, since partisan backing or the political orientation of a mayor is not always clear. The 1 June 1975 Register of the National Association of Progressive Mayors lists 120 members, down from 135 in July 1974, but by *Asahi shinbun* calculation the number increased slightly. The difference is explained in part by the failure of some mayors generally considered to be progressive to respond to the Secretariat of the National Association for reconfirming their membership. Interview with Nonaka Takashi, Secretary-General of the Chihō jichi sentā, the Secretariat for the National Association, 12 June 1975.

Table 6

Distribution of Major Local Executive Posts, April 1975

	Governors		Big City Mayors		Other City Mayors	
	No.	Percent	No.	Percent	No.	Percent
LDP	15		0		55	
Conservative Indep.[a]	19		3		397	
Total Conservative	(34)	72	(3)	33	(452)	71
JSP	0		1		14	
JCP	0		0		2	
Other Progressive[b]	0		0		6	
Progressive Indep.	9		5		110	
Total Progressive	(9)	19	(6)	67	(132)	21
Neutral Independent	4	9	0	0	50	8
Grand Total	47	100	9	100	634	100

[a] Progressive and conservative independents are distinguished by membership in the National Association of Progressive Mayors or the LDP's Mayoral Liaison Council or by the *Asahi shinbun's* assessment of the mayor's organizational backing. Those for whom such distinctions could not be made are considered to be neutral or "pure independents."
[b] Okinawan progressive parties.
SOURCES: *Yomiuri shinbun*, 15 April 1975 and *Asahi shinbun*, 29 April 1975.

natorial posts in Japan's most important urban areas that has brought "progressive local government" into national prominence and stimulated the kind of research represented by this volume.

In the next few pages, I shall briefly outline some of the major characteristics of local executive elections as they relate to partisanship, present an overview of postwar big city executive elections, and discuss the relationship between assembly and executive elections. Further details are presented in the section of this volume on progressive local government and particularly in Kurt Steiner's introduction to that section.[26]

Characteristics of Local Executive Elections

It will be sufficient for our purposes to describe two aspects of local executive elections: the extent to which they are partisan contests and the importance of the personal qualities of the individual candidates.

Partisanship and local executive elections. The vast majority of execu-

[26] See also MacDougall, *Dissertation*, and MacDougall, *Localism and Political Opposition in Japan.*

tive elections are today, as they were in the past, contests between or among independents. In 1975, only 32 percent of the gubernatorial posts and 12 percent of the city mayoral posts were held by persons who had run as the official candidates of particular parties. In this narrow sense, most executive elections, including those in the big cities, can be said to be "nonpartisan." But the term is misleading. Executive candidates avoid the partisan label even when they seek (or graciously accept) the backing of political parties, local assembly members, and other groups or organizations with clearly discernible partisan coloration or preferences. As indicated in Table 6, it is possible to characterize over 90 percent of all governors and city mayors as "progressives" or "conservatives" on the basis of their political ties or backing.

Why do most gubernatorial and mayoral candidates avoid the party label? In the first place, it is possible to have a party's backing without using its label and inviting some of the disadvantages of seeming to be "the party's man." Either an official candidate running under a party label (*kōnin*) or one with a party endorsement (*suisen*) can generally expect active campaign assistance from the party. Tactical calculations based on the partisan composition of the local electorate or the possibility of the joint backing of the candidate by another party help determine which of these forms of backing will be used. A candidate with only a pledge of support (*shiji*) usually cannot expect the same level of assistance, either because the party's backing is only lukewarm or because it has little local organization to activate on his behalf. But even an announcement of party support may help swing the votes of some groups and individuals to the candidate. "Endorsed" and "supported" candidates run as independents (*mushozoku*), as do others without formal partisan backing.

Related to the above tactical flexibility permitted an executive candidate is the practical consideration that in most cities and prefectures a candidate cannot expect to win simply on the basis of the aggregate level of support given to a single party. This is particularly true for a progressive candidate, since it is only in a few coal mining cities that the JSP can poll a majority of the votes in a national or local legislative election. Given the reluctance of each of the parties to supply any kind of formal backing to an official candidate of another party, an independent candidacy may facilitate the establishment of a loose "electoral coalition."

A large number of independent candidacies is also the result of divisions among local conservatives. These divisions can be seen in the establishment of more than one conservative group in a local assembly, affiliation of local conservatives with prefectural or national conservative politicians from competing factions of the LDP, and open competition between those conservatives in control of the local LDP branch and those who have little or no role in its affairs. Thus multiple conservative candidacies are frequent, especially in the numerous small regional cities where progressives may not have the resources to field a serious candidate, or any at all.

Finally, the expectation of a large part of the electorate that the governor or mayor should be "above party" and act in the interests of the whole prefecture or city may deter an executive candidate from running with a party label. A full explanation of this expectation is beyond the scope of the present article, but among the reasons for it are: (1) the heritage of depoliticization of the executive dating back to the prewar years; (2) a tendency to consider local government in terms of technical administration—there is no conservative or progressive way of building a school or laying a street; and (3) the great influence the Japanese perceive local governmental decisions as having on their daily lives.[27] A candidate need not be strictly "nonpartisan" in the sense of receiving no backing from political parties, but he should be "suprapartisan" in the sense of having no political obligations that might interfere with his tasks of maximizing the benefits that he will be expected to obtain for the prefecture or city and of distributing these in an equitable way.

In practice, most conservative candidates have not hidden their LDP-backing but have argued that it gives them a "direct pipeline to the center" that will facilitate their task of attracting funds and support for local projects from higher authorities. This was a powerful argument in the years when Japan was recovering from the war and beginning its rapid economic growth. Without control over the "center," progressive candidates had little choice but to attack local conservatives as lackeys of the central government and to claim their own special "direct pipeline to the people." More recently, however, by putting themselves on the side of "localism," progressive executive candidates have been able to tap both local pride and the increasing popular discontent with the excesses of the conservatives' rapid economic growth policy, which has disrupted traditional modes of life and despoiled the environment in many areas of the country.[28] This strategy is the more

[27] On these points, see Bradley M. Richardson, *The Political Culture of Japan* (Berkeley: The University of California Press, 1974), and Kurt Steiner, *Local Government in Japan* (Stanford: Stanford University Press, 1965).

[28] An excellent illustration of this process of progressive identification with localism is given in Ellis Krauss's study of the Ninagawa administration in Kyoto in Chapter 11 of this volume.

promising, since localism is a prominent aspect of popular sentiments in many areas. Identifying themselves with localism has broadened the appeal of many progressive executive candidates beyond the traditional JSP-JCP voter and has forced some local conservatives to make a tactical retreat from the "direct pipeline to the center" appeal. The consequent revitalization of localism seems to have reinforced the idea that the executive should be "above party" at a time when, paradoxically, the parties are involving themselves more deeply in executive elections.

Qualities of the candidate. "Party," as I have just argued, can play a significant role in the local executive election, but the personal qualities of the candidates may still be of decisive importance in determining the final outcome of the contest. The two points are related, since the composition of an electoral coalition may hinge on those personal qualities. For example, of two possible candidates, both closely identified with the JSP, one may be more acceptable to the JCP and the other to the CGP, DSP, or even antimainstream LDP conservatives. A background of union or leftist activism (or lack of it), demonstrated administrative skills, identification with local interests based on family background or local posts, style of political rhetoric, other factors related to personal stature and prestige, and the like will enter into the calculations along with an assessment of the partisan preferences of the electorate and the current state of relations between the various parties. In almost all cases, the JSP (along with local labor groups) plays the central role in negotiations. In principle, it would prefer to run its own official candidates, but lacking sufficient strength, it must usually seek the cooperation of other parties and face the dilemma that seldom is a candidate acceptable to both leftist and moderate progressive parties.[29]

Polls indicate that the Japanese electorate puts a high priority on "personality" in all kinds of elections, but especially at the local level.[30] The multimember district, single-entry ballot, electoral system facilitates such an emphasis on personality, since in most cases a voter will have a choice among a number of candidates from the same party. In an executive election, the range of choice is greatly narrowed, but personality still looms at least as large as in the case of local assembly elections. Earlier I described the importance of the candidate's appearing to be "above party." Whether local government is seen in terms of its

[29] For a more detailed description of electoral coalition formation and the central role of the JSP, see MacDougall, *Dissertation*, pp. 236-252.

[30] Ōkubo Tadayoshi, *Nihonjin no tōhyō kōdō* (Tōkyō: Shiseidō, 1974), pp. 60-62, and Kōmei Senkyo Renmei, *Dai-6-kai tōitsu chihō senkyo to yūkensha II* (Tōkyō: Kōmei Senkyo Renmei, 1967), pp. 66-71, 106-112, and 285-292.

function of soliciting funds and cooperation from higher authorities or in terms of responding to local needs and demands in an evenhanded way, the more important question for the voters in choosing a mayor or governor may not be which party supports the candidate but which candidate has the personal stature and prestige, as well as judiciousness, to fulfill most effectively the demands of the position. Although scholars may try to differentiate "progressive" from "conservative" local government, the Japanese voter is more likely to think in terms of "effective or ineffective" and "responsive and unresponsive" administration, with neither camp having a monopoly of the traits that make for effectiveness of responsiveness.

Take as an example what appeared to be one of the most highly politicized local executive elections ever, the 1967 Tokyo gubernatorial contest. The partisan lines were clearly drawn: the JSP and JCP recommended Minobe Ryōkichi, the DSP and LDP recommended Matsushita Masatoshi, and the CGP recommended Abe Kenichi. An immediate postelection survey of the voters indicated that only 32 percent voted on the basis of "party," while 49 percent based their vote on "personality," 17 percent on both, and 2 percent uncertain.[31] Those who placed some weight on personality were asked what particular candidate attributes most concerned them. The replies and their percentage distribution were: "He considers things from our standpoint" —38; "Personal character"—34; "Insistence on good principle"—15; "Good policy"—6; "Good political skill"—3; "Other"—1; "Don't know"—4. Although the precise meaning of these terms may not be entirely clear, there is sufficient consistency in this kind of survey to justify close scrutiny of the qualities of individual candidates and not simply their partisan backing. All the parties should take particular note that in both the 1967 and 1971 Tokyo gubernatorial election, the former a tight contest and the latter a landslide victory, the *winner*, Minobe Ryōkichi, won the overwhelming support of those who considered personality as paramount, while the *losers* garnered only a minority of the vote based on personality and had to rely mainly on partisan backers.[32] The lessons should be clear: careful candidate selection is essential, and the partisan distribution of the electorate gives only a rough estimate of the potential support base.

Thus, both in the big cities and elsewhere, gubernatorial and mayoral elections involve a combination of partisan activities on behalf of the candidates and the continuing importance of the personal qualities of

[31] Kōmei Senkyo Renmei, *Dai-6-kai tōitsu chihō senkyo to yūkensha II* (Tōkyō: Kōmei Senkyo Renmei, 1967), pp. 285–292.
[32] See Flanagan's Chapter 5 in this volume and the references in note 30.

the individual candidates. From the standpoint of partisan backing, most of these elections can be considered progressive-conservative contests. What difference the outcome of the contest will make is discussed elsewhere in this volume and in my own works cited in the footnotes. But it is important to keep in mind that, except for backing by the JSP or the LDP, there is no widely accepted definition of "progressive" and "conservative" in Japanese local politics. The continuing importance of the personal qualities of the candidates, as well as the exigencies of forming electoral coalitions with some sensitivity to the partisan preferences of the electorate, mean that these parties may back very different kinds of candidates in different areas. Whether the CGP or DSP aligns behind a "progressive" or "conservative" candidate in a given area will depend not simply on the variations in their policy positions in different areas but also on the tactical calculations of the major parties. Many of the ambiguities of the "progressive-conservative" dichotomy in Japanese national politics are found in local politics as well, but the divisions tend to be even less clear-cut at the local level. Local progressive-conservative competition must be considered on its own terms and not simply as a reflection of Japanese national politics. Indeed, elsewhere I have argued that this increased local progressive-conservative competition should be considered an independent variable that is changing the policies of Japanese national government and has the potential for reshaping national politics as well.[33]

Big City Executive Elections, 1947-1975

A total of 8 gubernatorial and 47 mayoral elections were held between 1947 and 1975 in Tokyo and the six large designated cities of Yokohama, Nagoya, Kyoto, Osaka, Kobe, and KitaKyushu. I have compiled virtually complete data on all but two of the elections. Candidates included 60 serious contenders, 15 who were politically significant but electorally minor (mostly official JCP candidates), and a large number of minor candidates who seldom received a combined total of more than 2 percent of the vote. What follows is focused on the 60 serious contenders, with some reference to the circumstances of minor JCP, CGP, or DSP candidacies. Figure 2 summarizes the results of all big city executive elections between 1947 and 1975.

Candidate attributes. It was possible to collect systematic data on only four attributes of the candidates: age, incumbency, education, and career background. There was no difference between progressive and conservative or between winner and loser by age: almost all have been

[33] See MacDougall, *Localism and Political Opposition in Japan.*

Figure 2

Big City Executives, 1947-1975

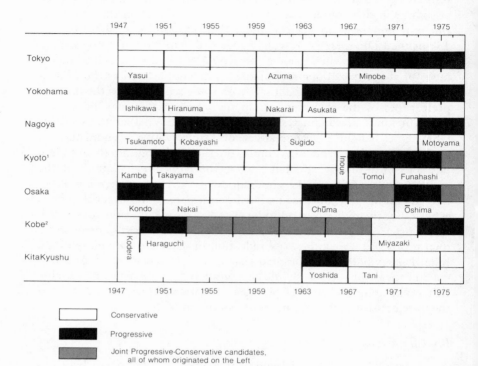

NOTE: Short lines indicate the reelection of the incumbent, and long lines dividing terms indicate the election of a new mayor.
[1] Takayama's organizational base of support changed from progressive to conservative after his first term.
[2] Miyazaki's organizational base of support changed from conservative to progressive after his first term.
SOURCES: *Asahi shinbun* and *Mainichi shinbun*, selected issues, 1947-1975.

in their mid-fifties to late sixties. Candidates (and especially successful candidates) outside this age range were rare. There has been no clear trend toward younger or older candidates. Incumbents faced reelection in 34 of the 55 contests and won in an overwhelming 30 of them, with the progressives and conservatives dividing the losses equally. The benefits of incumbency, including the publicity, prestige, and opportunities for rewarding one's supporters, seem to adhere to conservative and progressive alike and may account for a part of the importance of "personality" as a reason for supporting a candidate. Indeed, incumbents have tended to broaden their electoral coalition in their reelection bids and also to cut into the normal support base of the challenging side, whether it be conservative or progressive.[34]

Educationally, candidates for big city executive posts can be considered an elite: almost all had a college education, and close to half attended Tokyo or Kyoto University. There was no real difference between conservative and progressive candidates in this regard. Although the total numbers are too small to be fully confident of the findings, it would seem that education in one of the prestigious national universities was an advantage: close to two-thirds of the candidates from national universities, but only one-third of those from elsewhere, won election. Supportive of this interpretation is the fact that fully fourteen of the sixteen persons who have been elected as progressive governors in the postwar period received their education at famous national universities, eight of them at Tokyo University.[35] In a society that attaches great weight and status to education, it would appear that high educational attainments are an attractive quality in an executive candidate, at least at the big city and gubernatorial levels.

The career backgrounds of the candidates also indicate high attainments: 12 were national bureaucrats, 10 university professors, 8 local politicians, 5 journalists, 4 local bureaucrats, 4 engineers, 4 labor or socialist activists, 3 businessmen, 2 lawyers, 2 doctors, and 6 unaccounted for. Most strikingly, 25 of these, or 42 percent of the total, had been members of the National Diet, including 10 of the conservatives and 15 of the progressives. The importance of National Diet experience, however, is questionable: while 5 of the conservatives with such an experience won, only 3 of the progressives were successful, and even when they had National Diet experience, labor and socialist activists, journalists, and businessmen did not make viable executive candidates. Possibly such candidates simply did not have a broad

---

[34] Surveys documenting the growth of support for Governor Minobe Ryōkichi among LDP, DSP, and CGP voters can be found in Torōren, *Ryūdōka suru tomin no seiji ishiki* (Tōkyō: Tōkyō Tosei Chōsa kai, 1972), pp. 71-73, and Ōkubo Tadayoshi, *Nihonjin no tōhyō Kōdō*, pp. 66-68. For a comparison of the supporters of Yokohama Mayor Asukata Ichio in 1963 and 1967, see the surveys printed in *Asahi shinbun*, 15 April 1963 and 13 April 1967; these surveys indicate a broadening of his base to include normally conservative voters as well as progressives. His share of the vote increased from 42.8 percent to 62.0 percent.

[35] For their names and further details, see MacDougall, "Political Opposition and Big City Elections in Japan, 1947-1975," a paper delivered at the Conference on Local Opposition in Japan, Wrightsville Beach, North Carolina, 24-26 June 1976. The same paper contains further details on the educational and career backgrounds of big city executives.

enough appeal to form the grand electoral coalition necessary to win the office of mayor or governor. On the other hand, those associated with local administration, such as bureaucrats or professionals with advisory roles, won almost all their contests, while former national bureaucrats and local politicians were successful half the time. Successful conservative candidates most often had a background in the national bureaucracy, local politics, or the professions, while progressive winners came from local politics, local administration, education, or the professions. The thrust of the career background data seems to be that administrative experience of some sort or a successful political career that includes *both* local and national office are the important avenues to executive office in the big city. Note that these careers carry with them either the *quality of administrative experience* or the *development of a personal local support organization.* This interpretation is reinforced by a 1971 study of 47 progressive mayors; the study found that two-thirds of them had long experience in a legislative assembly, local bureaucracy, or administrative committee of the local government before being elected as mayor.[36]

Thus, an elite education, administrative experience, a personal local support organization, and the prestige, status, and other advantages of incumbency are some of the qualities of the successful big city executive candidates. Japanese voters in these areas are electing administrative or political professionals, not amateurs, to office.

Partisan backing of the candidates. Three-quarters of the 55 elections to big city executive office between 1947 and 1975 involved contests between major conservative and progressive candidates and were portrayed by the press as more or less struggles between the two camps. Most of the remainder consisted of a JCP challenge to a joint progressive-conservative candidate. Only about two-fifths of the elections were at all close, largely because of the strength of incumbency previously noted. Conservative candidates won 26 times, progressives 21, and joint progressive-conservative candidates 8. But since 1963, when progressives began to win these posts with some consistency, 8 conservative, 14 progressive, and 5 joint progressive-conservative victories have been registered. In each case, the joint candidates have been progressive incumbents who have broadened their support base to include the LDP. In all, 25 persons have held the Tokyo gubernatorial or big city mayoral positions since 1947, including 12 conservatives and 13 pro-

---

[36] Unfortunately, only one-half of the progressive mayors responded to the survey. Chihō Jichi Sentā, *Kakushin shichō shisei hōshin shū* (Tōkyō: Chihō Jichi Sentā, 1971).

gressives.[37] All of these points are illustrated in Figure 2, which also includes the surnames of the winners.

The partisan backing of big city executive candidates since the unification of the conservatives into the LDP in late 1955 is given in Table 7. A number of facts are immediately apparent. First, candidates with joint progressive-conservative support have always won. All 4 of these candidates (in 8 contests) have been progressives with long bureaucratic experience and could be considered administrative experts. The latter characteristic would seem to facilitate progressive-conservative cooperation in local politics. Second, the broader the coalition, the greater the likelihood of winning: only 13 of 31 candidates with single-party backing won, while 12 of 22 candidates backed by two parties, 8 or 9 candidates backed by three parties, all 3 candidates backed by four parties, and the 1 candidate backed by five parties were winners. An electoral coalition of some sort was particularly important for the progressives: only 5 of 13 candidates backed solely by the JSP and none of those backed solely by the JCP, CGP, or DSP won. Finally, it is clear that no single coalitional pattern predominates. But let us examine some of the major varieties.

Three alternative paths have been followed by the LDP in post-1955 big city elections. About half of the time (18 contests), it has been the sole backer of a conservative candidate. This has been the prevailing pattern in Tokyo and Yokohama. It is also the prevailing pattern in small- and medium-sized cities. Slightly less than half of these candidates won in the big cities, but their record elsewhere has been far better.

In another 9 of the big city contests, the LDP jointly supported a candidate with the DSP. Most often the candidate was an incumbent conservative who picked up DSP backing in his bid for reelection. Examples are former Nagoya Mayor Sugido Kiyoshi and KitaKyushu Mayor Tani Gohei. These are cities with considerable DSP strength and also of rivalry between Dōmei unions backing the DSP and Sōhyō unions backing the JSP. On three occasions, the LDP-DSP candidate was Socialist in background and was run in an attempt to be competitive with a JSP-JCP candidate in a leftist stronghold—for example, DSP Diet member Nagasue Eiichi was the LDP-DSP candidate in the

---

[37] One conservative, Kobe Mayor Miyazaki Tatsuo, ran for reelection with the backing of all four progressive parties and the opposition of the LDP. One progressive, Kyoto Mayor Takayama Gizō, ran for reelection with conservative backing and the opposition of progressive groups. Each is classified according to his original partisan backing, although the changes are noted in Figure 2.

Table 7

Political Backing of Major Big City Executive Candidates

	Candidates	Wins	Number of Parties	% Winning
Conservatives:				
LDP	3	1	1	
Ind. (LDP)	15	7	1	44
Indep. (LDP-DSP)	9	4	2	
Indep. (LDP-CGP)	1	1	2	50
Indep. (Other)[a]	1	0	–	0
Joint Progressive-Conservative:				
Indep. (LDP-JSP)	1	1	2	100
Indep. (LDP-JSP-DSP)[b]	4	4	3	100
Indep. (LDP-JSP-DSP-CGP)	2	2	4	100
Indep. (LDP-JSP-DSP-CGP-JCP)	1	1	5	100
Progressives:				
JSP	8	4	1	
Indep. (JSP)	5	1	1	38
JSP (JCP)	2	0	2	
Indep. (JSP-JCP)	6	4	2	
Indep. (JSP-DSP)	1	1	2	56
JSP (JCP-CGP)	1	1	3	
Indep. (JSP-JCP-DSP)	2	1	3	
Indep. (JSP-JCP-CGP)	2	2	3	
Indep. (JSP-DSP-CGP)	1	1	3	83
Indep. (JSP-JCP-DSP-CGP)	1	1	4	100

NOTE: For Tokyo governorship and Yokohama, Nagoya, Kyoto, Osaka, Kobe, and KitaKyushu mayoralships. Partisan backing for a candidate often changed from one election to another; each election bid is therefore counted separately. Official party or independent candidacy is given in the first column; endorsing or supporting party is given in parentheses.
[a] Backed by the DSP and local conservatives opposed to the mainstream LDP.
[b] In two of these cases, Kobe Mayor Haraguchi Chūjirō's 1965 and 1969 campaigns, the position of the JSP could not be fully determined from newspaper accounts available to the author.
SOURCES: *Asahi shinbun* and *Mainichi shinbun*, selected issues, 1955-1975.

1971 Kyoto mayoral election. In each case, the moderate lost. Outside the big cities the situation is similar. For example, in the April 1975 local elections there were 26 LDP-DSP electoral coalitions against progressive candidates. The LDP-DSP coalition candidate won in 23 of these cases, but 19 of the wins came in cities in which a conservative incumbent ran. Also, as was true for the big cities over a twenty-year period, the DSP more often cooperated with the LDP than with the other progressive parties. It would seem that the moderate political views of many DSP voters and the rivalries between Dōmei and Sōhyō unions make the DSP a natural coalition partner for the LDP in some areas. Coalitions between these two parties have increased in recent years, both in the big cities and elsewhere.

The third path followed by the LDP has been to jointly back a progressive-conservative candidate with the JSP and possibly other progressive parties. As previously noted, these candidates have always won. In the big cities they have all originated in the progressive camp, but in other cities they have sometimes come from the conservative camp. In a 1973 survey of progressive mayors (reproduced in Table 8), 13 of 103 progressive mayors had LDP backing. The candidates who

Table 8

Party Coalitions Backing Progressive Mayors

	Metropolitan Areas	Regional Cities	Total
JSP-JCP	18	14	32
JSP	5	13	18
JSP-JCP-CGP-DSP	4	7	11
JSP-JCP-CGP	3	6	9
JSP-CGP-DSP	1	5	6
Others[a]	9	18	27
Total	40	63	103

NOTE: Partisan backing of 103 progressive mayors in their last election prior to July 1973. All mayors were members of the National Association of Progressive Mayors in July 1973.
[a] These include the following frequencies of other coalitions: 4 JSP-DSP; 4 JSP-JCP-DSP; 4 JSP-DSP-LDP; 3 JSP-JCP-CGP-DSP-LDP; 3 JSP-LDP; 2 JSP-CGP; 2 JSP-CGP-LDP; 2 none; 1 JSP-CGP-DSP-LDP; 1 CGP-DSP-LDP; and 1 JCP.
SOURCE: Nihon Shakaitō, *Kokumin jichi nenkan, 1974-nenpan* (Tōkyō: Nihon Shakaitō Chūō Honbu, 1974), pp. 303-306.

have managed to receive support from both camps have usually done so only after being in office for one or two terms and having demonstrated considerable administrative competence and skill in representing the interests of the city. This is one example of how the element of localism might outweigh the usual progressive-conservative rivalry.

Finally, perhaps the most impressive aspect of conservatives in big city politics has been their ability to unite behind a single candidate. Only once in the twenty years between 1955 and 1975 have two major conservative executive candidates competed with each other. That was in the 1963 Yokohama mayoral election, and the result was the election of JSP candidate Asukata Ichio with a plurality of 43 percent. Asukata has been reelected three times, in each case with two-thirds of the vote. Given the large potential progressive vote in the big cities and the strength of incumbency, it is imperative for the conservatives to field no more than a single candidate. They have followed that imperative to an impressive extent. Outside the big cities, however, they have been less united, and their splits have sometimes resulted in the election of a progressive mayor in fairly conservative areas—for example, Asahikawa City in 1963 and Toyama City in 1971.

Unlike the big city conservatives, the four opposition parties have seldom been united. The JSP has been the most active of the opposition parties in backing candidates for big city executive office. On 13 occasions between 1955 and 1975, it ran an official or endorsed candidate on its own, but won only 5 of these contests. It did better when joined by the JCP (4 wins in 8 contests) or by the JCP with the CGP and/or the DSP (5 wins in 6 contests). As previously noted, the DSP has more often cooperated with the LDP than with the other progressive parties. Only from the late 1960s did the CGP begin to take an active role in local executive elections. At first its position was unclear, cooperating with the LDP on one occasion, running its own candidate on another, and entering a progressive coalition on a third. Following a major setback in the December 1972 elections, the CGP announced its decision to make its choice more explicit in local executive elections.[38] Since then, it has run a number of independent candidates, including one in the last KitaKyushu mayoral election, but more often the party has joined a progressive or progressive-conservative coalition. Today it is an official backer of progressive executives in Tokyo, Yokohama, Nagoya, Kyoto, Osaka, and Kobe.

The JCP has followed three different paths with about equal frequency in the big cities: making no announcement of support, running a separate candidate (usually as the party's official candidate), or joining a progressive coalition. As with the CGP, the JCP has increasingly abandoned the no announcement option. Its independent candidates have run most often as the sole opposition to joint progressive-conservative candidates, but on a few occasions, having failed to come to an agreement with the JSP, the JCP ran a separate candidate against the major progressive candidate, with from marginal to devastating impact on the former's vote-gathering ability. On the whole, a trend toward more frequent and more inclusive progressive coalitions is discernible.

[38] *Asahi shinbun*, 29 January 1973.

Although comparable national data are not available, it might be useful to compare the big city data with the patterns of partisan backing for progressive mayors noted in Table 8 and an *Asahi shinbun* survey of 89 electoral coalitions in the April 1975 mayoral elections.[39] As is the case in the big cities, the progressive mayors nationwide are almost all backed by the JSP. In practice, the JSP usually plays the central role in putting together a progressive coalition, and the JSP coloration of the National Association of Progressive Mayors, which since its founding in 1964 has provided a forum for the exchange of ideas, sharing of experience, and planning of action on common concerns, is still very strong.[40] The most frequent pattern (32 times) was a JSP-JCP coalition; such a coalition is particularly prevalent in metropolitan areas (in and around the big cities) where JCP organization is strongest. JSP-JCP electoral coalitions have not been as successful outside of these areas. In the April 1971 mayoral elections, there were 31 cases of JSP-JCP coalitions; of the 10 victories in these elections only 3 were in regional cities. By the April 1975 mayoral elections, the number of JSP-JCP coalitions dropped to 18 and their victories to 3, all incumbents in the metropolitan areas.

An increasingly frequent pattern of partisan cooperation in mayoral elections is that between the JSP and CGP, sometimes alone but more often with a third or fourth progressive party. This development is too recent to be fully reflected in Table 8, but, as previously noted, 6 of the big city progressive executives ran in their last elections with CGP backing. In the 1973 survey of progressive mayors, the CGP was a coalition member in 35 cases, 34 of which included the JSP. Of the 89 partisan coalitions in the April 1975 survey, the CGP was involved in 13 with the JSP alone, 23 with the JSP in a broader progressive coalition, 2 with the DSP alone, and 2 with the DSP and LDP. The total number of coalitions that included both the JSP and CGP exceeded that of the JSP and JCP; their rate of success was over fifty percent compared to one-third involving the JSP and JCP. The importance of the JCP for the success of progressive mayoral candidates should not be underestimated, but JSP cooperation with the CGP is a significant new alternative. If one of the center parties, the DSP, seems to have leaned to the right, the other, the CGP, has clearly leaned to the left.

[39] *Asahi shinbun*, 29 April 1975.

[40] One of its cofounders was the JSP mayor of Yokohama, Asukata Ichio, who also served as its chairman for fourteen years. Most of the other leadership posts are filled by JSP endorsees. In recent years, however, JCP and CGP representatives have attended some of its meetings, and a number of mayors without JSP backing have entered the association.

WILL PROGRESSIVE ELECTORAL SUCCESS IN
THE BIG CITIES CONTINUE?

The evidence presented in this chapter suggests that the progressive electoral success in the big city assembly and executive elections is not a transient phenomenon. Rather, this success appears to be rooted in basic social and economic changes accompanying urbanization and industrialization, including the heavy concentration of population in a limited area, extension of transportation networks into formerly isolated communities, greater residential mobility, and the diversification of formerly homogeneous communities. These changes have weakened a crucial basis of conservative electoral support—the solidarity of the local community—and created new urban and environmental problems that cannot be adequately handled by the older conservative style of areal representation and its standard formula of enlarging the economic pie and dividing the benefits. They have also multiplied the number and variety of communitywide leadership posts, an important avenue of advancement into local politics, and allowed for easier access to them by progressives, who had formerly taken a backseat to established local conservative elites. In addition, the JCP and CGP have used their organizational skills to mobilize large portions of the discontented urban population.

Conservative electoral decline in big city legislative elections is a result of these long-term factors and has occurred on both the assembly and National Diet levels. There is some evidence that the conservative decline is approaching, or has reached, its limits, but none that it will be reversed. Big city assembly elections will continue to be what they have been since the 1960s—highly partisan contests among all the major parties—and the assemblies themselves will be arenas for coalitional politics.

The sharp decline in conservative support in big city legislative elections since 1959 has been reflected in their losses of most of the big city executive posts as well. The broadened pool of voters for moderate-progressive and left-progressive parties in legislative elections is a distinct advantage to progressive executive candidates, but it does not translate automatically into a permanent progressive majority in executive elections. Ideological and policy differences and organizational rivalries among the progressive parties, as well as disagreements among their respective support groups, make agreement on a single candidate difficult. The defection of one of the moderate-progressive parties, most often the DSP, to support a conservative candidate is a constant problem, as is the possibility of a separate JCP candidate when that party is not satisfied with the JSP's preference. Personal qualities of the individual candidates also loom large in all executive elections. Neither progressives nor conservatives have a monopoly of candidates of high status and prestige, attractive personality, an appearance of responsiveness to local needs, administrative skills, and personal local support organizations—all important elements of success in executive elections.

But progressives do enjoy distinct advantages in the big cities, where their greatest concentrations of popular support and organizational capacity are to be found. Increased public awareness and concern with environmental and urban problems has provided a core area of agreement on issues of vital importance to local government that can serve as a basis for joint support of a single executive candidate. Progressive parties also have a desire to exploit the anti-LDP mood of the big city and may put aside some of their own differences to keep these important local governments out of LDP hands. Perhaps their greatest advantage is the incumbency of progressive executives in urban centers, especially where these incumbents are still young enough to remain in office for a few more terms. The most important of these positions, the Tokyo gubernatorial post, was, however, lost to them in the election of April 1979.

The moderate-progressive parties now occupy pivotal positions in big city local politics. Their cooperation in executive elections and in the assemblies is much sought after by both sides. These two forms of cooperation are related, since the partisan backers of a successful executive candidate are considered "parties in power" and tend to work fairly closely with the administration—although the JCP has on occasion quarrelled openly with some of the executives it has helped elect. The DSP is an important part of the "conservative" coalition that governs in KitaKyushu, while the CGP is the single largest component of three of the six ruling progressive coalitions of which it is a part in the big cities. In each of these cases, the moderate-progressive parties provide the vital margin to make an assembly majority for the executive's ruling coalition. The implication of this development for the functioning of big city assemblies and for administrative responsiveness and responsibility have not been adequately explored. This writer's initial impression is that it has been conducive to more responsive and responsible leadership for the big cities and, compared to the 1950s and the early 1960s, for greater initiative by these local governments. But a systematic study of the role of these parties in the big cities is sorely needed.

The prognosis for progressives in assembly and executive elections of cities and prefectures elsewhere is not as favorable as in the big cities. Most of the country is still, after all, a "conservative paradise." The citywide at-large system of elections for the assemblies of small- and medium-sized cities will continue to make it relatively easy to practice a nonpartisan and particularistic kind of politics in which the conservatives excel. Although the JCP and CGP have extended their organizations and developed support in many suburban, satellite, and regional cities, the pace of such changes is slow and the coverage uneven. The degree of disruption of local communities and social life and of severity of urban and environmental problems experienced in the big cities is not likely to be reproduced in many other cities. Thus, few cities outside the major metropolitan areas are likely to develop as competitive a partisan politics as the big cities.

The greatest room for future progressive inroads in local politics would seem to be in urban prefectural assemblies, which have an electoral system similar to that of the big cities, and in mayoral and gubernatorial elections, where local discontent with conservative leadership is great and progressive coalitions feasible. But even more so than in the big cities, progressive mayors and governors elsewhere will find it necessary to work with moderate and conservative assembly members and bureaucrats in order to carry out their functions as heads of their local governments.

CHAPTER 4

OPPOSITION IN THE SUBURBS

Gary D. Allinson

"THE engine of progressive government is steaming down the Chūō Line to sweep established groups from power and to replace them with popular, progressive administrations." In the early 1970s, this was the rallying cry of Japan's opposition parties in western Tokyo. The purported engine began moving along the Chūō Line in 1962, when the city of Chōfu elected a mayor who ran as a declared candidate of the Socialist Party. In the next year, voters in Musashino also elected a Socialist mayor. Subsequently, seven more progressives came to office in the area. By the mid-1970s, nine of the twenty-six cities in Tokyo's western suburbs had progressive mayors, a rate substantially above the nationwide average.

The ascent of the progressive mayor in Japan's urban areas has received wide attention in the media. Since the late 1960s, leading daily newspapers have given local elections wide play. Major magazines have published frequent articles dealing with progressive administrations. Scholarly publications have appeared that deal exclusively with local government and progressive rule. Television, too, has gotten on the bandwagon, and usually provides brief but incisive coverage of significant elections.

Most of this reportage is characterized by a common set of images. Progressives are seen as the bearers of a political mandate that will inevitably bring them to power. They possess a purity of purpose that will attract wide support from the voting public. Disenchanted with their incumbents and attracted by the participatory style of the progressives, the Japanese citizenry will cast the Liberal Democratic Party (LDP) out of office. Progressives will challenge the power of the bureaucracy that has controlled the affairs of Japanese cities from its

I want to express my appreciation to the Faculty of Arts and Sciences of the University of Pittsburgh and to the United States Educational Commission in Japan (the Fulbright Commission) for research grants in 1975-1976 that enabled me to collect the materials for this essay. I also wish to thank Kurt Steiner and Ellis Krauss for their frequent, stimulating comments as I wrote the essay, and Scott Flanagan for his incisive criticisms as I revised it.

perch in the national government, and they will finally place control of local government in the hands of the people.

As so often happens when such images are brought face to face with reality, they are wholly reshaped, if not completely shattered. Reality does not justify discussion of progressive local government in a context that is sharply polarized, the progressives standing in one clearly defined camp on the left arrayed against the conservatives behind their wall of power on the right. There is some truth in this portrait, for one can identify, in very broad terms, two points of attraction around which groups with different policies, organizations, constituencies, and methods seem to coalesce. But a polarized imagery does serious damage to both the complex reality of local government in Japan and to an understanding of the struggle in process between established and opposition parties.

In place of dichotomized conceptions, it would be useful if we could substitute a different imagery. We are dealing, after all, with a dynamic phenomenon. The legal structure, the economic conditions, and the attitudinal environment in which local governments operate change constantly, as do the governments themselves. This creates a fluid situation in which support and policies also change constantly. Therefore, rather than envisioning a left with its supporters and policies railing against an unmovable right with its adherents and their programs, it would be better initially to imagine a broad range of political behavior amidst which there are perhaps two discernible poles of orientation that exercise a shifting influence on the citizenry. While one pole may retain the persistent support of certain groups and individuals, they are only part of all the supporters that drift in and out of the web of influence cast by that pole of orientation. Moreover, although some groups and/or individuals do demonstrate rather persistent loyalty to the candidates and programs of one pole or the other, there is a panoply of groups and constituents that flow in the midst of this dynamic context. Sometimes the drifters flow toward one pole, sometimes toward another. And not infrequently they just drift, demonstrating no allegiance, only apathy.

Although it is perhaps overly abstract, this schema is a necessary antidote to the unduly crude image of local government cast up by popular discussions. The following essay has sought to adhere faithfully to the revised image of local government just articulated, but in this effort it has been only partly successful. The ease of typifying two groups for purposes of discussion is one reason for this lapse, but the major excuse rests on an important assumption. In the long run there may be considerable significance in a political competition where groups characterized as progressive eventually prevail over others styled conservative. If, in other words, the opposition parties force the LDP from power in the National Diet, or even make it form a coalition with another minority party, the Japanese political system could undergo substantial change. The forces at work in the political process at the municipal level may well contribute to the onset of this change. It is for these reasons that discussion couched in terms of progressives versus conservatives or opposition versus established parties is warranted.

SUBJECT AND METHOD

The purpose of this essay is to examine the electoral setting that fosters support for opposition party politicians. In other words, this paper will analyze the social, personal, organizational, and historical context in which progressive city council members, city mayors, and—to a lesser extent—National Diet members are elected. The essay will be concerned with how the Japanese, acting politically as individuals and as members of groups, have come to prefer opposition candidates in a particular kind of community setting—the suburban city.[1] Since the context of this study is as important as its basic approach, it is useful first to say something about the territorial referent—suburbia—on on which this analysis focuses.

Several reasons underlay the choice of suburbs as the focus of analysis. First, suburban communities in Japan have been among the fastest growing areas in the country since 1955 and have thus become home for a large share of the Japanese populace. Even a rough estimate of the size of Japan's total suburban population is treacherous because census data do not record the population in such fashion. Nonetheless, two examples are suggestive of the size of Japanese suburbia. In the Tokyo metropolitan area, which embraced a population of twenty-seven million people spread through four different prefectures in 1975, some 68 percent of the inhabitants resided in municipalities outside the twenty-three ward (*ku*) area. A similar portion of the metropolitan population of Osaka lived in suburban cities. Given the fact, therefore, that over half the residents of Japan's two largest metropolitan centers were suburbanites, and those suburbanites alone comprised about 24

---

[1] I wish to stress at the outset that my discussion of suburban cities is confined to separate and autonomous municipalities (*shi*) lying within the zone of socio-economic influence of Japan's two largest metropolitan centers, Tokyo and Osaka. Far more research is necessary to determine whether or not these findings apply to suburban cities in other regions of Japan.

percent of the nation's population, the demographic importance of suburban cities is evident.[2]

Second, Japan's suburban cities are socially important. Although they have not attracted populations as homogeneous as those drawn to postwar American suburbs, Japan's suburban cities have attracted in largest number those groups that personify postwar Japanese society: white-collar workers in the secondary and tertiary sector and industrial workers in large enterprises. Taken together, these groups form the largest segment of the Japanese populace. Their social, economic, and political behavior has been shaping and will continue to shape development in Japan for some time to come. In a political sense, especially, suburban behavior could well be prophetic of future trends.

This combination of demographic strength and social prominence provides the third reason for choosing the suburbs as a unit of analysis. Quite simply, the suburbs have become a very important field of political competition. In the suburban electoral districts surrounding Tokyo and Osaka, for example, the LDP won over half the votes and returned 55 percent of the members to the Lower House in 1958.[3] By 1977, its share of the suburban vote and its share of suburban seats had both fallen to about one-third. As demonstrated in the preceding chapters, it is primarily in the densely populated urban and suburban settings that the major shift in voting patterns has occurred at both the national and local levels. Finally, the content of the electoral reform of 1975 also attests conclusively to the newfound political strength of the suburbs. This legislation created twenty new Diet seats. Virtually all were the product of demographic shifts that sent people into the outlying areas of the Tokyo, Osaka, and Nagoya metropolitan centers, and fully sixteen of them were new seats in suburban areas bordering Tokyo and Osaka. In short, Japanese suburbia has assumed a political significance all its own.

This essay deals with just one part of Japanese suburbia, an area known as the Santama Region, which occupies the westernmost two-thirds of Tokyo Metropolitan prefecture. In 1976, it embraced twenty-

[2] These figures are taken from Sōrifu Tōkei Kyoku, *1975 Zenkoku todōfuken shikuchōson betsu jinkō gaisū* (Tōkyō: Nihon Tōkei Kyōkai, 1975), p. 7. Hereafter cited as 1975 Census.

[3] There were ten such suburban Diet districts in the two decades before 1975. They were: Chiba 1; Saitama 1; Tokyo 7; Kanagawa 1, 2, and 3; Osaka 3, 4, and 5; and Hyogo 2. Nishihira Shigeki, *Nihon no senkyo* (Tōkyō: Shiseidō, 1972), pp. 301-424. Following the 1975 reapportionment, Japan's suburban Diet districts were: Saitama 1 and 5; Chiba 1 and 4; Tokyo 7 and 11; Kanagawa 1 through 5; Osaka 3, 4, 5, and 7; and Hyogo 2. These sixteen districts returned 60 members to the Diet following the 1975 reapportionment, or 12 percent of the total.

six separate municipalities (*shi*) and six towns and villages (*chōson*). Like other suburban areas, the Santama Region has experienced fundamental changes in the postwar period. Its resident population nearly tripled between 1955 and 1976, growing from about one million to almost three million. People from all walks of life flowed into the region, but white-collar and industrial workers predominated. As opening comments suggested, this area witnessed political changes that matched its social and demographic alterations. Particularly conspicuous was the shift in support away from the established LDP toward the opposition parties at all levels.

Within the Santama Region, remarks in this essay focus on two different municipalities, the cities of Musashino and Fuchū. There are many reasons for the choice of these two cities but suffice it to mention here only the most important one. Since the early 1960s, the city administration in Musashino has been under the control of the Japan Socialist Party (JSP), whereas Fuchū has remained under the direction of the Liberal Democratic Party. By comparatively and systematically examining the circumstances that have brought these two administrations to office and kept them there, this paper will suggest the conditions under which the opposition has become a major force in the political life of Japanese suburbia.

The essay proceeds as follows. The next section briefly sketches political developments in the Santama Region, Musashino, and Fuchū since 1960, focusing on the level of participation and the shifts in party allegiance. A subsequent section explains why progressive political strength has flourished in Musashino, and conversely, why conservative strength has persisted in Fuchū under circumstances that are in many ways similar. That section, the core of the essay, will analyze four different phenomena: the socio-economic structure of the suburbs, the nature of individual candidacies, the organizational character of suburban politics, and the historical processes of suburban growth. A final section will draw conclusions from this comparative analysis and set them in a larger context for the purpose of illuminating the electoral conditions under which progressive suburban administrations seem to take root in Japan.

POLITICAL CHANGE IN THE SANTAMA, 1960-1978

In broad terms the most striking political change to occur in the Santama area in the postwar period has been the sharp decline in LDP strength and the commensurate increase in power witnessed by opposition parties. This decline has been especially conspicuous at the National Diet level, but it has appeared at prefectural and local levels also. This section illustrates explicitly some political changes that have occurred by portraying the results of Diet, mayoralty, and city council elections in Musashino and Fuchū between 1960 and 1975, stressing the shifts that have taken place in party support.

Before turning to a discussion of the results of recent elections, a word of comment on rates of participation in these two communities is in order. Turnout rates for elections of four different types appear in Table 1. The data in this table sustain the following general assertions. First, voters in Fuchū turn out at slightly higher rates in all types of elections than do voters in Musashino. Since high voter turnout is associated with rural districts in Japan, one might conclude from this comparison of voting rates that Musashino is significantly more "urbanized" than Fuchū. The differences, however, are negligible, except in the case of the city council elections, and hence the evidence is insufficient to warrant such a claim. Second, there is no clear trend illustrating a decline in levels of turnout over time, except in city council elections. This suggests that rather than a historic tendency toward disinterest in political elections, there seems to be a modest level of sustained, general interest that wavers from election to election, depending on issues, candidates, mood, campaigns, et cetera. Third and finally, these turnout rates conform to what Flanagan calls the emerging urban pattern. Thus in contrast with the pattern typically associated with rural areas, voters in these two cities have been most likely to cast ballots in elections for prefectural governor and least likely to cast ballots in local elections. Diet elections have attracted more voters than local elections, generally speaking, but less than gubernatorial campaigns.[4] The deeper meaning of these rates of participation, which are themselves a factor shaping the direction of political change, will be treated in subsequent sections of this chapter.

The year 1960 marked the first time in history that parties associated with the political Right failed to win more than half the votes in a Diet election in the Santama District.[5] The four LDP candidates who

[4] See note 56 in Chapter 5 of this volume. The unusually high level of interest demonstrated by these voters in gubernatorial elections is probably a result of the massive coverage given Tokyo gubernatorial campaigns by virtually all newspapers, magazines, and television stations.

[5] From the election of 1947 through the election of 1972, the Santama Region was coterminous with the Tokyo Seventh District. The election reform of 1975 divided the district to create two new ones, Tokyo Seventh (lying in the northeastern corner of the Santama) and Tokyo Eleventh (covering the remainder of the Santama). The old Seventh District returned five candidates; the two new districts each returned four.

Table 1

Rates of Turnout at Various Elections, Musashino and Fuchū: 1960-1975
(by percentage)

	National Diet		Prefectural Governor		City Mayor		City Council	
	M	F	M	F	M	F	M	F
1960	59	67						
1961								
1962						58		
1963	55	64	64	68	64		61	70
1964								
1965								
1966						48		
1967	67	67	67	66	NE[a]		54	65
1968								
1969	54	55						
1970						59		
1971			70	73	58		57	66
1972	60	64						
1973								
1974						60		
1975			67	67	NE		53	60

[a] NE = No Election.
Sources: Official electoral returns published by prefectural and local election commissions.

ran that year could only attract 49 percent of the vote. In the subsequent four elections, the LDP saw its share of the vote fall even more, to a low of only 28 percent in 1972. Despite this dramatic decline in public support, the party managed to retain its strength where it really counted. It was able to capture seats out of proportion to its electoral strength, three in the 1960 election and two in each contest thereafter. Therefore, despite often drawing less than 40 percent of the vote, the LDP still managed to retain 40 percent of the district's seats.[6]

While the LDP suffered, opposition parties witnessed clear improvements in their fortunes. Having captured 41 percent of the vote in 1960, the opposition parties were able by 1972 to capture fully 70 percent of the total. Largest among them was the Japan Socialist Party, which increased its vote from about 190,000 in 1960 to nearly 310,000 in 1972. However, its share of the total vote fell from 37 to 26 percent during the same period. Far more successful in collecting new voters

[6] For election results, see Nishihira, *Nihon no senkyo.*

during this period was the Japan Communist Party (JCP). Its supporters increased from about 30,000 in 1960 to nearly 210,000 in 1972, and its share of the vote increased from a mere 6 percent to a healthy 18 percent. This enabled its candidate to capture a Diet seat in 1969 and 1972. Both the Kōmeitō (CGP) and the Democratic Socialist Party (DSP) also increased their votes during this period, to such an extent that the former has returned a candidate to the Diet without defeat since 1967. Although this increase in electoral support has guaranteed the election of three opposition candidates in every contest since 1967, it has also created considerable instability. This has reflected most disadvantageously on the JSP, which elected three candidates in 1963, two in 1967, none in 1969, and one in 1972.

Diet election trends in Musashino and Fuchū (illustrated in Table 2) are a rather faithful reflection of trends in the Santama District as a whole. In both cities, the LDP decline has been significant and per-

Table 2

National Diet Elections, Musashino and Fuchū: 1960-1972
(by percentage)

	LDP		CGP		DSP		JSP		JCP		Unaffil-iated		Total	
	M	F	M	F	M	F	M	F	M	F	M	F	M	F
1960	37	42	—	—	13	12	42	40	8	6	—	—	100	100
1963	33	27	—	—	13	9	44	37	9	9	1	18[a]	100	100
1967	28	26	10	14	14	12	37	35	11	11	—	2	100	100
1969	28	30	13	17	17	13	24	21	18	19	—	—	100	100
1972	25	27	11	15	15	11	29	26	18	18	2	3	100	100

[a] These votes all went to a former LDP prefectural assemblyman from Fuchū who ran without party endorsement in 1963, so that they properly belong under the LDP column as "conservative" votes.
Sources: Official election returns published by the Administrative Office of the Lower House of the National Diet.

sistent; in both cities, the opposition parties have attracted a growing share of the vote. There are some differences in the rates of allegiance to the minority parties: the two Socialist parties are somewhat stronger in Musashino, while the Kōmeitō is somewhat stronger in Fuchū; the Communist Party attracts an almost identical share of the vote in both cities. Clearly, in electing candidates to the National Diet, voters in both these communities have largely turned their backs on the LDP.

In contrast with these findings, election results at the municipal level seem rather confounding. Table 3 illustrates the division of the

Table 3

Mayoral Election Results,
Musashino and Fuchū: 1962-1975
(by percentage)

	Musashino		Fuchū	
	Progressive	*Conservative*	*Progressive*	*Conservative*
1962-63	57	43	21	79
1966-67	No election		32	68
1970-71	78	22	33	67
1974-75	No election		32	68

SOURCE: Official election returns published by local election commissions.

vote between progressive and conservative candidates in Musashino and Fuchū on the occasion of the last four mayoralty elections. In Musashino, Gotō Kihachirō, a candidate of the JSP, has held office since 1963, having been returned on two occasions without opposition. In Fuchū, Yabe Takaji, a mayor associated with the LDP, has defeated both conservative and progressive candidates handily since his first election in 1962. Table 4 illustrates the rate of support for different parties in four recent city council elections. Owing to the dominance of the opposition parties in Musashino, they have been the "ins" (*yotō*) since Gotō's first victory in 1963. On the other hand, a coalition of unaffiliated conservative candidates and a few LDP adherents have always formed the governing party in Fuchū.

In both of these cities, local level election returns demonstrate that there is a far larger reservoir of support for conservative candidates

Table 4

City Council Elections,
Musashino and Fuchū: 1963-1975
(by percentage)

	Unaffiliated		LDP		CGP & DSP		JSP & JCP		Total	
	M	F	M	F	M	F	M	F	M	F
1963	18	76	38	4	14	8	30	12	100	100
1967	18	64	24	5	16	13	41	18	99	100
1971	21	57	19	6	15	13	44	23	99	99
1975	22	49	23	8	16	17	38	25	99	99

NOTE: Columns do not always add to 100 because of rounding error.
SOURCE: Official election returns from local election commissions.

than one would suspect from an analysis of national electoral figures. But what is most striking in Fuchū, of course, is the disparity between progressive strength in national elections and progressive weakness in municipal elections. The following section analyzes the reasons for this disparity, and in the process it explains the sources of progressive power —and impotence—in two Tokyo suburbs.[7]

THE ELECTORAL CONTEXT

In explaining why the two communities have developed politically as they have, four phenomena must be taken into account: the socio-economic structure of the two communities, the qualities of individual candidates and their opponents, organizations and organizational modes at work in the two cities, and the historical processes through which they have evolved. This section analyzes each of these phenomena in turn.

Socio-economic Structure

Several factors often alleged to influence the manner in which individuals vote include a person's age, level of education, occupation, residential mobility, and income. This section examines these five factors in order to determine how they might influence the degree of support for progressive politicians in Musashino and Fuchū.

For the past two decades, the composition of the voting-age populations in Musashino and Fuchū has been quite similar, approximating what might be termed a highly urban mode.[8] In other words, people between twenty and thirty-five have accounted for about 50 percent of the voters in both communities, followed by another 30 percent between thirty-five and fifty, with the remaining 20 percent over fifty. This differs from a rural mode, where one would find significantly fewer people under thirty-five and proportionately more in the two older groups. The large number of new industrial jobs for young people in Fuchū and the many singles dormitories and small rental

[7] One should note that candidates running without affiliation obscure precise party divisions in local elections. In Musashino, some unaffiliated candidates are actually progressives, so that the opposition's true share of the vote in that city is larger than it appears in Table 4. In Fuchū, virtually all unaffiliated council candidates seem to be conservatives.

[8] For data on socio-economic characteristics of Musashino and Fuchū, this paper relies on the official national census reports (*Kokusei chōsa hōkoku*), published at five-year intervals since 1950.

apartments in both cities accounts in large part for the predominance of the younger age group.

The presence of a large portion of younger people in a city is a mixed blessing for progressive politicians out to solicit their vote. In one respect, it is an advantage. Virtually all survey data from the recent past illustrate that younger people are more likely to support opposition parties than their elders. However, in another respect, having so many young people about is a disadvantage because they do not vote as faithfully as their elders. One example must suffice to illustrate this claim, although there is abundant evidence to buttress the assertion. In the 1974 mayoralty contest in Fuchū, only 48 percent of those between twenty and thirty-four turned out, while 68 percent of those between thirty-five and forty-nine and 72 percent of those over fifty voted.[9] Therefore, despite the prospective aid they could offer the progressive or opposition cause, younger people have been abandoning the field to their older, and often more conservative, compatriots. This enables older residents of a community to exercise disproportionate influence, especially in local elections where turnout rates are often lower, and it is one factor underlying the persistence of conservative voting strength at the municipal level.

A person's educational attainments play a somewhat mixed role in determining voting behavior in Japan. The LDP, for example, draws considerable strength from poorly educated persons, such as farmers who finished only elementary school during the prewar years, and some strength from well-educated persons, such as high-ranking business executives and government officials. In the same way, the two Socialist parties draw strength from people at both ends of the educational spectrum: industrial laborers with modest education and intellectuals with advanced degrees. The Kōmeitō and the JCP, on the other hand, seem to draw the bulk of their strength from people with high-school or grade-school educations. As a general rule, however, those with the highest levels of education are most likely to favor the Socialist parties.

This tendency underscores the observation that educational attainment is one social feature explaining differences between Musashino and Fuchū. In a nation where a majority of the populace had never finished high school, Musashino had attracted by the early 1970s a population that was exceptionally well-educated. Fully 65 percent of its residents aged fifteen and over had eleven or more years of education, while 18 percent of them (and 29 percent of the males) were

[9] Fuchū shi Senkyo Kanri Iinkai, *1974 Fuchū shichō senkyo no kiroku* (Fuchū: Fuchū shi Senkyo Kanri Iinkai, 1975), pp. 42-43.

college graduates. In Fuchū, by contrast, only 55 percent had more than eleven years of schooling, while only 11 percent of the adult population (and 18 percent of the males) had a college degree.[10] Given the likelihood of finding progressive party supporters among highly educated citizens, one can understand why the Socialist parties were relatively strong in Musashino.

Like most suburbs, Musashino and Fuchū both had occupational structures that differed significantly from the nationwide norm. While in 1970, 19 percent of the workers in the country were engaged in agriculture, less than 2 percent were so engaged in Fuchū and Musashino. Moreover, while less than half (47 percent) of the nation's workers were employed in the tertiary sector, fully 58 percent in Fuchū and 67 percent in Musashino were so employed. The two communities also differed from the nationwide average on a third count. With only 30 percent of its resident workers employed in manufacturing, Musashino was somewhat less industrial than the nationwide average (of 34 percent), but Fuchū was somewhat more industrial (at 40 percent). Both communities thus possessed an urban occupational structure, but they differed between themselves in that Fuchū had a larger percentage of industrial workers than Musashino.

In Japan, as in all other societies, a person's occupation has a direct influence on his voting behavior. Commonly, for example, industrial workers in large private firms, middleranking white-collar personnel in public and private organizations, and "intellectuals" support the JSP, while farmers, laborers in small firms, shopkeepers, owners of small companies, business executives, and highranking officials support the LDP. The DSP draws voters from the ranks of the intelligentsia and from among industrial workers and company owners. Finally, the CGP and the JCP have come to represent the "outs" in Japanese society, struggling shopkeepers, day laborers, alienated salarymen, et cetera. The JCP also draws support from organized workers, especially in public organizations. This is a somewhat crude characterization of the occupational traits of party supporters in Japan, but it bears a strong resemblance to reality.

Given these facts, one can understand why progressives were so dominant in both communities at the national level. Industrial workers, many of them employed in large enterprises, and white-collar personnel in commercial, industrial, and public organizations comprised well over half the occupied labor force in both cities. Such workers tended to support opposition parties, and we can assume, given the opposition

[10] Sōrifu Tōkei Kyoku, *1970 Kokusei chōsa hōkoku* (Tōkyō: Sōrifu Tōkei Kyoku, 1972), p. 161. Hereafter cited as 1970 Census.

vote in Diet elections in both Musashino and Fuchū, that they were doing so there as well.

These observations help to explain the relationship between occupational structure and party support in Diet elections, but they are less applicable at the local level, particularly in Fuchū. With a large complement of white-collar workers and a very large group of organized industrial workers, Fuchū should also have witnessed considerable support for opposition candidates at the mayoralty and council levels, but it did not. This suggests two things. First, one cannot reliably predict voting behavior in a community on the basis of its occupational structure alone. Second, one must therefore look elsewhere for an explanation of Fuchū's political character, in this instance toward organizational and historical factors.

The rate of residential mobility in a city is a demographic phenomenon that can exercise substantial influence on political conditions, especially in rapidly growing suburban areas. Musashino and Fuchū are excellent illustrations. Between 1960 and 1974, Musashino grew from 120,000 to about 140,000, while Fuchū exploded from 82,000 to over 180,000.[11] In both communities, a total of 35,000 to 43,000 people moved in or out of the community each year in that period. Although Fuchū experienced the highest rates of growth, Musashino witnessed the highest rates of mobility, for nearly 30 percent of the city's population was involved in inward or outward migration annually in the 1960s, while only 20 percent was so involved in Fuchū. In 1970, therefore, nearly one-half the residents of both cities had lived there for less than five years.[12] This is not to say that no one was a long-term resident in either city. By no means was this so, because in both cities at least one-third of the population had been in their present residence since 1959. Most of them were older people who owned the homes they occupied. These figures do indicate, however, that many people, for the most part young married couples and singles between twenty and forty (and some children), were constantly moving in and out of the suburbs until they found their own homes in which to settle permanently. The relatively large amount of rental housing (amounting to 66 percent of all housing units in Musashino and 58 percent in Fuchū) was a major cause of these high mobility rates.

Considerable evidence suggests that such high rates of mobility had an effect on rates of voter participation.[13] Mobility reduces the indi-

[11] 1975 Census, p. 46. [12] 1970 Census, p. 145.

[13] See especially the following attitude surveys conducted in Musashino and Fuchū in the early 1970s: Musashino shi, Kikaku bu, *Musashino shimin no jichi ishiki chōsa: 1970* (Musashino: Musashino shi, 1970), pp. 103-128, and Ukai No-

vidual's integration into a community and hence his participation in local politics. It is also associated with people in certain age and occupational categories—young apartment dwellers in the tertiary sector—who are also the least likely to vote in any election, especially local elections, owing to career pressure, an incomplete socialization into politics, and political disinterest. This provides yet another bit of evidence to explain the persistence of conservative power in municipal elections. The mobile residents who failed to vote were quite likely to support opposition parties, and by abstaining, they enabled conservatives to exercise strength at the polls out of proportion with their numbers. High rates of mobility had further implications as well, but these will be discussed later in the essay when it turns to an analysis of organizations and historical processes.

There is one point to be made regarding differences in income or wealth between Musashino and Fuchū and the political preferences demonstrated by their citizens. Simply put, comparison of these cities shows that the wealthier of the two, Musashino, was also the more likely to vote progressive at all levels. Its relative wealth was immediately evident to the naked eye, especially in the eastern portion of the city near Kichijōji Station. There one encountered three prestigious department stores, each in a gleaming new building, luring crowds of shoppers, among whom common figures were middle-aged suburban matrons with Pierre Cardin scarves draped conspicuously around their necks. In Fuchū, by contrast, one was most likely to encounter in its slightly run-down, middle-class department stores young, infant-toting mothers in their discount woolens. The types of shops, the quality of housing, and the general visual appearance of the two cities lent further support to the impression that Musashino was discernibly better off.

Underlying these subjective impressions are the actual differences in income levels between the two cities. Musashino happens to be one of the wealthiest cities in Japan. In 1973, it ranked third in the nation on the basis of its per capita taxable income.[14] With an index of 182 (where 100 equals the national average for all cities), Musashino stood well ahead of Fuchū, which scored 138.[15] Both cities were thus well above

bushige, ed., *Ningen to toshi kankyō: Daitoshi shūhen bu* (Tōkyō: Kajima Shuppan sha, 1975), pp. 207-215. Referred to hereafter as the Musashino Survey and the Fuchū Survey.

[14] Zenkoku Shichō kai, *Nihon toshi nenkan: 1975* (Tōkyō: Jichi Nippō sha, 1975), p. 161.

[15] The figure for Musashino is biased somewhat by the fact that wage earners made up a relatively large portion of its resident population, while in Fuchū children under fifteen were relatively overrepresented.

the national average. Musashino also had more very large income earners than Fuchū. Its residents with incomes surpassing 10 million yen per year in the early 1970s numbered 29 in every 10,000, while in Fuchū they numbered only 18.[16] This put Musashino in a class with such prestigious residential areas as Setagaya Ward, but it relegated Fuchū to the status of a working-class industrial district like Sumida Ward. Finally, although Fuchū had a population nearly 30 percent larger than Musashino's, both cities realized virtually the same total revenues from citizens' taxes (*shimin zei*), which were based largely on individual incomes.[17]

If Musashino were an American suburb, it would be strongly disposed to support the Republican Party. One might also expect, given the tendency of wealthy voters in Japan to support the LDP, that Musashino would be more supportive of conservative parties than it seems to be. But this problem must be viewed from a different perspective. Musashino is a city that has attracted a relatively high concentration of white-collar workers in the upper-middle income range. Although not rich, they make the city more wealthy than most, lending it an air of affluence. By virtue of their social attributes, these people tend to vote for Socialist parties in the Japanese context. Therefore, the relationship between wealth and partisanship in Musashino is not as puzzling as it might initially seem. When forty-year-old college graduates in middle-level white collar positions cluster in Japan, as they do in Musashino, they provide a logical base for opposition party support.

The foregoing analysis of the socio-economic structure of two suburban cities has helped to explain why they support opposition parties at the expense of the entrenched regime. Suburbs have attracted a large complement of relatively young, well-educated persons employed in the secondary and tertiary sectors. Over the past two decades, people with such attributes have shown a strong tendency to support the Socialist parties. While these individual traits do help to predict voting patterns to some degree, they nonetheless fail to provide plausible explanations for behavior at all levels of the political system. Therefore, I will seek to cast further light on political behavior in these suburbs by dealing with contextual and historical factors, beginning with a discussion of mayoralty candidates in Musashino and Fuchū.

[16] Kōjunsha, comp., *Nihon shinshiroku dai 62-han bessatsu furoku: Kōshotokusha meikan* (Tōkyō: Kōjunsha, 1973).

[17] Musashino shi, Shigikai Jimukyoku, *1974 Gikai yōran* (Musashino: Musashino shi, 1974), p. 40, and Fuchū shi, *Fuchū shi tōkei sho: 1974* (Fuchū: Fuchū shi, 1975), p. 32.

Candidates and Opponents

It would be valuable to assess how the qualities of candidates and their opponents have affected the political responses of the voting public in Diet, mayoralty, and council campaigns. Unfortunately space does not permit such analysis. Instead it is necessary to limit discussion to mayoralty candidates alone. But owing to their pivotal role as both keystones of support for Diet candidates and leaders of support for council candidates, this choice—however restricted—remains an important one.

Musashino's progressive mayor since 1963, Gotō Kihachirō, began his political career with a victory to the city council in 1951. At the time he was a thirty-one-year-old journalist who had attended Chūō University but left without a degree. Gotō became one of the central figures in the city's then small contingent of progressive councilmen. Over the next twelve years he watched progressive electoral strength in the city grow to majority proportions. By 1963, he was encouraged enough to run for mayor against a four-term incumbent named Arai.

At fifty-nine, Arai represented the city's "old guard" in two senses. As the son of a local landlord and former council member and the younger brother of a former council member, mayor, and head of the agricultural cooperative, he personified the character of conservative leadership that had controlled Musashino politics without interruption since 1889. As a mayor with ties to the LDP rather than the progressive parties, Arai also represented old guard party interests.

Gotō won the election easily, capturing 56 percent of the vote. On two other occasions he was able to retain office without having to campaign, since the conservative forces in Musashino could not muster a candidate to compete against him. When they managed to do so in 1971, the company president and frequently unsuccessful LDP candidate who did run could only attract 22 percent of the vote.

From a personal perspective, Gotō's tenure seems attributable to two factors. First, he was in a position to ride the tides of political change when he stood for office in 1963. Progressive parties had been increasing their vote steadily for the preceding decade, and by 1963, they could command a clear majority of votes in elections at the national, prefectural, and local levels. He was a leading figure in the local JSP and a logical candidate. Second, Gotō brought with him his own *jiban* or electoral base, referred to jokingly in the city as the *Sakai-tō* (or the party of the Sakai section of the city), as opposed to the *Shakai-tō* (or JSP). The Gotō surname is rampant on shop fronts and farm posts throughout Sakai, so that family ties were an important element in the mayor's base. So also were longstanding sectional interests. In prewar Musashino, the mayoralty rotated—albeit irregularly—between men from Sakai and Kichijōji, a more highly developed section of the city on the eastern extremity. Arai, Gotō's 1963 opponent, was a Kichijōji son, and his origins probably added fire to the ardor of Sakai residents who wanted to get their man in office. By contrast with his counterpart in Fuchū, Gotō did not seem by the mid-1970s to enjoy a widespread popularity. He was simply in the right place at the right time with the kind of supporters necessary to win nomination and partly sustain a candidacy.

In Fuchū, Yabe Takaji enjoyed a different public image, based on affection for a local son, trust in his integrity, and confidence in his ability. Yabe's reputation as a local son owed something to his father's political career, which, although brief, was rather dramatic. Yabe's father was the first man from Fuchū and one of the first in the entire Santama Region to run for national office as a candidate of a proletarian party. Although he was unsuccessful, Yabe's father did attract a large following in Fuchū, and not from tenants alone. He was a popular figure who could deal with entrenched as well as insurgent interests. Takaji inherited this ability, along with a deft sense of compromise and pragmatism. Confidence in Yabe stemmed from his long tenure as an official in Fuchū, which began in 1930 and continued without interruption until his election as mayor in 1962. In the intervening years, he wore virtually every hat available in local government and developed the broad skills he has demonstrated since 1962 in running the Fuchū city administration.

With such formidable attributes at his disposal, it is little wonder that Yabe enjoyed an edge over his campaign opponents. The edge was certainly not so great that it would account in full for the wide margin of his victories, but it certainly helped. Similarly the quality of his opponents aided him in securing his victories. Yabe's most difficult contest occurred in 1962, when he faced both a long-time conservative councilman and a candidate of the JSP. The former appeared more aggressive than competent in the eyes of the citizenry, and the latter had a base of support too small to challenge any conservative. Yabe captured 56 percent of the vote. In the next three elections, fusion candidates from the JSP and the JCP ran against Yabe. None had ever held office. Two were minor figures and one was an outsider with only tenuous ties in Fuchū. Moreover, the JCP took the lead in directing the opposition campaign. This made it easy for Yabe to draw DSP and Kōmeitō voters into his camp and to win three times running. Thus while organizational conflicts among opposition parties contributed to

Yabe's marked electoral successes, his own popularity also played a role in his victories.[18]

It is perhaps no more than a banality to point this out, but it must be noted that the personal qualities of candidates, whether they be council, mayoralty, or Diet aspirants, are factors determining the outcome of any election. It is easy to lose sight of this. There is the academic bias toward either microscopic, individually-centered factors, or toward macroscopic, sociological factors. There is also the popular bias toward ideological factors. All of these are important. But the personal factor must also be given a proper measure of attention. Indeed, it is quite possible to argue, when all other factors have been considered, that the personal stature of a candidate is often the decisive element in the victory of a progressive politician.[19] Conversely, as events in Fuchū demonstrate, it can also be a decisive element in the *defeat* of a progressive candidate.

In these two suburbs, as well as elsewhere in Japan, the significance of the personal factor stems from a candidate's ability to elicit support from voters nominally committed to the opposing camp. Thus, in Fuchū, Yabe's family's political history enabled him to appeal to Socialists on the basis of a common heritage of opposition to entrenched interests, and in a different way, in Musashino, Gotō was able to expand his nominal constituency by gaining support from farmers and shopkeepers in the Sakai area who would normally vote for an LDP candidate. The personal factor is thus a subtle blend of patrimony, localism, personality, and political skill operating in combination to alter the normal structure of political alignments in a community.[20]

Organizations and Organizational Modes

Perhaps the most arresting feature of Tokyo suburbs in the 1960s and early 1970s was their dynamism. Suburban cities were communities undergoing rapid evolution. Beside the mature, if not elderly, rural villages of the country, a suburb seemed almost like a blossoming and unruly adolescent. Growth and unruliness had important implications for the political process because they enormously complicated the task

[18] A discussion of the policies these mayors have implemented and of the popular reaction to them would be very much in order at this point. Unfortunately, considerations of space prevent this. The reader should, however, consult the essays in Part Four of this volume that cover the topic of policy implementation.

[19] See, for instance, Scott Flanagan's discussion of the Minobe victory of 1971 in Chapter 5.

[20] The chapters by Ellis Krauss on Kyoto and Jack Lewis on Mishima amplify the importance of the personal factor in opposition politics at the local level.

of getting people to the polls and persuading them to support one's candidate. In villages this was done as a matter of course by mobilizing people through personal networks that penetrated every aspect of daily life—social, economic, and religious, as well as political. In the suburbs, by contrast, personal networks embraced just a small part of the total populace because the mass of postwar newcomers were poorly integrated into the affairs of a community. This placed some premium on a candidate's ability to develop organizational modes that would bring him electoral success. It is the purpose of this section to examine several suburban organizations in order to cast light on their political roles. Four types of organizations will be treated in turn: political parties, candidate support groups (*kōenkai*), labor unions, and residential associations.

In a well-known and characteristically pithy comment, Robert Dahl has remarked that "politics is just a sideshow in the great circus of life."[21] This is an especially apt perspective from which to address the subject of Japanese political parties and their organizational behavior in the suburbs. As in Japanese society as a whole, suburban political parties are anemic organizations, with some exceptions. Their memberships are generally small, they are organizationally weak, and they enjoy negligible importance in the eyes of the public.

In the period covered by this essay, only three of Japan's five political parties had municipal branches that commonly registered with election officials in Musashino and Fuchū: these were the LDP, the JSP, and the Kōmeitō.[22] Of the three, the Kōmeitō was the newest party in both suburbs, having registered for the first time in 1970. Local branches of the other two parties were older. The LDP and JSP had both formed branches in Musashino in 1958 and in Fuchū in 1963. There was no stable DSP municipal branch in either city because the party enjoyed very little electoral support and had virtually no activists on the local scene, save an occasional council member. The JCP did have local organizations, generally in the form of liaison offices (*renrakusho*), but officially such organizations were a part of the party's Santama Regional Committee.

[21] Quoted in Robert E. Dowse and John A. Hughes, *Political Sociology* (London: John Wiley and Sons, 1972), p. 137.

[22] It is extremely difficult to speak with any assurance concerning such topics as membership, activities, and organization of local political parties in Japan. There is no central clearing house for such information, and the printed materials one does find are so formalized that they are not a faithful reflection of reality. The following comments are based, nonetheless, on some of this official information collected by city and prefectural election commissions and on interviews with knowledgeable officials and political activists.

Although parties established campaign headquarters during major elections, in the periods between elections they usually did not maintain permanent offices with professional staffs in either city. Rather, party branch offices changed locations with alterations in presiding personnel, usually finding a lodging place in the home of the local branch chief, a prominent party member, or a city councilman. Frequently, the location of such offices was a mystery even to the election officials whose responsibility it was to keep tabs on them. It must have been an even greater mystery for the average citizen who might have wished to contact the party branch about a political matter.

In reality, however, this seldom happened because, as organizations, municipal branches attracted little popular support and demonstrated little effectiveness. Citizen surveys showed that at most only two percent of respondents belonged to a political party, a rate that was even lower than the national average.[23] The JSP local branch in Fuchū, for example, had less than two dozen dues-paying members in 1976. Moreover, citizens did not use political parties as an avenue through which to express their grievances or articulate their political demands. Only 2 percent of the respondents in both cities claimed to go through party channels when trying to resolve a political matter, whereas most went directly to city hall, relied on a residential association, or imposed on a council member.[24] Most political parties thus did not serve effectively as organizations to integrate suburban residents into the political life of the community on a day-to-day basis. The LDP, JSP, and DSP foreswore such a role for themselves by failing to develop enduring, active organizations at the municipal level. Only the Kōmeitō and JCP made some attempt to do this, and it appeared by the early 1970s that the Kōmeitō was having some effect in both cities, while the JCP was becoming modestly entrenched in Musashino, though not in Fuchū. In conclusion, one must look elsewhere than toward political parties to find the organizations that were incorporating suburban voters into the political process.

One such body was the *kōenkai*, an organization established for the purpose of mobilizing voters to support a political candidate. In the absence of organizationally sound political parties, *kōenkai* function as party surrogates during election campaigns. Contemporary *kōenkai* trace their origins to the late nineteenth and early twentieth century and the *ingaidan*. These were extraparliamentary groups that frequently resorted to coercion and bribes as means of persuading voters to support their candidates. *Kōenkai* are a postwar phenomenon that differ

[23] Musashino Survey, p. 148; Fuchū Survey, p. 237.
[24] Musashino Survey, p. 148; Fuchū Survey, p. 248.

from their predecessors, especially by eschewing violence. To some extent, contemporary *kōenkai* function almost as miniature pressure groups, to elicit favors from government bodies for constituents who will in return provide financial and organizational support for a candidate. Not surprisingly given their pattern of evolution and their mode of operation, which relies heavily on personal contacts, *kōenkai* are most frequently organized by conservative politicians associated with the LDP. Opposition parties like the JSP have often spurned them as being traditional or feudalistic.

Although they originated to assist candidates for the national legislature, in recent years *kōenkai* have penetrated to the local level as well. They were conspicuous in both Fuchū and Musashino by the mid-1970s, although more so in the former than the latter.[25] In Fuchū, seventeen successful candidates for seats on the thirty-person council had *kōenkai*, while in Musashino eight of thirty-six successful candidates did. There was a striking difference between the two cities, however. Of the seventeen *kōenkai* in Fuchū, fully sixteen were organized to support conservatives, some of whom ran as LDP candidates but most of whom ran without affiliation (*mushozoku*). (The other Fuchū *kōenkai* belonged to a candidate from the JCP.) By contrast, in Musashino six of the eight *kōenkai* were organized to support candidates of the Socialist parties, while the other two supported conservative candidates. This distinction provides an important key to understanding the disparities in party strength at the municipal level in both cities. To put it bluntly, the conservatives are well organized in Fuchū, the progressives have the edge in terms of organization in Musashino.

It is not unusual to find that conservative political candidates in Japan possess good organizations. Despite popular images to the contrary, the LDP has shown an almost brilliant capacity to elicit the last ounce of strength from an electorate in which it possesses a steadily declining advantage. Effective campaign organizations assembled by its individual candidates have been one key to its success. The JSP, by contrast, has not been nearly as effective in marshalling supporters, in large part because it has just ignored people who were not union members or their relatives. It appears, however, that JSP candidates in Musashino have not fallen victim to this constraint. Only a small minority of the city's JSP council members are union activists who run with union support. Many of the others are private citizens who have formed electoral bases of their own by creating *kōenkai* that draw

[25] The following comments are based on materials examined and interviews conducted at the municipal election commissions in Musashino and Fuchū in March 1976.

support from a variety of sources, including residential associations, PTA groups, and sports bodies. Thus one important reason for Socialist success at the local level in Musashino has been the organizational skill its candidates have demonstrated by mobilizing voters not just in the union movement but from all walks of life. The significance of this organizational strategem is highlighted by the following comments on labor union activities in the two cities.

It is common knowledge that labor unions have provided the groundwork for opposition party strength in postwar Japan. Since the late 1940s, unions have lent indispensable organizational and financial assistance to the Socialist parties in particular, which have come to rely almost exclusively on their good services in election campaigns. Socialist parties have been especially reliant on large unions in the public and private sector that are aligned with the two major national centers, *Sōhyō* (the General Council of Japanese Trade Unions) and *Dōmei* (Confederation of Japan Labor Unions), or with their predecessors. Since its formation in 1950, *Sōhyō* has had especially close ties with the JSP, while *Dōmei* has had equally close ties with the DSP. A third national center, *Chūritsu rōren* (Liaison Council of Independent Labor Unions), has also been active in assisting right-wing, anti-Communist candidates of the JSP. By defining the affiliations of labor unions in a given community, one is sometimes able to anticipate how organized workers in that community will behave politically.[26]

There are striking differences in the national affiliations of local unions in Musashino and Fuchū, and these highlight one of the crucial explanations for the divergent political behavior in the two cities. In both cities, organized workers comprised about one-third of the local labor force, a rate similar to the national average. In Musashino, they numbered over 16,000 in a total labor force of nearly 50,000; in Fuchū, they accounted for some 23,000 in a local labor force of more than 63,000. Musashino's unions differed from those in Fuchū by being smaller: the largest union in Musashino had only 3,309 members, while there were two unions in Fuchū with over 5,800 members each. The greatest differences, however, rested on national affiliations. Of Musashino's more than 16,000 organized workers, 68 percent belonged to unions affiliated with *Sōhyō*, another 5 percent belonged to *Dōmei* affiliates, and the remaining 23 percent belonged to *Chūritsu rōren* and

[26] One such study that focuses on the political behavior of industrial workers in the auto industry near Nagoya is Gary D. Allinson's *Japanese Urbanism: Industry and Politics in Kariya, 1872-1972* (Berkeley: University of California Press, 1975).

nonaffiliated unions in equal proportion. In marked contrast, fully 63 percent of the union members in Fuchū, most of them employed in the city's two largest electrical manufacturing firms, belonged to *Chūritsu rōren*, a center that attracted only 11 percent of all organized workers nationally; conversely, just 17 percent of the organized workers in Fuchū belonged to *Sohyō* affiliates.[27]

Before appraising the political significance of these distinctions, it is necessary to digress a moment. The preceding figures enumerate the number of organized workers who belonged to labor unions with offices in the two cities. Many of these workers resided in the cities where they worked; some did not. Owing to the manner in which membership figures for labor unions are collected in Japan, there is no way of determining exactly how many organized workers reside in a given community, except to go through the membership lists of each and every union. Failing this, one can only make some educated guesses concerning what portion of local union members are local residents. On the basis of discussions with union officials and examination of union membership data in conjunction with census materials, it can be suggested that resident union members and their spouses comprised approximately 15 percent of the registered voters in Musashino and about 20 percent in Fuchū. In addition, there were other residents in the two cities who belonged to unions with offices outside the city, but it is virtually impossible to know what portion of the electorate they comprised.

These figures provoke one important observation. It is dramatically evident that union members and their spouses provide an electoral base far too small to support a majority party. This comment applies not only to Musashino and Fuchū; it is equally applicable to the national scene as well. JSP activists in Musashino have recognized this fact. By mobilizing voters beyond the narrow confines of the union movement, they have built an electoral base to support more than two decades of Socialist government in their city. Socialist candidates in Fuchū have recently begun to do the same thing themselves, but with only marginal success so far. However, the persistent weakness of the opposition in Fuchū was only in part a product of this failure to reach beyond the confines of the union base. Even more problematical, from the perspective of the opposition, was the political behavior of the union members themselves.

[27] The preceding figures are based on the 1975 labor union name lists (*rōdō kumiai meibo*) compiled by the Tokyo Prefecture Labor Affairs Offices in Mitaka and Tachikawa.

The majority of members in Fuchū's two large electrical unions thought of themselves as JSP supporters and generally voted likewise.[28] However, they preferred candidates from the right wing of the party if possible, and they shunned any association with the Communist Party, or even with a fusion candidate who had Communist support.[29] Therefore, in the last three mayoralty elections, when the Communist Party took the lead in promoting the opposition candidates, the city's major unions would not back them. Instead, they adopted a neutral position similar to George Meany's in the 1972 American presidential election. As a result, many of the city's resident workers in *Chūritsu rōren* affiliates supported Yabe Takaji. Although it is impossible to say exactly how many supported Yabe, it is safe to assume that any substantial defection to Yabe from the ranks of this normally Socialist constituency would have an important effect on an election because these voters numbered between 12,000 and 15,000. This was more than enough votes to swing an election decisively in either direction. The voting behavior of organized workers thus helps to explain in considerable measure why conservatives control the mayoralty in Fuchū.

Their behavior, however, produced different consequences in each election. In a citywide election for the mayoralty, many electrical union workers threw their support to Yabe and not his challenger. In a citywide election for the council, where a victor only needed 1,000 votes to win, union members distributed their votes among several candidates. In the 1960s and 1970s, some supported conservative, and others socialist, candidates.[30] In campaigns for the prefectural assembly or for the National Diet, by contrast, the impulse to elect genuine union candidates ran strongly.[31] Therefore, the Tōshiba union threw its

[28] Tōshiba Rōdō Kumiai, *Tōshiba kumiaiin no ishiki: Sono jittai to kōzō bunseki* (Kanagawa ken, Kawasaki shi: Tōshiba Rōdō Kumiai, 1973), pp. 149-150.

[29] This assertion is based on a lengthy interview in 1976 with the secretary of the Fuchū branch of the Tōshiba union and on discussions with other local politicians and political activists.

[30] The "conservatives" whom they supported were unaffiliated candidates who usually voted with the conservative-LDP majority on city council. They were former union officials employed in managerial positions in the Tōshiba factory. In their cases, workers supported them both because they were union associates and because they were neighborhood representatives, since both of them lived in the area near the Tōshiba factories where there were large company housing units. Some workers in the same area, however, undoubtedly voted for a declared Socialist council member.

[31] On four occasions in the 1960s and early 1970s, highranking, long-term officials in the Tōshiba union stood as candidates for the prefectural assembly. It seems safe to assume that they were perceived as candidates of the union and that they

support behind two former union officials in the 1960s and returned them to the Tokyo Prefectural Assembly on two of four occasions. Finally, in Diet elections, most electrical union members cast their ballots quite faithfully for Socialist candidates:[32] with two or more Socialists running, they always found one congenial with their position.

These observations help to explain why there is a disparity in opposition support rates in Fuchū between Diet elections and local elections. Ideological sentiments, organizational affiliations, and personal assessments of candidates promote distinctive electoral responses in campaigns at different levels. Under these circumstances, union members appear to vote loyally for Socialist candidates in national and prefectural campaigns, but they seem to split their vote between candidates of the Right and Left in municipal contests. In Fuchū, one thus finds a high rate of support for opposition parties in Diet contests but a lower rate in local contests.

There is a fourth type of organization whose political activities help further to explain distinctions between Musashino and Fuchū. This is the residential association, a rather abstract conception that actually encompasses a range of groups with widely differing purposes and characteristics. Broadly speaking, residential associations can be thought of as territorially-based, submunicipal, voluntary associations (if one sets aside for the moment the meaning of "voluntary"). Three different forms predominate: (1) *jichikai* or self-governing associations; (2) *chōnaikai* (or *chōkai*), the postwar successors of the prewar urban neighborhood associations; and (3) *shōtenkai*, or shop associations. *Jichikai* and *chōnaikai* are organized on the basis of one's residence. Commonly, the administrative subdivisions within a city (such as a *chōme*, or subward) each organize a *kai* for their area. The household is the basic unit of membership, and it is expected that each household will record itself on the group's name list, pay a small annual fee, and participate in the association's activities. Sometimes, especially in the case of associations bearing the name *jichikai*, a group is organized on the basis of a residential unit, such as a large public housing complex or a small privately-owned apartment building. *Shōtenkai* are a bit different. They are territorial bodies, in the sense that all members come from a certain street or section of the city, but they are more

therefore won a substantial portion of votes from union members living in Fuchū. At the national level, it is well-known that a long-time right-wing Socialist representative from the Seventh District has had close relations with the Tōshiba union in Fuchū.

[32] See the results of the Tōshiba union survey mentioned in note 28.

exclusive because they restrict membership to shopkeepers only. The other two groups expect everyone living in their area to join.

These associations undertake a diverse array of activities that fall into five discernible categories. First, they can serve essentially liaison functions, acting as a kind of administrative unit that represents the city government on the neighborhood level. In this capacity, residential associations do such things as send around official announcements, take part in insect eradication campaigns, and clean the streets after major public events. In the past, they sometimes collected local taxes as well, but this function is now conducted almost exclusively by officials in city hall. Second, associations can serve as voluntary organizations to complement the city's formal efforts at fire and police protection. They organize teams of men to patrol neighborhoods, for example, or send around criers to warn of fire dangers during the dry season. A third important function for many associations is to cultivate friendship (*chinboku*) and harmony (*wa*). Midsummer dance festivals, the sponsoring of hiking trips to the mountains, the support of women's and children's sections are indicative of activities in this capacity. Fourth, and more recently, some associations see as a primary activity the aggregation of resident's demands, either toward their landlord (who might well be a semipublic Japan Housing Corporation) or toward the local government. Finally, the *shōtenkai*, as a somewhat different kind of group, ordinarily devote their energies to commercial ends by sponsoring lotteries, decorating lamp posts in their area, and soliciting contributions for promotional purposes. By necessity, few if any groups undertake all of these activities, but all residential associations undertake at least some of them. This leads to the existence of a variety of groups whose activities vary radically in intent and character.

In Musashino and Fuchū, residential associations give expression to this diversity. These groups were far more common in Fuchū, where the city government continued to use them as the lowest level of administration. It relied on them to circulate city announcements and to help with fire and police protection. Fuchū thus had some 380 *jichikai* and *chōnaikai* in the mid-1970s. Over 80 percent of the residents questioned in an early 1970s survey declared membership in such an association.[33] There were far fewer associations in Musashino, where local administrations have disavowed their official use since the end of the war. Many that did exist in the 1970s were of the *shōtenkai* type, or they were *jichikai* in large apartment complexes (*danchi*). The *chōnaikai* type, organized around a neighborhood or section of the city, was

[33] Fuchū Survey, p. 240.

quite limited in number. The Musashino survey conducted in the early 1970s indicated that only 38 percent of the respondents belonged to such an association.[34]

Finally, residents in Musashino and Fuchū perceived the purposes of these groups differently. A third of the citizens surveyed in Musashino were either noncommittal toward or opposed to *jichikai*, while fully 76 percent of the respondents in Fuchū declared positive support for them. Moreover, there was a tendency for Musashino residents to value their services as demand-making bodies, while Fuchū residents tended to value more highly the historical functions of liaison, police and fire protection, and cultivation of good feelings.[35] This further supports the observation that a large share of the Musashino *jichikai* were organized by middle-aged, well-educated, white-collar workers living in *danchi* who were entirely willing to use them as political vehicles.

It is extremely difficult to define the extent to which these organizations were employed to sponsor (*suisen*) candidates from within and to mobilize their members to support them. Three successful candidates for the Musashino city council in 1975 stated membership in a residential association on their official campaign announcements. One was an LDP victor who belonged to a territorial *chōnaikai*; the other two were JCP and DSP victors, both of whom were heads of *jichikai* in public housing units. Only one Fuchū candidate, a Socialist who headed a territorial *jichikai*, listed ties to a residential association. How many others had such ties would be difficult to determine, but it may seem surprising that so many of those who did acknowledge their ties publicly were opposition party candidates. It is commonly thought that these bodies, which have a strongly indigenous and historical character, serve as the groundwork for conservative party support. In fact, contemporary conditions are very complex and lead to no simple conclusions.

At best, one can point to three different forms of political activity that might involve residential associations—activities that depend largely on the structure and membership of the group. It is possible to find territorial *chōnaikai* whose boundaries and memberships coincide with rural hamlets (*buraku*) that have been incorporated into a large city. These groups might well sponsor a candidate and give him rather fulsome electoral support. Thus, it is not a coincidence that the Yotsuya area in Fuchū, which was a *buraku* in one of the villages incorporated in 1954, had the largest *chōnaikai* in Fuchū and also returned two conservative members to the city council. A second type of residential association is one situated in an area where both long-term residents of

[34] Musashino Survey, pp. 146-147.   [35] Fuchū Survey, pp. 236-244.

a conservative persuasion and newcomers of progressive inclination live in mixed neighborhoods where single-family dwellings and apartments sit side by side. In such areas, there is a tendency to eschew any political activity. The conservative leaders of such groups recognize that they would antagonize the progressive newcomers if they backed one of their conservative friends under the banner of the association. So, in order to preserve harmony in the *jichikai* or *chōnaikai* itself, they try to keep politics out of their activities. Finally, a third form arises in the large housing units where *jichikai* are organized among college-educated, white-collar workers in their thirties and forties. One encounters a consonance of views on many matters in such developments, and such consensus can lend itself readily to unified political action. This seems to have happened in the large public housing developments in Musashino.

Residential associations in contemporary Japan thus have mixed effects politically. They can be mobilized for political purposes under particular conditions. In those cases, depending on the location, structure, and membership of the groups, they can serve as electoral bases for conservative politicians or they can help to elect opposition party candidates. It appears, though it is difficult to prove, that residential associations in Fuchū are one form of organizational support that helps in some part to elect so many conservatives to the city council. Conversely, the newer type of *danchi jichikai* that are common in Musashino seem to offer valuable electoral support to young opposition candidates in that city.

In conclusion, the four types of organizations discussed in this section have had a diverse influence on patterns of electoral behavior in Musashino and Fuchū. Of the four, political parties have probably had the least effect because they have been too small and too inactive to exercise very conspicuous influence. The activities of the other three organizations, however, have clearly contributed to some of the marked differences that are evident between the two communities. In Fuchū, *kōenkai* and residential associations have both provided relatively stronger support for conservative than opposition candidates, and they have thus helped to undergird persisting conservative rule in that community. Perhaps even more decisively, the political behavior of union members in Fuchū has contributed to the persistence of conservative power. Owing in some part, therefore, to distinctive patterns of political behavior adopted by members of these key organizations, Fuchū's recent political history has followed a course perceptibly different from that of Musashino.

Patterns of Historical Evolution

Any explanation of contemporary political conditions in Musashino and Fuchū would be incomplete without some understanding of the different paths of historical development these two communities have taken. This section analyzes in brief compass key aspects of the history of the two communities in order to explain their structural and organizational peculiarities.[36]

As sites of human settlement, both Fuchū and Musashino are quite old. The former dates from the seventh century and the latter from the seventeenth. However, 1889 might serve as a benchmark from which to define the historical character of today's settlements. When Musashino Village formed that year under the impetus of Japan's first local government codes, it was comprised of four rural settlements in which landlords with small holdings predominated. None of the villages had large commercial sectors, and none began to develop commercially until the 1910s. As a result, prewar politics in Musashino were characterized by squabbling among sectional interests within the community, and contests for power usually involved coalitions of landlords virtually all of whom were supporters of the Seiyūkai. As late as the 1930s, Musashino was less a unified community than it was a group of rural settlements living in awkward association under a common name.

Fuchū, too, was formed by amalgamating several settlements in 1889. But, unlike Musashino, they had a sense of community because most of them were mixed farm and commercial settlements clustered in close proximity at the crossroads of two rather heavily traveled thoroughfares, the Kōshū Road and the Kamakura Road. As in Musashino, there were also intracommunity squabbles, but rather than involving representatives of sectional interests from different parts of the community, they involved adherents of different party persuasions. From the 1880s onward, there were two political groups in Fuchū, one aligned with the Seiyūkai and the other with its conservative opponent. Although differences of opinion arose frequently, these disagreements focused on how to direct community development and who should do it. Thus, by contrast with Musashino, native inhabitants in Fuchū, especially political activists, possessed a rather strong sense of community. This would have significant implications once outsiders begin to arrive in large numbers.

[36] General accounts of the histories of the two cities are available in Fuchū shi Shi Hensan Iinkai, comp., *Fuchū shi shi*, 2 vols. (Fuchū: Fuchū shi, 1968-1974), and in Musashino shi Shi Hensan Iinkai, comp., *Musashino shi shi* (Musashino: Musashino shi, 1970).

The newcomers who initiated suburban development arrived at different times in the two communities, owing largely to their locations. The two cities actually sit quite close to each other on the western edge of the Tokyo ward area: the center of Fuchū is only five kilometers west of the center of Musashino. Thus, Fuchū is about 25 kilometers west of the Tokyo central district, and Musashino, about 20. However, thanks to the direct service provided by the Chūō Line, which opened through Musashino in the 1880s, in the mid-1970s one could get from Musashino to the center of Tokyo in only 30 to 40 minutes. By contrast, an express ride of the same duration out of Fuchū would only carry one to Shinjuku, where a transfer to another train or subway line was necessary to reach the central district, making a total trip of an hour or more. This relationship between geographic distance and commuting has had a critical effect on the timing of suburbanization in the two cities.

Given its relative proximity to the city center, Musashino began to develop as a residential community almost immediately after the Tokyo earthquake of 1923. A collection of sleepy agricultural settlements with a population of barely 5,000 in 1920 blossomed into an industrial and residential settlement of some 60,000 by the last years of the Pacific War. This wave of newcomers submerged native inhabitants numerically as early as the 1930s. Although the new arrivals by no means caused a revolution in local politics, they did create a society with educational, occupational, and intellectual traits discernibly different from those of the indigenous farm population. Owing to the very rapid pace at which Musashino developed, the community did not succeed in operating effective residential associations (*chōnaikai*) throughout the Pacific War and, when the war ended, only a few that survived it continued to function actively. Following the war, large numbers of newcomers, most of them from the ward area, moved to Musashino. They brought with them political positions developed in the highly charged atmosphere of the early postwar period. By the early 1960s, therefore, Musashino was on the way to becoming a mature suburban community of more than 100,000 residents, the bulk of them well-educated, reasonably prosperous, white-collar workers who had developed affiliations with opposition parties in the late 1940s and during the 1950s.

More distant from the city center and not as well served by rail lines until the 1910s, Fuchū's development as a suburb followed on Musashino's by several decades. The old post town did grow from 6,000 to about 25,000 between 1920 and 1945, but it was not until the late 1950s that Fuchū experienced significant growth. Some of its growth was artificial, taking place when the town of Fuchū amalgamated with two rural villages in 1954. This added about 14,000 persons to its population, the majority of whom, incidentally, supported conservative parties. But the great bulk of the population increase, which sent Fuchū soaring from about 60,000 in 1955 to over 180,000 in 1975, was the result of net in-migration combined with natural increases. Because the demographic expansion in Fuchū occurred so late, the vigorous residential associations that had functioned during the war both in the two villages and the old town were able to revive after the war. In Fuchū, leaders trying to perpetuate such groups did not confront the same indifference that their counterparts in Musashino did. Moreover, even among the newcomers there was some enthusiasm for the associations because many of the in-migrants were young factory workers from rural areas where similar organizations still flourished. Therefore, owing to the location of the city, the timing of Fuchū's suburbanization did not prove as disruptive to the continuity of prewar institutions as did the timing of Musashino's growth.

The timing of suburbanization in the two communities also shaped contemporary political conditions by sanctioning particular types of development. In the late 1930s, the Nakajima Aircraft Corporation built two large assembly plants in Musashino. American bombers attacked them frequently during the last years of the war. By the war's end, one factory was entirely destroyed and the other was just a skeleton. Although the sites were valuable as developed industrial properties, they were not used for that purpose. Rather, under the auspices of a national plan that sharply restricted the possibilities for industrial growth in Musashino, the sites were used for public housing complexes and for recreational purposes. Musashino was thereby able to preserve its character as a residential city. When the religion of economic growth swept the country after 1955, residents and politicians in Musashino were thus preoccupied with paving roads, building sewers, and constructing schools, not with attracting new industry. Their preoccupations created a positive image for the city, and it began to attract ever more young and middle-aged people anxious to find a home in a pleasant area where they could rear their families. Politically, they boosted the fortunes of the Socialist camp.

During the period of rapid growth, Fuchū, which had experienced virtually no bombing during the war, found itself with vast amounts of land available for development and a strong inclination on the part of local leaders to lure new industrial firms. The largest enterprise brought to the city in that period was the Nihon Electric Corporation, a firm whose workers belonged to *Chūritsu rōren*. It is possible to speculate that civic leaders may have found quite enticing a firm whose workers were not hard-line left-wingers. One cannot prove that Fuchū attracted Nihon Electric with this purpose in mind, but, the political consequences of its developmental efforts were to attract workers whose electoral behavior has helped, to some extent, to preserve the power of conservative interests in the local administration. Thus, developmental impulses shaped by the ideas current in two markedly different periods of Japan's recent history have played their role in determining contemporary political alignments.

Far more should be written to illuminate the historical processes that have shaped contemporary politics in Musashino and Fuchū, but the task awaits another occasion. This brief analysis must suffice to suggest some of the broad, evolutionary trends in the two cities. Musashino's relatively earlier development resulted in a somewhat earlier demise of indigenous interests, as these were never powerful enough to parry the political challenges brought by sweeping suburban growth. It also soured the local populace on industrial development and led to the emergence of a residential community that attracted the type of people who were more likely to support the opposition than the LDP. Having taken more time to develop as a suburban community, Fuchū confronted masses of newcomers with deeply rooted local institutions governed by men with a strong sense of community and a desire to preserve their control over it. Perhaps intentionally, they carried out a program of industrial development whose social and political consequences posed no serious threat to conservative interests on the local level. In summation, origins, location, timing, and aspirations have promoted different forms of urban development in both of these cities and in the process have led to the evolution of two distinctive political communities.

CONCLUSION

However distinctive Musashino and Fuchū might be politically, the fact remains that both provided substantial electoral support for opposition politicians by the 1960s, especially at the national and prefectural levels. This essay has cited a number of reasons why the opposition has become so strong. A fundamental explanation is that suburbs have attracted large numbers of people who by virtue of their age, their levels of education, their occupations, and their organizational affiliations have been strongly disposed to support opposition parties over the past two decades. Before concluding this essay, it will be useful to consider for a moment the broader implications of these findings.

First, however, one disclaimer is in order. The two suburbs under consideration are both situated near Japan's most important metropolitan center, Tokyo. It is well known that Tokyo is the center of the nation's economy, its cultural activities, and its political life. People in its vicinity are subjected to a barrage of information and a set of ideas that have had a kind of liberalizing effect on their political behavior when viewed in comparison with that of Japan's village residents. Suburbs that draw most of their in-migrants from this environment partake of its liberalizing atmosphere. One must bear this in mind when appraising the broader implications of political developments in Musashino and Fuchū. There is no reason why suburbs in other areas, particularly those near rustic, regional cities, should follow the same course that these two Tokyo suburbs have followed politically.

One observation suggested by a comparison of Musashino and Fuchū is that purely residential suburbs are more likely to support opposition parties than industrial suburbs. This would be especially true of residential suburbs situated in close proximity to a major metropolis, such as Tokyo, Osaka, or Nagoya. Such cities draw their new residents largely from the city center, where they have been exposed for at least some years to a political environment in which opposition parties enjoy a clear preponderance of power. This suggests that suburban migrants probably develop an affinity for an opposition party *before* moving to the suburbs and then carry that affinity with them into their new dwelling.[37] On the other hand, at least through the 1960s, industrial suburbs tended to attract many rural migrants in the form of younger workers joining factory labor forces. Although their work experience eventually conditions them to vote Socialist, that process requires many years, and in the interim such people provide a cushion for the persistence of conservative political influence, especially at the municipal level.

A second observation prompted by the findings of this essay is that the growth of opposition electoral strength depends heavily upon (1) the indigenous character of the community and (2) its location.[38] As the Fuchū case demonstrates, location is important because increasing distance from the metropolitan center favors preservation of indigenous institutions, such as residential associations. In older communities, these

[37] The question of when and where suburbanites develop their party affiliations is, of course, central in analyses of American suburban politics. Unfortunately, there is little material on this subject in Japanese that provides direct evidence of patterns of change. Foregoing comments are largely indirect inferences, based on exhaustive study of census data and attitude surveys.

[38] The findings of Ellis Krauss and Jack Lewis, reported in other chapters in this study, lend compelling support to the claim that a community's indigenous character can decisively shape its political alignments.

provide an organizational substructure that fosters support for conservative politicians. Therefore, if suburbanization occurs in an old community where prewar style residential associations persist and where conservative forces have been bolstered by the amalgamation of rural villages, progressive newcomers will usually encounter a well-entrenched regime. They will only overcome such established power with substantial organizational efforts on their own part, and this will take time.

Time itself draws attention to a third observation. If these two communities are at all representative, it appears that as suburbs age, they grow more disposed to support opposition parties. Table 5 provides rather compelling proof of this assertion. These figures demonstrate clearly that voters in both Musashino and Fuchū have given an ever increasing share of the vote to opposition candidates in elections since 1955. This trend is not evident in all cases, but it is certainly pervasive. Moreover, it is clear that support for opposition candidates penetrates more deeply into the political process over time. Opposition strength tends to grow first at the national level. Only later does it develop at prefectural and municipal levels, as the figures in Table 5 again illustrate. This trend is evident even in a community with a vigorous conservative base like Fuchū.

Table 5

Rise of Opposition Electoral Strength in Musashino and Fuchū
(by percentage of vote for all opposition party candidates)

Type of Election	Opposition Share in Musashino		
	1955	1963	1971-73
Lower House of National Diet	48	67	75
Prefectural Governor	55	53	70
Prefectural Assembly	57	69	60
Mayoralty	40	57	78
City Council	40	44	60
Type of Election	Opposition Share in Fuchū		
	1954-55	1962-63	1971-74
Lower House of National Diet	46	55	70
Prefectural Governor	55	53	66
Prefectural Assembly	45	47	48
Mayoralty	19	21	32
City Council	11	20	37

SOURCE: Official election returns from local election commissions.

It needs to be stressed that the growth of an opposition over time is not necessarily inevitable. A natural lag seems to occur during the process of suburbanization, so that conservative power persists at the municipal level during the first decade or two of suburban expansion. To a large extent, apathy on the part of newcomers permits this. Many newcomers do not begin to play an active role in local politics until they have been in a community for five to ten years. Thus, even though a once-rural city like Fuchū may be inundated within a ten-year period by one hundred thousand newcomers, they often fail to pose a political threat because at first they do not actively participate.

Once they have settled in, as they had in Musashino by the late 1950s, the (often progressive) newcomers begin to organize. It is this effort that promotes the rise in progressive fortunes at the local level. In Musashino, the organizational effort occurred during the 1950s and the 1960s, as Socialist council candidates and prefectural assembly delegates began organizing personal support groups to foster an expansion of opposition power. By the early 1970s, such efforts were occurring in Fuchū as well, directed with greatest success by Socialists and the Kōmeitō. In time, such activities might produce in Fuchū the same kind of broad and deep opposition strength found in Musashino as early as the 1960s.

In addition to mobilizing support for the opposition parties, organizational efforts serve an important ancillary function. They help bring to prominence men and women who can serve as viable, citywide candidates. This is no mean consideration in cities where the majority of residents are recent newcomers. The two cases under discussion have illustrated that successful mayoralty candidates share three attributes: they are native sons, they are moderates who can appeal to voters on both sides of the political spectrum, and they have substantial political experience—either as city councilmen or city officials. Some recognition based on public service at the municipal level is almost a necessity for a successful mayoralty candidate. By acquiring a reputation and building a base of supporters in such organizations as *danchi jichikai*, PTA associations, sports bodies, and possibly even civic action groups, prospective mayoralty candidates can win council seats that are often a springboard to higher office.

Ultimately, however, conditions in individual communities will depend substantially on political behavior in the national arena. Many well-educated younger people with good jobs and comfortable incomes despair of the Liberal Democratic Party largely, it seems, because of the anachronistic and venal image that its leaders project. Should the LDP find it possible to arrest its decline by reforming the party and bringing new faces to the fore, it is conceivable that some current opposition voters will switch to the LDP. There is thus no intractable guarantee that the kind of people who populate the suburbs in such number will forever shun the LDP. But given the dim prospects for reform in that party, their continued aversion does seem likely.

As important as the behavior of the LDP is the behavior of the opposition parties, especially the Socialist parties. Opposition growth in the suburbs depends not only on shifts in the socio-demographic character of a community. As the Musashino case has illustrated, it also stems from organization, usually in the form of mobilizing union members, party supporters, or personal *kōenkai*. By virtue of their age, their education, and their perspectives on the political process, many Japanese suburbanites are likely supporters of the opposition: whether they actually become opposition supporters will depend in large measure on the organizational efforts of the progressive parties and their candidates.

CHAPTER 5

NATIONAL AND LOCAL VOTING TRENDS:
CROSS-LEVEL LINKAGES AND CORRELATES
OF CHANGE

Scott C. Flanagan

In this chapter we will pursue two questions that were raised in the preceding chapters of Part Two. The first question concerns how we account for the long-term incremental growth of political opposition in Japan. In particular, we are interested in understanding why the erosion of one-party dominance is primarily an urban phenomenon, for it is this pattern of uneven opposition growth that has given rise to Japan's dual politics. The second question relates to the differences that are found in voting patterns between national and local elections. We have observed a general pattern of opposition growth on all three electoral levels—national, prefectural, and municipal—but while the rates of opposition growth reveal rough similarities, a gap in the percentage of the vote cast for progressive candidates often emerges between different electoral levels. In fact, we find consistent regularities in the tendencies for voters to shift their support from one political camp to the other between different levels and types of elections. Since both of these patterns are enduring phenomena, the underlying causes of the inconsistencies between urban and rural and between national and local voting trends become central questions for the analysis of Japanese electoral behavior.

Urbanization and the Growth of Opposition Support

Robert Dahl and Edward Tufte have advanced a number of hypotheses that relate the processes associated with urbanization to increased political competition.[1] In simplified form, we may say that their argument

The author would like to express his appreciation for the helpful suggestions and assistance he received at various points in the data collection, analysis, and writing stages of the preparation of this chapter to Kurt Steiner, Ellis Krauss, James White, Ronald Aqua, Michael McDonald, and Russell Dalton.

[1] Robert A. Dahl and Edward R. Tufte, *Size and Democracy* (Stanford: Stanford University Press, 1973), pp. 89-109.

proceeds along two lines. First, as the size of a community increases, its density increases. The greater the number of people that an individual comes in contact with, the more likely it is that he will find an ally. Small group experiments have shown that an individual is much more likely to voice his dissent if he finds support from some other members of the group. Also, as the scale of the occupational and institutional associations with which the individual is involved increases, the costs of dissent decrease. In small groups, dissent is difficult because it always entails personal overtones. Much more is at stake when dissent threatens to create antagonisms among people who must confront each other on a regular basis. In large-scale organizational settings, these costs are greatly reduced as conflict within and between groups becomes institutionalized and depersonalized. Increased scale and density, then, facilitate the identification of shared grievances, the organization of dissent groups, and the articulation of sectarian interests. Once established, dissent groups have an independent effect on increasing competition through the mobilization of potential clientele. This line of reasoning argues that increased size leads to increased density which in turn stimulates the organization of dissent groups and thereby results in greater political competition.

The second line of the argument is that as the size of the community increases, its diversity increases. As is well known, urbanization is associated with the processes of economic development—the growing size and complexity of production units, the differentiation and specialization of labor, and the increased distance between functionally specific roles (for example, management and labor). Thus when the size of a community increases, it not only enhances the chances of finding an ally but it also enlarges the number and diversity of interests that might potentially come into conflict. In short, diversity produces conflict, and conflict stimulates the polarization of loyalties and the mobilization of resources. Once again, the outcome is increased political competition.

On the basis of these arguments, Dahl and Tufte hypothesized that living in more densely populated areas and working in more modern, differentiated occupations (that is, nonagrarian occupations) would be associated with increased political competition. It was assumed that this increased competition would be manifested both in greater numbers of political parties competing in elections in proportional representation systems and in lower percentages of the vote won by the leading party in both plurality and proportional representation systems. They tested these hypotheses using data from the Netherlands, Switzerland, and the United States, and judging from their findings and similar analyses conducted in other countries, population density and occupational diversity are generally associated with higher levels of political competition.

In the Japanese context of one-party dominance, increased competition can only mean a decline in the Liberal Democratic Party (LDP) vote. We should then expect to find a number of demographic indicators associated with higher levels of opposition voting in Japan. Obviously the degree of urbanization would be one. A second would be the shift from traditional small-scale occupational categories such as farmers, small merchants, and retail store or street stall proprietors to blue- and white-collar workers in more highly differentiated modern organizations. Similarly, we might expect employees in large enterprises to be less supportive of the dominant party than employees in small shops and family concerns on the basis of the same arguments of density and diversity. Finally we would expect those who are organized into antistatus quo or antiestablishment groups such as labor unions to be less supportive of the dominant party.

Before we turn to the data, there is a third hypothesis relating demographic changes to a decline in one-party dominance that we might add to the density and diversity hypotheses. Both of the first two hypotheses suggest that some attitude of dissent, some consciousness of conflicting interests, or, at the least, some mobilization into an antiestablishment group is a necessary precondition to induce a voter to shift his support from the dominant party to an opposition party. However, much less conscious or structured processes of voting change may also be at work.

Research has shown that small group, face-to-face social networks tend towards homogeneity of political attitudes and partisan preferences. Most Japanese residential communities are characterized by a high density of such associational networks, particularly outside metropolitan areas. Moreover, historically these small-scale hamlet and neighborhood associations have been effectively utilized to maintain community solidarity and a consensual, communitywide approach to decisionmaking on important social, economic, and political issues. Thus we might expect community organizations to play an influential role in Japanese elections and a highly partisan one at that, since by and large these residential associations tend to be tied into conservative political networks. Indeed, as Terry MacDougall and Gary Allinson both argue in the previous two chapters, community associations are still used today, especially in local elections but also in national elections, to perpetuate conservative dominance.

Urbanization is associated with increased geographic mobility as well as increased density and social differentiation. The effect of increased mobility is to weaken the individual's integration into these kinds of conservatively oriented community associational networks. Mobility increases the citizen's anonymity and defeats the kinds of sanctions that communal groups have traditionally employed to ensure conformity. Thus in highly mobile urban settings, the associational infrastructure typically associated with residential communities in Japan is simply not as effective in reaching or influencing residents. As these more mobile residents increasingly slip through these conservative community mobilization networks, their voting patterns become more diversified by default. Clearly not all highly mobile Japanese conform to what has been called the "floating voter" syndrome (weak attachments to all parties and inconsistent voting behavior).[2] Nevertheless, this line of reasoning would suggest that increased mobility should be associated with a decline in support for the dominant party.

Unfortunately, there are no long-term panel survey studies that would enable us to precisely measure the effect of a change in occupation, a move to the cities, the joining of an antiestablishment organization, or the frequent changes of residence on an individual's voting preferences. Thus indirect tests must be used to evaluate the impact of demographic changes on the decline of one-party dominance and the rise in the opposition party vote. This involves a two-stage analysis. First, we will have to establish whether our causal variables are themselves on the rise. If there has been no substantial movement on our demographic indicators during the last twenty to thirty years, then demographics can hardly account for the voting trends we have observed. Second, we must substantiate that these same demographic variables are indeed associated with higher levels of opposition voting. This second stage of the analysis will be based on the 1967 Japanese Election Study.[3] While the survey data is limited to voting behavior in

[2] We can perhaps identify three types of independent voters in Japan: (1) the traditional type who is independent in the sense that he rejects any party label and identifies instead with a particular candidate, but who is frequently very regular and consistent in his voting behavior, supporting the same candidate in election after election; (2) the floating voter type who behaves much like the typical independent voter in the American literature—apathetic, inconsistent, and irregular in voting participation; and (3) a new type of independent voter who tends to be nonparty because he is highly critical of all parties and the condition of Japanese politics in general, but who is well-informed, concerned, and desirous of change. For a further discussion of this newer third type of independent voter, see Gary Allinson, "Japan's Independent Voters: Dilemma or Opportunity?" *The Japan Interpreter* 9 (1976): 36-55.

[3] The 1967 Japanese Election study was conducted by Robert E. Ward and Akira Kubota, and the data set was made available for secondary analysis by the Inter-University Consortium of Political and Social Research (ICPSR). This ex-

national elections, we believe that our analysis also pertains to voting in local elections. In other words, it is reasonable to assume that the causal variables we find associated with opposition voting in national elections are also associated with opposition voting in local elections.

Demographic Change and Opposition Voting

It is well known that Japan has undergone an unprecedented rate of urbanization and economic development throughout the twentieth century with all the attendant changes associated with those processes. Table 1, in fact, demonstrates that the movement of the population away from agrarian occupations and into the cities, while pronounced in the prewar period, greatly accelerated after 1950. From 1920 to

Table 1

Urbanization and Growth of the
Nonagricultural Labor Force in Japan

YEAR	% nonagricultural labor force	% living in cities of 100,000 or more
1920	46	12
1930	51	18
1940	56	29
1947	47	22
1950	52	26
1955	59	35
1960	68	40
1965	75	46
1970	81	52

SOURCE: Bureau of Statistics, Office of the Prime Minister, *Japan Statistical Yearbook*, 24th edition (Tokyo: Japan Statistical Association, 1974).

1940, the total labor force engaged in nonagricultural pursuits increased from 46 to 56 percent and the number of people living in cities of over 100,000 rose from 12 to 29 percent. In an equivalent postwar period, from 1950 to 1970, the nonagricultural labor force climbed from 52 to 81 percent and the urban population from 26 to 52 percent.

Along with the movement into blue- and white-collar/urban occupations has come a gradual rise in the scale of enterprises and in union

---

tensive national study consists of a pre- and postelection panel survey conducted at the time of the 1967 House of Representatives election. The analysis of the demographic and attitudinal correlates of opposition support presented in the three following subsections is based on this data set.

membership. For instance, from 1957 to 1972, the number of nonagricultural wage earners in the private sector employed in establishments engaging thirty workers or less decreased from 46 to 41 percent. During the 1955 to 1972 period, union roles have doubled from six million to twelve million members. The movement to the cities has also been associated with an increase in the mobility of residents. For instance, our survey data reveal that the number of renting as opposed to homeowning respondents increases dramatically from 14 to 33 to 48 percent as we move from rural areas to small and medium cities to metropolitan areas respectively and that even among homeowners urbanization is associated with more frequent moves.[4]

Turning to the second stage of our analysis, the findings reported in Table 2 show that each of our five demographic indicators is positively associated with higher levels of opposition voting. Only 24 percent of the farmers and 38 percent of the proprietor-managers voted for one of the opposition parties compared to 53 percent of the white-collar and 55 percent of the blue-collar workers; 34 percent of rural inhabitants supported the progressive parties compared to 59 percent of the metropolitan residents; and 43 percent of those engaged in medium and small enterprises voted progressive compared to 64 percent of those in large enterprises. Among those with low mobility (own their homes and have lived there over ten years) only 32 percent supported the opposition, while among those with high mobility (rent and have lived in their present dwelling ten years or less) 62 percent voted for an opposition party. Finally, only 36 percent of the nonunionized respondents voted progressive compared to 82 percent of those who were union members and 60 percent of those who, while not union members themselves, lived in a household with a union member.

While all five of these demographic changes are highly intercorrelated, elsewhere we have demonstrated that each has an independent and additive effect on a respondent's propensity to vote progressive.[5] One way to demonstrate the cumulative influence of these changes is presented in Table 3. The categories have been arranged in a logical sequence that might correspond to a pattern of change common to Japanese families experiencing the effects of modernization over one or more generations. Of course, the table does not prove a causal sequence

[4] For instance, the number of homeowners who had lived in their homes only ten years or less increases from 18 to 32 to 42 percent as we move from rural areas to small and medium cities to metropolitan areas respectively. Source: Secondary analysis of the 1967 Japanese Election Study.

[5] Scott C. Flanagan and Bradley M. Richardson, *Japanese Electoral Behavior: Social Cleavages, Social Networks, and Partisanship*, a Sage Comparative Paper in Contemporary Sociology, no. 06-024 (London: Sage Publications, 1977), pp. 1-93.

Table 2

Percentage of Vote for Opposition Parties
by Five Demographic Indicators

				Statistical Association (TAU)
Occupation	Farmer and Proprietor-Managers		White and Blue Collar Workers	
	29 (406)		54 (802)	.242
Urbanization	Rural Areas	Small and Medium Cities	Metropolitan Areas	
	34 (352)	45 (725)	59 (274)	.180
Enterprise Size	Medium and Small		Large	
	43 (659)		64 (287)	.190
Mobility	Low	Medium	High	
	32 (504)	51 (513)	62 (226)	.258
Union Membership	Nonmembers	Members in Household	Member	
	36 (903)	60 (183)	82 (142)	.279

SOURCE: Secondary analysis of the 1967 Japanese Election Study.

but only reports how respondents with different sets of attributes voted in 1967. Still the pattern that emerges is suggestive.

Among respondents classified as employed in a traditional occupation with a nonmetropolitan residence, a small- or medium-sized place of employment and low mobility, only 23 percent voted for one of the opposition parties. With each cumulative shift in one of these demographic attributes from a traditional to a modern characteristic, the percentage of those voting progressive increases successively to 38, 54, 71, and finally to 88 percent when all four attributes reflect modern characteristics. Had we added our fifth demographic variable, union membership, Table 3 would have reported an even wider gap between the extreme categories, but we could not introduce more than four independent variables because otherwise the number of cases per cell would have been too low.[6]

[6] While this paring down of the number of variables from the Table 2 type to the Table 3 type of analysis is unavoidable, we really do not lose very much.

Table 3

Percentage of Vote for Opposition Parties for Respondents
with Selected Demographic Attributes

Occupation	Urban-Rural Residence	Enterprise Size	Mobil- ity	% Voting Progressive
Traditional	Non- metropolitan	Small and medium	Low	23 (293)
Modern	”	”	”	38 (226)
”	Metropolitan	”	”	54 (54)
”	”	Large	”	71 (21)
”	”	”	High	88 (40)

SOURCE: Secondary analysis of the 1967 Japanese Election Study.

In short, the data would suggest that much of the rather substantial changes in aggregate voting patterns that have been reported in the earlier chapters of Part Two can be attributed to these five kinds of demographic change that we have been discussing. Urban, mobile, unionized wage earners in large enterprises are simply far more likely to vote for one of the opposition parties than are the rural, stationary, nonunionized, self-employed engaged in small-scale agricultural and commercial enterprises.

Attitude Change and Opposition Voting

In and of themselves, however, these demographic changes do not tell the whole story. Indeed, the density and diversity hypotheses suggest that important attitudinal changes accompany these demographic shifts. In order to gain a more complete understanding of Japanese voting trends over the last twenty to twenty-five years, therefore, we also need to consider how attitudinal changes within the Japanese electorate have contributed to the long-term shifts in partisan support that have occurred.

Here we shall not concern ourselves with short-term factors such as political issues or policy concerns, although MacDougall has shown a gradual shift in the priorities of urban voters from public works to environmental kinds of concerns.[7] Instead we will focus our attention

---

Since the impact of these variables is additive, when four out of five fall, for instance, on the modern side, the fifth has little further influence to add or subtract. Thus among those that were nonunion but modern on all four of the other demographic attributes, 83 percent still voted progressive.

[7] See Chapter 3.

on the changes that are occurring in voters' political orientations—in Japan's political culture. It is believed that in many cases it is these more fundamental attitudinal reorientations that lie behind voter shifts in public policy priorities. A number of studies have emphasized the passive, parochial character of Japan's traditional political culture, a culture that is still much in evidence in many sections of the country. Typically, this orientation is characterized by political apathy, deference to local influentials, and a low valuation of one's ability to exert any influence over political events. These passive parochials have a strongly local rather than national consciousness—they tend to be oriented more toward personalities rather than parties, to be preoccupied with special benefits for their local areas (*jimoto rieki*), and to be inattentive to the language and issues of debate over which national politics is being fought.

Our concern here is with the question of whether these attitudes are changing and, if they are, whether such changes are associated with a shift in partisan preferences. Our hypothesis would be that increased participation leads to increased competition. In other words, as parochial, apathetic, spectator orientations are replaced by cosmopolitan, attentive, participant orientations, we would expect that the citizen would become increasingly discriminating in his electoral choices and more aware of class and ideological concerns. These changes in political orientation would make it increasingly difficult for one party to successfully pose as the benefactor of every section of the population and hence should lead to a decline in one-party dominance and an increase in party competition.

There is also a second possible hypothesis relating certain kinds of attitude change to the decline in one-party dominance. This latter hypothesis concerns less explicitly political attitudes and more diffuse value orientations. Ronald Inglehart has shown that pronounced changes in value priorities are occurring in the advanced industrial societies of Western Europe.[8] Elsewhere I have shown that similar kinds of value changes are occurring in Japan and that at least in the Japanese context this value change can best be described as a shift from a *traditional*, austere set of value priorities that esteems frugality, piety, conformity, and devotion to authority to a *modern*, libertarian set of priorities that places more emphasis on self-indulgence, permissiveness, independence, and self-assertiveness.[9]

[8] Ronald Inglehart, "The Silent Revolution in Europe: Intergenerational Change in Six Countries," *American Political Science Review* 65 (1971): 991-1,071.

[9] Scott C. Flanagan, "Value Change and Partisan Change in Japan: The Silent Revolution Revisited," *Comparative Politics* 11 (1979): 253-278.

Our hypothesis would be that this traditional-modern value change is associated with greater political competition. There are several reasons for expecting this association to exist. First, the modern, cynical, self-assertive type is less likely to be awed by the symbols of authority and more likely to criticize performance failures. Thus we would expect these voters to be less likely to offer their unconditional support to the ruling party. Secondly, being more self-indulgent and permissive rather than austere and pietistic, their expectations for personal success and self-fulfillment would be greater. Thus, modern value types are both more likely to be dissatisfied with the realities of their life and social surroundings and at least partially to blame the government for the problems that they are experiencing.[10] This would also lead to higher defections from the ruling party. Thirdly, we would expect these more independent, assertive citizens to make heavier and more vocal demands on the government, once again making it more difficult for one party to adequately support and champion all the competing and in many cases conflicting demands being made upon it. Here again, the more vigorous assertion of new interests should lead to greater party competition. Finally, at least in the Japanese context, the dominant party is associated with a style of politics that is more consonant with the traditional set of values that we have been discussing. We would expect, then, that "modern" types would be less attracted by the style and rhetoric of conservative campaigns and more attracted to the progressives' appeals. In other words, voters with modern value orientations are less likely to be responsive to traditional campaign practices that are frequently employed by conservatives.

I have constructed a set of attitude scales to test the value change and participation hypotheses. These scales include a traditional-modern value scale, a deferential-assertive behavior scale, political interest and efficacy scales, and scales of class consciousness and ideological sophistication.[11] There is also a participation scale that counts the kinds of

[10] For instance, Inglehart finds substantially higher levels of socio-political dissatisfaction among his modern value type. Ronald Inglehart, "Value, Objective Needs, and Subjective Satisfaction Among Western Publics," *Comparative Political Studies* 9 (1977): 429-458.

[11] The traditional-modern value scale taps the four conceptual dimensions previously referred to, and it is identical to the traditional-libertarian scale introduced in Flanagan, "Value Change." The deference scale is a three-item scale indicating the respondent's deference to government officials, community leaders, and community opinion. Political interest is measured by a five-item scale covering the respondent's interest in the election campaign and politics in general, and efficacy is evaluated by the standard Michigan SRC four-item scale. Ideologues are those who use the concepts of Left, Center, and Right to order their political world

explicitly political acts and activities the respondent has engaged in beyond the simple acts of voting and attending the ubiquitous campaign meetings.[12]

Once again it is necessary to establish that a trend exists—that there is a consistent direction of change along these attitude and behavior scales. Naturally a number of the demographic trends that we have already discussed are promoting changes along these attitude dimensions, but here I will focus on two other kinds of changes that are strongly associated with shifting value and attitude orientations. These are generational change and education.

First we will consider the role of generational change. Inglehart argues that value priorities are acquired rather early in life as a result of the social context in which one's early socialization experiences take place. This early environment shapes the individual's basic values, and he tends to carry these values with him throughout the rest of his life. Thus, Inglehart has found that dramatic changes in the fundamental conditions of life in postwar Europe have brought about substantial generational change in value priorities. Elsewhere I have shown that in Japan, where the pace of postwar change has been even swifter, these generational value cleavages are even more sharply drawn than in Europe.[13] In Table 4, we note that the traditional-modern value scale is very highly correlated with age, with the younger generations far more likely to hold modern, libertarian values than the older generations. Thus as new generations emerge and replace older generations, the value priorities of the population as a whole shift in the modern direction. There is also a fairly substantial association between age and efficacy, with *younger* age cohorts professing a greater sense of political competence and assurance that their participation can make a difference. The other attitude scales, however, seem to be little affected by age.

A second factor promoting attitude change is education. In this regard it is important to note that in Japan education has changed dra-

---

and who can successfully classify parties as leftist and rightist, progressive and conservative. High class consciousness means that the respondent thinks in terms of class, rigid class lines (that is, the difficulty of class mobility), and class struggle.

[12] The participation scale taps such behaviors as working in campaigns, trying to persuade others to vote for one's preferred candidate, and giving campaign contributions. Attending political meetings was excluded because attending meetings is frequently more a function of personal or community loyalty than of political involvement, and the item was empirically found to correlate differently with the other scales and measures.

[13] Inglehart, "Silent Revolution"; Flanagan, "Value Change."

Table 4

Percentage Scoring High on Selected Attitude Scales by Education and
Correlation of Scales with Age and Education

Attitude Scales	*% Scoring High on Scales by Education*		*Statistical Association (TAU) of Scales with Age and Education*	
	Elementary	College	Age	Education
Modern Values	42	78	−.348	.264
Assertiveness (nondeferential)	44	72	−.066	.134
Political Interest	40	76	−.031	.215
Efficacy	31	70	−.168	.222
Class Consciousness	38	61	−.036	.120
Ideological Sophistication	40	75	−.040	.203
Participation	12	24	−.005	.058

SOURCE: Secondary analysis of the 1967 Japanese Election Study.

matically in the postwar period. First, there were important changes
in the content and context of education in Japan under the influence
of the occupation. In content, great stress was placed on teaching the
values of individualism and democracy; in context, education in the
schools changed from a hierarchic, authoritarian setting to one that
emphasized pupil participation both in the classroom and in extra-
curricular activities.[14] Secondly, there has been a tremendous expansion
in the average level of education in Japan. In the early postwar period,
compulsory education was extended from six to nine years of training.
Since that time, the proportion of junior high school graduates going
on to senior high school and college has steadily expanded. In 1950,
30 percent of the appropriate age cohort was attending senior high
school. By 1970, this had increased to 80 percent, and projections are
that it will reach 95 percent by 1980. Similarly, the proportion of the
college age population enrolled in an institution of higher education
has increased from around 9 percent in 1955 to about 25 percent in
1972, and it is expected to reach the 40 percent mark by 1980.[15]

Table 4 would suggest that these changes in the nature of and opportunities for education have brought significant changes in attitudes.
Modern values, political interest, efficacy, and ideological sophistication

[14] Ellis Krauss, *Japanese Radicals Revisited* (Berkeley: University of California
Press, 1974), pp. 68-76.

[15] See Office of the Prime Minister, Bureau of Statistics, *Japan Statistical Yearbook* (Tokyo: Japan Statistical Association, 1974).

are all strongly associated with educational attainment. As the frequencies show, on the average 36 percent more of the college educated are likely to score highly on these scales than are those with only an elementary education. The association between education and the assertiveness and class consciousness scales is somewhat lower, but still an average of 25 percent more of the college educated are likely to fall at the high end of these two scales than are those with just a primary education. Finally, the relationship between education and participation appears to be very weak, largely because the vast majority of all educational levels do not engage in these kinds of political activities. Nevertheless, we still find that the college educated are twice as likely to be active participants as those having only the lowest level of educational attainment.

Thus, despite being limited to using cross-sectional data, there is good reason to believe that considerable movement has taken place throughout the postwar period on these six attitude and behavior scales as a result of generational and educational change. The next question is whether these attitude scales are systematically correlated with political competition. If the value change and participation hypotheses put forward here are correct, we would expect the high ends of our scales to be associated with lower levels of support for the LDP.

As Table 5 demonstrates, we find significant positive correlations between all our scales and support for the opposition parties. The strongest relationships are found between opposition support and modern values, political interest, and class consciousness. On these three scales, the high and low categories differ in their support for the opposition parties by 40, 30, and 26 percent respectively. On the assertiveness, efficacy, ideological sophistication, and participation scales, the differences are 16, 16, 23, and 22 percent respectively. These findings would suggest that changes over time in the low to high direction on each of these attitudinal dimensions is associated with substantial shifts in partisan support, namely a movement away from voting for the dominant party and towards voting for one of the opposition parties.

One other variable is introduced in Table 5, and that is the respondent's expressed motivation for choosing the candidate for whom he voted. This variable is reflected by the scale for modern choice criteria. Regardless of whether the respondent said he chose his candidate on the basis of his relationship to the candidate or on the basis of the candidate's personality, or whether he supplied no specific reason or offered no codable response to the question, we find almost exactly the same levels of support for the opposition parties, namely 38 percent. In contrast, if the respondent indicated that he selected his candidate on

Table 5

Percentage of Vote for Opposition Parties by Attitudinal Variables

Attitude Scales	*Low*	*Medium*	*High*	*Statistical Association (TAU)*
Modern	28	46	68	+.228
Values	(187)	(992)	(144)	
Assertiveness	39	46	55	+.140
(non-deferential)	(580)	(294)	(405)	
Political	28	45	58	+.209
Interest	(215)	(842)	(293)	
Efficacy	41	50	57	+.119
	(651)	(364)	(164)	
Class	34	44	60	+.219
Consciousness	(421)	(541)	(368)	
Ideological	37	46	60	+.176
Sophistication	(587)	(490)	(274)	
Participation	42	58	64	+.107
	(1121)	(141)	(89)	
Modern Choice	38	—	72	+.274
Criteria	(1072)		(279)	

SOURCE: Secondary analysis of the 1967 Japanese Election Study.

the basis of the party label, ideology, or group interest, 72 percent voted for the opposition. The contrast here between the more traditional-apathetic and the more modern-participant orientations is readily apparent.

Table 6 demonstrates the cumulative effect of these attitudinal influences. Again, due to the severe restraint on the number of variables that can be introduced into this type of analysis, those scales in Table 5 that are more weakly associated with the vote (assertiveness, efficacy, and participation) were dropped. In addition, the class consciousness and ideological sophistication scales, which are highly intercorrelated, were combined into one class ideologue scale. All scales were dichotomized and, again as in Table 3, the variables were sequentially arranged in a somewhat arbitrary but nonetheless logical order. We note that as we move successively across the categories from traditional to modern values, apathy to interest, low class and ideological awareness to high class ideologue consciousness, and finally from a traditional, personalistic basis of making one's voting choice to a more modern, ideological basis, the level of opposition support monotonically rises from

Table 6

Percentage of Vote for Progressive Parties for Respondents
with Selected Attitudinal Attributes

Values	Political Interest	Class Consciousness and Ideological Sophistication	Voting Criteria	% Voting Progressive	N
Traditional	Low	Low	Traditional	24	(119)
Modern	"	"	"	36	(69)
"	High	"	"	37	(51)
"	"	High	"	62	(92)
"	"	"	Modern	87	(62)

Source: Secondary analysis of the 1967 Japanese Election Study.

24 to 87 percent.[16] Obviously there are other variables not considered
here that differentiate the voters in our extreme modern and traditional
categories and directly influence their voting behavior. Nevertheless,
our analysis strongly suggests that the kinds of attitude changes we
have discussed tend to undermine voter support for the LDP.

A Path Analysis of Voting Behavior

A complex connection of linkages interrelates the demographic and
attitudinal changes we have been discussing in this section and their
relation to voting behavior. In concluding this section, a path analysis
will be employed to identify these linkages. In order to simplify the
picture, several of the demographic variables were combined in single
indices. The *modern attributes* scale is based on age and education such
that college educated respondents in their twenties and thirties are at
the high end of the scale and those over 55 having only a primary
education are at the low end. In other words, younger generation respondents with high educational attainment are classified as having

[16] The particular sequence that we have chosen suggests that politically attentive nonclass ideologues do not behave very differently from apathetic nonclass
ideologues. On the other hand, if we had reversed the two middle variables reported in Table 6, the figures would show that attentive class ideologues *are* significantly more likely to vote progressive than apathetic class ideologues. The
particular sequence chosen for Table 6 represents the one that theoretically
seemed to most closely approximate the sequence of linked changes that we might
expect an individual to undergo over time rather than the sequence that empirically yielded the neatest results.

modern attributes. The *modern occupations* scale combines type of occupation with enterprise size. Thus blue- and white-collar workers employed in large enterprises constitute the high end of the scale, and farmers, proprietors, and managers engaged in small-scale enterprises are coded at the low end.

The four principal paths that emerge from Figure 1 seem to conform nicely to our five hypotheses. First we note that modern occupations lead to the organization of dissent groups (union membership) which in turn leads directly to opposition voting. This is the argument of the diversity hypothesis, and because urbanization is strongly intercorrelated with modern occupations, I assume that the density-organization-opposition voting developmental path is also partially confirmed. In any case, the density and diversity hypotheses are highly interrelated, and we could not expect a path analysis to generate an independent line from urbanization to dissent group membership unless such membership was not occupationally related, such as membership in a peace or a citizens' movement. Unfortunately such information on respondent memberships was not gathered.

A second important path leads through mobility and directly to vote. Urbanization, modern occupations, and modern attributes all tend to increase geographic mobility. Higher mobility is then directly related to decreased support for the dominant party. The interesting

Figure 1

Path Analysis of the Relationships Between Demographic and
Attitudinal Change and Increased Political Competition

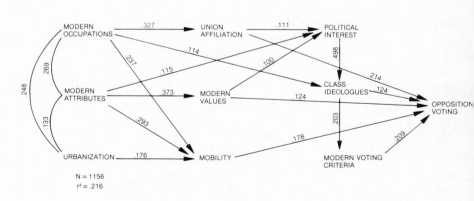

N = 1156
r^2 = .216

Note: All reported path coefficients significant at .001 level. Path coefficients under .100 not identified.

point that emerges here is that mobility is not related to attitude change.[17] This apparently substantiates the mobility hypothesis, namely that mobility weakens a voter's integration into community associational networks. We have argued that these networks induce conformity to traditional areal interests and that since these interests are almost uniformly represented by conservative candidates, community associational networks have predominantly boosted the fortunes of the conservative camp. The weakening of a citizen's integration into his residential community through increased mobility, therefore, can directly affect his voting behavior quite independently of any attitude change.

A third path goes directly from modern attributes to modern values to opposition voting. This conforms to the value change hypothesis. With the emergence of new generations socialized under new, more affluent circumstances and with the spread of more advanced levels of educational attainment, social values are changing. The more traditional, austere values are giving way to more modern, libertarian ones, and, for the reasons just discussed, this change is, apparently, directly and independently inducing voters to alter their partisan preferences.

The fourth and final path reflects the participation hypothesis and is somewhat more complex. Modern attributes, modern values, and union membership all lead to higher interest in and attentiveness to politics. This higher interest in politics is strongly related to the development of a more ideological and class conscious orientation to politics. Employment in modern occupational contexts also directly encourages a class ideologue orientation. The class ideologue orientation in itself leads directly to opposition voting but, even more importantly, it also alters the criteria of candidate selection which in turn strongly stimulates increased opposition support.

The path analysis, then, helps us to integrate our hypotheses and to begin to get a clearer picture of the ways in which a number of important postwar demographic and attitudinal changes have contributed to the rise of political opposition in Japan. Perhaps it bears emphasizing that the macrolevel, socio-economic processes of change that have been described here work as well as they do in predicting opposition voting because they are associated with microlevel changes. That is, demographic change is on the one hand associated with certain changes in voter attitudes and political orientations that weaken the appeal of

[17] When the attempt was made to introduce additional paths between mobility and each of the attitudinal scales respectively, in all cases the beta weights were extremely low (below .05), and none of these paths was significant even at the .05 level.

a dominant conservative party; on the other hand, it is also associated with reduced integration into small group community networks that tend to be conservatively oriented and with increased integration into antiestablishment organizations such as unions. It is this involvement or noninvolvement in informal small group and formal organizational networks that determines the magnitude and partisan direction of the most proximate and salient influence communications received for many Japanese voters. As discussed elsewhere, these kinds of social networks appear to play an important role in electoral choice in Japan.[18]

It should be clear, then, that demographics by themselves do not tell the whole story. Indeed, as with all macrolevel indicators, demographics are incapable of capturing much of the variance in experience at the individual level. Thus, for instance, some nonmobile, long-term residents are integrated into leftist oriented community networks and some unions support conservatively oriented candidates. A more comprehensive analysis of the voting behavior of any given community requires a more particularistic investigation, rich in the detail of community organizational structure, political history, and candidate qualities, as Gary Allinson's study has shown.[19] Here I have simply tried to identify the more general processes associated with increased opposition voting that are at work universally, if unevenly, throughout the country.

COMPARING NATIONAL AND LOCAL VOTING TRENDS

Thus far we have focused on the causes for the growth in the opposition vote in Japan over the last twenty to twenty-five years. While the analysis presented here was based on national election data, very similar relationships could be demonstrated for local electoral behavior. Indeed the growth of the progressive opposition vote has advanced consistently on all election levels since the early 1950s as a product of much the same set of developmental forces. However, while progressive strength in local assembly elections has risen, it has consistently lagged behind progressive strength at the national level. The progressives have been able to come to power in certain local areas due to pockets of great strength found especially in the metropolitan areas and due to their stronger drawing power in chief executive as opposed to assembly elections. As MacDougall has shown, it has been in the big cities that the pattern of convergence has been most pronounced in national and local levels of progressive support in the assembly type of election.

[18] See Flanagan and Richardson, *Japanese Electoral Behavior*.
[19] See Chapter 4.

Nevertheless, even in the big cities, the progressives continue to draw more support in national elections than in the prefectural and city assembly elections.

In their study of Japanese parties in the early 1960s, Robert Scalapino and Masumi Junnosuke drew attention to this phenomenon, noting that the political strength of the Socialists conformed to an *inverted pyramid*.[20] They showed that as of 1959, the JSP controlled 33 percent of the seats in the House of Representatives, 24 percent in the prefectural assemblies, 11 percent in the city councils, and only 2 percent of the seats in village and town councils in the countryside. Even when progressive independents were added in, the extreme weakness of the Socialists on the local level relative to their national strength was pronounced.

In Figure 2, I have drawn three sets of pyramids representing the mid-fifties, mid-sixties, and mid-seventies. Since we are interested here in voting behavior rather than parliamentary strength, I have used percentage of vote rather than percentage of seats. In addition, I have combined the total vote for special ward, city, town, and village assembly elections to enable us to look at the same electorate (the entire nation) on three different levels—national, prefectural, and municipal.

Figure 2 reveals that the Socialists' inverted pyramid of strength has persisted over time, while the LDP's local dominance has continued to rest on the support of conservatively oriented independents. The gap in progressive strength between national and local levels, however, does appear to have declined somewhat over time. For the Socialists, this decreasing national-local gap has been mainly a function of their declining strength on the national level rather than any substantial gains on the local level. In contrast, the other opposition parties exhibit rather even levels of growth on all levels. In fact, the Clean Government Party (CGP) and especially the Japan Communist Party (JCP) draw almost as much support on the local level as they do in national level elections. As MacDougall has pointed out, the JCP and CGP have paid a great deal more attention to local party organization and grassroots activities than either the JSP or the Democratic Socialist Party (DSP).[21] The Socialists and the DSP depend much more heavily on unions for organizational strength, and while unions are active in national and prefectural level politics, they are much less so in municipal politics. Thus while the JSP was polling 21-26 percent of the vote in national elections in the mid-seventies, their strength on the municipal

[20] Robert A. Scalapino and Masumi Junnosuke, *Parties and Politics in Contemporary Japan* (Berkeley: University of California Press, 1962), pp. 95-97.
[21] See Chapter 3.

Figure 2

Percentage of Popular Vote Received by Progressive and Conservative
Parties by Type of Election for the Mid-1950s, 1960s, and 1970s

Type of Election	Total Con.	LDP	Indep.	Other Prog.	JSP	Total Prog
1955-1956 ELECTIONS						
House of Councillors	56	48	7	4	38	42
House of Representatives	66	63	3	3	29	32
Prefectural Assembly	76	44	32	1	18	20
City, Ward, Town, and Village Assembly	82	14	68	1	8	9
1965-1967 ELECTIONS						
House of Councillors	49	44	4	18	33	51
House of Representatives	54	49	6	18	28	46
Prefectural Assembly	65	48	17	12	22	34
City, Ward, Town, and Village Assembly	74	18	56	14	11	26
1974-1976 ELECTIONS						
House of Councillors	44	40	5	29	26	55
House of Representatives	52	42	10	28	21	48
Prefectural Assembly	59	42	18	22	18	41
City, Ward, Town, and Village Assembly	67	14	52	22	11	33

NOTE: The independent category includes the NLC vote in the 1976 HR election
and excludes the small percentage that was cast for explicitly designated progressive
independents in the 1955 prefectural and municipal assembly elections. Otherwise
this category represents those who were simply designated as independents, nearly
all of whom can be assumed to fall on the conservative side of the conservative-
progressive dichotomy. Other progressive includes the Labor-Farmer, JCP, DSP,
and CGP vote. The minor party vote was excluded.
SOURCE: *Chihō Senkyo Kekka-chō* (Tōkyō: Election Bureau, Local Autonomy
Ministry), 1955, 1967, and 1975 editions; *Japan Statistical Yearbook*, 1974 edition.
The election years are 1956, 1965, and 1974 for the HC elections; 1955, 1967, and
1976 for the HR elections; and 1955, 1967, and 1974 for the unified local elections.

level was only 11 percent. In contrast, the JCP was polling about 10
percent on both levels.

Despite these differences among the various opposition parties, the
inverted pyramids in Figure 2 point to the phenomenon of delayed
politicization on the local level. Even today, the independent vote rises
from roughly 5 percent on the national level, to 15-20 percent on
the prefectural level, to over 50 percent on the municipal level. This
suggests that either (1) some voters who support progressive party

candidates in national elections shift their support to conservative independents in local assembly elections, or (2) progressively oriented citizens participate with greater frequency in national as opposed to local assembly elections and/or conservatively oriented citizens participate with greater frequency in local elections. The first hypothesis suggests that different stimuli are inducing voters to change the kinds of candidates they support from one level to the next, while the second hypothesis suggests that the different levels of elections mobilize somewhat different kinds of potential voters.

What we require, then, is some kind of theory that will explain why one or the other of these two possible effects might be occurring. In the next two sections, I will offer two possible explanations. The first relates district size to the *kankei* model of voter mobilization. The second focuses on the relationship between district age and the community integration model of citizen participation. In the Japanese context, both theoretical models appear to offer cogent explanations for the lower levels of politicization and the higher levels of support for conservative independents in local assembly elections. In explaining the district size and district age hypotheses, we will look closely at contrasting mobilization stimuli in different kinds of elections and see how they differentially affect the voter's attention to party labels and level of participation. Finally, we shall briefly analyze what kind of voter is most likely to be found shifting his vote between conservative and progressive candidates from one type of election to another.

POLITICIZATION AND DISTRICT SIZE

Dahl and Tufte argue that the smaller a community the greater its homogeneity. Since it is increased density and diversity that generates political competition, they hypothesize and empirically demonstrate that small communities are characterized by comparatively low levels of partisan competition. Indeed they suggest that, "in the politics of homogeneity parties scarcely exist."[22] It seems intuitively obvious that the greater the sense of community solidarity, the less partisan divisions will be reflected in the community's politics. Moreover, the smaller the community, the more politics will be conducted on an informal, face-to-face basis, and the weaker will be the tendency for politics to be resolved through formal, impersonal organizations. Thus in small communities, personalism tends to replace partisanship as the basis of political mobilization both because of the greater degree of proximity

[22] Dahl and Tufte, *Size and Democracy*, p. 97.

and familiarity with the personalities involved and the higher value placed on community solidarity. In the small community context, partisan divisions appear to be either irrelevant or inherently threatening to the peace and harmony of the community.

The other side of the argument, therefore, is the smaller the size of the community, the greater the emphasis on solidarity and personalism and the more nonpartisan will be its politics. We can apply this principle to the analysis of cross-level variations in electoral behavior. Here for the time being we will focus on the assembly type of election and exclude consideration of the local chief executive elections. In these assembly elections, the size of the electoral district decreases as we move from national to prefectural to municipal election levels. The smaller local constituencies, therefore, will have more homogeneous interests and more personal contact with their representatives than will the larger national election districts. It is important to clarify here that for the purposes of this analysis we are defining district size not in terms of legal boundaries and geographical areas but in terms of the number of votes necessary for victory in a given district in a given type of election. Thus an electoral district's size can be reduced either by narrowing its geographical boundaries or by increasing the number of seats that the single-entry ballot district vote is to elect. Due to the pattern of areal representation within the multimember districts discussed later in this chapter, a reduction in the number of votes necessary for victory does equate with a reduction in the size of the community being represented.

We should expect to find, therefore, that a shift from national to local elections is accompanied by a decline in partisan and an increase in personalistic orientations towards elections. Survey findings do in fact consistently report that Japanese respondents rely increasingly on candidate personality rather than on party in making their voting choices as the electoral arena shifts from the national to the prefectural to the municipal levels. For instance, if we look at the 1967 national and local election surveys, four times as many respondents chose personality as chose party (64 to 16 percent) as the basis for their voting choice in the city, town, and village assembly elections, while that ratio fell to 2.5 percent on the prefectural level and only 1.3 percent for the House of Representatives (HR) election. Looking across the KSR (*Kōmei Senkyo Renmei*) surveys from 1958 to 1976, we find personality has consistently played a far larger role in local as opposed to national elections. Perhaps the more surprising finding, however, is the sizable emphasis that has been placed on personality even in HR elections: from 1958 to 1976, personality has played as large or even a somewhat larger role than party in voting choices in HR elections.[23]

This raises the question of just what the respondents in these surveys mean by candidate personality. I would contend that there are at least two different phenomenon involved here. One is what we normally think of as candidate image. The voter develops images of the candidates through his exposure to them via the media, and he casts his vote for the one that he identifies with the most positive personal attributes —someone whom he feels is attractive, trustworthy, capable, and concerned. The other phenomenon deals with the voter's personal relationship with the candidate. It is this latter factor of personal connections that accounts for the strong element of personalism in Japanese elections and contributes directly to the lower levels of partisanship in local elections.

District Size and the Kankei Vote

A decade ago I introduced the concept of political *kankei* (personal connections) to describe the networks of ties arising from numerous different sources and contexts—kinship, geographical, occupational, patron-client, school, and other associational ties running the gamut from union to religious to recreational group affiliations—that operate to join diverse groups and individuals to a particular candidate through chains of personal relationships that claim the individual's loyalty quite apart from considerations of public policy.[24] Outside of the early interest of the Columbia school in the effects of social context and personal influences on voting behavior, social network explanations of voting behavior have received little attention.[25] The recent interest

[23] Kōmei Senkyo Renmei, *Dai-6-kai tōitsu chihō senkyo to yūkensha II* (Tōkyō: Kōmei Senkyo Renmei, 1967), pp. 66-69, 106-109; Kōmei Senkyo Renmei, *Dai-31-kai shūgiin giin sōsenkyo no jittai* (Tōkyō: Kōmei Senkyo Renmei, 1967), pp. 22-23. See also other similar KSR reports of their national and unified local election surveys conducted in conjunction with each House of Representatives and House of Councillors (local constituency) election and each round of prefectural, city, town, and village elections. The findings from the 1976 JABISS Election Study give a little clearer picture of the candidate-party mix in voting decisions: 25 percent said that they chose a particular candidate because he was endorsed by the party they support; 37 percent considered party but made their choice on the basis of candidate from among the parties that they took into consideration; and 26 percent indicated that party had little or no role in their choice and that they voted mainly on the basis of the candidate himself (see note 34).

[24] Scott C. Flanagan, "Voting Behavior in Japan: The Persistence of Traditional Patterns," *Comparative Political Studies* 1 (1968): 396, 399-410; Flanagan, "The Japanese Party System in Transition," *Comparative Politics* 3 (1971): 238-253.

[25] P. F. Lazarsfeld, B. Berelson, and H. Gaudet, *The People's Choice* (New

in a social network approach in the United States and Europe makes the Japanese case a particularly intriguing one to study, for several cultural factors appear to enhance the role that organizational and small group networks play in shaping the Japanese citizen's voting behavior.

First, Japan is still pervasively a personalistic society in the sense that people do things through known people: hence chains of connections play an extremely important role in the average citizen's daily life. The maintenance of these networks is based on the scale and frequency of exchanged favors and a culturally instilled consciousness of the need to repay favors and, so to speak, keep the books balanced. Thus if a candidate has done some past favor for one's family or community, this creates a sense of obligation in the voter to reciprocate with electoral support. Some voters may feel this obligation even if they have received nothing more than a towel with the candidate's name on it from an election worker.[26] Moreover, the exchange need not directly involve the candidate. Thus citizen A (a local influential, personal benefactor, work colleague, classmate, relative, or friend) may induce citizen B to support A's preferred candidate out of considerations concerning only past personal exchanges between A and B and having nothing to do with the candidate. Hence Japanese candidates have been able to build reliable electoral machines based on chains of personal relationships that tie candidate to local influentials to voters.

Second, hierarchic relations between people in different status positions are thought to be extremely important in Japan. Much has been written about various types of patron-client relations (*oyabun-kobun*,

---

York: Columbia University Press, 1944); B. Berelson, P. F. Lazarsfeld, and W. Mcphee, *Voting: A Study of Opinion Formation in a Presidential Campaign* (Chicago: The University of Chicago, 1954).

[26] The amount of small gift distribution by candidates in election campaigns is very extensive, and the costs of such activities are alarmingly high. In an effort to further control such activities, the new 1975 election law prohibits donations in the name of the candidate of cash, sake, wreaths, incense sticks, and other typically used gifts. Reportedly, however, many candidates are simply ignoring the new rules, while many of those that have attempted to comply are receiving a cold reception. For example, in the 1976 HR election, one Saga candidate reported that a rumor was being spread among his supporters that he had suddenly become a miser. An Iwate candidate related that his failure to send sake or some other offering to senior citizens gatherings had lead a number of those former supporters to openly declare their defection, while another campaigner who had stopped sending cash gifts to athletic meetings was asked if he had retired from politics. "New Election Law Plays Havoc Among Campaigners," The *Japan Times Weekly*, 6 November 1976, p. 10, and Iga Mamoru and Morton Auerbach, "Political Corruption and Social Structure in Japan," *Asian Survey* 17 (1977): 556-564.

sensei-deshi, sempai-kohai) and the vertical organizational structure of Japanese society.[27] Some scholars have even traced these patron-client relations to the concept of *amae* (the desire of an infant to passively receive love from its mother), which they believe is unusually strongly manifest in Japanese culture.[28] This work suggests that the very real material benefits that loyalty and service bring in a dependency relationship may be reinforced by a psychological need for such nurturing relationships. For whatever reason, hierarchic relations are important and can be exploited to deliver votes for a particular candidate.

The distinguishing feature of political *kankei* as an explanatory factor in Japanese voting behavior is that such influences motivating choice stem from personal loyalties and personal benefits rather than from ideological or partisan orientations or from preferred public policy outputs. From the *kankei* perspective, an unattached vote is a wasted vote. An attached vote, on the other hand, is one more exchange in the balance of favors and obligations that can be applied as payment against an obligation or invested as credit for future requests. In the case of several appeals for support, choice is based on both the *proximity* and the *power* of the tie—on the closeness of the source of the request for support to the source of anticipated payoff for the voter and the directness and magnitude of that payoff.[29]

The feasibility of relying on *kankei* in municipal assembly elections is made abundantly clear in Table 7. Since the competition ratio in Japanese elections averages at roughly two candidates per seat, on the average slightly over half of the votes cast per seat would be sufficient to ensure victory. This would mean that in the case of the town and village assemblies, an average of a little over 170 votes is generally sufficient to ensure victory. Even in the case of city and ward assemblies, somewhere around 1,200 votes on the average is all that is needed to win. In contests of this scale, we would expect personal relationships

---

[27] Nakane Chie, *Japanese Society* (Berkeley: University of California Press, 1970).

[28] Doi Takeo, *The Anatomy of Dependence* (Tokyo: Kodansha Int., 1973).

[29] If a hamlet (*buraku*) influential or a union boss requests his followers to vote for a certain candidate, no direct tie with the candidate is required because the influential or boss is the primary source of anticipated payoffs for his followers. If, on the other hand, a voter has no closer or more powerful a direct or indirect relationship with a candidate than geographical proximity and if two candidates are running from his *jimoto* (local district or hometown), he is likely to make his choice either on the basis of (1) the one who lives closer to him in order to place himself closest to the fruits of the candidate's future patronage (public works, roads, schools, etc.), or (2) the one who is more powerful judging from the candidate's connections, former positions, and supporters on the assumption that the more powerful candidate will be able to divert more funds to his *jimoto*.

Electoral Trends

Table 7
Type of Election by District Size

Type of Election	Total Votes Cast	Seats Won	Votes per Seat
Gubernatorial	49,600,000	47	1,060,000
HC—National Constituency	50,700,000	50	1,010,000
HC—Local Constituency	51,800,000	76	682,000
House of Representatives	56,600,000	511	110,000
Prefectural Assembly	51,200,000	2,796	18,000
City and Ward Assembly	31,900,000	13,957	2,300
Town and Village Assembly	8,200,000	23,810	340

NOTE: Votes cast and seats won were for the 1972-1976 gubernatorial elections; the 1975 prefectural assembly and city, ward, town, and village assembly elections; the 1976 HR election; and the 1977 HC election.
SOURCE: *Japan Statistical Yearbook, 1974 edition; Asahi shinbun,* and *Chihō senkyo kekka-cho* (Tokyo: Election Bureau, Local Autonomy Ministry, April 1975).

to play an important role. In House of Representatives, House of Councillors (HC), and gubernatorial elections, however, successful candidates must poll in excess of 50,000, 340,000 and 500,000 votes respectively. In these latter cases, we would expect the impact of personal connections to be greatly attenuated.

Table 7 illustrates one of the major differences between the local assembly and chief executive types of election referred to in Chapter 2. We note that there is a dramatic difference in district size between the prefectural assembly and prefectural governor's elections, with the former being among the smallest and the latter the single largest in Japan. In the case of the municipal chief executive and assembly elections, there is a similar marked contrast. The vast differences in the sizes of municipalities ranging from the small rural village to the huge urban metropolis, however, make it somewhat misleading to characterize the district size in municipal chief executive elections in aggregate terms. In the town and village mayoral elections, the number of votes required for victory is less than that needed in the prefectural assembly elections, and, indeed in the aggregate, the district size of municipal chief executive elections is somewhat smaller than prefectural assembly districts but substantially larger than municipal assembly districts. The big cities, however, deviate sharply from this general pattern such that in some big city mayoral elections, the winning candidate's vote total is of a similar order of magnitude as that found in gubernatorial contests. Therefore, we may characterize the district size as large in big city mayoral elections and as small in village, town, and small city mayoral elections. This means that the role that *kankei* plays in voting behavior is much more limited in gubernatorial and big city mayoral elections, and this fact sets these elections apart from other local elections.

Even in moderate to large size districts, however, social networks and personal connections may still play some role. This is because many of the same kinds of personal, face-to-face influences that we have noted in small community settings are also found operating within large Japanese organizations, and these influences may be used to mobilize support behind a particular candidate. For instance, many Japanese organizations still adopt the recommendation system (*suisensei*) by means of which the group attempts to mobilize its members to vote in a bloc for a particular candidate. The norms of group solidarity and conformity make this an effective vehicle of mobilization in certain kinds of organizational contexts in Japan. In addition, large organizations such as labor unions are likely to employ the "organization check" (*soshiki tenken*) procedure whereby each member is personally contacted in an attempt to assess whether his vote is secure and how many additional votes of family, relatives, and friends he can deliver. Frequently the sense of obligation and commitment is reinforced by inducing union members to sign their names to a *suisensho*, affirming that they, as members of the union, support the endorsed candidate. Such procedures not only solidify partisan support within an organization but also enable large organizations to count and distribute votes among the candidates of a particular party with a fair degree of accuracy. We also find machines of influentials and large-scale candidate support organizations (*kōenkai*) that are used to formalize essentially personalistic and informal exchange relationships between particular candidates or their core supporters and various individuals and groups within the community.

Kankei, then, spans a broad variety of relationships from the directly personal and strongly hierarchic type typically associated with rural areas to the organizational and more egalitarian type frequently found in the larger cities. At the former extreme pole, the candidate or local notable linked to the candidate maintains a kind of godfather relationship with the voter, participating in important occasions in the voter's life and taking care of difficulties that arise. Sometimes the form of the attachment is even more latent, an almost "invisible" tie sustained by the warp and woof of community life. The "lord" or "first family" of a local district is simply accorded the political office to which his ascribed status entitles him.[30]

[30] In many rural areas, the descendant of the district's feudal lord is still ad-

In the urban areas and increasingly even in rural areas, we find very different kinds of ties between candidates and voters. Urbanization, increased occupational mobility, and occupational diversity have decreased community solidarity and with it the basis of areal representation. Increasingly politicians have turned to organizations to formalize the voter-candidate relationship in the face of the declining salience of latent, community-based ties. This is accomplished in one of three ways: (1) the candidate approaches one or more existing areal or non-areal organizations and assumes a high office in it, generally in an advisory capacity; (2) the candidate establishes a network of supporters' organizations (*kōenkai*), enrolling local influentials and individual voters who are connected to him in some way; or (3) the candidate is a product and representative of an organization (perhaps a large organization, such as a labor union, company, or trade association). It is common for candidates to utilize all three forms of organizational ties.

Higher levels of education and various politicizing influences are also transforming the voter-candidate tie into a more egalitarian one. As the voter becomes aware of a greater variety of ways and more explicit means of making political *kankei* work for him, the candidate's role is transformed of necessity from that of patron or boss to that of caretaker or case worker. The increasing service orientation of incumbent politicians has been noted even on the local level.[31] Indeed the growing sophistication of Japanese voters should not be minimized. Thus we find voters exercising greater fluidity and flexibility in establishing and transferring voter-candidate ties, but we also see a weakening in the strength of these kinds of ties, especially where they are not reinforced by other considerations. One example of this on the progressive side is the case of labor unions. A number of unions, particularly in the big city areas, have found that the compliance of their rank and file to union endorsements has fallen from very high levels ten to twenty years ago to only 20 to 40 percent levels today.[32]

Despite the changes that are taking place in the forms and effective reach of political *kankei*, social networks and personal connections still

---

dressed as "lord" (*tonosama*), particularly by older people. See "Chihō jichi nikki," no. 5, *Asahi Shinbun*, 26 March 1967.

[31] For example, municipal assembly members coming from prestigious, upper-class families are more and more being supplanted by assemblymen representing various local associations. Ishida Takeshi, "The Direction of Japanese Reorganization," *Journal of Social and Political Ideas in Japan* 2 (1964): 26.

[32] Reported in discussions with Japanese colleagues Ogawa Kōichi and Kōhei Shinsaku.

play a substantial role in mobilizing Japanese voters, particularly in local level elections. Although it is difficult to directly measure the importance of considerations of *kankei* in the voter's decision, we can more easily document the prevalence of vote-soliciting activities. A series of national surveys for each of the five kinds of elections held in 1963 asked voters if in a specific election they had received an individual request or group recommendation from one or more of the following: a group or union to which you belong, a neighborhood association, a village association, relative, acquaintance, neighbor, person who usually takes care of you, election worker, or candidate. In Table 8, I have ordered the types of elections according to district size —that is, the number of votes necessary for a candidate to win.[33] The results indicate that there is a direct correlation between the number of votes necessary to win an election and the amount of personal vote-soliciting activity carried on in a campaign. Clearly the smaller the area and the fewer the number of votes required, the greater the feasibility of relying on personal ties to ensure success at the polls. Particularly in the city, town, and village assembly campaigns, personal connections appear to be extensively utilized, with over half of the respondents reporting that they had received one or more personal requests for their vote.

When these findings are combined with those from other surveys, two points become clear. First, requests for a respondent's vote almost invariably come from individuals that are well known to him, not from anonymous campaign workers. Second, this kind of personalistic vote-soliciting activity continues to be extremely extensive to this day and is perhaps even more pervasive than the data in Table 8 suggest. For instance, the recent JABISS National Election Survey found that in the 1976 House of Representatives election, when the question was

[33] As shown in Table 7, district size is largest in the gubernatorial elections and smallest in the town and village assembly elections. A comparison of prefectural assembly and mayoral election district sizes is somewhat complex. In the smaller towns and villages the mayoral elections require less votes for victory, while in the large cities they require more than the prefectural assembly elections do. Nationally, however, as of 1975 the Japanese elect 3,255 mayors compared to 2,840 prefectural assemblymen, or 15 percent more mayors. Due to the amalgamations of cities, towns, and villages over the last two decades, these differences are actually substantially smaller than they were at the time of the reported survey: for instance, in 1966 there were 30 percent more mayors than prefectural assemblymen. Thus, from a national perspective, the prefectural assembly districts are clearly larger. (See *Japan Statistical Yearbook*, 1974 edition.) In the case of the HR election findings reported in Table 8, the question-wording was changed slightly, with "local influential" and "superior at work" being substituted for the last four of the nine kinds of requesting groups and individuals cited.

Table 8

Percentage of Respondents Who Report Receiving Personal
Voting Requests

Type of Election	Number of Requests Received			Total	N
	One or More	None	DK-NA		
Gubernatorial	19	77	4	100	878
House of Representatives	27	73	—	100	2,107
Prefectural Assembly	33	63	4	100	1,838
Mayoral	37	59	4	100	627
City, Town or Village Assembly	52	45	3	100	1,349

SOURCE: Kōmei Senkyo Renmei, *Tōitsu chihō senkyo no jittai* (Tōkyō: Kōmei Senkyo Renmei, 1964), p. 16; Kōmei Senkyo Renmei, *Sōsenkyo no jittai* (Tōkyō: Kōmei Senkyo Renmei, 1964), p. 53.

asked more broadly—Did some friend or acquaintance ask you to vote for a particular candidate?—many more positive responses were given. Thus only 52 percent, instead of the 73 percent reported in Table 8 for the HR election, denied receiving any such request. Moreover, of those receiving requests, 54 percent were asked by two or three persons and 17 percent by four or more persons. Of the entire sample, 5 percent reported receiving such a request from a family member, 7 percent from a relative, 15 percent from someone at their place of work, 13 percent from a neighbor, 20 percent from some other friend or acquaintance, and 7 percent from some other known person.[34]

If this much personalistic vote-soliciting activity continues to this day in national level campaigns, the utilization of personal connections has to be extremely pervasive in local assembly elections. Frequently at the municipal level voting becomes primarily a matter of weighing the multiple tugs of *kankei* that converge on the voter at election time.[35] Naturally it is difficult to document the precise impact of

[34] JABISS is the acronym created to designate the 1976 Japanese election study conducted by J. Watanuki, B. Richardson, I. Miyake, S. Kohei, and S. Flanagan in conjunction with the December 1976 House of Representatives election. This nationwide pre- and postelection panel survey includes over 400 items, was fielded in successive waves in November and December of 1976, an realized 1,796 preelection and 1,556 postelection completed interviews.

[35] For instance, in the 1967 Sendai city assembly election, our maid and her family received personal requests from relatives, neighbors, acquaintances, and coworkers on behalf of five different candidates. In another example, Masumi reports, "In a town assembly election last April, my mother-in-law had three visitors: a grocer suggested a poultryman, an independent conservative candidate; a

these sorts of personal connections and other influence communications on the voter's decision, but fragmentary evidence suggests that the impact is substantial. For instance, results from the 1963 Mainichi and Yomiuri national surveys respectively demonstrate that 50 to 60 percent of the electorate affirmed that the recommendation of a group to which they belonged was an important referent in their voting decision. In the 1976 JABISS National Election Survey, among those who received a personal request for their vote, and voted, only 43 percent ignored the request and voted for another candidate, while 57 percent voted for the recommended candidate.[36] The important role that personal connections play in Japanese elections is born out by the perceptions of the candidates themselves. As one Yokohama city assemblyman reported in discussing the operation and functions of the twenty-three branches of his *kōenkai*, "People would not support me unless there was some kind of connection between me and them."[37]

---

neighboring widow urged the support of an independent socialist; while a Soka Gakkai widow recommended a butcher. On election day, two cars were sent to transport her to the voting booth. The grocer's car came a few minutes earlier, and won, although no one can be sure which candidate she voted for." Masumi Junnosuke, "A Profile of the Japanese Conservative Party," in *Cleavages, Ideologies, and Party Systems*, ed. Erik Allardt and Yrio Littunnen (Helsinki: Transactions of the Westermarc Society, vol. 10, 1964), p. 434.

[36] The 1963 Mainichi and Yomiuri national survey findings were reported in Kōmei Senkyo Renmei, *Tōitsu chihō senkyo no jittai* (Tōkyō: Kōmei Senkyo Renmei, 1964), p. 18. In the JABISS survey, respondents were asked to consider only the single-most important request they received in responding to the compliance question, and clearly the conformity levels were not overwhelming. The influence of personal requests for votes is rather subtle and difficult to tap by means of the opinion survey. Naturally, few voters will admit that a personal recommendation they received was the most important element in their voting decision, and undoubtedly arriving at a voting decision is a much more complicated process than an unthinking compliance to the requests of others. The very pervasiveness of this kind of vote-soliciting activity, however, vouches for its effectiveness in garnering support. Moreover, the most effective recommendations are likely to be those that are not recognized by the voter as outside requests at all—those that reinforce an orientation towards the candidate *our* group supports.

[37] Bradley M. Richardson, "Japanese Local Politics: Support Mobilization and Leadership Styles," *Asian Survey* 7 (1967): 866. These candidate perceptions have been reiterated in subsequent elections, including the 1976 HR contest. Despite the furor over the Lockheed scandal, it appears that the following maxim still holds—the farther you move away from Nagatacho (the political center of Tokyo), the less you hear Nagatacho topics being discussed. As one leftist candidate remarked, "human connection, and not policy measure, is the decisive factor." See "Lockheed is Not Issue in Rural Districts," *The Japan Times Weekly*, 4 December 1976, p. 5.

Areal Representation and Conservative Dominance

We have established that *kankei* plays an important role in voting behavior at all levels of election but a much more pervasive role in local assembly and small municipality mayoral elections that require relatively few votes for victory. In order to clarify the link between district size and the level of opposition voting, we now must clarify the relationship between *kankei* motivated voting and nonpartisan representation. MacDougall has identified the key factor here in his discussion of areal representation.[38] Areal representation and partisan representation are simply not compatible: the former is based on community solidarity and consensus, while the latter is based on division and competition. MacDougall and Allinson have discussed some of the ubiquitous kinds of community organizations found on the local level: neighborhood, fire-fighting, crime prevention, women's, young men's, PTA, and temple and shrine associations. Characteristically these kinds of community organizations tend to be all inclusive and to involve and represent, at least nominally, the community as a whole. Moreover, outside the large metropolitan areas we find greater numbers of these kinds of organizations, higher levels of resident participation in them, and a greater tendency for them to involve themselves in election campaigns.

In municipal elections, these community associations will generally try, where feasible, to elect someone from their immediate community to represent their area. In such cases, high levels of conformity to the recommendation of the neighborhood association are frequently achieved. Even in national level elections, particularly in the less heavily urbanized areas, these community associational networks can often be effectively mobilized by local influentials to deliver the vote for a specific candidate on the principle that as a man from our area he will best look after our interests. The Japanese call this phenomenon *enko*, which refers to a candidate's land and blood ties to his constituency. We can see the effects of *enko* graphically depicted in Figure 3. As I have drawn the figure, each full line represents 10 percent of the vote in one of the thirty-seven administrative subdivisions of Miyagi prefecture's second and predominantly rural election district in the 1967 House of Representatives election. The vote of the five LDP and independent candidates all exhibit the so-called "mountain" type voting pattern in which the candidate's greatest strength centers in his hometown (indicated by the asterisks) and decreases inversely as the radial

[38] See Chapter 3.

Figure 3

Graphic Depiction of the Pattern of Areal Voting in Miyagi Prefecture's
Second Election District in the 1967 HR Election

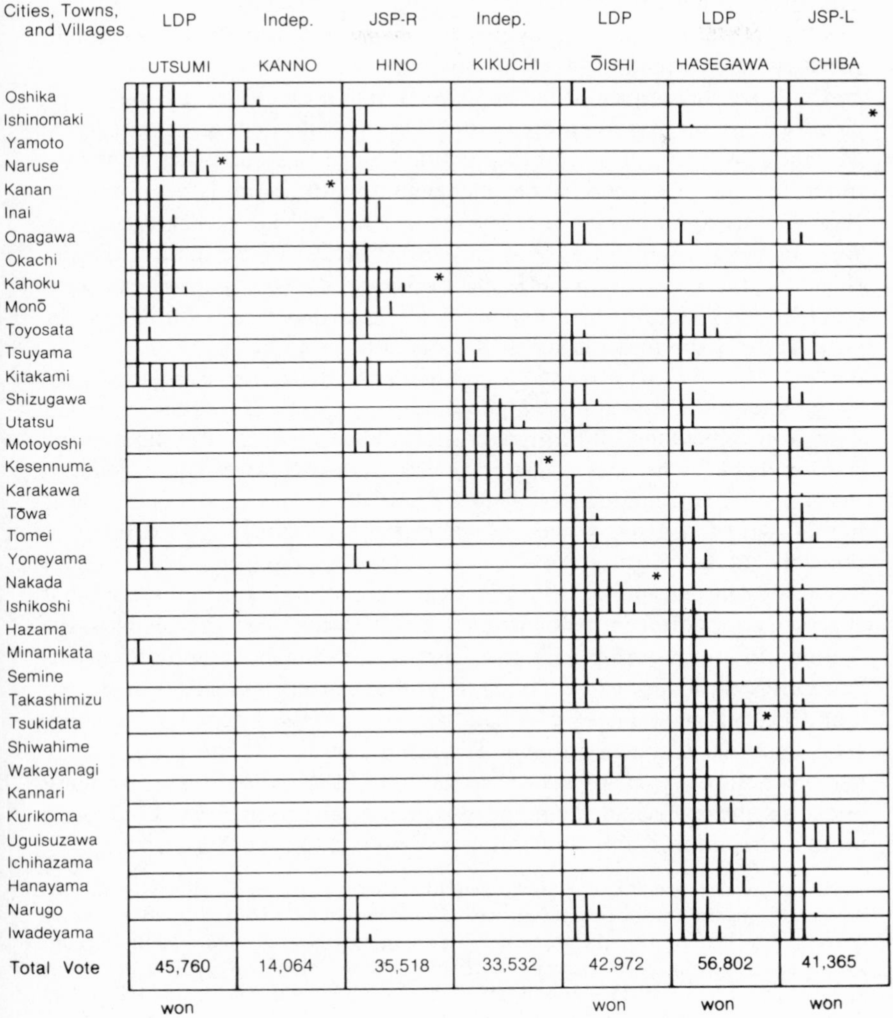

Cities, Towns, and Villages	LDP	Indep.	JSP-R	Indep.	LDP	LDP	JSP-L
	UTSUMI	KANNO	HINO	KIKUCHI	ŌISHI	HASEGAWA	CHIBA
Oshika							
Ishinomaki							
Yamoto							
Naruse							
Kanan							
Inai							
Onagawa							
Okachi							
Kahoku							
Monō							
Toyosata							
Tsuyama							
Kitakami							
Shizugawa							
Utatsu							
Motoyoshi							
Kesennuma							
Karakawa							
Tōwa							
Tomei							
Yoneyama							
Nakada							
Ishikoshi							
Hazama							
Minamikata							
Semine							
Takashimizu							
Tsukidata							
Shiwahime							
Wakayanagi							
Kannari							
Kurikoma							
Uguisuzawa							
Ichihazama							
Hanayama							
Narugo							
Iwadeyama							
Total Vote	45,760	14,064	35,518	33,532	42,972	56,802	41,365
	won				won	won	won

NOTE: The asterisk indicates the candidate's hometown, i.e., birthplace and family home. Each full line represents 10 percent of the vote in that city, town, or village. Thus two and one-half lines would be equivalent to 25 percent of the vote. A blank indicates that the candidate polled less than 10 percent of the vote in that municipality. R and L indicate the candidate's association with the right and left wings of the JSP respectively. An eighth candidate, Okutsu Hideo (JCP), also ran but failed to poll 10 percent in any administrative unit and hence is not reported.

distance from that center increases.[39] These five candidates captured from 41 to 74 percent of the vote from their respective hometowns, averaging 58 percent.

This pattern of areal voting emerges even more sharply at the prefectural assembly election level as shown in Figure 4. Ten of the towns and villages that appeared in the lower portion of Figure 3 for the HR election district together constitute *one* of the election districts for Miyage's prefectural assembly election. Since we are now viewing a much smaller area and since all seven of the candidates shown in Figure 4 were natives of the district, we must assume that these men were better known throughout this entire prefectural assembly district than was the case for the HR election candidates, six of whom were outsiders. We might, then, expect to find a broader distribution of the vote. Instead we find higher areal concentrations. Conservative candidates A, B, and G captured 68 to 88 percent of the vote in their respective hometowns, averaging 79 percent. The fourth conservative candidate from Kurikoma did not reap such impressive levels of hometown support because he had to share that support with two Japan Socialist Party (JSP) candidates who hailed from the same town. These three hometown candidates, however, accounted for virtually 100 percent of the vote in Kurikoma.

A close inspection of Figures 3 and 4 and other similar kinds of analyses conducted in other prefectures and elections reveals that the "mountain" type voting pattern is also typical for right-wing Socialists and DSP candidates as well (see the voting pattern for Hino in Figure 3 and D in Figure 4). In contrast, the vote of the left-wing Socialists (for example, Chiba Yoshio in Figure 3 and E in Figure 4) clearly exhibits a more "prairie" type distribution. This is due to the left-wing Socialists' heavy reliance on the organized labor vote that controls a more nearly uniform proportion of the vote throughout a district.[40]

[39] Any linear representation of the candidates' voting strength inevitably fails to present the true two-dimensional picture. Thus in Miyagi's second district, Oishi's strength was centered in the three northernmost towns of Nakada, Ishikoshi, and Wakayanagi, averaging 50 percent of the vote there. These towns lie adjacent to each other, although it does not appear so in the Figure 3 listing. Kurt Steiner also discusses this areal pattern of voting in *Local Government in Japan* (Stanford: Stanford Univerity Press, 1965), p. 434.

[40] Candidates of parties that depend more on non-areal organizations for their support, such as the JCP, CGP, and left-wing of the JSP, tend to draw their votes in a more even, prairie type of distribution. Thus in Figure 3, Chiba captured first place in the voting in only two towns. One was the heavily unionized mining town Uguisuzawa; interestingly, the other was the largely rural farming community of Tsuyama, the hometown of Chiba's faction leader Sasaki Kōzo.

Figure 4

Graphic Depiction of the Pattern of Areal Voting in a PA Election
District in Miyagi Prefecture in the 1967 Unified Local Elections

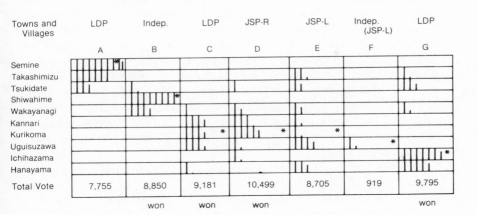

Towns and Villages	LDP	Indep.	LDP	JSP-R	JSP-L	Indep. (JSP-L)	LDP
	A	B	C	D	E	F	G
Semine							
Takashimizu							
Tsukidate							
Shiwahime							
Wakayanagi							
Kannari							
Kurikoma							
Uguisuzawa							
Ichihazama							
Hanayama							
Total Vote	7,755	8,850	9,181	10,499	8,705	919	9,795
		won	won	won			won

NOTE: The asterisk indicates the candidate's hometown. Each full line represents 10 percent of the vote in that town or village. Thus three and one-third lines would be 33 percent of the vote. A blank indicates that the candidate polled less than 10 percent of the vote in that municipality. R and L indicate the candidate's association with the right and left wings of the JSP respectively.

The smaller the district size and the closer the relationship of the candidate to the local area and its associational networks, the more pronounced the pattern of areal voting. Unfortunately, voting figures are not available for geographical subdivisions within the cities, towns, and villages for the municipal assembly elections. Thus we are unable to repeat the type of analysis presented in Figures 3 and 4 for the municipal level of election. It is well known, however, that the most extreme examples of areal voting are found in village assembly elections. In cases where one hamlet (*buraku*) has sufficient votes to elect a candidate of its own, it can frequently achieve virtually 100 percent compliance. Similarly, in municipal elections in the amalgamated cities, the vote often divides sharply along the lines of the village and town units from which the new city was formed. Even in the large cities, a pronounced pattern of areal voting commonly appears in municipal level elections in the old, established residential areas.[41]

[41] Allinson noted the pattern of areal competition in mayorality elections between the Sakai and Kichijoji sections of Musashino, and cases have been reported where this kind of intercommunity competition has assumed extreme proportions.

Throughout the electoral trends section, the authors have stressed that the conservatives have disproportionally benefited from this pattern of areal representation. There are several reasons for this. First, the positions of leadership in the neighborhood associations and other community organizations are generally dominated by members of the old middle class (upper- and middle-class farmers, retailers, small manufacturers and self-employed professionals), who tend to be conservatives either in terms of their values or their economic self-interests. They not only constitute the natural leadership of their communities in terms of family lineage, historical ties with the district, length of residence, position, and outside contacts but they also have the necessary time, wealth, and economic stake in their communities to act as the caretakers of district organizations and to manage district festivals, weddings, and funerals.

Secondly, the conservatives differentially benefit from land and blood ties and other forms of *kankei* because the conservative party occupies the positions of power that can best satisfy a community's desire for roads, schools, bridges, and other local benefits. The appeal of personal connections is not to an ideology or party label: the representative is viewed as a pipeline to the central sources of governmental largess. Thus when the voter decides which candidate to connect with, the principal questions are how large is a candidate's pipe (the candidate's power and influence) and how close is the voter to the tap (the voter's proximity to the candidate), not the political coloration of the pipe.

Thus progressive candidates are not defeated in the competition to exploit the traditional norms of areal representation simply because of their association with a leftist party. Rather, they can and do utilize the same kinds of personalistic approaches to the voters to gather a substantial portion of their support. For instance, left-wing Socialist Chiba, introduced in Figure 3, reported that when he entered politics in the early 1960s he organized a *kōenkai* in his hometown of Ishinomaki City. Although he had not lived there since his childhood, about fifty of his kindergarten and primary school classmates were still living there and

---

See Chapter 4; also Flanagan, "Voting Behavior in Japan," pp. 402-403. The neighborhood and hamlet associations (*chōnaikai* and *burakukai*) appear to play an important role in mobilizing their communities to vote on an areal basis in local elections, as is evidenced by the close association of local politicians with these assocations especially outside the major metropolitan areas. For instance, one survey of Sendai city assemblymen revealed that sixteen of the twenty LDP or conservative independent assemblymen and eleven of the fifteen JSP, DSP, and JCP assemblymen were presidents of or official advisors to their *chōnaikai*. Iesaka Kazuyuki, "Chōho toshi ni okeru shikai giin no katsudō to jumin soshiki," *Nihon Bunka Kenkyū Hōkoku* (March 1963), pp. 48-85.

by then held positions of relative importance as retailers, green grocers, small businessmen, and the like. He approached these people and, regardless of their ideological orientation, they uniformly agreed to help their former classmate and together established a *kōenkai* of some one hundred and fifty members.[42] So long as no conflicting ties are present, considerations of *giri ninjo* (obligation and human feelings) and the desire for close political connections guarantee such a response. Indeed numerous examples can be found where personal considerations have superseded partisan preferences in the voter's decision.[43] The point is that the progressive candidates as a whole do not tend to hold as prestigious positions in their communities or to have as influential ties with the center to enable the *kankei* mode of voter mobilization to work as effectively for them as it does for the conservatives.[44]

Even with the elaborately cultivated networks of face-to-face relations and chains of interconnected relations, personal connections can only reach so far. As the district size increases, the feasibility of relying primarily on personal connections declines. Thus if we may return to the case of Chiba Yoshio, he reported that in the 1967 House of Representatives election, of the 41,000 votes that elected him, only about one-quarter came through personal connections, while one-half came from his organized labor support, and the remaining one-quarter from the floating vote. Even on the municipal level, we find that, as a result of the larger district sizes and the higher rates of in-migration and residential mobility in the big cities, the effectiveness of *kankei* is limited. For example, a Socialist Yokohama city assemblyman reported, "One-third of my support comes from the unions, one-third comes from acquaintances and one-third from unattached votes."[45]

[42] While ties to former kindergarten classmates may seem rather tenuous at best in the American cultural context, they are accorded special significance in Japan and nurtured over the years through a sequence of reunions beginning six months after graduation and lasting throughout one's lifetime.

[43] See for example, Flanagan, "Voting Behavior in Japan," p. 402.

[44] The conservatives' greater ability to deliver to their constituents is reflected in the greater importance that they attach to such activities in securing their election. For example, in an Asahi survey of 481 of the 486 successful candidates immediately following the 1967 HR election, 47 percent of the LDP Dietmen felt that their active pursuit of *jimoto rieki* (benefits for one's local district, including both public works projects and individual case work) had been an essential factor in their election, compared to only 14 percent of the JSP Dietmen. "Minna no seiji gaku—zen daigishi ni kiku tōraku no kimete," *Asahi Shinbun*, 6 February 1967, pp. 5-6; see also five additional articles analyzing this survey in the issues of 7-10 February and 12 February of the *Asahi Shinbun*.

[45] Interview with Diet Representative Chiba Yoshio. On the Yokohama City councilman see Richardson, "Japanese Local Politics," p. 868.

Obviously, then, the greater the district size and the higher the level of residential mobility, the greater the number of floating voters that we would expect to find. Particularly in the major metropolitan areas, many voters fall through the *kankei* networks and at the same time are not strong partisans. Many of these individuals participate only infrequently in elections, but for those that do participate, we must examine the other dimension of "candidate personality"—the *image* of the candidate as projected by the media.

Large District Elections and the Role of Candidate Image

We would expect the role of candidate image to be most pronounced in those elections in which the reach of personal connections is most limited but at the same time the salience of party labels remains low. The gubernatorial and big city mayoral elections combine these two elements to a remarkable degree. As we have noted, the big city mayoral election districts are quite large, and the gubernatorial districts are virtually the largest in Japan.[46] This will limit the role that *kankei* can play. At the same time, party labels play a rather restricted role in these chief executive elections. One reason for this is because, as Mac-Dougall has shown, few gubernatorial and big city mayoral candidates run as official party candidates. Instead candidates run as independents, and we find a wide variety in the patterns in which parties combine to line up behind these independent candidates as well as a number of instances where a specific party takes a neutral position and declines to support any candidate.[47] Undoubtedly this reduces the clarity of partisan divisions in the voter's mind. Moreover, as the most important presidential types of contests in Japan, the gubernatorial and big city mayoral campaigns focus attention on the two major candidates who are given extensive media coverage. Particularly in these big city mayoral contests and those gubernatorial elections held in highly urbanized prefectures, we should expect to find increasing numbers of unattached voters relying on the mass media for information and imagery as guides to their voting decisions.

The 1971 Tokyo gubernatorial election is a good example of the role that candidate image can play in these kinds of elections. In this election, the incumbent governor, Minobe Ryōkichi, was endorsed by the

[46] Note that the district size thesis groups the gubernatorial with the HC national constituency elections and thus suggests a lower level of areal based voting and a higher level of floating voters in this "local" election than in even the national HR elections.

[47] See Chapter 3.

leftist JSP and JCP, while his opponent, Hatano Akira, was supported by the LDP. The DSP and CGP took a neutral stand, neither running a candidate of their own nor endorsing Minobe or Hatano. Judging simply from the party distribution of the vote in the four HR and Tokyo Metropolitan Assembly elections between 1969 and 1973, this should have been a very close election. In those four contests, the combined JSP-JCP share of the vote averaged 38 percent, while the LDP vote averaged 33 percent. Instead Minobe won a landslide victory, gaining 65 percent of the vote to Hatano's 35 percent.

A series of analyses of this election conducted by Yanai Michio yield some very interesting results.[48] His preelection survey of Tokyo voters in March of 1971 found that few voters placed great emphasis on party affiliation. Only 16 percent of his respondents thought party endorsements were very important, compared to 34 percent who attached some importance, and 40 percent who attached little or no importance to party ties. Indeed 52 percent of the respondents reported that they attached more importance to candidate personality than party, while only 28 percent stressed party over personality. In addition, the respondents were well aware of the names of the candidates (91 percent were able to name Minobe as a candidate and 86 percent were able to name Hatano) and also had well-developed images of these men. In fact, it appears that Minobe's margin of victory was attributable to his more favorable public image. Among those voters who said that they based their decision on party affiliation, 39 percent supported Minobe compared to 34 percent for Hatano. However, among those who said that they based their decision on the candidates' character (*jimbutsu*), 59 percent supported Minobe compared to only 8 percent for Hatano.

Several newspaper surveys conducted prior to the election employed the semantic differential technique and found that Minobe was viewed much more positively than Hatano on four dimensions listed here in order of the magnitude of Minobe's advantage over Hatano: (1) friendly and accessible versus cold and inaccessible; (2) conciliatory versus dogmatic; (3) bright versus dark; and (4) honest versus dishonest. On the other hand, Hatano was viewed as being more masculine and having a somewhat greater capacity to exercise leadership and get

---

[48] Yanai Michio, "Tōkyō-to chiji senkyo ni okeru image campaign," *Bulletin of the Faculty of Humanities* no. 8 (Seikei University, 1972), pp. 53-82; Yanai, "Tōkyō-to chiji senkyo ni okeru kōhōsha kettei yōin no bunseki (1)," in ibid. no. 9 (1973), pp. 37-38; Yanai, "Tōkyō-to chiji senkyo ni okeru kōhōsha shiji kettei yōin no bunseki (2)," in ibid. no. 11 (1975); Yanai, "Tōkyō-to chiji senkyo ni okeru mass media no taiō—'Minobe' 'Hatano' no shijiritsu ni kansuru shinbun hōdō o chūshin to shite," in *Shinbungaku Hyōron* no. 21 (April 1972), pp. 36-54.

things done.[49] The results from Yanai's survey, which are reported in Table 9, parallel these findings and demonstrate just how extensive Minobe's advantage was.

Table 9

Candidate Images in the 1971 Tokyo
Gubernatorial Campaign

Semantic Differential Pairs	Minobe's Image	Hatano's Image	Image Gap (Minobe—Hatano)
Gentle(+) Hard(−)	+78	−66	+144
Truthful(+) Scheming(−)	+72	−5	+77
Bright(+) Dark(−)	+86	+24	+62
Reassuring(+) Unreassuring(−)	+55	−5	+60
Active(+) Passive(−)	+44	+70	−26
Masculine(+) Feminine(−)	−42	+81	−123

NOTE: Candidate image scores were determined by subtracting the percentage of the respondents who identified the negative adjective in the pair with the candidate from the percentage who identified him with the positive adjective. The image gap score is simply Minobe's image score minus Hatano's score. Positive image gap scores indicate the extent of Minobe's advantage and negative scores the extent of Hatano's advantage on the image dimension.
SOURCE: Computed from item responses reported in Yanai Michio, "Tōkyō-to chiji senkyo ni okeru kōhōsha kettei yōin no bunseki (1)," *Bulletin of the Faculty of Humanities* no. 9 (1973), p. 42.

As might be expected, respondents who viewed Minobe more favorably reported that they intended to vote for Minobe, while those who saw Hatano in a better light intended to vote for him. This is not to say that there was no partisan political content to any of the voting behavior in this election. On the contrary, Yanai's multivariate analysis reveals that Minobe's supporters were more likely to be those who were satisfied with prefectural politics and opposed to the Sato Cabinet. Minobe's supporters were also more likely to have participated in a demonstration than Hatano's supporters, to agree that citizens can improve their livelihood through direct participation in prefectural politics, and to feel that politicians are not likely to make the Tokyo Metropolitan government better without the interference of people like themselves. In contrast, Hatano's supporters tended to be dissatisfied with prefectural politics, to be supporters of the Sato Cabinet, and to be

[49] *Tōkyō Shinbun*, 10 November 1970, and *Yomiuri Shinbun*, 25 March 1971; both reported in Yanai, "Tōkyō-to chiji senkyo ni okeru kōhōsha kettei yōin no bunseki (1)," pp. 41-43.

opposed to the policy of prefectural independence in disagreements with the national government.

Minobe's supporters, however, included a large segment of those who pay little or no attention to party endorsements and who had hardly any interest at all in either prefectural or national politics. Numerous cross-national studies have shown that independent voters tend to be marginal participants with low levels of interest, political awareness, and efficacy. Be that as it may, for the floating voters in this election, partisan politics and political issues were not the important concerns. Thus while for some, Minobe's popular image simply reinforced their partisan leanings, for others, considerations of candidate image superseded partisan politics. We find, for instance, that even among those who backed the Sato Cabinet, support for Minobe and Hatano was about equally divided and that even among those who disagreed with Minobe's policy of prefectural independence, a substantial majority supported Minobe. These voters were attracted not by Minobe's party affiliation or partisan policies but by the image he projected, an image of a friendly, accessible, honest, and concerned leader. Clearly Tokyo voters did not want the more dynamic but cold and perhaps corrupt steamroller politics associated with Hatano. At least in 1971, Tokyo voters found the more democratic, populistic style of politics represented by Minobe very attractive.[50]

What this section has shown is that there is a close association between district size and the level of opposition voting. With the increase in district size, the reach of personal connections and conservatively oriented community associational networks declines. In large districts, these personal and associational networks cannot blanket society as effectively as they can in the smaller districts. The result is a rise in the proportion of unattached voters and, as the voter-candidate tie weakens, a greater reliance on party labels or candidate images. These latter criteria of support are not as strongly dominated by conservative candidates as are the community associational networks, and hence increases in the proportion of unattached voters are associated with higher levels of opposition voting.

We may conclude that conservative candidates do better in local as opposed to national assembly elections due to the small size of the prefectural and municipal assembly districts. The large size of the gubernatorial and big city mayoral election districts, however, largely

[50] In Chapter 11 of this volume, Ellis Krauss also confirms the importance of candidate image, suprapartisan voting, and the floating vote in Kyoto's gubernatorial elections.

cancels the advantage that conservative candidates reap from personal connections and areal voting. District size, then, sets the local chief executive elections apart from the local assembly elections and, when coupled with the effects of candidate image, explains why progressive candidates have often captured a higher percentage of the vote in a given prefecture's gubernatorial race than in its prefectural assembly or even its HR election.[51] The district size thesis also seems to offer the best explanation of why the progressives on the national level have consistently done better in the HC as opposed to the HR elections (compare Table 7 and Figure 2).

Empirically, then, we have found that there is a high correlation between the number of votes necessary for victory in a given contest and the proportion of the vote that the progressives have been able to acquire. The explanation for this phenomenon, we argue, lies in the relationships among district size, *kankei*, and the floating vote. As the analysis of the 1971 Tokyo gubernatorial election has shown, it has been easier for the progressives to recruit sufficiently attractive candidates to capture the "candidate image" vote than it has been for them to develop the necessary organizational infrastructure to make *kankei* work as effectively for them as it does for the conservatives. The conservatives no longer have a monopoly on attractive candidates, at least in the big cities, but they still command a comfortable lead in the control of those community organizations that are so influential in local assembly elections and in small municipality mayoral elections.

COMMUNITY NETWORKS AND DISTRICT AGE

As we have seen, the size of an electoral district affects the strength of the opposition vote. In the smaller districts where only a few hundred to a few thousand votes are needed, personal connections and community representation on an areal basis assume their greatest importance. It is the principle of nonpartisan areal representation and a conservatively oriented local organizational infrastructure, therefore, that serves to impede the growth of opposition party support in local assembly and small municipality mayoral elections.

As Allinson has suggested, however, this need not always be so.[52] Indeed Allinson has shown that the process of urbanization and particularly high rates of in-migration tend to break down the effectiveness of traditional neighborhood associations as agents of political mobilization. The insights of what I shall call the community integration model of

[51] See Chapter 2.   [52] See Chapter 4.

political participation are quite relevant here. According to Nie and Verba, this model "predicts the decline of participation as citizens move from the smallness and intimacy of town and village to the massive impersonality of the city."[53] Moreover, as the community grows, particularly as a function of urban sprawl in a large metropolitan setting, it becomes less "bounded" in both the economic and social senses, as more and more residents commute to work and as recreational and educational facilities and governmental services are located outside the community. As community life becomes less bounded and community residents more mobile, we find a decline both in the integration of the community as a cohesive, self-sufficient environment and in the integration of the residents into the community's social networks. This leads to lower levels of participation in the political and social life of the community.

Thus the community integration model of political participation would predict that urbanization in Japan would be associated both with lower turnouts in voting and a decline in the capacity of community social networks to influence voting choices. It is intuitively obvious that residential associations such as the *chōnaikai* cannot effectively mobilize masses of newcomers who are only marginally integrated into their communities. Newcomers, therefore, are likely to either fall outside these conservatively oriented associational networks or attach less importance to their recommendations. Thus as was empirically demonstrated in the first section of this chapter, increased mobility in and of itself is directly related to lower levels of conservative voting.

Moreover, Allinson suggests that local community organizations need not always be dominated by conservatives. One effect of the influx of progressively inclined newcomers may be to eventually force many traditionally conservative community associations to adopt a neutral stance or to withdraw from politics in order to preserve harmony in the community.[54] But progressively oriented community networks can also be developed. Naturally, it takes time for the new

---

[53] Nie and Verba refer to this model as the "decline-of-community model." See Norman H. Nie and Sidney Verba, "Political Participation," in *Handbook of Political Science*, vol. 4, *Nongovernmental Politics*, ed. Fred Greenstein and Nelson Polsby (Reading, Mass.: Addison-Wesley, 1975), p. 33; Verba and Nie, *Participation in America: Political Democracy and Social Equality* (New York: Harper and Row, 1972), pp. 229-247.

[54] Allinson, in fact, found that a nonpolitical stance was typical for those *chōnaikai* situated in mixed residential areas containing substantial numbers of both established homeowners who tended to be conservative in their orientations and more recently settled and progressively inclined apartment dwellers. See Chapter 4.

arrivals to become fully integrated into their communities and to rise to influential positions in established community organizations or to organize new associational groups and networks. Thus there tends to be a lag between the arrival of progressively inclined residents and their effective participation in local politics. Allinson's comparison of Fuchū and Musashino, however, suggests that in time progressives too can develop the kinds of social networks necessary to make *kankei* work for them on the local level. Thus we find that in Musashino, his example of a community that experienced heavy early growth, the progressives were well-organized on the local level by the 1960s, and since 1967 the progressive parties have commanded a majority of the votes in the city assembly elections. Indeed he reports that among those successful candidates who had organized *kōenkai,* in the recent city assembly elections only 6 percent were progressives in Fuchu while 75 percent were progressives in Musashino.[55] Moreover, many of the neighborhood associations that were organized in Musashino were of the progressively oriented *jichikai* type.

What this suggests is that the *age* of a district is an important factor in explaining the lag in the growth of progressive support in local assembly and small municipality mayoral elections. In the older, more mature urban and suburban communities, we should expect to find a pattern of convergence between levels of progressive support in national and local elections. As progressively oriented political activists become integrated into their communities and organize their friends and neighbors, community associational networks should pose less and less of an obstacle to local progressive candidates. We might also expect to find a similar pattern of convergence in areas with more stable populations and far lower levels of urbanization. There we should see the more modest gains made by the progressives on the national level in the early postwar years gradually being reflected on the local level. In these more rural settings we would expect to find a more severe and prolonged organizational lag but a pattern of convergence nevertheless. In the younger urban areas, however, our district age hypothesis would lead us to expect to find a pattern of divergence. In national level elections, we would predict a rapid growth in opposition voting in response to the rapid influx of residents who are disposed by their occupations, age, and educational backgrounds to vote progressive. The impact of this population shift would be more weakly and gradually felt on the local level. This delayed local impact, therefore, should widen the national-local gap in progressive voting in these rapidly growing, young urban settings.

[55] Ibid.

I have attempted to test this district age hypothesis in a broader more national context than was possible within the confines of Allinson's case study by employing nationwide data aggregated at the prefectural level. The advantage of using this kind of aggregate data is that it tends to wash out the influence of idiosyncratic factors such as the candidate's personality and the special political history of the local setting. When we combine the data from several prefectures, we are aggregating the results of a vast number of local elections, and hence specific local conditions that tend to favor a particular progressive or conservative candidate tend to cancel each other out. The disadvantage of using data aggregated at the prefectural level is that it tends to somewhat blur the clarity of the very relationships we are examining. Even the most rapidly urbanizing prefectures contain rural pockets that have been relatively unaffected by the population shifts, just as predominantly rural prefectures contain urban types of voters. Thus inevitably the true strength of the relationships we are testing is somewhat diluted in the tables that are presented here. A more impressive and convincing analysis will have to await the collection and evaluation of further data aggregated at the city, town, and village level.

In order to facilitate testing the district age hypothesis, only those prefectures were selected that fit into one of five distinct patterns in terms of their postwar population growth (see Table 10). This yielded a sample of twenty-six prefectures out of an available total of forty-six. The first type labeled *mature urban* contains the four most highly urbanized prefectures: Tokyo, Kanagawa, Osaka, and Kyoto. In this group, an average of 84 percent of the prefectural populations live in densely populated areas. All four have exhibited high rates of urbanization since at least 1920, although the rates of growth have declined somewhat in recent years as these prefectures have begun to run out of space for further population expansion.

The next two categories of prefectures are substantially urbanized with an average of 56 and 58 percent of their populations respectively living in densely populated areas. The *stable urban* category is characterized by old urban communities, and in this sense it is like the mature urban grouping. These stable urban prefectures, however, experienced their most impressive rates of growth in the prewar and early postwar periods, and since 1955 they have tended to stabilize at comparatively low growth rates. In contrast, the *rapidly urbanizing* category represents the younger urban prefectures that have exhibited their most impressive rates of growth in the postwar period. Moreover, particularly in the cases of Saitama and Chiba, their rates of growth have tended to accelerate in the post-1955 period.

Table 10

Rate and Time of Population Growth for Prefectures

Prefectural Classification	Average % Population Growth Per Decade			% Densely Populated
	1945-55	1955-65	1965-75	
Mature Urban				
(Tokyo, Kanagawa, Osaka, Kyoto)	68.0	35.0	29.9	84
Stable Urban				
(Hokkaido, Fukuoka)	38.1	5.6	5.8	56
Rapidly Urbanizing				
(Saitama, Chiba, Aichi, Hyogo)	20.7	25.5	38.2	58
Late Urbanizing				
(Ibaraki, Tochigi, Gumma,				
Shiga, Nara)	1.9	0.7	16.1	28
Declining Rural				
(Akita, Yamagata, Fukushima,				
Niigata, Shimane, Tokushima,				
Kochi, Saga, Nagasaki,				
Kumamoto, Kagoshima)	14.1	−7.2	−3.1	29

NOTE: Growth rates for a prefectural class represent an average of the percentage growth rates for each prefecture in the class. The percent densely populated category represents the average of the percentage of each prefecture's population living in densely populated areas.

SOURCE: Computed from population data reported in the *Japan Statistical Yearbook*, 1974 edition.

The last two groups are predominantly rural, but here again we find important differences. The *late urbanizing* group represents those rural prefectures that experienced little or no growth until the post-1965 period, when relatively high levels of in-migration began occurring. These prefectures constitute the third tier beyond the mature urban and rapidly urbanizing prefectures in the pattern of growth emanating outward from Japan's major urban centers. The final category, the *declining rural*, includes all those prefectures that have experienced a continuous decline in their populations since 1955. These prefectures, therefore, are likely to be among those least affected by the processes of urbanization.

In Table 11, I have tested the district age hypothesis by presenting the average percentage of the vote cast for the progressive parties in each category of prefectures for three levels of election—House of Councillors, prefectural assembly, and combined city, ward, town, and village assembly elections—across three time periods: the mid-fifties, sixties, and seventies. Since it is increased district size that distinguishes

Table 11

Contrasting Rates of Growth in the Progressive Party Vote, 1955-1975

Prefectural Class and Election Years	% Voting Progressive			Difference in Progressive Voting Levels	
	HC Local Constituency	Prefectural Assembly	City, Ward, Town, and Village Assembly	National-Prefectural	National-Municipal
MATURE URBAN					
1955-56	45	31	21	14	24
1965-67	63	54	44	9	19
1974-75	64	59	53	5	11
STABLE URBAN					
1955-56	58	34	10	24	48
1965-67	55	45	23	10	32
1974-75	60	45	31	15	29
RAPIDLY URBANIZING					
1955-56	38	20	11	18	27
1965-67	54	35	25	19	29
1974-75	64	41	31	23	33
LATE URBANIZING					
1955-56	36	17	4	19	32
1965-67	40	23	14	17	26
1974-75	49	25	20	24	29
DECLINING RURAL					
1955-56	42	14	4	28	38
1965-67	45	28	17	17	28
1974-75	43	30	24	13	19

NOTE: The House of Councillors elections were held in 1956, 1965, and 1974, and the prefectural and municipal elections were held in 1955, 1967, and 1975.
SOURCES: *Chihō senkyo kekka-chō*, 1955, 1967, and 1975 editions; The Institute for Political Studies in Japan, ed., *Sangin senkyo—shiryo to bunseki* (Tokyo: Marketing Intelligence Corp., 1974); Nishihira Shigeki, *Nihon no senkyo* (Tōkyō: Shiseido, 1972).

voting behavior in national and local elections, I have chosen the HC Local Constituency election that has substantially larger districts than those for HR elections but still maintains the geographical territoriality of candidate campaigns not found in HC National Constituency elections. This selection should enable us to view national-local differences in their most pronounced form, since the number of votes required for victory in HC Local Constituency elections averages roughly 2,000 times that for town and village assembly elections, 300 times the number for city assembly elections, and 40 times those needed in prefectural assembly elections (see Table 7).

As we would expect, we find the strongest pattern of convergence displayed by the mature urban prefectures. A similar but less advanced pattern of convergence is also apparent in the stable urban and declining rural prefectures. In both of these latter cases, little change in population growth since 1955 is reflected in stable rates of progressive support in national elections and a general pattern of catching up on the local level. The rapidly urbanizing and late urbanizing prefectures, however, present the most intriguing patterns of change. In the former case, the very rapid rates of growth since 1955 in these younger urban prefectures are reflected in a steady pattern of divergence. In the case of the late urbanizing prefectures, we find a mixed pattern reflecting first convergence during the first decade when little growth was taking place and then divergence in the second decade when high growth set in.

The gap in progressive support across levels, then, is a product of the different ways in which the vote is mobilized in national and local assembly elections. National elections are characterized by large election districts that require many thousands of votes for victory, with the result that greater emphasis is placed on party labels and the media. Social networks are important in national elections as well, but here again we find more emphasis on large organizational networks. In this regard, the progressives with their heavy reliance on labor unions are not without a substantial organizational infrastructure at their disposal for the mobilization of voter support. In municipal assembly elections, unions are much less involved, and there is an increased reliance on smaller scale community associations and personal connections. Thus, the influx of new types of voters has a more direct and immediate impact on voting in national elections. On the local levels, the traditional associational infrastructure found in established communities impedes the mobilization of support for progressive candidates. Thus in the context of local assembly and small municipality mayoral elections, the new arrivals who are disposed to vote progressive in national elections may either be drawn into established community associations that endorse conservative independents or abstain from voting altogether.

Cross-Level Participation Rates and Voting Consistency

The gap between levels of progressive support in national and local assembly elections assumes that one or both of the following phenomena are occurring: (1) progressive and conservative voters exhibit different rates of participation in these national and local elections; and (2) some voters who vote progressive on the national level vote conservative on the local level. An analysis of voting turnout lends some support to the differential rate of participation hypothesis. Table 12 reveals that in the declining rural prefectures, the highest levels of participation are realized in municipal assembly elections, with participation rates successively declining in each higher level of election. This suggests the impact of *kankei* networks, the most forceful and pervasive expression of which we would expect to find on the municipal level.

Table 12

Percentage of Rates of Participation in National, Prefectural, and Municipal Elections, 1975-1976

Prefectural Class	House of Representatives	Prefectural Assembly	City Ward, Town, and Village Assembly
DECLINING RURAL	80.8	82.2	86.4
RAPIDLY URBANIZING	70.0	64.5	71.2
MATURE URBAN	65.8	65.2	63.2

SOURCES: *Japan Statistical Yearbook, 1974 edition; Chihō senkyo kekka-chō, 1975.*

As we move to the rapidly urbanizing prefectures with their large proportions of both urban and rural voters and finally to the mature, predominately urban prefectures, we see that the levels of participation consistently decline. More importantly for our purposes, we note that the order of involvement is reversed with the highest levels of voting in the mature urban prefectures occurring in national elections.

We may conclude that rural voters who are more likely to be motivated by personal connections participate most fully in municipal level elections, while urban voters who are more likely to be stimulated by the media participate most fully in national elections that attract the most attention. Once again we have somewhat weakened the relationships shown in Table 12 by using prefectures as our unit of analysis. At the town and village level, we frequently encounter participation rates that are 10 to 15 percent higher in municipal as opposed to national elections. Conversely, many urban districts show a more impressive emphasis on national elections than appears for the mature urban prefectures as a whole.[56] What this analysis suggests is that, regardless of their locale, voters who are mobilized by conservatively oriented *kankei* networks are more likely to participate in local as opposed to national elections, while those voters who rely more on the media or ideological orientations (the younger, more mobile and educated—that is, those categories of voters who tend to be progressive) are more likely to participate in national elections. To some extent, then, conservatively oriented voters may participate more heavily in local assembly elections, while progressively oriented voters may participate more heavily in national elections.

While variable participation rates may account for some of the national-local gap in levels of progressive support, undoubtedly there is a substantial category of voters who vote progressive in one kind of election and conservative in another. What are the characteristics of these floating voters? We have suggested that particularly in the rapidly urbanizing areas, a sizable number of voters support progressive candidates in national elections and conservatives in local assembly and small municipality mayoral elections. Unfortunately, we do not have any data on these progressive converts to local conservatism. However, James White's 1972 Tokyo survey does permit us to analyze the characteristics of voters who supported conservative candidates in the 1969 HR election but who shifted their support to the popular progressive Minobe Ryōkichi in the 1971 gubernatorial election.[57]

[56] This traditional rural pattern of voting as a function of community solidarity explains the anomalies of higher rural than urban and higher local than national election turnouts in Japan. The emerging urban pattern of more media oriented voting, however, more closely resembles what we find in the United States—higher turnouts in national as opposed to local elections. Table 12 shows that, for the rapidly urbanizing prefectures with high proportions of both urban and rural populations, the national and municipal election voting rates are nearly identical with much lower prefectural election rates, suggesting a mixing of the urban and rural patterns that assign highest importance to national and municipal elections respectively. Even in metropolitan areas, however, municipal election turnout rates frequently do better than a poor third due to the popularity of certain local progressive candidates or the efforts of citizens' movements. On voting turnout, see also Steiner, *Local Government*, pp. 382-390.

[57] I would like to express my thanks and appreciation to Jim White who was

Among White's respondents who reported voting for a specific party or candidate in both the HR and gubernatorial contests respectively, 42 percent voted consistently progressive, 28 percent consistently conservative, 29 percent voted conservative and then progressive, and 1 percent shifted from progressive to the conservative gubernatorial candidate. If we keep in mind that the key variable here is not national versus local level of election but district size, we will note that White's vote-switchers conform to the same pattern of higher support for conservative candidates in elections of smaller district size. In the smaller HR districts, we would expect conservative associational networks that tie the voters to specific candidates in some kind of exchange relationship to have a broader reach, while in the larger gubernatorial districts we would expect to find a higher proportion of unattached or floating voters who make their choice on the basis of party label or candidate image. What, then, are the characteristics of these voters who shift their support from conservative to progressive candidates as the electoral district size increases?

The inconsistent voters who moved leftward in the gubernatorial race looked very much like consistent conservatives in terms of their socio-economic status, their areas of residence, and their party identification. On several attitudinal dimensions, they did appear to fall between the consistent conservative and progressive voters, but the really striking contrasts are between all consistent and all inconsistent voters. From this perspective, inconsistent voters appear to be very much like nonvoters. That is, compared to the consistent voters, the inconsistent voters are more likely to be young, women, students, unemployed, retired, or shopkeepers, to have somewhat lower levels of education and political information, to mention fewer national problems, to feel politically powerless, and to have low political interest, low campaign participation, and no party preference. This is very similar to the 1964 Uji multilevel election survey finding that inconsistent voters tend to have a low sense of political efficacy, weak party images, and weak party support.[58] It is interesting to note, however, that while nonvoters had the lowest levels of media consumption, inconsistent voters exhibited the highest levels. This suggests that the media did play an important role in shifting marginal conservative supporters to Minobe. We

---

not only kind enough to share his 1972 Tokyo survey data but also conducted much of the analysis upon which the discussion of inconsistent voters is based. Naturally the responsibility for the interpretation of his data presented here is mine.

[58] Miyake Ichiro et al., *Kotonaru level no senkyo ni okeru tōhyō kōdō no kenkyū* (Tōkyō: Sobunsha, 1967), pp. 851-853.

may conclude that inconsistent or floating voters are by and large weak partisans who may be mobilized by one set of stimuli in elections of smaller district size (for example, conservatively oriented neighborhood associations or *kōenkai*) and a different set of stimuli in elections of larger district size (for example, the media or a union recommendation).

In summary, the second half of this chapter has tested two hypotheses—the district size hypothesis and the district age hypothesis—that seek to explain the gap in national and local levels of progressive support and the substantial reduction of this gap in recent years in the big cities. A close fit was found between aggregate voting statistics and the district size hypothesis. The smaller the district size, the higher the level of conservative support, and our discussion of *kankei* networks and areal voting have explained why this is so. In general, this means that the progressives do better in national than local elections. The district size hypothesis, however, also points to two important exceptions to this typical national-local imbalance—namely gubernatorial and big city mayoral contests. In these cases, we find district sizes that are as big or bigger than those found in the HR and HC elections. These exceptions have had a profound impact on advancing the progressive cause at the local level via the election of progressive chief executives.[59] The district age hypothesis views the national-local gap in a developmental perspective and predicts first divergence for communities undergoing rapid urbanization and finally convergence after these young urban communities have reached maturity. The empirical evidence also confirmed this hypothesis and points to the gradual disappearance of this national-local imbalance in progressive support, at least in the mature urban districts.

Conclusion

In conclusion, we come full circle to a point that is suggested by the five hypotheses introduced in the first part of this chapter. Urbanization in Japan has been associated more with a decline in conservative support than with an increase in long-term progressive identifications.[60]

---

[59] One measure of the difference between big city mayoral elections and other municipal chief executive elections is found in progressive rates of success. As of 1975, 67 percent of the mayors in the large designated cities were progressive compared to only 21 percent of the mayors of medium and small cities and virtually none of the town and village mayors. See Chapter 3.

[60] Both Gary Allinson and James W. White make this point, Allinson, metaphorically in the introduction to Chapter 4 and White in more direct, theoretical

It is important to keep in mind that all five of the hypotheses predicted increased political competition and not necessarily increased leftist voting. In other words, the progressives have been the beneficiaries of forces that make it increasingly difficult for one party to monopolize the political stage. Urbanization has produced increased diversity and competition that have led to lower levels of conservative voting. Moreover, urban voters are less likely to be highly integrated into their residential communities and hence both less likely to participate and less likely to vote conservative when they do. It is true that we have noted that in the older urban areas progressive organization has been taking place on the local level, and this is closing the gap between national and local levels of progressive support. Thus the maturing of urban districts as well as their growing size have undermined conservative dominance on both the national and local levels.

We should recognize, however, that much of the surge in progressive voting in urban areas over the last twenty years represents more of an enlargement in the proportion of floating voters than the socialization of strong progressive partisans. The urban voter is simply more inconsistent in his behavior than his rural counterpart, and in part this is because he is more likely to be motivated by changing national political events that are portrayed through the media than by local benefits and longstanding personal loyalties. As the voting statistics on national and local elections reported throughout Part Two have borne out, the demographic and attitudinal changes that accompany urbanization have proportionally penalized the leading opposition party almost as heavily as they have the ruling conservative party. Thus the growth of the big cities has meant a shift from a one-and-one-half party competition to a five-party competition, first on the national level and then gradually on the local level as the size (votes necessary for victory) and age of these urban local electoral districts has increased.

The continued very small size of local election districts in much of the countryside may well ensure that local politics will remain a conservative paradise in rural Japan for some time to come. Nevertheless, this analysis would suggest that the prolonged dominance of a single party cannot be indefinitely maintained. Indeed, as we have seen, growing political competition is rapidly undermining the basis of one-party dominance both in national and big city politics. Once that dominance is broken on the national level, we should expect further change along

terms in his "The Metropolitan Voter: Causal Patterns in Electoral Behavior in Tokyo," presented at the Conference on Local Political Opposition in Japan, Wrightsville Beach, N.C., 25-26 June 1976, pp. 39-43.

the demographic and attitudinal dimensions to have a new and different kind of effect. Just what kinds of new trends will develop will depend on the pattern of coalition government that emerges. If one dominant coalition with firm control of the Diet emerges over a prolonged period, as has been the case in several European countries, only peripheral turnover will be possible and we would expect electoral trends to be small, erratic, and largely meaningless. But if two distinct poles emerge around which viable coalitions can be organized, we might expect to see the present steady, gradual transfer of votes from the conservative to progressive camps replaced by something closer to the American pattern with larger fluctuations from election to election and movement in both directions. Once real turnover becomes possible, we should see the emergence of important swing groups of voters who shift their support from election to election in response to the government's success in handling economic, environmental, and other kinds of national problems.

In this regard, local level elections are serving an important intermediary role in preparing the nation for such an eventuality in two ways. First, the emergence of progressive governors and mayors in major urban centers is establishing the competence of opposition parties and candidates and their credibility as national administrators in the eyes of the electorate. Second, the presidential type of electoral system that pertains in these mayoral and gubernatorial contests is fostering a bipolarity of political tendencies. Although MacDougall has demonstrated that there is a great fluidity in the party coalition patterns related to these elections, as the strength and viabiliy of progressive candidates has increased over time, the frequency of mixed conservative-progressive coalitions has decreased. This movement towards a bipolarity in party coalition patterns is essential if a pattern of effective turnover is to be established on the national level. Hence, local level electoral developments have a number of important ramifications for national politics despite or perhaps because of the distinct dual pattern that has emerged between the levels.

PART THREE

CITIZENS' MOVEMENTS

CHAPTER 6

CITIZENS' MOVEMENTS:
THE GROWTH AND IMPACT OF ENVIRONMENTAL
PROTEST IN JAPAN

Ellis S. Krauss and Bradford L. Simcock

THE rise and growth of citizens' movements (CMs), particularly those protesting environmental pollution, is viewed by many observers as one of the most important and spectacular trends in contemporary Japanese history and politics. According to some surveys, there were at least 3,000 such movements based upon the mobilization of residents in a local area in 1973, a tenfold increase in the number of such groups since 1970. The protest activity carried out by these groups has also been significant: some estimates are that as many as 10,000 local disputes were being carried out in 1973,[1] and as early as 1971, local governments had received over 75,000 pollution-related complaints, almost double the number from 1969 and quadruple the number from 1966.[2]

The spectacular expansion of this movement has received wide attention by Japanese and American scholars and journalists. A few observers have seen citizens' movements as modern equivalents of the "peasant uprisings" (*hyakushō ikki*) common in Japanese history;[3] and some conservatives like to view them as merely front organizations for

We would like to thank Jack Lewis, Meg McKean, Kurt Steiner, and Scott Flanagan for the many very helpful comments, suggestions, and materials they have given us throughout the writing of this article. Susan Pharr's comments on citizens' movements at the conference from which this volume originated were also most helpful. Finally, a very special thanks to Professor Mayer Zald. Contact with Professor Zald (Krauss participated in an NEH seminar led by him in the summer of 1976; Simcock participated in a colloquium on social movement theory led by him in March 1977, both at Vanderbilt University) and his work have been major stimuli to our application of sociological theory to the study of citizens' movements in Japan.

[1] Kano Tsutomu "Peasant Uprisings and Citizens' Revolts," *The Japan Interpreter* 8 (1973): 279. This article by the editor of the journal cites an *Asahi Shinbun* report as its source (see 21 May 1973 issue).

[2] S. Prakash Sethi, *Japanese Business and Social Conflict: A Comparative Analysis of Response Patterns with American Business* (Cambridge, Mass.: Ballinger Publishing Co., 1975), p. 79.

[3] See "Peasant Uprisings and Citizens' Revolts."

the established Left—that is, as "old wine in new bottles." The more common and influential interpretation, however—one that dominates both English and Japanese language literature on citizens' movements and represents the predominant consensus as to their nature and significance—sees citizens' movements as a truly original and modern phenomenon. In this typical view, they are portrayed as loosely organized, democratically run groups spontaneously formed by individuals to protest against the "public hazards" (*kōgai*), such as environmental pollution, that have accompanied postwar economic growth. Rather than as a continuation of older peasant-movement or leftist-front traditions, most observers see citizens' movements as wholly new forms of political organization made up of ordinary men and women alienated by the failure of established organizations to respond to their concerns about the concrete problems in their daily lives (*seikatsu mondai*).[4] CMs are portrayed as rejecting the established Left's dogmatic ideology in favor of a nonideological but deeply moral belief in democracy. One observer has pithily described this common view:

> They are movements of "amateurs," based on relations of equality face-to-face, in small circles: complete democracy. Loosely knit and spurred solely by outrage against threats to daily life, the movements stem from the creativity of alarmed individuals.[5]

Many authors see such characteristics of CMs as a reflection of and as a contributor to the basic transformation of modern Japanese political culture.

> It seems undeniable, nonetheless, that *jūmin undō* suggest a new era of Japanese politics. They signify not only the rise of a new pattern of popular expectations, a new sense of political efficacy, and a new form of political action and participation, but also the emergence of a new political culture.[6]

Thus, citizens' movements signal the transition from traditional and deferential political culture and organizational modes to the "citizen

---

[4] Taketsugu Tsurutani, *Political Change in Japan* (New York: David McKay Company, 1977), pp. 191-192, provides a summary of this common view of citizens' movements. See also Matsushita Keiichi, "Politics of Citizen Participation," *The Japan Interpreter* 9 (1975).

[5] Takeshi Igeta, "Righteous Wrath of Residents' Revolts," *Japan Quarterly* 23 (1976): 141.

[6] Taketsugu Tsurutani, "A New Era of Japanese Politics: Tokyo's Gubernatorial Election," *Asian Survey* 12 (1972): 442. For a similar view, see also, Yasumasa Kuroda, "Protest Movements in Japan, A New Politics," *Asian Survey* 12 (1972): 949.

as autonomous man" and the institutionalization of grass-roots participatory democracy in Japan.[7] This transformation of political culture involves in part the resocialization of large numbers of individuals to a greater sense of political efficacy and to a new awareness of democratic action through the experience and example of participation in, and the success of, citizens' movements.

If the long-range implications of CMs are the emergence of new citizens, new organizational forms, and a new political culture, the short-run implications for Japanese politics lie in the creation of a new support base and electoral vitality for leftist parties and candidates, particularly in Japan's urban areas. CMs are deemed a major factor in the rise of progressive local executives in most Japanese cities during the last decade.[8]

A critical appraisal of the English and Japanese literature that has given rise to the previously described image of citizens' movements reveals some disconcerting elements, however. Most articles on the phenomenon consist of a series of sweeping generalizations with little attention paid to the diversity found in the myriad local movements that we collectively label "citizens' movements."[9] Many of these generalizations are based upon the stated goals of or the observer's hopes for the movement and not upon concrete case studies of the organization and process of movement activities. Assertions about the effect of participations in CMs on individual participants, political culture, and voting behavior have not been tested by survey research. Further, citizens' movements are treated as a uniquely Japanese phenomenon, with no attempt to deal with them as social protest movements, using the rich theory and comparative data on this subject available in the social science literature.

The significance of the two articles that follow this essay must be viewed in this context: Lewis's and McKean's thorough empirical research does much to make up for the deficiencies in prior treatments of citizens' movements. Jack Lewis's research is an in-depth case study of the development of the Mishima anti-*konbināto* (industrial complex) movement, one of the earliest and most famous citizens' move-

[7] Matsushita, "Politics of Citizen Participation," especially p. 453.

[8] See Kuroda, "Protest Movements," p. 950, and Tsurutani, "A New Era," passim.

[9] A recent exception to this and other critical generalizations is the collection of articles on citizens' movements appearing in *Chiiki Kaihatsu*, no. 154 (July 1977). The articles in this collection generally approach the phenomenon of citizens' movements with far more sophistication, realism, and objectivity than the typical literature in Japanese. Our thanks to Omori Wataru for bringing to our attention these articles by him and his colleagues.

ments that has often been cited in support of the typical generalizations about CMs in the literature and that has been called a prototype of citizens' movements. Through survey research and interviews among the leaders and followers of a number of citizens' movements, Margaret McKean has provided us with one of the first systematic studies of the effect of participation in such movements on the attitude and behavior of the individuals who take part in them. The two articles are probably the most sophisticated analyses yet to appear in English, and their findings allow us to test many of the widely held conceptions about citizens' movements.

Our task in the rest of this introductory essay will be to provide background to the two studies in order to place them in historical context and to present our own evaluation of the implications of their most salient findings for our understanding of the nature and significance of citizens' movements. This task will include an attempt to describe the development of both the "idea" and the practice of citizens' movements, to analyze the growth of the CM phenomenon in light of theories of social protest and the new evidence presented in this volume, and to evaluate the impact of CMs on local politics in Japan.

A Brief History of Citizens' Movements: The "Idea" and the Reality

The term "citizens' movements" (*shimin undō*) is a collective label for a social movement composed of many diverse types of organizations. There has often been some confusion as to what the term includes.[10] We use the term here to refer specifically to those groups that arose in the 1960s to protest the rapid economic growth policies of government and their consequences at the local level, particularly pollution and the deterioration of the quality of life. According to an *Asahi Jānaru* survey, ecology-oriented groups comprise about 60 percent of all "citizens' movements," with most of the remainder being

[10] Occasionally, this label has been used so broadly as to be synonymous with all "mass movements" in postwar Japan; in other cases it has been applied very specifically to refer to movements by citizens, usually against environmental hazards, that are not organized on the basis of local residence. The latter are then referred to as "*jūmin undō*," or "residents' movements." Our use of the term defines "citizens' movements" less broadly than all mass movements, but it includes *jūmin undō* as only one type of the more generic citizens' movements against pollution. See the section of this chapter entitled "The Diversity of Citizens' Movements" for more on *jūmin undō*.

antiwar and civil rights groups.[11] Consumer action groups have also
been viewed as expressing the same new spirit of citizen politics found
in the antipollution movement.[12] Our decision to focus here only on
the ecology and pollution-related movements is based on two factors:
(1) they are the most important of these participatory movements;
and (2) they are most directly connected to and have the greatest
impact on local politics.

The idea of citizens' movements and the phenomenon of antipollution protest initially followed two largely separate lines of development.[13] Although today the term citizens' movement is almost synonymous with antidevelopment and antipollution protest, this was not its
original meaning. It originally seems to have appeared in the conflict
surrounding the revision of the United States-Japan mutual security
treaty in 1960.[14] At the height of the widespread protest activity, significant numbers of "ordinary citizens" were also mobilized for demonstrations in addition to the organized left-wing political parties,
unions, and student movements that comprised the pillars of the leftist
subculture in Japan and the heart of antitreaty activity.[15] In defense
of the democracy that they saw threatened by the Japanese government's policies and actions, a leading group of progressive intellectuals
(primarily university professors) called for a national movement of
citizens (*shimin*) that would transcend the factionalism of the established Left and involve ordinary people in the protest against the high-
handed way in which the government had forced the treaty through
the Diet.

[11] Kuroda, "Protest Movements," p. 948.

[12] Maurine A. Kirkpatrick, "Consumerism and Japan's New Citizen Politics,"
Asian Survey 15 (1975): 235-246.

[13] Here we use the term *idea* to connote a symbolic image in distinction to *reality*; in the next section we argue that this idea also functioned as an ideology for
mobilizing movement participants.

[14] Mass level protest activity occurred before the 1960 crisis, of course, for example in the large scale "Ban the Bomb" and peace movements in Japan. We agree
with Takabatake, however, that the movement that arose in 1960 was distinguished
from previous mass level movements by the wider incorporation of normally
apolitical and nonactivists citizens and by its emphasis on activity in residential
areas. To this we would add that a new self-consciousness about being a "citizens'
movement" characterized the 1960 activity but had not been salient in previous
movements. See Michitoshi Takabatake, "Citizens' Movements: Organizing the
Spontaneous," *The Japan Interpreter* 9 (1975): 316-317.

[15] The following discussion on treaty crisis and its aftermath is based on George
R. Packard, *Protest in Tokyo* (Princeton: Princeton University Press, 1966), pp.
271-278, 318.

This *Shimin-ha* (citizens' faction) of intellectuals, and such spontaneously formed organizations as the "Voiceless Voices Association" (*Koe Naki Koe no Kai*), which attempted to become a vehicle for mobilizing the ordinary man and woman in the street into antitreaty protest activities, attracted a great deal of attention both during and especially after the treaty crisis. In the wake of this experiment with a "new" concept in Japanese political organization (it was not just the perennial, organized, established opposition groups but the spontaneously organized ordinary citizens who could mobilize to affect government policy), participants were urged to carry the spirit of political protest and reform back to their home communities. There they were to organize local citizens' movements to coordinate more permanent political opposition to the government.

During the summer of 1960, there was a brief flurry of such grassroots activity, mostly in the environs of Tokyo where the treaty demonstrations had been concentrated. But the visionary expectations that had been promoted by the proponents of citizens' movements never materialized, and the attempt to fundamentally change political activity at the local community level was a failure. The *idea* of citizens' movements had been born, but its incorporation into a viable social protest movement for fundamental change had to await an issue that aroused the interest and involvement of more than a small strata of concerned intellectuals.

For most Japanese, the beginning of the 1960s were years in which the conservatives' perceived abuse of power during the treaty crisis was more than offset by policies that were bringing economic growth and consumer prosperity. In the wake of the war's destruction, there existed a basic consensus in Japanese society on the need for economic growth and stability, particularly for higher employment, rising wages, and stable prices and for increasing food supply, clothing, and housing. The government was able to meet these basic needs (with the major exception of housing) and to stimulate the economy to rapid growth in a very short time by encouraging heavy investment in private industrial expansion and the development of new key manufacturing and export industries. Between 1955 and 1961, overall manufacturing production tripled, while machinery manufacturing multiplied seven times. Such development and its efficiency was fostered by encouraging the building of *konbināto* (from the Russian word *Kombinat*)—new clusters of interrelated industries built in close proximity to each other on planned sites.[16] These policies continued at an even more rapid pace

[16] See Norie Huddle and Michael Reich, *Island of Dreams: Environmental Crisis in Japan* (New York: Autumn Press, 1975), p. 57.

and with consequently more startling results throughout the 1960s in line with the government's declared aim of doubling personal income within the decade. In light of these accomplishments and the boost they were giving to employment and wage levels, few questioned the parallel emergence of a decision-making structure that involved the governmental bureaucracy and the big corporations in a symbiotic relationship with the ruling party and the conservative local power structure down to the neighborhood level but that excluded consistent citizen participation and input.

The consequences of such rapid, concentrated, and large-scale development, such as serious social overhead deficiencies and excessive environmental damage, soon began to be felt. Even as early as the beginning of the 1960s, some local government residents in areas targeted for regional development and some city dwellers began to raise questions about national priorities in economic development planning. Urbanites experienced a lifestyle made more affluent but also increasingly more inconvenient as concentrations of population and industry became excessive; the life of rural residents changed too as the viability of traditional communities and means of livelihood like farming and fishing were threatened by the expansion of industry into nonurban areas without adequate planning for social costs. All experienced the by-products of concentrated industry—industrial wastes—whose human and environmental impact was unknown or insufficiently assessed. In the face of these massive and rapid changes, the unchallenged consensus on national priorities that had allowed such development to proceed without interference or citizen participation began to be eroded.

The "Big Four" Pollution Incidents

The development of several particularly tragic incidents of pollution damage in the 1960s served as a catalyst for the erosion of this consensus and for a heightened awareness of environmental costs and consequences of unrestricted industrial growth. These "Big Four" incidents[17] produced uncustomary extended public conflicts and legal chal-

[17] These "Big Four" incidents and legal cases are discussed in Huddle and Reich, *Island of Dreams*; Margaret A. McKean, "Pollution and Policy-Making," in *Policymaking in Contemporary Japan*, ed. T. J. Pempel (Ithaca: Cornell University Press, 1977), p. 203 and pp. 231-234; Cynthia H. Enloe, *The Politics of Pollution in a Comparative Perspective* (New York: David McKay Company, 1975), pp. 231-232; and Frank Upham, "A Sociological Analysis of Four Japanese Pollution Suits," *Law and Society Review* 10 (1976).

lenges in the courts of Japan. In Minamata City in Kyushu, many people died and even more were permanently crippled as a result of eating fish containing high concentrations of organic mercury, the sources of which were eventually traced to factory wastes from the New Japan Nitrogen Company (*Chisso*) on the coast of Minamata Bay. The Minamata problem developed into a major controversy as the victims and their families, fishermen whose livelihood was threatened by the mercury in the bay, and a few independent scientific researchers attempted to make a stubbornly defiant company and a procrastinating and cautious national government recognize the link between the factory's wastes and the outbreak of the illness. This recognition would mean the acceptance of responsibility and the provision of a compensation. As the dispute raged on, a second outbreak of the disease was reported in Niigata in 1965, and another battle over responsibility and compensation began there too.

A similar issue emerged in Toyama prefecture when people along the banks of the Jintsu River contracted a very painful degenerative bone disease (*Itai-Itai byō* or "Ouch-Ouch disease") that resulted from eating rice contaminated with cadmium from the waste water and slag heaps of an upriver zinc refinery. The cadmium explanation for the disease was first offered in 1960; it was not until eight years later, however, that the Ministry of Welfare officially acknowledged the Toyama problem as a "pollution disease." As McKean notes, in the process of this dispute, the community was polarized, with victims and their families often under attack by established community organizations whose members, out of economic or traditional value motivations, wished the "deviants" to cease causing trouble in the community. Finally, along with the two mercury poisoning incidents in Minamata and Niigata and the cadmium problem in Toyama, the development of a particularly debilitating form of bronchial asthma due to air pollution from oil and chemical complexes in Yokkaichi City led to a fourth major struggle between local victims, this time supported by progressive labor unions and other groups, and corporate polluters. All of these struggles over responsibility and compensation entailed years of conflict and were eventually "resolved" only by court decisions between 1971 and 1973 in what has become known as the "Big Four Pollution Cases."

In all of the Big Four cases, the victims won; more importantly for the development of citizens' movements than the results of the trials was the extensive media coverage and publicity that had accompanied the entire extended process of local disputes between residents and companies, the investigations by national government agencies, and the court cases. This publicity, which extended from the early 1960s to the early 1970s, helped to produce a greater public awareness of the consequences of industrial pollution and to stimulate a concern for *prevention* of such occurrences among citizens in other parts of the country whose areas were slated for further industrial development.

The Mishima-Numazu Movement: A Watershed

The fact that media reports dramatizing the plight of the victims of pollution in the Big Four incidents sensitized residents of other communities to a concern for prevention of similar disasters is illustrated by the case of the first major prevention-oriented citizens' movement in Japan—that which took place in Mishima-Numazu in 1963-1964. There is no question that reports of severe pollution from oil and chemical plants in Yokkaichi City contributed to the mood of opposition among residents of Mishima City, and then later among residents of the adjacent Numazu and Shimazu areas, when the latter were targeted for a similar type of development complex. The success of this famous anti-*konbināto* prevention movement analyzed in Lewis's case study in turn attracted nationwide attention to both the environmental issue and to the citizen-based organization and strategy to oppose and prevent pollution. The movement became a symbol of the potential both for effective resident resistance to industrial development and for action to protect the local environment. Veterans of the Mishima-Numazu movements became "consultants" to residents of other nearby areas, travelled to advise other movements as far away as Kagoshima, and wrote articles for magazines.

In retrospect, the Mishima-Numazu movements appear to have been a watershed in the history of citizens' movements. Not only was the emphasis in movements after Mishima-Numazu to shift from a concern for compensation to a concern for prevention but the experience and example of the Mishima-Numazu movements served as an impetus toward merging the concept of "citizens' movements" and the "*shimin* ideal" with environmental activism. Even after the reports of the Big Four victims' movements first attracted attention, one could find articles in intellectual journals that discussed citizens' movements with no reference to antipollution protest;[18] but in the Mishima-Numazu movements, organizers made conscious use of the term *shimin* and *shimin undō* ("citizen" and "citizens' movement") to refer to their environment-conscious efforts to halt planned construction of an industrial

[18] See for example, Yamashita Hajime, "Chiiki jichi to shimin undō," *Toshi Mondai* 56 (1965): 81-90.

plant in their locale. The "idea" that had been born in the treaty crisis of 1960 of mobilizing average citizens to oppose government policy now had been wed to the burgeoning practice of organizing residents in specific local areas to prevent pollution.

Spurred by the example of Mishima-Numazu's successful grass-roots activism to prevent industrial development and by the media publicity given to the Big Four incidents and to the growing salience of the pollution issue abroad, the number of antipollution and antidevelopment movements increased dramatically during the following years. The extent of the growth of these movements in the late 1960s and early 1970s was indicated by the figures cited at the beginning of this article.

Perhaps as important as the astounding increase in the number of movements was the increased diversification in their goals, location, and organizational basis. As we have mentioned, in the early years, victims' movements seeking compensation for injured residents of rural areas predominated; after 1965, the movements were increasingly prevention-oriented, like the Mishima-Numazu prototype, and tended to take place in the urban areas of Japan. No type of community could avoid the conflicts attendant on the new concern for preservation and environmental protection, and local governmental and business elites suddenly met resistance where previously there had been acquiescence, demands where there had once been only support. In rural areas, regional developers found increasingly ineffective their attempts to use traditional methods of working through local leadership and merely going through the customary formula of "official announcement, explanation meeting (*setsumeikai*), and arbitration and compensation" to acquire the rural land for their projects. Their efforts were increasingly hampered by interference from organized residents, both farmers and ecologically conscious middle-class residents of semirural towns and smaller cities.

The case of Oiso, briefly described by McKean, is one example of the new prevention consciousness in rural areas. Even more spectacular and significant, though, was the veritable explosion of protest in urban and suburban areas. Suburban *danchi* (apartment complex) dwellers organized themselves to oppose industrial plants or highway interchanges in their areas and to demand from local governments the provision of services essential to the quality of life in their newly developed communities: sewers, parks, sidewalks. City governments, urban planners, and builders encountered frequent and persistent neighborhood level opposition to urban renewal and public facility construction from residents who no longer saw smoke, or even the vaunted "Bullet

Train," as symbols of progress but rather as invaders of their communities who deprive them of clean air and peace and quiet. In Tokyo, citizens' groups have even opposed the construction of tall buildings that deprive the inhabitants of neighboring dwellings of "the right to sunshine."

The Diversity of Citizens' Movements

As the movement's focus became increasingly prevention and urban-oriented, new types of organizations also began to appear. The "roving ombudsmen" of which McKean speaks, a small number of professional antipollution activists on the "Nader's Raiders" model who travel around and lend their technical, publicity, and political skills where they are needed, is one example. Ui Jun, a university researcher, and his colleagues comprise perhaps the most famous of these groups. "Imitation" citizens' movements, movements formed and sponsored by local governments, also grew up as progressive local executives sensed the changing political winds toward the idea of grass-roots citizen participation and attempted to legitimize their administrations with the appearance of citizen input and of environmental concern: the "Beautify the Kamo River" movement, sponsored by the leftist prefectural administration in Kyoto to both clean up and preserve the major river that runs through Kyoto City is one example.[19]

Both the professional "ombudsmen" type and the Mishima-Numazu type, with its coalition of a wide variety of local organizations mobilizing widespread support, helped promote essential elements of the *shimin undō* image: the pursuit of the common good and public welfare by the enlightened civic action of concerned citizens. Even the imitation type of movement, despite its lack of real grass-roots spontaneity, could be cloaked in the "*shimin* ideal." But not all instances of environmental protest seemed to share the wider vision of civic activism displayed by these types of citizens' movements. Indeed, in the late 1960s and early 1970s, there occurred a multiplicity of movements based exclusively on inhabitants of a particular residential area who sought redress for their own very specific, self-interested grievances. For example, in some areas, individual local neighborhood associations merely espoused a citizens' movement attitude to correct a particular local nuisance without really transcending their traditional roles and functions. McKean calls this type of movement a "converted neighborhood association" to indicate its basis in one preexisting local organiza-

[19] See Chapter 11 of this volume.

tion and its temporarily investing its energies in protest activity. Sometimes this type of movement even engages in activities that can be construed as being antithetical to a larger, or competing, "public good." In Tokyo, converted neighborhood associations, and even a converted ward assembly, engaged in a "garbage war" with each other and the progressive governor to prevent their areas from being the site of, or inconvenienced by, the construction of a garbage treatment facility desperately needed by the city.[20] The most affected neighborhood association and the ward assembly in Kōtō demanded compensation and revision of Tokyo Metropolitan Government plans for garbage disposal when local residents and associations in Sugimami ward demanded that a garbage incinerator plant not be built in their area. Even more narrowly interest-based were the urban "movements" that consisted of little more than a small group of individual "issue entrepreneurs"[21] who sought access to the media to publicize their own complaints. There are also a number of cases of "one-man bands"—a citizens' movement composed of a lone, but very vociferous, individual.

The expanded role of more narrow interest-based movement organizations such as these in the citizens' movement trend is probably reflected in the results of an *Asahi Shinbun* survey in 1973 on the relative size of citizens' movements.[22] About 2 percent of all CMs sampled had less than 10 members, another 15 percent between 11 and 50, and another 10 percent between 51 and 100. In other words, about a quarter of citizens' movements had less than 100 members. Another 28 percent of CMs were of more moderate size, with 100-500 members. As McKean indicates, although the independent citizens' movement of moderate to large size, often based on a number of existing community organizations with wide community support like the Mishima movement, remained the more common type, as the environmental issue percolated downward and the salience and legitimacy of citizen protest increased, the movement as a whole became more diverse and many particular local movements' size and goals had less an aura of public service than that of private complaint.

By the 1970s, terminology too began to reflect the presence of these more localized and narrow interest-based CMs. The term *jūmin undō*

[20] Alan J. Rix, "Tokyo's Governor Minobe and Progressive Local Politics in Japan," *Asian Survey* 15 (1975): 538-540.

[21] John D. McCarthy and Mayer N. Zald, "Resource Mobilization and Social Movements: A Partial Theory," *American Journal of Sociology* 82 (1977): 1,212-1,241.

[22] Sample was 627 groups. Cited in Nakamura Kiichi, "Jūmin undō no soshiki to Kōzō," *Chiiki Kaihatsu*, no. 154 (July 1977), p. 23.

became increasingly popular in referring to the latter. This term, as opposed to the more generic *shimin undō*, had connotations of resistance to authority based on extremely localized complaints arising out of individuals' concrete daily needs. If the term *shimin undō* symbolized a textbooklike civic action by a rational citizenry on behalf of the public good, *jūmin undō* contained implications of the "egoism" of protest that seeks a response to individual grievances with little regard to the complex problems and broader needs of the wider community.[23]

The proliferation and dispersion of citizens' movements, the attendant publicity they received, and the pressure they exerted was eventually felt at the national level as well as at the local level. Beginning with a session of the Japanese Diet in 1970, often called "The Pollution Diet," more than a dozen laws concerning the environment and pollution control were passed. Despite considerable watering down of the original stringent provisions of some bills due to the opposition of big business and factions within the ruling Liberal Democratic Party (LDP), the new laws contained some significant gains for the environmental cause: the creation of an Environmental Protection Agency, the provision of fines and jail terms for polluters who have been proven to cause hazards to life and health, and the delegation of greater powers to local governments in the control of water and other forms of pollution.[24] Combined with the favorable verdicts rendered in the following few years in the Big Four pollution trials and the effective role citizens' movements and the environmental issue played in achieving the election of sympathetic progressive executives in major urban areas of Japan during the same period, the passage of such legislation undoubtedly represents the high-water mark of the nationwide struggle by local residents to force a change in the priorities of local and national governments. Like the progressive movement in nineteenth-century America and the civil rights movement in twentieth-century America, citizens' movements against pollution in Japan achieved their greatest long-range successes when their values and aims were adopted and institutionalized by the established political elite.

Types of Citizens' Movements

We have attempted to bring some order to the diversity of citizens' movements described in the preceding historical sketch by classifying

[23] Omori Wataru, "Jūmin undō no tenkai katei," in *Chiiki Kaihatsu*, no. 154, (July 1977), pp. 13-14.

[24] Margaret McKean, "Pollution and Policy-Making," pp. 227-231.

them according to types based on the dimension of organizational autonomy, on the one hand, and the dimension of their goals (compensation versus prevention), on the other (See Figure 1).[25] The rows categorize CMs according to the basis of both their membership and the organization's dependence on existing organizations and local authorities. We begin at the top with the least autonomous type, the citizens' movement sponsored by local governments (McKean's "imitation" type), move through converted neighborhood associations and independent movements, which include many participants from established community organizations, to the completely autonomous individuals and small groups who form themselves into wholly new movements. The columns distinguish whether the goal of the movement involved an attempt to acquire compensation for, or remedy, past pollution damage, or to prevent construction of new facilities that would bring adverse environmental consequences. The cells of the typology contain examples from the movements we have mentioned above.

As one goes down the rows, perhaps the most crucial distinction is the jump from the "converted neighborhood association" type to the "independent" movement type. Both the "imitation" movement and the converted neighborhood association movement are almost totally dependent for their existence on the initiation and perpetuation of support from either local governmental authority or from a particular existing community or area association. The independent movement, on the other hand, may be based upon existing community associations and may rely on them to perform needed communication and recruitment functions, but it develops its own autonomous and separate movement structure. The final category are those movements not based on any existing groups at all but which have been spontaneously formed by individuals. As one goes from left to right, we proceed from those who have the most personal experience with the consequences of pollution and who protest to seek alleviation of a problem (either in the form of compensation for victims or of remedying the problem) to those who join movements to preserve the existing environment from

[25] Our typology is obviously based in part on that discussed by McKean in Chapter 7, but it differs from hers in at least two important respects: we have explicitly added the dimension of compensation versus prevention goals to our formal classification, and we have placed "independent" citizens' movements based on no existing organizational infrastructure into a separate category with the "roving ombudsmen" type of her typology. We have done the latter to emphasize the distinction between CMs based on existing local associations and those that are not, a distinction crucial to some of our later arguments about the significance of citizens' movements.

Figure 1
TYPES OF CITIZENS' MOVEMENTS

GOALS
ecological sophistication of members ➝

(vertical axis label, left side: autonomy from established organizations and authority)

ORGANIZATIONAL TYPE	Compensation/ Remedy	Prevention
"Imitation" (sponsored) CMs:	"Beautify the Kamo River" Movement (Kyoto)	
"Converted" Neighborhood Associations:	Tokyo "Garbage Wars": Kōtō Ward	Tokyo "Garbage Wars": Suginami Ward
"Independent" Movement (with associational infrastructure)	Yokkaichi	Mishima-Numazu "Right to Sunshine" (Tokyo)
Individuals and Small Groups	Minamata Victims and Families	"Ombudsmen" (e.g., Ui Jun)

future threats. The latter, as McKean points out, reflects their members' greater sense of ecological awareness.

Perhaps the most important aspect of this typology and of our brief review of the phases in the development of the citizens' movement phenomena are their implications concerning a disparity between the simplistic ideal image of citizens' movements and their reality. The *shimin undō* ideal and the literature on citizens' movements hitherto tends to portray CMs as being spontaneously formed by citizens who are both ecologically aware and without connections or access to established channels of influence. This ideal-typical image is actually only approached by certain types of movements (for example, the ombudsmen type in the lower right-hand cell of the typology), and these are but a small minority of all citizens' movements. In fact, many of the compensation movement participants have had but a limited ecological consciousness or sophistication; and, as both Lewis and McKean point out, the most important and prototypical movements are those that draw their members from, and utilize the resources of, established community organizations to build their own movement structure. As we shall discuss in the next section, this latter fact has important consequences for our interpretations of the growth and significance of these movements in postwar Japan.

Throughout this section we have intentionally emphasized the importance of distinguishing between the "idea" of citizens' movements and the phenomenon itself. The "idea" of citizens' movements was born in the 1960 treaty crisis with no relationship to the antipollution movement. It was not until the Mishima-Numazu movement in 1963-1964 that the CM ideal was grafted onto antipollution protest. The result of this merging was to endow the portrayal of most citizens' movements with the attributes of the *shimin* ideal, a simplistic yet influential characterization that has been applied whatever the realities and despite the diversity of movements.

It is our belief that the confusion of the "idea" of *shimin undō* with the reality of the movements against pollution has been primarily responsible for producing a view of citizens' movements that has been untested by systematic evidence and divorced from the insights provided by theories of social movements. Further, as we shall argue later, whatever its drawbacks as an accurate description of citizens' movements, the confusion of "idea" and reality has also performed an important function in the development of the movement itself. In the following sections, we will use the new and systematic evidence provided by McKean and Lewis to offer what we hope is a more realistic and theoretically significant view of citizens' movements.

THE GROWTH OF ENVIRONMENTAL PROTEST: THEORIES OF SOCIAL MOVEMENTS AND SOCIAL CHANGE

Citizens' movements have been implicitly viewed as an important social movement in postwar Japan, but rarely have they been explicitly analyzed as such. Our intent here is to apply social movement theory to McKean's and Lewis's findings in the belief that this approach will yield new insights into the growth of citizens' movements in postwar Japan and also bring a much-needed comparative perspective to our study of environmental protest in Japan.

Citizens' Movements as Social Movement Organizations

Social movements are collective, organized attempts to bring about change in society and in individuals.[26] Those who participate in social movements do so primarily to bring about the purposes for which the movement arose—the fulfillment of the values of the movement—and

[26] Rudolf Heberle, "Types and Functions of Social Movements," and Joseph R. Gusfield, "The Study of Social Movements," in *International Encyclopedia of the Social Sciences*, ed. David L. Sills (New York: Macmillan and Co., 1968).

only secondarily if at all from motivations of material gain or of the social-psychological benefits that membership might bring (for example, prestige or friendship).[27] Social movements are more enduring than mobs or crowds but less institutionalized than political parties, established interest groups, or bureaucracies.[28]

Although several of the earliest cases of citizens' movements were little more than episodic expressions of protest lacking a wider vision, most movements arising after the Mishima-Numazu movement (1963-1964) had the force and character of a social movement as defined by the preceding criteria. They arose as movements oriented toward social and political change: change in their living environments, change in government and corporate decisions and decision-making practices, change in the values of the elite, the general public, and the members of their community and movement, and frequently change in their elected officials and representatives. Although earlier victims' movement participants sought, among other things, financial benefits, certainly almost all of the prevention movements that have overwhelmingly predominated in the movement since the mid-1960s have mobilized their members by appealing to a broader set of environmental goals and values. In the latter movements, members participated primarily out of an interest in fulfilling the general aims of the movement, not from an interest in specific material or social rewards. CMs were unquestionably more organized and enduring than mobs, but, as almost all observers and participants have agreed, they were differentiated from more institutionalized political parties and conventional interest groups and were without the latter's primary emphasis on material incentives.

Similarly, the predominantly local nature of most movements and the lack of a single national coordinating body is not an impediment to considering them collectively as a single social movement: "A social movement may . . . be comprised of organized groups without having one over-all formal organization."[29] Most social protest movements arise from the grass roots, with many being predominantly local or re-

---

[27] Mayer N. Zald and Roberta Ash, "Social Movement Organizations: Growth, Decay, and Change," *Social Forces* 44 (1966): 329.

[28] Heberle, "Types and Functions of Social Movements," p. 439. Heberle does distinguish, however, between a "protest" movement and a "social" movement, seeing the former as having more limited goals and membership and a less comprehensive program or elaborate ideology than the latter. The distinguishing characteristics of the two are vague, however, and there is no separate body of theory or hypotheses concerning protest movements. We therefore use the terms interchangeably in this essay, as do many theorists, and often combine them, as in "social protest movement."

[29] Ibid., p. 439.

gional in character (for example, the progressive movement, the civil rights movement in the American South). Despite differences in the immediate target or problem they protested against, most of these local movements and their participants shared the general overarching aims of improving the quality of life, protecting the environment, changing government priorities, and increasing citizen input into local decisions. Thus, if citizens' movements qualify as a social movement, we no longer need to treat them as unique aberrations of Japanese culture but can view them as a Japanese variant of a universal sociological phenomenon. In so doing, we can both utilize the theoretical perspectives of social science to understand CMs in Japan and use Japanese citizens' movement experience to contribute to social movement theory.

Grievance and Organizational Resources Models

There are two general theoretical approaches to the study of social protest movements.[30] The classical approach has been to emphasize what may be called the "social-psychological grievance" model, in which rebellion and protest are seen to arise from the accumulated and severely felt grievances of individuals who experience the stresses of social structural change but have no access to conventional channels for the expression and alleviation of their discontent. The grievance model focuses attention on the "hearts and minds of the people"[31] and distinguishes between the rational, interest-seeking actions of those integrated into conventional groups, such as political parties, lobbies, and interest groups, and those excluded from them who have to engage in protest to express their distress.[32] One form of this view is the "mass society" theory of Kornhauser, in which the isolation of individuals and the centralization of political relations in societies without an extensive network of intermediary traditional and voluntary groups make

[30] Reviews of these two approaches are found in Gusfield, "Study of Social Movements"; William A. Gamson, *The Strategy of Social Protest* (Homewood, Illinois: The Dorsey Press, 1975), Chapter 9; Bruce Fireman and William A. Gamson, "Utilitarian Logic in the Resource Mobilization Perspective" (unpublished paper, Center for Research on Social Organization, Ann Arbor, Michigan, 1977); Donald Von Eschen et al., "The Organizational Substructure of Disorderly Politics," *Social Forces* 49 (1971): 529-544; Anthony Oberschall, *Social Conflict and Social Movements* (Englewood Cliffs, N.J.: Prentice-Hall, Inc., 1973), especially Chapter 4; and John D. McCarthy and Mayer N. Zald, *The Trend of Social Movements in America: Professionalization and Resource Mobilization* (Morristown, N.J.: General Learning Press, 1973).

[31] McCarthy and Zald, *The Trend of Social Movements*, p. 1.

[32] Gamson, *The Strategy of Social Protest*, especially pp. 130-134.

available the alienated, uprooted people who comprise those mobilized into mass movements.[33]

By contrast, the "resource mobilization" approach, a newer trend in social movement theory, argues that social protest movements tend to arise when structural conditions create both resources that facilitate the mobilization of participants into movements and the effective use of these resources to expand the movement's influence. Rather than the mere presence of severe discontent itself, it is the availability of resources—organizations, information, professional experts, money—that creates a protest movement. Indeed, it is this availability of resources that accounts for the movement's ability to grow rapidly. Those who engage in protest movements are no less "rational" or "interest-seeking" than those who engage in conventional politics; protest "is simply politics by other means."[34] In fact, because protest movements arise where there is a highly developed network of traditional and intermediary associations available for mobilization into the movement, many participants are not the isolated individuals portrayed by Kornhauser but those who are integrated into the conventional social and interest groups now being mobilized for different purposes.[35] If the grievance model focuses on discontent caused by social strains and a lack of organized grievance channels, the resource mobilization model focuses on the availability of organizational capabilities for protest through social development.

Most standard interpretations of citizens' movements in Japan have rarely been disciplined by anything nearly as systematic as the explicit use of one of these models; nevertheless, most seem to implicitly assume a "grievance model" of the origins and nature of citizens' movements. Thus, CMs have been viewed as a spontaneous populist insurgency of individuals, largely political novices, with genuinely severe grievances against the trend of socio-economic change in postwar Japan and with no connection with, or access to, established political organizations and groups.[36] A somewhat more theoretical variation of this view has been to see the grievances, isolation, and alienation of citizens' movement participants as specifically resulting from "postindustrial" change in which conventional political and interest groups, organized by the socio-economic cleavages of industrial society, were incapable of re-

[33] William Kornhauser, *The Politics of Mass Society* (Glencoe, Illinois: The Free Press, 1959). The best general critique of the Kornhauser model is found in Oberschall, *Social Conflict*, Chapter 4.
[34] Gamson, *The Strategy of Social Protest*, p. 139.
[35] See for example, Oberschall, *Social Conflict*.
[36] See the introductory section of this essay for specific examples.

sponding to a nondistributive issue like pollution that cuts across traditional socio-economic strata. Activists and leaders in CMs, it is argued, are primarily professional persons and newcomers to a locality who are unintegrated into traditional community interest groups and associations and who therefore have to express their grievances over pollution through the creation of new protest channels like citizens' movements.[37]

There is evidence for the validity of certain elements of the grievance/postindustrial view of citizens' movements in Japan. Some participants, especially the pollution disease victims and their families in the early compensation movements, have clearly been motivated to form and join movements as a result of pent-up frustrations and almost unbearable sufferings to which no one was responding. The pollution issue *has* been a cross-stratal one in that it has affected, and citizens' movements have mobilized, a wide cross-section of individuals from every socio-economic strata and political background, as the evidence of both McKean and Lewis bears out. And many of these antipollution activists (in McKean's sample, over half) are totally new to the protest scene.

Further, both the initial unresponsiveness of established political parties toward local residents' concern about pollution and the deep-rooted distrust toward political parties that is an element of Japanese political culture undoubtedly contributed to the formation of separate movement organizations. In the case of the ruling LDP, its sponsorship of development policies and its close ties to big business precluded an ability to respond to local residents' demands. The main opposition party, the Japan Socialist Party (JSP), was hampered, on the other hand, by lack of strong grass-roots organization down to the community level and by an ideological orientation that emphasized national, not local, issues. Once formed, citizens' movements reflected the distrustful view of many Japanese toward political parties as selfish and self-seeking organizations. Most citizens' movements feared their organization's being coopted, or manipulated, or their goals diverted by close association with any particular political party, and most tried to maintain a degree of autonomy from them. An *Asahi Shinbun* survey confirms the self-conscious distrust of particular parties and the attempt to maintain independence: almost 35 percent of the respondent movements said they had no relationship to any political party, and another

---

[37] The primary exponent of this interesting view is Taketsugu Tsurutani, *Political Change in Modern Japan*, pp. 193-198. Although we disagree in this essay with a number of the elements in Tsurutani's view of citizens' movements, it is by far the most theoretically sophisticated of the English-language treatments of citizens' movements and the one that most consciously attempts a comparative frame of reference.

24 percent said they maintained relationships with all parties.[38] Analysis of another survey found that in only a minority of cases opposition parties were listed as either constituent or cooperating organizations or that individual officials or politicians of these parties were involved in the movement in some capacity. Most of the latter cases were nonlocal resident based movements.[39]

Yet the grievance/postindustrial model of social protest is clearly inadequate as a total explanation of the rise and growth of citizens' movements in Japan. One of the great virtues of the two studies that follow is the evidence they provide that confirms the utility of the resource mobilization model in understanding the environmental protest movement in Japan. McKean identifies the CM that is originally formed by drawing upon participants in existing community organizations (even though it develops its own independent movement organization) as the most typical form.[40] Lewis gives us a vivid example of how the prototypical Mishima movement was formed from, and in many ways dependent for its success upon, existing conventional local organizations: a meeting of the Citizens' Council, an umbrella organization for the Mishima movement, included chairmen of forty neighborhood associations, fifty representatives of a wide range of local organizations, and only thirty individuals not affiliated with a component organization.[41] Further, McKean points out that conservative community leaders occupied a disproportionate share of the leadership positions in the CMs in her sample and that such persons provide needed respectability, political expertise, and leadership traits to movement organizations.[42]

It appears from this evidence that many CMs in Japan have relied on established community organizations and their leaders to form the organizational network that underlies the movement's activities.[43] And herein may lie one major explanation for the rapid and spectacular spread of CMs in Japan: it was not the availability of an isolated and alienated "mass" but the availability of an extensive web of community and associational organizations at the local level, together with the movement resources they can provide, that enabled the movement

[38] 21 May 1973; cited in Nakamura, "Jūmin undō," p. 24.

[39] The survey was conducted by the Japanese journal *Shimin*, and a reanalysis of the data presented was conducted by Bradford Simcock, "Citizens' Movements and Opposition Politics in Japan" (paper presented to the Conference on Local Opposition in Japan, Wrightsville Beach, N.C., 24-26 June 1976); see especially pp. 21-24.

[40] See Chapter 7.   [41] See Chapter 8.   [42] See Chapter 7.

[43] On this point, see also Daikichi Irokawa, "The Survival Struggle of the Japanese Community," *The Japan Interpreter* 9 (1975): 488-489.

against pollution to grow so rapidly, spread so widely, and exercise influence so greatly. In fact, it might be argued that variations in the number and characteristics of existing community organizations and groups among localities are at least potentially as important as the intensity of the pollution problem in different areas when it comes to finding an explanation for differences in the frequency and effectiveness of citizens movements.

Other elements in citizens' movements would also seem to be at variance with the grievance/mass/postindustrial society view that participants are the alienated, isolated, and unintegrated in their communities. Thus, for example, observers have noted the role of traditional folk beliefs[44] and traditional and community values[45] in the struggles and litigation of pollution victims and their families for compensation, and the role that a sense of community and the desire to protect their neighborhoods plays for CM participants in both old urban neighborhood and rural protests to prevent industrial development.[46] Still others have seen in citizens' movements the revitalization of traditional *buraku* (hamlet) community spirit and patterns of cooperation.[47]

Finally, one should note the important part played by professional experts, such as university and high-school teachers, scientists, and doctors in providing technical advice and aid to many movements and the important publicizing and organizing role played by professional "ombudsmen" in providing expertise and information to movements and to the public on behalf of movements. These activities coincide closely to what resource mobilization theorists argue is an increasing trend in social movements in the United States—the professionalization of protest.[48]

The Growth of a Social Protest Movement: Change and Continuity

Attention to the resource mobilization aspects of citizens' movements underlines the extent to which the movement is not only bringing about change in Japanese society and politics, a subject to which we will turn in the next section, but also the fact that it is itself a product

---

[44] Kazuko Tsurumi, "Social Price of Pollution in Japan and the Role of Folk Beliefs" (paper delivered at Princeton University, 8 March 1977).

[45] See Upham, "A Sociological Analysis."

[46] Margaret A. McKean, "Citizens' Movements in Urban and Rural Japan," in *Social Change and Community Politics in Urban Japan*, ed. James W. White and Frank Munger (Chapel Hill, N.C.: Institute for Research in Social Sciences, University of North Carolina, 1976), pp. 64-65.

[47] Irokawa, "Survival Struggle," especially pp. 487-491.

[48] McCarthy and Zald, *The Trend of Social Movements*.

of a complex intertwining of continuity and change in postwar Japan. Mobilization of ordinary citizens at the local level is not a new phenomenon in Japan. It took place on a mass scale under the wartime regime as it mobilized average citizens into neighborhood associations, fire brigades, and civil defense groups in support of the war effort. After the war, neighborhood associations were retained as informal extensions of local government.[49] With the new democratic political system, interest group activity was encouraged and legitimized, and there occurred a veritable explosion of such activity at the local level.[50] More widely and spontaneously than in the prewar period, people joined together with those of like interest: most farmers were organized into agricultural cooperatives, fishermen into unions, women into housewives' associations, parents into PTAs, city dwellers into neighborhood associations, and suburbanites into *danchi* organizations. Almost all of these organizations were tied via an extensive network of patron-client relations to conservative local politicians (and through them to LDP national politicians) and to conservative local government authorities.

Rapid economic growth in the 1950s and 1960s brought change familiar to citizens of all advanced industrial societies: urbanization, suburbanization, the expansion and dispersion of industry, and the creation of an educated, affluent middle class. But these universal socio-economic consequences of economic development had a particular Japanese pattern to them. Urbanization and suburbanization never destroyed the cohesiveness of Japanese inner cities, as it did in the United States, nor the extensive network of local organizations that keep neighborhoods true "communities." They did make Japanese residential areas far more socio-economically heterogeneous than those in American cities, however, partly because of the postwar housing and land shortage.[51] Urbanization brought many former rural dwellers to the cities, and suburbanization resulted in many urban middle-class white-collar workers living in suburban *danchi* in close proximity to farmers, fishermen, and small merchants. Rapid economic growth policies dispersed industry and industrial workers into rural areas throughout Japan. When the pollution issue arose, therefore, it was a problem that touched almost all: rural areas were affected as much as cities,

[49] Kurt Steiner, *Local Government in Japan* (Stanford: Stanford University Press, 1965), Chapter 10.

[50] Takeshi Ishida, "Emerging or Eclipsing Citizenship?—A Study of Changes in Political Attitudes in Postwar Japan," *Developing Economies* 6 (1968): 413-414.

[51] David H. Bayley, *Forces of Order: Police Behavior in Japan and the United States* (Berkeley: University of California Press, 1976), p. 17.

farmers and fishermen as much as urbanites, suburbanites as well as dwellers in factory towns.

Indeed, the dispersion of pollution and the heterogeneity of the affected local communities provides another insight into the sudden explosion of protest through local movements in recent years. Difficulty and expense of finding housing, and deep-rooted social, psychological, and economic ties to established communities, as well as the dearth of areas untouched by environmental hazards deprive many Japanese of the alternative of individual escape. Unlike many of their more mobile American counterparts, the Japanese cannot avoid environmental problems by fleeing to sheltered suburban enclaves and to completely undeveloped and isolated rural areas available in countries of much vaster land and space. In Hirschman's terms, lacking the ability to "exit," many Japanese could but "voice" their dissatisfactions and demands through political protest.[52]

If the particular pattern of socio-economic change in postwar Japan increased both the number and variety of people who had pollution- or development-related grievances and motivations to protest, it also ensured that many resources were available in the local environment from which a protest movement could be rapidly created and developed. The availability of a plethora of community and interest organizations could provide readymade recruitment and communication vehicles for such a movement; the presence of neighborhood and community leaders could provide leadership, respectability, and organizing skills; a heterogeneous population, all commonly affected by this issue, was available for mobilization, including in almost every community, educated, affluent middle-class residents with the leisure time, political consciousness, and communication skills to contribute to the movement.[53] It is neither the inherent cross-stratal nature of the pollution issue nor the severe impact of pollution alone, as many observers seem to imply, that automatically gave rise to a protest movement so rapidly developed and widespread: the structural pattern of socio-economic growth in postwar Japan also created the organizational resources necessary to mobilize such a movement in many locales.

Two major preconditions had to be met before the impact of the

[52] Albert O. Hirschman, *Exit, Voice, and Loyalty* (Cambridge, Mass.: Harvard University Press, 1970). On the inverse relationship between mobility and protest in American urban neighborhoods, see J. M. Orbell and T. Uno, "A Theory of Neighborhood Problem Solving: Political Action vs. Residential Mobility," *American Political Science Review* 66 (1972): 471-489.

[53] On the effectiveness of middle-class residents in using communication to further a citizens' movement, see Norio Tamura, "Mass/Miniature Communications and Citizen Participation," *Local Government Review*, no. 4 (1976), pp. 12-14.

pollution problem in local areas could result in the effective utilization of these resources to create a nationwide movement of antipollution protest. The first crucial intermediate stage was the diversion of the goals and concerns of many local community organizations from their previous nonprotest orientation and the loosening of their ties to established conservative politician/official patrons. As we have noted, most local community organizations, such as neighborhood associations and housewives' associations, have been pillars of conservatism in Japan, operating as local area pressure groups to receive distributive benefits from conservative local and national politicians, on the one hand, and as information and organizing adjuncts of local authorities and politicians, on the other. That many of these groups have individually converted themselves into quasi-citizens' movements or, more commonly, served in alliance with other such groups as the main organizational and communications base for a wider movement may represent a fundamental and significant development in local level politics.

The role of the neighborhood and housewives' associations and the attitude they choose to take toward an incipient pollution protest movement has been crucial to any local movement's development. In areas where such organizations and their leaders join the CM, the latter gains valuable human and organizational resources, as it obviously did in the Mishima case described by Lewis. Where neighborhood associations are hopelessly split by the pollution issue or are opposed to the movement's cause and remain closely tied to industry or conservative local governmental and political elites, citizens' movements face a constant uphill struggle for support, resources, and legitimacy. In this struggle, community solidarity norms are often invoked not to gain adherents for the movement but rather to discourage or intimidate prospective and actual movement supporters. McKean's descriptions of this problem in Oiso and Usuku illustrate both the obstacles that such a situation can create for the movement and the courage individual activists must have in trying to overcome them.

If this diversion of many and this resistance of some community organizations into the building-block units of citizens' movements is essential to understanding the process by which effective antipollution protest movements develop or fail to develop, it is also one of the least studied aspects of CMs. We do not yet understand clearly either the process by which the vertical organizational and patron-client ties of community associations to conservative power become weakened or transformed enough in many areas to make them available for diversion into a protest movement or the exact factors that determine whether such organizations will maintain their traditional roles or eschew them to join citizens' movements in a fight that often pits them against the very patron politicians and officials they had previously derived benefits from supporting. We suspect that important intervening variables may include the depth of residents' identifications with the local area, the perceived threat to the existing community, and the way in which association leaders resolve their conflicts between their loyalty to their followers and their loyalty to their own political values. In the latter regard, it is interesting to note McKean's finding that many conservative community leaders may continue to support the LDP at the national level while breaking ties with the conservatives at the local level in disgust at the latter's stance on a pollution issue that directly affects the neighborhood. We sorely need further studies of such neighborhood groups in the crisis created by the pollution issue, the changes they undergo, their internal politics and leader-follower relations, and their external links to both establishment and movement-related political activists.[54]

The second crucial precondition that had to be met before the accumulation of grievances could result in the effective mobilization of organizational resources into a social protest movement was the development and diffusion of a self-conscious set of related beliefs justifying and idealizing protest—the development of, in short, a "protest ideology."[55] We suggest that the *shimin undō* ideal described previously (that average citizens were spontaneously creating new forms of democratic organizations in the best traditions of grass-roots egalitarian democracy to gain control over their own destinies and work for the "public good") functioned as a protest ideology in the development of citizens' movements in Japan. Early victims' movement participants justified their actions using traditional values.[56] After the grafting of the *shimin* ideal to pollution protest and its first use in the Mishima-Numazu prevention movement, an image of citizens' movements was created and diffused that went far beyond the particular aims of each local movement and served to endow protest actions with a political consciousness and rationalization for action. It is no accident that the

[54] A welcome addition to the scant literature on neighborhood associations is White and Munger, *Social Change and Community Politics in Urban Japan*. Although these articles deal with the transformation of neighborhoods and associations undergoing social change, none of them deal directly with the specific research that we are suggesting is needed—a case study of a neighborhood association prior to and through the process of deciding whether to join or form a citizens' movement.

[55] The role of ideology in social movements is discussed in Heberle, "Types and Functions of Social Movements," and Gusfield, "Study of Social Movements."

[56] See Upham, "A Sociological Analysis," and Tsurumi, "Social Price."

crucial "take-off" stage in the spread and salience of citizens' movements occurred in the period between Mishima-Numazu and the early 1970s, by which time the *jūmin undō* characterization indicated an increasing awareness of the more complex realities of current environmental protest.

Whatever the elements of truth to the *shimin undō* ideal (and throughout this essay we are attempting to indicate where reality has conformed and where it has diverged from this ideal), it is important to note the functions that this image performed as a protest ideology. First, we can say that the *shimin undō* ideal helped to give each particular movement organization and its activists a sense of common purpose despite the different specific aims of each in different locales. In short, it helped to lend an image of common participation in a powerful universal cause to myriad local protests with different targets and different problems. In a fundamental sense, the *shimin undō* ideal helped to create *one* social movement from many local protest movements.

Secondly, endowing local actions against pollution with the *shimin undō* ideal made the protest against pollution more salient and appealing to the third parties, those that Lipsky calls "reference publics,"[57] whose support and aid are essential to the success of any protest. These third parties included the media, intellectuals, progressive politicians, and sympathizers nationwide. These "reference publics" first adopted and then helped to diffuse and perpetuate the image of local antipollution protest as being in the same tradition as the citizens' movements of the 1960 treaty crisis. With the help of a variety of politically knowledgeable and experienced "opinion leaders" both inside and outside the protest organizations (and these included local progressive activists, journalists, nationally-known intellectuals, and progressive candidates for the local executive in major urban areas), environmental protest was endowed with ideal qualities and the image of being a potentially significant political force on both the local and national scenes. In a nation like Japan, where nearly every community has its intellectuals and progressive activists and where the national media reaches even rural areas and is paid close attention to by most citizens, a massive infrastructure existed for the theoretical development and diffusion of the *shimin undō* idea.

Finally, and most importantly, the consequence of this propagation was to help legitimize participation in pollution protest for the average local resident and community leader. The *shimin undō* idea legitimized protest action on behalf of one's actual or potential interests as actions

[57] Michael Lipsky, "Protest as a Political Resource," *American Political Science Review* 62 (1968): 1,146.

for the *collective* good, and it legitimized political activities through noninstitutionalized channels and by direct action methods as being consonant with the best democratic ideals. In short, from the perspective of the individual local resident, the "citizens' movement idea" helped to decrease the potential "costs" of participating in a protest movement against authority, of being branded as a deviant or a rebel working for selfish ends—powerful psychological deterrents to participation in the context of Japanese culture. And it also served to increase the potential "benefits" of investing time and energy in the movement because it gave the image of increased likelihood of success and established participation itself as a worthwhile and worthy action for oneself and the community.

This is not to say that the civic activist ideal and the new ethic of participatory democracy in which antipollution protest became immersed has been either universally accepted or is an accurate reflection of many CMs: not all participants in protest have shared the ideological objectives and larger vision of the theoreticians or displayed the progressive characteristics ascribed to them by outside observers; and not all purveyors of the *shimin* ideal have sufficiently understood the more limited and self-interested livelihood and concrete personal concerns that have motivated many local activists. It is to say, though, that the *shimin undō* ideal has been more than merely an imperfect academic and journalistic description of the CM phenomenon: it has itself been a major *resource* in the mobilization of participants and the spread of the antipollution movement by universalizing individual local cases of protest, by attracting powerful allies to the movement, and by legitimizing the movement and removing potential social-psychological barriers to participation.

In our analysis of the growth of citizens' movements in Japan, we have emphasized the role of resource mobilization. We have done so to redress the balance in a literature that has emphasized both the nature and severity of the pollution problem itself and the deep grievances but enlightened political consciousness of individual citizens as sufficient to explain such a major phenomenon. Without negating the important role that individual grievances and discontent play in motivating protest, we are suggesting in effect that the realities of social movements in general, and of Japanese citizens' movements in particular, can best be understood and studied as a process by which a very real, but unformed, discontent is intensified by a particular pattern of prior socioeconomic development and is channeled and mobilized by ideological and organizational resources made available by that development. In sum, social protest movements are best understood by a sensitivity to both "shared grievances, interests, and aspirations" and to the conditions that make it possible to act on them collectively.[58]

THE IMPACT OF CITIZENS' MOVEMENTS ON LOCAL POLITICS

Social movements not only arise from a process of social change, they also seek and create change. Citizens' movements in Japan have been acclaimed by many observers as a major new force in Japanese politics that has helped transform the political process and political culture at the local level. The studies of McKean and Lewis are especially relevant to an evaluation of the impact of citizens' movements on local politics because one of their central aims is to analyze the consequences of movement mobilization for the individuals and local areas affected by it.

Richard H. Hall has suggested that organizations can be agents of change in three distinct ways: (1) by changing the organization itself; (2) by the changes the organization brings about in their individual members; and (3) by the changes it brings about in the larger society in which it operates.[59] We will use these distinctions as a convenient organizing framework for briefly evaluating and speculating on the consequences of citizens' movements for local society and politics in Japan.

Organizational Change

The studies that follow indicate that there is validity to the idea that CMs represent a new form of political organization in Japan in that their basis of recruitment seems less exclusive, their political stance more independent, and their internal decision-making processes more informal and less hierarchical than most established political organizations. For most of the postwar period, political support organizations and interest groups have recruited and mobilized their membership from relatively narrow strata of the population. And each local organization was closely linked to other similar organizations at higher levels in a series of patron-client ties. It was this characteristic—membership in community, religious, and occupational organizations tied into a vertical hierarchy of self-contained, opposing federations reaching up

---

[58] Fireman and Gamson, "Utilitarian Logic," p. 2.

[59] Richard H. Hall, *Organizations: Structure and Process* (Englewood Cliffs, N.J.: Prentice-Hall, 1972), pp. 328-342.

to the center—that formed one basis for the characterization of Japan as a "vertical society."[60]

Instead, as we have seen, citizens' movements have mobilized and recruited an occupationally and politically heterogeneous membership —farmers and professors, fishermen and white-collar workers, workers and housewives, progressive supporters and conservative partisans— that cuts across the main lines of socio-economic and political cleavage in postwar Japan. Whereas established political and interest group associations have tended to have a clearly differentiated leadership hierarchy in turn linked to higher leadership levels in a larger hierarchy with influence and power closely associated with organizational status, citizens' movements have tended to emphasize their independence from higher authorities and from partisanship, their lack of formal organizational structure, and their egalitarian decision-making processes.

These characteristics of citizens' movements, however, have often been thought to stem from the deeply held and shared beliefs of the participants in grass-roots democracy. No doubt this is true of some individuals. But Lewis suggests a somewhat different cause—that the open membership recruitment characteristics of CMs and their decision-making style are linked. The vaunted egalitarian consensual decision-making style and partisan independence of CMs and their frequent tendency to avoid establishing a formal leadership structure may well be a functional adaptation of the movement organization to its heterogeneous membership. Given the heterogeneity of the membership of CMs and their desire to mobilize as large a membership as possible in the context of the diversity of Japanese communities, decision-making processes and leadership roles that avoid dominance by any particular group or even by a majority over a minority and the avoidance of the appearance of linkages to any partisan organizations at higher levels may well be an organizational imperative. With such a diverse membership, any conflict over status, authority of leaders, or partisan issues would quickly split the movement along socio-economic or political lines. The appearance of openness, egalitarian decision making, political independence, and lack of formal leadership roles are not only moral values, therefore, they are also good organizational maintenance and mobilization politics.

The reader will note that in discussing the intraorganizational characteristics of CMs, we have been careful to use the word "appearance": organizations may be able to function without a formal leadership

---

[60] Chie Nakane, *Japanese Society* (Berkeley: University of California Press, 1970), passim. See also Scott C. Flanagan, "The Japanese Party System in Transition," *Comparative Politics* 3 (1971): 233.

structure, but few can function without informal leaders; organizations may avoid formal hierarchical roles, but they can rarely avoid an unequal distribution of influence on organizational decisions. To suggest that citizens' movements have somehow been able to insulate themselves completely from the strong status orientation in Japanese culture and from the typical social processes of all other organizations in Japanese society in which their members participate would be quixotic. Further, to neglect the fact that many conventional community associations are also relatively heterogeneous and openly consensual is to overdramatize the novelty of citizens' movements' organizational processes.[61] It is probably not without significance in this context that McKean reports that leaders of established community organizations occupy a disproportionate share of the identifiable leaders in citizens' movements. Perhaps the key, but unanswered, question becomes whether the *relatively* more heterogeneous, open, and nonhierarchical environment of citizens' movements is really developing a different mode of interaction between leaders and followers in Japanese communities and, if so, whether this experience is also helping to transform the innerorganizational dynamics and roles of traditional local associations.

Similar questions may be asked about the continued partisan affiliations of local community organizations that join citizens' movements. We have already noted the significant phenomena of neighborhood and housewives' associations formerly allied with the conservative power structure in local communities joining in antipollution protest. Is the apparent weakening of the links between these associations and their conservative politician and official patrons in many locales permanent? Or is the divergence of these organizations from their traditional roles temporary and issue-specific? The evidence is mixed, and it undoubtedly varies from area to area. McKean's findings that established community leaders who participate in CMs may continue their support for the national LDP, thus compartmentalizing their roles, would indicate that the influence of inclusion in citizens' movements may not permanently wean some neighborhood leaders and residents from their former political ties at all levels. Lewis's study of Mishima, on the other hand, gives a clear example of how a citizens' movement can bring about the long-lasting realignment of community associations and their leaders into the camp of opponents of the mainstream conservatives. Did the role of the mayor and maverick conservatives in Mishima in supporting the citizens' movement and the antipollution cause make

---

[61] However, see Nakamura, "Jūmin undō," p. 25, for a vivid illustration of neighborhood association hierarchy and CM openness coming into conflict.

it possible for community organizations to break their ties to mainstream conservatives without fear of jeopardizing—and perhaps even increasing—their leverage with city hall? Is a similar process occurring in large urban areas, enabling ruling progressive executives to institutionalize the diversion of community organizations to the opposition camp? Perhaps temporary diversion into the "opposition" camp and compartmentalization of protest and traditional roles is only necessary when mainstream conservatives control the trough at which community organizations feed and when the association is caught between its desire to act on the pollution issue and its desire to maintain connection to governmental benefits. The answers to these questions await the systematic compilation of evidence from numerous case studies in many different locales.

Changing Individuals

It is on this dimension of change that most of the literature has touted the impact of citizens' movements, particularly their alleged transforming of Japanese political culture through the resocialization of participants to more politically efficacious beliefs and participant behavior and through the conversion of formerly uninvolved or conservative citizens into progressive party supporters. McKean's study is especially pertinent to this claim because it is the first systematic survey to directly test these assertions. Her findings generally confirm the fact that CMs are important socialization agents for individual participants. As she notes, activity in citizens' movements often seems to bring about not only a greater awareness of conventional politics but frequently a disillusionment with it as well, and, may significantly alter attitudes toward and acceptance of open conflict in Japanese culture. She further finds that such participation can lead to a change in party support and voting preference toward the Left, although this change need not be accompanied by acceptance of doctrinaire ideology.

Perhaps as important as demonstrating that movement experience has an important socialization impact, her data also allows us to establish the conditions under which resocialization is more or less likely to take place. As she notes, movement participation is more of a "reinforcement" experience for the many CM activists who were already inclined to the Left; similarly, actual conversion from conservative to leftist support takes place primarily among a minority of participants —especially among conservatives who were ordinary members and not leaders in the conservative community associations or the movement. Further, conversion from conservative to leftist partisan support takes place more often among those in rural areas, among those with first-hand experience with pollution, and among those with prior protest experience in other contexts. These conditions warn us against un-critically accepting the portrayal of citizens' movements as primarily taking apolitical citizens and automatically converting them into opposition partisans. In their weakening of many participants' identifications with local conservatives and in their contribution to the creation of a larger "floating vote" in Japan's urban areas, however, citizens' movements undoubtedly have helped create a more volatile local electorate that has swept progressive executives into office in many cities.[62]

Changing the Political Process

Whatever the long-run implications of the changes citizens' movements have wrought in local level organizational forms and in the political culture, there is no question that they have been a major stimuli to change in the political process at the local level. A significant but often overlooked impact of CMs on local community power is their potential for bringing about political realignments and divisions within local political party branches and labor unions. Lewis's Mishima study is a vivid demonstration of this. Although a conflict between two conservative factions existed prior to the Mishima CM, the movement exacerbated the split and allowed the maverick faction led by the mayor to widen its support base and weaken the "mainstream" faction that had opposed the anti*konbinato* movement. Further, as Lewis points out, it even led to the maverick conservatives throwing their support to a socialist candidate for the Prefectural Assembly at election time. Lewis's conclusion that the significance of CMs may lie in their impact on political elites, rather than on the masses, and in the construction of new coalitions and majorities among these elites, deserves under-lining.

Citizens' movements have also exacerbated latent conflicts and divisions in other local organizations with political roles, particularly labor unions. The pollution issue and the mobilization of citizens into movements to combat pollution often poses a severe dilemma for labor unions. On the one hand, as "progressive" organizations with members who are also citizens in the community threatened by pollution, labor unions should be inclined to sympathize and play an active role in CMs. Since, however, the pollution issue and CMs often threaten the

[62] Gary D. Allinson, "Japan's Independent Voters: Dilemma or Opportunity?" *The Japan Interpreter* 11 (1976): 36-55, discusses both the rise of a new type of independent voter in Japan and the increase in the floating vote.

companies to which the local unions are closely connected through their enterprise-based organization and upon which the welfare of employees and families is dependent, local unions often find themselves under conflicting pressure. These pressures can lead to a split within the union, or even to a stance opposed to CMs.[63] On the other hand, because the national federations of labor unions have no vested interest in the welfare of local companies and are tied to opposition parties that support antipollution activities, they often take strong stands in favor of pollution control and CMs. Thus, CMs may well be helping to intensify the local-center divisions and problems long characteristic of the Japanese labor movement. In some areas, however, labor unions have been active in support of, or in alliance with, citizens' movements, for example in southern Nagoya and in the movement to clean up the Yodo River. As has been pointed out:

> How a given labor union will confront the problem of pollution will depend on various factors such as the history of labor-management relations at a given enterprise or factory, the nature of the enterprise itself, the ideology of the union leaders, the cultural and political characteristics of the local community, and the kind and seriousness of the pollution.[64]

Where citizens' movements are directed against an established industry, especially in "company towns," unions may be more likely to rise to the defense of their company and their own synonymous interests, as was the case in Minamata. When the target of the movement is to prevent the future location of an industry in the area or when the pollution problem is especially severe, local unions may be more likely to identify with the threat to their general community and support the movement. It should be noted that in the case of prevention movements, the enterprise-based Japanese union has much less of a vested interest in attracting new industry to the locale than their industrial or craft-based American counterparts who stand to gain more union members by the addition of new industry to their area. Conversely, where local unions are sympathetic to citizens' movements, the controversy over pollution stirred up by the movements has often provided both labor and managmeent with an issue to use in their own disputes: cases exist of management firing both union leaders and members too active in antipollution causes and of unions using a pollution issue publicized by movements to embarrass management.[65]

[63] Kazutoshi Koshiro, "Trade Unions and Industrial Pollution in Japan," *Japan Labor Bulletin* 12, no. 8 (August 1973): 7-8.
[64] Ibid., p. 8.   [65] Ibid., pp. 6-7.

The key question concerning the impact of citizens' movements, of course, is the differences they have made in the process and outputs of local and national governments. Perhaps the most important and obvious consequences of the rise of citizens' movements has been their contribution to the election of local progressive executives in Japan's major urban areas. Despite the sensitivity of most citizens' movements to manipulation or cooptation by the established Left, progressive candidates for local executive and citizens' movements are often natural allies. Participants in citizens' movements, both those with progressive sympathies to begin with and those whose experience in pollution politics has made them newly dissatisfied with the conservatives, have been eager to work and vote for a progressive candidate willing to embrace the environmental cause.

More importantly, citizens' movements have given progressive candidates in local executive elections a popular issue with which to attract the support of the many more voters who are not direct participants in movements. For years, progressive candidates have had little to offer their constituents in comparison to their conservative opponents who could point to the concrete benefits their city could anticipate by having a conservative with connections to the central government. In one stroke, the citizens' movement phenomena gave progressives the appealing themes of cleaning up the environment and responsiveness to citizen demands, thus changing the conservatives' major appeal into a handicap. "Blue Skies" for Tokyo could now be contrasted with the negative consequences of having a "direct pipeline" to the central government for development and the hazards that come in its wake. Thus, citizens' movements have contributed to revision of the local political agenda and, by raising the salience of environmental conflicts and redefining the meaning of past conflicts between conservatives and progressives, have helped to reallocate power in Japan's urban governments.[66]

New electoral themes and success in acquiring local power have also meant new priorities in local governmental outputs, generally in the seemingly positive direction of increased emphasis on much needed social services and on decreasing the gap between local administration and citizens' needs. Once elected, progressive executives have had to place priority upon antipollution and human service programs and also

---

[66] E. E. Schattschneider, *The Semi-Sovereign People* (New York: Holt, Rinehart and Winston, 1960), contains the most forceful argument that the essence of politics and power revolves around the skillful choice of issues to create new lines of cleavage and conflict in a society: "He who determines what politics is about runs the country, because the definition of the alternatives is the choice of conflicts, and the choice of conflicts allocates power" (p. 68).

attempt to institutionalize citizen input channels into local government. The explosion of "citizen consultation" offices in progressive local governments (and later in conservative administrations, as well) is one result.

The alliance of progressive local executives with citizens' movements also may have less positive results for efficient and democratic government at the local level. Local progressive executives who have publicly committed themselves strongly to letting citizen input determine policy have often found their decision-making process immobilized as they tried to satisfy contradictory demands. Tokyo's Governor Minobe, for example, having bound himself to a policy of "not constructing a bridge if even one citizen opposed it," often found his ability to carry out other programs for the public good severely slowed or even stymied by the opposition of small numbers of local residents demanding that he live up to his word. Whether it be garbage disposal plants, housing projects, or other needed social projects, the administration's ability to function efficiently has been hampered by the plethora of citizens' demands and the new ideology that CMs have created of listening to the voice of every citizen.[67] Other progressive executives who have taken a more flexible stance toward citizens' movements, such as Kyoto's Governor Ninagawa, have had better luck in reconciling local citizens' demands and oppositions with needed public projects.[68]

Even in Kyoto, however, as in all "progressive" administrations, bureaucrats have experienced the same conflicts between the progressive ideologies of their chief executives that emphasize responding to citizens' demands and the need for making choices in allocation based upon broader priorities and administrative planning. An interview by one of the authors[69] with a Kyoto bureaucrat illustrates these role conflicts that citizens' movements have helped to create. As "the consciousness of rights represented by citizens' movements has become extremely strong recently," said this official, "it is also a fact that there are appearing aspects of its having gone too far." Although it is not a question of suppressing their voices, he indicated, it does mean a dialogue (*taiwa*) with local residents in which the question becomes

[67] Kaminogo Toshiaki, "Kakushin jichitai no eikō to hisan," *Bungei Shunjū* 53 (1975): 101-106; an English translation of this article under the title "The Glory and Misery of Local Autonomies Under Progressive Control" appeared in *The Japan Echo* 2 (1975): 17-31.

[68] See Chapter 11.

[69] Krauss interviewed the head of the General Affairs Department of the Kyoto Prefectural Government on 22 April 1975.

deciding *which* of their demands will be implemented. He went on to say that it will be necessary for the bureaucracy to adopt a posture that, while keeping local residents primary (in allocation decisions), will not permit (resident) "egoism." In short, bureaucrats in urban areas under progressive rule must now cope with the explosion of demands created by citizens' movements to which their regime is pledged to respond but still carry out their responsibilities to the general welfare within the budgetary and procedural restraints faced by all administrative officials, a most difficult task. Whether these role conflicts result in a functional tempering of the tradition of bureaucratic dominance of governmental allocations with an attention to needs as perceived from the grassroots, or merely in the semiparalysis of decision making by an overloading of the system with numbers and types of demands with which it was not designed to cope, remains to be seen.

One potential negative consequence of "the new era" of citizen input into local administration has frequently been overlooked. Although citizens' movements have provided progressive local executives with the opportunity to form an alliance directly with "the people," bypassing the conservative community powerbrokers and business community that had often dominated local politics in the past, it has also allowed the political process to bypass local assemblies, which in Japan have always played the role of intermediary between local constituents and the executive's administrative bureaucracy. Although local assemblies continue to play this role and citizens' groups often continue to utilize all channels of influence available to them, the strengthening of direct links from local residents to local progressive executives in urban areas does involve the potential danger of further weakening the role of the local legislature in the political process. In short, "grassroots democracy" may well strengthen administrative power over legislative power and thus weaken representative democratic processes.[70]

Another more positive impact of CMs at both the local and national levels has been their influence in forcing both conservative and opposition parties to direct their attention and programs toward public, issue-specific, nonideological concerns. Perceiving their local power bases threatened by the new movements, conservatives must now pay greater attention to issues of the collective good rather than merely trying to satisfy special interests. Progressives have had to eschew their ideological crusades and deal with specific, pragmatic solutions to concrete problems such as pollution. For the first time in postwar Japan, both

[70] Murumatsu Michio, "Gyōsei katei to seiji sanka," in Nippon Seiji Gakkai, *Nenpō Seijigaku* (Tōkyō: Iwanami Shoten, 1974), pp. 53-59.

camps must now do battle in the arena of public interest issues in which performance is the standard by which they will be measured and by which they will gain or maintain support.[71] It is important to note that in these battles, progressives are not necessarily the inevitable winner: where conservatives at the local or national level perceive the changing patterns of politics and attempt to respond to citizens' movements and their constituents' new concerns, they can be successful in maintaining their power. Mishima is an excellent example of this. Further, progressive local administrations will also be judged by the same yardstick as were conservative incumbents—in terms of their performance. Where they do not measure up to expectations, citizens' movements can as easily direct their efforts against progressives as they can against conservatives. As McKean indicates, there is evidence that this is already occurring in some areas.

Our brief review of some of the impacts of citizens' movements on local politics has confirmed that they have served to resocialize numerous individuals to new orientations toward politics and, as a result, have partially contributed to the election of progressive local executives. These are changes in local political culture upon which the prior literature on CMs has concentrated. But we have also emphasized the impacts of citizens' movements on the structure and process of local politics: they have helped to alter the political ties and style of local community organizations and leaders, to create new political conflicts and alignments, and to redefine the priorities and strategies of local administrations and parties. And we have tried to indicate that these changes may have complex and sometimes ambiguous consequences for Japanese politics and democracy, for while they serve a number of potentially positive functions for democratic politics at the local level, they are not likely to automatically usher in a grass-roots democratic or progressive millennium.

THE FUTURE OF CITIZENS' MOVEMENTS

Organizational theorists since Michels have generally agreed on the inevitable fate of movement organizations in social protest: they either develop a permanent "bureaucracy" and institutionalized structure to maintain their organizations, or they soon decline and vanish. But the institutionalization of the movement would involve a transformation of its goals from protest to organizational maintenance. And the development of a permanent bureaucratic structure would create a more prag-

---

[71] Ibid., pp. 46-53. See also Chapter 7.

matic leadership with vested interests and a desire to accommodate the movement to the existing framework and values of the society: an "iron law of oligarchy" would operate to transform the movement in the direction of greater conservatism.[72]

Recently, however, Zald and Ash[73] have argued that oligarchy and its consequences are not an "iron law" but rather just one possibility among a number of alternative futures for a social movement. Whether movement organizations vanish or survive, change into more conventional organizations or maintain their original goals, depends upon a complex interaction of (1) the conditions and events in the larger society that maintain or decrease the movement's salience and support with (2) the type of movement organization itself. When the support and salience of the values of the movement continue and where the movement organization is "exclusive" (selective in its recruitment to create a homogeneous membership), is consciously more oriented toward changing its individual members than its environment, is not dependent on other organizations, and has numerous, broad social goals, the movement is likely to survive with its original goals or even become more militant: that is, the "iron law of oligarchy" is not a reliable predictor of the future of the movement.

However, the achievement of success or changing events may bring about a decline in the salience of the movement's values and its support. Under these conditions, the type of movement just described may survive, but a movement organization that is "inclusive" (open in recruitment and with a heterogeneous membership), is oriented more toward changing its environment than its members, is dependent on other organizations, and is relatively specific in its goals has a high probability of either disappearing or transforming itself into a bureaucratic and conventional organization with more conservative goals.

Applying this schema to citizens' movements in Japan, we should expect a variety of movement fates. In general, however, the latter conditions and consequent future seem more generally applicable, as citizens' movements and support for their environmental goals has waned since the movement reached its peak of local and national successes in the early 1970s. With the "oil shocks" of 1973, followed by a series of national political scandals involving top government officials and then a number of political crises over the redistribution of power within the ruling LDP and between the LDP and the opposition parties in the following years, there was a noticeable shift in media and public

---

[72] Zald and Ash, "Social Movement Organizations," pp. 327-328.

[73] Ibid. The subsequent discussion is based on this article's innovative hypotheses.

attention from the battle against pollution to the problems of economic and political stability,[74] and from the local to the national level. Both the salience and the level of environmental protest waned.[75]

These changes in the supporting environment had particularly great consequences for citizens' movements because of the nature of their organizations. Many CMs were oriented primarily toward a few specific goals related to environmental protection, were geared toward changing their local physical and political environments and not primarily toward molding their very heterogeneous (inclusive) membership, and were often dependent on their infrastructure of component organizations. With these characteristics, the success of local movements in attaining their aims and of the nationwide movement in achieving some of them, combined with the general decline in the salience of the ecological problem, deprived them of their reasons for existence and much of the motivation for participation of their members and constituent groups.

As Zald and Ash predict, under these conditions many such movements will either disband or begin to find new goals and in the process transform themselves into different types of organizations. Examples of both of these tendencies have already appeared in citizens' movements in Japan. Numerous citizens' movements of the 1960s and 1970s have arisen and then have quickly disappeared with the resolution of the particular local pollution problem with which they were concerned. Others have managed to maintain their organizational viability, or even grow larger, developing a permanent formal structure, but thence channeling their energies into institutionalized political activities rather than protest. Mishima is one example. As Lewis describes, having maintained a permanent coalition structure once it succeeded in its protest aims, the movement became primarily oriented toward electing "progressive" candidates. In other cases, CMs have grown to huge proportions enlisting many thousands of members and developing the coordinating apparatus such large organizations require and have then attempted to elect their own leaders or other sympathetic candidates to office.[76] In effect these citizens' movements have survived as organizations by transforming themselves into quasi-political parties and into electoral support machines, much as the nineteenth-century American progressive movement in parts of the Midwest (for example, Minne-

[74] Yasuhara Shigeru, "Jūmin undō ni okeru ri-da-sō no seikaku," *Chiiki Kaihatsu*, no. 154 (July 1977), p. 33.

[75] On the same problem in the United States, see Anthony Downs, "Up and Down with Ecology—The Issue Attention Cycle," *Public Interest* 28 (1972): 38-50.

[76] "Citizens' Movements," *Japan Quarterly* 20 (1973): 367-372.

sota) became less a social movement than a local political party, eventually being absorbed into the Democratic Party.[77] In other cases, citizens' movements have become more "administration oriented," participating in municipal programs and community development projects.[78]

But if Zald and Ash's hypotheses are correct, we can also expect that some citizens' movements in Japan, particularly those based primarily on a homogeneous group of individual intellectuals and middle-class professionals with strong progressive goals for broad social change and who explicitly conceived of CMs as potential resocialization agents— perhaps the "ombudsmen" type—may also survive the decline of the salience of the pollution issue but continue their protest goals and activities. It is also possible that as less devoted members dwindle and the established organizations that formed their base turn to other activities again leaving only a core of these kind of activists, other types of citizens' movements may actually *become* such militant organizations.[79]

Despite the current becalming of the movement against pollution, and whatever the fate of specific citizens' movements organizations engaged in the environmental cause, the citizens' movement phenomena may well rise again in another incarnation. If our analysis of the resource mobilization aspects of citizens' movements based on the evidence in the following studies is valid, a pool of mobilizable individuals and groups and their resources remain available for future mobilization at the local level. Should a new salient issue with grass-roots impact arise or be created by local, professional, or political elites, another such movement could develop. Thus, the civil rights movement in the United States demonstrated the availability of, and helped to create, a strata of grass-roots activists and organizational resources that later contributed to the growth of the antiwar and ecology protest movements. And, in Japan, if the *shimin undō* ideal that grew out of the 1960 treaty crisis movement could be used so effectively as a resource in the movement against pollution, it also remains available for application to other causes in other times.

[77] On the inherent limitations of CMs in replacing political parties at the local, and especially the national levels, see Tsurutani, *Political Change in Japan*, pp. 207-211.

[78] "Citizens' Movements," p. 371. See also the collection of articles on the theme of "Machi-Zukuri," in *Chiiki Kaihatsu*, no. 138 (March 1976).

[79] One of the crucial resources determining the effectiveness and fate of protest organizations is money; yet, virtually all studies of citizens' movements in Japan fail to discuss the question of the financial resources of movements. We very much need studies of the sources, amounts, and use of money by citizens' movements in their development as protest organizations.

CHAPTER 7

POLITICAL SOCIALIZATION THROUGH
CITIZENS' MOVEMENTS

Margaret A. McKean

THE emergence of citizens' movements (CMs) in Japan has led to
much speculation about their political significance, and claims have
ranged from the modest to the fantastic.[1] Some have argued that citizens' movements are a manifestation of a changing political culture in
Japan, incorporating new political attitudes and beliefs, a new popular
philosophy of citizenship, and the beginning of *kusa no ne* (grass-roots)
democracy.[2] Some also say that citizens' movements are achieving
more responsive and responsible local governments as well as greater
local autonomy.[3] Others have noted the parallel development of citizens' movements and progressive local governments, and they have
argued that these movements serve as a vehicle for the expansion of
new combinations of progressive forces at the local level[4] that in the

[1] One encounters two terms in Japanese: *jūmin undō*, or residents' movements,
which refers to locally organized protests by the residents of a particular region,
and *shimin undō*, which refers to those movements whose members are concerned
with citizenship and political rights. Having found that participants in most residents' movements are reasonably knowledgeable about politics and familiar with
democratic rhetoric, I have opted to use "citizens' movements" or CMs as an all-
purpose term.

[2] See Ishida Takeshi, "Emerging or Eclipsing Citizenship? A Study of Changes
in Political Attitudes in Postwar Japan," *Developing Economies* 6 (1968): 421-422;
Yasumasa Kuroda, "Protest Movements in Japan: A New Politics," *Asian Survey*
12 (1972): 949; Matsushita Keiichi, "Politics of Citizen Participation," *Japan Interpreter* 9 (1975): 462-465; and Taketsugu Tsurutani, "A New Era of Japanese Politics: Tokyo's Gubernatorial Election," *Asian Survey* 12 (1972): 442-443.

[3] For particularly well-known exponents of this theme, see Matsubara Haruo,
Kōgai to chiiki shakai: Seikatsu to jūmin undō no shakaigaku (Tōkyō: Nihon
Keizai Shinbunsha, 1971), passim, and Miyamoto Ken'ichi, *Kōgai to jūmin undō*
(Tōkyō: Jichitai Kenkyūsha, 1970).

[4] See "Citizens' Movements," *Japan Quarterly* 20 (1973): 368-373; Matsushita,
"Politics of Citizen Participation," p. 463; and Tsurutani, "A New Era," passim.
One of the most suggestive results of a CM has been the conservative-progressive
coalition government in Mishima. See Jack G. Lewis, "*Hokaku Rengō*: The Politics of Conservative-Progressive Cooperation in a Japanese City" (unpublished
dissertation, Stanford University, 1975).

future may provide the foundation for a coalition to replace Liberal Democratic Party (LDP) leadership at the national level.[5] More extreme conclusions include the assertion that citizens' movements are supplanting political parties altogether, or that they signify the "spontaneous" eruption of the democratic millennium for Japan.[6] Some hopeful leftist ideologues have also argued that these movements are preparing the masses to assume their appropriate roles as a revolutionary vanguard.[7]

But the bulk of the literature on citizens' movements at this early stage consists of semiautobiographical accounts by participants, of abstract theoretical discussions, or of individual case histories of well-known movements, particularly the much-publicized "Big Four" cases. Furthermore, little effort has yet been made either to ascertain whether the well-known examples are typical of the vast number of lesser-known movements or to discover what is actually happening to individual participants in citizens' movements.[8] Finally, most of this material is suspiciously enthusiastic about the potential significance of citizens' movements in terms of the authors' transparent philosophical preferences. One wonders if these writers are indulging in wishful thinking, instead of self-consciously compensating for any personal bias that might distort their observations: however much one might sympathize with some of the fundamental values of such writers, greater caution is necessary.

Thus, the literature on citizens' movements consists largely of sweeping generalizations based on spotty evidence and untested assertions. My research is an exploratory effort to evaluate empirically the recruitment and mobilization of individuals into citizens' movements and the impact of participation on their political attitudes. I examine a broad range of citizens' movements rather than a single example, in order to provide more reliable data to evaluate the significance of the phenomenon for Japanese politics and to test the assertions in the literature. I have attempted to assemble a representative variety of movements and to interview individual participants about their experiences.

My findings should also perform two broader functions in the larger

[5] Muramatsu Michio speculates on the conditions that would permit a reformist victory at the national level in "The Impact of Economic Growth Policies on Local Politics in Japan," *Asian Survey* 15 (1975): 815-816.

[6] See "Citizens' Movements," pp. 371-373.

[7] This tone is evident in discussions in popular magazines of movements that have been heavily aided by formal Socialist and Communist organizations or by the student movement.

[8] "Nihon Repooto," *Asahi Shinbun* (21 May 1973), p. 4, reports that there were probably 3,000 residents' movements in Japan at that time.

field of political science. First, looking at the socialization of CM participants can tell us a great deal about political socialization in general, a particularly compelling subject of study in Japan, where only thirty years ago the American Occupation surgically implanted democratic institutions into the Japanese body politic. Whether the system will reject or accommodate these institutions remains dependent at least in part on how successfully they are assimilated through the process of political resocialization of adults and political socialization of new generations. Although Japan provides a fascinating laboratory for the examination of political socialization, there are still very few such studies.[9]

Secondly, our investigation of the impact of participation on CM members is essentially a rather unusual one in the field of political behavior because we are looking at the *effect of behavior on attitudes.* Public opinion research is commonly a study of attitudes, and it is assumed or hoped by the researchers that attitudes are a reasonably reliable indicator of subsequent actual behavior, which is much more difficult to survey. Here, I will be examining attitudes and beliefs that those interviewed have themselves attributed to their participatory experiences in CMs.[10]

For the investigation of these several broad issue areas in Japanese studies as well as political science, we used three criteria to arrive at an operational definition of citizens' movements as grass-roots movements: they are (1) independently organized by their members and

[9] The pathbreaker in this area is Okamura Tadao, whose work on children has been continued and expanded by Joseph Massey. See Okamura Tadao, "The Child's Changing Image of the Prime Minister," *Developing Economies 6* (1968): 566-586; Joseph A. Massey, "The Missing Leader: Japanese Youths' View of Political Authority," *American Political Science Review* 69 (1975): 31-48; and Joseph A. Massey, *Youth and Politics in Japan* (Lexington, Mass.: Lexington Books, 1976). To date the only work dealing with adult socialization is Ellis Krauss's landmark study of student radicals, *Japanese Radicals Revisited: Student Protest in Postwar Japan* (Berkeley: University of California Press, 1974). See also, Akira Kubota and Robert E. Ward, "Family Influence and Political Socialization in Japan," *Comparative Political Studies* 3 (1970): 140-175.

[10] Of course there is abundant literature in social psychology on the effects of behavior on attitudes, the most well-known being studies of attitude change as a reaction to the cognitive dissonance induced by unaccustomed behavior. See Arthur Cohen, "Attitudinal Consequences of Induced Discrepancies Between Cognitions and Behavior," *Public Opinion Quarterly* 24 (1960): 297-318; Arthur R. Cohen, *Attitude Change and Social Influence* (New York: Basic Books, 1964), pp. 81-99; Leon Festinger, *A Theory of Cognitive Dissonance* (Evanston, Ill.: Row, Peterson, and Co., 1957), pp. 94-122; and Leon Festinger and James M. Carlsmith, "Cognitive Consequences of Forced Compliance," *Journal of Abnormal and Social Psychology* 58 (1959): 203-210.

not by external forces; (2) engaged in protest to obtain a redress of grievances against established authority; and (3) concerned about a local problem (such as pollution) that affects the livelihood or well-being of ordinary people. At the time I conducted field work in 1972, there existed only one comprehensive list of antipollution citizens' movements that included descriptive information about each group.[11] Assuming this list to be a representative sample of citizens' movements, I used a three-stage stratified sampling method, first to select particular movements that displayed the same range and variety in characteristics as did the sample as a whole, and then to select individual participants to be interviewed.[12]

As a result, in the fall of 1972 I interviewed a sample of sixty-four members from fourteen carefully selected citizens' movements (in both Greater Tokyo and more rural areas of Japan). Interviews were conducted in Japanese for two to three hours apiece, usually at respondents' homes, using a questionnaire prepared with the help of three Japanese political scientists. Replying largely to open-ended questions, respondents discussed their reasons for joining the movement, their political opinions and activities, the political activities of their group, their views on environmental problems, the response their group met from various political actors and institutions, their political beliefs, and their expectations for the future. To supplement the information that sample members themselves provided in interviews, additional material was obtained from discussions with the leadership and nonrespondent informants in each group, from their own collections of pamphlets and local newspaper clippings, and from the published sources concerning a few of the movements.

Because of the methods used, several kinds of sampling error have biased the final sample, although we have enough information about the direction of bias to compensate for these in examining the resulting data. Citizens' movements do not keep membership records, so that

---

11 "Zenkoku no shimin undō," *Shimin* 1 (1971): 1-82.

12 This method of cluster-stratified-judgment sampling is described in Russell L. Ackoff, *The Design of Social Research* (Chicago: University of Chicago Press, 1953), pp. 83-151. The representativeness of the *Shimin* list, stratification of the groups in that list into categories that differed along eighteen dimensions, as well as methods of contacting individual respondents through their organizations are discussed in Margaret A. McKean, "The Potentials for Grass-Roots Democracy in Postwar Japan: The Anti-Pollution Movement as a Case Study in Political Activism" (unpublished dissertation, University of California at Berkeley, 1974), pp. 211-265. Where individual respondents are quoted in subsequent sections of this essay, they are identified by their code designations (e.g., G4, I3, K2).

individual activists could not be selected through systematic random sampling. Rather, they had to be located through leaders of the movement, and, as persons known by name to the leaders, they inevitably constituted a more active sample of their movements than would have been desirable. Several group leaders themselves wanted to be included in the survey: this turned out to be a valuable source of unanticipated findings about the nature of the leadership itself. In addition to being top-heavy, the final sample also included a large proportion (58 percent) of supporters of the leftist parties and other progressive sympathizers, probably due to drawing most of the urban sample from the greater Tokyo area. According to both conservative and leftist informants, the majority of their respective movements were probably conservative in original party affiliation, so we may therefore conclude that the weighty presence of progressives in the sample constitutes sampling bias rather than an accurate portrayal of the political sympathies of CMs. Because the data we collected revealed a strong association between leftist partisanship and prior experience at political protest (*Tau-beta* = .412, p = .001), the sample appears to overrepresent veterans of protest as well as progressive party identifiers.[13]

These three types of bias—favoring highly active members of CMs, leftist partisans, and veterans of protest—inhibit our ability to generalize statistical findings to CMs as a whole, since we cannot be precise as to the extent of the bias. But we can certainly compensate for the direction of bias by paying special attention to the underrepresented groups: the CM participants below the leadership level, those who identified with the conservative party, and those who were relatively inexperienced at political protest. Because our concern here is with political socialization—the exposure of the formerly unpoliticized to the principles and practice of citizenship—these types of CM participants are of particular interest to us. In the ensuing pages, we will discuss the mobilization and recruitment of participants for CMs, the socialization of individuals, and changes in partisanship among CM members.

[13] The only way of obtaining a pure probability sample would have been to locate CM activists through a nationwide poll, to insert a set of closed-ended questions into the interview schedule, and to supplement these data with intensive face-to-face interviewing of the CM activists, a prohibitively expensive procedure beyond my resources. Where quantitative data is to be presented, I have used the nonparametric statistic *Tau-beta*, which is the most cautious of the *Tau* series and highly suitable for samples of less than one hundred. Although statistical inference should be used only for pure probability samples, we have also included p values to show levels of statistical significance, simply to assuage doubts that may be raised about the small size of the sample.

RECRUITMENT INTO CITIZENS' MOVEMENTS

Motivation of Activists

It is obviously important to understand what kind of people generally participate in CMs and what forces draw them into political activity. First of all, despite the fact that our sample was skewed in favor of leaders and activists, over half (58 percent) were participating in their first political protest by joining CMs. Only 17 percent of the sample could be classified as really experienced veterans of protest (with involvement in two or three previous protests of five years' duration). Thus CMs do not draw their supporters from the usual sources of protest in Japan—the leftist parties, radical labor unions and intellectuals, or the student movement.[14] If we could correct for sampling error, we would have undoubtedly found that CMs mobilize even larger numbers of people who are entirely new to the idea of protest—though not necessarily new to conservative "establishment" politics. Why have CMs appealed to so many people who have not previously felt it necessary to complain about government's activities? What were the motives and fears that jolted them into a pattern of political activity that was unfamiliar to them?[15]

Obviously, members of some of the most well-known *compensation-oriented movements* are recruited because pollution has taken on the proportions of a life and death issue for them. Asked why they took the fateful step of joining the lawsuit against Mitsui Mining and Smelting, *itai-itai* victims interviewed for this study each provided an identical explanation. Although the very idea of "going public" by turning their illness into a matter for litigation was anathema to all of them at the outset, they had exhausted every other device imaginable to obtain relief. In addition to the pain, the financial hardship, and the disruption of ordinary family life imposed on them by the disease itself, they and their families already suffered tremendously from social ostracism: (1) for being ill in the first place; (2) for accepting the idea that some external agent might in some way be responsible for their troubles; and (3) for drawing attention to the fact that agricultural products of the area might be contaminated and unsaleable. In this

[14] See Herbert Passin, "The Sources of Protest in Japan," *American Political Science Review* 61 (1962): 393-403.

[15] I have discussed the question of motivation in greater detail in "The Potentials for Grass-Roots Democracy," pp. 410-426, and in "Citizens' Movements in Urban and Rural Japan," in *Social Change and Community Politics in Urban Japan*, ed. James W. White and Frank Munger (Chapel Hill, N.C.: The Institute for Research in the Social Sciences, University of North Carolina at Chapel Hill, 1976), pp. 61-99.

situation, *itai-itai* victims decided that litigation could not make their lives any worse and that it was thus the only course left to take.[16] Once victims' movements view their problem as a question of survival, it is transformed into a political issue requiring public protest on their part.

Other CMs do not consist of victims at all but are aimed at *prevention*—usually opposing plans for the construction of highly polluting industries.[17] Some 60 percent of those sampled in this study reported that they never experienced pollution damage themselves and that their activism was based entirely on an interest in prevention. Another 24 percent were interested in prevention but also experienced some form of damage. Thus only 16 percent of the sample developed an interest in the issue solely on the basis of having suffered from pollution already and were concerned not about preventing future pollution but about dealing with an existing problem. Even a majority (59 percent) of the newcomers to protest were sufficiently moved to act without having any tragic firsthand experience with pollution, indicating that there is great potential for the development of prevention-oriented CMs. In fact, recent observers have pointed out that in contrast to the earlier skepticism regarding prevention-oriented CMs, the focus of attention for the bulk of CMs has shifted from compensation and relief to prevention.[18] This is an important development in view of the observation so frequently made during the early days of antipollution movements, by both Japanese and foreigners and by both movement participants and academic specialists alike, that the Japanese people simply lacked the civic consciousness that would be necessary for them to deal effectively with pollution.

Lest we give the impression that Japanese antipollution activists are self-sacrificing heroes, it is important to recognize that although many are concerned about preventing pollution that does not yet exist, the majority are quite pragmatically concerned with how the pollution issue affects their own lives. All of the respondents in our sample were initially interested in eradicating or preventing pollution that threatened them personally—their own health, property values, or life style —and 58 percent of the sample participated in CMs solely on the basis of their own material self-interest. But 42 percent of the sample (who

---

[16] For a discussion of the *itai-itai* victims' movement and lawsuit, see McKean, "The Potentials for Grass-Roots Democracy," pp. 104-116, 341-351.

[17] On the distinctions between compensation and prevention movements, see Bradford L. Simcock, "Environmental Pollution and Citizens' Movements: The Social Sources and Significance of Anti-Pollution Protest in Japan," *Area Development in Japan* 5 (1972): 13-22.

[18] See "Nihon Repooto," p. 4.

are labelled "altruistic") continued to be active in CMs even though they would not reap the material benefits of their efforts. One particularly interesting respondent became a full-time activist in Tokyo's sunshine rights movement after having met utter failure in her own case. Unable to obtain any substantial redress of her grievances, she was determined to use her own case history as an instructive example to prevent this from happening to others.

This problem of definition (self-interest vs. altruism) conceals a fact that is important to our interest in political socialization. The "altruists" were largely people who through participation developed a larger awareness of issues and a devotion to political activity based on an abstract issue-orientation rather than merely through an interest in their own personal well-being. In general, then, antipollution activists start out with a pragmatic but narrow concept of self-interest, not as heroes and martyrs devoted to high ideals. However, activism itself is a socializing experience that gives the altruists new commitments to abstract issues and principles.

We have established, then, that antipollution groups in Japan are indeed movements composed primarily of customarily quiescent citizens and not merely the regular, visible, active leftist opposition in new form. Antipollution activists, many of whom are entirely unfamiliar with political protest, are mobilized primarily out of personal fear based either on firsthand experience with pollution or on the ability to imagine the possibility of suffering such damage in the future.

Channels of Recruitment

Related to the question of motivation to join citizens' movements is the problem of how participants are channeled into their movements. In particular, do activists make a principled individual decision to become active, or are they gently but firmly guided into involvement by established organizations to which they belong, without having to make the intellectual effort of deciding on their own? This is an important issue at the heart of the rather regular insistence of environmental advocates in Japan that CMs may depend on established organizations only at their peril.[19] We must deal with this issue in an analysis of political socialization because an activist who engages in antipollution

[19] See Matsubara, *Kōgai to chiiki shakai*, pp. 179-191; Shōji Hikaru and Miyamoto Ken'ichi, *Osorubeki kōgai* (Tōkyō: Iwanami Shoten, 1964), pp. 194-196; Tsuru Shigeto, *Gendai shihon shugi to kōgai* (Tōkyō: Iwanami Shoten, 1968), pp. 271-286; and Ui Jun, *Kōgai no seijigaku: Minamata byō wo megutte* (Tōkyō: Sanseidō, 1968), pp. 198-210.

activity merely in the context of a membership in some other ongoing organization need not be self-conscious about his own behavior and need not undergo any change in belief or attitude to rationalize that behavior. This study indicates that established organizations can play a wide variety of roles vis à vis CMs, and that appearances can be quite deceiving. Movements that are widely acclaimed as diffuse, open, and entirely voluntaristic can turn out to be based on a framework of established organizations, as Jack Lewis has shown in his study of Mishima in this volume. But many movements built out of previously existing organizations nonetheless recruit members as individuals, without acquiring their support automatically.

Several factors appear to be involved in determining whether an individual participates in such a CM on the basis of a personal decision to be active. First of all, members of a movement composed of established organizations (political party branches, labor unions, neighborhood associations, merchants' associations, PTA, etc.) may think of the movement as a separate organization in its own right, with its own schedule of activities and its own structure, officers, and title. Participation in the more aggressive work of the CM (collecting money, circulating petitions during signature drives, attending study sessions, persuading others on behalf of the cause) is not automatic. Members of established organizations who do opt to participate in movement activities must decide to do so rather than to withdraw from them.

Precisely because of the work required of them as activists, participants may also *separate their roles* as members of component organizations and as energetic movement participants. They may conceive of their movement activities as protest, beyond the boundaries of those activities that are incidental to their membership in established organizations that comprise the CM. Regardless of whether they were channeled into the antipollution movement through prior memberships in other groups or not, all but three respondents in this study defined their activities as protest, and for the newcomers this required a major readjustment of their conception of their relationship with the political system.

This separation between role definitions is quite likely when many members of the established component organizations refrain from activity in the CM or when the established organizations disagree within or amongst themselves about the decision to form a movement. If the response of an established organization to the formation of a protest movement involves hesitation about joining or outright opposition to the protest, the members of that organization will probably have to engage in that debate personally and to decide individually whether to follow or to defy some or all of the organization's leadership. A few examples of the conflicting cross-pressures experienced by respondents in this study will illuminate how difficult and tormented the decision to become involved can be.

Although we have already referred to the community pressure exerted on *itai-itai* victims to prevent them from going to court, it is desirable to elucidate these techniques. Local influentials and officials, many neighborhood associations, and agricultural cooperatives were anxious to prevent the dispute from escalating into a public issue. They played on themes that could evoke guilt and embarrassment by arguing that the victims were just hypochondriacs (when their only visible symptom was intense pain) or irresponsibly accident-prone (when they began to experience frequent bone fractures)—that is, a detriment and a burden to their families. Respondents in this study reported that persons who were probably informers for Mitsui entered the victims' groups to foment disagreement, to demoralize the victims, and to break their will to persevere in court. (I3, I4)

Similarly, during the formation of a movement to prevent the construction of a chemical factory in Oiso (in Kanagawa prefecture), there was considerable disagreement expressed at neighborhood association meetings over the factory construction issue. One woman who decided to oppose the factory found her friends and neighbors accusing her of being an outsider (she had only lived in Oiso for twelve years), without the right to be concerned about the community or the right to object to the factory (because her land wasn't part of the projected factory site). These "friends" called her a Communist as well, and they threatened her with *mura hachibu* (ostracism). Although her husband did not prevent her activism, she also found his argument that opposition was hopeless quite demoralizing (G3). When other members of the women's division of her neighborhood association tried to pressure her into abandoning her opposition, she left the association entirely, along with many others in the antifactory movement. Another activist reported that the neighborhood and the PTA had been "effective and frightening" channels of pressure used against potential activists (G4).

Respondents in the Citizens' Council formed to prevent construction of an Osaka Cement Plant in Kazanashi, a fishing community within the boundaries of the city of Usuki (Oita prefecture), provided some of the strongest evidence about the difficulty of the individual decision to participate in a CM. Pressure to prevent people from joining came from the merchants' association, the chairmen of all of the neighborhood associations, the fire department (because of the personal predilections of the fire chief), and the agricultural and fishing cooperatives. One respondent, who first approached (unsuccessfully) the head of the women's division of her own neighborhood association, undertook the task of organizing opposition to the cement plant independently, eventually recruiting half of the women in her own *buraku* (hamlet) to form a separate women's group. This is her account:

"We created a new *fujinkai* (women's group), and conducted a signature drive to prove to the mayor that we did not all agree with his plan as he said. Maybe most of the *buraku* agreed with the factory plan at first, because the mayor always seemed to know what we were planning, even though our meetings were secret. So some among us must have been spies—that was the most painful period. . . . Someone was making secret tapes of the conversations at our opposition meetings and later we learned those people were on the pro-factory side. . . . The worst pressure we ever suffered from was the fact that the only strong opposition to Osaka Cement at first was just our little group. Our ward chief lied to us while telling us to wait for him to call a general meeting. He told us he was ill and wanted to postpone the meeting, but in fact he was proceeding with negotiations behind our back and was going to spring a completed agreement on us when he did call a general meeting. . . . I was very disappointed in the local teachers because they didn't help us. I went to Shibushi, and the teachers there were being very cooperative in that movement. But here, due to pressure from their superiors in the civil service, and from school principals, they don't help." (K2)

Another woman (K6) who had lived in Usuki for over twenty years was accused of being an "outsider" who had no business organizing any sort of political movement at all in the community, a very common argument used to make potential activists feel uncomfortable in their roles.

Another activist described the problem of ostracism that developed rapidly in the fishing hamlet of Kazanashi, located close to the proposed plant site. "All other kinds of pressure were minor compared to the effects of *murahachibu* and not having the services of our fishing cooperative. . . . All our money for repairing our boats, health insurance, bank loans, etc. comes from the fishing cooperative, and they said we couldn't borrow money any more" (K4). Another organizer of the Citizens' Council described the sort of atmosphere she faced when she began voicing her opposition to the factory:

238

"I have many friends and relatives on the pro-factory side, and they kept telling me to study so that I would agree with them. But it didn't matter to me. My son-in-law told me he couldn't be promoted at the school where he teaches, and my husband had the same situation too. . . . People called us red. My husband was . . . always on the management side in labor disputes . . . but he was against Osaka Cement. But all my friends and neighbors were mistaken, judging him by his career in labor problems, and thought he'd be in favor of the factory. They always tried to use that against me and tell me it was wrong for me to disagree with my husband. I told them we didn't disagree but that my opinions were my opinions in any case. . . . My friends tried to pressure me about cooperating more with my husband, and I told them that my husband doesn't object to my activities against Osaka Cement because he is also against the factory, and that my husband and I do not influence each other on politics. They were shocked and told me I was unruly, headstrong, disobedient, etc. . . . We got lots of phone calls from cranks telling me I was making trouble for my husband. . . . My son-in-law's brother was the winner of the city council election in August 1971 [the pro-factory candidate who narrowly defeated the Citizens' Council's own candidate], but nonetheless I stayed in the anti-factory movement." (K5)

One of the most notorious features about the antipollution movement in Usuki is that full-blown *mura hachibu* did develop in the hamlet of Kazanashi, and it has now persisted for several years:

"In Kazanashi there are 143 anti-factory and 33 pro-factory families. . . . We now ostracize each other entirely. We even have a different political structure (we have become different *buraku*), we don't take care of sanitation or garbage pick-up for the pro-factory families, and we're no longer in the same PTA or neighborhood association." (K2)

Relatives find themselves divided into different groups that no longer socialize with each other, the pro-factory families don't come outdoors or do their shopping when the rest of the town does, and people don't greet each other in the street.

Even where *mura hachibu* did not actually develop, it was a common threat used by the majority to silence an emerging antipollution minority in many other communities. The issue was far too controversial for people to join the antipollution movement accidentally, simply by following the dictates of some ongoing group to which they belonged. In almost every individual case in this study, pressure against participation—from one source or another—was sufficiently great to require activists not only to make a conscious decision to join the CM but also to continually reinforce that decision whenever they undertook special work for the movement.

A TYPOLOGY OF CITIZENS' MOVEMENTS: ORGANIZATIONAL STRUCTURE AND SOCIALIZATION

There is much debate in the literature on the relationship between CMs and ongoing organizations, but the bulk of this debate concerns tactical questions: whether dependence on established groups enhances or inhibits success, whether connections with other organizations can compromise the group or be valuably utilized, and thus whether such links are desirable at all. There is less discussion of what sorts of relationships between movements and other organizations actually exist and what significance this may have for questions other than the matter of success or failure. The following four categories provide a convenient way of summarizing more elusive characteristics of CMs and in turn seem to have some predictive utility. Naturally, all but the "Imitation CMs" meet our original definition of CMs (grass-roots origins, a protest orientation, and down-to-earth concerns); the criterion by which we differentiate them here is the nature of their relationship to preexisting organizations.

The Roving Ombudsman CMs

This first category represents one extreme of organizational independence, as Ombudsman CMs have no fixed geographical base and consist instead of free-floating individuals intensely concerned about pollution. However, they devote their efforts to the more typical residentially-based CMs, which they seek out. Citizens' movements as a whole are probably closer to issue-oriented voluntary associations as an ideal type than other Japanese social movements, but this characterization fits the Ombudsman CMs best of all. Our sample of three such groups (sixteen individuals) indicates that recruits to Ombudsman CMs have already developed a commitment to the pollution issue through earlier activities in hobby or study groups and that they also enter the movement with an intellectual belief in the importance of political participation, although they may not have previously put that belief into practice. Recent evidence indicates that Ombudsman CMs in the form of new national environmental coalitions are growing in number as they select new environmental issues as targets. This results in part from the frequently observed tendency for social movements to become institutionalized over time but more directly from the fact that as CM challenge projects that are part of the government's comprehensive national plans—particularly the construction of thermal and nuclear power plants and high-speed "bullet" railways (Shinkansen) all over Japan—CMs must operate at the national level.[20]

The Independent CMs

By far the vast majority of CMs (in our sample, eight groups or thirty-nine individuals) do have a geographical base and consist in part of coalitions of preexisting organizations utilized for recruitment, communication, and administration. But the movement itself is a new and independent structure, neither created nor controlled by other organizations. Its members do not have to be as strongly motivated as those in Ombudsman CMs, but they do have to make individual decisions about participating even if they do so within a component organization of the movement, as discussed earlier. Most of the general assertions about traits of CMs are intended to apply to this variety of CM but not to the others. To some extent, observers who exaggerate the significance of CMs as a new symbol of direct democracy confuse this kind of movement with the traits more often found among members of Ombudsman movements. Similarly, those who view CMs as a new label for an old phenomenon and who play down any significance they may have for political change tend to confuse this most prevalent type of movement with those based on neighborhood associations.

The Converted Neighborhood Association CMs

A third variety of CM—well-known but not really so common—is not merely based on preexisting organizations but is actually identical to them, in that a movement will coincide perfectly with an ongoing neighborhood association (our sample contains two such groups or seven individuals). The vast majority of neighborhood associations in Japan tend to be conservative, both in the strictly political preference of their leaders and also in their definitions of what issues constitute legitimate concerns and in the modes of action they consider appropriate. Their leaders ordinarily view their primary task as the cultiva-

[20] See "Citizens' Movements," pp. 368-373.

tion of harmonious links between the people below and the municipal government above. They are very unlikely to possess an adversary view of the relations between people and government, or to define their own position as a representative of local interests in a conflict.

Thus the common reaction among neighborhood leaders was to view pollution as a minor disruption and a necessary evil accompanying economic growth. To complain about pollution violated conventional political norms by rejecting the balanced and benevolent allocation by higher authority of development and pollution throughout Japan. For one particular area to refuse to go along with the master plan was unmitigated egoism, which most neighborhood association leaders regarded as their responsibility to eradicate. The bulk of the Japanese literature on CMs creates the regrettably erroneous impression that neighborhood associations inevitably react this way and cannot do otherwise. But in fact, when pollution threatens to be massive in its per capita impact on a particular area, even a conservative and conventional neighborhood leader can distinguish between the neighborhood's interests and the wishes of higher authority, adopt the role of defender of the neighborhood, and mobilize the local association around the threat, thus converting it into a CM.

The converted neighborhood CM conceives of its action as protest, thus implicitly defying many precepts usually binding on a neighborhood association. It may regroup and give itself a new name, important primarily as a symbolic gesture, that (1) awakens the community to the fact that the neighborhood has defined pollution as a threat, (2) plays upon the fears of local residents to evoke a more energetic response than a neighborhood association could normally extract from them, and (3) displays to the municipal government that the community has gone on the offensive. The group continues to carry out its daily business in the guise of a neighborhood association, but it conducts its antipollution protest in its new symbolic form as a CM.

The Imitation CMs

Finally we come to the controversial category of neighborhood associations that appear to be CMs because they are interested in the same sorts of issues (typically pollution) but do not meet our other definitional requirements (grass-roots origins and a protest orientation). Our own survey includes two interviews with leaders of one such group.[21] Frequently an Imitation CM will masquerade as a CM, hoping

[21] The statistical analyses presented here would be a more accurate reflection

that a bit of the CM reputation for strength, perseverance, and political sophistication will rub off on their own efforts.[22] The imitation CM does not form spontaneously but at the request of municipal authorities who may even subsidize the movement. The leaders do not conceive of their task as protest but as cooperation with these authorities, and members view their antipollution activity as one small part of the customary business of a neighborhood association that does not involve any effort beyond the normal call of duty. Members' primary orientation is toward their role in the neighborhood association, which is involved with many functions and problems other than pollution, and not as members of an ad hoc issue-oriented movement.

How can we use these categories to add to our understanding of CMs and in particular to address the issue of socialization? Unfortunately, we are hampered in our ability to reach firm conclusions by the realistic but uneven distribution of the sample among the four types. Statistical tests can determine whether predictions hold true within categories, but the low variance on some measures and the small sample size for the last two categories make it difficult to rely on tests involving comparisons between the categories. Nonetheless, additional evidence from open-ended interview material, informants other than survey respondents, and written sources on these and similar CMs, also support the following hypotheses.

First, there would appear to be a direct relationship between independence from established organizations and the scores that a CM might earn on a hypothetical "good citizen" index. That is, taking membership as a whole, the Ombudsman CM would probably possess the greatest and broadest knowledge of current affairs, politics, the law, environmental problems, and the greatest commitment to effective participation, along with the other traits usually considered important for democratic citizenship.[23] Imitation CMs would reveal the least. Our

---

of citizens' movements if these two cases were excluded from the data base, but often they appear as missing data anyway and thus do not affect our conclusions.

[22] There are cases when local authorities try to popularize a public works project—one that might actually arouse a good deal of citizen protest—by surrounding it with high-pressure advertising that describes the project as part of a CM. I encountered one such case in Ashio, where city leaders had erected banners over the main street saying: "Jūmin undō no chikara de ＿＿ tunnel [We can build the ＿＿ tunnel with the strength of the residents' movement]." In fact, of course, there was no "movement" at all.

[23] There is a long-standing consensus among political scientists as to what traits constitute good citizenship. See Bernard R. Berelson et al. *Voting* (Chicago: University of Chicago Press, 1954), especially pp. 305-323; Robert E. Lane, *Political*

questionnaire does not permit the construction of such a broad index, but we can examine surrogate measures that are available, as shown in Table 1. On the "isolation-sophistication index" (perhaps the closest we can come to creating a composite measure of citizenship), the Ombudsmen acquired very high scores, whereas the Independent CM activists provided the greatest number of "rural isolates," and none of the Converted CM members earned high scores on the index.[24] Other available evidence also indicates linear relationships in the predicted direction, as Ombudsmen CM activists are the most likely and Converted Neighborhood Associations are the least likely to display citizenly qualities. (Data for the Imitation CMs is spotty when extant and misleading in any case because our sample included no rank and file members of such groups.) Ombudsmen activists are the most likely to have broad goals, noble motives, high information and concern about pollution, and a clear preference for democratic political institutions. Having greater protest experience and a commitment to the environmental issue in the abstract, Ombudsmen are also most willing to protest pollution without having experienced damage personally. But members of Independent and Converted CMs are much more likely to require powerful tangible incentives to galvanize them into action.

A second use for these categories is that they appear to have some relationship to differences in political socialization within CMs, a hypothesis illustrated graphically in Figure 1. We initially delineated the categories in terms of the intimacy of a CMs' relationship to established organizations (represented by the vertical line). Based on knowledge of cases in our sample of how participants regard their activities in CMs, we superimposed a second dimension onto the typology (represented by the horizontal line)—participants' familiarity with the modes of action adopted by the group. Drawing upon theories of cognitive inconsistency and role strain from the field of social psychology, we may translate this typology of movements into a hypothesis of political socialization.[25] We would regard attitude and belief change to be least

---

Life (New York: Free Press, 1959), especially pp. 337-358; and Gabriel A. Almond and Sidney Verba, *The Civic Culture* (Boston: Little, Brown, 1965), pp. 117-135.

[24] For an explanation of how this index was constructed, see McKean, "The Potentials for Grass-Roots Democracy," pp. 826-832.

[25] On models of attitude change and cognitive inconsistency, see Arthur R. Cohen, *Attitude Change and Social Influence*, especially pp. 62-80; Jack W. Brehm and Arthur R. Cohen, *Explorations in Cognitive Dissonance* (New York: John Wiley and Sons, 1962); Leon Festinger, *Theory of Cognitive Dissonance*, especially chapters on the role of social support, pp. 177-259; and Shel Feldman, *Cognitive Consistency* (New York: Academic Press, 1966).

Table 1

Typology of Group Structure vs. "Good Citizenship" Indicators
(by percentage)

INDICATORS	OMB	IND	CONV	PHONY	TOTAL
A) Origin of Interest in Pollution (n=50)					
purely prevention-oriented	100	53	60	100	60
both prevention & experience	0	32	0	0	24
experienced pollution damage	0	16	40	0	16
B) Protest Experience (n=62)					
newcomers	44	54	100	—	56
veterans	56	46	0	—	44
C) Group Goals (n=64)					
specific only	31	87	100	100	75
general	69	13	0	0	25
D) Individual Motives (n=64)					
self-interested	13	72	100	0	58
altruistic	88	28	0	100	41
E) Pollution Information (n=62)					
low	0	13	0	—	8
medium	31	38	86	—	42
high	69	49	14	—	50
F) Pollution Concern (n=62)					
low	13	18	57	—	21
medium	38	33	29	—	34
high	50	49	14	—	45
G) Best Form of Government (n=58)					
popular sovereignty	81	61	25	—	64
balance between people and government	19	34	75	—	33
authoritarian guidance	0	5	0	—	3
H) Isolation-Sophistication Index (n=62)					
rural isolates	0	41	14	—	27
in between	13	38	86	—	37
urban sophisticates	88	21	0	—	35
TOTAL (N)	100 (16)	100 (39)	100 (7)	100 (2)	100 (64)

NOTE: OMB = Ombudsman CMs
IND = Independent CMs
CONV = Converted Neighborhood CMs
PHONY = Imitation CMs

likely where no new stimuli were present (that is, among Imitation CMs) and to be most likely where both the structure and the activities adopted by the CM were new and unfamiilar to participants (that is, Independent CMs).

Figure 1

A TYPOLOGY OF CITIZENS' MOVEMENTS

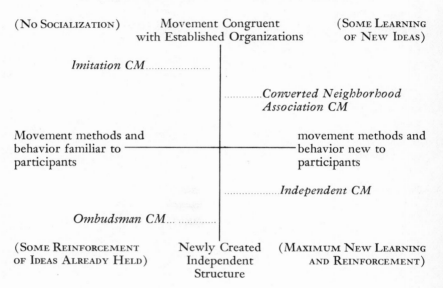

(No Socialization)   Movement Congruent   (Some Learning with Established Organizations   of New Ideas)

Imitation CM

Converted Neighborhood Association CM

Movement methods and behavior familiar to participants

movement methods and behavior new to participants

Independent CM

Ombudsman CM

(Some Reinforcement of Ideas Already Held)   Newly Created Independent Structure   (Maximum New Learning and Reinforcement)

To proceed methodically with the explication of this hypothesis and the evidence for it, Imitation CMs appear in the upper left quadrant of the typology because they are congruent with a preexisting organization and because their members encounter no stimulus to open their minds to new ideas, participating out of an ordinary sense of neighborhood esprit de corps and community responsibility, without any conflicting cross-pressures. Leaders do not need to resort to any novel rationalizations for the group's behavior, which remains quite conventional in the eyes of the membership. The only thing "new" about such a group may be the temporary adoption of a slogan that reflects the new citizenship theme popularized by real CMs, or the group's part-time interest in a pollution issue.

Converted Neighborhood CMs appear in the upper right quadrant because their members act within the comfort and security of a familiar cluster of friends but engage in unfamiliar activities as a protest organization. Although many participants are undoubtedly brought into the movement on the basis of a sense of obligation toward the neighborhood association and its leaders, not all of them remain immune to changes in role definition. Evidence from the two groups in this sample indicates that members undergo considerable change in order to adjust to the fact that pollution makes enemies out of superiors to whom they formerly felt great deference and that they have engaged in unconventional activities (sit-ins and demonstrations) to lend force to their protest. They sometimes find it necessary to cultivate their own home-grown democratic ethic in order to justify their protest and to remove the ugly taint of local "egoism" from their conduct.

The Independent CMs appear in the lower right quadrant of the figure because their members are involved in groups and activities new to them, and here we would expect to find the largest amount of attitude and belief change: in the acquisition of new views to replace previously held beliefs or to fill a vacuum and in reinforcement, the confirmation and amplification of existing beliefs.

Finally, the Ombudsman CMs appear in the lower left quadrant because they are totally ad hoc groups and because their members tend to have considerable familiarity with the notion of protest politics although they may be newcomers in terms of actual practice. The sixteen Ombudsmen in our sample spoke about having learned to put beliefs into practice, to build upon earlier simpler understandings of politics, and to become more realistic about methods appropriate for achieving their objectives.

Evidence from our sample also bears out our expectations. Table 2 displays the relationships between the type of CM and several variables that can be considered indicators of the extent to which participation in CMs was a jarring or instructive experience. As our hypothesis predicted, activists in Independent CMs were the most emotionally involved with the pollution issue. Furthermore, they contributed the largest number of defectors from the conservative camp, an important shift that will soon be discussed in detail. Similarly, members of the Independent CMs reported the greatest number of changes in belief (2.13 per person), followed in the predicted sequence by the Converted CMs (2.00 per person), and by the relatively unmoved Ombudsman CMs (1.31 changes per person). If we look at the nature of particular types of belief change, we find that members of Independent CMs were also the most likely to have reported learning about politics (54 percent) and to mention disillusionment and disappointment with the government (51 percent). These high levels of change support our prediction that the participants in Independent CMs would undergo the most intense socialization experience. A minor exception

Table 2

Typology of Group Structure vs. Belief Change
(by percentage)

BELIEF CHANGE	OMB	IND	CONV	PHONY	TOT.
(A) *Pollution Emotion (n=62)*					
low	38	28	100	—	39
medium	25	26	0	—	23
high	38	46	0	—	39
(B) *Partisan Change (n=64)*					
conservative standpatters	6	13	86	100	22
disillusioned switchers	13	28	0	0	20
reformist standpatters	81	59	14	0	58
(C) *Partisan Change Among*					
Conservatives (n=27)					
conservative standpatters	33	31	100	100	52
disillusioned switchers	67	69	0	0	48
Total	100	100	100	100	100
(N)	(16)	(39)	(7)	(2)	(64
(D) *How did your opinions change*					
as a result of the movement?[a]					
learned a lot about politics	25	54	43	—	44
grew disappointed, disillusioned					
in government	19	51	0	—	36
ideas substantively changed	19	26	71	—	28
became radicalized	31	21	29	—	23
grew hopeful about social					
change	19	8	0	—	9
average number of changes					
per type of group	1.31	2.13	2.00	—	2.00
(N)	(16)	(39)	(7)	(2)	(64

NOTE: OMB = Ombudsman CMs
IND = Independent CMs
CONV = Converted Neighborhood CMs
PHONY = Imitation CMs
[a] Figures represent the percentage of respondents falling *in a particular type of CM* who ported the change listed in the first column.

to this pattern is the fact that those most likely to report that the substantive content of their ideas changed were members of Converted Neighborhood CMs (71 percent of them mentioned this), but this actually confirms our expectations that there would be significant acquisition of new beliefs within this category.

Background material on the Independent CMs in our sample also supports our hypothesis. Those movements which faced hostile conservative local governments exposed their members to unanticipated disappointments and difficulties, thus creating a fertile field for sweeping changes in attitudes and beliefs.[26] Many of these activists acquired a new perspective on local politics that contradicted conventional wisdom on such matters, they learned new values about the expression of conflict and about methods for exerting political influence, and they acquired a new sense of self-reliance and citizenly assertiveness in their posture toward the local political structure.

In summary, there would appear to be a direct association between the potential for political socialization through a CM and the extent to which the movement has had to piece itself together within a hostile environment. The further away from conventional and established organizations a citizens' movement has to go and the more severe the social and political obstacles it encounters, the more difficult the acts of joining and participating become. Simultaneously, it becomes necessary for activists to adjust their attitudes and beliefs in order to interpret these unpleasant and unexpected experiences and to rationalize their own unconventional behavior. Similarly, the more energetically the movement has to concentrate on the pollution issue alone in order to achieve its objectives, the more likely that participants will have to justify their activism to themselves on the grounds of an intense personal concern with the issue rather than as behavior expected of them in return for the friendship and comradery of a group. Thus different movement structures can affect the likelihood that participants will change their attitudes and beliefs. My next task will be to investigate the process of political socialization at the level of the individual activist.

SOCIALIZATION AMONG INDIVIDUALS IN CITIZENS' MOVEMENTS

In order to examine the role of CMs in providing political socialization for their members, we will first look at the activists' own testimony as to the impact of participation on their attitudes and beliefs. Because this was not a longitudinal study with before-after data, but was instead gathered through interviews conducted at one time, we are forced to rely on respondents' subjective reporting. This raises the possibility of distortion through poor respondent recall, but it also includes the compensating advantage of providing a filter

[26] On the confrontation between CMs and hostile conservative local governments, see McKean, "Citizens' Movements in Urban and Rural Japan."

through which the respondents themselves remembered and reported the changes that were likely to be most salient to them. We will also examine the most interesting development resulting from activism, the phenomenon of change in partisan support.

Belief Change and Prior Experience with Protest

Although it was not possible to code and quantify every reply, almost every member of the sample reported some sort of change in attitudes and beliefs. Asked to describe how their ideas had changed as a result of participation in CMs, 80 percent of the respondents answered in some detail, as shown by the broad categories in Table 3. By far the most common reply (volunteered by 44 percent of the sample) was that they learned a lot about politics. This included remarks to the effect that participants began to appreciate the fact that politics could affect their lives, that they learned to be politically active, or that they acquired a deeper understanding of politics and the law. Thirty-six percent said that what they learned—about the LDP, about pollution, about how government and industry operated —was disappointing to them. Twenty-eight percent said that the experience had changed the substance of their ideas in some way (for example, they became more concerned with democratic values, or their ideas became more complex or more practical).

Table 3 also demonstrates that newcomers to protest reported considerably more change than did the experienced protesters. They did not glide through the activist experience impervious to what went on around them but instead felt the need to incorporate new information and adjust old ideas to fit accordingly. Newcomers were particularly more likely to mention that their ideas had changed in content or that they had grown disillusioned with the government, a threshold that previous protesters would obviously have passed already. Nonetheless, veterans to protest were susceptible to learning from CMs, and two patterns of belief change were clear within this group: the relatively mild-mannered veterans were inclined to report having been radicalized by the experience—shoved further leftward along the spectrum by yet another dose of what they'd experienced before—but those who had already located themselves on the extremist fringe were pleasantly surprised at the success of the movement and newly hopeful about the possibility of achieving social change within the political system.

Thus, a picture emerges of participants beginning their activism from different starting points and undergoing experiences that appear

Table 3

Changes in Ideas vs. Protest Experience

	NEW-COMERS	VET-ERANS	TOTAL
How did your opinions change as a result of the movement?[a]			
learned a lot about politics	46	41	44
grew disappointed, disillusioned in government	41	30	36
ideas substantively changed	32	22	28
became radicalized	16	33	23
grew hopeful about social change	8	11	9
Average number of changes in ideas in each category of protest	2.16	1.78	2.00
(N)	(37)	(27)	(64)

[a] Figures represent the percentage of respondents falling *in a particular category of protest experience* (either newcomers or veterans) who reported the change in ideas listed in the first column.

to bring their diverse views into closer alignment than before. Data from other measures indicate that the same pattern of convergence occurs not only with respect to ideas but also in relation to levels of political information and awareness. Veterans of protest invariably knew much more and exhibited greater concern and awareness about both politics and pollution, in absolute terms. Although the newcomers obviously did not begin to catch up to the veterans in some ways, they had adequate information about the particular pollution problem that concerned them and were quite emotionally troubled about it.

All activists were surprisingly well-informed about elections: 95 percent of the sample could remember and discuss at least one of the candidates they supported in the most recent elections for muncipal, prefectural, and national legislatures, 63 percent could recall and evaluate all three, and another 13 percent of the sample had actually run for office themselves. National surveys indicate that Japanese voters in general are well-informed, but from 16 to 65 percent of the respondents usually fail simpler tests of political knowledge that merely ask respondents to state whether they are or are not aware of a fact supplied in the survey questionnaire.[27] The campaign activity index indicates that newcomers to protest were involved in vigorous election

[27] See Bradley M. Richardson, *The Political Culture of Japan* (Berkeley: University of California Press, 1974), p. 149.

campaign work just as much as veterans were—particularly as a result of CM involvement in elections. Those movements particularly high in newcomers—the ones in rural areas—also tended to be those that found it practical and possible to exert influence by entering elections. Newcomers seemed a bit provincial and unpolished in contrast to veterans (which should not surprise us), but they were certainly acutely sensitive to their immediate surroundings and vigorously interested in politics—at least at the local level. Clearly, CMs provided newcomers with an opportunity to learn about politics in their own setting. In speculating about these patterns of convergence among newcomers and veterans, I do not mean to imply that convergence is the final product of continued activism. The point is that in a very modest way, the newcomers acquire some of the savvy of the more experienced, while the thick-skinned veterans feel restored by the naive energy of the newcomers.

Disillusionment

Although we do not have time or space to discuss the histories of the various CMs in this study, there is no doubt that most of the movements encounter unpleasant difficulties with community leaders and local government that embitter their members. Table 4 reveals the scores of newcomers and veteran protesters on four indices that summarize positive and negative attitudes toward different categories of political referents.[28] Here we see that newcomers' and veterans' political attitudes have very similar shapes, although the veterans' attitude profile has much more pronounced features, and the newcomers are not yet quite as jaded in their views of political objects as are the veterans. It is interesting that the feelings of both newcomers and veterans alike stem more from extreme disappointment and distaste for the conservative Right than they do from any comparable devotion to the Left: Japanese environmental activists are more "against" the establishment than they are "for" the leftist alternative. These figures alone lead one to toy with the possibility that many activists, including longstanding supporters of the leftist parties, might find continued conservative rule in Japan quite tolerable if it were only more responsive and open and if serious social crises were attended to sooner. At the same time, the

---

[28] Because many of the evaluations that comprise the measures were made in terms of a particular reference object's performance with regard to the pollution issue, we know that these measures consist in large part of atttiudes acquired through the activist experience, attitudes that were simply absent before the respondent became active in the antipollution issue.

Table 4

Hostility Toward Political Objects
vs.
Experience at Political Protest

		NEWCOMERS	VETERANS
(A)	Attitude toward the Political Right (RIGHT)[a]	−1.51	−2.52
(B)	Attitude toward the Political Left (LEFT)[b]	+ .38	+ .67
(C)	Net Preference for the Political Left (NET LEFT)[c]	+ .97	+1.59
(D)	Attitude toward Politics of both Left and Right (POL OBJ)[d]	− .57	− .93

NOTE: Each of the above scales runs from −3 (an extremely negative attitude) to 0 (a neutral attitude) to +3 (an extremely enthusiastic attitude). Each of these measures was based on indices built from over forty specific interview questions (asking respondents to evaluate several political reference objects—parties, political leaders, local politicians, pressure groups, and so on—on three different rating scales), along with every unsolicited evaluation of a political reference object that respondents provided during interviewing. All references to objects that could clearly be labelled conservative ("Right") or reformist ("Left") were taken into account. Each measure was then collapsed into seven categories, ranging from −3 to +3, with 0 representing neutral evaluations. Therefore these measures represent attitudes held after, and perhaps acquired through, the activist experience.
[a] RIGHT = attitudes toward all conservative and right-wing political referents.
[b] LEFT = attitude toward all reformist and left-wing political referents.
[c] NET LEFT = net preference for the political Left [(B−A)/2], with a negative score indicating a net preference for the Right and a positive score indicating a net preference for the Left.
[d] POL OBJ = summed attitude toward all political referents of both Left and Right [(A+B)/2], with a negative score indicating a dislike for politics and a positive score indicating a positive feeling for politics.

strongly negative scores earned by the conservatives also tell us that the LDP faces very long odds indeed if it does intend to try to win back any support from the swollen forces of discontent being mobilized by CMs because one of the most significant ways in which CMs provide political reeducation for their members is that half of those who join as conservative identifiers eventually become so disillusioned with the LDP that they switch to the progressive parties.

The Origins of Partisan Change

Our discovery that disillusioned activists in CMs may go so far as to switch partisanship requires a careful follow-up analysis to determine what kind of activist switches parties, why others do not switch, and what sort of a commitment switching signifies to each individual. The following discussion uses a trichotomy based on replies to the query, "Do you tend to support any specific political party?," aimed at determining party identification rather than voting habits (to which we will compare party ID later). Conservative standpatters are those who joined antipollution movements as supporters of the LDP and remained committed to the LDP. Disillusioned switchers are those who entered CMs as supporters of the LDP but who later became supporters of either the JSP, the JCP, or the opposition parties in general on the basis of the pollution issue (no respondent switched in the opposite direction). Progressive standpatters entered CMs as supporters of the JSP, the JCP, or the progressive parties in general, and remained so. It is important to note that this last category is quite large (58 percent of the sample), both because of sampling bias discussed earlier and because those who switched on the basis of an issue *prior* to participating in CMs have automatically been classified along with the reformist standpatters.[29] Therefore, we will concentrate on the twenty-seven members of the sample who joined CMs as conservatives and who are evenly divided between standpatters and switchers.

Table 5, Category (A) reveals a very strong association ($Tau-b =$ .412) between progressive partisanship and prior experience at protest, but we should avoid being carried away by the idea that CMs consist of seasoned leftists guiding conservative innocents toward the leftist parties. Forty-three percent of the newcomers themselves were already reformist identifiers (and, conversely, 43 percent of the progressive standpatters were newcomers to protest), indicating that many participants, even though they supported opposition parties, previously confined their views to the voting booth and avoided public protest. Citizens' movements thus mobilize two kinds of formerly "invisible" newcomers in large quantities: the progressives who have already developed an emotional sympathy with the Left (or at least a sense of disgruntlement with conservative dominance in politics) but have gone no further, and those who have previously supported conservative rule.

What can the data tell us about why the activist experience stretches the switchers' loyalties to the conservative party too far and turns them into progressives? A common finding in psychological studies of attitude and belief change is that people who change their views readily

[29] This is a very "clean" trichotomy, posing no problems in defining "conservative" or "reformist" because no respondent indicated support for either the centrist DSP or the Kōmeitō.

are unstable, vulnerable personalities. However, the available evidence in this case indicates that switching is a "rational" response to features of the activist experience (that is, predictable on the basis of what we know about the various movements) rather than a manifestation of the wobbly personality or the true believer syndrome.

First of all, Category (B) in Table 5 shows that rural CMs are twice as likely to produce switchers as are urban CMs. This difference is probably due to the fact that rural CMs are those that encounter the most trouble with conservative local governments and those that are more likely to run CM candidates (formally independent but often privately progressive) in local elections.

Members of movements that avoid electoral activity can presumably separate their public movement activities from their private political affiliations, often regarded as a delicate personal matter in Japan. But when a movement enters election campaigns in support of particular candidates or political parties, this compartmentalization obviously becomes difficult. As a consequence, the pressure to bring these two forms of political expression into agreement with each other undoubtedly forces many movement activists to change their partisan affiliation. On the other hand, a substantial number of the conservative standpatters come from urban areas where progressive parties are conspicuous at the local or metropolitan level. It would be a minor matter of cognitive readjustment for these conservative diehards to justify the act of political protest against a progressive local government while simultaneously maintaining a conservative political affiliation. Thus this pattern of partisan switching is a predictable reaction in terms of cognitive consistency theory both to concrete CM experience with a hostile conservative opponent and to movement involvement in elections.

There is also some evidence that switchers may have certain predisposition to change and that conservative standpatters are really more loyal in their partisan feelings in the first place than the conservatives who later switch. Table 5, Categories (C) and (D) display activists' orientations toward pollution problems. Progressive standpatters are the most likely to be active out of a pure concern for prevention, but the conservative standpatters are the most likely to have dragged themselves into action on the basis of direct damage from pollution itself. Similarly, progressive standpatters display considerable altruism in their goals, whereas conservative standpatters are overwhelmingly concerned with self-interest. In both cases, switchers are located in between the two extremes. It would appear, then, that conservative standpatters manage to become involved in protest against conservatives in power

Table 5

Traits of Antipollution Activists vs. Partisan Change

		CON-SERV	SWITCH	RE-FORM	TOTAL
(A)	*Protest Experience (n=64)*				
	newcomers	35	22	43	100%
	veterans	4	19	78	101%
	TOTAL	22	20	58	100%
	[*Tau-b* = .412; *p* = .001]				
(B)	*Residence (n=64)*				
	urban	25	15	60	100%
	rural	17	29	54	100%
	TOTAL	22	20	58	100%
(C)	*Origin of Interest in Pollution (n = 50)*				
	purely prevention-oriented	50	55	67	60%
	both prevention & experience	8	36	26	24%
	experienced pollution damage	42	9	7	16%
	TOTAL	100%	100%	100%	100%
	[*Tau-b* = −.203; *p* = .025]				
(D)	*Individual Motives (n=64)*				
	self-interested	79	62	49	58%
	altruistic	21	38	51	42%
	TOTAL	100%	100%	100%	100%
	[*Tau-b* = .228; *p* = .005]				
	(N)	(14)	(13)	(37)	(64)

NOTE: CONSERV = conservative standpatters
SWITCH = disillusioned switchers
REFORM = reformist standpatters

only because of immediate and powerful material incentives, whereas the switchers are vulnerable to mobilization on the basis of motivations and goals shared by reformists.

Additional evidence on the sources of respondents' anger about pollution, not shown in tabular form, tells us that 60 percent of the disillusioned switchers were absolutely fed up with their circumstances. They were poorer than average, having been bypassed by many of the benefits of postwar economic growth. For these people, pollution was the final blow in a long sequence of disappointments—the last straw that caused them to sever their allegiance to the ruling party. On the other hand, the conservative diehards were likely to lead more comfortable lives, to feel that they have shared in the benefits brought by LDP rule, and to regard pollution as their first major disappointment or the first problem that threatened to be beyond their control. The pollution issue was enough to move them to public protest when conventional methods failed but not sufficient to snap their bonds with the conservative party.

Thus far, then, it would appear that disillusioned switchers are different from conservative diehards both at the outset of activism and in their experiences during protest activity. Those destined to become switchers developed a fairly abstract interest in issues, drawing them into antipollution protest on the basis of concerns with prevention and not merely with immediate self-interest. The activist experience itself was also different for switchers, who tended to encounter greater difficulties at the hands of conservatives in power and who were more thoroughly immersed in direct political conflict with the local government.

Partisan Change and Belief Change

We have established that certain features of their circumstances are related to partisanship among diehards and switchers, but we should also investigate the relationship between ideas that activists acquired from participation in CMs and their decision to switch parties. Table 6 indicates that disillusioned switchers were quite different from both conservative and reformist standpatters in the content of what they learned: 54 percent reported having learned about politics in some way, and as many as 77 percent of the switchers volunteered the information that they had grown disillusioned and disappointed in government. A rather surprising 31 percent of the switchers termed their change in ideas a "radicalizing" experience, and they also reported a much larger absolute number of changes (2.69 per person) than either of the standpatter groups. Obviously, activism was a jolting but informative experience for the switchers, exposing them to much that was difficult to integrate with a conservative party affiliation and thus causing them to switch partisanship in order to reestablish cognitive consistency.

The fact that conservative diehards managed to mention the fewest changes indicates that they may have protected their partisan affiliation by isolating themselves from new ideas. If the primary distinction between switchers and conservative diehards is that switchers allowed

Table 6

Partisan Change vs. Changes in Ideas

	CON-SERV	SWITCH	RE-FORM	TOTAL
How did your opinions change as a result of the movement?[a]				
learned a lot about politics	29	54	46	44
grew disappointed, disillusioned in government	21	77	27	36
ideas substantively changed	36	17	30	28
became radicalized	14	31	24	23
grew hopeful about social change	0	8	14	9
Average number of changes in ideas	1.64	2.69	1.89	2.00
(N)	(14)	(13)	(39)	(64)

NOTE: CONSERV = conservative standpatters
SWITCH = disillusioned switchers
REFORM = reformist standpatters
[a] Figures represent the percentage of respondents falling *in a particular category of partisan change* who reported the changes in ideas listed in the left column.

themselves to become heavily involved in CMs while conservative die-hards remained peripheral, then we would expect to find switchers occupying positions of higher rank in their respective movements. As Table 7, Category (A) instantly reveals, this was *not* the case. In fact, none of the disillusioned switchers in the sample occupied positions of leadership, whereas 50 percent of the conservative standpatters—an enormously disproportionate number—were leaders of their movements. How can we reconcile the existence of conservative domination with the customary CM stance of opposition vis-à-vis a conservative local government (even in Tokyo, CMs usually had more trouble with conservatives at the ward level than with the reformist officials at the metropolitan level) and with activists' hostility toward conservative reference groups?

Our analysis must be devoted to two problems. First, why are so many movements led by conservatives (or, conversely, why do conservatives gravitate toward the upper ranks of CMs)? And secondly, how do these conservative leaders become deeply involved in CMs while maintaining an attachment to the party they are protesting? To begin with, CMs place great store by their claim to political neutrality. They must convince their opponents and the community around them

Table 7

Partisan Change and Leadership
(by percentage)

		RANK & FILE	OFFI-CERS	LEADERS	TOTAL
(A)	*Partisan Change (n=64)*				
	conservative standpatters	36	14	50	100
	disillusioned switchers	54	46	0	100
	reformist standpatters	62	27	12	100
(B)	*Protest Experience (n=64)*				
	newcomers	59	24	16	99
	veterans	48	33	19	100
TOTAL		55	28	17	100

that they are not tools of the leftist opposition but that they represent something much larger and more serious. In the second place, they must assure their own members that they will preserve neutrality within the group in order to maintain the allegiance of people, including even progressive partisans, who do not want to be part of an obstructionist radical leftist movement. Furthermore, citizens' movements, particularly those operating in hostile environments where confrontation and conflict are not quite acceptable, need as spokesman and figurehead a socially respectable community leader. Such a person can authenticate a movement's claim to decency and persuade members of the community, opposed to confrontation and conflict in general, and potential recruits to the movement that its objectives as well as its methods are reasonable. Similarly, as Table 7, Category (B) implies, veterans of protest do not have a monopoly on political expertise, as activists who gravitate toward the upper levels of CMs are almost as likely to be newcomers to protest as they are veterans. Clearly, conservative leadership can be an important asset to CMs by providing respectability and a useful knowledge of local conservative politics.

The question then becomes, why do such conservative newcomers to protest participate, and how do CMs find them? Or, even more perplexing, why do such persons often turn out to be motive forces in the creation of a CM? First, because of the enormity of environmental disruption in Japan, because pollution does not select its victims according to their partisan preferences, and because there are many reasons for even the most traditional conservative to object to pollution (the much-touted Japanese love of nature, affection for agrarian as opposed to industrial surroundings, etc.), even some conservatives with strong loyalties to the LDP are capable of objecting to LDP policies at times. Naturally, loyal conservatives who became protest leaders are made of tougher stuff than those who were too docile to raise their voices in objection to party policy or to higher authorities. An examination of individual CMs indicates that all of the conservative leaders in the sample were strong personalities, with a conspicuous streak of independence vis-à-vis other community leaders. They also tended to be extremely well-educated, generally with a degree from a prewar university, a credential held only by a very rarified group of older Japanese. Thus they were easily capable of cognitive manipulations permitting them to differentiate between conservative principles and conservative politicians, or between the national LDP and the local branch, retaining affection for the former while reviling the latter.

To return to the question of why switchers switched and why conservative diehards didn't, then, we clearly need to distinguish between movement leaders and the rank and file. I conducted a further analysis using a three-way comparison of switching, protest experience, and rank in the movement. Even though this analysis divides the sample into segments too small for statistical generalization, it helps to resolve the previously described inconsistencies. First of all, I found that none of the conservative movement leaders switched partisanship: they all fit the description of the strong-minded maverick. Secondly, I discovered that all but one of the conservative movement leaders were entirely new to protest. (Of course, as pillars of their respective communities they were not new to politics.) Presumably their ability to remain conservative hinged on the fact that they were not accustomed to being upset by conservative policies or politicians. Interviews supplied the strong impression that the very novelty of their feelings increased the magnitude of their rage at former compatriots in the local LDP establishment. Thus, if these leaders were to adopt the role of protester too often, they might indeed find their conservative loyalties going sour.

Among the rank and file activists who entered antipollution movements as conservative identifiers, there was a much greater vulnerability to changes in partisanship. All of those who had previously done a bit of protesting obviously had shaky loyalties already, and the pollution issue was all it took to drive them into the reformist camp. Even among rank and file activists who were entirely new to protest, vulnerability was high—53 percent of that subgroup abandoned the LDP as a result of participating in a CM. Those who stood firm with the LDP (47 percent) fit our description of marginally involved protesters who maintained conservative loyalties by insulating themselves from new ideas and uncomfortable thoughts. In summary, then, followers rather than movement leaders did all of the switching, and followers with previous protest experience were more vulnerable to switching than those who were entirely new to protest.

A final tool available to explain why switchers changed party ID is the set of hostility indices used earlier (see Table 4). Table 8 shows that switchers' attitudes toward the political spectrum closely resembled those of progressive standpatters—in other words, they switched parties in order to realign their partisan preference with their new political attitudes. Their hostility toward the conservative Right was intense, their preference for the reformist Left was substantial, but they were generally skeptical about political reference objects as a whole. The conservative standpatters, on the other hand, appear to have protected their partisanship by remaining relatively neutral on all of these dimensions, although it is interesting that insofar as they were inclined in any direction at all, it was always negative.

Because we have discovered important differences between conservative followers and leaders, Table 8 also provides scores on the hostility indices for the followers and leaders in each category of partisanship. Significantly, we find as we might expect that the only subset with a positive attitude toward the Right were the conservative standpatters who were officers or leaders in their movements. As we speculated earlier, these conservative leaders differentiated between "the Right" in general and the targets of their own particular protest. (Most of the items used to build these indices referred to national symbols, but the components that referred to local conservatives did elicit negative responses from conservative leaders.) On the other hand, conservative standpatters of the rank and file had an unusually negative attitude toward the conservative Right. They maintained these inconsistent attitudes by refusing to notice the inconsistency at all.

It seems fair to conclude, then, that activists who change their partisan affiliations through participation in CMs do so on the basis of their prior experience at protest, the already tenuous loyalties to the LDP that they bring with them, the degree to which they become immersed in CMs, and a reassessment of the behavior of their (usually) conservative opponents and reformist allies. Conservative CM activists are deviants vis-à-vis society because they are protesting against establishment politics, but they also remain deviant within their CM by maintaining a slim thread of allegiance (in the form of party ID) to the target of the CM's protest. The highly active conservative standpatters add complexity to their belief systems in order to rationalize their conflicting

261

Table 8

Partisan Change vs. Hostility Toward Political Objects

	RIGHT	LEFT	NET LEFT	POL OBJ
Conservative Standpatters	− .29	− .57	− .14	− .43
rank and file	−1.20	− .60	+ .30	− .90
officers and leaders	+ .22	− .56	− .39	− .17
Disillusioned Switchers	−2.38	+ .69	+1.54	− .85
rank and file	−2.57	+ .14	+1.36	−1.21
officers & leaders	−2.17	+1.33	+1.75	− .42
Reformist Standpatters	−2.41	+ .84	+1.62	− .78
rank and file	−2.30	+1.00	+1.65	− .65
officers & leaders	−2.57	+ .57	+1.57	−1.00
Total Rank and File	−2.20	+ .60	+1.40	− .80
Total Officers and Leaders	−1.62	+ .38	+1.00	− .62

NOTES: RIGHT = Attitude toward Right
LEFT = Attitude toward Left
NET LEFT = Net Attitude toward Left
POL OBJ = Attitude toward All Political Reference Objects
Each of the above scales runs from −3 (an extremely negative attitude) through 0 (a neutral attitude) to +3 (an extremely enthusiastic attitude). See note on Table 4 for further explanation.

allegiances; the marginal conservative standpatters compartmentalize their inconsistent views and thus ignore them. On the other hand, the switchers resolve their cognitive inconsistency and role strain by transferring their political allegiance from the conservative establishment to the progressive parties which, along with CMs, oppose that establishment.

Partisan Change, Ideology, and Voting Behavior

The data gathered in this study provide us with two measures (albeit rough indicators) to check changes in partisan affiliations against involvement in election campaigns and actual voting. Despite the problems with these two measures,[30] they still provide us with a fairly clear

[30] The measures of campaign activity and party loyalty in voting used in Table 9, categories (A) and (B) respectively are both cumbersome variables because respondents from different movements had to be lumped together. Different movements comprised different time periods that overlapped with regularly scheduled elections in very different ways, and some communities also had elections scheduled at irregular times or for special purposes. As a result, when respondents

message: that activists, including the switchers, actually voted according to their reported partisan identification. Table 9, Category (A) shows that, as we have already argued, disillusioned switchers were more involved in local election campaigns than were conservative standpatters, and Table 9, Category (B) shows that there was a very strong association between respondents' stated partisan preferences and their actual voting habits. Seventy percent of the conservative standpatters voted only for conservative candidates in the three most recent elections preceding the interview, and 74 percent of the progressive standpatters also voted loyally as reformists. The switchers reported the greatest quantity of mixed voting, reflecting both "cross-over" voting (progressives at the local level, conservatives at the national level) and a combination of elections occurring both before and after the change in partisanship. Eighty-one percent of the switchers had already demonstrated their commitment to the reformist parties in at least one election. Thus we come to the unavoidable conclusion that not only do CMs alter many participants' ideas, political attitudes, and partisan preferences but that they also lead to greater involvement in elections and a shift in voter alignment.

But what is the significance of a change in partisanship? Do switchers become doctrinaire ideologues or are they merely temporary protest voters? The only doctrinaire Marxists among the sample were already reformists before their environmental activism began, and switchers did not become very interested in leftist ideology. The switchers were quite familiar with the rhetoric of Marxism, almost always due to exposure to ideological arguments during their activism, but they did not rely on Marxist explanations. Even among progressive standpatters, some of whom had a long record of commitment to leftist causes, only 30 percent were strongly committed to a Marxist world view, aware of the finer points debated among different leftist factions.

An examination of respondents' own explanations for supporting progressive parties indicates that most of the nonideologues generally viewed their partisan preference as a matter of utility, not of emotional attachment or of ideological belief. Perhaps the activists themselves can describe these feelings the most accurately:

---

reported their campaign activity and voting in the three most recent elections in their community, they were referring both to different combinations of their participation in a CM and to their change in partisanship. There are cases where activists reported change in partisanship but had not yet had a chance to vote on the basis of the change or where an activist has not always had candidates of his own party to choose from.

Table 9

Behavior in Elections vs. Partisan Change
(by percentage)

		CON-SERV	SWITCH	RE-FORM	TOTAL
(A)	*Campaign Actviity (n=64)*				
	R merely voted, or indulged in passive campaign activities only (listening to speeches, belonging to a *kōenkai*, or talking to friends)	72	62	54	60
	R campaigned actively (passed out leaflets, put up posters, helped organize a *kōenkai*, worked in movement campaigns, spoke from campaign car with megaphone, or even ran for office)	28	38	46	40
(B)	*Party Loyalty in Voting (n=58)* Based on the Three Most Recent Elections Reported				
	voted conservative only	70	18	3	18
	mixed voting record	30	45	23	29
	voted reformist only	0	36	74	54
TOTAL		100	100	100	100

NOTE: CONSERV = conservative standpatters
SWITCH = disillusioned switchers
REFORM = reformist standpatters

"Right now I feel very confused, very angry about the LDP, but unable to settle on the JSP or JCP as a preferred choice, although I think the people in the progressive parties tend to be a lot more honorable." (B2)

"I have no particular party but if I had to vote I would make sure never to vote for the LDP." (C3)

"Our *kyōdō* is being ignored by everyone—mayors, Diet representatives, governors—so the people must unite and oppose this to get what we want. . . . We must protect our own community because no one else will do it for us. This is real self-government. . . .

I think the progressive parties should increase their seats in the national Diet in order to cause the LDP to worry more and be a better majority party." (J2, an LDP prefectural assemblyman)

"It's funny for me, a socialist, to say this, but I don't really think that progressive local governments will be a quick solution to anything. . . . You find more democratic types among the progressives, but I don't think they're all so good, nor do I think all the LDP politicians are so terrible." (K4, a labor organizer)

"I'm voting progressive only because it's bad for the LDP to have been in power alone so long. The reformists may not be any better when they're in power." (L1)

"I have left the LDP and am now voting mostly for the JCP, although sometimes I vote for other progressive parties too. . . . But I do not at all want the communists to win; I would hate to live in a country like Russia. But I think it would be good for the opposition to increase a good deal and make the LDP nervous so they'll try harder." (B5)

These comments give us the impression that CM activists share a consensus that the LDP is utterly irresponsible, perhaps because it is too powerful, that the JSP and JCP are much more interested in popular welfare and open government, and that a more even balance of power between conservative and reformist parties is desirable. Most such activists do not appear to favor toppling the national government, and many make a point of explaining that their support for reformists results more from a matter of tactics than a belief in socialism. What they want from the LDP is a more democratic style, a greater voice for ordinary people, and the decentralization of power.

Conclusion: Citizens' Movements and Local Politics

To summarize our findings, the experience of participation in CMs does have an impact on its members, and these effects seem to vary with the type of movement. The greater the independence from conventional or existing organizational structures and the more novel or unfamiliar the tactics adopted by a movement, the greater the change in members' political attitudes and partisan affiliations. Among the four types of CMs defined here, the Independent CM is not only the most prevalent variety but it is also the type in which we found the greatest magnitude of change—either as entirely new learning or as reinforcement, refinement, and development of old ideas. We may safely extrapolate from the multiplicative effects of these two findings that the total impact of CMs on their membership is great indeed.

Participation in CMs causes seasoned protest veterans to grow more hopeful than before about the possibilities of achieving limited goals within the system, but to the more numerous newcomers it brings disillusionment with conservative parties and politicians. CM activists are extremely disappointed and angry toward the right wing of the political spectrum and relatively (though by no means overwhelmingly) favorable in their views of the left, leading many to abandon the LDP and to support progressive parties instead. These views are based specifically on the pollution issue, and there is no indication of a major ideological shift within CMs. The more a movement becomes involved in local elections and the more bitter its encounter with local authorities, the greater the impact of participation upon members' political attitudes, party identification, and actual voting records. However, it is important to qualify this description by adding that conservative standpatters are disproportionately common in the leadership of CMs, indicating that the relationship between CM activity and progressive political tendencies is a complex one whose implications merit careful examination.

The Substance of Socialization

One important finding in this study is the fact that CMs provide their members with personalized training in effective citizenship. They learn to evaluate and criticize their local governments, to articulate their grievances, to exert influence successfully, and in short to post warning to local authorities that henceforth they will be judged according to more exacting standards of performance. Several respondents made the unsolicited point that CMs had opened their eyes to the meaning of the textbooks on democracy and the new constitution which their children studied in school and that they found their children's advice very helpful—political socialization in reverse gear in this instance. The fact that these new attitudes and beliefs develop out of experience and have an intense personal significance to each participant affords them some permanence.

It is also extremely important to note that CMs have brought people of varying beliefs and affiliations together to accomplish a common purpose—a meeting of minds quite unusual in Japan—the vertically structured corporatist society par excellence.[31] As we have seen, CMs are

[31] Chie Nakane, *Japanese Society* (Berkeley: University of California Press, 1970).

an amalgam of large numbers of progressive supporters and conservative leaders who both resort to cognitive acrobatics to integrate new principles of pragmatic, nonideological opposition with some of their old political beliefs. It cannot be overemphasized that the link between CM and leftist forces is an alliance of convenience to the movement, created on the premise that the CM will remain ideologically neutral.[32] Taken together, these two features of CMs—their creation of new channels of communication among progressives and conservatives who find themselves united in opposition to certain features of the status quo, and their pragmatism and independence of ideological rhetoric[33] —signify that CMs can apply the same standards of evaluation and criticism to progressive as well as to conservative governments.

My related findings on the impact of participation in CMs on partisan affiliation and voting behavior—that many activists, presumably a larger portion of them than the 20 percent in our heavily progressive sample, abandon the conservative party—do not necessarily mean that CMs will provide a solid foundation for progressive coalitions at the local or national level. Although this rate of partisan support change is significant, my evidence indicates that we should probably refer to our disillusioned switchers as the basis for a sophisticated floating vote. They are obviously sophisticated in that they have become political "gladiators," are knowledgeable about local elections, and report having learned a great deal about politics through CMs. Moreover, their new political preferences are based on practical experience and firmly held beliefs on specific issues, not on random vacillations or whimsy. They are floaters, however, rather than new converts to progressive parties because they display little interest in leftist ideology, a mixed pattern of voting (often in the form of cross-over voting at different levels of elections) for parties of both Left and Right, and only modest admiration for the progressive parties. It is significant that the switchers, along with the rest of our sample of CM activists, exhibit much more disgust for the conservative Right than they do enchantment with the Left;

[32] There is disagreement over whether self-interest and obtaining results are inadequate objectives, or whether all conservatives in Japan are bad or not. Takabatake Michitoshi argues that CMs serve the interest of conservative power because of their pragmatism, but Irokawa Daikichi suggests that the goals are quite honorable and that conservatives with such interests possess values that are conducive to democratic trends. See Takabatake Michitoshi, "Citizens' Movements: Organizing the Spontaneous," *Japan Interpreter* 9 (1975): 317, and Irokawa Daikichi, "The Survival Struggle of the Japanese Community," *Japan Interpreter* 9 (1975): 465-494.

[33] Muramatsu Michio, "Gyōsei katei to seiji sanka," in Nippon Seiji Gakkai, *Nempo seijigaku* (Tōkyō: Iwanami Shoten, 1974), pp. 46-53.

even conservative standpatters at the rank and file level of CMs reveal negative feelings toward the conservative end of the political spectrum.

If CMs continue to prosper and to grow in influence as they seem to be doing,[34] the key to political survival will be performance.[35] Indeed, according to Takabatake Michitoshi and Kano Tsutomu, CMs have not been satisfied with the policies of progressive administration recently.[36] It would appear, then, that CMs are affirming, and perhaps extending, their political impartiality and that progressive parties as well as the conservatives they have displaced must take heed. The issue orientation displayed by CMs affords opportunities to progressive and conservative parties alike to capture the floating vote, which in turn should create stronger forces for competition among the parties and presumably bring them closer together in policy and platform, even if they retain the appearance of polarized opposites. These results are already evident at the local level where CMs have been active.

New Patterns of Political Cleavage

Although we have dwelt upon political socialization within CMs, we should not ignore their external effects. One of the important findings to be gleaned from our sample of different CMs is that they appear to have long-term effects on the surrounding community as well. Just as we have noticed attitude change and partisan switching among CM members, it is important to note that similar changes occur among many nonactivist sympathizers, as evidenced by electoral outcomes after the emergence of a CM.

[34] According to a survey conducted in May 1973, 23 percent of Tokyo residents had observed a residents' or citizens' movement in their area within the preceding year. Forty-four percent of those who reported that there had been a movement in their area had also been directly involved in it, indicating that a grand total of perhaps 10 percent of all Tokyo residents had participated in a citizens' movement of some sort. By extension, then, perhaps 10 percent (or a good deal more over a longer period of time) of Japanese who live in congested urban areas have participated actively in such movements. Asked if they would consider involvement in a residents' movement in the future, 15 percent of the entire Tokyo sample said that they would become involved, and another 53 percent said that they might, depending on the circumstances. Quite clearly, participation in CMs has become legitimate in urban areas. *Asahi shinbun*, 15 June 1973.

[35] See Muramatsu Michio, "The Impact of Economic Growth Policies," *Asian Survey* 15 (1975): 812.

[36] Kano Tsutomu, "Peasant Uprisings and Citizens' Revolts," *Japan Interpreter* 8 (1973): 292, and Takabatake Michitoshi, "The Local Elections in 1975," *Japan Quarterly* 22 (1975): 202.

Citizens movement-endorsed candidates (usually progressive independents) often do well in local elections, either by acquiring more votes than opposition candidates have in the past or even by winning assembly seats and mayoral races. In our own sample alone, a Tokyo neighborhood group managed to elect three ward assemblymen, the Citizens' Council in Usuki successfully elected five city assemblymen and later their candidate for mayor, and a reformist independent was elected mayor of the community in Toyama prefecture where *itai-itai* victims are concentrated. The CMs in Oiso drummed their profactory mayor out of office and also managed to defeat him when he ran instead for a seat in the Kanagawa Prefectural Assembly, and the same group came within just a few votes of placing one of their own leaders into the town assembly in an election in which the reformists won many more votes than usual but divided them among too many contenders (three JCP candidates and one CM candidate), of whom only one JCP candidate won a seat. A broadly-based CM operation in an LDP stronghold in southern Japan (Shibushi Bay) campaigned energetically for leftist Diet candidates in the 1972 general election, and as a result the votes cast for the JSP and JCP from Kagoshima Third District increased from 26,662 votes (13.9 percent of the total) in 1969 to 42,284 votes (21 percent of the total) in 1972.[37]

CMs have not yet succeeded in removing officials from office through recall elections, but they have achieved the same objective by frightening those threatened with recall into premature retirement from politics. In what is perhaps the most impressive electoral accomplishment based solely on the efforts of a CM, the Citizens' Council in Usuki obtained signatures from a majority of the city's eligible voters demanding the recall of the mayor, and in the actual election that followed the Citizens' Council candidate narrowly missed victory with 11,647 votes (or 46 percent) out of a total of 25,093 votes cast (turnout was a record 92 percent).[38]

Clearly CMs are a catalyst for changes that go beyond their own membership. They considerably alter the style of local politics, replacing the customary LDP dominance with a more balanced form of competition based not upon left-right ideological differences but upon responsible political performance and practical results. This rearrangement of the patterns of political cleavage is clearer if we examine the impact of CMs on local political elites. Citizens' movements often de-

[37] *Asahi nenkan* (1970), p. 274; *Mainichi nenkan* (1972), p. 155.
[38] Matsushita Ryūichi, *Kazanashi no onnatachi: Aru gyoson no tatakai* (Tōkyō: Asahi Shinbunsha, 1972), pp. 45-49.

stroy the *kankei* networks that serve as the mainstay of LDP local organization. Many of the maverick conservatives who have gravitated toward the upper levels of the CMs were formerly LDP bosses. Because this study was carried out shortly before the general elections of December 1972, I witnessed several exchanges in which these LDP bosses-turned-CM-activists were approached by the local LDP branch office (which hoped desperately to obtain their customary electoral services) but adamantly refused to endorse LDP candidates or to deliver their normal quota of LDP votes. Thus CMs often create an organizational vehicle for mobilizing local opposition, while simultaneously depriving the LDP of one of its most important tactical advantages in local politics.

Citizens' movements also affect local elites by creating a new layer of opinion leaders, consisting of an unprecedented combination of (a) new recruits to political activism in the form of CM newcomers, (b) formerly complacent defectors from the establishment, and (c) reeducated veterans of opposition politics. The newcomers have learned to navigate in the political world for the first time, and those with prior political experience have learned to work more effectively with new methods to mobilize broader support. The result is to increase both the absolute size of the local elite and the variety of political opinions represented by the politically active members of the community, contributing to a much more fluid political atmosphere. A CM will sometimes provide a long-term channel for expression for this new elite by leaving a permanent organization behind to monitor local politics. The clearest example of a CM evolving into a permanent structure is probably the case of Mishima (described in Jack Lewis's contribution to this volume). The metropolitan government of Tokyo provides such a long-term channel for experience by actually recruiting former CM activists as citizen consultants on various committees.[39]

Lastly, a successful CM changes the ground rules and increases the channels of citizen participation in local politics. As evidence we may cite the precipitous increases, during the early 1970s, in the number of pollution lawsuits, in the number of pollution complaints filed with local government bodies, and in the number of antipollution contracts being concluded between municipalities and local industries.[40]

[39] See the annual publication of the Tokyo Metropolitan Government *Tomin no koe*, which describes with enthusiasm the contributions made by CMs to metropolitan plans.

[40] See McKean, "The Potentials for Grass-Roots Democracy," p. 150, and Kankyōchō, *Kankyō hakusho* (Tōkyō: Ōkurasho Insatsu Kyoku, 1974), pp. 370-375.

New Attitudes Toward Political Conflict

Muramatsu Michio suggests that the fundamental significance of CMs is not the contrast between their participatory orientation and the political past in Japan but rather an underlying pattern of evolution from consensus based on shared values to pluralistic and conflicting interests.[41] I would agree that one of the important changes wrought by CMs—not only among their own members but in the larger society that increasingly views such movements as legitimate avenues of political action—is the cultivation of a new orientation toward conflict. In most communities, the eruption of a CM is quite divisive, and the experience of conflict over the immediate issue exposes still other disagreements over more fundamental values: development vs. tranquillity, participation vs. withdrawal from politics, trust vs. skepticism toward politicians, conformity vs. independence as desirable traits in personal behavior, and most fundamentally of all, the quest for harmony vs. the tolerance of conflict.

A community faced with this situation must devise a process that restores the ability of different factions to accept decisions, even when disagreements are profound. Citizens' movements rapidly extend their concern with immediate policy objectives to include an interest in decision-making processes and come to advocate open decision making and more community participation (a traditional ideal as well, often lost as a community grows and differentiates). Because citizens may disagree violently among themselves and because politicians cannot read the minds of their constituents without guidance, workable compromises must be reached through open, not closed, bargaining and exchange. Political processes must be open for the participation of the community, including skeptical critics, because only then will the various factions of the community accept the product of the decision-making process as legitimate. Out of necessity, then, a CM that resorts to these arguments and methods to achieve its objectives moves imperceptibly toward the acceptance of conflict as a permanent feature of society, something that must be repeatedly resolved as issues arise but that can never be eliminated.

Modern democratic theory tells us that the ability to compromise, the agreement to disagree, and the capacity to tolerate dissent are very desirable features of democratic politics—they are obvious necessities for the protection of civil liberties that also lend stability to a system with large population, high participation, and high levels of "public

[41] Muramatsu, "Gyōsei katei to seiji sanka," pp. 59-67.

contestation."[42] To the extent that CMs have encouraged greater tolerance of political conflict, then, they are serving an extremely important function.

This discussion has been fraught with descriptions of disappointment, disillusionment, and hostility among participants in CMs. Taken in combination with the well-known fact that the Japanese are increasingly unhappy with political parties, we risk making the mistake of concluding that Japanese society is afflicted with the malaise that we hear so much about in analyses of postindustrial society. But I would regard these unhappy attitudes that we have found among activists as the natural and necessary ingredients of a healthy, positive orientation toward political participation, just as I view favorably their acceptance of conflict as a fact of life. Theoretically speaking, the possibility of misgovernment at best, tyranny at worst, is the suspicion on which democracy is justified. Disillusionment is the catalyst that makes it possible for budding citizens to make sense out of democratic principles. Or, in the words of one activist:

> "My ideas have changed tremendously because of this. I used to be 'deaf' about politics, but now I know how the city assembly works. This is true of all of us now. We all go to assembly sessions now because we don't know what they will do if they are able to fool us. We have to take an interest and go and ask questions and watch over them to see that they don't play any tricks on us. Now I always express my discontent and I don't listen to what others tell me without making sure of my facts first. This is sad, but I can certainly protect myself better this way." (K2)

Citizens' movements do not signify a problem so much as they provide a device for resolving issues that existing channels could not handle. Even though some activists are overtly hostile to the political establishment and describe themselves as "against the system," they plainly are more interested in transforming the system by participating in it than by tearing it apart. Citizens' movements have very rarely asked for impossible levels of perfection but instead have made demands that are within the physical capacity of the system to satisfy. All-or-nothing movements, such as the refusal of Sanrizuka farmers to allow the state

[42] Robert A. Dahl, *Polyarchy: Participation and Opposition* (New Haven: Yale University Press, 1971). From a broader perspective, Dean Jaros has emphasized that it is important for the political public to learn tolerance of dissent not only for the survival of democratic institutions but also in order to endure the stress created by the world's uncertain future. See Dean Jaros, *Socialization to Politics* (New York: Praeger, 1973), pp. 42-68.

to seize their land by eminent domain, which led to violence because both sides considered their positions to be nonnegotiable, are actually quite rare. *Threats* of extremism (destruction of property, sit-ins to the death) do occur, and some movements assemble a "suicide corps" of activists dressed in white who threaten to kill themselves if the group's demands are not met. But even in these cases, workable compromises are eventually created.

Furthermore, because so many CMs approach government with demands that focus on procedure and process, both national and local governments should find it possible to satisfy the movements by similarly focusing on procedure and process. It is clearly within the capacity of government to pay this much attention to movement demands, as demonstrated by the ability of so many local administrations to do so.

In conclusion, CMs have mobilized a sizable sector of the ordinary public to produce a new layer of issue-oriented participant citizens. By virtue of their effect on partisan change, they have also stimulated the growth of a floating vote among their own members. Extrapolation from aggregate election data indicates that there is a relationship between CMs and the rise of a floating vote in the general population as well.[43] Thus CMs have indirectly contributed to the increase in party competition and the emergence of new configurations of more responsive political leadership, they have contributed to a substantial increase in citizen participation and consequently to an increase in the variety, flexibility, and exchange of opinions represented in local politics, and, finally, they have shuffled and enlarged the political elite in many communities and provided for the emergence of a new common language among activists whose different political affiliations had formerly segregated them from each other. Both by socializing their own members to be skillful political actors and by legitimizing political conflict and providing a mechanism by which political decisions can accommodate greater diversity of views, CMs have done a great deal to strengthen democratic processes in Japan.

[43] Unfortunately, existing survey data does not permit us to test directly whether individuals in the general population have altered their voting patterns in response to the rise of CMs, and aggregate data is always vulnerable to the ecological fallacy. Nonetheless, Bradley Richardson observes an otherwise inexplicable shift to the left from 1960 to 1972 in at least thirteen semirural districts where CMs were strong, and he concludes that CMs are part of the cause of the rise of the floating protest vote that benefited the progressive parties at least until 1972. See Bradley M. Richardson, "Stability and Change in Japanese Voting Behavior, 1958-72," *Journal of Asian Studies* 36 (1977): 686-687.

CHAPTER 8

CIVIC PROTEST IN MISHIMA: CITIZENS'
MOVEMENTS AND THE POLITICS OF THE
ENVIRONMENT IN CONTEMPORARY JAPAN

Jack G. Lewis

To STUDENTS of mass politics in Japan, the recent emergence of citizens' movements is perhaps the most outstanding development in the postwar period. Many observers recognize a simple distinction between two types of citizens' movements involved in environmental politics: in *compensation movements* aggrieved residents organize to demand payment for injuries to their health resultant from pollution; in *environmental protection movements* residents organize to impede developments that may worsen the quality of the local environment.[1] Compensation movements such as the movement concerned with mercury poisoning in Minamata, with the "itai-itai" disease in Toyama prefecture, and with asthma and other air pollution related ailments in Yokkaichi have received more attention in the Japanese and foreign media than have environmental protection movements.[2]

I wish to acknowledge special indebtedness to Ellis Krauss for his extensive suggestions for revisions of this manuscript, to Kurt Steiner and Terry Edward Mac-Dougall for their support over the years on the project from which this study is taken, and to Hoshino Mitsuo and Hirahata Terayasu of the Tokyo Institute for Municipal Research who introduced me to Mishima.

[1] For the distinction between compensation movements and environmental protection movements, see Muramatsu Michio, "Gyōsei katei to seiji sanka," in Nippon Seiji Gakkai, *Nenpō Seijigaku* (Tōkyō: Iwanami Shoten, 1974), pp. 41-46; and Chapter 6 of this volume.

[2] The fact that the grievance is potential in prevention-oriented movements has implications for both media communications and citizen mobilization. A number of observers have noted that a major problem for prevention-oriented movements lies in convincing citizens of the potential ills involved. Thus, as in Mishima, Numazu, and Shimizu, an early stage in this type of movement is educative, oriented towards marshalling evidence of the potential ills and then towards communicating that evidence. Protection movements have received less publicity nationally than compensation movements because they have been less successful and thus merit less attention in a country where defeating those in positions of authority creates news. The Mishima-Numazu-Shimizu case is a relatively rare example of a major protection-oriented movement that achieved a clearcut victory of national importance.

The objective of this article is to test a number of the previously generated hypotheses on the nature of Japanese citizens' movements against an in-depth case study of an environmental protection movement that occurred in Mishima City in 1963-1964.[3] In this case, protest movements in Mishima and two neighboring communities eventually defeated plans of the central government, the Shizuoka prefectural government, and three major corporations to construct a massive petrochemical complex (*sekiyu kagaku konbināto*) in their communities. It is appropriate that in focusing on a single case Mishima is our choice, for Japanese specialists on citizens' movements have repeatedly used it as an example of a typical environmental protection movement that supports their generalizations on the nature of citizens' movements.[4]

[3] For a much more extensive treatment of local politics in postwar Mishima than that found in this chapter, see Jack G. Lewis, "*Hokaku Rengō*: The Politics of Conservative-Progressive Cooperation in a Japanese City" (unpublished dissertation, Stanford University, 1975); hereafter cited as Lewis, *Dissertation*.

[4] I am not contending here that this case somehow represents a "scientifically" better opportunity to probe the nature of citizens' movements than other cases. Concentration on a single case—and this was an early case in the history of such movements—invariably faces the problem of knowing whether it is sui generis or indeed "typical." I see this as the type of study that Arend Lijphart calls a *theory-confirming* or *theory-infirming* case study which, by its nature, can only marginally weaken or strengthen our faith in established generalizations. Only further in-depth case studies can further confirm or weaken the validity of the generalizations analyzed here. See "Comparative Politics and the Comparative Method," *American Political Science Review* 65 (1971): 692.

On the other hand, the importance of accounts of this particular case in shaping scholarly and lay understandings of the nature of Japanese citizens' movements should not be underemphasized. The attention given to this movement has been extensive. Descriptions of the Mishima movement—over forty books, chapters, and journal articles—continued to be published into the 1970s. Some of these sources cite the Mishima case as the prime example of environmental protection type movements. See Muramatsu, "Gyōsei katei," p. 42. Others stress the Mishima case as an example of how citizens' movements raise civic and political consciousness. See Ishida Takeshi, *Japanese Society* (New York: Random House, 1971), p. 60, or Akimoto Ritsuo, *Gendai toshi no kenryoku kōzō* (Tōkyō: Aoki Shoten, 1971), pp. 263-282. Others stress that the Mishima-Numazu-Shimizu victory was the first important defeat of national economic planning in postwar Japan and that the Mishima movement in particular was a critical link in the diffusion of prototype movement models throughout the nation. See, for example, Miyamoto Kenichi, "Chiiki hattatsu seisaku no sōgōteki hihan," *Sekai* 245 (April 1966), pp. 59-60; Miyamoto Kenichi, "Jūmin undō no riron to rekishi," in *Toshi mondai to jūmin undō*, ed. Miyamoto Kenichi and Endo Akira (Tōkyō: Yubunsha, 1971), pp. 59-60; Fukushima Tatsuo, *Chiiki hattatsu tōsō to kyoshi* (Tōkyō: Meiji Tosho Shuppan Kabushiki Gaisha, 1968), p. 16; and Kamioka Namiko, "Nihon shihonshugi no hatten to kōgai mondai," *Jurisuto* 458 (August 1970): 8-13.

As concerns the diffusion argument, this case is usually seen as the middle step in a three-step process of a growing national opposition to petrochemical com-

The degree to which these generalizations are in fact supported by this case will be examined in this chapter with particular focus on four categories of analysis: (1) characteristics of citizens' movement participants and leaders; (2) characteristics of movement organizations and decision making; (3) the nature of the relationship between citizens' movements and conventional local and national politics; and, (4) the impact of movements on postmovement local and national politics.

The chapter is divided into four parts. The first section describes the setting of the Mishima movement, including its relevant spatial, demographic, economic, and political characteristics. The second section briefly analyzes the temporal progression of the movement. Section three evaluates prominent generalizations on the nature of citizens' movements in the light of this case. The evaluation is based on survey data collected from movement participants, interviews with local political activists, local press accounts, and a variety of secondary source materials. Finally, in the fourth section I draw some general conclusions concerning the significance of the findings in the third section.

BACKGROUND TO THE MISHIMA MOVEMENT

Citizen mobilization and protest in Mishima was more successful than any previous movement in Japanese history. Never before had an industrial project of such scale with so much at stake for the nation's economic future been defeated. Under what circumstances did this successful instance of citizen mobilization occur? What features characterized the environment in which the movement occurred and perhaps contributed to its success?

Socio-economic Environment

Four aspects of Mishima's socio-economic environment appear to have particularly influenced its citizens' response to the petrochemical complex construction issue. First, Mishima is spatially compact, yet in 1963 its population was over 70,000.[5] Thus, the city is densely inhab-

---

plexes. First, Mishima, Numazu, and Shimizu residents observed pollution and its effects at the Yokkaichi petrochemical complex, then they organized to defeat the eastern Shizuoka complex, and, finally, movements modeled on this movement spread throughout Japan. I, too, believe this Mishima case to be important in many respects. Yet, at the same time, I think that many scholarly understandings of the nature of citizens' movements are incorrect because they are based on faulty, distorted, or incomplete accounts of this movement. For a comprehensive list of the sources on the Mishima movement, see Lewis, *Dissertation*, p. 231, n. 2.

[5] Of nineteen Shizuoka cities, for example, Mishima stood seventeenth in terms

ited, even compared to most other Japanese cities.[6] The compactness of Mishima and the contiguity of its population (both of which are factors that most likely facilitate interaction and citywide communications between political activists and between activists and others) probably contributed to the nature of its citizens' reaction to the *konbināto* issue. Whereas Mishima's population is large enough to support a diverse range of conflicting interests and interest groups, the tone of interest conflict in the city is probably moderated by the ease of personal communications and the extensive web of personal interrelationships existent in the city.

Second, although Mishima is spatially compact, residents think of it as divided into four districts. Like most of Japan's cities, Mishima is an "artificial" unit created by consolidating (*gappei*) a densely inhabited commercial core area (the old Mishima Town) with three more sparsely populated, agriculturally-oriented villages. In 1965, over 60 percent of Mishima's residents lived in its downtown district while the remainder lived in the other districts (Kitaue, Nishikida, Nakazato). Although these districts have no official status, residents continue to perceive Mishima as divided into four parts. Social organization and political behavior are affected by such perceptions. The local school system, agricultural cooperative system, neighborhood associations, women's groups, and a broad variety of other social and economic groups consistently utilize this division as a spatial basis for their organization. Although it is less than a five-minute drive on the city's congested roads, a city assembly candidate from Kitaue would not be foolish enough to trek all the way to Nakazato in search of votes. Thus, although small size facilitates citywide communication and interaction, intracity regionalism in the Mishima of 1963 would require special efforts to build a citywide response to the *konbināto* problem.

---

of area in 1965, in many cases half or less as large as cities of smaller population. Sōrifu Tōkei Kyoku, *Showa 40 nen kokusei chōsa hōkoku 4*, no. 22 (Tōkyō: Sōrifu Tōkei Kyoku, 1966), p. 3.

[6] Mishima's density was 1,152 persons per square kilometer as compared to the national city average of 760. Its downtown area, covering only 7 percent of the city's total area, had a density of 9,595 persons per square kilometer in 1965. This compares with Tokyo prefecture's density of 5,357 or the combined density of Tokyo's wards at 15,559 in the same year. In 1965, Mishima's downtown area was more densely populated than eight of ten Yokohama city wards. The contrast between this downtown area and the outlying districts is rather dramatic for, as compared to the inner-city figure of 9,594, the respective figures for Kitaue, Nishikida, and Nakazato were 695, 536, and 1,077 persons per square kilometer. See Mishima Shi Sangyōka, *1966 Mishima no Tōkei* (Mishima: Mishima Shiyakusho, 1966), pp. 8-10, and Sōrifu Tōkei Kyoku, *Nihon no jinkō*, Abridged Report, series 1, part 1 (Tōkyō: Sōrifu Tōkei Kyoku), pp. 230, 674, 690.

Third, while economic statistics indicate that by the early 1960s Mishima's agricultural sector was rapidly attenuating and that farm families were increasingly being integrated into city life by occupational and other changes, the rural areas continued to be of social and political importance. Thus, *konbināto* construction threatened a substantial rather than a marginal sector of the city's population, Nakazato's farmers. To be more specific, while in 1965 only 12 percent of the total city work force continued to be primarily employed in agriculture, its farm family population still stood at 9,350 of its 71,239 residents.[7] This constituted one-third of the population of the three outlying "rural" districts of the city. When coupled with their domination of various instruments of social control in these areas (for example, village associations, irrigation cooperatives, agricultural cooperatives, PTA organizations), this population base gave farmers a continuing and inordinately strong role in the city's social and political life. This was manifested in the fact that at least one-third of the city assembly seats during the 1950s and 1960s were occupied by farmers.

A final point relates to the structure and strength of Mishima's labor movement. Some have contended that unions and leftist parties are so weak outside of the major metropolitan centers that citizens' movements cannot depend on their aid in these areas.[8] Mishima, however, has historically been a city with a relatively strong union movement. As a result, the Japan Socialist Party (JSP) and the Japan Communist Party (JCP) have played a relatively significant role in its politics and were thus prepared to become involved in the *konbināto* construction conflict when it arose.[9]

[7] Mishima Shi Sōgō Hattatsu Shingikai Senmon Iinkai, *Mishima shi sōgō hattatsu keikaku ni kansuru chōsa hōkokusho* (Mishima: Mishima Shiyakusho, 1966), p. 79, and Sōrifu Tōkei Kyoku, *Showa 40 nen kokusei chōsa*, p. 351.

[8] On Mishima, see Margaret McKean, "The Potentials for Grass-Roots Democracy in Postwar Japan: The Anti-Pollution Movement as a Case Study in Political Activism" (unpublished dissertation, University of California at Berkeley, 1974), p. 29.

[9] The strength of the city's union movement can be attributed to the fact that a few large unionized firms employ a majority of the city's secondary sector employment. For example twenty-four firms of more than 100 employees supplied 56 percent of the secondary sector employment and, among these twenty-four, six firms of more than 300 employees employed 34 percent of such employment. See Lewis, *Dissertation*, pp. 47-48. This, combined with the fact that the transportation, education, and public service sectors (sectors with high levels of unionization) are important in Mishima, explains why Mishima is recognized as a city of relatively significant union and leftist party strength. Prefectural labor statistics corroborate this picture, indicating that in 1969 57 percent of the secondary and tertiary sector employees in the city were unionized. See Mishima Shi

Political Environment

Two aspects of Mishima's politics seem to have strongly affected its response to the petrochemical complex plan. First, whereas throughout the 1950s local politics were dominated by conservative politicians, in the early 1960s this dominance began to weaken. Second, by 1963 residents had experienced firsthand how the city government's successful efforts to lure large-scale industry could negatively affect their welfare.

Throughout the 1950s, local politics in Mishima were dominated by Liberal Democratic Party (LDP) branch politicians associated at the national level with Endō Saburō, a House of Representatives member from 1949 to 1972. This group of "mainstream" conservatives was opposed in city politics by other conservatives, some of whom were linked to other national level LDP politicians, by local branches of the Labor-Farmer (LFP), Socialist, and Communist parties, and in the 1960s also by branches of the Clean Government (CGP) and the Democratic Socialist (DSP) parties.[10]

From 1953 to 1961, Matsuda Yoshiharu, a businessman and former city assemblyman, served as Mishima's mayor with the support of the conservative mainstream. As mayor, Matsuda worked with a city assembly in which twenty-six to twenty-nine of thirty members were conservative and in which his own assembly faction numbered from eighteen to twenty-five members. A consistent objective of Matsuda-faction conservatives, mostly small businessmen and farmers, was to bring economic growth and prosperity to their city. This was to be

---

Keikaku Zaiseika, *Mishima no tōkei—1970* (Mishima: Mishima Shiyakusho, 1970), pp. 24-25, and Shizuoka Ken Shokugyō Taisakubu Rōseika, *Shizuoka ken rōdō kumiai meibo* (Shizuoka: Shizuoka Kenyakusho, 1970), pp. 123, 135.

[10] Progressive party strength in Mishima was not only an inner-city, working-class phenomenon. In 1963, Mishima had strong ties to the city's "rural" periphery, especially to Nakazato, for the upper Izu Peninsula, including the Mishima area, along with Okayama prefecture and certain parts of Hokkaidō, Mie, and Ishikawa prefectures, is unique in Japan as a pocket of strength of the Labor-Farmer Party (Rōdō Nōmintō) that seceded from the JSP in 1948 and rejoined it in 1957. In Mishima, the LFP's leader was Sakai Ikuzō. With the merger of the LFP and the JSP in 1957, Sakai became head of the Mishima Socialist branch and was therefore in a unique position to help bridge the gap between Nakazato farmers and labor and the progressive parties during the *konbināto* opposition movement. Labor-Farmer strength in the area also helps explain the relatively high level of interaction and cooperation between Socialists and Communists in the city, for the LFP repeatedly urged pragmatic united fronts with all those on the left including the Communists. See Allan B. Cole, George O. Totten, and Cecil H. Uyehara, *Socialist Parties in Postwar Japan* (New Haven: Yale University Press, 1966), pp. 289-290.

achieved by cooperating with the prefectural and central governments and by attracting industry to provide jobs and strengthen the local tax base. In his second term, Matsuda scored his greatest success by bringing Toyo Rayon's $33 million plant to Mishima and neighboring Nagaizumi Town. Later, Matsuda, his LDP branch associates, his city assembly faction, and their associates in the Chamber of Commerce and the Agricultural Cooperative leadership structures would be the most important local supporters of a Mishima *konbināto*.

To almost everyone's surprise, Matsuda was narrowly defeated in 1961 by a maverick "conservative," thirty-seven-year-old Hasegawa Taizō. Thus in 1963, it was Hasegawa who would be faced with the *konbināto* problem. Although previously an LDP branch member, Hasegawa was backed in his mayoral campaign by an unusual electoral coalition: the *Aishi Renmei* (League for City Love), his electoral support organization, was in fact a coalition of the local Socialist and Communist branches, *Sōhyō*-affiliated unions, certain prominent unaffiliated progressives, and Hasegawa's own personal supporters. In previous mayoral elections, progressives had developed a pattern of joint candidate support and even a willingness to look outside their parties for attractive candidates. In 1957, the *Aishi Renmei* had supported the mayoral candidate Koide Shōgō, a nationally prominent children's storywriter and unaffiliated Christian-Socialist. Koide narrowly failed to defeat Matsuda who was running for reelection, yet this campaign marked the birth of conservative-progressive local cooperation as Hasegawa and another maverick conservative city assemblyman joined Koide's campaign as treasurer and secretary, respectively. Hasegawa's support for Koide marked the public emergence of his personal and programmatic differences with LDP branch conservatives. Thereafter, he became a vocal critic of Matsuda, especially criticizing his efforts to bring Toyo Rayon to the area.

Progressives expected Koide to run for mayor once again in 1961. However, he declined and urged the *Aishi Renmei* to support Hasegawa.[11] After lengthy negotiations and agreement on a joint policy agreement (*seisaku kyōtei*), "conservative" Hasegawa found himself the candidate for the progressive camp. This policy agreement took on

[11] Koide saw his campaign in 1957 as educational, an effort to socialize citizens to the appropriate democratic citizenship values. Throughout his campaign, his constant theme was that democratic politics require that elections be won on the basis of voters' decisions on issues rather than on personalistic or monetary inducements. He steadfastly refused to spend any of his own funds on the election, pointing out that citizens who desired good government should themselves support good candidates. He also refused to offer alcoholic refreshments to visitors to his campaign headquarters, a service usually expected of candidates.

added importance with Hasegawa's surprise victory in January 1961. It required, first, that local autonomy and citizen welfare rather than plans for consolidation with other jurisdictions be stressed during the mayor's administration in anticipation of attempts to lure a petrochemical complex to the Mishima area. It also promised to protect Mishima's underground streams in the future, reflecting disenchantment with the Toyo Rayon project. Further, it promised that a Hasegawa administration would implement procedures for regular consultation with representatives of local citizen organizations and individual residents. Finally, it stressed that local autonomy could not be achieved by blindly following the wishes of higher levels of government or by relying too much on national subsidies to finance local government.

For the next two years the new mayor was confronted with a very hostile political environment. The national and the prefectural governments were controlled by friends of Matsuda-faction conservatives. Two-thirds of Mishima's city assemblymen were members of the LDP branch assembly faction. In the assembly, Hasegawa could count on the support of two Socialists and one Communist and the occasional support of one Democratic Socialist and some of the five "neutral" conservatives.

By the time that the *konbināto* problem arose, however, this situation had changed somewhat. First, the leader of the local Socialist branch was elected to one of Mishima's two prefectural assembly seats, breaking the mainstream conservative hegemony at this level. Second, the new mayor soon received additional support in the 1963 city assembly election. Three candidates who would form the core of the mayor's own assembly faction in the future were elected, and opposition parties were also more successful than in the past. Thus, the internal balance of the 1963-1967 assembly with which the *konbināto* opposition movement would have to deal was as follows: LDP branch faction (18); "neutral" conservative faction including three genuine mayor-faction conservatives (6); Socialists (2); *Kōseiren* (2); DSP (1); Communists (1).[12]

Thus, one major change that conditioned the city's response to the *konbināto* plan was a shift in the balance of the formal, positional power structure in the city. A second factor was Mishima's experience with large-scale industrial construction, which occurred immediately before the *konbināto* issue arose. Historically, Mishima is well-known as a city of beautiful clear streams and ponds. Mt. Fuji's lava flow stops in the middle of Mishima in a large, inner-city park. At this point the moun-

---

[12] *Kōseiren* was the precursor of the present Clean Government Party (*Kōmeitō*).

tain's underground runoff flows to the surface, creating natural ponds and streams which then flow through the city. Prior to 1962, this spring water was the sole source of residential water supply and was critical to Nakazato's irrigation system.

During Mayor Matsuda's second term in office, Toyo Rayon had been encouraged to locate its plant in Mishima and Nagaizumi on a spot that was directly between Mt. Fuji and downtown Mishima. By 1960, the first phase of this plant, which eventually employed 5,000 people, was completed and began to pump up large amounts of underground water for its production process. By 1962, the city's water supply had decreased markedly (the park's ponds began to dry up), and by 1963 the residential drinking water supply and Nakazato's irrigation system began to be severely affected. In the end, after prolonged citizen discontent and unsuccessful local government and citizen initiatives with company officials, the city government was forced to seek alternative water sources, investing large amounts of capital to transport it from distant above-ground sources. As a result, certain residents gained some experience in opposition movement tactics and others, not the least of all the Nakazato farmers whose crops had been threatened, were alerted to the dangers of massive plant construction. Further, by this time, Japan's media had begun to communicate to local residents the fact that Mishima's experience was not an isolated event but part of an evolving nationwide problem.

MOVEMENT DYNAMICS

The availability of flat farmland in Nakazato provided the opportunity for massive industrialization in Mishima. Previously, it had been largely passed over by the industrial growth that was sweeping Japan. The only exceptional postwar industrial construction was that of the "Mishima" plant of Toyo Rayon, which in fact was located more in neighboring Nagaizumi Town than in Mishima. The first indication that Mishima might become more involved in Japan's economic growth came in May 1960 with the announcement of Shizuoka prefecture's Sixth Comprehensive Development Plan. This plan reflected the desire of prefectural officials to shift Shizuoka's economy from its heavily agricultural orientation to greater industrialization in order to benefit more from national economic growth. It also reflected the efforts of the central government, through the Ministry of International Trade and Industry (MITI), to meet the nation's rapidly increasing energy and chemical needs. MITI's involvement in this sector had begun in 1953, and by the late 1950s it had led to the construction of massive petrochemical complexes in such places as Kawasaki, Iwakuni, Yok-kaichi, and Niihama.[13]

The prefectural government's plans were made more concrete in an announcement by Governor Saitō Ikio (LDP) in March 1961 that a number of firms planned to build a large petrochemical complex in the East Suruga Bay area.[14] Arabia Petroleum, which had been established in 1958 to develop the energy resources of Kuwait, wished to establish a port in Numazu City's Enoura Harbor from which its supertankers could unload Arabian crude oil. The surrounding area was ideal for the construction of facilities to process and utilize this crude oil, particularly the plentiful water supplies in Mishima and Shimizu Town and the three million square meters of undeveloped land in Nakazato. According to this first plan, Arabia Petroleum's bulk processing facility in Numazu would receive and process the crude oil and, in turn, supply plants owned by Showa Electric (Mishima), Sumitomo Chemicals (Shimizu), and Tokyo Electric Power (Izu-Nagaoka) for the production of electricity and by-products such as propane and gasoline.

This first plan for an East Suruga Bay complex was summarily dropped in early 1962, yet prefectural officials maintained their hopes for the area.[15] Saitō, in conjunction with the implementation of Prime

[13] Shibamura Yōgō, "Konbināto," in *Gendai nihon no dokusen shihon*, ed. Imai Noriyoshi et al. (Tōkyō: Shiseido, 1964), p. 176. See also, Yamamoto Masao, *Nihon no kōgyō chitai* (Tōkyō: Iwanami Shinsho, 1965), pp. 169-198. *Konbināto* consist of plants physically clustered together as suppliers of basic raw materials for one another. The companies to which the plants belong may or may not be related through capital, credit, management, and/or selling arrangements and, at least in the Japanese case, are always plural corporate undertakings. One finds these clusters primarily in the fields of chemicals—petrochemicals, which tend to be the largest *konbināto*, and iron and steel chemicals. Eleanor Hadley notes that the circumstances giving rise to *konbināto* are exceptional; gaseous chemicals, the raw materials of the complexes, are among the few raw materials that for the most part are not economically transportable and, as they result in interrelated end products, plants using them are grouped together. Eleanor Hadley, *Antitrust in Japan* (Princeton: Princeton University Press, 1970), p. 3.

[14] Fukushima, *Chiiki hattatsu*, pp. 22-23.

[15] For a number of reasons, the original plan faced increasing impediments, and Showa Electric finally withdrew its land-purchasing agent from the area. Numazu local government officials had become disenchanted after a land survey indicated that the Numazu site for the refinery was too unstable, and Arabia Petroleum began to plan for relocation in Nakazato. Without consolidation of the local governments concerned, Mishima would have benefited greatly at the expense of Numazu from this development (see Fukushima, *Chiiki hattatsu*). Tsuchiya Jūzan, a Mishima public employee, attributes the failure of the first plan to the lack of capital in the tight money market at that time, to intrafirm difficulties regarding

Minister Ikeda's 1960 "income-doubling plan," hoped to have the national government designate eastern Shizuoka as one of the districts that would receive massive central government development aid.[16] In July 1963, this area missed being designated as one of thirteen "New Industrial Cities" (*Shinsantoshi*). However, because of the intensity of competition for such designation, an additional category of "Special Industrial Development Region" (*Kōgyō Seibi Tokubetsu Chiiki*) was invented, and East Suruga Bay and five other areas were so designated.

Within five days, prefectural officials issued a formal call for Numazu, Mishima, and Shimizu Town to consolidate.[17] Consolidation was to occur as rapidly as possible. According to the prefectural government, the ideal plan would be for the respective local assemblies to vote their approval by January 1964 and for the merger to take place in January 1966. Formal preparatory negotiations between the four parties to refine the consolidation agreement drawn up by prefectural officials began in late November.[18]

The initial public reaction to the consolidation proposal was favorable. A survey conducted by four of Mishima's local newspapers in

---

the allocation of plant sites, and to the increasing opposition of Enoura fishermen. See his *Jūmin undō to hōshi* (Tōkyō: Nippon Seinen Hōshi Kyokai, 1970), p. 40.

[16] National economic planning in Japan increased considerably in importance with Prime Minister Ikeda Hayato's announcement of the "income-doubling plan" in 1960. The National Comprehensive Development Plan, set to begin in November 1962, was the first national development plan in twelve years and was intended to implement the income-doubling concept. In turn, the Law for the Advancement of Construction of New Industrial Cities (*Shin sangyō toshi kensetsu sokushinhō*) of the same year was designed to make concrete the details of these general plans and concepts, and it called for the designation of special districts (*shinsantoshi*) for special emphasis in the nation's future industrialization. For more discussion of national economic planning in this period, see Ketsujō Saigō "Wagakuni hattatsu seisaku no wadai—1," in *Shakai kagaku tōkyū* 37 (March 1968): 381-406.

[17] Mishima was already familiar with pressures for consolidation. Throughout the 1950s, the city had been urged by the prefectural government to join with one or more of its neighbors. Thus, as early as 1955, one can find an account of the Mishima City Assembly holding a special meeting to discuss consolidation with Susuno Town and Numazu. See *Mishima Minpō*, no. 407, 25 August 1955. Other efforts were made to consolidate Mishima with Nagaizumi and Kannami Towns. During the late 1950s, there was continued negotiation with neighboring Nagaizumi Town on consolidation in order to bring together under one local jurisdiction the land on which the massive Toyo Rayon plant was constructed.

[18] For a summary of the events surrounding the consolidation effort, see Hoshino Shigeo et al., "Numazu, Mishima, Shimizu (Nishi, Ichō) sekiyu konbināto hantai tōsō to Fuji shi o meguru jūmin tōsō," in Miyamoto and Endō, *Toshi mondai to jūmin undō* (Tōkyō: Yubunsha, 1971), pp. 79-82.

December 1963 found that 73 percent of the 500 respondents were in favor of consolidation with Numàzu and Shimizu, while only 22 percent were opposed.[19] Sixty-three percent favored consolidation with neighboring Nagaizumi prior to consolidation with Numazu and Shimizu. Further analysis indicated that the strongest support came from public employees (81 percent) while the weakest support came from farmers (62 percent). Among those who opposed consolidation, the major reason for opposition was the fear that consolidation was a preparatory step in the construction of a *konbināto*. Prefectural officials, however, denied that this was the case.

Many local politicians were also in favor of consolidation. However, important supporters of Mayor Hasegawa in his election victory of two years before urged him to act with caution and in accordance with his policy agreement with local leftist forces. The public statements of Socialist and Communist city assemblymen and other activists reflected their strong belief that city consolidation and *konbināto* construction were linked and part and parcel of the central government's master plan for increased political centralization and unbridled industrial growth at the expense of local autonomy and public welfare.[20] The Socialist and Communist parties and *Koseiren*, represented by their city assemblymen, opposed consolidation throughout the intercity consolidation negotiations, yet lacked a delegation majority.

This strong local leftist opposition in Mishima should be interpreted as a result of the intermingling of these two issues—consolidation and industrialization and its negative consequences. In the general context of Japanese politics at that time, this local Socialist and Communist opposition to consolidation was not unusual. Yet, although opposed in principle, leftist forces in local government politics seldom had the means to defeat proposed consolidations, given their lack of assembly seats or mayoral positions. The perceived tie between consolidation

---

[19] *Mishima Minpō*, no. 597, 1 January 1964.

[20] See Tsuchiya, *Jūmin undō to hōshi*, pp. 42-43. Leftist opposition to the plan was manifested in the behavior of progressive city assemblymen. For example, on December 13, before cautiously agreeing during negotiations with Numazu and Shimizu representatives and prefectural officials to move ahead with consolidation, Mishima's eleven-member Assembly Committee delegation voted on the consolidation policy statement proposed by prefectural officials. The final vote was split six to five with six assemblymen favoring the agreement on the condition that consolidation not move ahead "as swiftly as possible" as proposed in the original agreement. In favor of the consolidation agreement were four May Association (LDP) assemblymen, one independent conservative assemblyman, and one Democratic Socialist. Two Socialists, two Kōseiren asesmblymen, and the Communist assemblyman opposed the consolidation proposal. *Mishima Minpō*, no. 986, 15 December 1963.

and complex construction made this opposition all the more intense in Mishima. The concern with local industrialization and its negative consequences, which appears "advanced" for local leftist parties in the early 1960s, can be explained by a variety of factors: the character and principled, yet pragmatic leanings of the local leftist party leadership; the negative impact of Toyo Rayon plant construction as a socializing experience; the fact that complex construction would most likely occur in Nakazato where the Socialist Party had considerable links; the fact that Mishima's progressives felt strongly about the city's distinctive local history and physical environment and that they had little desire for Mishima to be overwhelmed by its much larger neighbor, Numazu (their opposition was, in this sense, "conservative"); and the fact that being a part of the incumbent mayor's support base, they had a decent chance to affect the outcome of this issue and a great stake, in terms of future elections, in how the outcome was viewed by local voters. There is no indication, on the other hand, that national-level Socialist or Communist politicians in Shizuoka played any particular role in opposing the conservative central and prefectural governments' plans for their local district.

The cautious attitude towards consolidation in Mishima was reflected in Mayor Hasegawa's mid-August call for a special meeting of former mayors and city assembly chairmen, all linked to the local conservative camp, to gain consensus on consolidation. Their own caution was reflected in the formal statement announced at the meeting's conclusion: "We support consolidation for the purpose of improving the welfare and lives of our people but we cannot agree to consolidation for the purpose of luring the petrochemical complex to this area because of our fear of *kōgai*."[21] The prefecture's response was that consolidation and specific measures for development were unrelated problems. Thereafter negotiations continued, and the result, announced on December 14, was a consolidation policy statement, modified at the insistence of the Mishima delegation, that was cautiously supportive of moving ahead with consolidation.

Given Mishima's reluctant mood, the prefectural government's next action is difficult to understand. Within hours of the consolidation deliberation committee's favorable recommendation, the head of the prefecture's Planning Department announced a new petrochemical complex plan. The construction site?—Numazu, Shimizu, and Mishima. Fuji Petroleum, a newly formed subsidiary of Arabia Petroleum, would construct a $72 million, 150,000 barrel naptha production center in the

---

[21] Tsuchiya, *Jūmin undō to hōshi*, p. 47.

Nakazato area of Mishima, Sumitomo Chemicals would build a $148 million plant in Shimizu to produce ethylene from the naptha, and Tokyo Electric would locate its $145 million generating plant in a coastal area of Numazu and generate approximately 1.5 million kilowatts of power.[22]

The prefectural government's announcement produced a swift negative reaction among many residents who had previously accepted the argument that consolidation and industrialization were separate matters. After December 14, general concern heightened and broader-based opposition to the prefecture's plans surfaced. Rather than include a lengthy narrative on the progression of events in Mishima following December 14, the following analysis briefly highlights major tendencies in movement dynamics.[23]

With hindsight, it is possible to identify three relatively distinct phases in the Mishima citizens' movement between December 1963 and October 1964 when plans for *konbināto* construction in eastern Shizuoka were finally defeated. The *first phase*, which lasted into early March, was characterized by the efforts of local activists to develop effective movement organizations and to educate residents on the potential ill-effects of petrochemical complexes. The *second phase*, which lasted from March until the end of June, commenced as the movement, now effectively organized and widely supported, turned to political action and protest. It ended with Fuji Petroleum's announcement that it had dropped plans for construction of its plant in Mishima in favor of a new Numazu site. A *third phase*, not discussed in the following pages, lasted from the end of June until October. Although citizens' movements in Numazu and Shimizu were active by spring 1964, and although the three movements kept in communication throughout the spring, until the end of June the Mishima movement was overwhelmingly preoccupied with the defeat of Fuji's Mishima plant rather than with the entire complex. After June, the movement turned its attention to aiding the Numazu and Shimizu movements so that a *kon-*

---

[22] At that time, there were only three other plants in Japan with capacities of over 100,000 barrels per day. Only Showa Petroleum in Yokkaichi at 180,000 barrels per day would have continued to have greater capacity than the Mishima installation. For complete details on the plan, see Fukushima, *Chiiki hattatsu*, pp. 27-29.

[23] This analysis is based primarily on my paper, "Civic Protest in Mishima: A Case Study of Local Opposition to Industrial Development with Observations on the Nature of Citizen Mobilization in Japan," presented to the conference on Local Opposition in Japan, Wrightsville Beach, N.C., 24-26 June 1976; see the appendix entitled "The Mishima Citizens' Movement—An Account of Movement Events."

bināto would not be constructed anywhere in the East Suruga Bay area.[24]

First Phase (December 1963-March 1964): Organization Building and Citizen Education

This phase of the movement was first characterized by organizational changes in the community that eventually resulted in the establishment of an effective, citywide liaison organization to coordinate the activities of individuals and groups opposed to the *konbināto*. It took almost three months after the prefectural government's December 14 announcement of the second *konbināto* plan for the full development of this organization. Prior to this time, the activities of concerned residents took place largely through the auspices of study groups and investigatory commissions instituted by either the city government or by established local organizations. In particular, the Federations of Women's Associations, the Federation of Neighborhood Association Chairmen, shopping district associations, and the local Chamber of Commerce actively pursued the issue.

One new, ad hoc group of individuals concerned with the city's future was established immediately after the announcement of the second plan. On December 15, approximately forty progressive and conservative city assemblymen, local activists, concerned residents and local civil servants, many of whom had actively supported Mayor Hasegawa through the *Aishi Renmei*, met to discuss the announcement of the previous day. The meeting's outcome was the establishment of an organization called the Mishima Regional City Problem Citizen Consultation Committee (*Mishima Koiki Toshi Mondai Shimin Kondankai*; hereafter, the Consultation Committee). The Consultation Committee's action policy urged all citizens to take part in its activities and promised full and open discussion in its meetings. Further, it promised that the Committee would refrain from taking a position on consolidation until it had thoroughly studied the issue. On the other hand, it indicated that the Committee had already resolved to oppose consolidation if it appeared that the prefectural government's intention was to lay the groundwork for *konbināto* construction.

The Consultation Committee continued to meet throughout December and January, primarily for the purpose of hearing from a number of specialists from various Japanese universities on consolidation and on petrochemical complexes. Its meetings, however, increasingly at-

---

[24] For a discussion of this third phase, see Hoshino et al., "Numazu, Mishima, Shimizu."

tracted the participation of individuals who were not involved in its initial December 15 meeting, especially representatives and officers of various established local organizations, such as neighborhood and women's associations. In the process, its functions increasingly expanded from education and discussion toward coordination of a public response to the *konbināto* plan. Finally, on January 25, the Consultation Committee changed its name to the Mishima Citizen Council on Policy Towards the Petrochemical Complex (*Sekiyu Kagaku Konbināto Taisaku Mishima Shimin Kyōgikai*; hereafter, the Citizen Council) to reflect participants' feeling that *konbināto* construction rather than consolidation was the critical issue in Mishima. By early March, the Citizen Council and its component organizations had come to explicitly oppose construction, and the Council had become the dominant vehicle through which the opposition movement was coordinated and furthered on a citywide basis. Other ad hoc movement organizations were also established during the early months of 1964. In particular, "opposition faction" Nakazato residents, who had initially worked through their neighborhood association, created their own independent movement organization on March 10. This Nakazato Area League for Opposition to the Petrochemical Complex worked closely with the Citizen Council in the months that followed.

The second major characteristic of the first phase of the Mishima movement was its effort to educate residents on the nature of petrochemical complexes and their potential hazards. Local interest groups everywhere frequently have difficulty dealing with environmental problems because of their technical complexity and the public's inability to digest technical information. Proponents of environment-threatening development, on the other hand, normally have an abundance of technical experts and publicists who utilize this information in the most favorable manner.[25] A rather distinctive aspect of Japanese environmental protection movements since the mid-1960s has been their thorough-going effort to right this imbalance through a wide variety of citizen-initiated research and study efforts. The Mishima movement's heavy emphasis on information gathering and public education during the early months of 1964 undercut the advantage held by *konbināto* proponents and served as a model for later Japanese movements. During the first phase of the movement, the effort to balance this information gap was furthered by actions of the incumbent mayor, by the local "invention" of mass investigatory "touring," and by the importation of outside technical expertise. Mayor Hasegawa's partisan-

[25] See Cynthia Enloe, *The Politics of Pollution in a Comparative Perspective* (New York: David McKay Company, 1975), pp. 65, 75.

ship had a particularly strong effect in these early stages. As a result of his commitment to open city government and the close political link between him and many of the movement's most active leaders, the early efforts of citizens to gain information on the *konbināto* were channeled through city-sponsored investigatory committees. Whereas in Numazu citizens faced a hostile mayor and city assembly, Hasegawa took an officially neutral position and included a broad cross-section of representatives of established organizations and parties in city-sponsored advisory groups.[26] However, after January, these city-sponsored activities took a back seat to the activities of established nongovernmental or quasi-governmental Nakazato residents' groups (for example, the two federations of neighborhood and women's associations and the Chamber of Commerce) and the Mishima Citizen Council.[27]

The most heavily utilized technique for educating residents on the nature of *konbināto* during these early months was the inspection tour wherein large groups of citizens visited the sites of established *konbināto* (especially those based in Yokkaichi). After early March, the frequency of "touring" fell off dramatically as the movement turned

[26] Hasegawa had, of course, promised openness in city government in his 1961 mayoral campaign. In fact, a major criticism of Matsuda by Hasegawa had been the "closed" atmosphere of his administration. Matsuda was accused of countenancing "entourage politics" (*sokkin seiji*). In January and February, in cases where Mishima held open meetings between company and prefectural officials and representatives of local government and city organizations, Numazu held similar meetings, but local government officials limited attendance to elected officials and civil servants. In these cases, it was reported that Numazu activists had to attend the Mishima meetings to gain information as to *konbināto* plans. See Hoshino et al., "Numazu, Mishima, Shimizu," pp. 100-101.

[27] It is clear that there was a general mood of relative openness and responsiveness to residents in Mishima after the 1961 mayoral election, leading local leaders and activists to feel that they must consider residents' feelings before taking actions. This was manifested in the extensive surveying of opinions carried out throughout this period in the city, beginning with the December postcard survey carried out by the five local newspapers. Thereafter, the Federation of Neighborhood Association Chairmen and the Federation of Women's Associations jointly carried out a house-by-house survey on *konbināto* construction, the results of which were announced on March 23 and used to justify the Citizen Council's claim for citywide opposition to the plan. The Nakazato resident's groups also carried out its own house-by-house poll of area families before resolving to fight the *konbināto*. This openness and responsiveness also contributed to the early decisions of the leftist parties and other activists within the Citizen Consultation Committee to begin by studying the issue rather than by immediately establishing an opposition movement. This stance meant the opposition movement began somewhat slowly, yet when the Citizen Council was finally formed it was broadly representative of citizens from across the partisan spectrum who opposed construction.

toward oppositional tactics, but prior to that time lengthy inspection trips sponsored by the Mishima Citizen Council, Nakazato residents, the Chamber of Commerce, and the Liberal Democratic Party took place no less than eight times from February 9 to March 10. On their return, representatives of these groups reported their observations to the Citizen Council, the federations of women's and neighborhood associations, or specific residents' associations. These reports were then further disseminated through the five local newspapers.[28]

The technical advantage of *konbināto* supporters was further narrowed because from the beginning, movement and local government leaders relied heavily on the technical expertise of outside experts from universities and research institutes to educate themselves and citizens on development, pollution, and local government finance.[29] Lectures by university professors from Tokyo, Nagoya, and Osaka and by a group of high-school science teachers were critical elements of this approach. Further, researchers from the National Genetics Research Institute (*Kokuritsu Idengaku Kenkyūjo*), which is located in Mishima, were included in city-sponsored investigatory activities, allowing the city to challenge the statements of prefectural and company officials from a technical standpoint. In the second phase of the movement, a committee appointed by Mayor Hasegawa and headed by the director of the Institute studied the *konbināto* problem and successfully challenged a similar research group that the Ministry of International Trade and Industry had established.[30] Further, the Citizen Council, aided by the

[28] One has the feeling that the Chamber of Commerce tour to Goi in Chiba prefecture had a fundamental impact on the movement as a whole, as the leadership structure of the Chamber of Commerce was partially interlocked with the top leadership strata of the local branch of the LDP. Regardless, the Chamber Committee, headed by an LDP branch member, concluded as early as February 29 that it could not support the luring of a *konbināto* to Mishima on the basis of its inspection trip discoveries. "Touring" was used by proponents as well as opponents, but if the local news accounts are correct, as a way of paying off individuals rather than for informational purposes. Whereas opponent's trips were paid for individually, the *konbināto* companies and the LDP are said to have foot the bill for the much more lavish trips taken by proponents, largely LDP branch members and "pro-*konbināto* faction" (*sanseiha*) individuals in the Nakazato area. See *Mishima Minpō*, nos. 994-1011, February-March 1964, passim.

[29] Mishima's openness to this type of aid may have resulted from the presence in the city of a university campus and the National Genetics Research Institute, from the influence on Mishima Citizen Council of "elder statesman" Koide Shigō who is well-connected in national academic as well as literary circles, from the presence of a number of other university-educated individuals among influentials in the Citizen Council, and from the mayor's own high level of education. Such expertise had previously been used during the Toyo Rayon problem.

[30] See Hoshino et al., "Numazu, Mishima, Shimizu," pp. 143-155.

science teachers from Numazu Technical High School who were also involved in the Numazu opposition movement, gathered data and audio-visual materials and carried out an intensive educational campaign throughout this period primarily through the neighborhood associations. The coordination of this campaign, in fact, may have been the Citizen Council's most important initiative during this period.

Second Phase (March 1964-June 1964): Opposition, Protest, Pressure

In early March, the character of the movement changed dramatically towards straightforward opposition to the *konbināto* and actions designed to block its construction. As a local journalist noted, "In the last few days since March 10th, the strength of opposition towards the proposal for a petrochemical complex has completely changed, growing much stronger."[31] By this time, the Mishima Citizen Council had come out explicitly against construction, the Chamber of Commerce had reversed itself to vote unanimously against the plan, and Nakazato residents had changed their initial study group into a Nakazato League for Opposition to the Petrochemical Complex.

Mishima's protest movement was carried out as much by established organizations as by the Mishima Citizen Council. In Nakazato, the new Nakazato opposition group was organized by residents. Outside of Nakazato, partly due to the progressive parties' decision to keep a low profile by working through the Citizen Council, the main vehicles of opposition were the Federation of Neighborhood Association Chairmen, the Federation of Women's Associations, and the Citizen Council. A survey by this author wherein movement activists were asked to list organizations that had contributed to the opposition victory found that the following were seen as the most influential: Nakazato residents' groups (25 percent of the total responses), the Mishima Citizen Council (16 percent), neighborhood associations and the Federation of Neighborhood Association Chairmen (16 percent), and women's associations and the Federation of Women's Associations (12 percent).[32] The progressive parties received fewer mentions.

Protest was aimed at two targets, and different tactics were utilized

---

[31] *Mishima Minpō*, no. 1002, 15 March 1964.

[32] For further information on this survey, see Lewis, *Dissertation*, pp. 124-143. Respondents were allowed multiple responses (total responses = 147). There were no significant differences in the first four ratings between conservative and progressive activists. Also listed were unions (10 percent), the JSP (9 percent), the National Genetics Research Institute (5 percent), *Kinrōkyō* (a nonparty "workers" support group organized by Socialist leader Sakai Ikuzō—3 percent), the JCP (2 percent), and the Chamber of Commerce (5 percent).

in each case. First, movement tactics were shaped to influence the outside world that had brought the problem to Mishima. The targets here were the *konbināto* firms (especially Fuji Petroleum) and government officials (Governor Saitō and central government decision makers, especially the ministers and bureaucrats in MITI and the Health and Welfare Ministry). In this case the dominant tactic might be called *supplicant petitioning*—leaders of the Citizen Council, neighborhood associations, and women's organizations traveled to Shimoda City and Tokyo for rather ritualized presentations of petitions and reports on local conditions to officials.

The second target was local government. Here, the movement sought to pressure Mayor Hasegawa and the city assembly to formally oppose the *konbināto*. Hasegawa found himself in a difficult position. On the one hand, his election in 1961 had depended on the same individuals who formed the early core of the opposition movement. To wait too long to announce his position on the plan would seriously hurt his prospects for reelection in 1965. On the other hand, the mayor was under tremendous pressure from the prefectural and national governments and his friends and enemies in the LDP.[33] In the face of this pressure, on May 23, Hasegawa followed the dictates of both political expediency and personal conviction and announced his opposition to the *konbināto* before a rally of 1,500 residents and the national media.

A much more difficult task was to break the will of *konbināto* proponents in the Mishima City Assembly. When the spring meeting of the assembly convened on March 18, all seventeen members of the May Association, an assembly block tied to the local LDP branch, still supported the complex. As long as this majority group stood firm, proponents of construction could claim that the assembly, not the citizens' movement, was the true expression of residents' feelings on the issue. The movement moved to change these votes. Its tactics differed considerably from those used against the outside targets, as they now resorted to aggressive pressure and protest activities. Farmers, unionists, women, and neighborhood association leaders engaged in heckling from the assembly gallery, badgered and physically confronted May Association members in the hallways of City Hall, and cooperated in a variety of pressure tactics—mass meetings, parades, recall movement

[33] Hasegawa had, in fact, acted as the official election representative for Governor Saitō in 1959. He also faced significant administrative and political sanctions in deciding to support the opposition movement. These worries are reflected in his statement to city employees on May 27 that they should not worry as he had full hopes that the prefectural government would approve all of the upcoming city budget. However, in mid-1964, the prefectural government declared Mishima to be insolvent and put its budget under prefectural supervision.

planning sessions, signature drives, fund drives, private contacting, and the like.

May Association members found allies against this onslaught in members of the local LDP branch, their LDP-affiliated prefectural assemblyman, Governor Saitō, Endō Saburō, the national government, and the *konbināto* companies (which were rumored to be materially enriching those taking the "correct" position). Local LDP officials had always stressed that the city's economic health depended on keeping an open "pipeline to the center"—in other words, on consistent LDP dominance from the local government up to the national government so that Mishima could reap the benefits of national economic planning and *largesse*. Association assemblymen maintained this stand despite mounting opposition until June 8. Then, even they capitulated to the movement, as May Association's representatives joined other members on a special assembly *konbināto* investigatory committee in sending a draft resolution of opposition to construction to the assembly floor. This resolution passed the full assembly on June 18. On June 25, Fuji Petroleum's managing director informed Hasegawa that his firm would not build in Mishima. On August 3, Fuji announced plans to construct its plant on a nearby site in Numazu. But in Mishima, at least, the movement had finally succeeded.

CHARACTERISTICS OF CITIZENS' MOVEMENTS

The most important objective of this study is to use the Mishima case to assess the adequacy of present understandings of the nature of citizens' movements. One category of generalizations about these movements concerns the social backgrounds of the participants and leaders of the movements, on the one hand, and their political backgrounds, on the other. The primary contention of these generalizations is that such movements reflect generalized discontent in local society and that participation in them is not limited to specific social strata or types of individuals already active in Japanese conventional politics or political protest. On the contrary, participants in citizens' movements are said to be "ordinary citizens" or "middle Japanese," and their mobilization is said to constitute a belated explosion of mass participation in Japanese democracy. Thus, in the case of the social backgrounds of movement participants, this means that women as well as men are said to participate actively, that middle or older aged citizens become mobilized (not just young radicals), that the level of educational achievement of participants is similar to the Japanese population in general (that is, these are not movements of college students and intellectuals), and that middle-class individuals, especially the new middle class of white-collar workers and professionals, often participate.[34]

Another aspect of this description relates to movement participants' prior political participation. Citizens' movements are usually portrayed as spontaneous, grass-roots eruptions of previously passive, politically uninvolved residents. Such movements are said to mobilize various strata that have heretofore been peripheral to the process of political demand making in Japanese politics. Furthermore, the movement initiators are "ordinary" local residents threatened by pollution rather than perennial political participants from the left-leaning strata, for example, students, intellectuals, or labor union activists. There is less discussion in the movement literature on the backgrounds of movement leaders. Some authorities, in fact, have stressed the "mass" or "democratic" character of these movements, by which they mean that they tend to lack hierarchy and, by inference, leaders. Residents are seen as directing these "ad hoc, transitory" organizations by their own unskilled hands.

Discussion of the nature of movement organizations is important, as it is often assumed that inclusion in a movement organization is a critical adult socialization experience through which participants learn participatory orientations and democratic decision-making patterns. Generalizations on this subject relate to the nature of movement members' linkage to movement structures, the character of the structures, and modes of decision making. First, movement structures are said to be formed by "individuals" participating voluntarily. Movement participants are issue-oriented and have common objectives. They are public-regarding and thus do not join as a result of preestablished diffuse or traditional relationships with community influentials.[35] Citizen movements are rarely pictured as coalitions of preexistent groups because the building blocks of these movements are individuals. Second, the structure of movement organizations is said to be different from other Japanese organizations: they are less hierarchical and less inclined to

---

[34] See, for example, Margaret McKean, "Urbanization and Citizens' Movements," paper presented at the 1975 Association for Asian Studies meeting, p. 1, and Taketsugu Tsurutani, "A New Era of Japanese Politics: Tokyo's Gubernatorial Elections," *Asian Survey* 12 (1972): 433. The argument that citizens' movements reflect a flowering of mass participation and civic consciousness in Japan is made, among others, by Ishida, *Japanese Society*, p. 60.

[35] McKean, "Urbanization and Citizens' Movements," pp. 3-6, sees differences in factors motivating participation according to the site of the movement. Her feeling is that the more rural the movement, the more the movement activist becomes involved because of private or collectivity-regarding motives (self-preservation/personal health, community health, threat to the agrarian way of life), while the more urban the movement, the more the activist responds because of threat to his general political rights.

formalize an internal authority stratification system.[36] A final, related contention is that movements employ more "democratic" modes of decision making than is normally the case in Japan. Here democratic decision making is usually equated with lack of hierarchical structure, full and open discussion of the issues before decisions are made, and decisions by consensus.[37]

The literature generally fails to describe the relationship between citizens' movements and the dynamics of conventional politics and to pay sufficient attention to the impact of movements on local politics. The descriptions of the link between movements and established factors in local politics that exist, most of which relate to the citizens' movement-progressive party relationship, are contradictory. One contention is that citizens' movements have developed as a result of the paralysis of established political parties.[38] Movements are said to supplant or by-pass established political forces and may become involved in electoral politics to achieve their ends. Other accounts suggest that the relationship is much more complex, with movements accepting the aid of local branches of the opposition political parties and of labor unions while striving to maintain political neutrality and continuing to be wary of dominance by leftist groups.[39] Finally, as movements are said to activate large numbers of new participants into political participation, it is usually assumed that conventional politics in the future will be affected: we can expect "civic" politics from this new generation of the active, participant, public-regarding middle-class that are free of the taint of association with the older generation of politicians and established parties.

[36] Ui Jun succinctly summarizes some of these points: "The fifth principle is that an organization based on concentration of power at the center is generally not only useless in solving pollution problems, but is often a stumbling block when viewed over the long run. When we analyze the movements against pollution which have succeeded in the past, we find that every one of them was the result of each participating individual giving the fullest play on a voluntary basis to his own creativity." See his "The Singularities of Japanese Pollution," *Japan Quarterly* 19 (1972): 287.

[37] For an excellent discussion of the meaning of democracy in Japan, see Joseph Massey, *Youth and Politics in Japan* (Lexington, Mass.: Lexington Books, 1976), pp. 51-64.

[38] As Tsurutani says, "In short, the existing political parties, and the political process they partake of, have proven incapable of providing meaningful measures and needed leadership for tackling the fast worsening problems of a virtually post-industrial society." See his "A New Era of Japanese Politics," p. 431.

[39] Margaret McKean, "The Potential Political Impact of the Japanese Environmental Movement," paper presented at the Center for Japanese and Korean Studies, University of California at Berkeley (June 1974), pp. 7-8.

Participants and Leaders

How well do these generalizations square with my findings on the Mishima movement? While there are some important similarities, there are also important discrepancies between the social and political background "model" just described and the Mishima case. It is possible to identify at least four levels of movement involvement in Mishima: movement sympathizers, mass action participants, movement activists, and movement leaders. While sympathy with the opposition movement came to be extremely widespread—82 percent of the residents surveyed in early March by the women's associations and the neighborhood associations indicated opposition to the *konbināto*—the proportion of residents actively taking part in mass pressure activity at any time throughout the movement probably constituted less than 10 percent of the city's adult population. For example, the largest gathering of movement participants, a rally in the Mishima Civic Auditorium, is said to have been attended by 2,000 people, about 4 percent of the adult population. Although this puts the absolute size of the Mishima mobilization into some perspective, it is important to recognize that this is still a higher level of active mass involvement in politics than is normally found in democratic systems.[40] Unfortunately, data that would allow analysis of the backgrounds of these "mass action participants" is not available. However, by extrapolating from the fact that this and other large opposition rallies were sponsored in part or wholly by the neighborhood and women's associations, we can assume that these participants came from both sexes, that they represented all areas of the city, and that many had been involved in social and civic activities of established community organizations prior to the opposition movement.

More is known about the two remaining strata of movement participants, "movement activists" who participated regularly in the day-to-day *konbināto* opposition activities and top "movement leaders." In 1971, I surveyed the one hundred fifteen members of the Mishima Improvement Association (*Mishima o Yokusuru Kai*), an organization that evolved directly from the Mishima Citizen Council in October 1964. Seventy-five of the eighty respondents claimed to have opposed the *konbināto*, and fifty-five indicated that they had "positively participated in the movement." What were the backgrounds of these fifty-five movement activists? Were they "ordinary citizens" or "middle

[40] See Lester W. Milbrath, *Political Participation* (Chicago: Rand McNally, 1971), pp. 16-22, and Sidney Verba and Norman H. Nie, *Participation in America: Political Democracy and Social Equality* (New York: Harper & Row, 1972), pp. 25-32.

Japanese"? Were they new initiates into political participation? My findings indicate that, on the whole, Mishima activists came from a rather broad cross-section of social backgrounds but that they were a rather unrepresentative group in terms of their level of organization or political participation in local society prior to the opposition movement.

More specifically, it is possible to say that this movement was a city-wide effort, as the residences of these activists closely mirrored the distribution of the city's population during that period.[41] Furthermore, the movement was not dominated by workers, students, intellectuals, or other groups often associated with protest activities in Japan. Activists came from a wide spectrum of occupations. Over half can be said to have been "middle Japanese" in the sense that 52 percent held white-collar occupations. Another 38 percent were farmers or blue-collar workers.[42] The education and age data also seems to be supportive, in general, of the "ordinary citizen" model. While activists were somewhat more educated than the Japanese population as a whole, all levels of education were represented, and university graduates (24 percent) were not heavily overrepresented.[43] Young people were clearly not overrepresented, as only 6 percent of these activists were under thirty-two years old at the time of the movement. Two-thirds of the activists were between thirty-three and fifty-two years old at the time, in other words, they were middle-aged Japanese. The most important discrepancy between the social-background-related generalizations and this case regards participants' sex. Specifically, only eight of these fifty-five activists were female, indicating that most women participated in

[41] Movement activists resided in Mishima's downtown area (66 percent), Nakazato (20 percent), Nishikida (9 percent), and Kitaue (6 percent). The city population distribution for the same period was: the downtown area (61 percent), Nakazato (14 percent), Nishikida and Kitaue (12 percent each). There is indirect evidence that the underrepresentation of Nishikida and Kitaue may reflect private or collectivity-regardingness (that is, a "rural localism" hypothesis) in these two semirural parts of Mishima where the personal interests of the inhabitants were not directly threatened. While 80 percent of the Nakazato area respondents and 78 percent of the inner-city respondents actively opposed the *konbināto*, only 47 percent of the Nishidida and Nakazato respondents actively opposed the *konbināto*. While 80 percent of the Nakazato farmers opposed actively, only 46 percent of the Nishikada and Kitaue farmers did so.

[42] Twenty-nine percent held managerial positions in private or public enterprises, 27 percent were farmers, 16 percent were professionals, 11 percent were blue-collar workers, 9 percent were housewives, and 7 percent held sales positions.

[43] Seventy-two percent had graduated from junior or senior high school and 24 percent from a university.

the Mishima movement indirectly through women's associations, neighborhood associations, or other such established organizations.[44] The eight female activists all held leadership positions in local women's organizations.

The most striking discrepancies between the backgrounds of the Mishima activists and the preceding generalizations relate to their prior organizational and political activities. It is clear that Mishima movement activists were not initiated into civic activism or local politics as a result of the antipetrochemical complex movement. Eighty percent of these activists were serving as leaders of established local organizations— neighborhood associations, women's groups, PTA, unions, the Chamber of Commerce—at the time of the movement.[45] Furthermore, many of these activists had participated in prior citizen protest activities, and most were well acquainted with partisan political activties, having actively campaigned in local or other levels of elections prior to the anti-*konbināto* movement.[46]

Some accounts of citizens' movements stress their lack of hierarchy, their spontaneity, and their antileadership orientation. In retrospect, it is clear that the Mishima movement had leaders, although in the fol-

[44] Mishima natives or long-time residents are also overrepresented in this group of activists. Fully 64 percent of the activists were born in Mishima, while another 26 percent were born nearby somewhere in eastern Shizuoka. Only three of the fifty-five activists had lived in Mishima less than twelve years, while 54 percent had lived in the city from thirteen to forty-two years and 40 percent for more than forty-three years. These data indirectly support the contention of some chroniclers of the Mishima movement that leaders of the movement were motivated by a fundamentally conservative instinct to keep the city from change, either in regards to its natural beauty or its perceived place as a regional *bunka toshi* (cultural city) rather than a commercial or industrial center.

[45] Fifty-one percent were officers in one organization, 16 percent in two, and 13 percent in three or more organizations. Twenty of the fifty-five activists held leadership positions in neighborhood associations in the Federation of Women's Associations. Others included: Worker's Association (*Kinrōkyō*)-8; labor unions-7; Chamber of Commerce-4; PTA-3; and many miscellaneous others.

[46] Movement activists were *politically experienced*. Thirty-five percent reported being members of the *Aishi Renmei*, the progressive-conservative electoral coalition in 1957 and 1961. Forty-two percent were members of the *Mishima Yosui o Mamoru Kai*, an organization formed to protest Toyo Rayon's overuse of the underground water supply. These activists evidence a long history of involvement in local progressive and conservative causes. In 1953, of the 41 respondents answering the question, 68 percent indicated actively campaigning for or otherwise aiding a mayoral candidate and specified the candidate for whom they had worked. In 1957, 41 of 48 (85 percent) indicated the same. Ninety-four percent of the 54 respondents answering the question indicated the same for the 1963 Prefectural Assembly election and 70 percent indicated they had supported Socialist Sakai Ikuzō.

lowing pages I suggest that the leaders of the Mishima movement were especially sensitive to questions of consensus and accountability. Although the Citizen Council avoided appointing individuals to the customary formal leadership positions found in most Japanese groups, there were movement leaders in Mishima in two senses. There were *positional* leaders in the prior established organizations that participated in the Council: the Federation of Neighborhood Association Chairmen, the Federation of Women's Associations, the Nakazato Area League for Opposition to the Petrochemical Complex, the Nakazato Area Alliance Against the Sale of Farmland, the local Sohyō-affiliated union federation, and the Socialists all had formal leadership structures. The movement also had *reputational* leaders. Survey respondents were asked if they could name individuals who had exercised a special amount of influence in bringing about an end to the petrochemical complex plan,[47] and there is a high level of coincidence between these evaluations and positional leaders in the movement.

Who were these reputational leaders? Do their backgrounds deviate from that of most Japanese? Analysis shows that the occupational and educational backgrounds of these thirteen individuals were distinctly higher than most Japanese. Movement leaders either owned their own business, had extensive agricultural holdings, or were intellectuals of national stature.[48] Over half were graduates of a university or higher technical school. Their average age was over forty-nine. Further, like movement activists, movement leaders had been deeply involved in local associational life, most holding a top leadership post in at least one organization and in local politics prior to the movement.[49] Five of these thirteen individuals had held or were holding local elective positions;

[47] Respondents had an opportunity to name up to five individuals. Altogether, thirty-one individuals were named at least once. For this analysis, a cutoff point of three mentions by the eighty respondents was used to ensure that as broad as possible a picture of movement leaders is presented. One individual (JSP Chairman Sakai Ikuzō) was named more than thirty times, two individuals (Mayor Hasegawa and Koide Shōgō, former mayoral candidate of the *Aishi Renmei*) were named more than twenty times, and two were named more than ten times.

[48] Six of thirteen owned their own businesses, and two were farmers with considerable land holdings.

[49] Among the organizational positions there were: two vice chairmen of high-school alumni associations, present and past chairmen of the Mishima Youth Association, chairman of the Mishima Furniture Sales Association, chairman of the Mishima Christian Association, national chairman of the Japan Association of Juvenile Literature Authors, two officers in agricultural cooperatives, at least three Neighborhood Association chairmen, chairman of the Mishima Federation of Labor Unions, chairman of the Mishima Federation of Women's Associations, chairman of a PTA, and others.

three were party or party faction leaders; only two had not been active in partisan political battles in the city.[50]

Organizations

In what manner did Mishima residents organize to combat the petro-chemical complex plan? How was the citizens' movement structured? How did citizens make collective decisions for action against the complex? First, it should be stressed that the residents' actions were not encompassed or orchestrated by a single organization. The movement consisted of individuals *and* organizations. Movement organization evolved over time. Eventually, an umbrella coalition mechanism was established to coordinate the activities of various organizations in the city, yet it was not a highly formalized organization, and it lacked strong sanctions over its constituent groups. Furthermore, the organizations that were represented in its activities differed in structure, in their initial functions in the community, and in their level of involvement in the opposition movement.

The development of the Citizen Consultation Committee into the Mishima Citizen Council was paralleled by changes in organizational role and participation. The Consultation Committee was organized as a study group, and its members participated as individuals rather than as official organizational representatives, even though most were active in the JSP, the JCP, the local union movement, or other local associational activities. In part, the Consultation Committee focused on study activities and minimized the role of established local organizations to overcome fears that it would be seen as a front for the progressive parties and thus not be able to attract broadly-based participation.

On January 25, the Consultation Committee was disbanded in favor of a new organization, the Mishima Citizen Council. The Council increasingly developed into a decision-making forum and movement coordinating mechanism for a wide variety of local organizations that were moving towards formally opposing *konbināto* construction.[51] At

---

[50] Four usually supported Socialists in national electoral politics, two supported Communists, and five supported the LDP (two unclear). In local politics, seven of thirteen had been active in the *Aishi Renmei*, which had supported Koide in 1957 and Hasegawa in 1961. Six had actively campaigned for Koide in 1957, while three others had actively supported a conservative candidate (one had not campaigned; there was no data on three).

[51] The most important tasks performed by the Citizen Council during the movement were to organize meetings to bring together organizational representatives and concerned activists, to provide a place (the Council secretariat) where information on the activities of movement groups could be collected, to assist in the

the same time, even though the meetings of the Citizen Council were open to anyone in the city, its business was increasingly dominated by representatives of these local organizations acting in their official capacities. The March 6 meeting of the Citizen Council, for example, was attended by approximately forty of the city's one hundred neighborhood association chairmen, fifty other officers of local organizations, and thirty citizens participating as individuals. These individuals represented the following organizations, among others, that were active in the Council at some point during the movement:

Federation of Neighborhood Association Chairmen
Federation of Women's Associations
Nakazato Area League for Opposition to the Petrochemical Complex
Nakazato Alliance Against the Sale of Farmland
Mishima Area Trade Unions (Sōhyō affiliated unions)
Nakazato Youth Association
Mishima Federation of Youth Associations
Japan Socialist Party-Mishima Branch
Nōheibushi Promotion Society
Worker's Association
Japan Communist Party
Mishima Federation of Children's Groups
National Genetics Research Institute
Mishima Chamber of Commerce
Mishima Cultural Association

On March 6, the Council considered the matter of its internal structure for the last time. A suggestion that a chairman and other officers be selected was turned down on the suggestion of Socialist leader Sakai Ikuzō and the mutual agreement of those present. Thereafter, Council meeting agendas were drawn up by the Council staff and decisions were arrived at through a process of discussion and consensual agree-

---

coordination of joint actions by constituent organizations, to organize explanation and study sessions (*gakushūkai*) between residents' groups and the Citizen Council's environmental pollution explanation team (which included science teachers from Numazu Technical High School), and to coordinate Citizen Council activities with the activities of similar organizations in Numazu and Shimizu. Although such services were provided by the Citizen Council, in many cases affiliated organizations cooperated in movement activities without the active intercession of the Council or its secretariat. Many movement activities were organized by officials of Federation of Neighborhood Association Chairmen and the Federation of Women's Organizations who, in turn, kept the Citizen Council secretariat informed.

ment of those in attendance. The Council administered its activities collectively. At first, three individuals, who had been chosen to balance the secretariat politically shared responsibility without compensation. They included a union federation leader, an *Aishi Renmei* activist with political connections to both the JCP and local antimainstream conservatives, and a former youth association leader close to Mayor Hasegawa. By mid-February, the latter individual took up full-time duties in the Citizen Council office, yet he continued to be aided by others in the secretariat.

Thus, there were two general types of linkage between residents and the Mishima Citizen Council and two types of organizations represented in its deliberations. Some individuals were linked *directly* to the Council through their participation in its planning sessions as official representatives of organizations, as autonomous individuals, or as a result of their position of prominence in some organization (for example, neighborhood associations). Yet, most movement participants were linked to the Citizen Council *indirectly*, never personally participating in its meetings; they were mobilized into movement activities by leaders of the established local organizations who were active in Citizen Council affairs. It is also clear that two types of organizations took part in Citizen Council activities: preexistent social, economic, or political organizations and new, ad hoc, residentially-based movement groups (for example, the two Nakazato area protest groups). As compared to the Citizen Council, neither type of participating organization evidenced particularly innovative structural characteristics. Both types had formalized, differentiated leadership structures that sometimes met in executive session to make decisions for their members. It is interesting that both of the new Nakazato movement organizations quickly developed a system of officers (chairman, multiple vice-chairmen, secretary, treasurer, and representatives [*yakuin*] for each of the fifteen Nakazato neighborhoods) that closely resembled the pattern of organization of long-established local organizations.

Modes of decision making in the constituent organizations of the Citizen Council approximated those utilized prior to the movement. The more ad hoc Nakazato movement organizations reached decisions after thorough discussion on the basis of consensus, although status differences and differences resulting from these organizations' decision to select a formal hierarchy of officers affected the degree to which influence was distributed equally. Decision making in the Citizen Council was more "open" than in its constituent parts. Meetings were chaired by one of the three members of the organization's staff. Otherwise, the 60-120 participants in these meetings technically had equal status in its deliberations. There is some indication, however, that participants who represented important local organizations carried more weight in deliberations than others. Decisions were made by open and lengthy debate among those participants until consent or recognition of consent was achieved.

In some settings, this kind of procedure could have lent itself to manipulation by a strident minority or by those to whom others deferred. However, participants in the Council were highly experienced in public settings, representing widely divergent interests and willing to defend their preferences. Thus, while the Council's meetings lasted as long as six hours, decisions genuinely appear to have been arrived at through compromise and "unanimity." Sakai Ikuzō's suggestion on March 6, which was accepted by members of the Citizen Council, most adequately reflects its procedures:

> When the Council was established, it was put together by interested citizens (*shimin yūshi*) independently (*jishuteki ni*) on a supra-partisan (*chōtōha*) basis. Now, interested neighborhood association chairmen, members of women's associations and youth groups, etc., and representatives of the Culture Association and the Mishima Area Trade Unions, etc. participate. Let's continue by a process of mutual consent (*kyōgisei de*) without having a chairman or group representatives (*daihyosha*). We can consider the problem of officers (*yakuin kōsei*) in the future.[52]

Parties and Politicians

The citizens' movement literature tends to picture movement participants as political amateurs and often suggests that such movements represent a threat to established parties and politicians in the local arena. The Mishima case suggests that this type of generalization is deficient in a number of respects. From its earliest stages, the Mishima movement was thoroughly interrelated with established political forces at both the individual and organizational levels. In retrospect, it is clear that divisions between early opponents and proponents of a petrochemical complex significantly paralleled partisan divisions in the mayoral election of 1961. Local Sōhyō-affiliated unions and unionists, the JSP and its members, the JCP and its members, a few important unaffiliated progressives and Hasegawa-faction conservatives were responsible, along with some others, for the initiation of the movement and its early development. Although fear existed among both conservatives and progressives that

[52] *Mishima Minpō*, no. 1001, 10 March 1964.

the movement would be accused of being a leftist front, it should be stressed that Mishima's outstanding progressive activists were an integral part of the movement from its earliest stages.[53] On the opposing side, support for the complex came most significantly from the LDP and those individuals who worked for Mayor Matsuda in the 1961 election. As the potential dangers of a Mishima *konbināto* became more apparent, however, LDP branch activists became increasingly isolated by their backing of the project, and support patterns in the 1961 mayoral election became an increasingly weak indicator of citizens' movement activism.

In Mishima, progressive forces had long been inclined towards moderate tactics when they helped build a broader-based coalition of citizens. Both the Consultation Committee and the Citizen Council took pains to ensure that they be seen as an independent citizens' organization rather than an alliance of established progressive parties and unions, and the progressives flexibly adapted to this policy. A critical point in the movement regarding this problem came in early January when Koide Shōgō, Mishima's independent progressive elder statesman, met with his close friend Sakai, other JSP leaders, and union officials to secure a promise that the JSP would not inject itself divisively into the activities of the movement.[54]

There was a significant overlap in personnel between Citizen Council activists and conservatives who had supported Hasegawa against the LDP incumbent in 1961 as well. Especially in the earliest stages of the movement, those conservatives who worked aggressively to further the movement—neighborhood association chairmen, former youth group leaders, women—had also supported Hasegawa and Sakai in 1961 and 1963. Some Hasegawa conservatives, of course, did not participate in these early stages. Yet, after early March, these individuals and many others who had previously been close to the mainstream LDP faction became active in the Citizen Council. Thus, the movement became

---

[53] Part of the explanation for the ease of interaction across partisan lines in Mishima relates to the fact that JSP and JCP leaders are not outsiders but long-time residents who are significantly integrated into the community. Sakai, for example, is said to receive as much support from conservative partisans in his inner-city district and from his high-school cohorts as from progressives. JSP city assemblymen and union leaders play leadership roles in the city's PTA's, neighborhood associations, sports organizations, etc. One Socialist assemblyman who led the Congress of Mishima Area Labor Unions at the time of the *konbināto* protest, for example, also served as a neighborhood association chairman and a PTA vice-chairman. Furthermore, he is the brother of the wife of the conservative mayor who was defeated by LDP branch leader Matsuda in 1953.

[54] Interview with meeting participant, 5 April 1971.

increasingly *cross-partisan* as it proceeded. Movement leaders, on the other hand, would suggest that it is more appropriate to say that the movement was nonpartisan throughout and merely became increasingly inclusive. In either case, many movement activists were hardly amateurs, and established local politicians and political groupings played an important—and increasingly larger—role in movement activities.

The Impact of the Movement on Local Politics

What impact did the movement have on Mishima politics? Although this type of question is difficult to answer with complete certainty, a number of observations can be ventured with confidence as to the impact of the citizens' movement on local politics in Mishima. It is clear, for example, that the defeat of the complex plan led to intensified conflict between the Hasegawa administration and the LDP. Tension between Hasegawa and the local LDP branch had arisen as early as 1957, during the Matsuda administration. With the failure of Mishima's city government to support the plan, however, Hasegawa became the target of LDP wrath from the local to the national level. The attack on the Hasegawa administration was manifested in a variety of ways. For example, on 24 May 1964, only one day after the mayor had formally announced his opposition to the plan, officials from the prefecture's Local Affairs Bureau visited the Mishima City Hall for a three-day inspection of local finances.[55] In August of the same year, after Fuji Petroleum had announced its withdrawal from Mishima, prefectural officials publicly announced that they were preparing a more thorough study of the city's finances, hinting that they had found some potential irregularities in the manner that the city had borrowed money. In the newspapers this story was headlined, "Mishima's Unsound Local Finances."[56] These inspections were preliminary steps to declaring Mishima's local government financially insolvent and therefore subject to direct budgetary supervision by prefectural officials. While the inspections never resulted in these measures, it is a reasonable interpretation of these prefectural actions that the threat of supervision was a sanction against the city for its position during the opposition movement struggle and that the prefectural LDP was developing an issue that could be used in the forthcoming mayoral election.[57] In addi-

[55] *Mishima Minpō*, no. 1035, 30 August 1964.
[56] "Fukenzen no Mishima no zaisei," in Ibid.
[57] In fact, Mishima was in debt in 1964 as is not unusual for Japanese cities, yet in less debt in 1964 than during the administration of the previous LDP-backed mayor. From 1960, the last year of the Matsuda administration, to 1964, the city's debt as a proportion of its income dropped from 23 to 14 percent. See Ibid.

tion to the prefectural government's sudden interest in Mishima's local finances, throughout the fall of 1964 Governor Saitō became much more deeply involved than usual in the local LDP branch's preparations for this election, pressuring the reluctant former incumbent mayor to again enter the mayoral race against Hasegawa.

On the other hand, the citizens' movement clearly strengthened Hasegawa's electoral support base and the progressive orientation of the Hasegawa administration. First, the JSP and JCP felt much more confident in their 1961 decision to support a mayoral candidate from outside their ranks. One participant observer has noted, for example, that the joint involvement of Hasegawa-faction conservatives and progressives in the opposition movement heightened trust between these individuals and for the first time provided an opportunity for their mutual discussion of Mishima's future.[58] Furthermore, as a result of their participation in the movement alongside conservatives and progressives who had supported Hasegawa in the 1961 election, a number of important leaders of predominantly conservative local organizations in the city (neighborhood associations, women's associations, cultural groups) came for the first time to actively support the Hasegawa administration. They were among the conservatives who worked for Hasegawa in the 1965 mayoral elections and who thereafter organized the mayor's personal, predominantly conservative electoral support group, the *Taizōkai*. Finally, after the *konbināto* victory, Hasegawa increasingly committed himself to the role of a progressive mayor. He was one of the earliest mayors to join the newly established National Association of Progressive Mayors (*Zenkoku Kakushin Shichōkai*) and came increasingly to support the policies recommended by this organization. By 1965 or thereabouts, while the politically knowledgeable among Mishima's oldtimers remembered Hasegawa's conservative origins, the average citizen (and outsiders, such as national level newspapermen or scholars) identified the mayor with the defeat of the *konbināto* and with *kakushin shisei* (progressive local government).

The battle lines were thus clearly drawn for the January 1965 mayoral election in which Hasegawa faced Matsuda for the second time. Hasegawa had been a surprise victor in the previous election, the lowest mayoral election turnout in the city's history, attesting to the LDP branch's lack of concern about his candidacy at that time. This election was different in tone, if not in result: after a vicious campaign in which the LDP attacked Hasegawa on three fronts (the *konbināto* defeat, financial irresponsibility, the red scare), the mayor was again

[58] Tsuchiya, *Jūmin undō to hōshi*, p. 44.

elected by a small margin. Thereafter, Matsuda retired from active public involvement, and, Hasegawa, again supported by his conservative-progressive electoral coalition, twice defeated other LDP-affiliated mayoral candidates by larger margins.

The Hasegawa administration lasted for sixteen years. Yet, over such an extended period of time new problems arise and accomplishments fade in the memories of older generations and are unknown to younger generations. In December 1976, the mayor, having failed to receive the support of the Socialist Party for a fifth term, announced that he would retire (at the age of fifty-three). In January 1977, amid local progressive and Hasegawa-faction conservative confusion and lack of cooperation—three candidates including the JSP chairman, a Hasegawa-faction city assemblyman, and a LDP branch candidate entered the election—the LDP again secured the mayor's office.

Regardless of these recent events in Mishima, it is clear that the *konbināto* conflict contributed to the deterioration of the position of the LDP in the city. Mishima was without an LDP-affiliated mayor for sixteen years. The dramatic drop in the strength of the LDP city assembly group can also be attributed in part to the anticomplex struggle. It went from eighteen members in 1964 to nine in 1967 and then to five in 1971. By contrast, by the late 1960s, Mayor Hasegawa had managed to construct an assembly majority coalition consisting of ten' mayor-faction conservatives and eight opposition party assemblymen.

My survey of anticomplex movement activists further supports the argument that movement involvement affected the electoral support patterns in the city. As already noted, these data show that a number of conservative organizational leaders switched their support from the LDP candidate in 1961 to Hasegawa in 1965. It also shows that conservative movement participants also came to support Socialist Sakai Ikuzō in prefectural assembly elections after the movement. Forty percent of these movement conservatives report actively supporting Sakai in his first successful campaign in 1963. In 1967, after the movement victory, 62 percent say that thoy worked in the Sakai campaign. Although in 1971 the level of support dropped below the 1967 level (an antimainstream conservative had independently entered the race), Hasegawa and his closest conservative supporters continued to campaign for Sakai.

The movement also led to the formation of a permanent "citizens' movement" organization in the city. When the defeat of the *konbināto* seemed assured, movement leaders decided that some type of organization should continue to study local policy problems and to recommend directions for the city's future development. Thus, the Mishima Improvement Association (*Mishima o Yokusuru Kai*) was established and continues to exist to this day, even after the problems of the 1977 mayoral election.[59] This organization has met regularly each year since 1964, and it has conducted numerous special study sessions as problems have arisen in the city. Its chairman is the same intellectual, former independent progressive mayoral candidate who urged the local progressive party branches to support Hasegawa for mayor in 1961. The chairman of the Federation of Neighborhood Association Chairmen, the chairwoman of the Federation of Women's Associations, and the chairman of the Congress of Mishima Area Labor Unions (that is, *Sōhyō*-related local unions) have each always held one of the three positions as vice-chairman. The executive secretary of the Association is the same person who during the movement served as the full-time staff member of the Mishima Citizen Council and who continues as Hasegawa's main political confidant. The Mishima Improvement Association opens its door to all Mishima citizens and is officially nonpartisan, yet its purpose has always been to further progressive or, from the perspective of its leaders, citizen-oriented policies in Mishima. Its importance in Mishima since 1964 has been felt in many ways, including its contribution to conservative-progressive coalition maintenance, its role in mayoral elections, its push for the early development of a master plan to guide the city's future growth from the mid-1960s, and its central role in a number of more recent "movements" related to local development and pollution problems.

CONCLUSION

The Mishima citizens' movement provides an excellent opportunity to assess the adequacy of our current understanding of citizens' movements. How well do the generalizations stand up against this test? First, it is clear that the movement reached occupational strata not generally associated with protest activities in Japan. Activists came from a variety of occupations. A majority can be classified as middle class (managers, professionals, salesmen), while others were farmers or unionists. However, while it is often said that the most important long-term effect of movements on the future of Japanese politics is the initiation of new participants into politics, Mishima movement activists were not new initiates into associational or political activity. Furthermore, the most influential individuals in the movement were not only politically experienced but also more active in associational activities, more highly

[59] Koide Shōgo, "Shimin sanka no jittai: Mishima shī shimin iinkai no baai," in *Toshi Mondai* 58 (1967): 49-61.

educated, and from higher status occupations than Mishima citizens in general. As a result, one cannot say that this movement contributed a sizable new group of individuals to the city's pool of political activists.

As regards the dynamics of citizen involvement in civic protest movements, personal "choice" must have played some role in differentiating participants from nonparticipants, but characterizations of movement involvement as being solely the result of autonomous personal decisions appear inadequate. True, decisions to participate must have entailed some individual rational calculation of the potential benefits of participation and a *konbināto* defeat (for example, a pollution-free environment, protection of the economic, demographic, and political status quo, defeat of "monopoly capitalism" and the LDP) against the personal costs of involvement (for example, expenditure of time, potential dislocation of friendships, disruption of business, or associational relationships). Yet, at the activist level, given the information available in this case on the prior organizational and political attachments of participants, many individuals may have been strongly influenced in their decisions to become involved by extensive reference group pressures, resulting from family or residential attachments (for example, Nakazato residents), organizational attachments (for example, women's association leaders or neighborhood association chairmen), and prior political obligations. Clearly, at the level of mass action participation, many citizens participated at the behest of group leaders and in conformity with reference group expectations. Thus, both individual choice and group expectations probably play a role in motivating participation.

Authoritative observations ring somewhat more true in the case of the nature of movement organization and decision making. The most outstanding case is that of the Mishima Citizen Council. Although most fundamentally a coalition of organizational representatives and organizational leaders acting in a quasi-representative manner rather than an organization of unattached individuals, the Council strived for openness in its deliberations (all meetings were publicly announced and everyone was urged to attend), equality of representation (formally speaking, all participants were assured an equal voice), and decisions based on the consent of all participants (a decision-rule based on unanimity rather than majoritarianism). It is possible to view these organizational patterns as reflecting a progressive or liberal democratic ideology. Many movement analysts tend to accept this type of interpretation, implying that these patterns evidence a fundamental transformation in the orientations of movement participants. One might also suggest an alternative interpretation, however—that these patterns were also a necessary and rational response to the organizational imperatives that the Citizen Council faced. In other words, the disparate, mixed nature of the coalition, the high status of many of the participants, and the threat that the organization would be taken over by an active minority necessitated openness and a consensual decision-making style.[60]

The Mishima case also suggests that more attention should be focused on the relationship between citizens' movements and conventional politics in the local political arena. In this case, there was a complex interplay between the movement, established associational life, and parties and political interest groups in the city. In fact, the movement was successful in great part because of its incorporation of all these forces.

The impact of the movement on the future of Mishima politics was substantial. Although cross-partisan mayoral electoral cooperation emerged in the city prior to the movement, the movement solidified the alignment between the JSP, the JCP, and Hasegawa conservatives, and it contributed to the incorporation of more and more conservatives, previously supporters of the LDP branch mainstream, into Hasegawa's organization. This, in fact, may be the most important lesson of the Mishima case. Some authors have stressed that the most significant effect of citizens' movements on the future of Japanese democracy lies in their impact on the socialization of increasing numbers of Japanese into participatory political roles. This case leads one to think that this emphasis may be misplaced. Perhaps one ought not to search so intently for change at the mass level: politics is moved by elites. In this case, a movement of tremendous proportion seems to have failed to bring about any significant increase or shift in incumbent elite roles, but it did help to create new political alignments and elite coalitions and to serve as a learning experience for the activist elite.

The Mishima case lends evidence to the oft-made point that environmental pollution or the threat of environmental pollution, a problem that affects all individuals in a community in a relatively equal manner, is a unique type of issue that represents in local politics an opportunity for what E. E. Schattschneider has referred to as "displacement of conflicts" and a new "mobilization of bias."[61] Schattschneider reminds us that what happens in politics depends on the way in which people are divided into factions, parties, and groups. In the formation of majorities in democratic systems, the outcome ultimately depends on which of the multitude of possible conflicts or cleavages within the polity gains a dominant position. In the end, people and their leaders must choose

[60] I am indebted to Ellis Krauss for this observation.
[61] E. E. Schattschneider, *The Semisovereign People* (New York: Holt, Rinehart & Winston, 1960), pp. 60-75.

which battle they most want to win because issues, cleavages, or conflicts compete with each other for dominance. When a choice is made, there follows a new "mobilization of bias" in the form of a coalition based on this interest.

In most urban communities, postwar alignments have reflected national partisan alignments—a "mobilization of bias" related to what Watanuki has called the "cultural politics" cleavage.[62] Environmental issues confront communities with the question of whether they wish to support national industrialization and the policies of the hegemonic Liberal Democratic Party at the expense of personal or local welfare. This question represents an overlay of a new issue-dimension on existent political cleavages. In Mishima, the environment issue was so salient that it afforded an opportunity for a flexible minority, the local progressives, to consolidate a new coalition with antimainstream conservatives and for this new dominant "mobilization of bias" to broaden its base among other conservatives in the community.

Such new coalitions of experienced community activists and their organizations require opportunities to learn how to deal with others previously perceived as political enemies. Citizens' movements provide this opportunity, facilitating personal interaction that breaks down walls between political subcultures and creates trust. Through movement participation, activists' attitudes on the *scope of permissible political cooperation* were transformed. Cooperation in the anti-*konbināto* movement taught pivotal actors in the Socialist, Communist, and conservative camps that it was possible to agree and work together for a "public good." While progress to this point had already begun before 1963, with the development of antimainstream conservative and progressive electoral coalitions in Mishima, this movement furthered and fundamentally solidified cooperation. Progressives learned that conservatives were interested in more than an electoral coalition supportive of their leader, Hasegawa; conservatives saw that progressives had kept their promise not to use the movement for partisan advantage.

One final observation. Conventional wisdom has it that in the Japanese case, as in other "unitary" systems, local government doesn't "make a difference" and that therefore partisan control of local political roles whether progressive or otherwise is relatively inconsequential. The Mishima case should serve as an example that such observations oversimplify reality. In the case of large-scale industrial construction projects, the cooperation of local governments is critical to the interests

---

[62] Watanuki Jōji, "Patterns of Politics in Present-Day Japan," in *Party Systems and Voter Alignments*, ed. Seymour M. Lipset and Stein Rokkan (New York: Free Press, 1967), pp. 456-460.

involved. Where the local public is hostile and where local government cooperation is not forthcoming, such powerful interests as Sumitomo, Arabia Petroleum, and Tokyo Power, even when backed by the national government, can be made to bow to the wishes of the people. Furthermore, the nature of the local administration and the political elite can make a difference. The Mishima movement succeeded in part because it dealt with a city that had an open and sympathetic local government and could attract the support of maverick conservatives. Had it been otherwise, it may well have been defeated.

PART FOUR

PROGRESSIVE LOCAL ADMINISTRATIONS

PROGRESSIVE LOCAL ADMINISTRATIONS: LOCAL PUBLIC POLICY AND LOCAL-NATIONAL RELATIONS

Kurt Steiner

In the preceding parts of this volume we looked first at the electoral trends that led to the rise of progressive local governments and their relationship to electoral trends at the national level. We then discussed the character and effect of citizens' movements. In the part that follows, we focus on the progressive local administrations themselves. The chapter by Ellis Krauss is a case study of the leftist Ninagawa administration in Kyoto prefecture. Ronald Aqua's paper deals with the important questions of whether and to what extent the progressive political coloration of local administrations is reflected in their policies, and it investigates these questions in the context of medium-sized cities on the basis of budgetary and other aggregate data.

In the present chapter, we give an overview of the increase in the number of progressive administrations at the prefectural and city levels and then present sketches of two particularly important administrations —that of Mayor Asukata in Yokohama and that of Governor Minobe in Tokyo—to supplement the more detailed case studies in this volume. Finally, we take a more general look at the effect of progressive administrations on local public policies as well as on Japan's system of intergovernmental relations. In exploring the effect on local-national relations in the case of Japan, we also set the stage for the final chapter, in which we attempt to discuss the effect of local political opposition on the political system in more theoretical and comparative terms.

The Meaning of "Progressive Local Administrations"

In theory, it might be possible to distinguish local administrations on the basis of the policies they espouse. Thus administrations that are

In writing this chapter the author was greatly aided by material made available to him by Terry MacDougall. He also benefited from the valuable comments of Scott Flanagan, Ellis Krauss, and Terry MacDougall on an earlier draft. All this help is gratefully acknowledged.

innovative in their welfare policies, in their dealing with environmental problems, and in their responsiveness to such new forms of participation as citizens' movements may be considered "progressive," while the others may be called "conservative." In practice it would be difficult at best to make this distinction, and we do not attempt to do so. Rather, we take our first clue from the prevalent usage of the two terms "progressive" (*kakushin*) and "conservative" (*hoshu*) as they are applied to parties at the national level. At that level it is customary to refer to the Liberal Democratic Party (LDP) as conservative and to the opposition parties—the Japan Communist Party (JCP), the Japan Socialist Party (JSP), the Clean Government Party (CGP), and the Democratic Socialist Party (DSP)—as progressive. In other words, we start by distinguishing between conservative and progressive local administrations on the basis of partisanship or political orientation, leaving the question of the correlation between progressive partisanship and progressive policies open to investigation.

More specifically, it is the partisan or political orientation of the chief executives—governors or mayors—that according to common usage determines the character of the local administration. To put it differently, the characterization of local administrations is independent of the political composition of the local assemblies. In fact, to categorize local administrations on the basis of the political composition of the local assemblies would be close to impossible. It could perhaps be done in the case of prefectural assemblies, of big city assemblies, and of the assemblies of the twenty-three Tokyo wards, all of which are highly politicized. But in the assemblies of medium- and small-sized cities and, above all, in town and village assemblies, independent assemblymen predominate and party affiliated assemblymen are in the minority.[1] To establish the political profile of an assembly one would thus have to determine in each case how many of the independent assemblymen are really conservative or progressive in their orientation, allowing also for a residual category of "pure independents." Fortunately it is not necessary to do so. A local administration is considered progressive as long as its chief executive is progressive, regardless of the coloration of the assembly majority.

[1] Thus in 1975, only 409 of the 2,864 prefectural assemblymen were independents, while 2,455 had some party affiliation, all but 52 with a party represented in the Diet. In designated cities, 65 of the 650 assemblymen were independents, but in other cities independents held 12,699 of the 20,086 assembly seats (see Chapter 3, Table 1). In the Tokyo ward assemblies, 1,019 of the 1,073 assemblymen were party affiliated as of 31 December 1976. In town and village assemblies, 42,961 out of 48,010 seats were occupied by independents. See *Local Government Review*, no. 4 (1976), Statistical Appendix, p. 64.

Chief executives are directly elected and are thus in this sense independent from the assembly majorities. In other words, at the local level, Japan has a presidential system rather than a parliamentary system of democratic government. This arrangement, anchored in the 1947 Constitution, is of fundamental importance.[2] Since conservatives predominate in most assemblies, it is no exaggeration to state that under a system of indirect election by the assemblies the rise of progressive local administrations would have been stifled.[3] Various institutional factors and related attitudinal factors affecting the elections of assemblymen and chief executives differentially explain why progressive governors and mayors so frequently face conservative local assemblies.[4]

A number of reasons justify categorizing local administrations as progressive or conservative in accordance with the political orientation of the chief executive. The chief executive holds a preeminent position in local government and politics: executive dominance over the assemblies is a tradition going back to the local government laws of the Meiji period.[5] Although the local government reforms of the Occupation aimed in part at establishing a balance in executive-legislative relations by providing that the local assembly may under certain circumstances achieve the resignation of the chief executive by a vote of nonconfidence,[6] the institution of the presidential system at the local level had the contrary effect of strengthening executive leadership. Being directly elected, the chief executive can claim a mandate that enhances the legitimacy of his position; while the members of local assemblies are seen as representatives of areal interests within the community, the chief executive represents the community itself. He convokes the assembly, initiates local policy, and presents bills and the budget to the assembly. The latter, which are drafted with the aid of the local bureaucracy, are usually approved by the assembly. The chief executive

[2] Constitution of Japan, Article 93, paragraph 2, provides that "the chief executive officers of all local public entities, the members of their assemblies, and such other local officials as may be determined by law shall be elected by direct popular vote within their several communities." The "presidential system" at the local level contrasts with the "parliamentary system" at the national level where the prime minister is designated by a resolution of the Diet (Article 67).

[3] See Takagi Shosaku, *Jūmin jichi no kenri* (Tōkyō: Hōritsubunkasha, 1973), p. 2. As Takagi points out, at the time when the occupation's local government reforms were under consideration, the Home Ministry opposed a direct election system. See also Kurt Steiner, *Local Government in Japan* (Stanford: Stanford University Press, 1965), p. 85.

[4] For a discussion of the factors involved in the election of the assemblies of big cities, see Chapter 3.

[5] Steiner, *Local Government*, pp. 43-63.

[6] Ibid., pp. 365-371.

then promulgates the by-laws and where required issues enforcement regulations. As agent of the national—and, in case of the mayor, also the prefectural—government, he carries out a multitude of assigned tasks without any reference to the assembly. As chief administrator, he is charged with the management of the local entity's property and establishment, with the receipt and payment of funds, and with the levying and collection of taxes. He supervises public organizations within his local entity and coordinates their activities. He also represents the local entity in contacts with higher levels of administration. These contacts include, of course, the important negotiations to secure grants and subsidies or permits to float bonds, but, given the various forms of national guidance or control over the local entities, they concern a wide spectrum of local activities. In addition, the individual inhabitant's contact with local government is primarily through the local bureaucracy, which is headed by the chief executive. Thus the chief executive's style influences the inhabitant's perception of and their attitudes towards their local government. For all these reasons it is understandable that by common usage the definition of "local progressive administration" hinges on the orientation of the mayor or governor.

However, to state that a progressive local government is one that has a progressive mayor or governor is only the first—and easiest—step in our quest for a definition. As just noted, at the national level the LDP constitutes the conservative camp, while the opposition parties are considered progressive. At the local level, a problem arises because most chief executives are not affiliated with any party but for a variety of reasons prefer to compete in elections as independents. Thus, as of December 1976, 32 out of 47 governors were independents, 14 belonged to the LDP, and 1 position was vacant. In other words, not a single governor was affiliated with a progressive party. Of the 644 city mayors, 575 were independents; so were all of the 23 chiefs of the Tokyo wards and 2,520 of the 2,607 town and village mayors.[7] Some of these independents (such as most town and village mayors) are conservatives, and their administrations should be so classified; some of them, being neutral or pure independents, defy allocation to one or the other camp. Our next task is to find criteria for distinguishing those independent governors and city mayors who are "progressive independents."

The criterion commonly used is electoral support by one or more

[7] Forty-seven city mayors belonged to the LDP, 15 to the JSP, and 7 to groups not represented in the Diet. The corresponding figures for town and village mayors were 77, 6, and 4 respectively (see *Local Government Review*, 1976).

of the progressive parties. In the case of the city mayors, our task is facilitated by the existence of the National Association of Progressive Mayors, because it is commonly accepted that membership of the mayor in that association qualifies the city administration as "progressive."[8] As MacDougall states, almost all members of the association were backed by the JSP, although most of them were not the party's official candidates.[9] Of course, backing by the JSP alone is normally insufficient to carry the day in an election. Thus most successful progressive candidates for city mayor are supported by a varied, loose, and fragile electoral coalition of progressive parties (usually including the JSP) to which they add other groups such as personal supporters' associations or citizens' movements.

The situation is similar in the case of progressive governors. There is as yet no counterpart to the National Association of Progressive Mayors to facilitate categorization, but the number of cases being smaller, it is somewhat easier to determine existing support patterns of successful progressive candidates. If we take the gubernatorial election of 1975 as an example, these patterns range from support by a single progressive party (such as the JCP in case of the governor of Osaka), through support by both JSP and JCP (as in the case of Kyoto) and support by three progressive parties (as in the case of Tokyo), to support by all four opposition parties (as in the case of the governor of Kanagawa).

There is a residual category on both levels—the joint conservative-progressive candidate. This category includes the candidate who manages to obtain the support of the LDP and all four opposition parties

[8] As Jack Lewis indicates in Chapter 8, this is the case even if the mayor himself belongs to an LDP faction that is in opposition to the mainstream of the local party organization. According to a survey of 103 progressive mayors in 1973, 13 were backed by coalitions, including the LDP (see Chapter 3). Membership in the National Association of Progressive Mayors is a somewhat imprecise criterion. Some mayors who are backed by the JSP do not become members of the association: local conditions may make it inadvisable to do so because the association is too strongly identified with the JSP, and some mayors want to avoid the cost of membership, which is allocated according to the size of the city and is paid out of the funds of the mayor. On the other hand, some mayors who are not backed by the JSP or by labor unions are invited to become members of the association if they have taken a stand against centralization, and some of them do join. The net effect of the imprecision of the criterion is an underestimation of the number of mayors who could be called "progressive" if some other criterion were used.

[9] See Chapter 3. The difference between candidates running under a party label and candidates endorsed or supported by parties while running as independents is also explained there.

or, more frequently, the support of the LDP, DSP, CGP, and JSP against a JCP-supported challenger. Clearly the categorization of local chief executives as progressives or conservatives involves a substantial element of judgment. But, as MacDougall notes, in spite of their supposed independence, it is possible to characterize about 90 percent of all governors and city mayors as either progressive or conservative.[10]

THE DEVELOPMENT OF PROGRESSIVE PREFECTURAL AND MUNICIPAL ADMINISTRATIONS

Progressive candidates for gubernatorial and mayoral positions achieved rather spectacular successes in Japan's most important urban areas in the sixties and seventies. These successes, dramatically highlighted by the election of Governor Minobe of Tokyo in 1967, focused public attention on the phenomenon of progressive local government. However, the phenomenon was not altogether new. In the following we shall sketch the development of progressive local government at the gubernatorial and city mayoral level, tracing the mixed fortunes of the progressives since the first unified local election in 1947.[11]

The Gubernatorial Level

The gubernatorial elections of 1947—the first in the history of Japan —reflected the initial postwar upsurge of leftist parties in general that at the national level made the JSP the strongest single party in the House of Representatives at the time. In these elections, all forty-six gubernatorial positions had to be filled. Typically for this early period, the four progressive governors emerging from the election in Hok-

[10] Ibid. Two problems make the task difficult in the case of governors, and these account for slight discrepancies in the inclusion of a specific individual among the progressive independents. One is the problem of categorizing the conservative-progressive independent candidates competing only against a JCP candidate. In the absence of other considerations they are excluded in the following account. The other problem is a shift in political ties of the same candidate over a number of elections. Notes 13, 14, and 17 of this chapter illustrate this problem.

[11] This section is based on the following works: Terry MacDougall, *Political Opposition and Local Government in Japan: The Significance of Emerging Progressive Local Leadership* (unpublished dissertation, Yale University, 1975), Chapter 5, and on an earlier draft of the same author's contribution to the present volume; Steiner, *Local Government*, Chapters 15 and 16; Nishihara Shigeki, *Nippon no senkyo* (Tōkyō: Shiseido, 1972), pp. 179-212 and pp. 473-520; and various issues of *Senkyo nenkan*. I am grateful to Carl Walter for his assistance in research for this and the following sections. MacDougall's work will hereafter be cited as MacDougall, *Dissertation*.

kaido, Nagano, Fukuoka, and Tokushima all won as JSP candidates. The Liberals and the Democrats elected an equal number, three posts were captured by smaller parties, and thirty-one went to conservative independents, many of them exgovernors formerly appointed by the Home Minister and now returning as "the people's choice." In 1950,. Governor Ninagawa began his long term of office in Kyoto as a progressive independent, thus bringing the total of progressive governors to five. In the 1951 election, when thirty-one posts were contested, three Socialists were reelected in Hokkaido, Nagano, and Fukuoka, bringing the total—including Governor Ninagawa of Kyoto—to four. From then on their number hovered between two and four until the late sixties. The prefectures with progressive governors were in general areas with strong labor movements, especially in coal mining prefectures such as Hokkaido and Fukuoka, or areas with a tradition of progressivism, such as Nagano and Kyoto. Hokkaido, Japan's "frontier," may also have been receptive to progressive appeals or less receptive to conservative mobilization methods because of its distinct social and political history.

But as on the level of national politics, the initial postwar momentum that had propelled progressives into power soon began to wane. The advantages of incumbency and other factors such as personal appeal kept some progressive governors in office for a while.[12] Thus in 1955, the incumbents held on in Nagano and Hokkaido, but the progressives lost the governorship of Fukuoka, so that after the elections there were three progressive governors, including Ninagawa.[13] When Miyagi elected a JSP candidate in a bielection in 1956, the total rose to four.[14] In 1959, the conservatives were finally able to win the gubernatorial elections in Nagano and Hokkaido. But the Socialists regained Fukuoka under Uzaki, a "second generation" progressive candidate,. so that to-

[12] The reelection success ratio of incumbent governors is about 70 percent. See Nishihara, *Nippon no senkyo*, pp. 198-199.

[13] In 1955, Oita elected the independent Kinoshita who, according to some evaluations, is to be counted as a progressive. The fact that he ran in 1963 against an LDP candidate gives some credence to this, at least as far as his third term is concerned. See also Chapter 10 regarding his friction with the LDP at that time. In 1959 and 1967, however, he ran only against the JCP candidate and may thus be considered a progessive-conservative independent. Also in 1955, the independent Hara won against a Liberal Party candidate in Tokushima. Being reelected without contest in 1959, he ran in 1963 as the LDP candidate. He thus may be counted as a conservative independent.

[14] In another bielection in 1956 in Toyama, the independent Yoshida beat an LDP opponent and may thus be counted a progressive during his first term. But in subsequent elections (in 1960, 1964, and 1968) his only opposition was a JCP candidate and he may thus be counted as a conservative-progressive independent.

gether with Miyagi and Kyoto, progressives occupied three governorships. When Miyagi was lost in 1960, this number dwindled to two. The 1963 election brought no improvement for the progressives: at this point, the Socialist Uzaki in Fukuoka and the independent Ninagawa in Kyoto were the only progressive governors.

If we compare this earlier period with the period after the 1967 elections, the following differences stand out: the number of progressive governors increased, but these progressives rarely competed under the JSP label.[15] The gubernatorial positions they occupied were of greater national visibility, and the incumbents showed greater staying power. Thus, the number of progressive governors increased from two in 1963 to nine in 1975, a figure that included the governor of Okinawa, who was reelected after the island was returned to Japan in 1972 as her forty-seventh prefecture; nearly all of the successful candidates in the intervening period had run as independents, most of them backed by a coalition that included the JSP and JCP. In 1967, Fukuoka reverted to conservative rule, but the progressives under Minobe captured the most visible gubernatorial post, that of Tokyo Metropolis. Osaka prefecture elected a progressive independent, Kuroda, in 1971, so that the prefectures of Tokyo, Osaka, and Kyoto—Japan's political, economic, commercial, educational, and cultural centers—were all in progressive hands. When Saitama and Okayama, in addition to the new prefecture of Okinawa, elected progressives in 1972, the number of progressive governors rose to six. In 1974, the rural prefectures of Kagawa and Shiga elected progressive governors, to be followed in 1975 by one of the major urban prefectures, Kanagawa. This brought the total of prefectures with progressive governors up to the unprecedented number of nine, including—as noted—Tokyo, Kyoto, and Osaka. Ninagawa of Kyoto had been in office since 1950; Minobe of Tokyo, since 1967; and Kuroda of Osaka, since 1971.[16]

The Municipal Level

On the city level, the phenomenon of an early progressive upsurge can be seen in the initial victories in the original five designated cities,

[15] See Chapter 3 for the reasons for this phenomenon in the case of gubernatorial and big city mayoral elections.

[16] Ninagawa retired in 1978, and in the election of that year a conservative candidate became governor of Kyoto. Minobe retired in 1979, and Suzuki Shunichi, who was supported by the CGP, DSP, and LDP, won the gubernatorial election in Tokyo. In Osaka, the incumbent governor, Kuroda, was defeated in his reelection bid in 1979 by his vice-governor Kishi Sakae, who was supported by all parties except the JCP.

Yokohama, Nagoya, Kyoto, Osaka, and Kobe. But conservatives soon won over Yokohama and Osaka, Mayor Takayama of Kyoto turned conservative (which enabled him to remain in office for four terms), and Mayor Haraguchi of Kobe enlarged his support base to include conservatives so that he remained in office for five terms, being opposed only by the JCP. Only in Nagoya, Mayor Kobayashi was reelected for three terms as a progressive. However, when he retired in 1961 he, too, was succeeded by a conservative. This was a low point in progressive fortunes in the big cities. But the tide soon began to turn. In the 1963 mayoral elections, Yokohama elected the Socialist Asukata and Osaka elected the independent progressive Chuma. Kyoto reverted to a progressive administration in 1967, and Nagoya and Kobe followed course in 1973.[17] Once again the original five big cities were under progressive leadership. Kitakyushu, amalgamated into a new designated city in 1962, elected a Socialist mayor in 1963, but he failed in his bid for reelection in 1967. Of the three cities designated in 1971—Sapporo, Kawasaki, and Fukuoka—only Kawasaki elected a progressive. Thus, after 1973 six of the nine designated cities were in progressive hands.

While this development at the gubernatorial and big city levels in Japan's most important urban areas brought progressive local administrations into national prominence, the rise of progressive local administrations in other cities was equally spectacular. The progressive wave of 1947 had barely reached the small- and medium-sized cities. Only twenty of these cities, many of them in the coal mining regions of Hokkaido and Fukuoka, elected progressive mayors in that year. Some of these mayors showed considerable staying power, but their number at first remained small. The number of progressive mayors rose, however, in the period between 1955 and 1962, that is at a time when progressive strength in gubernatorial elections still stagnated. The new progressive mayors were elected in small- and medium-sized cities in the Tokyo and Osaka metropolitan areas and in regionally important cities in the Tohoku region. Urawa and Omiya in Saitama prefecture, Yokosuka in Kanagawa prefecture, as well as Uji and Maizuru in Kyoto prefecture and Hirakata in Osaka prefecture fall into the first group; Sendai in Miyagi prefecture and Akita in the prefecture of the same name are examples for the second group. Many of these progres-

---

[17] The case of Kobe again demonstrates the fluidity of the categorization of progressive chief executives. In 1969, Mayor Miyazaki was elected with the backing of the LDP, DSP, and the JSP delegations in the city assembly. Early in his term he began to work closely with progressive big city mayors, and in 1973 he was backed by all four opposition parties in his reelection bid against an LDP candidate. Thus the Kobe city adminstration is to be considered progressive after 1973.

sive mayors continue in office today. While the number of progressive mayors in Fukuoka and Hokkaido has dwindled (this trend could be seen in Fukuoka in the sixties and in Hokkaido more recently), the number of progressive mayors in the metropolitan areas has further increased since 1963, and progressive city administrations have spread to almost every region of the country. Thus, in 1973 progressives held the mayoral posts in 138 out of 643 cities, including sixteen of the forty-seven prefectural capitals; the 135 cities with progressive mayors as of 1 July 1974 included 38.2 percent of the city population nationwide.

In summary, we find certain similarities in the patterns of progressive successes in gubernatorial and big city elections. The postwar upsurge of leftist parties was reflected in the first election, but the momentum could not be sustained on either level in the second half of the fifties. However, a new period of progressive successes began in the sixties, culminating on the prefectural level with nine progressive governors in 1975 and on the city level with progressive mayors in all of the five original big cities in 1973. The picture for small- and medium-sized cities is more mixed. As we noticed, except for a few cities with great labor concentrations, they were largely unaffected by the progressive upsurge of the first postwar years. Over time, progressive support dwindled in the areas where it existed in the beginning. However, as early as the second half of the fifties, at the time that progressive support still stagnated at the gubernatorial and big city levels, progressive support began to rise in the rapidly growing cities of the metropolitan areas and in some regions where it used to be conspicuously weak, such as the Tohoku region. By the late sixties, progressive mayors could be found in every region and, in fact, in nearly every prefecture of the nation.

The Progressive Administrations of Mayor Asukata of Yokohama and Governor Minobe of Tokyo

In retrospect, the election of Asukata Ichio as mayor of Yokohama in 1963 and the election of Minobe Ryōkichi as governor of Tokyo Metropolis in 1967 appear particularly significant in this development. Both men served as pace setters for progressive administrations elsewhere, so that a few comments about their administrations seem appropriate.

In 1963, Asukata "descended" from his position as a JSP member of the House of Representatives in his fourth term to compete in the election for the mayor's position in Yokohama. Running as the JSP candidate and benefiting by disunity within the LDP, he was able to wrest the mayoralty from the conservatives who had held it ever since 1951. Asukata's step in turning to a local position was both the result and symbol of a changing evaluation of the importance of local governments on the part of the Socialists, of which he himself was the leading exponent.[18] The weakness in the progressive movement and the depth of the social basis of conservative support were exposed by the outcome of the antisecurity treaty struggle and the Miike coal miners' strike of 1960. Conservative electoral successes of that year—in elections for the House of Representatives and in various local bielections—made it clear that the greatest mass movement in Japan's political history had made no dent in the conservative dominance. Since this dominance rested on a solid foundation of local power, it appeared to some that the JSP would have to put a higher priority on local politics. Thus, in its 1961 Action Program, the JSP recognized that its activities had been centered too much on national politics, and it set itself the goal of expanding the party's representation in local government by appealing to the people in terms of local problems. These themes were echoed and made more specific at the 1962 party conference. The establishment of the local politics bureau at JSP central headquarters indicated an increased commitment to local politics in terms of finances and personnel.

Asukata's action in 1963 is to be seen in this context. While a change in the national leadership of the party—specifically the loss of leadership by Eda Saburo, head of the party's moderate Structural Reform Wing, to his left-wing rival Sasaki Kozo in 1965—arrested these tendencies for a while, the disastrous defeat of the Socialists in the 1969 House of Representatives election reawakened them. In conjunction with objective circumstances such as the declining JSP fortunes in national elections that contrasted with the rising tide of progressive local government, the increase in the salience of urban problems, and the growth of local citizens protest movements, the ideas of Asukata again exerted considerable weight.[19] His influence was further bolstered

[18] The following statements are based mainly on MacDougall, *Dissertation*, pp. 287-325.

[19] This is not to say that Asukata's views on the relationship between local autonomy, democracy, and socialism articulated in his speeches and writings were shared by the party's leadership as a whole. MacDougall finds that there was substantial agreement on the tactical importance of progressive local governments in the JSP's struggle with the LDP, but little agreement on its long-range strategic importance. Many JSP leaders insisted that the essential energy for social and

by the National Association of Progressive Mayors, which he had co-founded in 1964 and which he headed for fourteen years. Asukata became a vice-chairman of the JSP in 1974, and he assumed the chairmanship of his party in December 1977, relinquishing his position as mayor of Yokohama. Nevertheless, his tenure as mayor of that city between 1963 and 1977 remains a landmark in the development of progressive administrations.

Asukata always competed as a JSP candidate but, as his continuing success indicated, he attracted many other voters. During most of his tenure, he benefited from the backing of the DSP and CGP in the city assembly. While his lead over the conservative incumbent in 1963 was small (43 against 41 percent in a close, three-man race in which the conservatives were disunited), by 1967 he was able to win a lopsided victory with 62 percent against one conservative candidate's 34 percent and one communist candidate's 4 percent. In 1971 he attracted nearly 70 percent of the vote, while his LDP-backed opponent received barely 30 percent, the remainder of less than 1 percent going to an independent.[20] In 1975 he won against an LDP-backed independent by 65 to 33 percent, with the balance split between two other independents.[21]

Aside from the fact that Asukata ran as a JSP candidate, it should be noted that the JSP retained a lead over the JCP in the Yokohama city assembly. This contrasted with the situation in the Kyoto city assembly, as well as in the Kyoto prefectural assembly and the Tokyo metropolitan assembly, where the JCP passed the JSP and assumed a greater leadership role.[22]

As mayor of Yokohama, Asukata initiated some policies that are frequently associated with progressive administrations. Already in his 1963 campaign he was emphasizing the "principle of direct democracy," an idea that since then has been echoed in official JSP pronouncements. Starting with the premise that grass-roots democracy requires that the people articulate their needs and demands among themselves and in a two-way dialogue with their local government, he called for a "meeting of ten thousand citizens." To facilitate the dialogue with

---

political change had to come from the struggle of the working class against the capitalist order. See MacDougall, *Dissertation*, pp. 315-321. On Asukata's views, see also ibid., pp. 299-303, 321-325.

[20] Ibid., pp. 255-257.

[21] In the 1975 election, Asukata received the official backing of the CGP.

[22] On the distinction between this "Yokohama pattern" and the "Kyoto pattern" of leftist support, see Terry MacDougall, "Japanese Urban Local Politics: Toward a Viable Political Opposition," in *Japan: The Paradox of Progress*, ed. Lewis Austin (New Haven: Yale University Press, 1976), pp. 40-41. See also Chapter 11.

the city administration, he instituted consultation windows in City Hall and in ward offices and established consultation desks in shopping districts and railroad stations, some of which he occasionally manned himself. He also initiated campaigns to encourage the writing of letters to the mayor and to city officials.[23]

The Asukata administration was also identified with innovations of a more substantive sort in the area of pollution control, namely voluntary pollution control agreements between local governments and private industry. This "Yokohama formula" initiated by an agreement with the Electric Power Development Company on 1 December 1964 spread to other municipalities and prefectures, including some under conservative control, as is typical for the new policy competition that has emerged. By December 1970, thirty prefectures and 100 cities, towns, and villages had entered agreements with 574 companies. Yokohama was also particularly active in enforcement of national and local antipollution ordinances. To this end, the Asukata administration expanded its organizational capacity by establishing a Public Hazards Center, a Public Hazards Policy Liaison Conference (to coordinate the activities of various administrative bureaus), and a broad-based Public Hazards Policy Council.[24]

When Minobe Ryōkichi won the gubernatorial election in Tokyo Metropolis in 1967, the progressives achieved their most visible success.[25] Until 1965 the Tokyo governorship as well as the Tokyo metro-

[23] MacDougall, *Dissertation*, pp. 336-340. Other local administrations, including some controlled by conservatives, established similar public hearing mechanisms. Some local administrations have gone beyond consultation devices in attempts to involve citizens in the activities of groups such as Kyoto's Association for the Beautification of the Kamo River (see Chapter 11) or in participation in city planning activities.

[24] MacDougall, *Dissertation*, pp. 392-398. On the number of pollution control agreements, see Watanuki Yoshimoto, "How the Environmental Pollution Problem is Handled by the Court, the Public Authority, and the Citizens' Group of Environmentalists in Japan," a paper that appeared originally in the Tokyo Kyoiku University's *Journal of Social Sciences*, no. 20. I am grateful to Professor Julian Gresser of the University of Hawaii School of Law for bringing this article to my attention.

[25] This section is based on: MacDougall, *Dissertation*, pp. 256-259; Ide Yoshinori, *Chihō jichi no seijigaku* (Tōkyō: Tōkyō Daigaku Shuppankai, 1972), especially pp. 278-292; and Asahi Shinbunsha, *Chihō kenryoku* (Tōkyō, 1974), pp. 14-40. On the 1971 election, see also Yanai Michio, "Tōkyō-to chiji senkyo ni okeru Image Campaign," in *Bulletin of the Faculty of Humanities*, Seikei University, no. 8 (1972), pp. 55-82. See also Chapters 3 and 5 of this volume on the importance of "personality" in the 1967 and 1971 Tokyo elections. The account of the 1975 election is based mainly on various issues of the *Japan Times* and *Japan Times Weekly* between 16 February and 19 April 1975.

politan assembly were firmly in Liberal Democratic hands. The first defeat of the LDP occurred in the special assembly elections of that year. The election was precipitated by a corruption scandal that involved several LDP assemblymen, a recall movement, and the hasty passage by the Diet of a special law regarding the dissolution of local assemblies.[26] Two years later in the gubernatorial election of 1967, Minobe, the son of the eminent constitutional law professor Minobe Tatsukichi and himself a professor of economics who had gained considerable media exposure by popularizing his criticism of the national government's economic policy on T.V., became the progressive candidate. He ran as an independent with the joint support of the JSP and JCP, competing with Matsushita Masatoshi, a middle-of-the-road candidate supported by the DSP and LDP, and with a candidate recommended by the CGP. There were also seven minor candidates. Minobe's victory with 44.5 percent of the vote against 41.7 percent and 12.2 percent for his two major competitors was hardly overwhelming. He may well have owed it to the fact that the CGP candidate drew off votes from the joint LDP-DSP candidate.

However one may judge Minobe's performance in office during his first term, the LDP's campaign scare tactics in 1967 evoking the spectre of a "red flag over the metropolitan government building" and of a "people's republic of Tokyo" had clearly overshot their mark. By 1971 Minobe's administration had achieved a certain legitimacy for itself, and in the campaign of that year the LDP fell back on a more conventional "direct access to the center" argument, promising huge infusions of national funds for urban reconstruction if its candidate were elected. Since the DSP and CGP neither nominated nor supported a candidate in 1971, the contest was between the progressive incumbent, Minobe, and the LDP-backed candidate, Hatano Akira, a former chief of the Metropolitan Police Board. The LDP spared neither effort nor money to dislodge Minobe in this election, which it considered crucial for Japan. The campaign was in part an "image campaign," conducted on the basis of research by public relations firms, especially on the part of Hatano, who hoped to gain votes by contrasting his "virile" image to Minobe's "soft" image. Still, much of the campaign dealt with issues. Minobe emphasized his record on welfare, proposing "ten main poli-

[26] See Chapter 3, Table 3 for the prior strength of the LDP in assembly elections and the subsequent drop in 1965; see also MacDougall, *Dissertation*, pp. 266-275, and the report, *Shūchōshugi to chihōgikai*, published by the research division of the office of the Tokyo metropolitan assembly in 1973. Although the LDP made a comeback in the 1969 metropolitan assembly elections, conservatives did not regain the majority in the assembly until the election of July 1977.

cies" for its continuation; Hatano termed Minobe's rule "an administration for old people, women and children," offering as an alternative
a detailed "Tokyo development plan" embodying his "vision for Tokyo."

Above all, the campaign was a high-pitched battle between the conservative and progressive camps. Minobe stressed the national significance of the election, adopting "Stop Sato!" as one of his slogans
(referring to the current LDP prime minister). Hatano, on the other
hand, at times attempted to avoid being too closely identified with the
national government and the increasingly unpopular LDP, a maneuver
at odds with the promises of financial support from the center in case
of election. In targeting Sato as the antagonist, Minobe relied on the
citizens' awareness that local self-government implied potentially antagonistic relations of local government with the center.[27]

The base of Minobe's support was the cooperation between the JSP
and the JCP in his main campaign organization, the "Committee for
Creating a Bright, Progressive, Metropolitan Administration." This support was supplemented, however, by a bevy of smaller groups representing various areas of the metropolis and various professions, such as
the Tokyo Private Taxi Union and the "Abacus Party" for businessmen.[28] In addition to the LDP organization, Hatano also had a looser
organization, "The Heart of Tokyo Inhabitants' Liaison Committee,"
to influence religious, business, and industrial groups. In the election, an
unprecedented 72.3 percent of the eligible voters cast their ballots.
Minobe was reelected by a wide margin, gaining 64.8 percent of the
vote to Hatano's 34.7 percent.

Minobe's attractiveness to alienated voters and even to some LDP
voters is often attributed to his personality and his style, but his stand
on substantive issues also attracted certain groups across the political

[27] In polls conducted in anticipation of the election in the fall of 1970 and in
the spring of 1971, 46.1 percent of the respondents agreed that local government
"must take a strong stand vis-à-vis the central government and at times oppose
and fight it," while 22.9 percent did not agree and 24.3 percent were undecided.
See Ide, *Chihō jichi no Seijigaku*, p. 283. Earlier, Minobe had revealed his unconventional concept of local government for Japan by the use of the term *"chihō
seifu"* instead of the traditional term *"chihō jichi."* An LDP assemblyman called
his use of the term a "grandiose overstatement . . . resulting in the impression
of dual political authority which is a denial of the present structure of the state"
(ibid., pp. 3-5).

[28] Some of these groups had their roof organization in the "Ganbare, Minobe-
san!" Citizens Groups Liaison Committee. See Ide, *Chihō jichi no seijigaku*, pp.
280-286. The term *"Ganbare"* is used by fans in sporting events to spur on a con-
testant to still greater effort. On the 1971 election campaign, see also Chapter 5.

spectrum. This stand was reflected, for example, both in his interpretation of Article 25 of the Constitution as it affects the activities of local
government and in his propagation of the concept of a "civil minimum." Article 25 reads:

> All people shall have the right to maintain the minimum standards
> of wholesome and cultured living. In all spheres of life the state shall
> use its endeavors for the promotion and expansion of social welfare
> and security, and of public health.

In 1967 the metropolitan government released a "Tokyo Medium
Range Plan for 1968" with the subheading "How the Civil Minimum
Can Be Achieved." The basic consideration advanced was that the national implementation of Article 25 through subsidies and grants fell
short of the actual minimum requirements of urban life, so that the
metropolitan administration had to set its own minimum standard—the
"civic minimum" as differentiated from the national minimum—based
on the felt and expressed needs of the citizens for such amenities as
parks, institutions for the handicapped, and the like. The "civic minimum" was to be achieved by a series of three-year plans on a rolling
system: each year a new three-year plan was to be produced, developing the ideas of the previous plan. The long-term goal was to progressively increase the ratio of funding for each of the minima until eventually 100 percent of each was provided for.[29]

In the field of social welfare, Minobe popularized the concept of free
medical care for the aged. Other prefectures and cities had initiated
similar, if somewhat more restricted, programs before Tokyo, but Tokyo's program added a new impetus to the concept. Its application
spread first to a number of other local governments, both progressive
and conservative, and then in 1973 to the national level with a revision
of the Old People's Welfare Law. Similar advances were made in regard
to childhood allowances. The national government had worked on a
plan for such allowances since 1960. By 1967 local governments started
to set up their own programs, beginning with Musashino, a city within
Tokyo prefecture that had a JSP mayor, supported by a progressive
city assembly majority. Tokyo's program was instituted in 1969. The
national government's program finally came into effect in three stages
between 1972 and 1974, but as in the case of free medical care for the

[29] MacDougall, *Dissertation*, pp. 305-310; Takagi, *Jūmin jichi*, pp. 74-79. Since
existing administrative and financial constraints limited the feasibility of the realization of these plans, it was natural for Minobe and other progressive chief executives to call for an expansion of the scope of local autonomy through a new
distribution of functions and finances.

aged, Tokyo's system was more liberal.[30] There was, of course, a strong connection between these policies, Minobe's humanitarian image, and the style of his administration, on the one hand, and his ability to attract certain voters who did not identify with one of the progressive parties, on the other hand.

The atmosphere of the 1975 gubernatorial election was different from that of earlier elections in a number of respects. The 1973 assembly election had disappointed the hopes of the progressive camp; the LDP had actually gained slightly in popular vote, obtaining 51 seats, followed by the CGP with 26 seats. The JCP had substantially increased its vote and had become the third strongest party with 24 seats. The big loser was the JSP, which dropped to fourth place in the assembly, with 20 seats. This reversal in the strengths of the JCP and JSP led to tensions over their respective influence that surfaced before the gubernatorial election of 1975 in a controversy over the issue of allocation of funds to two competing *burakumin* organizations. As the Socialist-Communist core of Minobe's support showed signs of disintegration, he announced that he would withdraw his candidacy. The rift between the two parties was hastily papered over, and Minobe stayed in the race, but his vacillation only a month before the election hurt his image and diminished his appeal to the floating vote. To counter this trend, Minobe emphasized his distance from the parties supporting him by claiming to draw his primary support from what he called the *Tominto*—the Metropolitan People's Party—an ambiguous and innocuous denomination for a wide variety of potential supporters, including white-collar workers, housewives, students, and others. Minobe's main opponent was the novelist Ishihara Shintaro, who ran as the LDP candidate. Ishihara, a member of the House of Councillors, had gained the largest personal vote in the national constituency in 1971 and was a relatively new face in conservative politics. He presented a clear political profile because in the Diet he had led an LDP faction known as the *Seirankai*, or Blue Storm Society, which—in contrast to the line of the LDP prime minister, Miki Takeo—represented the far right of the party. Since Minobe had reached an accommodation with the CGP halfway through his second term, his only other opponent was the DSP candidate, Matsushita, who had run unsuccessfully against Minobe as the DSP-LDP candidate in 1967 and who, in 1975, joined the race only after Minobe had reentered it.

[30] MacDougall, *Dissertation*, pp. 366-368, and 380-386, points out the policy competition between the national government and the Minobe administration in these years. Thus Minobe's announcement of a plan for free medical care for children with cancer quickly led to national action, so that both plans came into effect in 1971.

Perhaps most troubling for Minobe was the change in the economic situation. Subsequent to the oil crisis of 1973, a recession had ended the high growth rate of the Japanese economy and ushered in a period of retrenchment. Minobe had always been critical of the government's high growth policy. Somewhat paradoxically, the end of that policy meant a sharp reduction in the revenues of Tokyo Metropolis, so that in 1975 its budget, drafted before the election, was actually smaller than its 1974 counterpart. As a consequence, the realization of programs long advocated by Minobe had to be temporarily abandoned. In addition to attacking Minobe for the untrustworthiness he had shown in the temporary withdrawal of candidacy, Ishihara promised to liberate the Tokyo administration from the fetters of the Socialists and Communists. But much of his fire was directed at Minobe's financial administration. Echoing conservative criticisms of progressive local governments in general, he claimed that Minobe's policies were bankrupting Tokyo. In response, Minobe blamed Tokyo's financial problems on inflation and recession, on the unfair system of revenue-sharing, and on the excessive fiscal burdens imposed on local governments by the central government, at the same time promising to further improve his welfare-oriented metropolitan administration. Minobe won a narrow victory with 50.5 percent of the votes over Ishihara's 44.3 percent and Matsushita's 5.2 percent, but clearly some of his support had eroded during his second term in office.

Like other progressive chief executives, Minobe was expected to be sympathetic to the demands of citizens' movements for environmental improvement. "Blue Skies for Tokyo" had been one of his popular slogans from the beginning, and in his first term he aggressively attacked the pollution problem by sponsoring a tough environmental pollution control ordinance and by establishing a Pollution Bureau within the metropolitan government. But, as is also true for other progressive chief executives, Minobe found that his relationship to environmental groups was not free of friction. In 1972 he compounded his problems by announcing his "philosophy of the bridge." Carrying his responsiveness to citizens' desires to an extreme, he quoted the Algerian revolutionary Frantz Fanon to the effect that "if there is a single opponent, a bridge shall not be built." This philosophy made it difficult, for example, to reject the opposition of property owners who demanded the abandonment of public housing projects that threatened to deprive them of an assumed "right to sunlight" or a "right to an unobstructed view." Costly delays were the consequence. Minobe was plagued by similar problems with groups in Nerima and Toshima wards on the issue of highway construction.

Another clash with local citizens' movements became known as the "garbage war." The disposal of garbage is unquestionably a great problem in Tokyo. Minobe announced an attack on the problem in September 1971, and over the next two years he strengthened the relevant administrative departments in terms of both personnel and budget. However, organized movements based on neighborhood associations in Suginami and Koto wards opposed the establishment of garbage plants within their areas and refused to be placated by "dialogues" with the governor or by conciliatory proposals. Ultimately, the policy of peaceful negotiation was abandoned, impairing the credibility of Minobe's philosophy.

Minobe's rocky relations with such citizens' groups illustrate his difficulties in following simultaneously the concept of a "civil minimum" as well as the "philosophy of the bridge"—of adjusting the fulfillment of the needs of a greater number of people to the often equally strongly articulated needs of a minority.[31] More generally, they point up the fact that the expectations regarding responsiveness raised by progressive local administrations potentially increase the level of demands as much as the level of support. The situation of progressive local administrations in this regard is not very different from that of conservative local administrations that run into the opposition of citizens' movements. Taking a larger view and considering the diffusion of the policies of progressive administrations in other fields to local administrations under conservative control, one is confronted with the question, how much impact does political coloration have on local public policy?

PARTISANSHIP AND LOCAL POLICY

In reviewing the scholarly literature on urban politics, James Q. Wilson wrote more than a decade ago: "Who governs? is an interesting and important question; an even more interesting and more important question, it seems to me is *what difference* does it make who governs?"[32]

---

[31] Taketsugu Tsurutani considers the insistence on such rights as the "right to sunshine" or the "right to an unobstructed view" as examples of the "trivialization of politics." See his *Political Change in Japan: Response to Postindustrial Challenge* (New York: McKay, 1977), p. 55. Kaminogo Toshiaki argues that the two concepts mentioned in the text are essentially incompatible. See his "Glory and Misery of Local Autonomies under Progressive Control," which first appeared in *Bungei Shunjū* 53 (1975): 106-116, and then was translated in *Japan Echo* 2 (1975): 17-31. For a response to that argument, see Takagi, *Jūmin jichi*, p. 196.

[32] Quoted from James Q. Wilson, "Problems in the Study of Urban Politics," in *Essays in Political Science*, ed. Edward H. Buehrig (Bloomington: Indiana University Press, 1966), p. 133. (Emphasis in original.) Much of the following is based

In the present context we may paraphrase this question: Are the policies of progressive local administrations in Japan different from those of conservative local administrations?

The question whether partisanship significantly influences policy choices or whether the influence of other factors—especially socio-economic factors—renders the effect of political factors comparatively negligible has been repeatedly investigated in other countries such as the United States and Britain. The findings are decidedly mixed. Many studies find that political variables such as partisan control are much less important than environmental variables such as the socio-economic structure of the community. Other studies find that partisanship has a substantial effect on policy output, at least in certain areas of local policy, such as public housing.[33] In a paper presented at the Conference on Local Opposition in Japan, Richard Samuels reviewed the literature that considers the relative importance of partisan political influences on policy choice and found that the researchers' choice of methodology plays a substantial role in the determination of the results. Intranational aggregate comparisons usually elevate socio-economic variables to an all but overpowering importance. They are normally based on budgetary data for both revenues and expenditures as measures of policy output, and this facilitates comparisons. But these studies tend to ignore the policy process that is more likely to reveal the influence of political decisions. Case studies are more sensitive in this respect, and consequently they are prone to result in the elevation of political variables. They are also more likely to recognize that some outputs that may not be reflected in budgetary data, such as symbolic outputs, can nevertheless be relevant to the question of whether it makes a difference who governs. Such outputs may, for example, influence the citizens' perception of their local government's performance, increasing their satisfaction and thus the support level of that government, and this in turn may give a greater leeway for policy innovation by local officials.

---

on Richard J. Samuels, "Partisanship and Local Public Policy: A Review of Cross-national Evidence and Propositions," Wrightsville Beach, North Carolina, June 1976.

[33] For example, in the British context, the studies of Oliver and Stanyer, Danziger, and Ashford found no significant positive relationship between Labour Party control and local expenditures, while Alt, King, and Boaden found that local authorities, controlled by the Labour Party, spent more on housing, education, and health services. Research regarding other countries, such as Italy, Norway and Germany, produced a similar variability of assertions. For a short review of the British literature, see also Dilys M. Hill, *Democratic Theory and Local Government* (London: Allan and Unwin, 1974), pp. 106-108.

This is not the place for resolving the contradiction between the findings in these two branches of the literature. From a common-sense perspective we may, however, make the following observation: even if aggregate budgetary data were to reveal that, taking Japanese cities as a whole, the output of progressive city administrations is not clearly distinguished from that of conservative city administrations, this would not mean that the policies of, say, Yokohama are not different from that of any city with a conservative mayor. And having found that the policies of a progressive city such as Yokohama are in some way distinctive, we need not assume that the policies of all progressive cities are equally distinctive.

Of course, there cannot be any distinctive local politics and thus no influence of partisanship on local policy in local entities that lack local autonomy to such an extent that their policy agenda are set by the central government. Thus, there is an antecedent question that needs to be answered: Is this the situation in present-day Japan? In the chapter that follows this introduction, Ronald Aqua answers this question by studying changes in revenue and spending priorities for eighty-eight medium-sized Japanese cities between 1962 and 1974 and by comparing these changes with those at the national level. He finds that "the noticeable lack of congruence between national and local priorities in major issue areas suggests that the impact of central policy on local priority-setting is less significant than the simple catch phrase '30 percent local autonomy' would seem to indicate" (pp. 371-372). The variability in the changes in revenue and spending patterns among cities for the same policy or between policy areas for the same city points in the same direction. There thus exists a degree of local autonomy in present-day Japan that permits both distinctive local policies and an influence of partisanship on local policies. Potentially, then, politics can make a difference.

In proceeding to test the latter influence, Aqua notes first that "when the separate effects of organizational [decisional] and socio-economic conditions are compared, organizational factors seem to account for greater internal variation in local policy outcomes" (p. 372). But he finds no confirmation of a significant influence of the partisan identification of the mayor on changes in the pattern of revenue acquisition and the pattern of priority setting. Thus the measures he uses indicate that the relationship between local decision making and formal partisan ties seems to be tenuous and even inconsequential.

In the beginning of this chapter we distinguished between conservative and progressive local administrations on the basis of partisanship or political orientation, and we stated that the question of the correlation between progressive partisanship and progressive policies remains open to investigation. Aqua's investigation failed to detect any strong association between the two factors in his sample cities. This negative finding implies at least an important caveat against the facile assumption that progressive chief executives necessarily pursue progressive policies and that only progressive chief executives do so—a caveat that does not seem to be taken into account sufficiently in much of the Japanese and Western literature, which tends to depict the progressive chief executives rather indiscriminately as struggling for more autonomy, more governmental responsiveness, and more humane social and environmental goals. As Aqua intimates at the end of his chapter, progressive as well as conservative mayors gain and hold office in a context of localism. We must remember that many progressive city administrations are headed by progressive independents who derive their support from a coalition of local forces of which the branches of progressive parties—themselves operating in a context of localism—are only one part.

For these reasons, Aqua's findings are unexpected only when examined against the background of the rather indiscriminate assumptions of some of the literature. At the same time we must note that Aqua deals with medium-sized cities, and in the absence of further investigations we must not prematurely extend the scope of those findings to big cities and to prefectures.[34] Without anticipating the results of such investigations, we may state that the imagery of progressive administrations previously referred to is derived principally from the performance of these more conspicuous units, such as Tokyo, Kyoto, and Yokohama. These units are perceived as the forerunners (*sakidori*), pace setters, and models for progressive administrations elsewhere.[35] For this and other reasons, case studies of such units are important.

[34] The findings that local entities at present have more policy leeway than the conventional wisdom assumed and that partisanship and policy are not strongly associated are somewhat different in their inferences. It seems reasonable to assume that the former finding, although derived from an investigation of medium-sized cities, applies also—and perhaps even more strongly—to big cities. In the case of the second finding, such an assumption would be difficult to justify. Since the partisan character of politics increases with city size, the association between partisanship and policy may be stronger in big cities (see Chapters 3 and 5). It should be noted that Aqua excluded cities created by more or less recent amalgamations of towns and villages, thus strengthening his findings.

[35] It is widely recognized that innovative policy initiatives on the part of these units tend to become diffused to other local units, often including units controlled by conservatives. Over time, this tends to weaken any association between policy and partisanship. As MacDougall noted in the conference discussion, it would be

In the present chapter we touched on some policies of the Asukata and Minobe administrations. The chapter by Ellis Krauss that follows focuses on the support mobilization techniques of the Ninagawa administration in Kyoto prefecture and on the adaptation of this progressive administration to the local milieu, but it also affords insights into some of Ninagawa's policies. Thus we learn that in 1960 he created a source of independent revenue for the prefecture by instituting an automobile acquisition tax, and that this example was followed by many other prefectures. His policy of aiding small- and medium-sized enterprises is to be noted in juxtaposition to the conservative government's emphasis on big industry. An element in his policy is the program of large-scale loans, unbacked by collateral, enabling small- and medium-sized enterprises to modernize their machines, strengthen their management, and diversify their products. This program also has been copied by other local governments.[36] Ninagawa's emphasis on education is reflected in the budget and in turn in a low teacher-pupil ratio compared with other prefectures.

But the case study of Kyoto also calls our attention to the importance of measures that are not necessarily reflected in budgetary data. Krauss notes the steps taken by Ninagawa to assert control over the prefectural bureaucracy, including an administrative reorganization and a "purge" of department heads and section chiefs. While such steps may be seen as assertions of gubernatorial power vis-à-vis the bureaucracy, a likely underlying motivation is to assure more forceful implementation of policies thought to be uncongenial to the "purged" local public ser-

---

useful both to determine the initiatives for specific policies and their starting dates, and then to map their diffusion on a time line.

An example for such pace setting—as well as for its limitations—was the movement to abolish publicly operated racing and gambling establishments as a source of revenue. This movement was initiated by Governor Minobe in 1969. Mayor Asukata and other progressive chief executives favored the policy, and the JSP officially endorsed it. In the first stage of the process, some racing establishments operated by Tokyo Metropolis were abolished. A number of prefectures and cities, including some that were not administered by progressives, followed Tokyo's example, converting racing establishments into sports arenas or parks. But later the stringency of local finance militated against the abandonment of revenue sources. As a result, some cities—including a number of progressive cities within Tokyo Metropolis—continued to operate racing facilities or even to establish new ones, and the movement lost its original momentum. See Ide, *Chihō jichi no seijigaku*, pp. 214-235.

[36] While not immediately reflected in the budget, the protection of small shopkeepers against competition from supermarkets and department stores is also apparent in matters of zoning. See Chapter 11; also Asahi Shinbunsha, *Chihō Kenryoku*, p. 54.

vants. Although an increase in the size of the staff engaged in the enforcement of a given policy is likely to have budgetary ramifications, this need not be the case for the more qualitative aspects of staffing. The head of a department may achieve that position by seniority within the department or by transfer to a higher position within the administration that happens to have become vacant, but he may also have been selected, perhaps from outside the administration, because of his known enthusiasm for the specific policy he is to implement. To cite examples: in the area of environmental protection, Tokyo and Yokohama not only have relatively large agencies for the enforcement of water pollution standards but Governor Minobe's and Mayor Asukata's commitment to environmental policy has led them to handpick administrators with a similar commitment from outside the metropolitan administration.[37] It can be expected that such matters as the commitment of elected officials and the attitude of administrators towards their programs are closely linked to variations in implementation.[38]

As the study by Krauss also points out, at an early period Ninagawa opposed rapid economic growth policies through large-scale industry, was accessible to demands from organized progressive interest groups, and juxtaposed his insistence on self-rule with the government's desire for more centralized control. Since he was one of the earliest progressive chief executives of national prominence, it is not surprising that he is perceived as one of the pace setters for such policies.

In terms of symbolic outputs, Ninagawa's slogan "let's make the constitution live in our lives" is more significant than may appear at first glance. It must be remembered that the enthusiasm of conservatives for the basic law is somewhat subdued; after all, they tried for years to revise it. The central government stopped marking Constitution Day (May 3) soon after the end of the Occupation. Local administrations had followed the central government's lead in celebrating the day; now they followed that lead in disregarding it. Recently, however,

[37] Allan B. Campbell, "The Implementation of Water Quality Legislation: Comparative Case Studies in Japan" (unpublished dissertation, Rutgers University, 1977), pp. 239-271. Minobe picked a man to whom the press had bestowed the title "pollution of the sea G-man" as his Water Control Department chief, luring him away from a department chief's position in the Maritime Safety Agency; Asukata appointed members of the medical profession to head the Pollution Control Bureau, and it was their leadership that led to the "Yokohama formula" of pollution control by pollution prevention agreements.

[38] Ibid., p. 399. On a larger question, Campell finds that despite various constraints on their local autonomy, Japanese cities and prefectures exhibit a significant amount of variation in their policy outputs. This view is similar to that held by Aqua (see Chapter 10).

progressive local administrations (Kyoto being one of them) began to celebrate Constitution Day on their own initiative, while the day is still overlooked by conservative administrations.[39] Ninagawa's slogan thus reflects the attitude of some other progressive chief executives.

The emphasis on devotion to the constitutional principles including the "principle of local autonomy" strengthens the perception of the difference between progressive and conservative administrations and, incidentally, rationalizes and legitimizes antagonistic attitudes toward the center that may have their origin in localistic thinking and feeling. While more research on the citizens' perceptions of their local government—as distinguished from the actuality of its performance—needs to be done, a poll conducted in 1973 indicates that Tokyoites considered the Minobe administration as distinctive. While the respondents evaluated this administration differentially—43 percent positive, 32 percent negative—only 17 percent felt that it was "no different from a conservative administration."[40]

Conservative critics do not deny that such a difference exists. What distinguishes progressive administrations, they assert, is a lack of fiscal responsibility. They accuse progressive administrations in particular of excessive spending in both their welfare programs and their personnel policies. In the latter regard, they consider the expansions of the staff and the upgrading of salary levels and fringe benefits, such as retirement payments, to be extravagant, and they point to the fiscal rigidity that these policies create or reinforce. They also contend that the rather indiscriminate responsiveness to the demands of certain unions, such as local public service unions and teachers' unions, as well as to citizens' groups add unduly to the financial burden of progressive local entities. All together they feel that these policies lack a sense of realism, especially when coupled with opposition to policies of higher economic growth that could enlarge the local revenues. When carried out at a time of decreasing revenues, they must inevitably lead to financial disaster. However, while it can hardly be denied that local administrations are once again approaching a state of financial crisis, progressive politicians and commentators see the cause for the crisis not in specific progressive policies but rather in inflation (involving higher material and personnel costs) and recession (involving a slowdown in the rate

[39] Takagi, *Jūmin jichi*, pp. 1, 7.
[40] *Sankei shinbun* poll of 14 May 1973, cited in Kodaira Osamu, "Jimoto no rieki de erabareta kyōsantō," in *Kakushin* (September 1973). The Minobe administration scored high in terms of its effectiveness in increasing welfare and citizens' participation but relatively low in its effectiveness in solving problems of garbage disposal, traffic, and housing.

of increase in tax revenues). They point out that deficits are as rampant in conservative prefectures and cities as they are in progressive ones. In addition to the present economic situation of the country, they blame the government and the ruling party for maintaining a system of local finance that has failed to keep step with the changes and to cope with the problems created by increasing urbanization. They therefore call for reform of the local finance system specifically and for tax reform more generally.[41]

Without attempting to evaluate these contradictory views, we may note that the local finance system became a major issue in the local elections of 1975. This in itself is a development of great significance that may not have come about but for the emergence of local political opposition.

LOCAL POLITICAL OPPOSITION AND LOCAL-NATIONAL RELATIONS

In the preceding section we have been concerned principally with the question of whether the partisan coloration of individual local governments makes a difference for the inhabitants, but, as the previously mentioned demands for reform of the local finance system indicate, the growth of progressive local administrations also has effects on central-local relations. In Chapter 1 we suggested that the salience of institutional opposition as a reflection of a natural tension between the state and subnational units on issues of corporate autonomy is heightened by political local opposition. This is consonant with Muramatsu's scheme of three different patterns of central-local authority relationships, which is cited by Aqua in Chapter 10. Increasing politicization of these relationships, first reflected in the conservative "direct pipeline" argument, ultimately led to an antagonistic pattern, spearheaded by some progressive local administrations. The point we wish to make here is

[41] In "Glory and Misery," Kaminogo refers to "the common pattern, most typically represented by Minobe, of putting forth a lofty ideal, then pathetically appealing to people that realities are so hard that it is not easy to realize the ideal, and finally calling on the public to join them in blaming the central government for their difficulties." For a response, see Miyamoto Kenichi, "The Financial Crisis of Local Governments," translated from the April 1975 issue of *Sekai* in the April 1975 issue of *Japan Echo*, pp. 32-43. To single out progressive administrations for the excessive costs of their personnel policies seems unwarranted. An Autonomy Ministry survey showed that progressive and conservative localities could not be differentiated in this regard and that among the cities with the highest salary levels, conservative and progressive cities were equally represented. See Ronald Aqua, "Politics and Performance in Japanese Municipalities" (unpublished dissertation, Cornell University, 1979), pp. 30-33.

that in this antagonistic pattern, the system of central-local relations itself has become an issue of great significance.

One element in this development is the greater exploitation of the possibilities for autonomous local behavior within the existing system. Progressive chief executives, eager to establish a political profile and willing to benefit by the latent tension between localism and centralization found loopholes for autonomous local behavior in the fuzzy system of distribution of functions.[42] The planning for a "civil minimum" in Tokyo, the measures in support of medium- and small-sized enterprises in Kyoto, and the "Yokohama formula" of pollution control are only a few examples of changes of attitude within an essentially unchanged institutional system. Another element is the rejection of guidance and control from above, which may be exemplified by Mishima's refusal to amalgamate with Numazu and Shimizu and success in thwarting the establishment of a petrochemical complex in the area.[43] The issue there was one of submission to or rejection of guidance rather than of control, because the central and prefectural governments lacked a legal instrument to enforce their desires.

The issue in the case of Tagawa City was different. The function involved in that case was that of alien registration (specifically the alien registration of Korean aliens)—a function in which the mayor was to act as an agent of the national government. The progressive mayor of Tagawa refused to obey administrative directives in regard to this delegated function, and a legal remedy in the form of a sort of *mandamus* procedure based on Article 146 of the Local Autonomy Law was available to the central government.[44] An order requiring the mayor to execute the law as directed was issued, and the invocation of Article

[42] Earlier literature emphasized the exploitation of the same fuzziness by the central government to enlarge the scope of its guidance and control. See, e.g., Steiner, *Local Government*, Chapters 11 and 13.

[43] See Chapter 8.

[44] On this procedure, see Steiner, *Local Government*, pp. 313-315. On the Tagawa case, see MacDougall, *Dissertation*, pp. 412-489 (on which much of the present section is based). The issue involved Japan's relations with South Korea and was thus politically charged. But one line of the argument of the progressive mayors was that the directive went beyond the scope of the basic statute, the Alien Registration Law, and violated the constitutional "principle of local autonomy." It may have been this line of argument that in time persuaded conservative mayors to follow Tagawa in disobeying the Justice Ministry's directive. The Tagawa case was only the culmination of efforts by progressive local administrations to change the directive. A number of progressive mayors also refused to comply with a Health and Welfare Ministry directive, denying welfare payments to families that owned certain household appliances. In this case the ministry withdrew its directive. See MacDougall, *Dissertation*, p. 474.

146 was threatened at an early stage. The order was disobeyed by the mayor. The second step in the procedure would have been a request by the minister with jurisdiction in the matter (in this case the Justice Minister) to the courts for a ruling that would have permitted execution of the matter in place of the recalcitrant mayor and his removal from office. This step was never taken. In the face of a successful national campaign to encourage other cities to follow Tagawa's example, a legal confrontation was avoided. Instead, a political settlement closed the case in a manner that was at least partially a victory for the mayor of Tagawa and other mayors who had followed his lead. The case is noteworthy because of the prominent role played by the National Association of Progressive Mayors in supporting the challenges to the central government directives. It raised the novel question of whether a local chief executive who is to perform a national function by way of agency delegation may exercise his discretion in interpreting the law on which the delegation is based. In doing so, it focused attention on the larger problems involved in the entire system of agency delegation.

In the Tagawa case it was the national government that had the option of recourse to the courts, although it preferred not to exercise that option. But recently local governments have themselves used litigation to assert their rights vis-à-vis the central government. This new development is connected with value changes in Japanese society at large. Japanese tradition in general is not hospitable to the insistence on rights and the use of the courts as a conflict-solving mechanism.[45] During the period when local government was a "conservative paradise" and conservatives set the mold for intergovernmental relations, local government cases dealing with intergovernmental issues were a very small proportion of all administrative cases reaching the courts. In 1965 it could be stated that "the progressive local leader . . . has not yet learned to entrust his protection in case of deviance to the law and to the courts, which would elsewhere serve as his logical shield."[46]

[45] See, for example, Kenzo Takayanagi, "A Century of Innovation: The Development of Japanese Law, 1868-1961," in *Law in Japan*, ed. Arthur Von Mehren (Cambridge: Harvard University Press, 1963), p. 39; Takeyoshi Kawashima, "Dispute Resolution in Contemporary Japan," in ibid., pp. 43-45; and Takeyoshi Kawashima, *Nihonjin no hōishiki* (Tōkyō: Iwamami, 1967), passim. An analysis of contemporary surveys on the law consciousness of the Japanese was published by the Nippon Bunka Kaigi, also under the title *Nihonjin no hōishiki* (Tōkyō: Shiseido, 1973). See especially pp. 88-90.

[46] Steiner, *Local Government*, p. 328. According to Supreme Court statistics, only 4.8 percent of all administrative cases between May 1947 and December 1957 were "local government cases" and probably very few—if any—dealt with intergovernmental issues.

The use of litigation in public affairs in general has become more prominent in recent years. For example, the "four major pollution cases" had among other effects a substantial impact on the climate of public opinion regarding the importance of the judicial process. The use of lawsuits by local entities in the era of the "antagonistic pattern" of intergovernmental relations is part of this emerging picture. The lawsuits deal primarily with the existing financial arrangements between the center and the local entities.[47]

In the suit brought in 1973 by Settsu, a city in Osaka prefecture headed by a progressive mayor, the issue involved the central government's payment of its share for the construction of day nurseries. The share was prescribed by the Local Finance Law and the Child Welfare Law.[48] According to the latter law, this share was to be 50 percent, and the plaintiff asserted that this amounted to about 45.5 million yen. Since the government had paid only 2.5 million yen, the city sued the

[47] In May 1975 the legal journal *Hōritsu Jihō* published a special issue on local finance and litigation. The documentation of four cases was published by the All-Japan Union of Local Public Government Workers in 1976 under the title *Chihō zaisei kakuritsu no saibantōsō*. I am indebted to Professor Takagi Shosaku for having provided me with this and other pertinent material.

In a broader sense, cases in which local entities are willing to face a lawsuit and to rely on the vindication of their position through the judicial process are also indicators of a heightened law consciousness and rights consciousness. In addition to the Tagawa case, two cases involving the city of Kushiro in Hokkaido may be mentioned. The plaintiffs in these cases were a milk products company and a paper company that had established themselves in the city at a time when, like many other cities, it had a policy of attracting industry by supportive measures. Following the election of a progressive mayor in 1965, the city's policy changed, and it passed a by-law withdrawing further support for the enlargement of plants. The two companies sued the city, but the Kushiro District Court rejected their claim, and when the paper company appealed to the Sapporo High Court, the appeal was rejected. See Wada Hideo, "Jichitai, Jūmin Undō to shihōsanka," in the May 1975 issue of *Hōritsu Jihō*, p. 24. In 1977, Governor Minobe's intention to sue the central government on the issue of its granting or withholding permits for the floatation of local loans was thwarted when he did not obtain the required resolution of the Metropolitan assembly. On this issue, see also Chapter 10, n. 26.

[48] The Settsu case highlights one reason for the "excess financial burden" borne by the local entities, namely the failure of the central government to contribute its share of certain expenses in accordance with the Local Finance Law and other laws. About the relevant provisions of the Local Finance Law, see Steiner, *Local Government*, pp. 284-286. On other reasons, including the system of agency delegations, see MacDougall, *Dissertation*, pp. 83-91. Although recourse to lawsuits such as that of Settsu affect central-local relations in general, a successful outcome affects first and most immediately the local entity in question. To the extent to which progressive local entities are more likely to bring such lawsuits, the political coloration of the local administration may also matter to the inhabitants.

state for the difference of about 43.9 million yen. The government asked for rejection of the suit because the city had failed first to obtain an allotment decision of the Minister of Health and Welfare that was a prerequisite for a suit in accordance with a recently enacted Law for the Appropriate Implementation of the Budget. In December 1976 the Tokyo District Court rejected the suit on procedural grounds. Until that decision is changed on appeal or until the procedural flaw is remedied, the substantive issue remains in abeyance. But the mayor of Settsu, Inoue Issei, achieved sufficient exposure through the lawsuit to run successfully in the Diet election in 1976. Moreover, he was succeeded as mayor by his brother. Thus it seems that a significant portion of the local electorate no longer considers lawsuits against the national government as a sort of dangerous insubordination or as an unharmonious and in a sense un-Japanese undertaking, but on the contrary as a somewhat heroic defense of local interests. A similar though more complex suit, dealing with the financial support for the expenses of the management of nursery schools, was brought in 1974 by the progressive mayor of the city of Kokubunji in Tokyo Metropolis. In this case, too, the government asked for dismissal on procedural grounds. The case is now pending in the Tokyo District Court.

A different challenge was presented to the government by the suit that the city of Omuta brought to the Fukuoka District Court in 1975. The city, headed by a conservative mayor, attacked a provision of the Local Tax Law as unconstitutional, claiming that it violated the constitutional "principle of local autonomy." The provision exempts certain large industries from paying a local tax on electricity consumption. The lawsuit, based on the State Indemnity Law, demanded indemnity for tax revenues lost because of the exemption of the Mitsui Corporation's aluminum and chemical works situated in Omuta. The suit has not been decided as yet in the courts, but it has already had its effect in a political sense: the Autonomy Ministry submitted a bill to the Diet, eliminating a number of exemptions from the Local Tax Law.

The number of suits is still small. If they are not used more frequently, it is probably because of calculations of the chances of success and of the time and costs involved rather than because of traditional inhibitions or a belief in the need for nonconflictive relations between levels of government. The potential usefulness of litigation has now been recognized, and in 1975 the National Association of Progressive Mayors, which had lent its support to some of the mayors involved in the past, considered expanding the number of such suits.

Although the use of litigation is by its nature a type of resistance

346

to the central government within the existing institutional system of central-local relations, there have also been efforts to change these relations. Here, too, intergovernmental financial arrangements and, in particular, the excess financial burdens resulting from agency delegation are central issues.[49] The existence of the problem of excess financial burdens has been confirmed by surveys of the Finance and Autonomy Ministries. A number of activities illustrate its salience. Thus, appeals for alleviation of the problem have been made to the government by the semiofficial National Association of Governors and National Association of Mayors for many years. In 1969, fourteen progressive mayors used a provision of the Local Finance Law for the first time to submit an opinion on the matter (*ikensho*) to the Cabinet.[50] In 1970, a meeting of the National Association of Progressive Mayors passed a resolution calling for a thorough study of agency delegation. The Local Self-Government Center in Tokyo, which functions as the secretariat of the National Association of Progressive Mayors, the all-Japan Union of Local Government Employees, a research group in Hokkaido, and others conducted their own research.[51] Furthermore, the Tokyo Metropolitan government has repeatedly presented plans for financial reform, and Yokohama, Kobe, and Kawasaki have taken similar steps. Late in 1974 the six semiofficial local government associations organized a Special Committee to Eliminate the Excess Burden on Local Authorities, and they later released a report sharply critical of the central government's lack of action in the matter. In late 1974 progressive mayors demonstrated in Tokyo and, in a visit to the prime minister's residence, demanded immediate measures to eliminate excess burden, threatening a sit-in. The annual Conference of Governors of 1975, held at the prime minister's residence, was marked by an air of distrust bordering on hostility in regard to this issue. The government admits that some adjustment is needed—a three-year program to ease excess financial burdens was actually launched in 1969—but adamantly insists that many local governments have interpreted certain functions,

---

[49] From a progressive viewpoint, in the long range reform is needed to decentralize the decision-making structure; more immediately, concerns are with facilitating the redistributive policies of progressive entities, especially in the welfare field. But inasmuch as the issue of intergovernmental financial relations affects the solvency of local governments in general, progressive and conservative local governments are on the same side.

[50] MacDougall, *Dissertation*, pp. 87-89.

[51] Ibid., p. 488. Some of the findings of the All-Japan Union of Local Government Workers are contained in its report *Kikan ininjimu to zaisei futan* (Tōkyō, 1975).

especially in the area of welfare services, too broadly and have engaged in irresponsible spending programs.[52]

In the background looms the application of the Law to Provide Special Measures for the Promotion of Local Finance Reconstruction of 1955, which would increase central government control over deficitary local governments. As stated, the issue of financial reform is not new. It first came to the fore in the early fifties, and the Special Measures Law of 1955 was the result. In this context, the opinion was expressed that the crisis of that time was only a symptom of a malaise inherent in the local finance system and that local finance reconstruction dealt only with the symptom while the system remained unchanged. This is true even today, but the emergence of progressive local administrations has given a new salience to the issues involved, and a new climate of public opinion provides greater resonance for demands for change.[53]

Attempts to change another aspect of the local government system in the direction of fuller implementation of the constitutional "principle of local autonomy" were successful. At various times they involved direct demands as a form of direct democracy, the use of the judiciary, and the support of a progressive chief executive. The issue was the mode of selection for the chiefs of Tokyo's twenty-three "special wards." These "special wards" in Tokyo Metropolis, comprising the most densely inhabited areas, constituted the city of Tokyo before 1943. When the city of Tokyo was abolished as a governmental unit in that year, the wards continued as subdivisions of the newly created Tokyo Metropolis, side by side with cities, towns, and villages within the metropolis.[54] The Local Autonomy Law of 1947, enacted as one of the major occupation reforms in the area of local government, stated that, except as provided for in cabinet orders, special wards were to be treated as cities. This meant that they elected their chief executives—the ward chiefs—directly. But, as part of the "reverse

[52] See Aqua, "Politics and Performance," pp. 17, 48, 50f., and Miyamoto, "The Financial Crisis," p. 41.

[53] Steiner, *Local Government*, p. 297. The change in the attitudes of local administrations is reflected in the obsoleteness of an earlier observation based on interviews at the time: "One would expect that local officials would oppose this system [of assigned functions]. However, many of them are so used to carrying out primarily assigned functions with revenues from 'above' that they find it difficult to envision a state of affairs in which their main task would be to carry out local projects with locally raised revenues. Their eyes are firmly fixed on obtaining more and greater national shares. . . . The effect of this on their sense of local responsibility needs no comment" (ibid., p. 286).

[54] See Chapter 1, and also Steiner, *Local Government*, pp. 61; 194-195.

course," the Local Autonomy Law was amended in 1952 to provide for the indirect election of the ward chiefs by the ward assemblies, subject to the approval of the metropolitan governor. The amendment that left the ward inhabitants at a political disadvantage compared with the inhabitants of cities, towns, and villages occasioned violent protest by progressives in some ward assemblies, but these tactics were of no avail.[55]

A different tactic was first applied by citizens of Nerima ward in 1968. Since a revision of the existing Local Autonomy Law could not be obtained from the LDP cabinet, a citizens' group calling itself the Association of Ward People to Elect a Ward Chief proposed a by-law for the ward according to which, in electing a ward chief, the assembly would have to do so "on the basis of the vote of the ward residents" in a preliminary election. The group intended to make this proposal the subject of a direct demand as provided in the Local Autonomy Law, but when the group submitted the proposal to the acting ward chief to initiate the direct demand procedure, he refused to do so on direction of the Autonomy Ministry, stating that a by-law of this content was not covered by the provisions of the law and that it would deprive the ward assembly of its independence in a matter under its jurisdiction. The administrative lawsuit brought by the group was successful in the Tokyo District Court as first instance and in the Tokyo High Court as second instance, but in the end, the Nerima ward assembly failed to enact the desired by-law.

The second attempt to change the system was made in Shinagawa ward in 1972, with an entirely different outcome. The by-law, passed unanimously by the Shinagawa ward assembly, stated that the assembly would select the ward chief "having reference to the results of the preliminary election," thus softening one of the legal objections raised in the Nerima case. On the ward chiefs' request for reconsideration, the assembly passed the by-law—again unanimously. As provided by the law, an investigation was then requested of the next higher au-

---

[55] The constitutionality of the amendment was attacked in two cases that ultimately reached the Supreme Court. In the first case, in 1956 the Supreme Court refused to rule on the question of constitutionality, finding that the plaintiff lacked standing in an actual controversy concerning his concrete legal rights. In the second case, which arose in connection with the bribing of ward assemblymen by candidates for the position of ward chief, in 1963 the Supreme Court quashed a contrary decision of the Tokyo District Court and found that the provision of Article 93 of the Constitution requiring direct election of local chief executives did not apply to Tokyo's wards because they were not independent local entities in the sense of that article. The Court decided, therefore, that the amendment of 1952 was not unconstitutional. See Steiner, *Local Government*, pp. 123-124.

thority, the governor, who could have rescinded the assembly's action. But Governor Minobe refused to do so, stating that "it was natural that the people in the wards demand the return to the principle of local autonomy as far as it is possible."

The first preliminary election in Shinagawa was held in December 1972, and a number of other wards passed similar by-laws during the next two years. Shortly after Minobe's refusal to act, the Local System Investigation Council, a consultative government organ established by law, met to deliberate the issue and presented a report favoring reform. A bill amending the Local Autonomy Law to provide for the public election of ward chiefs was passed by the Diet in 1974. The government's willingness to restore the situation existing prior to the amendment of 1952 was probably influenced by a political consideration: the number of special ward assemblies with LDP majorities was decreasing, and this created the possibility that, if united, the opposition parties in the assemblies could elect progressive ward chiefs as had already happened in Chuo ward in 1971.[56] The first direct ward chief elections were held in April 1975. The successful candidates in all wards were independents, supported by a variety of coalitions: in seven wards that coalition included the LDP and the JSP, CGP, and DSP.

What we have attempted to demonstrate in the present section is that the salience of local autonomy is heightened when institutional local opposition is reinforced by political local opposition. This point is stated well by a critic of "the first generation progressive heads of local governments," such as Governors Minobe of Tokyo and Kuroda of Osaka and Mayor Motoyama of Nagoya. Dealing with the "Glory and Misery of Local Autonomies Under Progressive Control," Kaminogo Toshiaki wrote in 1975:

> [A] Significant achievement of the first generation progressive heads of local autonomies is that they have made citizens conscious of the existence of autonomy. For example, Tokyo prefectural policies were seldom treated as big news prior to Governor Minobe.

[56] The amendment of 1974 also had important consequences for the status of the wards as local entities and for their relationship to the metropolis in terms of functions, personnel, and finances. See Takagi Shosaku, "Kuchō kōsensei no fukkatsu to tokubetsuku no jichi," in *Shakaihendo to gyōseitaiō*, Nippon Gyōsei Gakkai, pp. 187-229, and "Kūchō kōsen to jimuigō," in *Toshi Mondai* 65 (1974): 27-37; also Wada, "Jichitai," pp. 21-23, and Tokubetsukusei Chōsakai, *Tokubetsuku no arikata ni tsuite* (Tōkyō, 1975).

Aside from the political consideration mentioned in the text, the government may also have been willing to amend the law in order to forestall the proliferation of spontaneously created ward by-laws, putting the management of preliminary elections into the hands of private groups.

This is not to say that making headlines is a good thing in itself, but had there not been a rush of progressive controlled autonomies, we would not have taken to the "study of autonomy," nor would many people have given thought to the subject of "what autonomy is."

Kaminogo concludes: "Is this not the essential significance of progressive controlled local autonomies?"[57]

To summarize the preceding two sections of this chapter: if we ask whether or not there is any difference between the policies of progressive and conservative administrations on the mayoral and gubernatorial level, we find that the evidence is somewhat mixed. When viewed from the perspective of aggregate budgetary data, conservative-progressive distinctions tend to become blurred. We noted one of the reasons in passing: the diffusion of certain policies initiated by progressive local entities to conservative local entities by way of demonstration effect. In some areas, the policies of progressive local administrations were a spur to national action. This horizontal and vertical diffusion of policy initiatives has narrowed the distances between progressive and conservative administrations. Thus it bears repeating that just as it is unwarranted to assume that all progressive chief executives are progressive in their policies, so it is no longer warranted to assume that there are no conservative chief executives with progressive policies.

The differences become more marked when we enlarge our perspective to encompass issues not necessarily reflected in budgetary data. In this context, we note questions of a more systemic nature that loom beyond the question of whether the partisan coloration of individual local governments makes a difference for the inhabitants in terms of local policy. One of these questions concerns the effect of the emergence of progressive local governments on central-local relations. There is little doubt about such an effect. The issue of local autonomy has acquired a new salience in regard to initiatives for institutional reform in terms of both the actual behavior of local officeholders and in terms of popular awareness.

There remains the question of the impact of the emergence of progressive local governments on the political system more generally. There are indications that due largely to the initiatives taken by highly visible progressive administrations in social welfare and environmental protection policies as well as in the area of government-citizen relations, a link has been established in the public mind between progressive administrations and progressive policies. This mass perception of

---

[57] Kaminogo, "Glory and Misery," pp. 30-31.

a difference between progressive and conservative administrations is likely to have important political consequences. Thus a number of progressive local chief executives have won considerable public approbation in a country in which opposition to those in national power has not been a popular stance heretofore and in which politicians are generally seen in unusually negative hues. Many local elections have become more "marginal" in the sense that alternation in local control has become more feasible. The influence of personality and of image building on campaigns notwithstanding, the mass perception of a difference between conservatives and progressives indicates that to many voters electoral contests present a more meaningful choice than before. In short, in public policies, intergovernmental relations, citizen-government relations, and mass attitudes towards politics, at least on the local level, the impact of the emergence of local progressive administrations has been considerable.

CHAPTER 10

POLITICAL CHOICE AND POLICY CHANGE
IN MEDIUM-SIZED JAPANESE CITIES, 1962-1974

Ronald Aqua

IN a variety of ways, the contributors to this volume analyze the localistic forces that have challenged the authority of the central government in recent years. It is important to remember, however, that subnational policy processes need to be discussed in the context of the policies and programs of the central government in Tokyo. Several of the authors have already indicated that local policy makers confront many structural and political constraints when setting local priorities.[1] Thus, as progressive administrations assume office in many areas and citizens' movements thwart important developmental initiatives of the central government, a shift in the flow of political resources between different tiers of government is occurring. Still, most observers are reluctant to admit that the traditional pattern of "leadership from above" has changed in any fundamental sense.[2] Proponents of the local reformist movement point with pride to their achievements in such areas as environmental protection and social welfare—and yet, they find it difficult to relate these initiatives to the acquisition of real power in the Tokyo-based national political system.

Not surprisingly, then, a certain degree of vacillation has marked much of the scholarly literature on this subject.[3] While few scholars feel at ease with the contradictory notions of local reformism and a high degree of centralization, there has not been a concerted effort to resolve these conceptual difficulties through careful and systematic empirical research. One unfortunate outcome of this scholarly impasse has been a distinct failure to rise above rigid partisan positions or to

The author gratefully acknowledges the support he received from the Social Science Research Council's International Doctoral Research Fellowship Program to conduct the research for this study.
[1] See Chapters 1, 9, and 11 of this volume.

[2] The phrase "leadership from above" is used by Ide Yoshinori in his discussion of the central government's regional development programs. See his *Chihōjichi no seiji-gaku* (Tōkyō: Tōkyō Daigaku Shuppankai, 1972), pp. 51-93.

[3] See, for example, Ide Yoshinori, "Toshi seiji kakushin no kadai," in Iwanami Kōza, *Gendai toshi seisaku III* (Tōkyō: Iwanami Shoten, 1973), pp. 16-20.

explore the implications of localistic political activities for the larger political system.[4]

The purpose of this essay is to examine these issues by attempting to find the answers to two important questions:

1. To what degree do local policy priorities reflect the priorities of the central government? Here we shall hypothesize that even in a system where the notion of "leadership from above" is still very strong, legal constraints and financial dependency relationships do not *by themselves* constitute any compelling proof of central domination over the local decision-making process. Just as the capacity to decide on basic goals is a critical component of local autonomy, so the absence of that capacity must be incorporated into a truly meaningful definition of "centralization."

2. If we establish that localities set their major priorities independently and free from any significant central intervention, what forces operate locally to influence the direction of local priorities? In particular, we shall test the common assumption that local administrations can be considered either progressive or conservative and that this partisan-based dichotomy is significant in accounting for local policy outcomes.

Muramatsu Michio has suggested that three different patterns of central-local authority relationships are intrinsically linked to the degree of partisanship in the Japanese political system.[5] In Muramatsu's schema, these patterns are united in both a chronological and a developmental sense. Furthermore, they do not necessarily seem to be mutually exclusive. In the following discussion, we shall present the outline of Muramatsu's very useful observations, relating how they have led us to derive several hypotheses concerning the relationship between local autonomy and the partisanship of city mayors.

The first pattern of "cohesive" central-local relations developed from the reconstructed remnants of the prewar administrative structure. Above all, central officials strove to provide a comprehensive and rational framework for postwar reconstruction efforts, as exemplified in the passage of the National Land Comprehensive Development Law

[4] Relevant discussions of this problem include Douglas Ashford, "Theories of Local Government: Some Comparative Considerations," *Comparative Political Studies* 8 (1975): 90-107, and Mark Kesselman and Donald Rosenthal, *Local Power and Comparative Politics*, Sage Professional Papers in Comparative Politics 5, series no. 01-049 (Beverly Hills and London: Sage Publications, 1974).

[5] See his "Sengo Nihon no chihō seiji," in *Gendai seiji to chihō jichi*, Muramatsu et al. (Tōkyō: Yūshindō, 1975), pp. 67-77. See also his "The Impact of Economic Growth Policies on Local Politics in Japan," *Asian Survey* 15 (1975): 799-816.

of 1950.[6] The dynamics of decision making centered around in-house ministerial investigations and deliberations, with some degree of input from appointed advisory commissions, paid consultants, and local officials. Localities were tightly bound to the central government through the system of delegated functions and its accompanying categorical grants-in-aid structure, as well as through personnel policies that assured a central government "presence" at the local level. In a larger sense, there was a distinctive "administrative dynamic" that required a considerable degree of local petitioning during the annual budget-drafting season in the central ministries.

A widely cited example of the effectiveness of this cohesive structure, and one provided by Muramatsu, is the postwar wave of amalgamations of smaller local authorities into larger entities. This program grew largely out of central government (and Occupation authority) initiatives. From 1940 to 1960, for example, the total number of local entities decreased from 11,232 to 3,511, while the number of cities rose from 166 to 556.[7] Also at the behest of the central government, local authorities passed ordinances that provided attractive conditions for industries wishing to relocate or construct new facilities. By 1966, almost 70 percent of all cities had passed such ordinances.[8]

By 1955, a merger of parties in both major ideological camps had resulted in a united Socialist Party and a conservative and business-oriented Liberal Democratic Party. The LDP and its business allies quickly set out to expand their influence over many bureaucratic aspects of the ongoing regional development program. This effort was enhanced by the presence of former central bureaucrats in the ranks of both the major corporations and the LDP. Within a few years, the earlier "rationalistic" model of bureaucratic decision making evolved into a system dominated by narrowly construed partisan interests.

---

[6] On the basis of this law, prefectures took the first small steps toward establishing their own development agencies. The central government coordinated their efforts, however, and was chiefly responsible for drawing up plans for "resource regions" that were to serve as the basis for resource mobilization during the postwar reconstruction. See Haruo Nagamine, "A Memorandum on Regional Development in Japan: The Case of Aichi Prefecture" (United Nations Center for Regional Development, October 1972).

[7] Kurt Steiner, *Local Government in Japan* (Stanford: Stanford University Press, 1965), p. 182.

[8] Muramatsu relates that "these incentives typically included the following provisions: (1) the incoming industries would be exempt from paying local property taxes for three to five years; (2) the industries would receive land as a gift; and (3) the local government would promise to construct public facilities in support of business activities." See his "The Impact of Economic Growth Policies," p. 805.

Masumi Junnosuke has observed that during this period, the "normal pattern" of decision making all but excluded the opposition parties, organized labor, local civic action groups, and other organizations seeking a voice in the decisions affecting their localities.[9]

In the election campaigns of that period, many LDP candidates for office openly promised a "direct pipeline to the center" if they were elected.[10] Whereas this direct pipeline presumably entailed numerous tangible benefits for localities that consistently elected conservative candidates to public office, it could more properly be regarded as a double-edged sword. Public criticism of the LDP or failure to publicly identify with it was thought to expose an "offender" to a wide range of sanctions and countermeasures by the central government, as several well-documented cases will serve to illustrate. In 1958, the governor of Chiba prefecture found it expedient to join the LDP prior to the gubernatorial campaign of that year in order to overcome certain bureaucratic obstacles that impeded his prefecture's industrial development plans.[11] In another instance, the Socialist mayor of Koriyama City in Fukushima prefecture left his party and joined the LDP to facilitate the designation of Koriyama as a new industrial city under the New Industrial Cities Construction Act of 1962. On the other hand, the progressive governor of Oita prefecture refused to travel to Tokyo to petition the central government for a "New Industrial Cities" designation for the city of Oita. Because the act of petitioning was thought to represent a gesture of local subordination to central authority, the LDP indicated that the governor's behavior was "impertinent." This same governor also failed to greet a visiting LDP cabinet officer at the train station during an election campaign, and for this transgression, the LDP warned of harsh retaliatory action.[12]

The politicization of bureaucratic decision making was epitomized in the events surrounding the announcement of the Comprehensive National Development Plan of 1962. This master plan was originally intended to direct the allocation of capital investment for industrial development in areas along the Pacific coastal belt that were already

[9] Masumi Junnosuke, *Gendai Nihon no seiji taisei* (Tōkyō: Iwanami Shoten, 1969), p. 414.

[10] According to Hoshino Mitsuo, this slogan was first strongly emphasized during the unified local election campaign of 1959. See Isomura Eiichi and Hoshino Mitsuo, *Chihō jichi dokuhon* (Tōkyō: Tōyō Keizai Shimpōsha, 1966), p. 37.

[11] See the account in Ōhara Mitsunori and Yokoyama Keiji, *Sangyō shakai to seiji katei* (Tōkyō: Nippon Hyōronsha, 1965), pp. 116-119. See also Masumi, *Gendai Nihon*, p. 254.

[12] For an account of these cases, see Matsubara Haruo, *Nihon no shakai kaihatsu* (Tōkyō: Fukumura Shuppan, 1968), p. 119.

highly developed. Strong-willed and vociferous intervention by rural LDP Dietmen, however, succeeded in having that intention considerably revised. In its final form, the plan addressed itself to the problem of regional disparities in income levels and promised more investment in depopulated or underdeveloped rural areas. This promise was soon fulfilled in the passage of the New Industrial Cities Construction Act to which we have already alluded.[13]

According to Muramatsu, a new pattern of central-local relations seemed to emerge during the implementation of various regional development programs in the early 1960s.[14] He regards this as a period of "cooperative" relationships between central and local authorities, for by this time, most prefectures had established special "development agencies" attuned to the needs of industrial firms operating in their areas, and local "development councils" that consisted of representatives from business, the national and local branches of the LDP, and prefectural and municipal governments served in an advisory capacity to "development bureaus" within the prefectural governments.[15] Local civic action groups were generally not represented in these councils.

Several structural deficiencies in this cooperative structure eventually came to haunt the advocates of direct pipeline politics. Muramatsu recounts how an antagonistic relationship gradually began to develop between the conservative central government and many newly elected "progressive" local administrations. In one famous case, a well-organized locally run campaign in three small Shizuoka prefecture communities succeeded in forcing the cancellation of central government plans for a major new petrochemical complex.[16] This success spawned many similar campaigns throughout the nation. Furthermore, a series of favorable decisions for the victims of industrial pollution in four widely publicized lawsuits established the principle of corporate responsibility in cases where industrial polluters caused damage to personal health and livelihood.[17] Many local activists in the environmental movement read-

[13] For a description of the famous "war on petitions" that accompanied the quest for designation as a "New Industrial City," see Satō Atsushi, "Shin-sangyō-toshi no rinen to genjitsu," in *Hōgaku seminaa*, December 1963-April 1964 issues. See also Masumi, *Gendai Nihon*, pp. 412-413.

[14] These programs instituted laws to promote industrial developments in underdeveloped areas (1961), in mining areas (1961), in special designated areas (1964), in remote areas (1965), in depopulated areas (1970), and in rural areas (1971).

[15] See Masumi, *Gendai Nihon*, pp. 250-251. For a detailed account of local reorganization in Chiba prefecture, including the problems associated with that reorganization, see Ōhara and Yokoyama, *Sangyō shakai*, pp. 66-85.

[16] See Chapter 8.

[17] These cases are the Minamata, Yokkaichi, Niigata, and itai-itai disease cases.

ily found allies in candidates for local office who promised a "direct pipeline to the people" rather than a "direct pipeline to the center."

The complex relationship that developed between locally based "citizens' movements" and the national opposition parties can be traced in part to certain reorganizational measures undertaken by the progressive camp after the Ampo demonstrations of 1960. Many Socialists felt that their movement had failed to mobilize ordinary citizens at the grassroots level and that future efforts should focus on the local political arena. Local progressive administrations could then administer programs in a manner consistent with socialist principles and, at the same time, in a way that would serve to undermine the support bases of conservative politicians. Certain socialistic policy goals could thus be achieved on a piecemeal basis without the necessity of attaining an absolute majority in the national Diet.[18] The actualization of this new strategy is best reflected in the resignation of Socialist Asukata Ichio from his Diet seat to stand for election as the mayor of Yokohama in 1963. He was elected and thereafter initiated a reformist program that many regard as a model of progressive local administration.[19]

More than a hundred local governments are led by progressive chief executives at the present time. According to compilations of policy statements assembled by the National Association of Progressive Mayors, these progressive leaders strive to democratize local political life by incorporating the opinions of ordinary citizens into the local decision-making process.[20] This concept of "direct democracy" strongly interferes with the normal pattern of cooperative decision making, and it is not hard to understand why Muramatsu calls this third pattern of central-local relations "antagonistic." This pattern is still in its developmental stage and is not yet clearly demarcated from the cooperative pattern in many localities.

See Norie Huddle and Michael Reich, *Island of Dreams: Environmental Crisis in Japan* (New York and Tokyo: Autumn Press, 1975).

[18] See Terry E. MacDougall, "Political Opposition and Local Government in Japan: The Significance of Emerging Progressive Local Leadership" (unpublished dissertation, Yale University, 1975), pp. 287-294 and pp. 315-325 (hereafter cited as MacDougall, *Dissertation*).

[19] Asukata has been a driving force in the establishment and development of the National Association of Progressive Mayors, an effective lobbyist organization for the local progressive cause. He has also figured prominently in developing programs for greater citizen participation in city government and for greater city control over industrial polluters. See ibid., pp. 295-296, 340, and 392-399.

[20] See the annual publication of the National Association of Progressive Mayors entitled *Kakushin shichō shisei hōshin shū* (Tōkyō: Chihō Jichi Sentaa).

Based on Muramatsu's analysis we are now able to propose several statements that relate the degree of local autonomy to the degree of local partisanship. In the cohesive pattern of local-central relations, local control over the setting of developmental priorities is very low, and the potential influence of partisan-based organizations over local decision making is correspondingly minimal. The dominant features of the cohesive pattern are low corporate autonomy and a "rationalistic," depoliticized decision-making structure throughout the system.

In the cooperative pattern, central agencies are responsive to partisan pressure and tolerate a measure of local flexibility in reshaping program requirements to fit local conditions. Localities engage in strenuous competition for highly specific grants-in-aid and other discretionary benefits. Central agencies are faced by a scarcity of resources to be allocated, and they find themselves increasingly unable to follow wholly nonpartisan criteria for the allocation. Consequently, certain localities acquire a degree of bargaining leverage vis-à-vis the center, and localities with access through the conservative party network stand to derive the greatest material benefits from a cooperative relationship with the center.

The third, or antagonistic, pattern of local-central relations is certainly the most complex. Discontented citizens exert pressure on their local leaders to reassess central government policies and to respond to local rather than national needs. Local administrators come to realize that carefully planned and well-timed resistance to particular central plans, backed by local citizen support, does not necessarily entail severe retaliation, as the central conservative elite can punish particular localities only at the risk of seriously undermining its own electoral support base. The criteria for resource allocation set by central administrators become increasingly standardized in response to demands for nonprejudicial treatment and this, in turn, reinforces the ineffectiveness of partisan-based retaliation by the LDP. Local affairs become increasingly politicized at the same time that local partisan ties to central party elites become strained. Local politicians depend on locally derived support for important policy initiatives, though not necessarily in the context of sterile ideological debate. Central-local authority relationships reflect this new local assertiveness as grass-roots democracy is finally implanted in Japanese soil.

Our extrapolation from Muramatsu's analysis must remain tentative and somewhat incomplete, insofar as this is not the appropriate place to present a more detailed commentary on his approach. The boundaries and chronological ordering of Muramatsu's three patterns

359

of central-local relationships are not carefully defined, nor is much empirical evidence mustered in support of his assertions. Muramatsu does provide us, however, with a comprehensive framework that incorporates many of the conventional arguments raised with respect to the relationship between local autonomy and partisanship in postwar Japan. From this perspective, the analysis is well-suited to serve as a guide in the construction of a number of testable propositions.

We shall hypothesize that low local autonomy is most strongly associated with a low degree of partisanship in local politics, moderate autonomy with moderate partisanship, and high autonomy with strong partisanship. To test for the strength of these relationships, we studied partisanship and policy performance in eighty-eight medium-sized Japanese municipalities. The cities in this particular size-range displayed the following attributes: 1) they were located throughout Japan and not necessarily in the greater Tokyo or Osaka metropolitan regions; 2) they varied considerably with respect to their socio-economic and industrial structures and the degree to which they have experienced demographic change; 3) they had large enough populations to have experienced substantial competition in local and national electoral contests; and 4) the sample size was sufficiently large to filter out some of the idiosyncratic factors that influence smaller samples.[21]

In the next part of this study we shall attempt to measure local autonomy by studying changes in revenue and spending priorities for the cities in our sample. Revenue and spending decisions do not, of course, constitute a universe of the major policy decisions for a city administration in a given year. Certain regulatory or organizational questions (including a decision to incorporate more direct citizen participation into the local policy process) are also critical parts of any mayor's program. Nonetheless, revenue strategies and spending decisions certainly constitute singularly important political acts for a local chief executive. Adjustments in local tax rates or changes in the pattern of spending commitments can reveal how city leaders respond differentially to pressures from higher administrative tiers or to other political forces operating at the local level.[22]

21 Those cities that had a "densely inhabited district" (DID) population of between 100,000 and 500,000 according to the national census of 1970 were included here. This served to exclude many smaller cities that had been created through the amalgamation of smaller villages during the 1950s. Several of the eighty-eight cities in the sample experienced further major amalgamations during the time period under study here, and two of the cities were actually incorporated after 1962. These two cities therefore have not been included in certain parts of the analysis that utilize longitudinal data.

22 See the related discussion in Valerie Bunce, "Elite Succession, Petrification,

The time frame for our analysis will be 1962 to 1974. The first time point coincides with the release of reliable local financial data, the emergence of reformist chief executives in local elections, and the implementation of major new developmental programs initiated by the central government. The end point of the analysis marks the beginning of a new economic era for Japan, as inflation and unemployment reached high levels, governmental revenues plummeted, and the growth rate of the economy slowed considerably.

CENTRAL POLICIES AND LOCAL PERFORMANCE

The central government provides one-fifth or more of total revenues to the cities in our sample in the form of categorical grants-in-aid. These funds would seem to represent an important mechanism for higher-level control over the local policy process. If we accept the argument that central spending policy is a key determinant of local policy outcomes, then even a slight adjustment in the level of central spending for a particular program would be felt throughout the entire local government system. In order to test for the effects of changes in central spending commitments on local priorities, we shall first examine changes in the overall structure of central spending and then compare these to changes in spending at different subnational levels. If the assumption regarding the relationship between financial dependency and policy domination is correct, we could expect a degree of congruence between the patterns of change among different levels of the system.

Table 1 shows the structural composition of central government spending by the percentage breakdown of various spending categories for 1964 and 1973. These figures are generally supportive of John Campbell's contention that a notion of "balance" among competing central agencies results in little change in the allocation of funds from year to year.[23] The share of central government revenues reverted to localities through a system of local equalization grants (called "local finance" in Table 1) increased slightly during this period, as did outlays for social security (many of which were administered locally). Neither gain is indicative of a major shift in national spending priorities. By contrast, spending for industrial development increased consid-

and Policy Innovation in Communist Systems: An Empirical Assessment," *Comparative Political Studies* 9 (1976): 10.

[23] John C. Campbell, "Japanese Budget *Baransu*," in *Modern Japanese Organization and Decision-Making*, ed. Ezra F. Vogel (Berkeley and Los Angeles: University of California, 1975), pp. 98-99. Campbell used different accounting procedures and a different data set for his analysis. See his notations in Tables 1 and 2.

Table 1

General Settled Accounts of the National Treasury, 1964 and 1973
(by percentage)

	1964	*1973*
National Administration	8.7	6.1
Local Finance	19.3	22.0
National Defense	8.5	6.5
Disposition of External Affairs	0.8	1.4
Land Conservation and Development	18.4	16.1
Industrial Development	8.0	13.5
Education, Culture, and Science	12.3	10.7
Social Security	15.6	16.8
Pensions	4.5	3.3
National Debt	1.4	4.6
Other	2.3	0.2

SOURCE: Japan, Office of the Prime Minister, Bureau of Statistics, *Japan Statistical Yearbook*, 1967 and 1975 editions.

erably. Campbell also notes this increase and attributes it to the growing financial burden incurred by the central government in its rice price-support program.[24]

Table 2 presents a slightly different perspective on these same general trends. Percentage rates of change for several of the most important items were computed, and then a "coefficient of priority" was calculated by dividing each separate item's percentage rate of change by the percentage rate of change for the total expenditure. The coefficient of priority thus indicates the extent of change above or below a "normal level" of "1"—a score of "2" for a particular item indicating, for example, that the item increased at twice the rate of total expenditures. Since we regard spending change as an indicator of policy priorities, the higher the coefficient of priority, the higher the priority given to a particular item over a number of years. As Table 2 shows, three categories of central spending failed to keep pace with change in the level of total expenditure: national defense, land conservation and development, and education, culture, and science. Spending for industrial development, however, increased at nearly twice the normal rate.

Still another way to analyze the structure of central government spending is by ministry or agency, which Table 3 does for several of the central ministries that have the most extensive contacts with local authorities. Among these, the Ministry of Health and Welfare and the Autonomy Ministry increased their share of total central spending,

[24] Ibid., p. 99.

Table 2

Percent Rates of Change and Coefficients of Priority
for General Settled Accounts of the
National Treasury, 1964-1973

	Rate of Change(%)	*Coefficient of Priority*
Total Expenditure	346	
Local Finance	409	1.18
National Defense	242	.70
Land Conservation and Development	291	.84
Industrial Development	647	1.87
Education, Culture, and Science	288	.83
Social Security	380	1.10

NOTE: Coefficient of Priority $= \dfrac{\%\ \text{Rate of Change for Item}}{\%\ \text{Rate of Change for Total Expenditure}}$

SOURCE: See Table 1.

Table 3

Expenditures of Selected Central Government Ministries:
Composition by Percentage Breakdown, 1964 and 1973;
Percent Rates of Change and Coefficients of
Priority, 1964-1973

	Composition (%)		*Rate of Change (%)*	*Coefficient of Priority*
	1964	1973		
Education	12.1	10.1	268	.78
Health and Welfare	12.3	14.9	434	1.27
International Trade and Industry	1.5	1.4	304	.89
Transportation	2.4	4.2	680	1.99
Construction	12.1	10.8	293	.86
Autonomy	19.9	22.4	399	1.16
Total Expenditure (All Ministries)			342	

SOURCE: See Table 1.

while the Ministry of Education and the Ministry of Construction lost
ground during the same period. These findings reinforce and confirm
those in Tables 1 and 2. A major discrepancy between changes in the
Ministry of International Trade and Industry (MITI) spending (Table
3) and changes for the "industrial development" category in Tables 1
and 2 can be explained by the inclusion of large primary sector outlays
under the "industrial development" heading, although these are not

within MITI's purview. A substantial increase in expenditures by the Ministry of Transportation reflects the central government's efforts to develop an integrated transportation network as part of the regional industrialization program.

The first three tables have indicated priority spending areas at the central government level during a recent ten-year period. We shall next compare changes in central level spending to changes at the subnational level. First we shall examine spending changes for all local authorities and for all municipalities. Then we shall turn to spending changes in the smaller sample of eighty-eight medium-sized cities. If the impact of central spending on local performance is significant, we should expect the direction of central priorities to be reflected in local priorities as well.

Table 4 summarizes changes in spending patterns for all local government bodies and all cities in Japan for the years 1964-1973. These figures may be directly compared to those in Tables 2 and 3. Both groups of local entities in Table 4 increased their total spending at higher rates than the central government, with cities far surpassing the larger sub-

Table 4

Composition by Percentage Breakdown, Percent Rates of
Change, and Coefficients of Priority for Selected
Expenditure Items for All Local Government
Bodies and for All Cities, 1964-1973

	Composition (%)		Rate of Change (%)	Coefficient of Priority
	1964	1973		
All Local				
Governments				
Social Welfare	7.0	9.9	552	1.55
Sanitation	5.8	6.5	419	1.17
Industrial Promotion	12.3	12.4	362	1.01
Public Works	21.2	23.4	405	1.13
Education	26.7	24.6	323	.90
TOTAL			357	
All Cities				
Social Welfare	10.3	15.4	703	1.61
Sanitation	7.2	7.7	475	1.09
Industrial Promotion	9.5	8.6	386	.88
Public Works	19.7	22.8	523	1.20
Education	19.1	19.3	443	1.01
TOTAL			437	

SOURCE: Japan, Autonomy Ministry, *Local Finance Statistical Yearbook*, 1975 edition (*Chiho zaisei tokei nempō*).

group in this regard. Furthermore, cities devoted a much larger share of their spending to social welfare and gave it greater priority than did the larger subgroup. Cities seemed slightly less burdened by educational and public works expenditures than did local governments as a whole, while their sanitation expenses ran slightly higher. In general terms, social welfare spending received more priority locally than at the national level. This was also true for spending in construction and education.

In the more restricted sample of eighty-eight medium-sized cities, six revenue items have been included in the analysis to indicate changes in the composition of the local resource base. In addition, more specific expenditure items have been substituted for the broad expenditure categories shown in the previous tables. The percentage rates of change and coefficients of priority for six local revenue sources and nine specific expenditure categories appear in Table 5.[25]

We find, first of all, that total spending in the medium-sized cities increased at a much higher rate than spending either by the central government (see Table 3) or by all cities (see Table 4). Revenues rose at a correspondingly high rate. Local taxes were inadequate to meet these sharply rising costs, however, and many cities turned to other local revenue options: borrowing through the sale of bonds and the establishment of new public enterprises such as gambling facilities ("miscellaneous revenues") generated much of the revenue that was needed. Neither of these revenue sources is tied to specific central programs (unlike categorical grants-in-aid), and a greater reliance on them might indicate a relative loss of central control over the formation of local spending priorities.[26]

On the expenditure side, spending for social services for children and the elderly increased at very high rates, reflecting in part the introduc-

[25] The items shown in Table 5 and the following tables represent only a portion of all the revenue and expenditure categories given in the financial accounts of cities. We selected these items on the basis of their presumed sensitivity to the political factors we shall be discussing.

[26] Program control is, of course, a matter of degree. The central government imposes restrictions on the uses to which funds are generated through borrowing may be applied. Nonetheless, such funds are not necessarily earmarked for specific central programs at the time they are borrowed, and the use of borrowed funds for "questionable" purposes has occasionally surfaced as a political issue. See *Asahi Shinbun*, 1 April 1975, for an account of the Autonomy Ministry's objection to Tokyo's utilization of certain bond-generated revenues. Progressive localities often claim that the bond procedure is too rigidly controlled, but among the data being examined here we have not detected any patterns of systematic discrimination in the Autonomy Ministry's approval of bond authorizations. The approval procedure seems *pro forma* provided that certain conditions are met.

Table 5

Percent Rates of Change and Coefficients of Priority for
Selected Revenue and Expenditure Items for 88
Medium-Sized Municipalities, 1964-1973

	Rate of Change (%)	*Coefficient of Priority*
Revenues		
Local Taxes	435	.77
Local Allocation Tax	6683	11.83
Treasury Disbursements	682	1.21
Prefectural Disbursements	731	1.30
Bonds	1277	2.26
Miscellaneous	1025	1.82
Total Revenues	565	
Expenditures		
Social Welfare	741	1.34
Old-Age Welfare	3544	6.42
Child Welfare	1772	3.21
Sanitation	647	1.17
Roads-Bridges	667	1.21
Land Adjustment	423	.77
Elementary Schools	723	1.31
Middle Schools	687	1.25
Total Expenditures	552	

NOTES: *Local Allocation Tax* is the general equalization grant administered by the Autonomy Ministry. *Miscellaneous* revenues include receipts from locally operated enterprises such as gambling facilities. *Social Welfare* expenses here include those expenditures not included in either the *Old-Age Welfare* or *Child Welfare* categories. Ordinary public assistance is not included under any of these headings. *Sanitation* refers specifically to the operation of sewerage and refuse treatment services. *Land Adjustment* includes projects that upgrade properties for residential housing construction and also involves improvements to existing public facilities. SOURCE: Japan, Autonomy Ministry, Finance Bureau, *Toshi-betsu kessan jōkyō shirabe 1964* and *Shichōson-betsu zaisei jōkyō shirabe 1965-1973*.

tion of new national programs in these areas during 1972-1973.[27] Local authorities implemented such programs on behalf of the central government, but many cities surpassed the performance standards set by the center or initiated entirely new programs on their own.[28] In many instances, local officials responded to local needs at a different level

[27] See MacDougall, *Dissertation*, pp. 362-386.

[28] See ibid., pp. 371 and 377, for comparisons of the Tokyo and national programs for free medical care for the aged and childhood allowances.

of spending and with a different sense of urgency than their counter-part central agencies. This also holds true for the other spending categories.[29]

We have offered some indication that central and local priorities have been less than perfectly aligned during the period 1964-1973. Even if priorities were different, however, there is still the possibility that certain strong "systemic" (centralizing) influences were significant in restricting the range of variability among cities in various policy areas. Furthermore, in cases where purely "nonsystemic" (localistic) forces influenced local policy making, it would be necessary to sort out the separate effects of "environmental" factors (such as changes in the socio-economic composition of the population) and "decisional" fac-tors (such as mayor's partisan support base or the activity level of local civic action groups). By examining variations in policy performance among and within policy categories, we can learn the extent to which systemic or nonsystemic factors predominate.

Let us first consider the relationship between rates of change in the separate revenue and expenditure items. If the different categories changed in roughly parallel ways (or if the items responded in similar ways to changes in overall revenue and expenditure levels), then we could hypothesize that certain systemic factors exerted a strong influ-ence among all of the separate items. Table 6 presents the mean revenue and expenditure levels and the percentage rates of change in these levels over three successive time periods for the eighty-eight sample cities. In general, we find little congruence between rates of change for the separate items. In fact, there appears to be a highly differentiated pat-tern of response to changes in the total resource base. Certain items expanded relative to shrinking local tax bases, while other items dimin-ished in importance even as overall spending increased. At least *among* the categories then, systemic factors do not appear to be significant determinants of policy change.

We next consider the degree of consistency in changes within spending categories over time. Evidence from studies of other political

[29] The sharp divergence of views between the central government and the lo-calities regarding suitable levels of subsidization for programs that both sides rec-ognize as necessary is well illustrated in the "excess burden" problem. (See the discussion in MacDougall, *Dissertation*, pp. 83-91.) The "excess burden" assumed by many localities reflects more than the central government's failure to provide adequate subsidies—it is also reflective of *different* standards being set for the "same" programs by different localities. In some instances, localities argue that their priorities are being thwarted through undersubsidization by the center, par-ticularly for such social services as day-care centers.

Table 6

Mean Per Capita Revenue and Expenditure Levels and Percent Rates of Change in Mean Per
Capita Revenue and Expenditure Levels for Selected Revenue and Expenditure
Items of 88 Medium-Sized Municipalities, 1964, 1967, 1970, and 1973

	Per Capita Level				Rate of Change (%)		
	1964	1967	1970	1973	1964-67	1967-70	1970-73
Revenue Levels							
Total Per Capita Revenues	15.5	22.7	39.9	71.4	46.5	75.8	78.9
Local Taxes	7.7	10.9	16.9	29.1	41.6	55.0	72.2
Local Allocation Tax	0.7	1.1	3.6	6.0	57.1	227.3	66.7
Treasury Disbursements	2.1	3.1	5.0	10.1	47.6	61.3	102.0
Prefectural Disbursements	0.5	0.8	1.5	2.8	60.0	87.5	86.7
Bonds	1.1	1.9	4.1	8.3	72.7	115.8	102.4
Miscellaneous	1.5	2.5	4.4	7.5	66.7	76.0	70.5
Expenditure Levels							
Total Per Capita Expenditures	15.2	21.7	38.7	68.9	42.8	78.3	78.0
Social Welfare	0.3	0.5	0.9	1.8	66.7	80.0	100.0
Old-Age Welfare	0.1	0.2	0.3	2.1	100.0	50.0	600.0
Child Welfare	0.4	0.7	1.5	3.7	75.0	114.3	146.7
Sanitation	0.9	1.3	2.2	4.1	44.4	69.2	86.4
Roads-Bridges	0.7	1.3	2.4	3.7	85.7	84.6	54.2
Land Adjustment	1.1	0.8	1.7	3.4	-27.3	112.5	100.0
Elementary Schools	1.1	1.9	3.7	5.8	72.7	94.7	56.8
Middle Schools	0.6	0.9	1.6	2.9	50.0	77.8	81.3

NOTE: Per capita level is expressed in ¥ 1,000s.
SOURCE: See Table 5.

systems indicates that change within spending categories is usually incremental from one time period to the next.[30] Incremental spending reflects the preponderance of routine spending decisions built into most bureaucratic structures. Steplike increments are, in turn, based upon long-term plans and commitments in particular program areas. Central government or systemic influence over well-established local spending patterns may be inferred from relatively uniform incremental changes in a particular policy area among *all* of the subunits. This reflects the local implementation of centrally determined program guidelines or standards. Such changes would not necessarily be tied to the overall level of resources, since increased spending for a new program may be offset by reductions in other spending areas.

Table 7 shows the simple correlation coefficients for the per capita revenue and expenditure items for three successive time periods. Except for three of the revenue items, very high autolinear coefficients (.90 or above) do not appear to exist. Instead, we find only weak relationships from one time period to the next for such important local programs as old-age welfare and middle-school education. If changes in spending patterns for old-age welfare in one city are unrelated to changes for a similar program in another city, then the effects of centrally imposed standards or other systemic forces must be very weak indeed. This low impact of systemic or centralizing effects on program change, either through an adjustment in overall resource levels or through the implementation of uniform standards, raises the possibility that distinctly nonsystemic forces affect local policy outcomes.

If we limit the search for such nonsystemic determinants to two broadly defined areas called "local environment" and "local organization," a possible test of the relative impact of local environmental and organizational forces would be to measure the degree of variability among the eighty-eight cities in terms of both the structural composition of spending (the percentage allocated to each program) and the level of spending (the per capita expenditure for each program). We hypothesize that structural change is most closely associated with organizational forces (including decisions made by the city's leadership), while change in spending levels is most closely associated with environmental changes (including changes in a city's overall level of resources due to changing local economic conditions). Thus, if the extent of

[30] See Douglas E. Ashford, "The Effects of Central Finance on the British Local Government System," *British Journal of Political Science* 4 (1974): 197-214, as well as his related "A Research Note: Longitudinal Analysis of Policy Variables for Comparative Local Government Studies," *Political Methodology* (1975), pp. 319-330. See also Bunce, "Elite Succession," p. 14 and especially note 7.

Table 7

Simple Correlation Coefficients for Selected Per Capita Revenue and
Expenditure Items of 88 Medium-Sized Municipalities,
1964, 1967, 1970, and 1973

	1964 and 1967	1967 and 1970	1970 and 1973
Total Per Capita			
Revenues	.76	.59	.67
Local Taxes	.93	.91	.89
Local Allocation Tax	.86	.90	.92
Treasury Disbursements	.81	.93	.92
Prefectural Disbursements	.49	.50	.85
Bonds	.22	.53	.64
Miscellaneous	.89	.66	.78
Total Per Capita			
Expenditures	.75	.58	.69
Social Welfare	.34	.49	.36
Old-Age Welfare	.44	.23	.03
Child-Welfare	.81	.74	.88
Sanitation	.60	.64	.53
Roads-Bridges	.70	.57	.58
Land Adjustment	.53	.63	.65
Elementary Schools	.52	.62	.64
Middle Schools	.43	.26	.39

SOURCE: Compiled from Table 6.

structural change exceeds the extent of change in spending levels for
the same revenue or spending item, we would conclude that organizational (decisional) factors are more significant than aspects of a locality's social or economic structure in determining what type of change
occurs. If, on the other hand, spending level changes are greater than
structural changes, the opposite would be true.[31]

In Table 8 we test this hypothesis by showing "coefficients of variability" (standard deviation divided by the mean) for percentage rates
of change for the revenue and expenditure categories in terms of both
per capita spending levels and structural composition. Coefficients of
less than "1" indicate a smaller degree of variability, while the higher
the coefficient, the greater the internal variation. In every instance,

[31] We do not argue that one type of change is necessarily more significant than
the other. We are only interested here in the more basic issue of *where* the greater
change is taking place.

Table 8

Coefficients of Variability for Selected Revenue and Expenditure Items
of 88 Medium-Sized Municipalities, 1964-1973

| | Coefficient of Variability | |
	Change in Structure	Change in Level
Revenues		
Local Taxes	1.08	.23
Local Allocation Tax	3.46	2.81
Treasury Disbursements	1.77	.39
Prefectural Disbursements	2.18	.65
Bonds	1.64	.96
Miscellaneous	4.08	1.77
Expenditures		
Social Welfare	2.57	.86
Old-Age Welfare	.53	.46
Child Welfare	.97	.85
Sanitation	2.74	.54
Roads-Bridges	2.85	.70
Land Adjustment	3.71	1.08
Elementary Schools	2.35	.59
Middle Schools	5.25	1.12
Total Revenues		.25
Total Expenditures		.27

NOTES: Coefficient of Variability $= \dfrac{\text{Standard Deviation}}{\text{Mean}}$

Change in Structure = Percent Rate of Change in Percent Composition of Item
Among Total Revenues or Expenditures, 1964-1973.
Change in Level = Percent Rate of Change in Per Capita Level of Item, 1964-1973.
SOURCE: See Table 6.

there was greater structural variation than variation in spending level changes. This leads us to suspect that decisional or organizational factors induce more differentiated responses in local spending than do environmental factors, although the proof offered here is certainly indirect. Our major concern is to introduce the possibility that variation in spending practices among cities is considerably more responsive to local political conditions than has previously been recognized.

We are thus able to derive the following conclusions from the findings in this section. First, the noticeable lack of congruence between national and local priorities in major issue areas suggests that the impact of central policy on local priority-setting is less significant than the simple catch phrase "30 percent local autonomy"[32] would seem to indicate; and second, when changes in revenue and spending patterns are compared among cities for the same policy or between policy areas for the same city, there is far less consistency than one would expect to find in a nation that is usually regarded as highly centralized. Furthermore, when the separate effects of organizational and socio-economic conditions are compared, organizational factors seem to account for greater internal variation in local policy outcomes.

Viewed in the context of Muramatsu's analysis, our findings indicate that by the late 1960s the degree of local autonomy in postwar Japan appears well within the high, "antagonistic" category. Based on the hypotheses we derived from the Muramatsu argument, a high degree of local partisanship should be associated with high autonomy in determining local performance. We shall test for the validity of that assumption in the final section.

PARTISANSHIP AND LOCAL PERFORMANCE

Earlier we indicated that several competing paradigms have been proposed to explain the role of partisan politics in local government. Proponents of the "direct pipeline to the center" model contend that it still constitutes an effective rallying cry for conservative candidates in local and national elections, while progressives feel otherwise. The conservative "pipeline to the center" and the progressive "pipeline to the people" also claim distinctly different types of linkages to higher-level political actors, of course, and these different linkages are in turn thought to have important distributional consequences at the local policy level. We must be prepared to question how useful these stereotypes are in explaining the relationship between local politics and policy making.

Interestingly enough, many students of Japanese politics seem to accept the validity of the pipeline to the center notion without subjecting it to more rigorous testing. Richardson relates, for example, that Diet candidates from the rural areas and smaller cities "nurture their constituency," in part by procuring "grants-in-aid and subsidies to build roads and schools or various other items on the agendas of local wants."[33] Thayer describes how LDP Dietman Nakasone Yasuhiro "is called upon by the towns and villages to assist them in obtaining funds

[32] This commonly heard expression refers to the fact that on the average roughly a third of local government revenues are derived from local tax sources.

[33] Bradley M. Richardson, "Party Loyalties and Party Saliency in Japan," *Comparative Political Studies* 8 (1975): 50.

from the government" for roads, bridges, sewage systems, gymnasiums, and train stations.[34] Japanese scholars also make similar references to the same phenomena.[35] Nor do conservative politicians themselves fail to affirm their faith in the efficacy of the pipeline in election after election. Stockwin cites the example of Kobayashi Takeji, Minister of Justice in the Satō Cabinet, who stated during an election campaign (1971) that

> every prefecture, town and village must count on the central Government. This cannot be helped. It follows that the Government run by us, the Liberal Democratic Party, will be willing to accommodate the wishes of mayors and governors if they are affiliated to our party.[36]

Kobayashi added that cities and prefectures under progressive control could not expect to be similarly rewarded. Despite such claims, however, there is little evidence to indicate that localities run by conservative chief executives are treated better by the central government than those run by the progressives.

Of course many local administrations are no longer able to boast of access to the LDP's direct pipeline by virtue of the fact that their voters have elected a progressive mayor or governor. Progressive leaders will frequently assert, however, that their localities have not particularly suffered as a result. On the contrary, they claim that with solid community support behind their programs, they can maintain a strong bargaining stance vis-à-vis the central government. The center, in turn, cannot help but respond to their requests in a relatively even-handed manner. Japan is too small a place and too conformist in nature, it is argued, for communities to be deprived of a secure financial base merely because their leaders do not share the ideological inclinations of the ruling LDP.[37]

Within the context of a "dual-pipeline" approach to analyzing local partisanship, it is conceivable that the two types of "pipelines" reinforce different attitudes toward the selection of local priorities. Conservative local officials who prefer to rely on revenues generated through particularistic channels might shape their priorities to satisfy

[34] Nathaniel B. Thayer, *How the Conservatives Rule Japan* (Princeton: Princeton University Press, 1969), p. 94.

[35] See, for example, Muramatsu, "Sengo Nihon," p. 69; Masumi, *Gendai Nihon*, pp. 8-11; and Ōhara and Yokoyama, *Sangyō shakai*, p. 108, to cite only the works previously mentioned in this chapter.

[36] J.S.A. Stockwin, *Japan: Divided Politics in a Growth Economy* (New York: Norton, 1975), p. 210.

[37] These observations are based on personal interviews conducted by the author in a number of progressive cities.

the expectations of their higher-level benefactors. Progressive officials who are unable to capitalize on such personal connections must turn to alternative revenue sources and in doing so presumably shed some of the obligations incurred by conservatives. Since conservative "pipeline politics" are often thought to be tied to subsidies for conspicuous and expensive public works projects, we might expect conservative localities to express a preference for such capital-intensive projects.[38] Progressives, on the other hand, frequently concern themselves with upgrading the quality of social services such as day-care centers and nursing homes or with expanding the scope of transfer payment programs for groups such as the handicapped and the mentally retarded. These types of redistributive measures are often tied to nondiscretionary and rather standardized formulas for the allocation of central government subsidies.

Earlier we posited that local organizational forces seem to be strongly associated with local policy outcomes. From this perspective, our present discussion of an admittedly stereotypical dichotomization between (a) conservative=discretionary subsidization=capital intensive public works or (b) progressive=nondiscretionary subsidization=redistributive social services nonetheless provides a useful framework within which to describe the relationship between local autonomy and local partisanship. If we can demonstrate that the partisan affiliation of the mayor has a strong influence over local policy outcomes according to the dichotomy we have proposed, we can conclude that this type of local partisanship is an important "organizational" factor operating at the local decision-making level. If, on the other hand, our tests of association fail to confirm a significant relationship between mayoral partisan identification and local performance, other measures of the effect of local partisanship should also be explored.

The construction of a meaningful typology of mayoral partisan identification is complicated by the fact that mayors frequently choose not to establish formal ties with one of the national political parties. However, they do tend to indicate their membership in either the progressive or the conservative camp, and they readily accept party endorsements during election campaigns. Party records and newspaper accounts of these endorsements are often inconsistent, and mayors occasionally change their affiliations in mid-career.[39] In terms of this study,

---

[38] See MacDougall, *Dissertation*, pp. 90-91.

[39] The five-term Socialist mayor of Mitaka, Suzuki Heizaburō, left the progressive camp during his last term in office (although many still considered his policies progressive); and mayors in several cities have consistently avoided any clear identification with either camp: included in this group are Hitachi, Himeji, Akashi, and Matsuyama.

mayors have further eluded simple classification because many cities experienced one or more changeovers in office between 1962 and 1974. In spite of these complicating factors, however, we ultimately arrived at the following classificatory scheme: all mayors who held office in the 1962-1974 period were designated as either "conservative" or "progressive" according to their respective classifications in newspaper reports of election results, and these newspaper accounts were subsequently verified through comparisons with official results compiled by local election commissions.[40] Because newspapers generally based their classifications on progressive party endorsement, or, after November 1964, on membership in the National Association of Progressive Mayors, mayors who did not receive a progressive party endorsement or who failed to join the NAPM were classified as conservative.[41]

The cities in the sample were then divided into four groups according to the nature of conservative or progressive leadership. The first group contained only cities with conservative mayors during the entire period (the number of actual officeholders varied from city to city). In the second group of cities, there was a temporary changeover from conservative to progressive mayoral leadership and then a reversion to the conservative pattern. The third group of cities changed from conservative to progressive local rule with every indication that the change was more than temporary, or at least that a local "two-party system" had developed. The fourth group of cities had only progressive mayors during this period (again, with some variation in the actual number of officeholders from city to city). There were forty-four cities in the first, "straight conservative," group; ten in the second, "predominantly conservative," group; twenty-seven in the third, "progressive leaning," group; and seven in the fourth, "straight progressive," group. The distribution of cities within these groups is thus rather skewed, with half of the cities having no progressive mayoral history and less than a tenth of the cities lacking any conservative mayoral leadership at all.

We should expect the partisan identification of the mayor to influence changes in both the pattern of revenue acquisition and the pattern of priority setting. To test for the influence of mayoral partisanship on

[40] Newspapers were consulted first, since official election results do not indicate "progressive" or "conservative" affiliation if a candidate is formally listed as "independent." Newspapers rely either on party endorsement or the lack of a specific progressive party endorsement in classifying candidates. The author gratefully acknowledges the assistance of the Chihō jichi sōgō kenkyūjo in obtaining a complete record of official election results for the eighty-eight cities in the sample.

[41] There were several cases in which a mayor was endorsed by one of the progressive parties but failed to join the NAPM. In such cases, they were listed as "conservative" in order to avoid an even more complex classification scheme.

these two aspects of local performance, we shall consider data from an expanded version of Table 5. In this case, percentage rates of change and coefficients of priority have been calculated for the fourteen revenue and expenditure categories according to our fourfold typology of mayoral leadership. Cities with more conservative leadership ought to prefer revenue sources that reflected their direct pipeline connection. These same cities would then emphasize the construction of an infrastructural support base related to industrial expansion. Progressive administrations that lack access to pork-barrel arrangements for the financing of local projects should be expected to search for such alternate revenue sources as borrowing through the sale of bonds or increased reliance on prefectural grants-in-aid. Spending priorities would presumably reflect their "procitizen," "antimonopoly capital" social welfare ethic.

Table 9 shows the percentage rates of change and the coefficients of priority for the four groups of cities. Turning first to the revenue side, we find that major increases in revenues from the Local Allocation Tax (the nondiscretionary system of equalization grants administered by the Autonomy Ministry) favored the two middle groups, while the two outer groups fared best in the prefectural disbursements category. In the all-crucial category of treasury disbursements (thought to contain subsidy programs with the highest discretionary element), the difference between gains in the conservative and progressive camps was insignificant. Much the same could be said for borrowing through the sale of bonds. One distinct variation was detected in the miscellaneous revenues category. A number of smaller cities, many of them led by progressive mayors, have in recent years established new municipal gambling facilities in order to raise badly needed revenues for new educational and construction projects. Partisan interest would seem to be less salient in accounting for this phenomenon than sheer economic necessity. It is thus apparent that none of the anticipated patterns emerge from the revenue side of Table 9. The size of increases in total revenues did not vary markedly from group to group, and in the single most important category of local revenues—local taxes—the differences were inconsequential.

Turning next to expenditures, there is only the slightest indication that the partisan identification of the mayor really makes a difference in setting local priorities. In the case of child welfare spending, the leaning progressive group does display a tendency to give heavier priority to this item. This performance is not matched, however, by the straight progressive group for the same spending category. And in a category most closely associated with the local progressive movement,

Table 9

Percent Rates of Change and Coefficients of Priority for Selected Revenue and Expenditure Items for 88 Medium-Sized Municipalities, 1964-1973, by Partisan Identification of Mayor

	Straight Conservative		Predominantly Conservative		Leaning Progressive		Straight Progressive	
	%RC	CP	%RC	CP	%RC	CP	%RC	CP
Revenues								
Local Taxes	454	.78	371	.88	419	.72	461	.76
Local Allocation Tax	6244	10.73	6936	16.40	8714	15.02	1822	3.02
Treasury Disbursement	744	1.28	411	.97	685	1.18	670	1.11
Prefectural Disbursement	845	1.45	484	1.14	585	1.01	886	1.47
Bonds	1291	2.22	800	1.89	1457	2.51	1230	2.04
Miscellaneous	962	1.65	370	.87	1538	2.65	528	.87
Total Revenues	582		423		580		604	
Expenditures								
Social Welfare	785	1.39	695	1.73	680	1.18	750	1.25
Old-Age Welfare	3425	6.07	3168	7.90	3879	6.71	3637	6.08
Child Welfare	1526	2.71	1291	3.22	2514	4.35	1359	2.27
Sanitation	677	1.20	428	1.07	677	1.17	637	1.07
Roads-Bridges	761	1.35	642	1.60	544	.94	549	.92
Land Adjustment	351	.62	264	.66	583	1.01	372	.62
Elementary Schools	786	1.39	509	1.27	695	1.20	737	1.23
Middle Schools	711	1.26	576	1.44	579	1.00	943	1.58
Total Expenditures	564		401		578		598	

NOTES: RC = Rate of Change
CP = Coefficient of Priority

old-age welfare, the highest gains were recorded by cities with predominantly conservative mayoral leadership.[42]

One spending category did meet our original expectations. Changes in spending for roads and bridges increased at much higher rates in the two conservative groups than in the two progressive groups. We feel uneasy in generalizing from this single finding, however, because of a lack of corroborating evidence from the other public works categories (sanitation and land adjustment). It may well be that as in the case of the miscellaneous revenues category just discussed, other circumstances have accounted for this "deviation."[43]

A mayor's partisan affiliation is only one of several possible indicators of local partisanship. Another important measure, and one that is closely related to the direct pipeline argument, is the partisan preference of the local electorate for candidates in Diet elections. Many cities that elect progressive mayors also send LDP candidates to the Diet in election after election. Presumably the presence of a strong conservative representation in the Diet can help to offset some of the disadvantages that may be associated with having a progressive local administration.

To test for the relationship between local performance and this second aspect of local partisanship, we first developed an indicator of the central-local conservative connection. We decided that the total percentage of votes received by all conservative[44] candidates in eight Upper and Lower House elections of the national Diet held during the period from 1963 to 1974 would constitute a suitable measure based on

[42] A possible reason for this is that larger proportions of elderly people reside in more rural areas where voting patterns are more conservative. Younger, more progressive voters tend to be overrepresented in the newer suburban cities in the Tokyo and Osaka metropolitan regions.

[43] Among these is the basic factor of *need*. A secondary analysis of these data, not presented here, indicates that many of the cities with conservative mayoral leadership are older industrial areas with lower than average income levels, depressed economies, and frequently deteriorating public physical plants. In these cities, emphasis must necessarily be given to the replacement and maintenance of essential public facilities such as roads and bridges. In a sense, these cities are the victims of their developmental legacy in terms of the spending decisions they must make.

[44] "Conservative" here will mean either all Diet candidates formally affiliated with or endorsed by the Liberal Democratic Party or unaffiliated "independents" (*mushozoku*). In most cases, independent candidates are in fact associated informally with the LDP or join the party after election. In an unsystematic perusal of election results and postelection party ties in the Diet, we found that the number of independents who were actually progressives was quite small.

the following rationale. Japanese elections statistics reveal that conservative incumbents are more likely to win elections than new conservative "faces," thus testifying to the advantage of incumbency in attracting higher numbers of votes consistently over several election periods.[45] We can infer that the greater the number of conservative votes polled in a particular election district, the greater the likelihood that those votes will go to long-term incumbents. We also know that within the ruling Liberal Democratic Party, there is a strong association between repeated electoral success and appointment to Cabinet posts and other high positions.[46] Thus, election districts that send the same LDP Dietman to Tokyo in election after election enable that person to expand his personal network of obligations and loyalties. Although it is true that there has been a decline in the level of support for LDP candidates in recent years,[47] in spite of this fact, cities with strong conservative voting records continue to give relatively high levels of support to LDP candidates, even in the face of overall decline.

After we computed a "total conservative score" for each city, the cities were classified as "strong conservative" (those with scores higher than one standard deviation above the mean), "weak conservative" (those with scores lower than one standard deviation below the mean), and "moderate conservative" (those with scores within one standard deviation from the mean). The mean score for the sample was 358.3, or an average of 44.8 percent conservative votes per Diet election per city. The lowest score in the sample was 177.8 (or an average of 22.2 percent per election), and the highest was 517.4 (64.7 percent per election). Eighteen cities were classified as strong conservative, fifty-five as moderate conservative, and fifteen as weak conservative.

In order to compare the influence of partisanship as reflected in Diet voting patterns with the influence of mayoral partisan identification in accounting for local policy performance, we have again reconstructed

[45] See Thayer, *How the Conservatives Rule Japan*, pp. 125, 127.

[46] Former Prime Minister Miki Takeo, for example, is a fifteen-term incumbent who in 1972 polled the most votes among ten contenders for five Diet seats, outdistancing his nearest rival by more than 24,000 votes. Fukuda Takeo and Nakasone Yasuhiro come from the same Diet district and, in 1972, together polled more than 70 percent of the vote. Fukuda is a ten-term incumbent, Nakasone a twelve-term incumbent. Ōhira Masayoshi is a ten-term incumbent who outpolled his nearest rival in 1972 by more than 32,000 votes. Statistics are from Seiji Kōhō Sentaa, *Seiji Handobukku*, January 1975 edition.

[47] During the period of the four Lower House elections included here, the percentage of total LDP plus independent votes declined from 59.44 percent in 1963 to 51.97 percent in 1972 nationwide. See ibid., p. 328.

the data in Table 5, this time grouping the cities according to the strength of their conservative Diet vote. The results of this computation are presented in Table 10.

It is apparent upon examination of these new data that this alternate method of measuring local partisanship does yield important insights into the structure of policy outcomes. Rates of increase in both revenues and expenditures are higher as we move from more to less conservative on the Diet voting scale. This difference is particularly pronounced between the "moderate" and "weak" groups, possibly indicating a marked difference in aspects of socio-economic development that is normally associated with a change in administrative capacity. The fact that cities in the least conservative group seem to be undergoing the greatest degree of administrative expansion is not surprising given the close relationship that is said to exist between urbanization and progressive electoral strength in postwar Japan.[48]

In terms of specific items, the weak conservative group shows the highest rate of increase in revenues generated from bond sales and miscellaneous sources and the lowest rate of increase in revenues generated through local taxes or prefectural and central treasury disbursements. This same group also led in the expansion of child welfare services and in spending for middle-school construction. These two characteristics can easily be associated with policy making in rapidly urbanizing areas where the need for such services is predictably the greatest. Spending for major construction projects such as sanitation facilities and roads and bridges, on the other hand, received much greater emphasis in strong conservative areas.

In this final section of the paper, we have been unable to detect any strong association between party identification and local performance. This does not mean that such a relationship does not exist, of course, but merely that our particular measures of these two concepts have not yielded findings of a positive nature. Nevertheless, we have learned that the notion of a conservative-progressive split in local politics is an inadequate device for analyzing the substance of local policy making. We are not yet prepared to discount the significance of political forces as important determinants of policy outcomes, but we do wish to indicate that the relationship between local decision making and *formal partisan ties* seems to be tenuous and even inconsequential. The concept of a direct pipeline to the center may have a special symbolic value at election time, in much the same way that the direct pipeline to the people claimed by progressive candidates can be a positive factor in regions where "guilt by association" with the LDP often spells electoral

[48] See Chapters 2 and 5.

Table 10

Percent Rates of Change and Coefficients of Priority for Selected Revenue and Expenditure Items for 88 Medium-Sized Municipalities, 1964-1973, by Strength of Conservative Diet Vote

	Strong Conservative Diet Voting		Moderate Conservative Diet Voting		Weak Conservative Diet Voting	
	%RC	CP	%RC	CP	%RC	CP
Revenues						
Local Taxes	411	.84	424	.82	499	.61
Local Allocation Tax	2677	5.49	7841	15.20	6707	8.15
Treasury Disbursements	605	1.24	623	1.21	980	1.19
Prefectural Disbursements	626	1.28	700	1.36	956	1.16
Bonds	999	2.05	998	1.93	2595	3.15
Miscellaneous	671	1.38	585	1.13	3017	3.67
Total Revenues	488		516		823	
Expenditures						
Social Welfare	670	1.41	699	1.40	970	1.19
Old-Age Welfare	3065	6.44	3414	6.81	4534	5.54
Child Welfare	1168	2.45	1403	2.80	3772	4.61
Sanitation	677	1.42	625	1.25	696	.85
Roads-Bridges	720	1.51	701	1.40	485	.59
Land Adjustment	455	.96	363	.72	611	.75
Elementary Schools	510	1.06	734	1.47	911	1.11
Middle Schools	421	.88	588	1.17	1336	1.63
Total Expenditures	476		501		818	

NOTES: RC = Rate of Change
CP = Coefficient of Priority

failure. Neither catch phrase in and of itself evokes any meaningful explanation for the conduct of local administration, however.

Our findings have also given us impressive evidence that the allocation of central government resources to localities is generally nonpartisan and nonpunitive in its effect. Although more careful longitudinal studies are needed to determine if this is in fact a historical phenomenon, it would seem in any case that the conventional assumption of partisan control over the distributive policies of the central government needs to be reconsidered.

The findings of this study have hinted at an abundance of complex factors that make medium-sized cities in Japan so different from each other. In particular, we feel certain that political differences abound and that these influence the course of local affairs in ways as yet undetermined. We also suspect that strands of political development intrinsic to each separate locality are more significant in affecting local performance than national political currents or even many conspicuous socio-economic factors. Strongly held beliefs about territorially based political identity reinforce insular decision-making processes, and it is in this mutually reinforcing relationship that we can point to the soundness of Muramatsu's "high autonomy and high partisanship" argument. Partisanship in this sense is *not* the partisanship of party or of state but of locality and of place. It is the partisanship of territory, and we have every reason to believe that it thrives in Japan today.[49]

[49] This theme receives extensive consideration in my doctoral dissertation, "Politics and Performance in Japanese Municipalities" (Cornell University, 1979).

OPPOSITION IN POWER:
THE DEVELOPMENT AND MAINTENANCE OF
LEFTIST GOVERNMENT IN KYOTO PREFECTURE

Ellis S. Krauss

KYOTO AS A CASE STUDY

BY almost any measure, Kyoto prefecture has deserved its reputation as the "stronghold" (*toride*), "beacon" (*tōdai*), and "source" (*genten*) of leftist local government in Japan. Its former governor, Ninagawa Torazō, was first elected to office in 1950, but unlike other progressive local executives who came into office on the tide of leftist sentiment in the immediate postwar years, Ninagawa survived its ebb in the 1950s and early 1960s.[1] By the time of his retirement in 1978, he had been reelected seven times, a record for Japanese gubernatorial incumbents. The twenty-eight years of his prefectural administration represent the longest continuous progressive local government in Japan, with many observers seeing Ninagawa's administration as a forerunner of the numerous local progressive administrations and Ninagawa him-

I would like to thank the many individuals and organizations who aided in the research for this paper. Professor Fukushima Tokujurō of Kyoto University was my advisor and teacher throughout the field research, and his aid was invaluable. Ms. Noguchi Yasuko was a conscientious research assistant during the interviewing process, and Mr. Isono Tōru was helpful in initiating contacts for a number of the interviews. Kurt Steiner, Scott Flanagan, and Gary Allinson offered many helpful suggestions, criticism, and information during the research and writing process. J.A.A. Stockwin, Terry MacDougall, and Yanai Michio were particularly selfless in their willingness to share information and data from their own previous local level research in Japan. Carol Draper Krauss, my wife, helped in the editing of earlier drafts. I am grateful to the Japan Foundation, the Social Science Research Council, and Western Washington University for the grants that funded the research. The Bureau for Faculty Research, WWU, provided draft manuscript typing services. I appreciate all this aid. The responsibility for the contents of this paper is entirely my own.

[1] Terry Edward MacDougall, "Political Opposition and Local Government in Japan: The Significance of Emerging Progressive Local Leadership" (unpublished dissertation, Yale University, 1975), pp. 217-225, describes the periods in the emergence of progressive local executives.

self as a prototype of the local leftist executives that came to be elected in Japan in the late 1960s and early 1970s. Kyoto thus has great symbolic significance in the history of local opposition in Japan because the Ninagawa government proved that the left could attain and maintain power and effectively govern a major local area.[2]

It has been said that Kyoto may well be a model in another respect as well. The local and national growth of the Japan Communist Party (JCP) vote in legislative elections throughout Japan's urban areas in the 1970s occurred earliest and most strikingly in Kyoto. The fact that the JCP has now surpassed the Socialists as the major leftist party in Kyoto leads other observers to see in the Ninagawa administration a competing pattern to such Socialist strongholds as Yokohama in the struggle for leadership of the Left at the local level.[3]

Finally, Kyoto may also deserve the distinction of being a forerunner in the negative sense. In the 1978 gubernatorial elections following Ninagawa's retirement, a conservative candidate recaptured the governor's seat for the first time in almost three decades, a fact that many see as a harbinger of a conservative resurgence at the local level throughout Japan.

Kyoto's value as a case study of local opposition in Japan is apparent and provides the aims of this article. As has just been emphasized, it has been the Left's strongest base of support at the local level in the postwar era. Whether Kyoto in Japan or Bologna in Italy,[4] one must analyze an opposition's major power bases in order to understand the nature of local opposition, the relationship between a particular local environment and leftism, and the more general factors underlying opposition politics in a political system. The long-lived Ninagawa administration provides the unique opportunity to analyze the development through time of a leftist local government in Japan. Although newer progressive administrations can tell us much about how the Left attained power at the local level in recent years, Kyoto's long history as a leftist stronghold can tell us more about the techniques by which

[2] See Sasaki Tadasu, "Kyōto fusei to kakushinteki 'mura-kōzō': Kafuchō to Kyōsantō to no yuchaku," in *Kyodai tōshi: Sono genjitsu*, ed. Noguchi Yūichirō et al. (Tōkyō: Keisō Shobō, 1972), p. 432, and Sankei Shinbun Chihō Jichi Shuzai-Han, ed., *Kakushin jichitai: Sono kōzō to senryaku* (Tōkyō: Gakuyō Shobō, 1974), p. 11. Both works discuss the arguments for the significance of Kyoto as a case study.

[3] MacDougall, "Political Opposition," pp. 182-183, and Sankei Shinbun, *Kakushin jichitai*, p. 11.

[4] One of the major studies in English of a local leftist stronghold is Robert H. Evans, *Coexistence: Communism and its Practice in Bologna, 1945-1965* (Notre Dame: University of Notre Dame Press, 1967).

leftist executives can *maintain* themselves in power over time.[5] Similarly, the ultimate failure of the Left to perpetuate its long rule in Kyoto after 1978 can tell us much about the limitations of those techniques.

Most importantly, an analysis of Kyoto politics enables us to evaluate a number of assumptions about leftism in postwar Japan. The organized support of leftist parties, their Marxist orientations, and the general tenor of the rhetoric of national politics would lead one to expect that the Japanese Left would be particularly dependent on Marxist blue- and white-collar workers and intellectuals, that it would mobilize support through appeals to ideology and class-oriented issues, and that it would seek to bring about a restructuring of society through redistributive policies once in power. Are such assumptions necessarily true at the local level and where the Left actually attains power?

I will utilize a wide variety of methodologies in analyzing these issues and questions. Because of their importance, both Ninagawa and Kyoto politics have been the subject of hundreds of journalistic and scholarly articles that provide a valuable, if often subjective and redundant, source of secondary materials.[6] In analyzing Kyotoites' political orientations and behavior, I will rely on official prefectural statistics and the results of survey research conducted by Japanese social

[5] See J.A.A. Stockwin, "Shifting Alignments in Japanese Party Politics: The April 1974 Election for Governor of Kyoto Prefecture," *Asian Survey* 14 (1974), Don Oberdorfer, "It's a Joyful Spring for the Tiger of Kyoto," The *Washington Post*, 17 March 1974, p. C3. Both of these articles are the only two accounts of Kyoto politics in English, and neither traces the history of the Ninagawa administration in any detail.

[6] The most comprehensive and useful bibliographies on Kyoto prefecture's government and politics are the two issues of Kyōto Furitsu Sōgo Shiryōkan, *Shūshū shiryō geppō: Gyōsei shiryōhen*, no. 8 (November 1973) and no. 11 (January 1974). Together, these list a total of 33 books and manuscripts and 240 journal and magazine articles on Kyoto politics and government (not counting newspaper articles and government publications), and this is still not a complete listing of everything published on the topic. Among the books and articles that will often be referred to in this paper are the works cited in note 2, which afford critical or fairly objective views of the Ninagawa government. Others include: Kyōto Fusei Kenkyūkai, ed., *Sengo ni okeru Kyōto fusei no ayumi* (Kyōto: Shobunsha, 1973), which provides a sympathetic but thorough account of the policies of the Ninagawa administration; Yamaoka Ryōichi et al., *Nihon no kao: Kyōto* (Tōkyō: Rōdō Junpōsha, 1970); Jichitai Mondai Kenkyūsho, *Kyōto minshu fusei: Sono tōtatsu to kadai* (Tōkyō: Jichitai Kenkyūsha, 1974); and Katayama Kyōsuke, *Kamogawa: Ninagawa fusei no nijūnen* (Tōkyō: Tosei Shinpōsha, 1972), which are all pro-Ninagawa works. Yamaguchi Yasashi, "Ninagawa fusei o meguru futatsu no hyōka," *Shimin*, no. 7 (March 1972), is sympathetic to Ninagawa while also affording one of the best scholarly analyses of the subject.

scientists.[7] Additional data will be provided by the interviews I conducted in 1975 with prefectural politicians, officials, and interest group leaders.[8]

THE CONTEXT: SOCIO-ECONOMIC STRUCTURE AND POLITICAL CULTURE

Kyoto is one of Japan's most important prefectures, not because of the size of its population (its roughly two million, three hundred fifty thousand people make it only the thirteenth most populous in the nation)[9] but because of its capital city's history and significance. For a thousand years the emperor's residence as well as the center of Buddhism in the nation, Kyoto City thrived as a city of artisans, priests, and courtiers, but after the Meiji Restoration and the transfer of the emperor and capital to Tokyo, the prefecture never developed industrially as did so many other areas during the modern period.[10] Yet the city continued to be considered the cultural and spiritual capital of Japan even as Tokyo became its administrative capital and Osaka its

[7] Among the books and articles based on systematic survey research to which I will refer are: Miyake Ichirō et al., *Kotonaru reberu ni okeru tōhyō kōdō no kenkyū* (Tōkyō: Sobunsha, 1967); Miyake Ichirō, "Seitō shiji no dōkō to seiji kōdō no henka—Kyōtoshi (Kyōto ikku) no bāai," *Toshi mondai* 64 (1973); Miyake Ichirō, "Zenkoku senkyo to chihō senkyo: Kyōtoshi ni okeru kōsa tōhyō," *Toshi mondai kenkyū* 26 (1974); Okamoto Kōji et al., *Gendai seiji to ningen—Kyōto shimin no seiji ishiki* (Kyōto: Mineruba Shobō, 1971); Kodaira Osamu, " 'Jimoto no rieki' de erabareta Kyōsantō: Kyōto shimin no seiji ishiki chōsa kara no kōsatsu," *Kakushin* (September 1973); Ōkubo Sadayoshi, *Nihonjin no tōhyō kōdō* (Tōkyō: Shishōdō, 1974); Sudō Shinji, "Kyōtofu chijisen no shōin-hai'in: Kyōto shimin no seiji ishiki to tōhyō kōdō," *Toki no kadai* (February 1971); Yoshino Kenji, "Ninagawa nanasen to jūmin no ishiki: Asahi Shinbun no yoron chōsa kara," *Asahi ja-naru* 15 (1973). The *Kyōto Shimin Ishiki Kenkyūkai*, a group of Kyoto political scientists, have published a long series of articles based on the results of their 1971 survey of Kyoto City voters. Two of these articles will be cited in this paper: Muramatsu Michio, "Kyōtoshi ni okeru shimin ishiki (2): Komyunitei ishiki," *Hōgaku ronsō* 91 (1972), and Miyake Ichirō, "Kyōtoshi ni okeru shimin ishiki (7): Ippanteki seiji taido," *Hōgaku ronsō* 94 (1973). Many other surveys have been carried out by the Kyoto Election Committee and other groups.

[8] Eighteen separate interviews involving twenty-three respondents were carried out between February and June 1975 by the author and his assistant (who took comprehensive notes during the sessions). They included interviews with top prefectural officials, executives of leftist parties and interest group organizations, leaders of the prefectural assembly, and scholars.

[9] Kyōtofu Sōmubu Tōkeika, *Kurashi no shiori: Kyōtofu, 1975* (Kyōto: Kyōtofu Sōmubu Tōkeika, 1975).

[10] Takeo Yazaki, *Social Change and the City in Japan* (Tokyo: Japan Publications, Inc., 1968), pp. 318-319.

economic capital. Today the city is Japan's fifth most populous with over one million, four hundred thousand inhabitants (1974), and together with its suburbs it dominates much of the southern part of the prefecture. To the north, the prefecture, which spans the mountainous center of Honshu, stretches all the way to the Japan Sea where small port cities such as Maizuru and Miyazu (97,000 and 30,000 population, respectively) are heavily engaged in fishing, tourism, and overseas trade. Tea growing and rice farming are two of the major agricultural activities in the rural parts of the prefecture.[11]

The socio-economic structure of the city and prefecture reflects its historical development, its geography, and the policies of its twenty-eight years of progressive administration. Although a thriving tourist, craft, educational, and religious center, Kyoto houses little heavy industry or giant enterprise within its boundaries: the large enterprises that are represented in Kyoto are primarily branch companies whose main offices are located elsewhere.[12] Rather, Kyoto prefecture may well lay claim to the title of the "small and medium enterprise capital of Japan," with about 84 percent of all its commercial and industrial facilities employing less than four people (far above the national average of 72 percent). Similarly, of any of the major cities of Japan, Kyoto City has the largest percentage of manufacturing enterprises that employ such a small number of persons. Among these enterprises are many skilled traditional industries, such as the famed Nishijin textile artisans.[13]

One other aspect of Kyoto's socio-economic structure deserves special note: the high proportion of intellectuals and medical personnel. Kyoto is one of the great educational centers of Japan, with Kyoto City ranking second only to Tokyo in the number of its university

---

[11] Kyōtofu Sōmubu, *Kurashi no shiori*, contains basic information and statistics on most aspects of the prefecture's population, socio-economic structure, etc.

[12] See Kyōtofu Kōhōka, ed., *Fusei yōran*, 1974 edition, p. 426. This work contains a chart which shows that only nineteen large enterprises are Kyoto-based and only three of these may be considered giant enterprises of over 5 billion yen capital. On Kyoto's lack of large enterprise, see also Ōhashi Ryūken, *Nihon no kaikyū kōsei* (Tōkyō: Iwanami Shinsho, 1971), pp. 197-198.

[13] About 77 percent of manufacturing enterprises alone employ four persons or fewer compared to a national average of about 50 percent. Employees in these small enterprises comprise about 20 percent of all employees in manufacturing, whereas they comprise only 7 percent of all employees in manufacturing nationwide. Sixty-one percent of all persons employed in the prefecture work in firms of less than thirty persons, a number equivalent to about 20 percent of the entire population of the prefecture. See Kyōto Fusei Kenkyūkai, *Sengo ni okeru Kyōto fusei*, pp. 43-44. Fifty-three percent of Kyoto's industrial establishments are textile firms. See Okamoto, *Gendai seiji*, p. 212.

students and university educators and first in the nation on a per capita basis. The prefecture also has the highest per capita number of doctors in the country.[14]

We thus find a prefecture whose economic activities revolve around small commercial establishments, light manufacturing, and educational and professional services. This is reflected in the figures for employment in industrial sectors: in 1970 9.5 percent of the prefecture's population was employed in primary industries (compared to 19.3 percent nationwide), 38.8 percent in secondary industries (compared to 34.1 percent nationwide), and a majority of 51.7 percent in the sales and service jobs that make up the tertiary sector (compared to 46.6 percent nationwide).[15] And even without heavy industrialization, the prefecture is a wealthy one, ranking about fifth in Japan in income per capita.[16]

Despite the lack of heavy industry, the prefecture is highly urbanized. According to the 1970 census, about 80 percent of the total population lived in areas designated as "cities" (*shi*).[17] The 63 percent of the prefectural population that lives in Kyoto City is a far higher percentage than that of the other major designated cities' proportion of their prefecture's population.[18] More important than its extent of urbanization, though, is the character of the population within the city: it is remarkably stable. There has been little population increase compared to other major cities in Japan, and most of that increase has been due to natural increase and not migration.[19] According to one survey, 52 percent of the residents have lived in the city since birth and another 36 percent for over ten years. The same survey found that 86 percent of its respondents had relatives in the city.[20] For the prefecture as a whole, an *Asahi Shinbun* survey found that 75 percent of its respondents had lived in Kyoto since birth,[21] a higher percentage than in other major urban areas.

[14] See Okamoto, *Gendai seiji*, pp. 207-208. Kyōtofu Sōmubu, *Kurashi no shiori*, p. 38, gives the figures of 187.3 doctors per 100,000 persons in Kyoto compared to 116.7 per 100,000 nationwide.

[15] Kyōto Fusei Kenkyūkai, *Sengo ni okeru Kyōto fusei*, p. 42. Kyoto City alone has a higher proportion of persons engaged in the tertiary sector than any major city except Tokyo. See Okamoto, *Gendai Seiji*, pp. 209-210.

[16] Kyōtofu Sōmubu, *Kurashi no shiori*, p. 111.

[17] Calculated from figures provided in the section on Kyoto prefecture in Sōrifu Tōkeikyoku, *Kokusei chōsa hōkoku, Shōwa 45* (Tōkyō: Sōrifu Tōkeikyoku, 1970).

[18] Kyōto Fusei Kenkyūkai, *Sengo ni okeru Kyōto fusei*, p. 40. Yokohama is the closest to Kyoto, with 41 percent of Kanegawa prefecture's population.

[19] Okamoto, *Gendai Seiji*, p. 208.   [20] Muramatsu, "Kyōtoshi," pp. 56, 63.

[21] Yoshino, "Ningawa nanasen," p. 33.

This unique and remarkable stability has resulted in a population with intense local identification, pride, and community consciousness. Indeed, Kyotoites themselves, as well as other Japanese, see as one of their dominant characteristics "exclusiveness" (*haitateki*) to outsiders.[22] The self-sufficiency and independence of the Kyoto community is also touted by Kyotoites.[23] These characteristics led one author rather accurately to describe Kyoto as a city with a "village" structure,[24] for more than any other large city in Japan (indeed possibly in the urbanized world) Kyoto preserves a community structure and spirit more like a small town than the modern city and prefecture that it is.

As in other local areas with their own intense pride and tradition, such as Bologna or Florence in Italy, there are shared values, myths, and symbols that create a distinctive local political culture. In the case of Kyoto, this local political culture is a significant element of the context in which the longest running leftist local government in Japan arose and survived. These myths and traditions also provide insight into how Kyotoites themselves account for their leftist proclivities. According to common wisdom, Kyotoities have never forgiven Tokyo for stealing the emperor away from them after the Meiji Restoration. Still considering themselves the cultural and spiritual center of Japan, they resent the power and prestige that has concentrated in the administrative center of the nation to the north. With an economy made up largely of small and medium enterprises, there is also some hostility both toward the concentration of large capital and industry in nearby Osaka and the influence of big business on the central government in Tokyo. In short, the local political culture supposedly contains strong anti-Tokyo, anticentral power, antibig money elements upon which a leftist opposition can build.[25]

Anticenter sensitivities are invariably given in explanation of the fact that Kyoto's progressive tendencies predate the present postwar Ninagawa administration. Before World War II, Kyoto was known as one of the most liberal of all local areas and sent two of the first representatives from socialist parties to the Diet.[26] Marxist scholars, such as

[22] See Muramatsu, "Kyōtoshi," pp. 60-62.

[23] One hears of this character trait widely, and it was emphasized by Mr. Inada Tatsuo, comptroller (suitōchō) of Kyoto prefecture and one of Ninagawa's most important advisors (interview, 25 February 1975).

[24] Sasaki, "Kyōto fusei," p. 433.

[25] See, for example, Ōkubo, *Nihonjin no tōhyō*, pp. 1-2, 22-24; Okamoto, *Gendai seiji*, pp. 205-206.

[26] See Yamaoka, *Nihon no kao*, p. 244, for this and other examples of Kyoto's liberal and radical traditon. See also George Oakley Totten III, *The Social Democratic Movement in Prewar Japan* (New Haven: Yale University Press, 1966), pp. 301-303, 414-415.

Kawakami Hajime who taught at Kyoto University, helped make Kyoto a prewar intellectual Mecca for the Left.

What was a small beginning in the prewar period became a dominant characteristic in the postwar period when Kyotoites tended to give their vote to the leftist candidate Ninagawa in gubernatorial elections and, to a lesser extent, to the Communists and Socialists in legislative elections. Figure 1 depicts post-1950 voting tendencies in Kyoto at the gubernatorial level and post-1958 voting tendencies in the elections for the Prefectural Assembly (PA) and the House of Representatives (HR). It is obvious from the chart that Ninagawa's support has always exceeded the combined support for the Japan Socialist Party (JSP) and the Japan Communist Party in legislative elections. Further, the especially rapid rise of the Left in the PA in the late 1960s and early 1970s is also apparent. Actually, combining the leftist vote masks another important trend: the increasing share of the vote captured by the Communists. As we will indicate later, while the JSP's voting support has declined steadily at both levels, the JCP's share of the vote rose steadily in the HR through the 1960s and early 1970s, and it grew precipitously between the 1967 and 1971 PA elections.

Taking a closer look at the Ninagawa vote, an analysis of the gubernatorial vote between 1958 and 1974 (in which all fifty-two voting districts in Kyoto were classified on an urban-rural continuum) reveals that Ninagawa's strongest base of support against conservative candidates was usually in Kyoto City.[27] For example, in the three elections in which Ninagawa ran against Liberal Democratic Party (LDP) and Democratic Socialist Party (DSP) opponents, all of Kyoto City's nine ward districts gave him vote percentages above the prefectural average. In these same elections, his weakest support was not, as one might expect, in the usually conservative rural districts but in the small semiurban cities in the northern part of the prefecture.[28] Suburbs and rural

[27] The nine wards of Kyoto City made up the first category, and these have a population density of over 750 persons per square kilometer. Suburbs were those thirteen voting districts surrounding Kyoto City with population densities above 350 persons per square kilometer, semiurban were the fourteen voting districts in the northern part of the prefecture—away from Kyoto City—with population densities of over 125 persons per square kilometer, rural were the sixteen voting districts with less than 125 persons per square kilometer. Thus categorization was based both on population density from the 1970 census figures and on geographical location in the prefecture. These categories were then run against vote percentage in gubernatorial elections in which districts were categorized as being above or below the prefectural average for Ninagawa.

[28] Thus in 1962, 1966, and 1970, 72 percent, 86 percent, and 86 percent of the

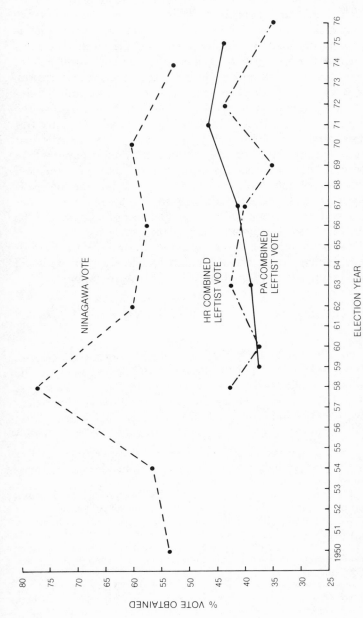

NINAGAWA VOTE

HR COMBINED
LEFTIST VOTE

PA COMBINED
LEFTIST VOTE

% VOTE OBTAINED

ELECTION YEAR

Note: Percentage for combined leftist vote in both legislative elections are not given pre-1958 because of the JSP split into left and right Socialists prior to 1955. The right Socialists became the DSP after 1959, and including pre-1958 figures would have prevented any real comparison between percentages before and after the split. Sources: Publications of the Kyōto Senkyo Kanri Iinkai (Kyoto Election Administration Committee); 1975 PA election from *Kyōto shinbun*, 15 April 1975, p. 3.

districts were in between, with suburban districts tending to support Ninagawa more than rural districts.[29]

Surveys reveal the sources of Ninagawa's support against conservative candidates by occupation, education, and income level. Ninagawa had his strongest support (over 60 percent of each category) among blue-collar workers in small and medium as well as large enterprises, white-collar workers in large enterprises, and the self-employed (including students), among the more highly educated and among the lower-middle income groups. Although many of these groups are traditional sources of leftist support in Japan, what is significant is that Ninagawa also did very well among almost all other groups, where he garnered a majority of all occupational groups (except farmers and executives) and of all educational and income levels but the highest.[30] Clearly, the governor's success in elections rested on his ability to gather votes from a wide variety of strata, and his strength could not be explained solely by socio-economic correlates of electoral behavior. During the following analysis of the development and maintenance of the Ninagawa administration, we will look more closely at the political factors that account for this remarkably broad base of support.

The Development of the Ninagawa Prefectural Government (1950-1965)

In terms of electoral alliances, leftist goals and ideology, political and administrative problems, and policy initiatives, the development of the Ninagawa administration can be rather clearly divided into three stages: terms 1 and 2 (1950-1958), a conservative phase following initial electoral victory; terms 3 and 4 (1959-1965), a transitional leftist phase; and terms 5, 6, and 7 (1966 to 1978), a "mature" leftist phase.[31]

---

semiurban districts, respectively, were below the prefectural average in voting support for Ninagawa.

[29] Interestingly, however, different support patterns appear in the two elections in which Ninagawa ran against more progressive candidates (in 1958 against a JCP candidate and in 1974 against a maverick JSP candidate). In these elections we find a suburb, rural, Kyoto City, semiurban order of support for Ninagawa. This might indicate that Ninagawa picked up the votes of normally conservative supporters in rural and suburban districts who prefer an incumbent to another "progressive" nonincumbent.

[30] See Okamoto, *Gendai seiji*, pp. 322-323; also, Yoshino, "Ninagawa," p. 33.

[31] Sasaki, "Kyōto fusei," pp. 437-438, characterizes Ninagawa's relationship with the leftist parties using the same periodization. Kyōto Fusei Kenkyūkai, *Sengo ni okeru Kyōto fusei*, tends to use ten-year periods (1950s, 1960s, and 1970s) to discuss the policy emphases of the Ninagawa administration. Ninagawa's former

Foundations, 1950

The Ninagawa prefectural government was born in the chaotic days of late Occupation Japan immediately prior to the Korean War and indeed may well owe its existence to the unique conditions of that time and to some fortunate accidents of history.[32] In 1950, despite Kyoto's prewar leftist tradition, both the prefecture and the city had conservative executives with a year remaining to their terms. When the mayor of Kyoto City resigned to take an appointed office, the Socialists, Communists, and leftist labor unions formed a united electoral front, *Mintōkaigi* (*Zen-Kyōto Minshu Sensen Tōitsu Kaigi*, All Kyoto Democratic Front Unity Conference), and they supported a common candidate, Takayama Gizō. Takayama won a handy victory over a conservative candidate whose supporters were still divided over a bitter nomination struggle. In March of 1950, the conservative governor also resigned suddenly and, bouyed by their success in the mayoral election, the *Mintōkaigi* searched for a suitable gubernatorial candidate who could maintain their united coalition. They found him in Ninagawa Torazō.

Born (1898) and raised in the working class *shitamachi* section of Tokyo, Ninagawa graduated from prestigious Kyoto University where he studied economics and was influenced by such prewar left-wing intellectuals as Kawakami Hajime. After graduation, he stayed on at Kyoto University to teach and do graduate work, and during this period he also went to Germany to study economic statistics. On his return to Kyoto, Ninagawa wrote a Ph.D. dissertation that became an influential book in the field of economics, and he eventually rose in the academic hierarchy of the university to become a full professor (1939) and then chairman of the economics faculty (1945). Ninagawa's political views during the Pacific War are the subject of controversy today, with his critics, particularly in the new Left, claiming he wholeheartedly supported Japan's war effort. He resigned his chairmanship and his teaching post at the end of the war, however, ostensibly to allow for the "democratic reconstruction" of the faculty. In

---

vice-governor and then JSP Diet member from Kyoto's second district, Yamada Yoshiharu, offered a 1950-1963, 1963-1972, 1972-present periodization in an interview on 2 May 1975, primarily based on policy initiative criteria. All periodization is arbitrary to some extent, and none is completely clear-cut. The periodization adopted in this paper is based upon my belief that it makes the most sense in terms of political, ideological, and policy changes.

[32] The following discussion on the 1950 election and Ninagawa is based on Sankei Shinbun, *Kakushin jichitai*, pp. 32-36; Sasaki, "Kyōto fusei," pp. 433-434; Yamaoka, *Nihon no kao*, pp. 243-254; Katayama, *Kamogawa*, pp. 17-28.

1948, after a hiatus of three years, his friend and political mentor, Mizutani Chōsaburō, Minister of Commerce and Industry in the Ashida cabinet and a leading figure in the Socialist—and later Democratic Socialist—Party, chose him as the first head of the newly established Small and Medium Enterprise Agency. Ninagawa remained in that position despite the transition to the conservative Yoshida cabinet, but he was soon embroiled in a controversy within the government that had more than a little relevance for his later career as governor of Kyoto. The unsettling economic conditions of the time—due in part to the "Dodge Line" retrenchments in government spending—were causing difficulties for many small and medium enterprises. In February 1950, when Ninagawa circulated his "March Crisis" thesis which stated that government policy was soon to cause widespread bankruptcies among small and medium enterprises, he was forced to leave his post.

By coincidence or design, the *Mintōkaigi* had a perfect candidate in this famous Kyoto intellectual who had stood up to the conservative government in defense of small enterprises. When he arrived at Kyoto station on 10 March, *Mintōkaigi* representatives and supporters gave him a hero's welcome and petitioned him to run for the governorship as the leftist candidate. Ninagawa's entrance into the race was delayed by a dispute between the Socialists and Communists over the form that support for Ninagawa should take, but he eventually filed his candidacy under a compromise solution of JSP "nomination" (*kōnin*) and *Mintōkaigi* "support" (*suisen*).[33]

The campaign was hard fought, the chief issues involving communism, unemployment and layoffs, and central government domestic and foreign policy. Ninagawa won with a margin of about 33,000 votes out of the more than 600,000 cast. Thus Kyoto became the first major urban prefecture in Japan with a leftist governor and also the first with both a governor and a mayor of its chief city from the leftist camp.[34]

The victory, however, was heavily dependent on a combination of fortuitous circumstances, less a precedent for leftist unity and strength than a high-water mark in the early postwar years of a Left soon to enter a period of serious decline at the local and national level. The "accident" of two conservative executives suddenly retiring made the

[33] Today there are different versions of the ways in which Ninagawa accepted the candidacy and the problems involved in working out a suitable formula for party endorsement. See the references in the previous footnote.

[34] Katayama, *Kamogawa*, p. 28. See also MacDougall, "Political Opposition," pp. 218-220, for a brief description of leftist executives elected in this early period.

mayoral and gubernatorial elections possible, and Ninagawa's sudden departure from his central government post provided the Left with an appealing candidate at that exact moment. Despite increasing factional disputes within the JSP—that were to result in the following year in its split into Right and Left Socialists—and a trend away from cooperation with the Communists, the Kyoto Socialists had managed to remain together and agree to cooperate with the JCP in the two local executives' elections. The fragility of this alliance became apparent only a few months later with the break-up of the *Mintōkaigi*. Further aiding Ninagawa's election, the "Dodge Line" and the "Red Purge" in labor had created the environment of serious economic difficulties, unemployment, and anticommunism that stimulated the Kyoto Left to overcome their differences and temporarily unite, as well as to pick up strong labor support. The Communists, junior partners in the leftist camp but gaining strength up to this point, were themselves soon to have their leadership purged by the Occupation, to enter into their "militant" phase of the early 1950s, and almost to disappear as an electoral force for at least a decade.

In short, as some have noted, had the gubernatorial election been held at its appointed time a year later, it is highly unlikely that the Ninagawa administration would have come to power in Kyoto.[35] This point is important not because it highlights the importance of the "accidents of history" and the role of political climate in the 1950 victory but because it illustrates the fragility of the Left's power base in Kyoto and in Japan in the 1950s and helps to explain the character of the Ninagawa administration in its first two terms in office.

The First Stage (terms 1 and 2), 1950-1958

The conservative character of the Ninagawa administration in its first terms in office was largely determined by the political and administrative challenges it faced within the prefectural government and by financial difficulties that decreased its flexibility vis-à-vis the conservative central government. One should not, however, ignore the possibility that Ninagawa himself was not thoroughly committed to leftist policy and causes at this time.[36] But whatever Ninagawa's per-

[35] Sankei Shinbun, *Kakushin jichitai*, p. 36; some of the preceding arguments are from this work.

[36] See ibid., pp. 34-35. There are a number of arguments that support this contention: first, the suspicions about Ninagawa's wartime views; second, his willingness to stay on in the central government even after Yoshida and the conservatives came into office. Finally, the conservative parties were also considering him as a candidate in the 1950 gubernatorial election.

sonal views in this period, it is likely that the political, administrative, and financial constraints the governor faced would have tempered strong tendencies toward the Left in any event.

The major events of Ninagawa's first term in office revolved around his attempts to assert control over his own bureaucracy and to attain majority support in the Prefectural Assembly.[37] Upon taking power, he confronted a prefectural bureaucracy that was conservative, was partially staffed by former central government bureaucrats brought in by the previous governor who was himself a former central official, and was split by factionalism. Particularly, the General Affairs Department (*Sōmubu*) concentrated both personnel and financial matters within its purview, and factional competition, seniority norms, and personal connections dominated its operations.

Ninagawa moved step by step to break the power of this bureaucracy and to assert his control over it. In June of 1951, he created the Office of the Governor (*Chiji Kōshitsu*) and transferred personnel functions to it, thereby weakening the *Sōmubu*, separating personnel from financial functions, and concentrating actual power over bureaucratic staffing directly in the governor's hands. In 1955, this new office was to become the present Planning and Administration Department (*Kikaku Kanribu*), an office that, according to many observers, lies at the heart of the Ninagawa administrative system and exercises power over personnel, information and planning, and coordination of local areas within the prefecture. On 1 May 1952, Ninagawa's second step was to carry out a grand "purge" of recalcitrant conservative high-level bureaucrats in his administration, "retiring" or demoting four department heads (*buchō*) and three section chiefs (*kachō*). Soon after, in February 1953, Ninagawa went even further: he fired his own vice-governor, Tamura Yoshio.

Tamura originally had been chosen as vice-governor because it was thought his conservative connections could smooth Ninagawa's relations with a hostile assembly in which the conservatives maintained a wide majority over Ninagawa's leftist supporters, thirty-six seats to twenty-one. Any legislative repercussions from Ninagawa's act were mitigated by another "coup" he carried out in the assembly only two weeks after Tamura's dismissal. Using the lure of "pork barrel" bene-

---

[37] Following discussion on Ninagawa's first years in office is based upon Sasaki, "Kyōto fusei," pp. 434-435; Sankei Shinbun, *Kakushin jichitai*, pp. 44-53; Katayama, *Kamogawa*, pp. 36-43, 65-76; Asahi Ja-naru, ed., "Kyōto Kyōsuke to Ninagawa taisei: Soshiki to kafuchō," *Asahi ja-naru* 12 (1970): 11; Toyama Shirō, *Kakushin chiji* (Tōkyō: Kokusho, 1975), pp. 44-46; Asahi Shinbunsha, eds., *Chihō kenryoku* (Tōkyō: Asahi Shinbunsha, 1974), pp. 49-53.

fits and the post of assembly speaker as bait, Ninagawa managed to get eight conservative assemblymen to bolt their parties and join four Socialists in forming the *Junsei Kurabu* ("Pure Club"). In one stroke, the governor had managed to attain a slim majority of one in the assembly. Until the April 1975 Prefectural Assembly elections, the supporters of the administration were to retain a majority over the conservative parties through the cooperation of leftist parties and various groups of independent conservatives.[38]

Despite making a start toward control over bureaucracy and assembly in the first term and being reelected to a second term in 1954 with 56 percent of the vote, the Ninagawa administration maintained a conservative posture in policy and rhetoric throughout its first two terms. The continued weakness and divisions of the Socialists and Communists at both the local and national levels, the dependence on a large group of conservative independents of unknown reliability to maintain a slim assembly majority, the continuation of conservative influence on the bureaucracy despite personnel and structural changes, and the isolation of Ninagawa as one of the few progressive executives in the country during the 1950s may have all played a role. But in addition, the prefecture was in severe financial difficulties, as were many local areas during this era. Kyoto's financial problems were exacerbated by severe flood damage in the early 1950s, the rebuilding costs of which added to the prefecture's burdens. In 1956, Kyoto was designated the first "Financial Reconstruction Entity" (*Zaisei Saiken Dantai*) under a new law designed to aid the increasing number of prefectures and cities with large fiscal deficits.[39] This made possible special national subsidies, but it also put the prefecture's financial affairs under stringent central control and investigation. Under these circumstances, dependence on government aid and maintenance of good relations with the center were essential. No major leftist policy initiatives were taken, and no real or symbolic challenges to the national government were made during this period. Indeed, even after the bureaucratic and legislative "purges" in Ninagawa's first term, so little did the conservatives feel threatened by this "progressive" administration that they offered to support Ninagawa for reelection to a third term in 1958.

All progressive local executives in Japan confront the same two problems that Ninagawa did after taking office from conservatives: those

[38] For power balances in the Prefectural Assembly over time, see especially the Sasaki and Katayama references in the preceding footnote.

[39] On the Financial Reconstruction Law, see Kurt Steiner, *Local Government in Japan* (Stanford: Stanford University Press, 1965), pp. 296-297. See also all of Chapter 12 of that work on the general financial problems of local governments.

of extending their influence over predominantly conservative bureau-cracies and over assemblies in which they lack a majority. These two problems are usually interrelated, since they arise from the close alli-ance of local officials, conservative politicians, and business/farm or-ganizations that compose the community power structure in most local areas. In addition, in times of financial difficulty, this alliance may find a willing ally in a wary conservative national government and its po-tential for applying pressure and withholding aid. Few progressive local executives—and Ninagawa was no exception—can completely free themselves in their first terms from the power of this conservative local alliance, the dependence on national financial aid in times of fiscal crisis, and the constraints that both of these forces impose on policy making and symbolic political challenges. Where Ninagawa was exceptional was in his ability to greatly weaken conservative dominance of the bureaucracy and assembly early in his administration, thus laying the groundwork for greater flexibility in politics and policy when financial conditions improved in subsequent periods.

The Second Stage (terms 3 and 4), 1958-1965

The 1958 gubernatorial election proved to be a major turning point in the Ninagawa administration.[40] By the late 1950s, in some local areas the LDP and the Left had managed to reach a *modus vivendi*, allowing conservative support of the more flexible incumbent progressive execu-tives. In 1958, Ninagawa too met with LDP leaders and in return for promising to carry out a "neutral" administration received their promise of support in his bid for a third term. The JCP, however, reacted strongly against the idea of conservative support for Ninagawa and, when Ninagawa declined to formally reject the LDP's offer of support before filing day, ran their own candidate against him. Ninagawa handled this problem by the tactic of not accepting the LDP's official letter of support when it was sent to him, thus neither publicly rejecting nor accepting the LDP's backing. In so doing, he managed to prevent the LDP from opposing him and simultaneously to limit the impact of the Communists' disaffection and electoral opposition. Ninagawa was reelected with 77 percent of the vote, while his JCP opponent received less than 7 percent. The maneuver, however, permanently soured Ninagawa's relations with the conservatives and also apparently convinced him that joint JSP-JCP support at election time was desir-

[40] The following discussion is based upon Sankei Shinbun, *Kakushin jichitai*, pp. 54-65.

able. In his next election bid in 1962, he once more secured the support of the JCP and publicly backed their candidates for the House of Councillors.[41]

By 1962, Ninagawa's rapprochement with the Communists was easily achieved because he had taken a leftward turn during his third term in office, initiating both leftist policies and closer relations with leftist unions and interest groups. Soon after the 1958 election, for example, he had pressured the superintendent of education to resign when he pushed for actions opposed by the leftist Teachers Union. In 1960, Ninagawa intervened to avert a confrontation between the Prefectural Employees Union (*Fushokurō*) and the police.[42] Such actions early in his third term were the beginning of a relationship of mutual benefit between leftist unions and interest groups and Ninagawa that continued to 1978: they provided electoral support in exchange for the administration's support and protection on concrete policy and political matters.

In policy too, Ninagawa moved leftward. By 1961, Kyoto had finally overcome its financial deficits and ceased to be a Financial Reconstruction Entity. Fiscal recovery, combined with the maintenance and strengthening of his coalition of leftist parties and pro-Ninagawa independent conservatives in the assembly, freed him to initiate innovative policies. Even before the formal end of financial restrictions, Ninagawa had shown his potential for such innovation. In 1960, he introduced and, dangling the promise of more revenue for rural development in front of rural conservatives, pushed through the assembly an "Automobile Acquisitions Tax." This tax, the first of its kind in the nation, provided only a small source of independent income for the prefecture, but it was successful enough to be imitated by many other prefectures.[43]

More important policy initiatives were to follow. Throughout the 1960s, for example, Ninagawa consistently opposed the central government's policies that favored large industry and rapid economic growth. Although his administration was active in building dams, schools, and roads, in mechanizing agriculture, and in aiding small and medium enterprises in response to constituents' demands, he rejected "development that serves the interest of large enterprises" while "ignoring small

[41] *Kyōto minpō* (the newspaper of the JCP in Kyoto), 21 February 1962, p. 1, contains the Communist report of their meeting on 17 February that led to the official rapprochement.

[42] See Sasaki, "Kyōto fusei," pp. 439-440, and Sankei Shinbun, *Kakushin jichitai* pp. 59-62, on these two incidents involving the unions.

[43] Sankei Shinbun, *Kakushin jichitai*, p. 65.

and medium enterprises and farm, timber, and fishing enterprises."[44]
"Protecting the life and livelihood" (*kurashi o mamoru*) of citizens became a slogan of the Ninagawa government, as did the phrase "invisible
construction" (*mienai kensetsu*), which implies that emphasis must be
placed on coordinating economic, social, and cultural human relationships through local initiative if people are truly to reap the fruits of
"visible construction." Thus, instead of following the national policy
of large-scale rapid growth at all costs, Kyoto followed an independent
course of more balanced economic development through local control.[45] And, unlike almost all other local executives who engaged in a
mad scramble to attract large industry and government aid to their
areas during this period, Ninagawa attempted to protect traditional
small-scale industries while refusing to petition the central government
for benefits.

The "ideology" of the Ninagawa administration was also established
in the early to mid-1960s. Essentially, it was founded on the symbol
and principles of the American-inspired 1947 Constitution rather than
on the overt use of the rhetoric and saints of Marxism. Although Ninagawa claims he has been emphasizing the Constitution since 1950, it
was in 1965 that he made a concerted effort to establish it as the major
symbol of Kyoto government. In that year, a pocket edition of the
Japanese Constitution was issued from funds allocated in the budget
to "protect and diffuse the Constitution," and some two hundred thousand copies were widely distributed to prefectural employees and citizens. The slogan, *"Kenpō o Kurashi no naka ni Ikasō"* (Let's Make
the Constitution Live in Our Lives) hung on banners from major
prefectural official buildings and adorned official envelopes.[46]

Thus, by the mid-1960s, the major themes of Kyoto progressive local
government could be clearly discerned: emphasis on leftist unity, on
independence from the central government in economic and develop-

[44] Kyōto Fusei Kenkyūkai, *Sengo ni okeru Kyōto fusei*, p. 216, quoting from
Fusei dayori, 1 May 1962.

[45] Ninagawa also criticized the central government's regional development plans
because he felt they served large capital's interests in Osaka, strengthened
national control over local areas, and failed to seek enough input from governors in their planning process. Although later to use the term *"kurashi o
mamoru"* in the title of two of his many books, Ninagawa seems to have used it
as early as 1960 in the same article in which he first referred to *"mienai kensetsu."*
On Ninagawa's policies and his attitudes toward economic development, see Kyōto
Fusei Kenkyūkai, *Sengo ni okeru Kyōto fusei*, pp. 215-216, and passim. Jichitai
Mondai Kenkyūsho, *Kyōto minshu fusei* (part 2), and Yamaoka, *Nihon no kao*
(parts 2, 3, and 4), are general favorable descriptions of the governor's policies
regarding development and pollution.

[46] See, for example, Katayama, *Kamogawa*, pp. 48-51, 54-59.

ment policies, on protection of small and medium enterprises, on hostility to large industry and the LDP, and on local autonomy and the Constitution. That Kyoto was following such a program during the nationwide period of conservative dominance and rapid economic growth by large industry and prior to the era of "pollution politics" and disillusionment with GNP at any cost truly marks it as a distinctive experiment in opposition politics at the local level. But only after the 1966 election did the political development of the Ninagawa administration attain. its "mature" form: new styles of electoral coalition, increasing dominance of the JCP, and concern for institutionalizing progressive government in an era of citizen participation.

THE MAINTENANCE OF POWER (1966-1978)

The New Coalition

Fundamental changes in the style of leftist policies in Kyoto took place in the 1966 gubernatorial election, Ninagawa's attempt at a fifth term in office. The Democratic Socialists, first as part of the JSP, later as the "Right Socialists" of the early 1950s, and finally as a separate party after 1959, had comprised a major element in the leftist coalition that had supported Ninagawa. But in 1966, the DSP broke completely with Ninagawa and turned permanently to the conservative camp. Wooed by the LDP and disenchanted with the increasingly leftward course of the prefectural administration, they put up their own candidate to oppose Ninagawa, a candidate also supported by the LDP. The two parties mounted an all-out campaign to unseat the governor. Although a maverick group of DSP assemblymen refused to support their party's policy and continued to work on behalf of Ninagawa, the progressive administration had lost a pivotal, if small, element in the coalition that had kept it in power.

Only the JSP and the JCP remained as the core of Ninagawa's electoral organization, and relations between the right-wing faction of the JSP and the Communists had become increasingly strained as a result of disputes in the 1966 Kyoto mayoral election. Although the JSP decided to continue its joint support of Ninagawa, the right-wing of the party seemed to give only nominal support and did not exert itself on his behalf.[47] In short, Ninagawa's organized and active party support had dwindled to only the left-wing JSP and the JCP.

[47] On both the 1966 mayoral election in which the JSP insisted on running a known anti-JCP scholar and on the 1966 gubernatorial race, see Asahi Ja-naru, "Kyōto Kyōsuke to Ninagawa taisei," pp. 11-12; Sasaki, "Kyōto fusei," pp. 437-438; Yamaoka, *Nihon no kao*, pp. 264-265.

The Left responded to the greatest threat to its control of the Kyoto prefectural government by giving the Communists equal status with the JSP in their electoral alliance and by creating new support organizations that included a wide range of interest groups and citizens' organizations. On 14 March, a month before the election, the JSP, JCP, and pro-Ninagawa DSP splinter group entered into a formal electoral alliance to support (*suisen*) Ninagawa as their gubernatorial candidate and to work for his "overwhelming victory" through the reconstruction of *Minshufusei Kyōgikai* (Council for a Democratic Prefectural Government; *Minkyō* for short), the coalition organization that had sponsored Ninagawa in the 1962 election. But whereas in 1962 the JCP had supported and had participated in *Minkyō* but had not signed a formal electoral agreement with the JSP, in 1966 it was a joint signator and a formal equal partner with the Socialists for the first time. Further, the 1966 agreement was unusual in that it called for the creation of a *Minkyō* organization that would bring under its purview all political *and* nonpolitical groups and individuals who supported Ninagawa and that could serve as a liaison between the diverse participating organizations.[48]

One basis for the reconstituted *Minkyō* coalition had been laid a few weeks before the March 14 announcement with the founding of the Kyoto *Fushimindantai Renraku Kondankai* (Kyoto Prefecture-City People's Organizations Liaison Committee; *Fushimindantai* for short). Responding to the crisis in the progressive camp caused by the loss of the DSP and its labor union allies to the conservatives, 65 organizations—including small and medium enterprise organizations, women's groups, clubs of artists, craftsmen, intellectuals, and religious and social welfare associations—had answered the call of two doctors' associations for an organizational alliance to support Ninagawa.[49] In short, both the new *Fushimindantai* and the reconstructed *Minkyō* were created as supraparty bodies for the 1966 Ninagawa campaign to coordinate and mobilize nonaligned voters after the loss of the DSP had severely weakened and isolated the coalition.

The strategy of unity between leftist parties and interest groups in a grand coalition worked, as Ninagawa fought off the conservative challenge and won with 53 percent of the vote, albeit his lowest margin

---

[48] See *Kyoto minpō*, 23 March 1966, p. 1, for the text of the formal agreement; see also Asahi Ja-naru, "Kyōto Kyōsuke to Ninagawa taisei," and Yamaoka, *Nihon no kao*, pp. 264, 269.

[49] On the formation of *Fushimindantai*, see Yamaguchi, "Ninagawa fusei," pp. 56-57, and Yamaoka, *Nihon no kao*, pp. 267-268.

since 1950. The significance of the 1966 election was far-reaching, for it established the pattern of the 1970 and 1974 elections as well, which included polarized confrontations between the left and all other parties, supraparty campaign organizations, and increasing dependence on the JCP and interest group activities and activists to get out the vote. Thus in 1970, Ninagawa won a sixth term (with 56 percent of the vote), opposing an LDP candidate also supported by the DSP and *Komeitō*, using the same type of campaign organization—now called the *Akarui Minshu Fusei o Susumerukai* (Association to Advance a Bright Democratic Prefectural Government; *Susumerukai* for short)—and relying heavily on Communist and interest group-citizen organizations for vote mobilization. After the sudden retirement and death of the LDP incumbent in 1967, the same coalition campaign organization and mobilization style succeeded in electing a progressive mayor in Kyoto City for the first time since 1950.

The Techniques of Support Mobilization

A closer look at the "new coalition" that emerged after 1966 shows us how its participants' support for Ninagawa had been attracted, mobilized, and sustained using organization, policy and patronage, personal appeal, and ideology. The *"Susumerukai"* style coalition was basically an alliance between the *Fushimindantai* and related groups, public employee unions, and the leftist parties. The *Fushimindantai* was a unique interest group-citizens' group coalition that, even if reproduced in form in other progressive local areas, achieved major success only in Kyoto. After its role as an electoral organization in the 1966 gubernatorial campaign, the *Fushimindantai*'s constituent organizations decided to make their federation permanent and to attempt to serve as "a pipe to have the desires and opinions of its various groups be reflected in the prefectural and city governments"[50]—that is, to become a permanent interest group federation with access to the progressive governments in the prefecture. These two complementary roles—electoral campaign organization to mobilize independent voters for progressive executives and pressure group federation—remained central to the organization's goals as it grew from the original 65 founding groups and individuals to 132 "member groups" (1975) and 252 "supporting groups." To these it added a third role: go-between between the Socialists and Communists. One of its major functions was also to maintain unity among the progressives and, with the leftist labor union fed-

[50] Yamaoka, *Nihon no kao*, pp. 274-275.

eration *Sōhyō*, to mediate disputes and tensions between the two leftist parties.[51]

The pillars of the federation were doctors' associations and small and medium enterprise groups, the former providing much of the operating expenses of the organization and the latter a large number of its member groups.[52] One of *Fushimindantai*'s most important executives was a trusted friend and political advisor to Ninagawa, Horie Tomohirō, a small and medium enterprise leader, and the other, Nakano Nobuo, was an executive in the major doctors' associations in the prefecture.

That doctors and small and medium enterprise groups should be important in the political life of a prefecture that tops the nation in doctors per capita and whose economy is based on small and medium enterprise is not surprising. That doctors and small business people who generally tend to support the LDP or DSP should be two pillars of a progressive governor does require some explanation. Although the Communists do have medical front organizations that mobilize the minority of leftist doctors, the majority of doctors in Kyoto are not necessarily more leftist than doctors elsewhere. A survey of Kyoto Medical Association (*Kyōto Ishikai*) members conducted by the association actually showed a minority (about 30 percent) supporting the JSP or the JCP, with the majority (about 60 percent) supporting either no party or the LDP.[53]

The Kyoto Medical Association and the Insurance Doctors Association, the two main medical groups in the prefecture, supported Ninagawa actively at election time primarily for two reasons: they saw the national government trying to keep down medical fees and insurance claims and they derived prefectural government benefits from their support for Ninagawa. Ninagawa once got rid of a head of the insurance section of the prefectural government who had been opposed by

---

[51] The best article on the *Fushimindantai* and the role it plays in Kyoto politics is Yamaguchi, "Ninagawa fusei," especially pp. 56-57. Information on the federation's member groups, executives, and procedures is found in *Kyōto fushimin dantai kyōgikai dai-23kai zentaikaigi shiryō* (Kyōto, 10 June 1974). In interviews with executives of the organization, these were also the roles emphasized as central to the federation's purpose.

[52] *Kyōto fushimin dantai*, p. 30, shows that medical groups provide almost half the group's dues. Page 22 indicates that 58 out of the 132 member organizations and 128 out of the 252 cooperating organizations are small and medium enterprise groups.

[53] Interview with Nakano Nobuo, 14 March 1975. Nakano is an executive in the two major medical federations in the prefecture, president of the national organization of the Insurance Doctors League (*Hōkeni Dantai Rengokai*), secretary-general of *Fushimindantai*'s assembly, and a representative to the *Susumerukai*.

the *Ishikai,* and since that time the governor solicited in advance the approval of candidates by that organization before making appointments to this important post that oversees the medical insurance system in the prefecture. In addition, because of their support for Ninagawa in elections, the doctors' organizations had direct access to this office in making requests.[54] This access seems to have served them well, since Kyoto has a higher rate of medical insurance claims per capita than any other prefecture in the country.[55] The policy and patronage benefits they received from the Ninagawa administration attracted and maintained the support of doctors who played a crucial leadership and organizational role in the *Fushimindantai* and in elections for leftist executives in Kyoto.

Similarly, small and medium enterprise received substantial benefits from supporting Ninagawa either through the *Fushimindantai* or in conjunction with *Minshō,* the JCP-influenced small and medium enterprise federation. The administration's consistent policy of emphasizing economic growth by developing local infrastructure rather than by attracting and encouraging large enterprise obviously found favor with Kyoto's many shopkeepers and small, skilled manufacturers and their employees. In addition, Kyoto was the first local administration in the country to begin a program of large-scale loans to small and medium enterprise unbacked by collateral, a program since copied by other local governments. In matters of zoning and constructing supermarkets and department stores, the Kyoto government also sought to protect the interests of the small shopkeeper against competition from large business. The government's encouragement and protection of Kyoto's traditional culture, crafts, and industries helped it attract support. Finally, the JCP-related *Minshō* gave aid and advice to shopkeepers, including help on tax matters. And, it was said that tax forms turned into the prefectural government from *Minsho*-member businesses were not looked at too closely.[56]

[54] These policy, protection, and access benefits are openly discussed by the organization, both in personal conversation with its leaders (interview with Nakano Nobuo, 14 March 1975) and in the literature they send to members. See for example, *Kyōto hokeni shinbun,* 4 November 1974, especially pp. 13-17, and the 22 July 1974 issue, which is entirely devoted to doctors and the Ninagawa seventh-term victory. The basis for this cooperation between doctors and Ninagawa was laid in a signed memorandum agreement in 1964. See Sasaki, "Kyōto fusei," p. 442.

[55] Sasaki, "Kyōto fusei," p. 442.

[56] The policy benefits and protection of the Ninagawa administration of small and medium enterprises were emphasized to me by Isono Tōru, an executive of a small and medium enterprise organization and of the *Fushimindantai,* 24 February 1975. See also Kyōto Fusei Kenkyūkai, *Sengo ni okeru Kyōto fusei,* Chapter 1; Jichitai Mondai Kenkyusho, *Kyōto minshu fusei,* Chapter 2; the special collection

Because of the *Fushimindantai*, the JCP front organizations, and the judicious use of policy, patronage, and access, Ninagawa was able to mobilize and maintain the allegiance of groups traditionally associated with conservative bases of support. The active support that he received from public employee unions, particularly the Kyoto Teachers Union (*Kyōkyōso*) and the Public Employees Union (*Fushokurō*), was less surprising. Yet here too, policy, benefits, and patronage helped to reinforce the usual leftist inclinations of the public unions. Ninagawa placed great emphasis on education in this education and culture-oriented area. He stressed "Three Principles of Education" (coeducation, primary school [neighborhood] districts through high school, and general education rather than technical education) to preserve the egalitarian education reforms of the Occupation and to deemphasize the competitive "examination hell" preceding college. Teachers also supported Ninagawa because he sought to protect them from interference by the Ministry of Education and by local educational administrations. Thus, for example, he managed to prevent implementation of the Teachers Efficiency Rating System, which was initiated by the Kishi government in the late 1950s and was strongly opposed by the Teachers Union and the Left.[57] Less symbolic benefits came as well: Kyoto now has a low teacher-pupil ratio compared to other prefectures, and both teachers' salaries and those of general prefectural employees are high.[58]

---

of articles entitled "Jichitai to chiiku sangyō," in *Keizai*, no. 83 (March 1971), pp. 140-164; Yukimachi Shirō, "*Chihō jichitai to kōgyō—Kyōtofu no bāi*," in *Toshi mondai* 64 (1973). On *Minshō* (*Kyōto Minshu Shōkokai*, the Kyoto Democratic Commerce and Industry Association), see Sasaki, "Kyōto fusei," p. 441; Asahi Ja-naru, "Kyōto Kyōsuke to Ninagawa taisei," p. 9. In English, see Oberdorfer, "It's a Joyful Spring," and the interesting discussion of JCP activities and relations with such interest groups, especially in rural areas, in George O. Totten, "The People's Parliamentary Path of the Japanese Communist Party (Part 2: Local Level Tactics)," *Pacific Affairs* 46 (1973).

[57] On the "Three Principles" and Ninagawa's educational policy, see Yamaoka, *Nihon no kao*, pp. 222-240; on the Teachers' Rating System dispute, see Sasaki, "Kyōto fusei," p. 439.

[58] These benefits of Ninagawa's educational policy are recognized by Kyoto Teachers Union leaders (interview with the secretary-general, secretary, and assembly chief of Kyōkyōso, 19 May 1975). Almost a third (32.1 percent) of Kyoto's budget disbursements in 1973 went to education, and most of this went for personnel expenses. The percentage of personnel expenses in the education budget in Kyoto between 1970 and 1973 (about 88 percent) was higher than in Tokyo and Osaka and higher than the national average. The average salary of prefectural employees in Kyoto was higher than in Tokyo and Osaka and higher than the national average (1973), and the proportion of personnel expenses for

In addition, both teacher and prefectural employee unions are strongly influenced by the JCP. Although the Communists have succeeded in penetrating public employee unions in other areas, they have succeeded perhaps to the greatest extent in Kyoto. Executives of both unions claim independence from the JCP and a desire primarily for unity between leftist parties. Nonetheless, their public policy positions are usually quite close to the JCP's. The Teachers Union policy toward teachers striking is the same as the JCP's (negative), for example, even though this goes against the national union's position. And, as one of the largest unions in Kyoto *Sōhyō*, the Teachers Union was instrumental in getting the federation to become the first prefectural local in the country to advocate the union's freedom to support parties other than the JSP (that is, the JCP). Executives of the union estimate that while only about 20 percent of high-school teacher members are actual JCP members, about 80 percent support the JCP's policies. The executive committee of the union is also dominated by JCP sympathizers.[59]

As each gubernatorial election approached, support groups like the *Fushimindantai* and the labor unions joined the JCP and the JSP to initiate the *Susumerukai* coalition. In 1970, 24 such groups sent out a call, and eventually over 2,000 groups responded by becoming participating members and another 2,000-plus groups by becoming "supporting organizations" (*suisen dantai*)—enough organizations to potentially mobilize 950,000 votes.[60] This formation of the *Susumerukai* was by no means easy or automatic and often required intensive negotiations and bargaining between the JCP and the JSP, with *Sōhyō* and *Fushimindantai* acting as go-betweens. For example, in 1970 the JCP would have preferred a "Minobe-style" simple unified front for the two parties, but the JSP refused to join unless the election coalition agreement (*kyōteisho*) included a wide variety of organizations. The two parties also disagreed on the division of leadership positions in the campaign organ-

---

prefectural employees of the total budget, on a per capita basis, was also higher in Kyoto than in Tokyo, Osaka, and in the nation as a whole. See Kaminogō Toshiaki, "Kakushin jichitai no eikō to hisan," *Bungei shunjū* 53 (1975): 106-116.

[59] Interview with secretary-general, secretary, and assembly chief of Kyōkyōso, 19 May 1975. About half of the approximate quarter million organized workers in the prefecture are members of *Sōhyō*, about half of members are blue-collar workers, and nearly all are small and medium enterprise employees. Among members, about two-thirds are estimated to be JSP sympathizers and about one-third JCP sympathizers. Interview with Yachiguchi Kōji, secretary of *Sōhyō*, 4 April 1975. On the Prefectural Employees Union's programs and political positions see Kyōtofu Shokuin Rōdō Kumiai, *Dai-43kai teiki taikai giansho: 1975 nendo*. On the JCP penetration of the union, see also Sasaki, "Kyōto fusei," p. 441.

[60] Yamaguchi, "Ninagawa fusei," p. 56.

ization, a problem eventually resolved by Ninagawa's interceding to support a compromise.[61]

Once the *Susumerukai* was formed, the participating organizations divided campaign mobilization responsibilities, and even the JCP agreed to place itself under their leadership. But the weak grass-roots organization of the JSP meant that actual vote mobilization of progressive voters was mainly carried out by the Communists and the labor unions. In addition, in the hard-fought 1970 election, the parties recognized that they had to capture the "floating" independent voter, and they encouraged the "nonpartisan" citizen-interest groups to carry out much of the publicity and overt campaigning.[62] Indeed, when I asked one of the leaders of the *Susumerukai* why this kind of organization and campaign style was necessary, he replied honestly that it was because of citizens' mistrust of political parties.[63] The *Susumerukai* style of campaign organization in Kyoto thus served a dual function: it indirectly allied the JCP and JSP but under the rubric of a suprapartisan organization that could appeal to floating leftist, nonaligned, or even conservative voters who wished to support Ninagawa.

The ability of the progressive prefectural government to maintain itself in power was in great part due to its ability to mobilize these normally conservative or independent voters who were attracted to Ninagawa's personality or by his long incumbency and policy accomplishments. Survey research conducted by Japanese social scientists at both the city and prefectural levels in the 1970 and 1974 gubernatorial election reveals that Ninagawa obtained the support of a large percentage of the voters with no party identification (perhaps as much as three-quarters of that vote) and that perhaps as much as a third of his total support was obtained from this type of voter.[64] One reason for Ninagawa's 1970 election victory was his ability to get normally politi-

---

[61] Ōta Masao, "Kyōtofu chiji—Ninagawa rokusen to tōitsu sensen," in *Asahi ja-naru* 12 (1970): 136-138.

[62] Ibid.

[63] Interview with Nakano Nobuo, 14 March 1975.

[64] The figures vary according to the timing and methodology of the surveys. Ōhashi, *Nihon no kaikyū*, p. 195, Okamoto, *Gendai seiji*, pp. 324-325, and Sudō, "Kyōtofu chijisen," p. 73, present data which shows that about seventy-five percent of those who support no party preferred Ninagawa. A recalculation of data presented by Ōkubo, *Nihonjin no tōhyō*, p. 229, and Yoshino, "Ninagawa nanasen," p. 33, give the figure at closer to 40 percent; but these two latter surveys are both preelection surveys and they include many respondents who had not made up their minds yet, so that it is likely that the actual percentage is closer to the three-quarters figure. Sudō, "Kyōtofu chijisen," p. 73, found that about 31 percent of Ninagawa's total vote came from those who supported no party, the largest single bloc of voters supporting Ninagawa.

cally uninvolved and independent voters to the polls and to obtain their vote because of their attraction to his personality, their unwillingness to turn out an administration with no apparent corruption or major failures, or their fears of the changes that a conservative administration might bring.[65] In addition, Ninagawa received the vote of between a quarter and a third of LDP supporters and an even higher percentage of DSP supporters.[66]

It was not only the independent and conservative voters, however, that supported Ninagawa as a person or as the incumbent rather than for party or ideological reasons. Most surveys agree that although political party identification played the greatest role in determining Kyoto voters' choices in national level elections, the role of personality and policy factors increased in local—including prefectural—level elections. These same surveys show that much of Ninagawa's overall support was predicated on the latter factors. As many as half of those who voted for him may have done so on the basis of "personality" rather than party support factors, and when given a choice of "personality," "policy," or "party" to explain their reasons for voting, Ninagawa supporters chose "party" least frequently. Further, it was often the progressive party identifiers, particularly the supporters of the JSP, who tended to vote more frequently on the basis of personality factors, while conservative party identifiers, particularly those of the *Komeitō* and LDP, often cast their ballots for Ninagawa's opposition on the basis of party affiliation.[67] The elements of Ninagawa's personal appeal that were cited by Kyoto voters, conservatives, independents, and progressives alike, were his "reliability" (*tayori ni naru hito or tayorigai*), his "clean and uncorrupted (*seiketsu*) image," and the belief that he worked hard for the local area (*jimoto no tame ni tsukusu*).[68]

Similarly, despite the polarization of center and conservative parties against the Left since 1966, gubernatorial elections have been fought with little controversy over the parties' programs or their ideologies. Rather, they have revolved around two types of issues: the personalities

---

[65] Sudō, "Kyōtofu chijisen," p. 72.

[66] Again the actual figures vary in the surveys that were cited in note 64. The figures for DSP supporters voting for Ninagawa given by Ōhashi, Okamoto, Sudō, Ōkubu, and Yoshino, respectively, are 31 percent, 41 percent, 43 percent, 43 percent, and about 30 percent.

[67] See Okamoto, *Gendai seiji*, pp. 331-332, 337; Kodaira, "'Jimoto no rieki'," pp 74-76; Ōkubo, *Nihonjin no tōhyō*, pp. 3-13; Sudō, "Kyōtofu chijisen," p. 74. For a slightly different view, see Miyake, *Kotonaru reberu*, pp. 409-412, and his "Zenkoku senkyo to chihō senkyo," pp. 49-50.

[68] Okamoto, *Gendai seiji*, p. 338; Ōkubo, *Nihonjin no tōhyō*, pp. 3-4; Sudō, "Kyōtofu chijisen," p. 74.

and policies of Ninagawa, and the relationship of Kyotoites to the central government. The Left's campaign literature[69] emphasized the man himself, with photographs and cartoons invariably portraying his famous grin and his relationship to the common man. The Communists conducted the campaign overtly as a crusade to "protect" Ninagawa and his progressive government, which in turn was portrayed as protecting and aiding Kyoto citizens, their constitutional rights, their interests, and their welfare. The opposition often attacked Ninagawa's age, his too-long incumbency, his too-close relationship with the Communists, and the negative aspects of his leftist policies, particularly an alleged decline in educational standards.

The theme of protection and benefit versus the costs of leftist government emerged even more clearly in the second major type of issue. The Ninagawa campaign inevitably sought to portray the conservative opposition as puppets whose strings are pulled by the corrupt LDP and big business outsiders seeking to destroy a progressive government that has protected its citizens' tradition, welfare, and environment. Kyotoites of all political persuasions were constantly reminded in the course of a campaign that Ninagawa represented independence, self-rule, community pride, and the protection of their heritage. The conservatives often seemed to play into the hands of the Left by running campaigns emphasizing the future material benefits of "direct pipeline" (*chokketsu*) to the center of a conservative governor. The extent to which this kind of campaign rhetoric directly influenced votes, however, is difficult to gauge. Indeed, surveys have shown that most Kyotoites would have preferred their governor to be *more* solicitous of receiving national government aid and that opinions on this question were not related to support or nonsupport of Ninagawa at the polls.[70] Rather than the issue of independence from, or the seeking of, benefits from the LDP government, it is likely that, along with personal appeal and incumbency, the governor's stance of preserving and aiding local interests and of protecting Kyotoites from industrial development were the more important campaign issues that worked to his advantage at election time.

[69] See, for example, Akarui Minshu Fusei o Susumerukai, '70 *Kyōtofu chiji senkyo no kiroku* (Shukusatsuban; 1970). On the 1970 election, see also Ōta, "Kyōtofu chiji," pp. 135-136, and Itokawa Seiichi, *Senkyo sendensen—Kore ga jōhōka shakai no senryaku da* (Tōkyō: Kubota Senden Kenkyūsho, 1971), Chapter 5.

[70] See Yoshino, "Ninagawa nanasen," p. 35; Sudō, "Kyōtofu chijisen," p. 75; Okamoto, *Gendai seiji*, p. 249. By contrast, according to Yoshino, p. 33, 70 percent of Ninagawa's supporters who thought he was doing a good job mentioned protection of the environment as a reason.

The Rise of the Communists and the Growth of Citizen Participation

The "new coalition" that helped maintain Ninagawa in power after 1966 was integrally related to two other major changes: the rise of the JCP and an increasing emphasis on institutionalizing progressive government while responding to new demands for citizen participation. After 1966 and with their enhanced role in the Ninagawa coalition, the JCP experienced a remarkable growth in electoral support at the prefectural and national levels that was to make it the main leftist party in Kyoto by 1975. Table 1 shows the percentage of votes obtained by the JSP and the JCP since 1958 in the House of Representatives and Pre-

Table 1

JSP and JCP Vote, Combined Vote, and JCP Proportion of
Combined Vote Obtained in House of Representatives
and Prefectural Assembly Elections in Kyoto
1958-1976
(by percentage)

	JSP	JCP	COMBINED VOTE	JCP AS PROPORTION OF COMBINED VOTE
Prefectural Assembly				
1959	31.6	6.5	38.1	17.0
1963	27.0	10.2	37.2	27.4
1967	28.1	13.3	41.4	32.1
1971	23.7	23.0	46.7	49.2
1975	17.6	25.5	43.1	59.1
House of Representatives				
1958	37.0	5.8	42.8	13.5
1960	29.3	8.9	38.2	23.2
1963	29.4	13.5	42.9	31.4
1967	25.7	14.4	40.1	35.9
1969	15.3	20.4	35.7	57.1
1972	19.0	24.6	43.6	56.4
1976	14.8	21.0	35.8	58.6

SOURCES: Publications of the Kyoto Election Administration Committee (*Kyōto Senkyo Kanri Iinkai*). 1975 PA percentages calculated from voting results in *Kyōto Shinbun*, 15 April 1975, p. 3; 1976 HR percentages calculated from *Yomiuri Shinbun*, 7 December 1976, p. 3.

fectural Assembly elections and also the increased proportion of the leftist vote that has gone to the Communists as the Socialist vote has declined. As the table shows, although the combined leftist vote has not consistently or significantly increased since 1958, the JCP has increased its proportion of that vote from 13 percent to 58 percent in HR elections since 1958 and from 17 percent to 59 percent in PA elections since 1959. The JCP in Kyoto has gained electoral support for their candidates beyond that in all other local districts and far beyond the national average. By 1972, Kyoto's first House of Representatives district was the JCP's top district in the country in terms of voting percentage. The second district was the JCP's tenth best in the nation.[71] After the 1975 local elections, the Communists were the largest leftist party and the second largest party overall in both the prefectural and city assemblies.[72] For the first time in Japan, one of their members held the vice-speakership in the Prefectural Assembly.

Although a complete analysis of the causes for the rise of the Communists and the decline of the Socialists is beyond the scope of this paper, we may note a few of the factors contributing to this phenomena. First, the JCP's electoral mobilization capabilities are much more formidable than the JSP's. The Communists have a grass-roots and professional party organization, while the Socialists rely almost exclusively on labor union activists, many of whom are now being wooed by the JCP. Further, the JCP has had a great deal of success recently in building candidates' personal support organizations (*kōenkai*), thus matching the JSP's previous advantage in this form of voter mobilization. As a consequence, JCP supporters are more likely than any other party identifiers except those of the *Komeitō* to vote consistently for their party and to be willing to undertake activities on its behalf.[73] Perhaps more importantly, between elections the JCP has been active in organizing the rising daily demands of citizens and neighborhoods. The party has also been active in allying themselves with citizens' movement causes.[74]

---

[71] Shiratori Rei, *Nihon ni okeru hoshu to kakushin* (Tōkyō: Nihon Keizai Shinbunsha, 1973), p. 172.

[72] The JCP maintained 13 seats, while the JSP dropped from 14 to 10 seats in the 63-seat Prefectural Assembly. The LDP is first with 21 seats. In the city assembly, the JCP gained one seat to bring its total to 20, second only to the 25 seats of the LDP. The JSP dropped from 11 seats to 8 out of the 72-seat total. The *Komeitō* advanced in these elections from 9 to 11 seats in the city assembly and 2 to 6 seats in the PA. See *Kyōto shinbun*, 14 April 1975, p. 1.

[73] Kodaira, " 'Jimoto no rieki'," p. 74.

[74] Interview with Hirota Yoshio, vice-chairman, Kyoto JCP, 13 May 1975; see also for example, Sankei Shinbun, *Kakushin jichitai*, pp. 22-23.

This grass-roots organizing and attention to citizens' everyday demands, combined with their image as the most incorruptible of Japanese parties, has enabled them to gain the support of voters unconcerned with ideology in addition to those attracted by it. At least one survey showed that JCP supporters were more likely to give the "purity" of the party as a reason for their support than any other party identifiers and more likely to give "local interests" as a reason for support than any party identifiers except those of the LDP.[75] Because Ninagawa was known to be accessible to demands backed up by organized groups, the JCP was able to take advantage of the trends toward rising demands and collective participation and to establish a reputation as having a "pipe" to the governor.[76]

Thus, beginning with the formation of the "new coalition" in 1966, there was a mutually beneficial relationship between Ninagawa and the JCP whereby increased access to the governor helped the party to attain electoral success which in turn increased its importance as an element in the Ninagawa coalition and so gave it even more access. Indeed, this prefectural administration-JCP relationship had become so far advanced by late 1973 that it caused the strain between the right wing of the JSP and Ninagawa to break out into the open in the preparations for the 1974 gubernatorial elections. The right-wing faction of the Socialists, who at this juncture controlled the leadership of the prefectural JSP chapter, decided not to support Ninagawa for reelection to an unprecedented seventh term. When the national executive committee of the JSP refused to sanction this decision lest it jeopardize its attempt to run joint candidates with the Communists in the 1975 nationwide local elections, the prefectural chapter defied the decision and announced the candidacy of its chairman, Ohashi Kazutaka. He was expelled from the national party but ran against Ninagawa anyway, with the formal backing of the DSP and the tacit support of the LDP and *Komeitō*. By the strenuous efforts of the JCP and other remaining elements in the coalition, Ninagawa won the election by a mere 4,000 votes.[77] More than ever before, the governor was now dependent on the Communists and his "nonpartisan" organizations such as the *Fushimindantai* for support.

As the JCP's enhanced role in electoral politics in 1966 was a forerunner of a subsequent change in the relative influence of the leftist

[75] Kodaira, "'Jimoto no rieki'," pp. 74-75.

[76] On the advantages that Ninagawa's administrative style gives the JCP, see Miyake, "Seitō shiji no dōkō," pp. 26-27.

[77] See J.A.A. Stockwin, "Shifting Alignments," for an excellent account of the intra- and interparty conflicts leading up to the election.

parties in the prefectural government, so too did the increased participation of interest-citizens organizations like the *Fushimindantai* in gubernatorial elections herald the coming of a new era of concern with
the political participation of the ordinary citizen. In 1966, one of the
first major citizens' movements against pollution in Kyoto occurred,
protesting the construction of a concrete factory in the environs of
Kyoto City. Like most other regions of Japan, Kyoto was to witness
many more of these movements in the late 1960s and early 1970s, although these were to be directed primarily against utilities, private
industry, or proposed construction by the central government rather
than against the consequences of existing polluters or against the prefectural government itself. The Ninagawa administration's previous policies discouraging the development of private heavy industry in the
prefecture had mitigated the frequency, consequences, and severity of
the type of pollution problems occurring elsewhere. Also, Kyoto City's
status as a "designated city" meant that the prefecture itself was spared
becoming the main target of movements over issues that more directly
fell under the jurisdiction of the city government.

The Ninagawa administration's response to these movements was
somewhat atypical: it neither resisted the new movements, as some
conservative governments initially did, nor invariably agreed with their
aims and championed their cause, as many progressive governments
newly elected on the wave of citizen protest did. Rather, while championing the principle of listening to the voices of protesting citizens,
the administration was flexible in its actual reactions to the movements,
attempting not to become involved in some until it had to, acting on
behalf of others, and seeking to arbitrate the conflict of still others.[78]
The governor's policy was not to ignore citizens' desires or force them
to accept projects they opposed but to decide each case considering
the well-being of the prefecture as a whole.[79]

Along with the flexible attitude toward spontaneous citizen's movements, however, the Ninagawa government actively sponsored the
formation and growth of other types of "citizens' movements." As
early as 1964, the prefecture actively encouraged the formation of a
"Beautify the Kamo River Movement" (*Kamogawa o Utsukushuku
Suru Undō*) to clean up the large river running through the heart of

[78] See the *Asahi shinbun* (Kyoto edition) series, "Yobōsen o miru—Kutabare
kōgai, dai-nibu" (part 2; 24-29 November); Aiba Jūichi, "Keiji baipasu hantai
undō no genjō to kadai," *Shimin*, no. 1 (March 1971); Yamaoka, *Nihon no kao*,
Chapter 2; Asahi Ja-naru, "Kyōto Kyōsuke to Ninagawa taisei," p. 12.

[79] Interview with Fujinami Kiyoshi, head of the Public Information Section
(*kōhōkacho*) of the Kyoto prefectural government, 18 April 1975.

Kyoto City, to build parks along its banks, and to educate citizens to preserve this natural resource. As part of a 1972 prefectural government campaign to "Protect Our Homeland" (*Furusato o Mamoru Undō*), the Kamogawa movement allied itself with other citizens' societies to preserve Kyoto rivers and canals.[80] Commencing in 1966, the administration directly sponsored a campaign to organize rural residents into community associations called *Robata Kondankai* ("Hearthside Circle Meetings") to raise their local consciousness and mobilize them to join with the administration in discovering and solving community problems.[81]

By sponsoring these "citizens' movements" the administration attempted to adapt its progressive ideology to the new nationwide concern for resident's initiative and citizen participation. In addition, these efforts to initiate or patronize citizens' groups and the "Let's Put the Constitution in Our Lives" movement were attempts to create such a concern where it did not exist in order to institutionalize progressive government in Kyoto at the grass-roots level. Indeed, that these campaigns were sponsored as early as 1964-1966 suggests that the desire to socialize citizens to progressive goals and to institutionalize progressive administration and policy in anticipation of Ninagawa's eventual retirement may well have been as important as the desire to conform to new definitions of the meaning of progressivism.

In 1975, the attempt to institutionalize progressive administration, Kyoto style, was threatened by a return of the same problems that beset it soon after its inauguration in 1950: a fiscal crisis and unstable assembly support. Like all other local governments in Japan, the Ninagawa administration desperately tried to stave off large financial deficits that might once again have forced it to become a Financial Reconstruction Entity. And, as a result of huge losses by the Socialists, the stabilization of Communist gains, and large increases by the *Komeitō* in the 1975 prefectural assembly elections,[82] the JCP-JSP-independent majority that had been so dramatically inaugurated in 1953 and stabilized in the 1960s was broken. Only by working with the previously antagonistic *Komeitō* was the governor able to gain majority support for the passage of his policies in the last years of his final term. The wounds of the 1974 gubernatorial election remained deep as well, and the JSP

[80] See Yamaoka, *Nihon no kao*, Chapter 1; Kamogawa o Utsukushiku Suru Kai, "Kamogawa o utsukushiku suru undō no ayumi" (pamphlet distributed by Kamogawa o Utsukushiku Suru Kai, June 1967).

[81] Interview with Sakamoto Keiichi, scholar and consultant to the *Robata Kondankai*, 21 February 1975; see also his article, "Shimin ishiki no haitatsu—Robata kondankai," in *Toshi mondai* 62 (1971).

[82] See note 72.

itself remained reluctant to support Ninagawa for another term or to cooperate again with the JCP.

Although surveys indicate that a majority of Kyotoites preferred the continuation of a progressive government,[83] the retirement of Ninagawa and the failure of the Left to support another joint candidate in 1978 allowed the conservatives to recapture the greatest local stronghold of the opposition in postwar Japan.

Conclusion

I have described the long history of the Ninagawa administration in terms of three relatively distinct periods: 1950-1958, 1959-1965, and 1966-1978. The first period was dominated by problems of asserting control over the bureaucracy and assembly, with few attempts to initiate progressive policies or to oppose the national government. The second stage was one of increasing leftism, characterized by attempts to initiate policies, programs, and ideology that gave the administration both a more stable base of power and a distinct (leftist) identity. Finally, the third stage emphasized the institutionalization of the leftist government through the modification of alliances and the creation of new organizations to mobilize the vote, to mediate the increasingly conflictual JCP-JSP alliance, and to socialize citizens to administration goals.

Since the end of the first period, the Ninagawa regime demonstrated its capacity for innovative policies and politics that have provided an alternative model to conservative rule in Japan. Some of these innovative policies and political strategies—for example, the rejection of centrally planned, large-scale industrialization in favor of preservation and development of the existing economic structure and of social services, the development of a political ideology based on local autonomy and democratic rights, and the formation of a coalition of leftist parties and citizens' groups under the leadership of a popular scholar with a suprapartisan appeal—proved to be a prototype of the leftist governments that sprang up in other urban areas of Japan in the late 1960s. Others, such as the ability to command a stable assembly majority and the creation of citizens' movements to institutionalize the regime's goals, seemed to be more developed than in many of the newer progressive local administrations.

Yet, reviewing the quarter century of leftist rule in Kyoto, one is

[83] Yoshino, "Ninagawa nanasen," pp. 34-35, found that 48 percent of his respondents wanted progressive government to continue and only 20 percent wanted a changeover to conservative government.

struck as much by a consistent and limited aspect to its policy outputs and style as by its changing stages and innovation. To put it in terms of Lowi's typology of public policies,[84] throughout its evolving stages the progressivism of the Ninagawa regime manifested itself more in *distributive* and *regulatory* policies than in the *redistributive* ones we might expect of a leftist regime. The administration engaged in a re-ordering of the priorities of local government rather than in calling for accomplishing a massive reallocation of local resources or extensive changes in the socio-economic or political structure. Its priorities have been symbolized and implemented primarily by granting selective access and allocations (as in its loan programs for small and medium enterprise, its attention to the interests of education and medical personnel, and its use of "pork barrel" benefits to secure support in the assembly) and by favorable regulatory and appointive decisions to supporting local interests and associations (as in its relations with the medical associations and its administrative protection of small industries and traditional handicrafts). Its policy style has been that of *incrementalism* rather than utopianism, making "adjustments in existing reality," not attempting abrupt large-scale transformations to a preconceived ideal.[85] Further, many of its outputs have been symbolic, thus its emphasis on local pride and history, constitutionalism, and responsiveness to citizens' needs. To the extent that "redistribution" has been emphasized, it has been at this symbolic level where welfare and populist egalitarian values are embedded in much of its public rhetoric.

A partial explanation for this pattern of policy and policy-making style lies in the limitations and demands imposed on a progressive administration by the local autonomy system and political culture in Japan. Dependence on central government subsidies and grants for a majority of its funds together with a limited ability to develop large new sources of independent revenue undoubtedly impose major constraints on a leftist administration's capacity to develop sweeping new redistributive programs. While this was most obvious in the first period of the Ninagawa administration when Kyoto was a "Financial Reconstruction Entity," the limits of authority, the lack of independent sources of revenue, and the potential, if not the actuality, of central government reaction to "radical" programs for change was a restricting factor even during the latter two periods. In the case of a prefectural administration with a major city within its boundaries, policy is further

[84] Theodore J. Lowi, "American Business, Public Policy, Case Studies, and Political Theory," *World Politics* 16 (1964), especially pp. 690-691.
[85] Robert A. Dahl and Charles E. Lindblom, *Politics, Economics, and Welfare* (New York: Harper & Row, 1953), pp. 82-85.

constrained by the division of functions set by law. Designated cities, such as Kyoto City with its almost two-thirds of the prefecture's population, have primary responsibility for many welfare services ordinarily exercised by the prefecture.[86]

Yet, the Ninagawa regime also faced the necessity of responding to the demands of local interests (an expectation both widespread and widely legitimated in postwar Japan) and of providing some concrete manifestations of its "leftism." The result of constraints, on the one hand, and pressures, on the other, was a mixture of "programmatic" policy that emphasized symbolic outputs and bureaucratic "patronage" via selective access and favorable but limited regulatory, appointive, and allocative decisions on behalf of supporting interest groups.

To see the nature of leftism only in terms of a progressive regime's goals being thwarted by the parameters of the local autonomy system, however (as many Japanese progressives and Kyoto politicians and officials tend to do) is to overlook the real significance of the Ninagawa government, which was that its policy outputs and style also represented a successful political strategy for maintaining power by adapting[87] leftism to Kyoto's pluralistic socio-economic and fragmented political environment.[88] To understand this strategy is to answer the question of why and how a progressive administration became so firmly entrenched in Kyoto for most of the postwar period.

A search for the sources of Ninagawa's success in institutionalizing his leftist administration in Kyoto might plausibly lead one to the socio-economic trends of postwar Japan that have created a larger strata of voters amenable to the appeals of the Left—the trends of urbanization, mass higher education, and unionization described elsewhere in this volume.[89] Indeed, many of the environmental characteristics associated with leftist support are present in Kyoto, which is one of Japan's most

[86] On funding of local governments and financial dependence on national government, see Steiner, *Local Government*, Chapter 12 and pp. 323-326. On designated cities' functions in public service areas, see ibid., pp. 181-182.

[87] On the difference between a leftist party's active "adapting" versus passive "adjusting" to its environment, see Alan Stern, "Political Legitimacy in Local Politics: The Communist Party in Northeastern Italy," in *Communism in Italy and France*, ed. Donald L. Blackmer and Sidney Tarrow (Princeton: Princeton University Press, 1975), pp. 221, 257.

[88] The discussion in this conclusion is loosely based on Sidney Tarrow's suggestion that the "instruments of state power" available to a government, the nature of the social bases underlying political support, and the strategies of party leaders can largely explain the stability of a political system and the pattern of policy and exchange within that system. See Sidney Tarrow, "The Italian Party System Between Crisis and Transition," *American Journal of Political Science* 21 (1977).

[89] See Chapters 3 and 5.

highly urbanized prefectures, with a high proportion of intellectuals and students in its population. Further, public employee unions, a major pillar of leftism in Japan, played an important role in supporting the Ninagawa coalition.

These characteristics in the Kyoto environment, however, are but a necessary precondition for leftist power; they are hardly a sufficient explanation of its strength and longevity. Other aspects of Kyoto's socio-economic structure are not predictably suited to undergird the greatest local bastion of the Left in Japanese history. If highly urbanized, Kyoto also has undergone relatively little of the demographic changes of other urban areas of Japan: its population density is but a fraction of that in other urbanized prefectures, it has few in-migrants, and it possesses a remarkably stable population with strong traditional social ties. Furthermore, Kyoto has experienced little of the kind of industrial development and its consequences that is often said to account for leftist strength in urban areas. Thus it has few of the industrial workers and salarymen in large private enterprises who frequently vote for the leftist parties but many of the shopkeepers and small and medium enterprise workers who typically cast their votes for conservative or middle-of-the-road parties; yet Ninagawa was to capture significant electoral support from the latter strata.

Thus a sufficient explanation of leftist strength and success in Kyoto must take into account how Ninagawa was able to mobilize both the usual sources of leftist support in Japan *and* the normally conservative or moderate strata and groups that make up a larger percentage of Kyoto's population than of the population of most urban areas of Japan. Indeed, the ability of the Ninagawa regime to maintain itself in power for twenty-eight years depended on its ability to bridge this dualism of postwar Japanese political culture by devising a strategy for appealing to the heterogeneous social and political bases of the Kyoto electorate. This strategy has involved: 1) successfully integrating leftist ideology with the Kyoto milieu via the themes of localism and protection; 2) skillfully engaging in the politics of coalition building; and 3) utilizing a variety of appeals to attract and mobilize the widest possible range of voters.

The goals and rhetoric of leftist politics in Kyoto represented the unfulfilled aims of the American Occupation:[90] the institutionalization

---

[90] There is no denying Ninagawa's sincere belief in Marxism or that many of his supporters are Marxists. My point here is only that Marxist ideology plays a relatively small role in mobilizing support for the Ninagawa administration among Kyoto citizens and that the public ideology of Kyoto politics would not seem alien to a non-Marxist American liberal.

of the postwar Constitution, the enhancement of local autonomy, emphasis on social welfare and mass democratic education, and the championing of the "little man" against corporate and national government power and corruption. In the 1960s, these basic values of the postwar Left in Japan became combined with the newer progressive causes of environmental protection and of responsiveness to citizen input into administration. The accomplishment of the Ninagawa administration was to take this abstract progressive ideology and give it concrete meaning in terms of Kyoto's cultural and socio-economic context and political reality: the values had to be adapted to a locale with a small and medium enterprise and professional-dominated socio-economic structure and with unique historical traditions and myths. Thus the anticentral government and big business and the prosocial and political democracy and local autonomy elements in the ideology were identified with and given embodiment in rhetoric and decisions to preserve the local traditions, environment, and arena of decisions, to defend and aid small and medium enterprise against a distant central government and its big business allies, and to stress the need for social services and the professionals and public employees needed to carry them out.

Linking leftist ideology with the Kyoto environment are the themes of localism and protection. Ninagawa was the first progressive politician in Japan to realize that local pride and tradition, latent hostility and fear of the great concentration of political, economic, and cultural power in Tokyo, and the advancement of local interests by local government could be used by the Left against the conservative LDP: localism need not be a resource left only to the conservatives to exploit through a complete identification of conservatism with tradition and of the LDP with benefits to local interests. In the context of a political system in which conservatives enjoyed seemingly perpetual control of the central bureaucracy and were committed to policies of rapid economic growth, change, and big business expansion, what a progressive local government could offer its citizens was protection—protection of their "life and livelihood," of their rights, and of their unique tradition. The legitimation and maintenance of leftist government in Kyoto was aided by identifying progressivism not with massive redistribution policies to alter social stratification, rapid change, and greater centralization but with orderly growth, preservation, and local initiative.[91]

---

[91] The importance of allaying fears of massive change in conservative environments is illustrated by Giacomo Sani's speculation that much of the continued suspicion and distrust of the Communist Party of Italy (PCI) in Italy may be due to this factor. See his "Mass-Level Response to Party Strategy: The Italian Electorate and the Communist Party," in Blackmer and Tarrow, *Communism*, p. 489, n. 36.

In this respect, the Kyoto "model" invites comparison to the stronghold of local opposition in Italy—Bologna. Despite fundamental differences in the context and operation of politics in the two areas,[92] underlying general similarities exist: in both Kyoto and Bologna, leftist administrations successfully adopted the themes of local tradition and resentment of central interference and adapted their policies and ideologies to a local social structure based on light industry, smaller commercial organizations, and professionals.[93] In both cases, a degree of ideological purity was sacrificed, but this sacrifice purchased the additional support necessary to gain the unaccustomed benefit of maintaining and exercising power.

In addition to integrating progressive ideology with the Kyoto environment, power was maintained by the administration's ability to build organizational coalitions and to mobilize a wide strata of voters. The JCP thrived in Kyoto because of its own strategy of responding to local interests, its superior organizational abilities, and its direct access to the administration. Yet the party may have reached, at least temporarily, the limits of its growth in the prefecture, as the 1975 assembly elections indicated.[94] The JSP is organizationally weak and torn by factionalism. Either singly or in alliance, the two leftist parties cannot command a majority of votes. Indeed, the total vote for the two parties has not expanded much in the last fifteen to twenty years—only the proportion received by each party has changed drastically. The alliance itself has

[92] Among the obvious differences are the following: the executive is not directly elected in Bologna, as it is in Kyoto; voting turnout is much higher in Bologna and surveys find relatively high political interest, whereas the opposite is true in Kyoto; leftist support in Bologna is partially based on large-scale urban migration from surrounding "Red Belt" areas, whereas we have already noted Kyoto's phenomenal stability in demographic patterns and there is no surrounding "Red Belt"; the Communists are the overwhelmingly dominant partner in the leftist coalition in Bologna, but they are more evenly matched with the Socialists in Kyoto. On these characteristics in Bologna, see Evans, *Coexistence*, pp. 20, 35-41; see also Sani, "Mass Level Response," p. 503, and Stern, "Political Legitimacy," p. 236, in Blackmer and Tarrow, *Communism*.

[93] One can assert the equivalence of Bologna's anticlericist tradition and its resentment of interference from the Vatican in politics with Kyoto's antipower, anti-Tokyo traditions. See Evans, *Coexistence*, pp. 3-4, 54-63, 182. The Bolognese Communist administration also has evolved special appeals and policies for small merchants and light industry because of their importance there. See Stephen Hellman, "The PCI's Alliance Strategy and the Case of the Middle Classes," in Blackmer and Tarrow, *Communism*, pp. 392-398.

[94] See note 72. Many of the potential supporters of the JCP may already have been convinced, and the remainder of the electorate holds strong antipathies to the party. According to surveys, as many as 24 percent of Kyoto voters identify the JCP as the party they most dislike. See Okamoto, *Gendai seiji*, pp. 280-285.

become more, not less, riven with conflict with the passage of time. It was just such tensions between the two leftist parties that led to their failure to agree on a joint gubernatorial candidate in 1978 and to the return of the prefecture to the conservative column for the first time since 1950.

The foundation of leftist power in Kyoto therefore rested only in part on the institutionalization of the two leftist parties. The retention of power and effective governing required the skillful construction, during gubernatorial election campaigns and in the Prefectural Assembly, of a grand alliance of the leftist parties and other progressive organizations with independents and sympathetic conservatives. The key to Ninagawa's ability to keep this alliance together and to mobilize the support of the many nonaligned voters, who were without strong party identification or were distrustful of established parties, was the development of organizational devices like the *Fushimindantai* and *Susumeru-kai*. The *Fushimindantai*'s performance in electoral mobilization and in interest group and alliance politics made it a unique and significant experiment as a cross between an independents' party, a citizens' movement organized along functional lines, and a progressive liaison office. More than anything else, it was really the governor's *kōenkai*, his personal support organization that loyally delivered votes to him in exchange for access to his administration, and which also served as his go-between and buffer in managing the JCP-JSP alliance's many tensions and conflicts.

The administration thus attracted a wide strata of voters to support it at election time by some of the very appeals and techniques of electoral mobilization that have helped sustain the LDP in power at the national level for so many years. Much of the electorate, for example, was influenced by the attractions of personality, incumbency, and stability; organized group support was maintained by allocating governmental benefits and patronage; electoral campaigns were fought by appealing to concern for the preservation of deep-rooted cultural values and local interests, by organizing a leader's *kōenkai*, and by mobilizing nonpartisan and apolitical voters in addition to leftist partisans. Much more research on other major urban areas in Japan is necessary to determine whether some of these same appeals and techniques have also been responsible for the electoral success of newer progressive executives.[95] But in Kyoto at least, they enabled the Left to mobilize

[95] Surveys of Tokyo gubernatorial elections reveal that Minobe also received a large degree of support from moderates, conservatives, and independents, not just progressive party identifiers, and that personality played a large role in rea-

strata of the electorate that hitherto have been considered the baili-
wick of the conservatives and to add their support to that of progressive sympathizers attracted to the leftist parties and to the regime's
symbolic rhetoric, priorities, and antagonism to the LDP.

Observers of Japanese politics noted in the late 1960s that the Left
"seemed content to wait until the 'natural' growth of their support
concomitant with the urbanization process puts them into power."[96]
Since that time, the Left has taken advantage of the "natural" growth
of their support to take power in many urban areas of Japan besides
Kyoto. The Ninagawa administration reminds us (whatever opportunities are created or not created by socio-economic trends) of the importance of political resources, especially of political leadership. For it
is such skills as those of symbol manipulation, coalition building, and
the ability to transform pressure group demands into policies and those
policies into electoral support that are essential to maintaining power
once attained.

The problem of the Left in contemporary Japanese political culture
is that in order to gain and maintain power it must transcend class and
ideological appeals and mobilize support from formerly apolitical or
conservative interest groups and voters. It can do this by running attractive suprapartisan local executives, by maintaining unity between
the Socialists and the Communists, by eschewing Marxist symbols and
rhetoric for vaguer "progressive" ones, and by delivering concrete
benefits to important, even nonleftist, local interest groups. This is the
formula that proved so successful for so long in Kyoto. But as the
Kyoto "model" also demonstrates, these requirements for attaining and
maintaining power themselves help to transform any radical or redistributive goals into pragmatic, instrumental, and incremental policies.

Further, no matter how successful this "Kyoto formula" has been,
two of its key elements—the personal appeal of the local executive and
leftist unity—are potentially vulnerable. When the popular executive
incumbent retires and/or the always tenuous JSP-JCP alliance breaks
apart, conservative or Center-Right candidates can recapture even progressive strongholds, as happened in Kyoto in 1978. Leftist strategies

---

sons for vote. On the other hand, there appears to be a relationship between dis-
approval of the prefecture having a "direct pipeline" (*chokketsu*) to the national
government and vote for Minobe, a relationship lacking in Kyoto. See Yanai
Michio, "Tōkyō-to chiji senkyo ni okeru kōhosha kettei yōin no bunseki (1),"
Bulletin of the Faculty of Humanities, no. 9 (1973), pp. 39, 50, 53.

[96] Scott C. Flanagan, "Voting Behavior in Japan," *Comparative Political Studies*
1 (1968): 410.

such as those followed during the Ninagawa administration in Kyoto may maintain leftist local control for a long time, but they do not guarantee power in perpetuity.

And this is the final lesson of the Ninagawa administration in Kyoto: structural constraints, political opportunities, and vulnerability to alternation of regimes create a leftist opposition in power very different from that hoped for by the Left's most fervent supporters or feared by its staunchest critics.

PART FIVE

CONCLUSION

CHAPTER 12

THE PARTISAN POLITICIZATION OF LOCAL
GOVERNMENT: CAUSES AND CONSEQUENCES

Scott C. Flanagan, Kurt Steiner, and Ellis S. Krauss

THE various sections and chapters of this book have demonstrated that a great variety of fundamental changes have been taking place within the local political arena, including the expansion of the opposition party vote in local elections, the growth of citizens' movements, and the rise of progressive administrations. In short, we are witnessing a *politicization* of local politics in Japan. We will conclude this study of political opposition and local politics with a discussion of the broader system effects of the intrusion of oppositions and partisan political contestation into local politics. Traditionally most observers have strongly opposed the politicization of local politics, and we will review their arguments on the presumed ill effects of local politicization. We will then analyze more closely a number of the effects that partisan politicization on the local level in Japan appears to be having on local autonomy, the policy-making process, government responsiveness, system support, system stability, and evolving party coalition patterns.

POLITICIZED VERSUS NONPOLITICIZED LOCAL GOVERNMENT:
TWO MODELS OF REPRESENTATION

In its simplest sense, the term "politicization" refers to the decline in the number of successful independent candidates and the concomitant rise in partisan candidates and partisan competition. In Chapters 3 and 5 it was shown that below the national level this politicization process was most pronounced at the prefectural and big city municipal election levels but that it was also sufficiently widespread to characterize local electoral trends within the nation as a whole.

The rise in partisan labels and partisan competition, however, is simply the most visible macrolevel indicator of the politicization process. Underlying these electoral changes are microlevel attitudinal and behavioral changes in the citizens themselves. Thus the politicization of local politics also refers to changes in the consciousness of Japanese citizens—a rise in the awareness of citizen rights, in expectations of government responsiveness, and in a recognition of the legitimacy of demand making. In turn, these kinds of attitude changes are not only altering citizen behavior at the polls but are also stimulating new modes of citizen participation, such as involvement in local residents' movements. As a result of this politicization process, undifferentiated support at the local level is increasingly being replaced by differentiated demands. Moreover, the process appears to have policy implications, as local politicization has been accompanied by a rise in progressive administrations and by a shift in the style and policy priorities of many local governments, conservative as well as progressive.

To suggest that local politics is becoming politicized in Japan is not to assume that the prior condition was apolitical or that local inhabitants were totally excluded from any form of political participation. Certainly the exercise of politics was more private and personalistic, but one can nevertheless identify political input processes. Thus in our terminology, local politics was not apolitical but nonpoliticized. In drawing a distinction between a politicized and a nonpoliticized local politics, we direct our attention once again to the dual quality of Japanese politics outlined in Chapter 2. In that context, we noted a duality in styles of politicking and in the political consciousness of the citizenry. It was also suggested that the Japanese electorate could be characterized in terms of two distinct galleries—a traditionally oriented and a more modern gallery. To say that we can conceptualize Japanese politics in terms of two types of voters and two styles of politics suggests that there are two contrasting modes of representation. In its most fundamental sense, therefore, dual politics implies dual models of democracy.

We might label the older, more traditional model *patron-client democracy* and the newer, more modern model *pluralist democracy*.[1] The patron-client democracy model is based on localism, areal voting, and a traditional value system—that is, a value system that stresses community solidarity, repression of internal dissent, deference to community leaders, conformity to group decisions, and a resignation to the way things are. Voting in the context of this model becomes an expression of community will and communal duty. The payoffs for the voter take the form of direct benefits for himself, his family, and

---

[1] Nobutaka Ike describes Japan as a patron-client democracy in his *Japanese Politics: Patron-Client Democracy* (New York: Knopf, 1972). The concept of pluralist democracy has been treated extensively in the writings of Robert A. Dahl, including his *Who Governs?* (New Haven: Yale University Pres, 1961) and *Pluralist Democracy in the United States* (Chicago: Rand McNally, 1967).

the immediate community, bestowed by a personal benefactor, either the candidate the community supports or some local notable.

While participation in this patron-client model is more an affirmation of community membership or personal loyalties than an expression of political interest and involvement, the model is not without merit. Built on community solidarity, the model encourages and frequently achieves virtually 100 percent voting participation within a given village hamlet or city neighborhood and thus ensures maximum representation of that locality and works to its benefit as a whole.[2] The model also provides for the incorporation of the citizen without requiring a great deal of knowledge or sophistication on his part regarding national politics.

Patron-client democracy, however, does have serious shortcomings. Moreover these deficiencies assume greater proportions with the advance of economic development, which causes the periphery to be increasingly affected by decisions made at the center. As seen in the schematic depiction of our two models in Figure 1, the patron-client model short circuits the input-output loop normally associated with the policy-making process in democratic political systems. Thus in Model I, the accountability loop is simply a personal one between the voter and his representative. The voter extends his support in return for individual and local community benefits. This model, however, bypasses the public policy process and denies the voter any check on the actions of the Diet and the cabinet. The representative as patron simply plies his influence with the appropriate bureaucrats, party leaders, and other power brokers on behalf of his constituents. So long as community benefits keep flowing down the pipe, partisan politics, national issues, and even political corruption are quite beside the point.

The pluralist model of democracy as depicted in Figure 1 presents an alternate mode of citizen representation. We note that in this model, voting affects incumbency which in turn affects policy decisions and government performance and on around the loop on the output side to the impact of government policy and performance on citizen attitudes and behavior which in turn affect voting. Here we see that the accountability loop provides for two-way interaction between the decisions of government policy makers and the supports and demands of articulate opinion leaders, interest groups, and protest

[2] For a discussion of the social mechanisms that operate to ensure village and neighborhood solidarity and a pattern of areal voting, especially in the context of municipal assembly elections, see Kurt Steiner, *Local Government in Japan* (Stanford: Stanford University Press, 1965), pp. 377, 409-415, 418-427.

Conclusion

Figure 1

Two Models of Democracy

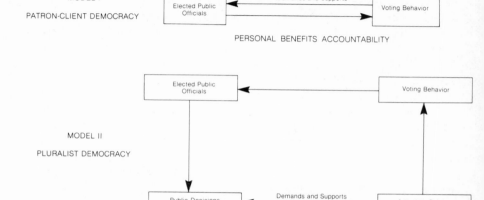

MODEL I

PATRON-CLIENT DEMOCRACY

PERSONAL BENEFITS ACCOUNTABILITY

MODEL II

PLURALIST DEMOCRACY

PUBLIC POLICY ACCOUNTABILITY

movements within the mass public. The pluralist model, therefore, is based on conflict and contestation in the public policy arena.

The causes for the shift from the patron-client to the pluralist mode of representation in Japan were discussed in some detail in the electoral trends section. On the one hand, we noted that the processes associated with modernization and urbanization were raising the political consciousness of citizens and creating a greater diversity of interests. These changes have opened the door for a more competitive, less holistic mode of representation on the local level, and the response has been a growing policy differentiation and resort to partisan labels among local politicians.

On the other hand, and perhaps even more fundamentally, these same developmental processes have been destroying the very communal solidarity upon which the patron-client model was based. For instance, it has been reported that the solidarity of many established communities in urbanizing areas has been weakened by the arrival of large numbers of newcomers and the erection of high-rise apartments that cater to a highly mobile, transient clientele.[3] Other studies report more extreme examples, where old neighborhoods are dissected by new

[3] See Chapter 4.

highways or simply annihilated by development projects that dislocate many long-standing families.[4] Moreover, the large suburban apartment complexes tend to isolate residents from their neighbors, with husbands commuting long distances to work and wives and children confined to physical spaces poorly designed for community interaction.[5] Thus many local residents in urban neighborhoods in present-day Japan are simply not available for mobilization by traditional community networks either because of the inability of these networks to effectively integrate many new residents into the mainstream of community opinion or because the greater diversity of interests that have invaded the neighborhood render a holistic, areal mode of representation inoperative.[6]

We have, then, a push-pull model of the politicization of local politics. On the one hand, politicization is a function of pressures coming from within the mass public in the form of heightened political consciousness, increased demands for government services, and participation in citizens' movements. These pressures have made local politics more competitive and increased the salience and viability of partisan labels in local elections. On the other hand, politicization is being stimulated by the political elites themselves who are forced to rely increasingly on party labels and policy stands to win the support of a growing portion of the electorate who simply can no longer be reached by traditional modes of voter mobilization. Both factors are enhancing the partisan politicization of politics, and it is this expanding partisan dimension to political competition on the local level that is altering the mode of representation from Model I to Model II.

The consequences of this process are predictable: we see lower levels of nominal involvement but higher levels of meaningful citizen participation. The pluralist model requires significantly higher levels of

[4] G. R. Falconeri, "The Impact of Rapid Urban Change on Neighborhood Solidarity: A Case Study of a Japanese Neighborhood Association," in *Social Change and Community Politics in Urban Japan*, ed. James W. White and Frank Munger, Comparative Urban Studies, Monograph no. 4 (Chapel Hill, N.C.: Institute for Research in Social Science, 1976), pp. 31-59.

[5] Christie W. Kiefer, "Leadership, Sociability and Social Change in a White Collar *Danchi*," in ibid., pp. 15-30.

[6] We are not suggesting that Japanese society is becoming anomic or increasingly characterized by social isolation but only that the old, communal, areal-based forms of social organization are increasingly being replaced by more diverse, nonareal associational forms. There are, of course, also many cases where the more traditional forms of community organization survive, particularly when they successfully adapt themselves to new functions and purposes as discussed by Krauss and Simcock in Chapter 6.

information and political sophistication for incorporation than does the patron-client model. Participation depends more on an awareness and evaluation of individual self-interest, and this in turn requires a higher degree of issue salience in order to surmount a higher threshold of apathy in a context in which the citizen is receiving far fewer cues from his immediate environment. As a result, the vehicles of citizen action—local organizations—are also changing in the direction of becoming both less areal and all inclusive in nature, while more spontaneous, issue-specific, and of a more limited duration.

The shrinking of the independent vote in local elections, as charted over the last twenty to twenty-five years in Part Two, is a macrolevel indicator of the politicization of local politics in Japan. We have already noted that this process has been further stimulated by the Occupation's establishment of a "presidential" type of election system for chief executives on the prefectural and municipal levels. Because the districts in the elections of local chief executives are substantially larger (in terms of votes needed for success) than are the districts in the local assembly elections, these "presidential" contests have provided the progressives with their most promising point of advance. We have also noted that the progressives have made steady encroachments on conservative majorities in the prefectural and municipal assemblies to the point of completely reversing the balance in many of the big cities. This rise in the progressive vote in local level elections is not only a response but also a stimulus to the politicization of local politics, as many former conservative independents have reacted to the changing contours of local politics by adopting the LDP label.

There are, however, questions as to how far this process of partisan politicization can proceed. In some areas, particularly in the countryside, we still find a preference for nonpartisan, areal representation, and in many cases localism inhibits politicization. We also find, even in the more politicized settings, progressive as well as conservative candidates exploiting localism to expand their base of support. Thus as noted in Chapter 5, the two modes of representation we have discussed are not mutually exclusive but rather are frequently both incorporated into the appeals of progressive and conservative candidates alike. Regardless of how far the politicization of local politics is likely to proceed in Japan, it has advanced sufficiently in some areas to evaluate its effects, for good or for bad, on local government and national politics. We shall begin our discussion of these effects with a review of the theoretical arguments for and against the politicization of local politics in reference to the question of local autonomy.

Politicization and Local Autonomy

Questions regarding the politicization of local government have been raised in the literature for a long time. Is such politicization desirable? Is it beneficial or destructive of local autonomy? Most early writers concerned with these issues viewed the prospect of politicization with alarm; later writers decried politicization when it had become an accomplished fact and advocated means to reverse the trend. The contrary viewpoint has found few advocates.

The discussion is by no means only of historical interest. The notion that local government can and ought to be "apolitical" or at least nonpartisan is still influential in many countries. In France, local candidates and officeholders engage in a "rhetoric of *apolitisme*," either because they believe in it or because they consider it to reflect the popular view. In Japan, many local candidates run as independents, even when they receive partisan support. In the majority of American cities, the nonpartisan ballot is in force.[7]

The arguments against politicization antedate the rise of party politics in local government. We shall deal first with the more general argument that politics in the broad sense of a conflict of interests has no place in local government. In the next section we shall discuss the more specific argument that partisanship of the kind that characterizes national politics is not only out of place in local government but is also destructive of local autonomy. Underlying both arguments is the ideal of the self-contained local government. Finally, we will present the counterargument—namely that the politicization of local politics can actually enhance local autonomy.

The Myth of the Apolitical, Self-Contained Local Government

The general argument against politicization on the local level starts out with the image of local communities in which decisions are based on common agreement. Thus, de Tocqueville extolled the townships of New England because "the commotions of municipal discord are infrequent." Bryce considered it a virtue of local government in rural areas that it formed the habit of "maintaining those friendly relations which befit neighbors."[8] In Japan, villages have long been praised as

[7] On France, see Mark Kesselman, *The Ambiguous Consensus* (New York: Knopf, 1967), pp. 136-149; on the United States, see Fred I. Greenstein, "The Changing Patterns of Urban Party Politics," in *Subnational Politics*, ed. Joseph F. Zimmerman (New York: Holt, Rinehart and Winston, 1970), p. 282.

[8] Alexis de Tocqueville, *Democracy in America*, Borzoi edition (New York:

"communities of cooperative life" (*seikatsu kyōdōtai*), embodying in their absence of conflict and their stress on the interests of the collectivity important elements of the traditional value system. In this view, politicization is to be avoided because it introduces conflicts of interests and divisions concerning public matters and thus disrupts the community's solidarity and harmony. As we will note later in greater detail, Bryce felt that the extension of national parties through the local level in particular furthers local divisiveness and is a "perversion" of local government.

It appears to us that the image of community life conjured up by these writers is a nostalgic idealization rather than a realistic description. To put it drastically, we share Dahl's suspicion that "the village probably never was all that it is cracked up to be."[9] More often than not, harmony and solidarity are only a thin veneer to cover unrepresentative government by local oligarchies. We believe that "politics is found wherever people debate issues of public import," and we thus view the local community inherently as a political arena.[10]

Those who see the virtue of local government in its assumed non-conflictual character also argue that it has to be self-sufficient and insulated from national politics in order to remain apolitical. As we noted in the introduction to this volume, the desirability of this insulation was stressed by de Tocqueville and Bryce.[11] The assumption that local government can be so insulated may have had some plausibility in the past. The New England townships of de Tocqueville's time may have been relatively insulated, certainly more so than their counterparts of later times. But the plausibility of insulation recedes with the increasing penetration of society by government. Whether a political system of today is centralized or decentralized, its government and politics are linked in many ways. The issue of centralization versus local autonomy concerns only the location of the local governments in a given country along a continuum, the end points of which— complete centralization or complete autonomy—cannot be found in reality. On a purely theoretical level, the notion of a completely insulated and autonomous subnational entity contradicts the idea of national sovereignty: subnational entities are by definition not sovereign.

Knopf, 1945), vol. 1, pp. 62-68; James Bryce, *The American Commonwealth* (New York: Macmillan, 1899), vol. 1, pp. 589-649. See also his *Modern Democracies* (New York: Macmillan, 1921), vol. 1, p. 147; vol. 2, pp. 435-445.

[9] Robert A. Dahl, "The City in the Future of Democracy, *American Political Science Review* 61 (1967): 961.

[10] Roscoe Martin, *Grass Roots* (New York: Harper and Row, 1957), p. 39.

[11] See Chapter 1.

In practice, governmental linkages from above to below take many forms. Thus, in Britain local authorities can only do what Parliament expressly allows them to do, and they have to ask for every extension of their functions: the division of powers is enforced through the judicial doctrine of *ultra vires*; district auditors who are national civil servants supervise the legality of local expenditures; and the main sources of revenue, aside from the local tax, are controlled by the center. In the cases of France and Italy, the system of tutelage provides for state approval of local decisions, and linkage mechanisms not provided by law (such as "preclearance" of municipal projects) have developed out of this system. In the case of Japan, we may mention the various types of administrative guidance, the system of financial grants, and the assignment of national functions to local governments.[12]

But it is not only penetration by the national government as such that impinges on the insulation of local entities. In Japan, public corporations—some national, others regional in scope—have proliferated since 1955 when the Japan Housing Corporation was established. The activities of these extralocal agencies often involve supportive local measures and expenditures.[13] There are also linkages with private extralocal actors. Whether United States Steel in Gary, Indiana, or Showa Denko in Yokkaichi in Mie prefecture in Japan, big corporations with headquarters outside the locality may sigificantly influence the lives of inhabitants. And even if the articulated corporate policy does not stress involvement in specific local problems, these firms have to be reckoned with by local officeholders. Where only one major company is situated in a locality, its influence on local government and politics may be even stronger.[14]

Political linkages also take a variety of forms. One of these is the recruitment of local officeholders as members of the national legislature. In some countries—France, the Netherlands, Belgium, Norway,

[12] These linkages became especially apparent in the effect of national plans for economic growth on local government. The transition from a "cohesive" to a "cooperative" and to an "antagonistic" model of relationships posited by Muramatsu indicates their increasing politicization.

[13] For example, when the Japan Housing Corporation builds houses, related public facilities such as schools or water and sewage lines have to be constructed by local government. See Norie Huddle and Michael Reich, *Island of Dreams* (New York: Autumn Press, 1975), pp. 95-96; on the effect of public corporations on local government in general see, for example, Jichi Kenshū Kyōkai *Kuni to chihō no atarashii kankei* (Tōkyō: Jichi Kenshū Kyōkai, 1977), pp. 7, 27.

[14] On Toyota's influence on Kariya, compared with General Motors' influence on Ypsilanti, Michigan, see Gary D. Allinson, *Japanese Urbanism* (Berkeley: University of California Press, 1975), pp. 251-256.

and Sweden among them—they may hold local office and national office simultaneously.[15] In other countries local officeholders become candidates for offices at successively higher levels of government. This pattern of recruitment exists for instance in some areas of the United States, and it is also emerging in India. Under either pattern, those who attain a position at the national level are commonly expected to represent the interests of their locality in the national arena and to become spokesmen for local grievances as well as sources of local patronage. In Japan, some national parliamentarians enter politics directly at the national level, but others "step up" from subnational positions.[16]

The recruitment of local officeholders to national positions strengthens the integration of local and national politics. It is not a precondition for such an integration, however. Where national and local offices are held by the same person—where the system of *cumule* exists—the locality has the most direct access to the center. Where this is not the case, national and local officials are often linked at least by the exigencies of politics, and they can help each other in many ways. Thus services rendered to local interests by national officeholders may be exchanged at election time against support by local officeholders, or a national officeholder may support a local candidate in anticipation of similar support when his own election comes up. Linkages may also exist between elected officials and informal local leaders who are power brokers, especially where particularistic client-patron relations are strong.

In many countries local governments are linked to the national level through national associations. Germany has its League of German Cities and France its Association of French Mayors. Japan has six

[15] It should be noted that in the French system and in French political thought, the integration of local and central politics is more widely accepted than in many other countries. The majority of the members of the French Senate—for example, 168 out of 283 in 1969—are mayors, and many others are departmental or municipal councilors. A 1971 poll indicates that a majority of the respondents (54 percent) considered the cumulation of the office of mayor with the position of deputy desirable, while only 24 percent were opposed. See Jack Hayward, *The One and Indivisible French Republic* (New York: Norton, 1973), pp. 31, 71, and Mark Kesselman and Donald Rosenthal, *Local Power and Comparative Politics* (Beverly Hills: Sage Publications, Comparative Politics Series, 1974), pp. 24-25. While in France and in some other countries the recruitment is upward for candidates from the old style centrist parties who start as notables with a local base, deputies of the better-organized parties also acquire local links by "parachuting" into a position at the local level.

[16] Kesselman and Rosenthal, *Local Power*. As MacDougall indicates in Chapter 3, there is also some "parachuting" into local positions in Japan, although without cumulative officeholding.

such associations—all established by law and all suprapartisan in character—three for chief executives at the prefectural, city, and town and village levels, and three for the assembly chairmen at these levels. One of the main purposes of such associations is to defend the interests of local governments vis-à-vis the national government, although centralistically inclined governments may try to use them more as downward communication channels.[17] Once the politicization of local government has reached an advanced state, separate associations linked to parties or political tendencies may be formed. Most French political parties sponsor their own associations of local officeholders, and in Japan there is a National Association of Progressive Mayors.

To summarize, whether we consider the politically insulated local government a reality of bygone days or simply a figment of a romantic imagination, there can be no question that it no longer exists in the developed countries of the world. While local governments probably never were "apolitical," their fuller integration into national politics and partisan politicization are of more recent origins. Today local government is, de jure and de facto, not insulated from the national arena, and with the increasing penetration of local affairs by national bureaucracies, corporations, and political elites, it is becoming increasingly politicized. We have thus established a trend, but we have not as yet evaluated the impact of that trend for good or for bad. We shall begin that evaluation with an assessment of the primary danger that partisan politicization is thought to pose for local autonomy. In this context, the arguments against local politicization focus on the role of national party organizations and their presumed interference in local affairs.

Party Organization and Local Autonomy: The Negative Argument

Of all the linkages between the local and national levels, the linkage through political parties has been the object of the most vigorous and sustained criticism. Long after the debate regarding the legitimacy, desirability, or necessity of parties in a democracy had been stilled at the national level, it continued—and continues—on the local level. Parties may be taken for granted at the national level, but—so one argument runs—they have no place in local government.

As we noted earlier, Bryce viewed the extension of national party issues to the local level as a "perversion" because they introduced an

---

[17] In France the government attempted unsuccessfully to replace the Association of French Mayors, which frequently opposes government policies, with a new organization of its own creation. See Kesselman, *Ambiguous Consensus*, pp. 105-111. For Japan, see Steiner, *Local Government*, pp. 316-317, 364.

element of divisiveness into local councils. At the time, partisan politicization had already made inroads into local government both in
England and in the United States. In England the extension of the suffrage in 1867 had led to the development of local party organizations,
and elections in large towns were being fought along party lines between Conservatives and Liberals. Because of differences in the party
system, partisan politicization in the United States took a somewhat
different form, leading to the dominance of some cities by political
bosses. Viewing this development with great distaste, Bryce in his
Modern Democracies sympathized with efforts of municipal reformers
to curb such excesses by depoliticizing municipal government. He accepted the notion that partisan politics at the local level was not only
deleterious but also superfluous because "municipal administration has
become more and more a business matter for experts in such sciences
as sanitation and engineering." Political considerations had no place
in the decision of such technical questions.

We find little merit in this argument against the politicization of
local government. Local government is more than the technical administration of services. The stock phrase that "there is only a right
way and a wrong way of paving a street" neglects for instance the decisions of whether resources should be applied to the paving of streets,
and if so, which streets should be paved. In a situation of scarce resources, differences over priorities and over areas or groups that should
receive benefits inevitably occur. Almost all technical decisions follow
a political decision.[18] When parties articulate their views on such decisions they perform the important function of organizing the public
will.

It appears rather obvious to us that Lord Bryce's strictures against
the intrusion of party politics into local government are an extension
of his distaste for party organization in general. A parallel may thus
be drawn between Bryce's thinking and that of Yamagata, a conservative, who considered the issue in a different setting. Both distrusted
parties as such and, faced with the ineluctable fact of their existence
at the national level, tried as a sort of last ditch stand to prevent them
from infecting local government.

The argument that party politics have no place in local government
received an additional impetus when a new type of party, differing
from the old style party of notables, came into existence—namely the
programmatic, organized, and disciplined party, especially the one on
the left of the political spectrum. To earlier contentions, the fact that

[18] J. G. Bulpitt, *Party Politics in English Local Government* (New York:
Barnes and Noble, 1967), pp. 2-3.

partisanship is divisive and alien to the tasks of local government as a provider of services was now added the argument that partisan local officeholders would become party delegates, mandated by and responsive to a distant party headquarters. This would pervert local self-government because local issues would no longer be decided on their merits or in accordance with the best interests of the locality. In England, these arguments were advanced especially after 1919 as a defense mechanism against the Labor Party. When in the 1930s the Labor Party produced a set of Model Standing Orders for the organization of party groups on local councils, Conservatives, Liberals and independents claimed that this confirmed their fears that the interest of local tax payers were being subordinated to directives emanating from central party headquarters.[19]

Although the argument is not without a certain plausibility, it has rarely been subjected to a rigorous analysis. Such an analysis would have to raise questions, such as: Do parties in a given political system have organizations that extend to the local level? It would seem that the argument has little force where local notables constitute the basis of so-called caucus parties. As officeholders, they are not likely to jeopardize their local power base by subservience to outsiders whose assistance is of little or no value to them. More generally, one would have to investigate the influence on local candidacies of formal party organs at the national level. Is their endorsement a prerequisite for candidacy? Do they provide financial support for candidates? Negative answers would deprive the argument of much of its force, but even positive answers would only present a sort of circumstantial evidence regarding the possibility of influence by party headquarters.

The most important question is, of course, whether these headquarters in fact interfere in local policy making. Such interference should be distinguished from the influence on the selection of local candidates, on the formation of local alliances, or on the organization of party groups within assemblies or councils. There is also a difference between the issuance of broad policy guidelines and the handing down of directives to local officeholders on specific issues before them. Even where such directives exist, the argument would be confirmed only if they are being obeyed rather than being ignored with impunity.

[19] See Dilys Hill, *Democratic Theory and Local Government* (London: Allen and Unwin, 1974), p. 67, and Bulpitt, *Party Politics*, p. 7. After 1945 when Conservatives also competed increasingly as party candidates, the argument subsided (see Hill, *Democratic Theory*, p. 133). The argument is normally raised in relation to the municipal rather than some intermediary level, such as departments, prefectures, provinces, or regions. The following remarks are, therefore, meant to apply to the municipal level.

Some recent research in European countries deals with these questions either directly or at least tangentially by analyzing the relations of partisan local officeholders to their parties more generally. In England the question of headquarters' directives and their influence became especially salient with the issuance by the Labor Party of the previously mentioned set of Model Standing Orders. The Standing Orders were "models"—that is, they were not mandatory. But gradually the majority of labor groups in councils adopted them, either in a "strict" or a "loose" fashion.[20] It is important to note, however, that they deal with organization and procedures rather than policies. A. H. Birch states that "local parties are highly individual, conditioned more by their environment than by directives from central office and largely independent in managing their business"; the case studies of J. G. Bulpitt support this finding.[21] A study of councilmen in the Netherlands (where party influence may be expected because city councils are elected from party lists on a proportional representation basis) comes to the conclusion that in spite of this emphasis of party in recruitment, even local party executives (where such a group exists outside the caucus of councilmembers) do not seem to perform an important role in supervising the day-to-day functioning of the city councils. Survey responses indicate that only a small minority of councilmen perceive their role as related to a party program, and even among this minority many see themselves as "party trustees" (launched by the party and expected to conform to his own conception of party positions and principles but still accountable to the voters at large) rather than as "party delegates" (responsible directly to the party).[22]

Communist parties epitomize the type of well-organized, disciplined, and centralized parties to which the argument should apply with the greatest force. Studies of local governments in which the Communists play a significant role are thus of particular interest in the present context. If the argument that central party headquarters influence local

[20] On the difference in interpretation of the Standing Orders, see Bulpitt, *Party Politics*, p. 17.

[21] A. H. Birch, *Small Town Politics* (Oxford: Oxford University Press, 1959), p. 44, and Bulpitt, *Party Politics*, p. 97.

[22] Galen A. Irwin, "Party, Accountability, and the Recruitment of Municipal Councilmen in the Netherlands," in *Elite Recruitment in Democratic Politics*, ed. Heinz Eulau and Moshe M. Czudnowski (New York: John Wiley, 1976), pp. 183-185, 201. In France, local sections of the Communist Party avoid getting absorbed in the nitty-gritty of local affairs. See Jerome Milch, "The PCF and Local Government: Continuity and Change" in *Communism in Italy and France*, ed. Donald L. Blackmer and Sidney Tarrow (Princeton: Princeton University Press, 1975), p. 362.

policy decisions does not hold true for the relationship between Communist party headquarters and local officeholders, it is highly improbable that it will hold true for other parties. The view that local officeholders belonging to the Communist party follow party directives is based on the expectation that they are militants, dedicated to the party's program. Fortunately we have a number of studies of French and Italian local politics that pay particular attention to Communist local officeholders, especially mayors.[23] While there are significant differences in the *modus operandi* of mayors in these two countries, in both countries, although they may have obtained their position as party activists, Communist mayors are no longer ideologically impassioned militants but rather policy brokers, working through the administrative network in France and through the partisan network in Italy. In regard to Italian mayors who are Christian Democrats or Communists, Sidney Tarrow states:

> Italian party activists are neither rootless agents of the national party system, inactive spectators of local public life, nor politicians whose contacts are limited to those made available by their own party organization. They are essentially political entrepreneurs with a wide network of contacts in both local and national political systems who use their party affiliations to open up a network of contacts in seeking resources for their communities.[24]

In France, where the Communist Party changed its municipal strategy after 1945, the Party has become increasingly conscious of the need for greater flexibility in the day-by-day operation of local government, for a separation between party and local government, and for allowing more freedom to local officials.[25]

There is hardly any research on such questions in the case of Japan. In his study of the LDP, Fukui notes that local politicians are "remarkably free from regularized and effective controls by the national

[23] Communism in both countries belongs to the category recently dubbed "Euro-Communism." As the case of the Japan Communist Party suggests, this denomination may be too restrictive geographically. We do not have studies dealing with our questions for a broad spectrum of Communist parties outside of the Soviet orbit.

[24] Sidney Tarrow, *Between Center and Periphery: Grassroots Politicians in Italy and France* (New Haven: Yale University Press, 1977), p. 182.

[25] Milch, "The PCF and Local Government," in Blackmer and Tarrow, *Communism*, p. 349. On the attitudes of French partisan local officeholders towards their parties more generally, see Mark Kesselman, "Political Parties and Local Government in France: Differentiation and Opposition," in *Comparative Community Politics*, ed. Terry N. Clark (New York: John Wiley, 1974), pp. 124-129.

parties."[26] There are a number of facts which support this observation and which strongly suggest that the arguments against partisan politicization of local government have little validity in Japan. With the exception of the Japan Communist Party (JCP) and the Clean Government Party (CGP), Japanese parties are poorly organized. The Liberal Democratic Party (LDP) is still essentially an old-style caucus party: Only in 1963 did it begin to induce candidates below the prefectural level to become members. In terms of election support, including financial support, formal party organs are less important than informal groups of factions. In addition, the importance of personal supporters' associations fortifies the independence of local officeholders: many conservative local candidates get elected as independents and join the party later. In their case, party discipline cannot be expected to override their localistic commitments. The Democratic Socialist Party (DSP) is also an alliance of notables whose power base includes moderate local unions; and even the Japan Socialist Party (JSP) is anything but a monolithic and centralized party with a strong network of local organizations below the prefectural level. In terms of its candidates' personal supporters' associations, party factions and local trade unions are also more important than the central party leadership.

In general, the tendency to consider officeholders as party delegates is stronger in leftist parties than it is in conservative parties.[27] In spite of its organizational feebleness, this tendency is not entirely absent in the case of the JSP. Thus, JSP headquarters seems to concern itself occasionally with local policy in general, as when it favored abolition of public racing or gambling establishments as a source of local revenue or when it opposed the employment of the "users' charge system" for local improvements. But such general pronouncements can hardly qualify as instructions. Moreover, many local officeholders do not consider these pronouncements as binding but simply ignore them.[28]

[26] Haruhiro Fukui, *Party in Power* (Berkeley: University of California Press, 1970), pp. 72-73 and passim.

[27] Maurice Duverger, *Political Parties* (New York: John Wiley, 1954), pp. 352-372.

[28] See Chapter 9; also Ronald Aqua, "Politics and Performance in Japanese Municipalities" (unpublished dissertation, Cornell University, 1979), Chapter 3. In Chapter 11, Krauss mentions that in 1974 JSP headquarters refused to sanction the decision of the Kyoto prefectural chapter not to support the election of Governor Ninagawa. This conflict did not concern a specific issue of local policy making but rather the issue of local alliance-formation in which party influence may be expected to be stronger, especially at the prefectural level. Still, the chairman of the chapter, Ōhashi Kazuo, defied the party and ran against Ninagawa anyway. In this case the only recourse the national JSP headquarters had was to expel Ōhashi and his followers from the party.

There remain the two parties that are relatively well-organized, namely the CGP and the JCP. In their cases, the degree of organization may well be sufficient to permit some central control of local officeholders. But in contrast to the case of the Communist Party in France and Italy, the question of whether such controls are exercised and complied with in Japan is somewhat academic. As of 31 December 1976, there were no local chief executives belonging to either party.[29]

In our view, these general observations militate strongly against the argument that the partisan politicization of local government results in a control of the actions of partisan officials on local policy issues by party directives. It has often been stated that the devolution of functions from the national government to the local governments has the advantage of preventing "apoplexy at the center." No national government can make the decisions on the myriad of local issues in a large and developed country. For national party headquarters to involve itself in the policy problems of individual local entities would invite such apoplexy.[30]

A second observation concerns the potential for compliance with central party directives by local officeholders. We noted that local officeholders sometimes disavow their partisanship, running as independents, or deemphasize it, engaging in a "rhetoric of *apolitisme*." One of the reasons for this is their perception of an electorate which fears that outside influences may subvert the officeholders' concern for the well-being of the community—in other words an electorate in which substantial sections agree with the argument against partisan politicization. A certain localism is undoubtedly shared by many officeholders who have lived in the community for some time and are involved in a local network of associations. Partisan officeholders are

---

[29] *Local Government Review*, no. 4 (1976), Statistical Appendix, p. 64. A Communist Party Member running without support of the Socialists was elected mayor of Shiojiri, Nagano prefecture in 1967, and he held office until 1971. We are indebted to Professor George O. Totten III for this information. To our knowledge, this is the only case of its type, although JCP members may have run successfully as independents. In addition, it should be noted that neither of the two centralized Japanese parties (JCP and CGP) has anything even approaching majority control in any prefectural or municipal assembly. Thus in contrast to a situation such as exists in Italy, these centralized Japanese parties can only hope to gain power as part of a much larger coalition, thereby further limiting the ability of a national party headquarters to dictate local policies.

[30] Milch, "The PCF and Local Government," in Blackmer and Tarrow, *Communism*, p. 349, states that the French Communist Party advocates greater decentralization on the municipal level in part on grounds of greater efficiency, reasoning that "one cannot harmoniously and rationally administer the country by decisions made at the summit."

not necessarily immune to an affective orientation toward their communities. But, whether they are or not, those who consider themselves accountable to their local constituency and who need the support of voters beyond the local party membership in order to be reelected cannot ignore the impact of localism on the electorate. There is a danger that a strong identification with a political party would alienate more voters than it would attract. For this reason, parties and officeholders cannot allow themselves to be pressed into a straightjacket of partisan conformity. They are inhibited in assuming the role of party delegate and have to play other roles that involve the notion of accountability to the voters at large. Thus even partisan officials commonly stress their concern for the local public interest rather than for the interests of a single clientele group. They attempt to demonstrate the efficiency of their stewardship in terms of practical results for the community, and—as the case of France and Italy indicate—they use whatever avenues are available to them to achieve such results and to fulfill local expectations.

Finally, we should remember that most local governments are not ruled by a local branch of a national political party. The more frequent pattern is rule by a local coalition of diverse forces formed by local candidates and officeholders with little reference to national coalition patterns. The accommodations necessary for the formation and maintenance of such coalitions serve to further inhibit subservience to a distant party headquarters in the day-by-day decisions on local issues.

These observations suffice to indicate that the argument against partisan politicization of local government rests on a very weak basis of analysis and empirical research. Thus, in the absence of further evidence that such politicization diminishes local autonomy because local officeholders become party delegates, the verdict must be: "not proven." The contrary assumption that partisan politicization may acturally enhance local autonomy has rarely been considered. We now turn to a discussion of this unconventional assumption.

Political Competition and Local Autonomy: The Positive Argument

Perhaps the main argument in favor of the politicization of local government is that it helps to institutionalize the principle and practice of local autonomy by creating groups with vested interests in the defense and actualization of that principle. Especially since the Weimar Republic and its model democratic constitution failed to withstand easy destruction by the Nazi movement in Germany, political scientists have become acutely aware that providing legal democratic forms and rights in a constitution is by itself a fragile and superficial defense against authoritarianism. Rather, a society's social processes and values must be relatively congruent with its constitutional ideals and political institutions, and the society's elites and a fair proportion of its citizens must identify with these constitutional principles and institutions.[31]

Viewed from this perspective, it is often said that the maintenance of democracy in postwar Japan is due to the American Occupation's acknowledgment of the need to change both the culture and social norms of Japanese society as well as its political structure. Indeed the legal guarantees of political, economic, and social rights were buttressed by large-scale resocialization campaigns and a thorough restructuring of the educational system aimed at changing political orientations, economic relations, and the status of women. This kind of social engineering, however, requires a fundamental change in cultural values, a change that requires considerable time, often one or two generations. Perhaps the real key to the short-run success of the Occupation reforms, then, is to be found in the Occupation's encouragement of the formation of "clientele" who would defend the Constitution and the new rights it guaranteed after the Occupation ended. Thus, political parties had a vested interest in protecting parliamentary government, and labor unions, farmers, and women were primarily concerned with defending newly won economic and social rights.[32]

In some areas, however, "where the reforms made no contact with genuinely felt Japanese needs and when there was no well-organized, coherent clientele they tended to lapse or be turned about."[33] Local autonomy is one example of such an area. Given both the tradition

---

[31] This is of course the basic assumption underlying the field of political culture. See, for example, Lucian W. Pye and Sidney Verba, eds., *Political Culture and Political Development* (Princeton: Princeton University Press, 1965), especially the introductory and concluding articles by the editors. Harry Eckstein, *A Theory of Stable Democracy*, Center of International Studies, Research Monograph no. 10 (Princeton: Woodrow Wilson School of Public and International Affairs, 1961), similarly argues that the authority patterns of a society and its political system must be relatively congruent to ensure stability.

[32] See Herbert Passin, *The Legacy of the Occupation of Japan* (Occasional Paper of the East Asian Institute, Columbia University, 1968), especially p. 14; also Kazuo Kawai, *Japan's American Interlude* (Chicago: University of Chicago Press, 1960), especially Chapter 12. Kawai puts more emphasis on the Occupation releasing latent interests and forces for change inherent in Japanese society. Robert E. Ward, "Reflections on the Allied Occupation and Planned Political Change in Japan," in *Political Development in Modern Japan*, ed. Robert E. Ward (Princeton: Princeton University Press, 1968), pp. 528-532, labels this method of change "the creation of new vested interests."

[33] Passin, *Legacy of the Occupation*, p. 14.

of central control in the Meiji period and the Occupation's failure to ensure adequate independent financial resources, local politicians and officials had little incentive to defend the provisions of local autonomy in the Constitution, but they had a great deal of incentive to revert to acting as units of government subordinate to the center in exchange for financial and public works benefits from the national government. As long as conservatives held power at both levels of government, community identifications and norms of harmony further encouraged local politicians to cast themselves as independents so as to be in a better position to lobby the center as suprapartisan representatives of the entire local area. Their constituents also had little reason to understand or appreciate the concept of local autonomy but many reasons to appreciate the benefits that a nonantagonistic relationship with the central government could bring.[34] Opposition to those in authority for the sake of a principle seemed inadvisable. Thus, lip service was given to the principle of local autonomy in abstract terms, but the realities of intergovernmental relations and the underlying attitudes and behavior patterns remained incongruent with it.

Today the politicization of local politics is breathing new life into the local autonomy principle. Progressive chief executives and their supporters have an increased stake in local autonomy and an incentive to translate their political opposition into institutional opposition. For example, since it is the Constitution that made their ascent to power possible by providing for the direct election of local chief executives, they have a vested interest in defending it and in propagating a belief in local autonomy. It is no accident that many progressive local executives have made the local autonomy principle a key element in defining and legitimizing their distinctive stance vis-à-vis the conservative central government. For the first time in postwar Japan, there exists a "clientele" who benefit enough from the Occupation's local government reforms and the values underlying them to attempt to defend and utilize them.

Indeed, progressives have attempted to go beyond mere defense of the ideal of local autonomy by trying to expand local power. We previously noted that local officeholders who are in political opposition to the center have a political interest in expanding local autonomy, that is, in loosening the potential constraints on their activities by the center,[35] and we have illustrated this phenomenon for the case of Japan. To recapitulate, first of all, in Japan progressive chief executives have exploited the possibilities for autonomous local behavior within

[34] See Steiner, *Local Government*, especially pp. 447, 470-475.
[35] See Chapter 1.

the existing system of intergovernmental relations to a much higher degree than was ever attempted when governments at all levels were of the same conservative persuasion. For example, they have discovered within the existent structure of these intergovernmental relations hitherto undiscovered areas in the fields of welfare, environmental protection, and the protection of small business in which they can act with some independence. They have also found it possible to reject guidance and control from above in such matters as amalgamations and the establishment of unwanted industries within their jurisdiction. Secondly, they have learned to enforce such local rights as the constitution grants them by recourse to the courts. Finally, they have engaged in efforts to change the institutional system, especially, but not exclusively, in the areas of the distribution of financial resources between various levels of government.[36]

The politicization of local government has also served to resocialize ordinary citizens to attitudes supportive of local autonomy. The media has played a major role in directing attention to this principle. Tending to define conflict and drama as news,[37] the media suddenly rediscovered local government and politics as conflicts and competition arose between progressive local executives and the central government and among political parties more evenly matched in some local areas. For the first time in the postwar period this media coverage has stimulated ordinary citizens to consider the appropriate role and limits of local and national governments. As Kaminogo has put it, "Had there not been a rush of progressive controlled local entities, we would not have to take the study of autonomy now nor would many people have given thought to the subject of what autonomy is."[38]

Many progressive local executives have attempted to spur this interest by manipulating media coverage. Thus, Tokyo's Governor Minobe, himself a former television personality, used the media to great advantage to create a popular political image and to focus attention on local issues.[39] Other local executives have staged "media events" to dramatically direct public attention to problems of local autonomy. In October 1974, Kyoto Mayor Funahashi and twenty-three other progressive mayors made demands at the Prime Minister's official residence, threatened sit-ins, and distributed leaflets on the street over the issue of the excess burdens of mandated responsibilities imposed on local

[36] See Chapter 9.
[37] This is true in Japan as elsewhere. On the phenomenon in the U.S., see Edward J. Epstein, *News From Nowhere* (New York: Random House, 1973).
[38] Kaminogo Toshiaki, "Glory and Misery of Local Autonomies Under Progressive Control," *Japan Echo* 2 (1975): 30.
[39] See Chapter 5.

447

governments by the central government without adequate financial compensation.[40] Still other progressive local executives have supplemented the use of mass media by mobilization campaigns in order to more directly resocialize constituents. A prime example is Governor Ninagawa of Kyoto's sponsorship of a "Let's Put the Constitution in Our Lives" movement and his distribution of vest-pocket copies of the Constitution and Local Autonomy Law.[41]

Both the rise of citizens' movements against pollution and media coverage of this phenomenon has also done a great deal to bring about mass level attitude change toward local government and local autonomy—forcing residents to consider the environmental damage to their local communities of unquestioned central government policies, leading many local conservatives to reevaluate their identification with the ruling party, and raising basic questions about who should have power and how policy should be determined on issues affecting the lives of local inhabitants.[42] Goals such as citizen input and grass-roots democracy have entered the vocabulary of public discourse as a result of citizens' movements and consequently helped to stimulate mass public concern for the essential values and concepts that underlay the Occupation's reforms in the area of local government. In concrete form, this concern has also been translated into administrative devices like citizen consultation offices in local bureaucracies to better process and alleviate residents' complaints.

In summary, the politicization of local government may be belatedly completing some of the work of the Occupation by helping to bring Japan's local political culture and process into greater congruity with the ideals embedded in its Constitution. The rise of local opposition in Japan has contributed to the resocialization of citizens towards local government and local autonomy (increasing political knowledge, raising the salience of the autonomy issue, and changing attitudes) and has created an elite and mass clientele with a vested interest in defending and expanding a principle that most theorists have judged to be beneficial to a healthy democracy.

LOCAL POLITICIZATION AND PUBLIC POLICY

We have argued that the politicization of local politics is likely to enhance rather than to decrease local autonomy. We may also ask, however, what impact this change in the local political arena is likely to have on other aspects of the Japanese polity. In the remaining sec-

[40] *Kyōto Shinbun*, 3 October 1974, p. 1.   [41] See Chapter 11.
[42] See Chapters 6 and 7.

tions of this chapter, we will shift our argument somewhat and suggest that, at least for the case of Japan, partisan politicization on the local level is having a number of other positive effects, particularly on public policy, mass socialization, and the hegemonic and polarized character-istics of the party system. In this section we will focus on the impact of local politicization on public policy.

There have been a number of warnings by observers of Japanese politics that politicization may entail unexpected costs that may nega-tively affect the quality of local policy outputs. On the one hand, some have argued that politicization will lead to too intense a preoccupation with parochial interests while, on the other hand, other voices have warned that it will lead to the total disregard of these interests. The first argument revolves around what Tsurutani calls "the trivialization of politics."[43] Increased partisan competition and the rise of citizens' movements may stimulate citizens to overly high expectations of a local government's ability to respond to their needs. Because of these high expectations, many minor problems, of concern to only a narrow strata of citizens, often became conflictual issues in the political arena. As an indication of a trend in this direction, we can cite the so-called "Tokyo Garbage War." The seemingly administrative question of placement of a garbage facility that affected only a small number of Tokyo residents became a major issue in Governor Minobe's second term. The explosion of demands makes it difficult for executives and bureaucracies to limit the scope of their decision-making responsibili-ties, to set priorities, and to respond to any demands at all. The triviali-zation of politics, in other words, can potentially immobilize local government as many interests and demands are politicized but few are aggregated.[44] This danger can be viewed, however, as just one aspect of the demand overload problem that faces national as well as local governments as levels of citizen awareness and participation in-crease. To the extent that parties can aggregate these sorts of demands and evaluate them from the perspective of programmatic priorities, the partisan politicization of local politics may actually simplify the tasks of administrations in dealing with the rising level of citizen de-mand.

The second argument takes the opposite position, suggesting that the politicization of local politics may lead to a decline in the degree of official attention paid to purely local issues. According to this argu-ment, politicization may lead political parties and candidates to use

[43] Taketsugu Tsurutani, *Political Change in Japan* (New York: David McKay, 1977), pp. 53-56, 206-207.
[44] See Chapter 6.

local contests to mobilize support for their views on national and international issues and consequently to disregard local issues. Should this occur, the burgeoning development of local autonomy consciousness and the institutional and attitudinal changes just described may be short-circuited. In these circumstances, politicization and party competition at the local level will succeed more in "nationalizing" local politics in a different form than in creating greater attention to local autonomy.

This argument is a corollary of the previously stated argument that the intrusion of partisan competition into local politics will lead to the control of local politics by national party directives. It is hard to imagine, however, that a progressive local chief executive would ignore the needs and concerns of his local constituents and address his attention primarily to national issues, at least not so long as the conservatives remain in power at the national level and the source of his political strength rests on localism. This suggests that it is the peculiar juxtaposition of conservative power on the national and progressive power on the local level that we find in Japan and several Western European nations that is responsible for the strong positive associations found between partisan politicization and increased demands for local autonomy. Thus it could be argued that if the progressives were to come to power on the national level, their enthusiasm for enlarging the scope of local autonomy might wane, and we might find a role reversal with conservative local chief executives raising the banner of local autonomy. In general, however, we may conclude that the more the pattern of partisan competition and turnover is established on both the national and local levels, the greater the possibility that national and local governments will not be consistently controlled by the same party, and hence increased partisan politicization on the local level should continue to serve the cause of local autonomy.

We would argue, then, that the partisan politicization of local politics is not likely to obscure the salience of local issues. In a sense, however, there is a valid point underlying the fear of local politics becoming "nationalized." In our discussion of the classical case for local autonomy, we pointed out that the ideal of the insulated, self-contained local community was not to be found in advanced industrial societies. Rather a great variety of national-local linkages draw local communities into national political affairs. This is particularly true of the public policy-making sphere of politics. In modern societies, the nature of problems and the wider sphere of expectations toward governmental solutions to those problems creates a "seamless web of politics." An issue seemingly local in character is often the consequence of national decisions and nondecisions and cannot be resolved in purely local fashion. Nor is it usually possible to contain demands and the consequences of problems within watertight compartments of particular locales: local problems have a way of becoming national issues. But, as this discussion suggests, the interaction is two-sided rather than one-sided. If in some cases municipalities must contend with a localization of national issues as a result of the impact of national policy decisions on their communities, in other cases they may benefit from a nationalization of local issues, providing their local issues with a national audience and forcing national officials to treat such issues more seriously.

A perfect example of the "seamless web" of national and local politics and issues in postwar Japan was the circular development of the problem of economic growth and the environment. It was both conscious central government policy encouraging rapid economic growth and central government nondecision in the area of regulating the consequences of that growth that created environmental hazards and pollution diseases such as those that occurred in Minamata or Yokkaichi. These occurrences in turn gave rise to local incidents and movements that helped to create an "environmental issue." Both media attention to these local problems and the existence of an infrastructure of intellectuals and activists contributed to the development of environmental consciousness and the creation of similar issues in other locales. Finally, the spread of local movements and issues became so diffused that they became a major national problem with which the central government had to deal.

Another example is the area of demographics, housing, and welfare. Mass migration from rural areas into cities, in part created by a central government agricultural policy that encouraged the importation of foreign foodstuffs and the lack of an effective national housing policy, helped to create overcrowded inner cities. Rapid economic growth policies simultaneously contributed to the rise of an affluent urban middle class in creating a more pleasant environment in the cities as well as in the suburbs, since some of that class moved there to escape the overcrowded cities. The pressure on local governments to respond to these demands—a response often beyond their resources to provide —has tended to be passed on to the central government, thus making these problems into national issues.

When the opposition controls local government, the tendency for "local" issues to become an input into national policy is probably intensified. In part this arises from a "demonstration effect." Knowledge of successful attempts by citizens' groups to get sympathetic local governments to respond to their demands, together with the "showcase"

policies of some progressive administrations, lead citizens in other locales to demand similar responses from their own local governments.
Both conservative and progressive administrations in other areas feel
themselves under pressure to conform to a new standard of performance.[45] Thus, both through the diffusion of local policies to other areas
through the examples of models in some locales and through the pressure brought on the center by local entities for aid in solving problems
beyond the control of a single local government, local opposition intensifies the creation of national issues of public policy from what
were seemingly "local" problems.

We have argued, on the one hand, that the politicization of local
politics helps to actualize the principle of local autonomy; on the
other hand, we have also argued that the functional consequences of
local autonomy assumed by its traditional proponents, of increased
local handling of problems and the insulation of the center from local
demands, are unrealistic in the modern age. Rather, in regard to policy
the politicization of local politics helps to integrate local and national
politics. Does this mean that the rise of local opposition creates the
conditions for real local autonomy while simultaneously depriving it
of any real meaning? We think not. We would argue instead that the
institutionalization of local autonomy created by the politicization of
local politics merely functions in the modern world in a different manner than was expected by its proponents in another age but that it is
no less functional for democratic politics.

If it does not ensure local solutions to "local" problems or the insulation of the central government from excess demands, the actualization
of local autonomy in the context of the "seamless web" of policy
making does lead to the creation of new independent and powerful
actors in national politics—local governments and interest groups. By
simultaneously developing local administrations and citizens concerned
about local autonomy who attempt to initiate policies independent of
the central government and by stimulating the integration of local
elites and policies into national politics, the politicization of local politics makes central decision making more pluralistic. The domination of
national politics by the ruling party, large industry, opposition parties
and large labor federations, and the national bureaucracy is rendered
less effective. Local opposition governments and movements and the
issues they raise create countervailing inputs into national policy making that ensure a broader policy agenda, more attention to the needs
of average citizens, a wider variety of interests represented, and po-

[45] Kaminogo, "Glory and Misery," p. 25.

litical debate over problems of public interest and not just ideology. In short, the politicization of local politics can contribute to the creation of a more pluralistic policy-making process at both the national and the local levels.[46]

SOCIALIZATION EFFECTS: POLITICAL DISAFFECTION AND SYSTEM SUPPORT

In this section we shall argue that the politicization of local politics is also helping to build support for Japan's postwar political institutions. In order to evaluate the socialization effects of local politicization on the Japanese citizen, however, we must first consider the socializing impact of national politics over the last two decades. We have discussed the notions of a duality of political styles and dual modes of representation. We have also suggested that the Japanese

[46] One caveat to this optimistic assessment is the argument that the expanded role that the progressive chief executives have given to the administrative as opposed to the legislative side of the policy-making process may have some negative side effects. For instance, Muramatsu Michio has warned that the direct alliance of progressive executives and their bureaucracies with citizens' groups may further weaken representative legislative power at the local level in Japan (see Muramatsu Michio, "Gyōsei katei to seiji sanka," *Nenpō Seijigaku* [1974], pp. 53-59). In most industrialized countries there has been a tendency toward the development of the "corporatist state" in which citizens and interest groups are tied ever more closely into a client relationship with the government bureaucracy. In Japan, this phenomenon that tends to accompany the rise of the welfare state also receives strong cultural and historical reinforcement from the tradition of bureaucratic power, status, and leadership.

While from the perspective of Japan's bureaucratic tradition the danger may be very real, it is perhaps too early to properly assess the consequences of local politicization on this aspect of the policy-making process. We might point out, however, that "pluralistic corporatism" (as distinct from the fascist variety) is not necessarily antidemocratic. In a number of European countries it appears to be providing a useful supplementary input channel for incorporating interest organizations and citizens' groups more directly into the political process and indeed it is not inconceivable that in the future some form of "functional representation" may replace our present geographical mode of representation. See James Douglas, "Review Article: The Overloaded Crown," *British Journal of Political Science 6* (1976): 483-505. Moreover, the development of public advisory bodies and citizens' councils is far advanced on the national level in Japan and hence cannot be attributed simply to local politicization. See Ehud Harari, "Japanese Politics of Advice in Comparative Perspective," *Public Policy 22* (1974): 537-577. While it is true that the rise of progressive administrations has drawn greater public attention to the executive as opposed to the legislative input channel, it should also be pointed out that legislative assemblies typically represent special interests better than they do the common good and that directly elected chief executives are more likely to address issues from a comprehensive perspective.

electorate can be conceptualized in terms of two galleries, each viewing the political parade through a different cognitive lens. For the moment, then, let us picture this electorate in terms of two principal polar types—the more traditional and passive *parochial spectator* and the *modern participant*. The parochial spectator evaluates Japanese democracy on the basis of the patron-client model. In that model the representative is responsible not for his actions in the Diet but for the distribution of special services and favors for his constituents. In contrast, the modern participant applies the standards of the pluralist model and tends to relate to politics in terms of idelogical or class orientations, national issues, and nonareal, associational group or partisan identifications.

To the extent that the norms of the patron-client model prevail, they render the pluralist model inoperative and to the extent that the norms of the pluralist model predominate, they portray the operation of the patron-client model as corrupt and undemocratic. In other words, when both models are operating side by side as they are in Japan, the day-to-day political transactions of the patron-client type not only undermine the legitimacy of the political process in the eyes of the modern participant but also frustrate his efforts to achieve public policy accountability, reform, and turnover. We might expect, then, that the citizens of the modern participant type would be found among the most disaffected elements in Japanese society. The analysis presented in Chapter 5 along with the findings of a number of other studies demonstrate that the modern participant type of citizen is found in greater proportions among the young, the urban, and the educated. It is among these cohorts that we find the highest levels of modern values, class consciousness, ideological (Left-Right) political perceptions, and political interest. Thus it is quite significant that other studies have found that it is these very same cohorts who are more critical of Japanese society, politics, and political leaders and who are more likely to participate in protest meetings and demonstrations.[47]

There are at least two reasons why we might expect to find high levels of dissatisfaction with national level politics among modern participants. First, as shown in Chapter 5, modern participants tend to disproportionally support the progressive parties and, we can assume, progressive goals for the reform of Japanese politics. For these citizens, the 1960s was a decade of frustration. The May-June incidents of 1960

[47] See NHK Hōsō Seron Chōsa-jo, ed., *Nihonjin no ishiki: NHK seron chōsa* (Tōkyō: Shiseido, 1975); Kokumin Seikatsu Center, *Nihonjin no seikatsu ishiki*, vol. 2 (Tōkyō: Shiseido, 1973); and Ikeuchi Hajime, ed., *Shimin ishiki no kenkyū* (Tōkyō: Tōkyō Daigaku Shuppankai, 1974).

mobilized hundreds of thousands of demonstrators to protest the crisis in parliamentary government brought on by Prime Minister Kishi's strong-armd tactics in ramming the ratification of the United States-Japan Security Treaty through the Diet. The demonstrators found, however, that their protest accomplished little. The ruling Liberal Democrats continued to amass large majorities at the polls, and the political consciousness of the general populace outside the big cities appeared unchanged. Predictions made during the 1950s that the gradual, steady decline in LDP electoral support would bring a dramatic change in power by 1970 came to naught as the decline of the Right was matched by a fragmentation of the Left. The 1967 election focused on a nationwide media campaign directed against corruption in office, but several key figures in the scandals were returned to office with even higher levels of support than before. This demonstrated the LDP's seeming imperviousness to reform movements and the willingness of the parochial spectator type of voter to forgive indiscreet and even illegal acts on the part of *his* representative so long as such corrupt practices enhanced that representative's power to deliver benefits to the folks back home. In a similar vein, the media uproar over "money power" elections, the "Tanaka Watergate," and the Lockheed Incident in the seventies have done little to stimulate the institution of safeguards against corrupt practices, to reform the perceived unresponsiveness of the LDP establishment, or to alter the electoral balance of power in national elections.[48]

Even among modern participants who are not of a leftist hue, however, we might expect to find great dissatisfaction with national politics. These voters are not frustrated so much by the failure of the progressives to come to power as by the dilemma with which national politics confronts them. While they abhor the corruption and unresponsiveness of the ruling party, they are equally repelled by the ideological dogmatism, factional infighting, and irresponsibility of the Left. Although they cannot approve of the performance of the LDP regime, neither can they place any confidence in the ability of the progressive parties to run the country and to stabilize the economy. For some, the policies of the left-wing Socialists and Communists seem too risky and threatening, while for others, the inability of the progressive parties to harmonize their differences and present a united front frustrates the realization of a viable alternative to continued LDP control.

[48] These recent scandals have prompted some reform attempts such as the new 1975 election law (see Chapter 5, note 26), but so far the impact of these efforts has been minimal.

For many of the modern participant voters, then, none of the available alternatives on the national political stage are attractive, and they find themselves choosing between the lesser of two evils. This dilemma may in part explain the decline in the rate of descent in the LDP vote noted in Chapter 2, as the conservatives approach the point of losing control of the Diet. It would appear that a significant portion of the electorate casts its votes for one of the opposition parties more as a protest vote against the corruption and mismanagement of the LDP regime than out of any desire to see a leftist coalition assume control of the national government. Indeed some voters have freely admitted to pollsters that although they voted for an opposition party, even in some cases the Communist Party, they do not want the LDP to lose its majority but only hope to make the voice of opposition and criticism stronger in the Diet. A typical expression of this sentiment was the respondent query, "How can LDP candidates be elected with the lowest possible vote?"[49]

The events of the 1970s seem to have made Japanese voters more wary of any abrupt political change. The oil crisis, the fishery rights issue, recession, and inflation have combined to focus public attention on problems of energy, national resources, and the economy—all issues that recommend the continued experienced management of the ruling conservative party.[50] Thus many protest votes that were cast against the LDP in the 1960s, when it was "safe" to do so, may have returned to the conservative fold in the 1970s and thereby slowed the LDP rate of decline. The results of a 1977 NHK national survey just prior to the House of Councillor's (HC) election, however, suggests that an anomaly still exists between voting behavior and preferred election outcomes. While less than 50 percent of the voters actually cast their ballots for conservative candidates (LDP, NLC, and independent), 62 percent of the survey respondents wanted the election to result in an LDP or conservative majority compared to only 38 percent who preferred a progressive or opposition party majority.[51] It would appear that a number of those who vote for one of the progressive parties in national elections are not yet ready to see the progressives come to power on the national level.

[49] Arai Kanji, "Tories Face Rough Going in Kansai," The *Japan Times*, 24 January 1967.

[50] Like the oil crisis, the fishery rights issue is a resource access problem. The advent of the "age of the 200-nautical-mile economic zones" has posed a serious threat to the Japanese fishing industry and embroiled Japan in a series of stormy negotiations with the Soviet Union. See Kohei Shinsaku, "Reversal of the Balance of Power Thwarted," The *Japan Echo* 5 (Special Issue, 1978): 109-120.

[51] Ibid., p. 113.

Thus far our analysis would suggest that modern participants of both political persuasions have good cause to be strongly dissatisfied, if not totally disaffected, with national politics. But what of the parochial spectator type of citizen? It is, after all, the more traditional and localistic orientations of these citizens that is responsible for much of the system's unresponsiveness to the modern participants' reform attempts. Is the passivity of this Japanese "silent majority" an indicator of their satisfaction with national politics?

A great deal of further investigation is needed here, but we shall tentatively offer the following observations. Under the best of conditions, the patron-client mode of representation only marginally integrates the voters into the system. Constituents are tied to a particular Diet member by direct or indirectly mediated personal connections (*kankei*).[52] These ties are based on the Dietman's support of local interests, his dispensing of personal favors, or simply an amorphous sense of connectedness, and they have little to do with how that legislator votes on national issues or with what most of the rest of his party does. For the parochial spectator, national politics remains a distant play, and the Diet is a political arena in which only one or two parliamentarians are seen as supporting his interests and the other 500 plus House of Representatives (HR) members and roughly 250 HC members are viewed as standing in varying degrees of opposition to those interests. Thus Lee Farnsworth has found that Japanese voters tend sharply to differentiate between politicians in general who are seen as uniformly bad and their man in the Diet who is still pictured in glowing terms.[53] The parochial spectator, then, is hardly a vigorous supporter of national political elites, processes, or institutions. At best, he is a kind of neutral bystander.

For a number of reasons, however, we might expect to find dissatisfaction with and criticism of the central government spreading even among the spectator type of citizen. First, the media coverage of stories of corruption in government and big money elections has noticeably increased in recent years, beginning with the 1967 black mist scandals. As a result, the press, magazines, and other media have consistently instilled negative images of party politics and politicians throughout the populace. Second, with increased urbanization, the patron-client approach to integrating voters into the political system has been breaking down. In the more impersonal, fluid, and economically diverse urban environments, many people simply slip through the politicians'

[52] On *kankei*, see Chapter 5.
[53] Orally reported results of an unpublished survey conducted by Lee Farnsworth.

networks of personal ties and hence feel excluded and alienated in a traditional sense because no one is taking care of them. Finally, patron-client democracy only works effectively when the ruling party has the resources to distribute on a grand scale to a wide variety of interests. During the 1950s and 1960s Japan's phenomenal economic growth rate enabled the LDP to increase subsidies and other government benefits, keep wages high and consumer prices down, and lower taxes all at the same time. Now with the energy crisis, the flattening of Japan's growth curve, and inflation, the government will no longer be able to satisfy everyone. The result is likely to be that conservative patrons will begin losing clients.

All segments of Japanese society, therefore, have reason to be un-happy with national politics, and indeed recent surveys report astound-ing levels of political dissatisfaction in Japan compared to those levels typically found in Western democracies. Overwhelming majorities of the Japanese respondents report dissatisfaction with Japanese politics. Most Japanese view the national government and political leaders as unresponsive to the people's needs, and most distrust national politics. Most give the government poor marks in its performance on domestic issues and are far less sanguine about being treated equally by a gov-ernment office or the police than are the nationals of most Western European countries. Few feel that public officials care about people like themselves, and indeed the popular image of Japanese politicians, as revealed through the semantic differential technique, appears to be unrelentingly negative. Finally this picture of citizen alienation from national politics in general is being reinforced by an emerging trend towards the rejection of all established parties and the appearance of flash parties.[54]

Partisan Local Politics and Positive System Affect

In this context of high dissatisfaction with Japanese politics, a po-liticized local politics plays an important role. By themselves, the high levels of political disaffection that are revealed in Japanese public opinion surveys evoke images of political instability and regime col-lapse. Yet despite these consistently cynical and negative evaluations of national politics, there are no signs that the Japanese are inclined

[54] For an extensive review of survey findings on political disaffection in Japan, see Scott C. Flanagan and Bradley M. Richardson, "Political Disaffection and Political Stability: A Comparison of Japanese and Western Findings," in *Com-parative Social Research*, vol. 3, ed. Richard F. Tomasson (Greenwich, Conn.: JAI Press, 1980).

to abort the democratic experiment. Rather, Japan has emerged during the postwar period as a paragon of political stability in the midst of a sea of Asian turmoil. In the remainder of this section we will show that Japanese citizens have more positive attitudes toward local as opposed to national politics and suggest that these more positive evaluations of local politics and politicians serve to compensate for their alienation from national politics. In other words, local politics, and particularly a politicized local politics, is playing an important role in legitimizing the political process.

We will argue that partisan politicization on the local level is helping to build support for Japan's postwar democratic processes and institutions in two ways. First, for the modern participant, the politicization of local politics has made possible the transfer of administrative power from the ruling LDP to the opposition parties in a number of prefectures and cities. These opposition party successes on the local level have helped to diffuse the discontent of those modern participants who have long been frustrated by their failure to effect any regime change on the national level. The rise of progressive local administrations has not only ushered in a new era in which turnovers of power have become a reality on the local level but also along with it a new style of politics. The face of local politics has changed in Japan such that we find a growing responsiveness to citizen concerns that has been manifested in many important symbolic as well as tangible ways. Perhaps one of the earliest clear signals of the changing tone of local politics was the successful recall movement launched by Tokyo citizens in the summer of 1965 in response to the uncovering of a vote-buying scandal involving seventeen Liberal Democrats in the Tokyo Metropolitan Assembly. This movement paved the way for the subsequent election in Tokyo in 1967 of a progressive governor, Minobe Ryōkichi, but more importantly it put local Japanese politicians on notice that a new citizen accountability was becoming a reality on the local level, at least in urban Japan.

The politicization of local politics, therefore, has led not only to a circulation of partisan elites in office but also, as a result, to a new responsiveness that has gained favor among many Japanese long disturbed by the unresponsiveness of national politics. We would argue that politicization leads to greater political competition which in turn increases officeholders' vulnerability to electoral sanctions. It has been found, for instance, that partisan politicization on the local level tends to increase the number of contested elections.[55] The resulting increased

---

[55] On local electoral competition in Japan, see Steiner, *Local Government*, pp.

threat of defeat is likely to induce politicians of all political stripes to court their constituents' support more assiduously. Thus the politicization of local politics is directly associated with a rise in the responsiveness of local governments which in turn should raise the level of citizen satisfaction with politics at least on the local level.

There is a second way in which the politicization of local politics has helped to legitimize the political process. Here we turn our attention to the parochial spectator gallery. For these citizens their localistic orientations tend to insulate them from the frustrations of national politics. So long as all is well in their immediate environment, they are not likely to be too deeply disturbed by the scandals and irregularities that plague national politics. While their images of national politics are likely to be negative (unfamiliar, distant, and hence suspect) their affective involvement will be slight. Hence positive orientations towards local politics can easily compensate for negative images of national politics. Even more importantly, for the parochial spectator a politicized local politics serves as an important training ground for socializing these citizens into the meaning and relevance of party identifications as opposed to mere personal attachments to local influentials. Local politics is more familiar and manageable and as such provides the parochial spectator with a more accessible point of entry into various political input processes beyond the simple act of voting. Through such experiences, these citizens may gain the skills and perspective to involve themselves more fully in national politics. Moreover, their socialization into partisan politics in a local setting is more likely to instill positive evaluations of the political·process than would their initiation to partisan participation in the more conflictual national political arena.

The evidence would suggest that local politics is playing the kind of role that we have outlined. We find many more positive orientations toward local politics on a whole number of dimensions. The sense of involvement and efficacy are higher on the local level. The evidence indicates that Japanese are by and large more aware of and concerned about local as opposed to national problems and take a more active, participatory role in local issues. We also find that there are substantially higher levels of trust towards local as opposed to national politics and growing levels of trust in local chief executives and chief executive elections as opposed to assemblymen and assembly elections. Respondents also feel that local government officials and

390-395. J. G. Bulpitt notes that the Labor Party's entry into local government increased the number of contested elections (see Bulpitt, *Party Politics*, p. 9).

assemblymen better understand and reflect the needs and wishes of the people than national political leaders and public officials. For instance, one survey of citizen perceptions of government responsiveness found high, positive levels for governors and city mayors, substantially lower, moderate levels for municipal and prefectural assemblymen, and very low levels for the Diet and national government.[56]

Our conclusion echoes Joseph Massey's suggestion that "local-level support may serve as a surrogate for national-level alienation."[57] But, as we have argued, it is partisan politicization that has enhanced the potential for local politics to perform this role. At least to date, local politicization seems to have contributed significantly to increased citizen participation, greater responsiveness by local governments, and more positive citizen evaluations of certain elected offices and political processes and as a result to a general strengthening of the legitimacy of the political system.

SYSTEM STABILIZING EFFECTS: THE INTEGRATION OF PRINCIPLED OPPOSITIONS

Political contestation is one criterion of democracy. It distinguishes authoritarian, noncompetitive, monocentric systems from open, competitive, polyarchic ones. The form the competition assumes, however, is also vital, for healthy democracies are based on a delicate balance between consensus and dissent. If a nation's politics is too consensual, there will be no real accountability check on the behavior of political elites, and the system is likely to drift into unresponsiveness, corruption, and decay. If, on the other hand, there is too much competition, the system will become immobilized or torn asunder in a violent upheaval.[58]

The first deficiency has to do with the resource balance. If the asymmetry in the distribution of resources too strongly favors the incumbent regime over a long period of time, its opponents will be

[56] See Sakamoto Yoshiyuki, "Chōsa—'Shimin' no jitsuzo: Ishiki to undō no aida," *Jiyū* (March 1973), pp. 69-75; Tororen Kakushin Tosei Kakuritsu Iinkai, *Ryūdōka-suru tomin no seiji ishiki* (Tōkyō: Tōkyō Shisei Chōsakai, 1972); Ikeuchi, *Shimin ishiki*, pp. 255-261.

[57] Joseph A. Massey, *Youth and Politics in Japan* (Lexington, Mass.: Lexington Books, 1976), p. 47.

[58] For an extensive elaboration of these theoretical ideas, see Scott C. Flanagan, "The Genesis of Variant Political Cultures: Contemporary Citizen Orientations in Japan, America, Britain and Italy," in *The Citizen and Politics*, ed. Sidney Verba and Lucian W. Pye (Stamford, Conn.: Greylock Publishers, 1978), pp. 129-165.

too weak to present a viable challenge, thereby removing any effective check on the behavior of incumbent elites. Balanced competition, therefore, enhances the sound functioning of democratic institutions, while unbalanced competition undermines the accountability of the incumbent regime. The second deficiency is related more to the nature of the issues that divide government and opposition. If the differences are too fundamental, if they involve value or valence issues rather than distributive economic issues, negotiation and compromise become impossible, and the opposition will begin to view both the incumbent regime and the institutions and processes by which authoritative decisions are made as illegitimate. Thus the nature of the issues defines the nature of the opposition. Oppositions of principle arise when policy preferences become polarized and raise fundamental systemic questions. Such principled oppositions pose much more serious problems for representative democracies than do pragmatic oppositions.

In a peculiar way, several postwar democracies such as Italy, France, and Japan have been plagued with both kinds of problems simultaneously—unbalanced competition and principled oppositions. Moreover, when both of these conditions are present, they tend to reinforce each other. Robert Dahl notes that in polyarchies, massive differences in the political resources of groups are sources of discontent.[59] This discontent leads to frustration and political alienation when the resource deprivation relegates dissenting groups to a permanent minority status in elected representative bodies. If the differences in political resources between incumbents and challengers were truly massive and not just artificially engineered through repression, the challengers would pose little threat to the regime. But in a majoritarian system, opposition parties can hold a substantial proportion of the resources and still be locked out of power. In such cases, the opposition's exclusion can become the central issue and precipitate an attack on the political system and its constituted rules of political competition.

Issue polarization and large permanent oppositions, therefore, constitute a potentially destabilizing combination. Continued exclusion of the opposition increases its ambivalance towards the institutions of representative democracy with the result that the incorporation of the opposition through a turnover of power comes to assume more and more the proportions of a revolution. Thus exclusion intensifies issue polarization and issue polarization reinforces exclusion. We may conclude that the long-term viability of democratic institutions in such a

[59] Robert A. Dahl, *Regimes and Oppositions* (New Haven: Yale University Press, 1973), pp. 18-20.

situation depends on the narrowing of the issue polarization while the opposition is gradually given political power.

Enter local politics. Subnational prefectural and municipal governments represent relatively safe political arenas in which the transfer of power to intransigent oppositions may be started. Moreover, given the prior conditions of issue polarization and permanent opposition status, the circulation of elites on the local level can promote a number of reinforcing healing processes that enhance the integration of the opposition into the political system and the stability of the system as a whole.

First, as we have already noted, the circulation of elites on the local level can defuse discontent. It furnishes the opposition with concrete victories and encourages the expectation among opposition supporters that in time total victory is possible through the system. This anticipation that local victories mark an important step towards national success is reflected in such slogans as "From Kyoto the dawn of Japan" and "Today Rome, tomorrow Italy." Naturally, should the pattern of continued control by one group on the national level and opposition control in some local enclaves be perceived as permanent, its integrative potential would be weakened. But the postwar experience of Italy and France suggests that an opening to the left on the local level can exert a positive integrative influence over a relatively long period of time.

Second, the circulation of elites on the local level gives the opposition a greater stake in the system. The capturing of "redoubts" (safe areas) and "beachheads" (new hopes) on the local level assures the survival of the opposition. It also enables an opposition party to build a grass-roots base and local organizational infrastructure to broaden its contact with the mass public and to put to rest the "ghost party" image.[60] In addition, local level electoral victories create an opposition elite whose success and power has come from working within the system. In time this means a shift from a class of political agitators who feel insecure and threatened regarding their future to a class of successful politicians who have a vested interest in the political system. In Japan we noted that progressive chief executives, especially, have a wide range of administrative and regulative powers that enable them to win new supporters and build a stronger power base through the

[60] The Japan Socialist Party, for example, has been referred to as a ghost party particularly during the 1950s and 1960s because of its extreme weakness in local level elections and its lack of a strong local organizational base. See Robert A. Scalapino and Masumi Junnosuke, *Parties and Politics in Contemporary Japan* (Berkeley: University of California Press, 1962), pp. 95-97; also Chapter 5 of this volume.

exercise of their office. Thus Krauss's discussion of Ninagawa's grand purge is an example of the appointive and patronage power that a progressive chief executive can utilize, just as his discussion of the special favors and benefits his administration bestowed on doctors, teachers, and small and medium businessmen illustrates the pork-barrel dimension of the office.[61] As opposition parties gain greater access to the political reward structures on the local level, their stake in the system increases.

Finally, the circulation of elites on the local level leads to a change in the perception of the opposition's role. Opposition control of a number of important municipal and prefectural governments enhances the legitimacy of the opposition parties in the public eye by demonstrating the ability of these parties to govern as well as criticize. It also gives them a chance to prove that they can do better and to show that what party is in power does make a difference. As we have noted, in the Japanese case progressive local governments have placed considerable effort on projecting a positive image as open administrations, pipelines to the people, and administrations with a heart. The innovations that these administrations have introduced in political style and policy priorities have frequently won them new supporters.

The desire to maintain and expand this enlarged base of support, coupled with the socialization experience derived from the exercise of power, tends to temper the posture of opposition politicians and their own perception of their role. As a result, ideological rigidity and the "resistance struggle" (*teikō kōsō*) mentality give way to pragmatic problem solving. At the same time, power brings accountability and quickly stifles the irresponsible opposition tactic of outbidding, which tends to polarize the electorate by stimulating unrealistic expectations. Power also brings experience and expertise and develops the politician's negotiating and coalition formation skills. Hence, the circulation of elites on the local level can both provide an important socialization and training experience for opposition politicians and create a reservoir of popular leaders who can be tapped for major national roles, such as Willy Brandt's move from Mayor of Berlin to Chancellor of West Germany or Atsukata's move from Mayor of Yokohama to Chairman of the Socialist Party.

In short, the circulation of elites on the local level contributes to a change in the opposition's role from that of a vehicle for articulating the voice of frustration to that of a vehicle for bringing concrete benefits for its supporters. This is an important step in the full integration of permanent oppositions into the political system. Through the long-

[61] See Chapter 11.

term socialization process just described that accompanies the transfer of power on the local level, intransigent, principled oppositions may in time be transformed into loyal, pragmatic oppositions and finally into full partners in the governance of the nation through the regularized turnover of power on the national level.

Projections: Long-Term Effects on Coalition Patterns in Japan

Giovanni Sartori identifies the central tendency of polarized multiparty systems as centrifugal.[62] Extreme policy disagreements lead to irresponsible outbidding, and the incumbent regime becomes immobilized by antisystem oppositions. This results in growing citizen disaffection and a long-term decline in the electoral fortunes of the incumbents. The predicted outcome of this centrifugal system dynamic is eventual regime collapse and constitutional upheaval. We have suggested that the only way that polarized multiparty systems can avoid this unhappy fate is if the decline in the strength of the incumbent regime can be matched with a narrowing of the distance between government and opposition. This seems to have been what has been happening in Japan, and it would appear that the partisan politicization of local government and the resultant rise of progressive local administrations have played an important role in this integrating process.

Sartori argues that a pattern of bipolar competition is essential if the destructive outward drives of the polarized multiparty system are to be replaced by the integrative, center-seeking dynamics associated with two-party systems and a healthy pattern of turnover.[63] In this regard the presidential format of the local chief executive elections, which require candidates to seek majority support rather than direct their appeals narrowly to particular clientele, is helping to both establish a bipolar pattern of competition and to draw the Left and Right towards more central, consensual policy positions. The mayoral and gubernatorial elections in Japan have forced the opposition parties to adopt a more flexible, conciliatory pattern on the local level and to participate in a broad variety of different coalition patterns—with other progressive parties in those areas where opposition majorities were possible and with conservatives in those areas where opposition majorities were not possible.

We are also witnessing the emergence of a growing cluster of centrist parties in Japan, particularly in local big city elections where

---

[62] Giovanni Sartori, *Parties and Party Systems: A Framework for Analysis* (London: Cambridge University Press, 1976).

[63] Ibid., pp. 131-185.

these parties are much stronger relative to the JSP and the Left as a whole than they are nationally in the Diet. In these cities, the CGP and DSP alone control 25 to 30 percent of the vote, making the Center the deciding swing vote between the Left and Right. As a result, we are beginning to see the centrist parties take the lead in the local chief executive elections in these areas in the selection of candidates and supporting party coalitions.

Nationally, the Communist Party has consistently been the stumbling block that has frustrated the formation of a united coalition of progressive parties. In several of the big cities, however, it has now become possible for the political Center to achieve a majority by forming a coalition with either the conservatives on the right or the Socialists on the left. For instance, in the April 1978 mayoral election in Yokohama, a coalition of three centrist parties (DSP, CGP, and NLC) jointly put forward the candidacy of Saigo Michikazu, a former classmate of a prominent Yokohama DSP Dietman. While both the LDP and Socialists had wanted to put up their own candidate, this move effectively outflanked them. If the Right put up an independent candidate, the Left would throw its support to the centrist candidate and defeat the Right, and vice versa. The outcome was that both the LDP and the Socialists eventually threw their support to the centrist candidate to avoid losing face in an election defeat and antagonizing the future mayor and being totally shut out of his administration.[64] In a different example, in the 1974 Kyoto Gubernatorial election, the Communist-Left Socialist backed incumbent, Ninagawa, received his stiffest competition from a Center-Right Socialist candidate in a three-way race.

The local chief executive elections, therefore, appear to have had a moderating effect on political competition in Japan. These elections have forced Japan's ideologically fragmented parties to form coalitions and to seek areas of agreement with other parties. They have also helped to establish a pattern of competition of conservative versus progressive, and they are now increasingly helping to set up variations on the pattern of Center-Right versus Left or Center-Left versus Right. This latter form of bipolarity makes real turnover possible without entailing radical policy departures.

We have noted that one of the major obstacles to the rise of a progressive administration on the national level has been the Japanese public's hesitancy to entrust the reigns of government to an untried

[64] Shimizu Minoru, "A New Trend in Local Government Elections," *The Japan Times Weekly*, 28 January 1978, p. 5; Shimizu, "Komeito's Yano in Limelight," *The Japan Times Weekly*, 25 March 1978, p. 5.

and divided opposition. The results of a 1977 NHK election survey, however, suggest that the various experiments in coalition government on the local level may have been having an effect on building popular acceptance for their institution on the national level. When asked, "What type of government would you like in the near future?" only 10 percent chose an exclusive LDP government. We also note that only 26 percent desired a government that totally excluded the LDP, suggesting that the Japanese are not yet ready to completely entrust the government to the opposition. But 44 percent wanted to see some form of coalition government that included the LDP and one or more of the three centrist parties (the DSP, CGP, and NLC).[65] What we are now seeing, then, is an opening to the Center, and once a Center-Right coalition pattern is established on the national level, the possibility of a future Center-Left coalition will be greatly enhanced. Thus the rise of progressive administrations on the local level has been not only a forecast of a coming trend on the national level but also an added catalyst that has worked to legitimize such a move.

The rise of local progressive administrations, however, is not likely to be monotonic. For one thing, the emergence of a Center increases the fluidity of coalition patterns and the volatility of election outcomes. For another, the office of local chief executive is not based on firm parliamentary majorities, as is the case in some other countries such as Italy where the office is elected by the local assembly. In contrast with local assembly elections that exhibit smaller, more gradual changes from election to election, we have noted that the chief executive elections are characterized by much sharper fluctuations due to the effects of candidate image. In our analysis of electoral trends, it was also argued that the demographic and attitudinal changes that were responsible for the decline in conservative support pointed towards higher levels of political competition in the future rather than a long-term transition to progressive dominance. Thus we may, from time to time, witness reverses in the fortunes of progressive local chief executives, even in established progressive strongholds.

Recent local elections illustrate the trends we have noted: there is an increased politicization at the local level in general and an increased competition among parties. In local executive elections in particular, coalitions have become crucial, so that the centrist parties assume a role of strategic importance. Together with the growing role of the candidates' personality, this leads to a greater variability in the results of executive elections than is the case in assembly elections.

In executive elections in major urban areas in 1978 and 1979, the

[65] Kohei, "Reversal," p. 113.

Left lost all three of its major "showcase" prefectural governments in Tokyo, Kyoto, and Osaka. The retirement of Ninagawa in Kyoto (1978) and Minobe in Tokyo (1979) deprived the Left of two incumbents with wide suprapartisan appeal. In Tokyo and Osaka (1979), centrist parties (and in Osaka, the JSP as well) jointly supported a successful candidate with the LDP. In these races, the centrist parties took early initiatives in candidate searches and were joined by the LDP to form a winning coalition.[66] In Kyoto, the alliance of centrist parties with the JSP against both an LDP-NLC candidate and a JCP candidate provoked a three-way race, allowing the conservative Hayashida to win, but with less than a majority of the votes. These results suggest that at least in urban areas, "the LDP cannot win gubernatorial or mayoral elections any longer on the basis of its own strength, without backing from other parties."[67] Rather than a conservative resurgence, the leftist loss of these governorships represents the increasing competitiveness of local politics, the vagaries of alliance strategies in executive elections, the partial substitution of centrist opposition power for leftist opposition power, and the failure of the Left to run candidates with the same broad-based appeal as retiring incumbents.

In local assembly contests in 1979, the fragmentation of the vote continued. There was no significant change in the distribution of the relative strength among the parties. In Prefectural Assembly contests overall, the LDP increased its vote percentage by less than 1 percent over 1975, the JSP and JCP both declined fractionally (by 1.5 percent and 2.5 percent, respectively), and the centrist parties remained virtually the same. In terms of seats, the LDP increased its proportion of seats by only about a quarter of a percent, the JSP declined by over a percent and a half, the JCP increased by less than half a percent, and the centrist parties remained almost unchanged. In the eight big cities, excluding Tokyo and Kitakyushu, the lack of change was even more striking: in comparison to the 1975 elections, no party gained or lost more than six seats out of the almost six hundred being contested in 1979. In these big cities, the LDP lost three seats overall, while the

[66] In Tokyo the successful candidate was Suzuki Shunichi, a former vice-governor. Originally selected by the CGP, and supported by the DSP and LDP, he defeated the joint JSP-JCP candidate, Ohta Kaoru. See The *Japan Times Weekly*, 14 April 1979, p. 2.

[67] Ibid. It should be noted that in the 1979 elections the LDP entered gubernatorial candidates of its own only in a few of the most rural prefectures. On this point and the important role of the Center in reversing leftist trends, see also The *Japan Times Weekly*, 28 April 1979, p. 4, and Richard J. Samuel's article on the elections, The *Japan Times Weekly*, 21 April 1979, p. 5.

JSP gained three and the JCP gained six.[68] In other words, the LDP managed to arrest its decline, but the Left continued to make marginal inroads in the big cities.

Despite the Left's loss of key urban administrations, therefore, there is no return to the conservative paradise of the past. With the establishment of a more competitive pattern in many Japanese cities, an important watershed has been crossed. The results of this transition seem to be having beneficial effects on the Japanese political system, its political leaders, and its citizens.

[68] Prefectural Assembly results calculated from data in *Mainichi Shinbun*, 15 April 1975, p. 2, and *Yomiuri Shinbun*, 10 April 1979, p. 2. Big city assembly election results were provided by Terry MacDougall and are based on his calculations of results in newspaper reports.

CONTRIBUTORS

Gary D. Allinson is Professor of History at the University of Pittsburgh who holds a Ph.D. degree from Stanford University (1971). He is the author of *Japanese Urbanism: Industry and Politics in Kariya, 1872-1972* (1975), *Suburban Tokyo: A Comparative Study in Politics and Social Change* (1979), and numerous articles on Japanese history.

Ronald Aqua serves as staff to the Joint Committee on Japanese Studies and the Joint Committee on Korean Studies at the Social Science Research Council. He recently completed his Ph.D. dissertation at Cornell University on politics and policy making in Japanese cities. His current research interests include regional development policy and the relationship between corporations and local governments in Japan.

Scott C. Flanagan is Associate Professor in the Department of Government, Florida State University. He is coeditor (with Gabriel Almond and Robert Mundt) of *Crisis, Choice and Change* (1973), and coauthor (with Bradley Richardson) of *Japanese Electoral Behavior* (1977). He is also author of numerous articles on Japanese parties, political culture, and voting behavior.

Ellis S. Krauss is Associate Professor of Political Science and East Asian Studies, Western Washington University, and in 1978-1979 was an Honorary Research Associate in East Asian Studies, Harvard University. He received his Ph.D. from Stanford University, and is the author of *Japanese Radicals Revisited: Student Protest in Postwar Japan* (1974) and coauthor (with James Fendrich) of articles on comparative political socialization processes in the United States and Japan. Currently, he is engaged in research on conflict regulation between government and opposition parties in the Japanese Diet.

Jack G. Lewis is Field Director of the Konan-Illinois Center at Konan University in Kobe and Visiting Assistant Professor of Asian Studies at the University of Illinois. He is presently conducting research for both a coauthored volume on the politics of urban growth in Yokohama and Kobe and for his own study of mayoral recruitment and elections in Japanese cities.

471

Terry Edward MacDougall is Associate Professor of Government and Acting Executive Director of the Japan Institute at Harvard University. He is the author of *Localism and Political Opposition in Japan* (1980) and is currently working on a study of political leadership focused on Asukata Ichio, Chairman of the Japan Socialist Party, in addition to coauthoring a volume on politics and urban growth in Yokohama and Kobe.

Margaret A. McKean is Assistant Professor of Political Science at Duke University. She has written numerous articles on the environmental issue in Japan and has recently completed a book on the environmental movement, *Japan's New Citizen Politics* (forthcoming). She is now involved in a study of common property rights in Japan and other industrial democracies.

Bradford L. Simcock is Assistant Professor of Sociology, Miami University (Ohio). He received his Ph.D. from Harvard University and is the author of several articles on environmental problems and protest in Japan.

Kurt Steiner, Professor of Political Science (Emeritus) at Stanford University, is the author of *Local Government in Japan* (1965) and *Politics in Austria* (1972). He contributed to J. M. Maki's *Court and Constitution in Japan: Selected Supreme Court Decisions, 1948-1960* (1964) and to Robert E. Ward's *Political Development in Modern Japan* (1968). He has also published several articles on Japanese local government and on Japanese law.

Index

local politics and government (*cont.*)
on, 212, 215-24, 265-73, 296, 306-309,
311; coalitions in, 444, 465-69;
Communist parties in, 440-41, 443n;
as "conservative paradise," 3-7, 14,
18, 56-57; dual nature of, 41-45;
linkages to central government, 5,
7-16, 19, 354-59, 434-37, 438-39, 450-
51; meaning of "conservative" and
"progressive" unclear in, 83; myth
of, as insulated, apolitical, and
conflict-free, 12-14, 16, 433-37, 438,
450-51; opportunity structures in,
25; party activity in, and local
autonomy, 434, 437-44, 449-50;
political styles in, 52-53, 70; positive
citizen attitudes toward, 459-61;
recruitment of officials from, to
national positions, 436-37. *See also*
politicization of local politics
local public policy: central government priorities and control as determinant of, 354-69, 371-72, 382, 450-
53; CMs' impact on, 221-23; effect
of partisan allegiance on, 335-42,
351, 354-61, 372-82; Ninagawa's
incrementalism in, 416-24; nonsystemic local forces affecting, 354,
369-72, 374; in patron-client democracy, 429, 430 fig.; in pluralist
democracy, 429-30; and politicization of local politics, 448-53; and
shifts in electoral interest, 70, 71
table, 74-75

Maas, Arthur, 10n
MacDougall, Terry Edward, 30, 31,
42, 43, 53, 54, 133, 138, 148, 149, 162,
168n, 182n, 184, 319n, 321, 324n,
329n, 330n
McKean, Margaret A., 21n, 23n, 31,
189, 190, 194, 196, 197-98, 200n,
201, 202, 206, 207, 211, 212, 215,
217, 218, 224, 295n, 448n
Massey, Joseph, 461
Masumi Junnosuke, 149, 356
Matsuda Yoshiharu, 279-80, 282, 290n,
305, 306, 307-308
Matsushita Masatoshi, 82, 330, 333,
334

May Association, 293-94
mayoral elections, 77-92; big city
trends, 83-91; candidate attributes
in, 83-86; candidate image in, 168-72;
candidate qualities in, 81-83; CMs'
impact on, 269; coalitions in, 465,
466, 467; district size and, 156-57,
160 table, 171-72; *kankei* and, 156-
57, 160 table, 171-72; partisanship
in, 78-81, 86-91; progressives in,
4, 6-7, 42-44, 77-92; suburban trends
in, 100, 101 table, 102-103, 110-12
media: and candidate image, 168-72;
CMs and, 213; coverage of corruption by, 457; and publicity about
pollution incidents, 195; and resocialization for local autonomy, 447-48;
and voter participation, 179-80
merchants' associations, 236, 237-38
Metropolitan People's Party
(*Tomintō*), 28, 333
Miike coal miners' strike, 327
Miki Takeo, 333, 379n
Minamata: CM in, 274; pollution
incident in, 194, 220, 451
Ministry of International Trade and
Industry (MITI), 282-83, 363-64
Minkyō (Council for a Democratic
Prefectural Coalition), 28, 402
Minobe Ryōkichi, 28, 82, 85, 112n,
317, 322, 324, 326, 329-35, 459, 468;
antipollution policies of, 333-34, 340;
candidate image of, 168-72, 341; CMs
and, 222, 333-34; on local-central
government relations, 331, 332;
media used by, 447; policies of, 222,
332-33, 334-35, 339n, 340; support
base and coalition of, 331-32, 333,
422-23n; and Tokyo Garbage War,
449; voter appeal of, 180-82, 331-32,
333, 341; on ward chief selection,
350
Minshō, 405, 406
Minshufusei Kyōgikai, see *Minkyō*
Mintōkaigi (All Kyoto Democratic
Front Unity Conference), 393, 394,
395
Mishima, 17n, 31, 112n; assembly elections in, 281; coalitions in, 28n;
conservatives in, 279-80, 281; con-

480

Library of Congress Cataloging in Publication Data

Main entry under title:

Political opposition and local politics in Japan.

Based on a conference sponsored by the Joint
Committee on Japanese Studies of the American
Council of Learned Societies and the Social Science
Research Council.
1. Local government—Japan—Congresses.
2. Opposition (Political science)—Congresses.
I. Steiner, Kurt, 1912-   II. Krauss, Ellis S.
III. Flanagan, Scott C.
JS7372.P64   320.8'0952   80-7555
ISBN 0-691-07625-1
ISBN 0-691-02201-1 (pbk.)